Writing As

Writing As Resistance

The Journal of
Prisoners on Prisons
Anthology
(1988–2002)

Edited by
Bob Gaucher

Canadian Scholars' Press Inc.
Toronto

Writing As Resistance:
The Journal of Prisoners on Prisons Anthology (1988–2002)
edited by Bob Gaucher

First published in 2002 by
Canadian Scholars' Press Inc.
180 Bloor Street West, Suite 1202
Toronto, Ontario
M5S 2V6

www.cspi.org

CSPI gratefully acknowledges the financial support of the Government of Canada through the Book Publishing Industry Development Program for our publishing activities.

National Library of Canada Cataloguing in Publication Data

Writing as resistance : the Journal of prisoners on prisons anthology
(1988-2002) / edited by Bob Gaucher.

Includes bibliographical references.
ISBN 1-55130-220-9

     1. Imprisonment. 2. Criminal justice, Administration of. 3. Prisoners writings, Canadian (English). 4. Prisoners' writings, American. 5. Prisoners' writings, English. I. Gaucher, Robert

HV8301.W75 2002   365   C2002-903478-7

Page design and layout by Brad Horning
Cover design by Heidy Lawrance Associates

02 03 04 05 06 07   7 6 5 4 3 2 1

Printed and bound in Canada by AGMV Marquis

Canadä

*Dedicated to Ian Roger Taylor and Little Rock Reed,
comrades who are dearly missed.*

Table of Contents

PART IV: IN THE HANDS OF THE STATE

Women Prisoners

PART V: RESISTANCE STRATEGIES FOR SURVIVAL

PART VI: TALKING BACK: COUNTER-INSCRIBING THE PRISON INDUSTRIAL COMPLEX

PART VII: APPENDICES

EDITOR'S ACKNOWLEDGEMENTS

Many people have contributed to the *Journal of Prisoners on Prisons*. First, I would like to acknowledge Professor Ian Roger Taylor, whose work as a radical criminologist in the 1960s inspired me to engage in critical criminology. My academic interest in prison writing started in the 1970s with the encouragement of Professor Ioan Davies, whose work in this area stands as a benchmark. Henry Cyr, Jr., Ron Westad, Claire Culhane and Art Solomon taught me the importance of active resistance, and the resistance of Little Rock Reed and Rob Brydon provided the inspiration to undertake the work.

Over the fifteen years of the *JPP's* publication, editorial board members, prisoner contributors, and fellow travellers were instrumental in its success. Fellow editors: Howard Davidson, John Lowman, and Liz Elliott; guest/co-editors: Little Rock Reed, Gayle Horii, Curtis Taylor, Mícheál Mac Giolla Ghunna, Stephen Reid, and Jay Jones — all devoted time and energy, ensuring that success. Brian MacLean, Kim Cunnington Taylor, Marcia Stentz, and Jay Jones laboured on the production, contributing countless hours. Most inspiring were the prison writers, whose manuscripts set the tone of the journal and whose continued encouragement and support kept it going. Of special note were Jo-Ann Mayhew, Paul Wright, Little Rock Reed, Victor Hassine, Jon Marc Taylor, Charles Huckelbury, Gerald Niles, Steven King Ainsworth, James V. Allridge III, and Thomas Mann. The determination and support of Ruth Morris and Kim Pate provided encouragement throughout the journey. All contributed to the struggle against state repression that is the focus of the *JPP*.

Writing As Resistance

PART I

INTRODUCTION

The Journal of Prisoners on Prisons:
An Ethnography of the Prison
Industrial Complex in the 1990s
Bob Gaucher

T he 1990s were characterized by the massive growth of prison
populations and the expansion of penal control and carceral
institutions throughout Western societies (Garland, ed., 2001; Weiss
and South, eds., 1998). Though the extent of this expansion varies according
to the society, the trend is best represented in the alarming growth of the
prison-industrial complex in the U.S.A., where there are now more than
two million prisoners, and in the equally unsettling growth of prison
populations in the Netherlands, the former bastion of social tolerance and
liberal criminal justice policy (Downes, 2001).[1] In this decade, the conjunction
of the rhetorics of retribution and deterrence defined public and political
discourse, and the resultant social and criminal justice policy of most Western
nations. Previous societal and legal concerns for proportionality between
the crime (social harm) and the punishment were often submerged by these
punitive demands, as expressed in "the war on drugs", mandatory sentences
(e.g., "three strikes" legislation), longer sentences with reduced parole
opportunities, and harsh prison conditions. These developments were
accompanied by the growth in the industrialization and privatization of penal
control. Despite the academic debate over the extent of these changes and
their significance (Burton-Rose et al., eds., 1998; Christie, 1993; Currie,
1998; Garland, ed., 2001; Parenti, 1999; Taylor, 1999), the growth of the
prison-industrial complex produced real changes in most jurisdictions. The
impact of these changes on the carceral commodity, the prisoner, has often
been extreme.

   The analysis and commentary of prisoners in this anthology represent a
counter-inscription to these developments and the arguments that legitimize
them. Located firmly within the long-established tradition of prison literature
(Gaucher, Part II), they collectively represent the prisoner-intellectual's
responses to the current conjuncture, as informed by the experience of
criminalization and incarceration in the 1990s. Many contributors have spent
over twenty consecutive years in the "belly of the beast" and their
understanding is grounded in first-hand experience of the hard realities of
these changes (e.g., Part IV, Hassine).

These accounts and representations of the experience of incarceration
and carceral culture differ significantly from that found in most academic
studies, state reports and research documents, and from that of the dominant
mass media and attendant public discourse. This is true over time and across
jurisdictions. Working as a professor of criminology for the past twenty
years, I have been repeatedly struck by the incongruity between the accounts
and analysis of prison intellectuals and those of state and academic authorities.
The prison, as described and analyzed by contemporary prisoners, does not
resemble the image of the "accredited penal institution" of the American
Correctional Association (ACA) (see Part VI, Cahill et al., and Reed and
Denisovich) nor the model institution suggested by the Correctional Service
of Canada's (CSC) guiding "Mission Statement" and CPAC (Canadian Public
Access Channel) television presentations (see Arbour, 1996). It most certainly
differs from the punitive lobby's depiction of mollycoddled prisoners lounging
in "club fed" prisons as commonly portrayed by right-wing political
commentators (Harris, 2002) or the mass media.

In both research and teaching, I have found that this contradiction is a
good site from which to approach, read, and understand the prison and its
relationships. If we are to understand the prison institution, and the culture
and order it contains, then we must investigate the positions, relationships,
and "sense"/accounts of all participants in this complex organization, especially
those of the silenced majority—the prisoners. To make sense of the dynamic
complex organization of the total institution (i.e., prison) (Goffman, 1961),
it is necessary to explore the everyday routines, fears, and concerns of
prison life and prison culture. Prison writers can part the mists that shroud
carceral life and cast light upon the realities of the pains of imprisonment
and the formative power of the prison. They can map the changes produced
by penal policies and enlighten us as to the consequences that are seldom
part of the dominant discourses. The contributors to this anthology
accomplish this for the 1990s.

A random sample of the vast array of literary and artistic work by prisoners
immediately indicates that the experience of criminalization and imprisonment
is disorienting, threatening, and total. The quest for relief from its
claustrophobic sameness often takes the form of writing, painting, or some
other creative "escape" (see Cohen and Taylor, 1977), and in those quiet
moments the landscape of the prison flows from their pens and paintbrushes
with acuity, insight, and pathos. This is the prison I have encountered, with
its constant noise, smells, and atmosphere of sterile control. How can we

possibly make sense of those we criminalize and the end results of incarceration without listening to their accounts of being processed as a carceral commodity? Fortunately, there seems to be a renewed interest in the expertise and understanding of prisoners and former prisoners by academics. For example, current books by Victor Hassine (1996, 1999); Mumia Abu-Jamal (1997); Daniel Burton-Rose, Dan Pen, and Paul Wright (1998); and Laurence McKeown (2001) are being widely used in university courses. The recent *Convict Criminology* initiative of John Irwin, Stephen Richards and Jeffery Ian Ross (2002)[2] promises to add to the debate in the United States. In Canada recent CSC initiatives such as *LifeLine*[3] indicate that at least some CSC managers are aware that the understanding and expertise acquired by prisoners through years of incarceration do have value and utility.

. . The essays in this anthology illustrate the spirit of resistance that characterizes the survival strategies of most prisoners, especially prison-bound writers and intellectuals. In Part II, their considered resistance is evident in their understanding of "being a writer in prison". In their analyses of the sociological context and contemporary utility of penal control (Part III), they search for explanations for the evident and growing disaster that is unfolding around them. Political economy, class, race, gender, and ethnicity are addressed as significant factors. In Part IV, the overwhelming and threatening experience of incarceration within the gulags of the 1990s is portrayed from clearly located positions that carry forward the themes of the previous section. In Parts V and VI, discussion of strategies for surviving the violence and debilitating effects of prison life lead to the refutation of the "fairy tale" of social justice as illustrated in the U.S.A.

The *Journal of Prisoners on Prisons*

Franklin (1998) refers to the 1960s and 1970s as an age of literary renaissance in American prison writing. A new wave of prison writers and their literary forms and styles transcended the traditional classifications, transforming them into a new prison-focused narrative (Part II, Gaucher). Above all these new forms were imbued with the political consciousness that came to inform convict culture and the discourse of convict intellectuals in Western societies. It is this literary tradition that the *Journal of Prisoners on Prisons* strives to represent.

The first International Conference on Prison Abolition (ICOPA) was held in Toronto, Canada in the summer of 1983 (Finateri and Saleh-Hanna, 2000) and drew together grassroots activists, radical academics, NGOs, and a solid representation of prisoners. ICOPA II was held in Amsterdam in 1985 and was much more academic in its program and participation. A group of Canadians — Claire Culhane, Art Solomon, Ruth Morris, Liz Elliott, Howard Davidson, and myself — discussed the lack of representation of grassroots activists and prisoners, and this discussion resulted in ICOPA III being jointly hosted by the Université de Montréal and Université d'Ottawa at the Université de Montréal, Canada. In redressing the perceived imbalance of ICOPA II, we included strong participation in the program of grassroots organizations such as Anarchist Black Cross groups and the Leonard Peltier Defense Committee, and we were pleased about the involvement of Art Solomon and Canadian Aboriginal communities. It is difficult to get prisoners out of prison to attend penal abolition conferences and though we had some (former) prisoner participation, we extended their participation by presenting papers written by current prisoners (Davidson, 1988). The positive reception they received led directly to our broader discussion of the importance of prisoners' input into official and academic discourse, and eventually the creation of the *Journal of Prisoners on Prisons* (*JPP*). As Howard Davidson noted in the first volume, "for the prisoners and former prisoners who would welcome an opportunity to engage in the production of knowledge about crime and punishment, the barriers to participation remain formidable" (1988, 1:1, 3). The *JPP* was intended as a vehicle for the accounts and analysis of prisoners "to bring the knowledge and experience of the incarcerated to bear upon ... academic arguments and concerns, and to inform public discourse about the current state of our carceral institutions" (Gaucher, 1988, 1:1, 54). Our intent and expectations for the journal were informed by penal abolitionist arguments and strategies (see Culhane, 1979, 1985; Hulsman, 1985; Kneen, 1994; Mathiesen, 1974; Posluns, 1990). I addressed this intent in my "Response" to the first issue:

> ... if the prison abolitionist argument that the goal and necessity of
> the outside critic should be to empower the disenfranchised, then
> providing the opportunity for prisoners to state their case, to identify
> the major problems, and to provide us with up to date information
> and analysis about what is actually occurring in our prisons is a

necessity. Amongst the diverse group of people who serve as the carceral commodity there are many with extraordinary talents and insights, whose contributions can revitalize this barren area of study (i.e., corrections). ... as a teacher I am constantly in search of ethnographic materials which will provide insight to my students and will help to combat the "monster" stereotypes of the criminalized and incarcerated which dominate public and academic discourse. So there is clearly a role to be played by prisoners and a need for them to try and take back a small measure of control of their destinies by actively engaging the concerned public and by defining the dominant problems of the current situation (Gaucher, 1988, 1:1, 54).

The extent to which we succeeded may be judged by the essays presented in this anthology.

Commencing as a biannual in the summer of 1988, the *JPP* has published twelve volumes, including fourteen single and five double issues. As of Volume 11, the journal is being published as an annual. The editorial group has maintained the independence of the journal by depending upon the contributions of editorial group members and contributors to produce it, and upon subscriptions and university sales to finance its production and distribution. In serving as a legitimate academic forum for prisoners, we thought that maintaining our independence was of primary concern. We were already aware of the problems of prison writers mingling with staff and administrators of the prison-industrial complex and how this led to compromise, misrepresentation, and absorption (Mathiesen, 1974:13–36). We also wanted to assure contributors that they could feel free of the censorship and publication problems that shadow prison writers and intellectuals.

The manuscripts selected for publication have been peer reviewed and edited. The *JPP* publishes essays of commentary and analysis of criminal justice issues by prisoners and former prisoners. The work of associated non-prisoners (fellow travellers) has been included as "Responses" to particular volumes or as co-authorship. Contributors to the *JPP* — such as Jo-Ann Mayhew, Little Rock Reed, Gayle Horii, Jon Marc Taylor, John Perotti, Ronald Del Raine, Victor Hassine, Gerald Niles, Paul Wright, and Charles Huckelbury — all helped in the composition and production of these volumes, whether through general discussion or direct involvement. Indeed, with the assistance of Lisa Morgan, Little Rock Reed edited Volume 4:2 (1993, on special handling units) from within Lucasville (Ohio) Penitentiary; Gayle Horii co-edited Volume 5:2 (1994, on the imprisonment of women) shortly after being paroled, and Jon Marc Taylor, imprisoned in Missouri, is currently co-editing Volume 13 (2003, on educational issues). These are "joint" productions.

   One of the most enjoyable editorial tasks is choosing the art for *JPP* covers. The drawings, paintings, carvings, and sculpture featured on *JPP* covers is representative of the long tradition of prison art. For most, prison was where the artists first engaged their art and developed their skills.

THIS ANTHOLOGY: *JPP* 1988 – 2002

I am of the opinion that the *JPP* has been successful in achieving the original intention of providing a formal academic publication in which prisoners can state *their positions and discuss and debate their issues*. We have also assembled a portrait of the 1990s prison, as well as the crime-control industry and its legitimating moral panics and dominant narratives. Over its thirteen years of publication, the *JPP* has mapped many of the major concerns of prisoners and provided the supportive evidence and argument that they present to legitimate their assessments. Collectively these essays represent an ethnography of the prison-industrial complex in North America in the 1990s. In this decade the increasing reliance upon penal forms of state control to manage the growing social disorder and widening class divisions of post-industrial societies produced an alarming expansion of prison populations.

   Prison writing fundamentally represents the relationship between the prisoner and the prison. In this age of the "great confinement" with the massive expansion of prison facilities and the proliferation of industrialized institutional models and styles, the *prison* can take many forms and regimes. Most of our contributors have been serving long-term, life, or death row sentences and are or were housed in high-security facilities, some for many years. Steven King Ainsworth and Mumia Abu-Jamal endured nineteen years on death row, and James V. Allridge III and Johnny Byrd have spent more than a decade under its oppressive reality. Ronald Del Raine, Victor Hassine, Danny Homer, Charles Huckelbury, and Jon Marc Taylor have all served more than twenty consecutive years. Hassine, Homer, Gayle Horii, Jo-Ann Mayhew, Gregory McMaster, and Gerald Niles are all life-sentence prisoners. These writers speak from the experience of long-term incarceration under maximum-security conditions.

Even within maximum security there is a great variation in the regimes and extent of isolation. Conditions include the extreme isolation of high-security units (see Rosenberg, Part IV), the experimental deprivation and isolation model of Marion[4] (see Del Raine, Part IV; Griffin, Part IV) and Pelican Bay (see Morris, Part IV), and the ghost train model of transfers from one institutional special handling unit (SHU) to another (see Niles, Part IV). Many of our long-term contributors (Abu-Jamal, Hassine, Niles, Perotti, and Taylor) have been transferred a number of times and over the past decade have spent periods in solitary confinement and special handling units, often as reprisal for their political activities. They deconstruct the argument that Marion's style of close confinement is reserved for the "most dangerous" and show it to be mere legitimating rhetoric that masks prison bureaucracies' attempts to break their collective and individual resistance. Their analysis suggests that though the walls of the cage may narrow and the isolation become extreme, their spirits remain strong.

Regardless of the conditions under which they are incarcerated, writers in prison bring the urgency of survival and resistance to their task. In Cohen and Taylor's (1972:138) *Psychological Survival: The Experience of Long Term Imprisonment*, British prisoners note that understanding where you are and what is happening to you is the first rule for surviving criminalization and incarceration, and a necessity for resisting metamorphosis into a helpless convict. Writers in prison engage the demands of survival by locating, deconstructing, and analyzing the dominant and directing narratives of their carceral world. In their counter-inscriptions prison writers engage the prison by knowing it and resisting it. Intertwined in the narratives that collectively and universally compose the oral and written traditions of prison culture is a generality that Davies (1990) refers to as the "ur-epic", and a specificity of subjective history and location, as illustrated by Franklin (1978) in his study of Afro-American prison literature. The ur-epic aspects represent the cultural history of the prison and its self-informing oral traditions, stories, language/argot, and value expressions. The everyday reality of carceral life is dominated by the structure and organization of the confining total institution. The prison becomes the lens through which the prison writer reads and relates to the inside and outside worlds. The antecedent experiences of writers frame their understanding of the carceral, but it is the carceral that dominates their attention regardless of their class, race, or gender location. Surviving carceral brutalities and resisting the conformities of the total institution are universal needs shared by all prisoners.

In this light, I have organized the essays within a framework that broadly addresses the conditions of incarceration in the 1990s. These conditions are understood sociologically as reflecting the emergence and development of the prison-industrial complex (foremost in the U.S.A.) and the consequences of the industrialization of punitive control for those criminalized and incarcerated (Burton-Rose et al., 1998; Christie, 1993, 1999; Churchill and Van der Wall, eds., 1992; Hassine, 1996, 1999; Parenti, 1999). This framing allows for the inclusion of essays that focus on traditional themes of prison writing: class, race, gender, capital punishment, isolation (marionization), suicide, prison disturbances, prison violence, and victimization. These traditional themes were also prominent themes in the prison writing of the 1990s.

Part II: Writing As Resistance: Writers in Prison
This anthology opens with a general introduction to prison writing (Gaucher) and considerations "on being a writer in prison today" by Charles Huckelbury, Victor Hassine, and Gregory McMaster, all established prison writers and contributors to this volume. They illustrate the domination of the prison and the need to know, understand, and deconstruct it as a formative aspect of their decision to write and as an influence upon their development as writers. Writing and artistic expression become resistance, a means of survival and a testament to surviving the dislocations of prison life. Irish Fenian political prisoners Mícheál Mac Giolla Ghunna and Paddy O'Dowd extend the discourse in their discussion of the Drama Project in the H-Blocks of Long Kesh as "a continuation of a long history of jail cultural struggle". Their adaptation of "Bobby Sands' epic trilogy of poems" as the stage production *The Crime of Castlereagh* was understood to be more than "merely an act of resistance". It also helped to fulfill their "wish to give voice to the pain of their people and articulate the need for radical change to end this pain" (p. 71). Ghunna understands this desire as embodying their revolutionary spirit. "It has become almost a defining feature of political prisoners that they engage in cultural struggle" (p. 71). Paul Wright illustrates Ghunna's

"cultural resilience" in the history of *Prison Legal News* (1990–2002), a politicized and critical chronicle(r) of the development of the prison-industrial complex in the U.S.A. Though composed, written, and edited within prison, *PLN* is published outside and therefore avoids many of the censorship problems that beset prisoners/ writers. However, its circulation within prisons continues to encounter the type of censorship problems addressed by Abu-Jamal in "Revolutionary Literature = Contraband".

Part III: Control of the Dangerous Classes
The complex organization of punitive state control formally commences with the processes of surveillance, designation, arrest, and criminalization. In this selection of essays, prisoners address the growth and development of the crime-control industry, and identify the marginalized as its preferred targets/designated criminals. In doing so, they provide ample evidence of the health of its entrenched biases and discriminations. Jon Marc Taylor analyzes "The Resurrection of the 'Dangerous Classes'", a product of the shift from social welfare to punitive criminal justice state policy as an industrialized crime-control response to the threats to capitalist social order posed by a growing surplus labour group composed of the marginalized and disenfranchised. Paul Wright casts "three strikes" legislation as producing "fast-tracked" transformation of the marginalized petty criminal into a lifetime carceral commodity with complete disregard for such legal niceties as proportionality between the crime and its punishment. In "Slaves of the State", Wright portrays the prison-industrial complex's growing interest in the utilization of these carceral commodities as an organized industrial workforce producing Third World-style products (e.g., textiles) at sweatshop prices.

   The importance of race, class, and gender to the actual workings of criminal justice is borne out in the composition of prison populations, where the poor and people of colour are significantly overrepresented. Juan Rivera and James Morse discuss possible collective responses to the overrepresentation of Afro-Americans and Hispanics in New York State's prisons. They both highlight the need to break the current cycle in which the carceral commodity is released onto the mean streets of specific disorganized inner city areas and later, lacking opportunity or possibility, are recycled back to the prison (see also Currie, 1993, 1998). The prisoner organized and operated "non traditional community specific educational program" Rivera (Part III and 1995) presents is directed at arming these minority community prisoners through analyzing and relocating the prison, their communities, and therefore *themselves* and their relationships (roles and responsibilities) to them. While Morse appreciates prisoners' use of education as a means of understanding, resisting, and overcoming institutionalized racial discrimination through criminalization, he argues that the solution cannot be found within the carceral. Rather, solutions must be achieved through social and economic policy that overturns racial segregation and discrimination, and by re-establishing community within the prisoner-specific enclaves from which most of the recycled carceral commodities are drawn.

In "Corrections Is a Male Enterprise" Jo-Ann Mayhew argues that imprisonment is a patriarchal response that is inappropriate for women. Mayhew describes her own initial disorientation and adjustment to carceral control and its relationship to her traumatizing experiences as representative of many women's encounter with incarceration. Melissa Stewart explores this theme further in her discussion of the *invisible minority* of women at Kingston Prison for Women who have previously suffered serious emotional, sexual, and physical abuse. Mayhew and Stewart understand the prison response as denying and exacerbating these problems, as evidenced in the suicides and self-destructive behaviour of many women prisoners. Many of these women are Aboriginal, for whom imprisonment produces even greater cultural dislocation. Ms. Cree reflects on the result as "Entrenched Social Catastrophe".

Steven King Ainsworth discusses class and race as they relate to his analysis of judicial homicide and human rights, arguing that social and economic factors are most instrumental in who is charged and who is convicted of a capital offence.

The stigmatization of the criminalization process extends from prisoners to their families and relations. In their dealings with police and correctional authorities, family and friends are often treated with distaste and suspicion. It is in this relationship that we can see the conjunction of class, race, and gender combining to affirm official definitions/stereotypes as to their shared status as members of the "dangerous classes". The struggles of prisoners and their families to maintain relationships and a sense of connectedness inside and outside the walls is addressed by Amy Friedman, and by an Irish republican prisoner's wife whose relationship to the prison is also expressed as resistance.

Part IV: In the Hands of the State
As editors of the *JPP*, we are accustomed to receiving long letters/short essays from people who have been criminalized and incarcerated for the first time. They cannot believe what is going on around them and what is actually happening to them. Hoping not to sound too jaded, we thank them for submitting their manuscripts and try to explain that what they are encountering is "par for the course" and "old hat" to our contributors and readership. However, such initial responses to incarceration are widely shared by prisoners and highly indicative of the carceral experience. In a keen update of traditional prison "kidding on the square", Seth Ferranti's "The American Dream: Free Enterprise" describes his sense of powerlessness, awe, and amazement at finding himself in the hands of the state.

Prison conditions vary according to time and place, but a relative constant is the disorder created by overcrowding. The first U.S.A. prison model, the Quaker "East Pennsylvania" system, broke down because of its inability to deal with the rapid increase in prisoners in the late eighteenth century and eventually was displaced in the United States and Canada by the competing "Auburn" (New York) congregate labour prison model. The rapid worldwide expansion of prison populations in the past two decades is exemplified in the frenzied prison construction and overcrowding of existing prison facilities throughout the U.S.A. The rate of expansion of the prison population in the 1990s outstripped the prison bureaucracies' ability to manage their prison systems and facilities. Victor Hassine describes the "loss of control and organizational disorder" produced by chronic overcrowding and underfunding from the perspective of the prisoner, whom he portrays as a passenger on a runaway train. In the process of coming to terms with these unstable and disorienting surroundings, the prisoner has to also deal with the imposition of the stigmatized and marginalized status of criminal and convict.

Huckelbury's general discussion of the impact of the negative transformation into the convict social identity provides a basis for further consideration of the debased status of prisoners. Little Rock Reed extends the analysis of prisoners' social status to prison rehabilitation programs such as Alcoholics Anonymous and Narcotics Anonymous. According to Reed, these "programs" serve to legitimate the discreditation of the Native

American prisoners' social identity through the imposition of European cultural norms and values. Stephen Reid, in "A Clockwork Grey", explores his recent reacquaintance with being risk assessed and having his thoughts and personality probed. In his Kafkaesque post-rehabilitation prison, the struggle is over the power-knowledge to define the prisoners and assess their worth and destination as carceral commodities. Gerald Niles, in "A Decade of Diesel Therapy in the Floriduh Gulag", reminds us of the raw conditions and punitive regime of many prisons in the United States. In the words of the Auburn, New York, penitentiary's first agent (warden), Gresham Powers, "Reformation by horror, constant hard labour, and the breaking of the spirit, was the Auburn method" (quoted in Lewis, [1922] 1967:93). Despite a comic Theroux-style narrative logging his prison travels, Niles elicits our understanding of the prisoners' lost sense of control and self-determination, and the anxiety of the transported who can only fear the future.

For those serving extremely lengthy and natural life sentences, the spectre of aging, deteriorating, and dying in prison generates anxiety, a heightened sense of the loss of control over one's life, and a resultant fatalism or hopelessness. As Victor Hassine portrays in "Monochromes from over a Prison's Edge", the constant and unrelenting stress of prison life accelerates normal physical and mental deterioration. Prisoners who have lost or are losing their minds are part of the everyday sounds, images, oral history, and stories of prison life, and they serve as a constant reminder of the dominating and threatening power of prison and the powerlessness of the prisoner.

Women in Prison

Working together on *TightWire* (1986–88)[5], Jo-Ann Mayhew and Gayle Horii transformed the framing of the magazine's content by feminizing its focus and discourse. They exposed this period in the history of Kingston P4W as characterized by mutilations, self-destruction and suicide, prison disturbances, and an institutional reliance on solitary confinement. A connecting theme of these three articles by women prisoners is the impact of prison deaths and suicides, and their desire to intervene and stop the pain. Melissa Stewart and P. Dunford discuss the extent of the problem in Canadian women's prison facilities and argue for innovative responses to address the particular needs relevant to the profile of past abuse and marginalization that characterized much of the prison population at P4W. Rather than inappropriate punitive patriarchal approaches such as segregating suicidal prisoners, they argue for suicide lifelines and non-institutional counselling available twenty-four hours a day. Mayhew shares the sadness and anger created by the futile and demeaning deaths of friends. In their words we feel their sense of helplessness and readily understand the traumatic impact these deaths and related events had upon the women prisoners at P4W. An American prisoner, Dawnya Ferdinandsen, exposes another needless death in "One Prison, One Death, One Mass Coverup", emphasizing that in the hands of the state, one's life is in peril.

Marionization

Whether justified by traditional penal rationales such as the safety of society, risk management, institutional control, or by modern control adaptations like rehabilitation and behaviour modification, the full powers of the coercive arm of the state are most evident in the regimes of lock-down prisons of the Marion type (*JPP*, 1993, 4:2; Churchill and Van der Wall, eds., 1992). The extent of the panoptic control and Skinnerian processes of behaviour modification that can be imposed upon prisoners is unlimited. With total control and relatively unlimited resources, the state's "administrators of pain" are constrained only by their consciences and there is little evidence to suggest that this is sufficient (see, for example, Jackson, 1983:72–83). As Christie (1999) argues, the new industrial-style management, with its rationalized and technologized administrative control processes, transforms the delivery of pain into a dehumanized business enterprise in which the prisoner is the commodity. Eddie Griffin, in "Breaking Men's Minds: Behaviour Control and Human Experimentation at the Federal Prison in Marion, Illinois", historically grounds the Marion model within the post-Korean War experimental brainwashing program and methodology of Dr. Edgar H. Schein. The willful and focused psychological attacks endured under this regime is also addressed by another former Marion prisoner, Ronald Del Raine. He provides an Orwellian analysis of the purposeful use of Marion's Long-Term Control Unit as a means of isolating and destroying prisoners who resist the transforming power of the prison through their intellectual, political, and leadership activities.

The parameters of coercive carceral power are further explored in Susan Rosenburg's report on political prisoners being "buried alive" in the women's high-security unit at Lexington, Kentucky. Their isolation accomplishes the dual purpose of silencing their voices and punishing their dissent. John H.

Morris III attests to the proliferation of Marion-style behaviour-modification regimes in his descriptive analysis of the then newly opened and technologically superior Security Housing Unit at the maximum-security prison at Pelican Bay, California. The prison authorities' power to define prisoners as criminal incorrigibles, "the most dangerous of the dangerous", and on this basis subject them to destructive isolation and coercive psychological deprivation "management", is undeniable and irresistible. The threat of long-term isolation is a *constant* in the lives of prison writers.

Capital Punishment

   Like the public spectacles of terror in the age of the European aristocracy (Foucault, 1977), judicial homicide displays the extent of the state's power and its monopoly on the use of extreme violence. The United States of America is the only Western democratic society that retains and utilizes capital punishment. Despite the massive evidence refuting its deterrent capabilities and outlining the inequities of class, race, and circumstance that influence its use, and the myriad of wrongful convictions interspersed through the files, since the reinstatement of capital punishment in 1977, more than 500 state executions have taken place. How does a prisoner relate to such a fate?

   Writing from death row in San Quentin, California, Steven King Ainsworth considers the unfathomable question of whether or not death row prisoners should have a choice in their method of execution; this is an unfathomable decision for the person forced to choose the method of their own execution. Johnny Byrd chronicles his thirty-five hours in the death house at Lucasville, Ohio, and his last-hour reprieve. The spirit of solidarity with his fellow prisoners and his concern to ease the pain of his family and relations shine through as a testament to the human spirit. In "A Commemorative Celebration in Honour of Ronald Keith Allridge" James V. Allridge III, writing from death row Ellis Unit at Huntsville, Texas, reflects on the execution of his brother Ronald the past summer and how his refusal to go quietly has encouraged James to continue the fight for his own life. Allridge III recognizes the pain and needs of crime victims and their families, but also recognizes the humanity of those awaiting sentence and the pain of their families and relations.

   State penal institutions possess an awesome power over their captives and a willingness to demand and coerce compliance to their dictates. The traditional themes of race, gender, close confinement, prison brutality, and death addressed by the writers in this section are framed by the 1990s' context of the emerging prison-industrial complex and its managerial drift toward the industrialization of the delivery of pain (Christie, 1999).

Part V: Resistance Strategies for Survival

The dominance of the prison is sustained through controlled routines, numbing boredom, relative deprivation, and violence, primarily state-managed violence. Surviving the prison demands that you understand where you are and what is happening to you; that you resist the changes in self and self-identity forced upon you by carceral life, and avoid falling casualty to the impending and often predictable violence of prisoners and staff. The management of violence by prison authorities as both a security problem and an opportunity to destabilize prisoners and the prison population is exemplified in the essays in this section.

These essays address prisoners' collective struggles against the oppression and violence of the prison. John Perotti describes the overcrowded, deplorable conditions and institutional violence that led to a full-blown riot at Lucasville, Ohio, in 1993, and analyzes the ways in which the riot could have been avoided. As a result of his support for prisoners' rights and their struggles at Lucasville, ten years later, John remains caged in a high-security isolation unit. Experienced long-term prisoners understand the futility of anti-institutional violence and, wherever possible, try to avoid the prison's long-term repressive response to it. The growing disorder and instability of the maximum-security Indiana State Reformatory and the open combat between prisoner and guard gangs that characterized the facility in 1991 provide the context for Jon Marc Taylor's "The Unity Walk". In his essay he analyzes prisoners' attempts to transform a situation that is ripening toward rebellion into a peaceful and socially responsible demonstration of prisoners' grievances and solidarity. In Taylor's account, the role and calming influence of older convicts (many of whom had educated themselves in prison) created the consensus needed to produce a responsible and non-violent response to increasing repression. The institutional response to their efforts — defining the older, moderate prisoners trying to cool out the situation as "criminal predators" and subsequently segregating and isolating them — suggests that institutional authorities have an interest in maintaining a threatening and violent prison atmosphere.

The universality of the immutable power-repression relationships of the prison (Breytenbach, 1984:339) is also attested to in subsequent articles that address collective strategies employed to resist the violent domination of the prison. Despite differences in perspective and location (Canada, Northern Ireland, United States), the experiences and responses are remarkably similar.

In presenting the history of the Millhaven, Ontario, prisoners' initiative, Prison Justice Day (August 10), Gaucher chronicles the development of this "nonviolent response to prison repression" as played out through the worse decade (1970s) of prison violence and disturbances in Canadian penal history. The violent riot at Kingston Penitentiary (Ontario) in April 1971 led to the premature opening of the new supermaximum penitentiary at Millhaven later that year. From the violent post-riot reprisals visited upon the first prisoners transferred into its special handling unit (SHU) (Swackhammer, 1973), a reign of terror characterized its operation (Culhane, 1979; McNeil and Vance, 1978; MacGuigan, 1977). Like the organization of "Unity Walk" in Indiana fifteen years later, older long-term convicts tried to construct a way of resisting institutionally instigated violence while still drawing attention to their serious grievances. In 1975, prisoners at Millhaven organized a memorial day commemorating those who have died in custody, and held it on the year anniversary of Eddie Nalon's death in the SHU. It succeeded in drawing public attention to prisoners' grievances and exposing the conditions at Millhaven. With the outside support and publicity provided by social justice critics, especially Claire Culhane, within five years, Prison Justice Day was observed in virtually all Canadian penitentiaries.

Robert Brydon describes his experience of a memorial gathering at Stony Mountain penitentiary (Manitoba) in 1988, the tenth year of Prison Justice Day observances. Mary McArdle, in "Remembering Women in the Struggle", reports on an Irish Republican celebration of Prisoner Day and its memorial for women who had given their lives to "the struggle". Ned Flynn, in "Birth of the Blanket Protest" provides a history of this internationally renowned Fenian strategy. In the construction of organized convict protest and resistance, some form of education generally plays a part. Jacqueline Dana and Seán McMonagle discuss the creation in the H-Blocks of Long Kesh of "a system of self-education where the ideas of a revolutionary movement can be developed, tested through discussion and passed on to others within the movement" (p. 415). These articles on Northern Ireland attest to the universality of institutional repression and prisoners' organized resistance to it. Danny Homer, in "Sweet Grass in the Iron House", reiterates these themes in his discussion of Aboriginal prisoners' struggles to rediscover their culture and its spirituality as a means of restoring their sense of self-identity, self-understanding, and inner peace.

Part VI: Talking Back:
Counter-inscribing the Prison-Industrial Complex
This section features the critical deconstructions of the criminal "just-us" system and its legitimating issues and discourses by five major contributors to the *JPP*.

A driving force behind the increasingly punitive approach to social problems in the United States and Canada has been the political organization of the crime victims' lobby (Elias, 1993; Gaucher and Elliott, 2001; Roach, 1999). Paul Wright, in "Victims' Rights as a Stalkinghorse for State Repression", analyzes the designation "crime victim" as selectively applied to those cases and victims that reinforce right-wing punitive justice ideology. In relocating the discourse on victimization, Wright identifies and distinguishes the dominant ideological utilization of the "victim" designation, and extends the parameters of this concept to include violent victimization by the state and victimization of the underclass by distributive injustice. Victimization of the marginalized and disenfranchised by the state is of particular significance for the incarcerated and their families. The crime victim lobby's attack on prisoners' human rights as reducing the rights of crime victims is analyzed by Charles Huckelbury in "Victims' Rights: The Fallacy of the Zero-Sum Solution". Huckelbury maintains that the civil and human rights of both parties are guaranteed by the American constitution and are not in conflict. Dan Cahill explores the relationship of prisoners' victimizing criminal activity and their subsequent victimization by the state. Arguing that overly punitive responses of the state are counter-productive, Cahill suggests mediation and restitution as alternatives that will reduce the brutalizing effect of imprisonment and the subsequent cycles of recidivism that result. These authors all deconstruct the major narratives of this issue as crude political discourse that both legitimates and masks the inequities of the criminal "just-us" system.

The elite of the prison-industrial complex in the U.S.A. are well represented in the American Correctional Association (ACA) whose "code of ethics" requires members "to respect and protect the civil rights of all clients". In

"The American Correctional Association: A Conspiracy of Silence", Reed and Denisovich attack "the fraudulent" and "profitable" process of accreditation of prison institutions provided by the ACA. The accreditation of the penitentiary at Lucasville, Ohio, shortly before a major riot in that institution (see Perotti, Part V) forms the backdrop for their analysis. The authors explore the connecting lines of interest of the ACA executive and locate them as major players in the prison industrial complex in the U.S.A. They note that their careers and their businesses are advanced by this industrial association. Four years later, Dan Cahill et al., also writing from Ohio, update and advance this analysis in "The ACA Accreditation Fraud". The authors monitored the October 5–7, 1998, ACA accreditation audit of an Ohio prison (Orient) and logged its inadequacies. Their investigations led them to conclude that the accreditation "was predetermined months before this audit", and that "This was not hard to figure out since the DORC (Department of Rehabilitation and Corrections) director is also the ACA president" (p. 473).

The anthology ends with counter-inscriptions of issues that are highly illustrative and characteristic of the dominant criminal justice politics and public discourse of the 1990s in North America. Though the issues discussed are located in the U.S.A., cuts in educational opportunities (Glaremin, 1993:32), moral panics over youth crime, and citizens dying at the hands of out-of-control, militarized police forces (Pedicelli, 1998) all played a part of criminal justice discourse in Canada and internationally during this decade (I.R. Taylor, 1999; Weiss and South, 1998).

Jon Marc Taylor, who in the 1990s established himself as an authority on prison education issues in the U.S.A.[6], analyzes the passage of legislation eliminating Pell Grant support for prisoners' pursuit of higher education, and warns of the ramifications for prisoners and society. Taylor counters the rationales that justified these cuts by establishing the extent of educational needs among prisoners, and the past success and future promise indicated by academic research that has assessed the effects of college education on post-release reintegration. In opposing these misguided and counter-productive cuts, he reveals the mean-spirited mindset of those on the American right who advocate the "get tough on crime" ideology that dominated the decade.

In a subsequent essay, "Where Have All the Superpredators Gone?" Taylor deconstructs the decade-long moral panic over youth crime. In his analysis of the pronouncements of the "foreboding prognosticators", the "prolifically vocal triumvirate of the 'lock 'em up and throw away the key' school of criminology" (professors J.A. Fox, J.Q. Wilson, and J.J. Dilulio), he notes that the "impending tidal wave of dangerous, violent *superpredators* terrorizing an unprepared nation", which was predicted in 1994, had failed the test of time. Fox defined this addition to the "dangerous classes" as "the young and the ruthless". Taylor notes that though the evidence indicates a steady decrease in youth involvement in violent crime since 1993, the moral panic still served to justify increasingly repressive legislation, higher rates of transfers of youth to adult court, and higher rates of imprisonment. Similar scenarios have also recently been played out in Britain (see I.R. Taylor, 1999:ch. 3), Canada, and France. The victims, of course, are the youth caught in the expanding web of the crime-control industry. Taylor's example also illustrates that moral panics constructed to forward the repressive political agendas of the punitive right continue to have serious impacts on public discourse and legislation, regardless of how groundless the fears generated may be (see also Cohen and Taylor 1972; Gaucher and Elliott, 2001; Hall et al., 1978).

The gunning down of a peaceful and unarmed West Indian immigrant by the police in New York City on February 4, 1999, is symbolic and representative of the "war on crime" mentality that flourished throughout the decade. Huckelbury, in "Life and Death in America: The Killing of Amadou Diallo", provides his own dire vision of the end results of the current trend toward the militarization of police forces. This case illustrates that the conjunction of institutionalized racism/classism and militarized forms of civil policing inevitability leads to such tragic deaths. As poignantly elaborated by Al-Jamil (1993) in "who killed mcduffie", this is an old story and so the beat goes on!

The rapid expansion and intensification of the "master pattern" of carceral surveillance and control (Cohen, 1985) in the 1990s was legitimated by the type of criminal justice narratives deconstructed and counter-inscribed above and throughout this volume. Behind the moral camouflage of the ideology "liberty and justice for all", behind concerns for the rights of crime victims and the fears for the future of an "unprepared nation", lies the prison-industrial complex with its own agendas. From its heartland in the United States, the international growth and development of the prison-industrial complex escalated throughout the decade (Burton-Rose et al., 1998; Christie, 1999;

Parenti, 1999; I.R. Taylor, 1999; Weiss and South, 1998). The moral panic generated by the September 11, 2001, attacks in the U.S.A. is now being used to garner support for even greater reliance on punitive state control and less concern for human and civil rights throughout the world. This trend darkens the horizon of the future. Joe Miceli fantasises the *industrial profits* awaiting the entrepreneur who creates "Reality TV" featuring prison violence as the "hook". Certainly current penal conditions in the United States are ripe for such exploitation.

In editing and composing volumes of the *JPP*, there was always a desire to include more of the myriad of essays, commentary, letters, and personal "cases" prisoners sent us. As I look over the composition of this anthology, I feel bombarded by the interesting and relevant essays not included, which would enrich and elaborate this portrait of the "workings" of the prison-industrial complex over the past decade.

However, this anthology does provide a representative account of issues and concerns of prison writers in the 1990s. This "mixed composition" of prison philosophy, critical insight, and analysis is written from the heart. Stephen Reid notes that it takes "heart" to be a writer, to be able to bare your soul in public. For prisoners, this task is further burdened by their stigmatized status and public antipathy toward them (Huckelbury, Part IV). For writers born in prison, their initial "coming out" can be a major step toward reclaiming their humanity (Hassine; McMaster, Part II). The contributors to this volume exhibit their "heart" and their place in humanity by sharing their carceral experiences, unravelling their meaning, and relating them to the dominant narratives that mask the realities of criminal justice.

I thoroughly enjoyed the opportunity to reread the past issues of the *JPP* and to work with this selection of manuscripts. Producing and distributing the *JPP* has meant constant dealings with a wide variety of *recalcitrant prisonocrats,* taking on more work than we could manage and the squabbles that resulted, and, oh, those worrisome deadlines. Yet I always enjoyed receiving letters and manuscripts from prisoners, especially from those who became regular contributors and with whom I felt I had developed a friendship over the years of our correspondence. Many are contributors to this volume. They always amazed me with their keen awareness, the resilience of their spirits, and the willingness to engage a subject. Their energy served to motivate me!

They have also made two important contributions to my work as a professor of criminology that I would like to note. On the one hand, they have kept me up to date as to what is actually happening in prisons, especially in the U.S.A. In my "Response" to the first issue of the *JPP* (1988), I noted the fertile relationship between politicized academics and radicalized prisoners that existed in the 1960s and 1970s, and its influence upon the development of the new critical criminologies within universities. With special mention to Little Rock Reed, our contributors have kept me connected to the current realities of prison life and aware of vital issues as they arose, often long before (if ever) they surfaced in the mass media or were addressed in academic journals. As illustrated by the essays in this anthology, prisoners are front-line workers who encounter the problems first and whose expression of concern is often later taken up by academics and official bodies.

When first teaching criminology, I was struck by the barriers of mass media stereotype and imagery that shroud the subject matter I was trying to address. Especially problematic was the demonized portrait of the criminalized and incarcerated that dominated our discourse. No one was going to get too upset by the prison's torment of a violent child molester. I brought prisoners to my classes as guest lecturers and involved students with prisoners' groups, all in an attempt to rehumanize students' constructions of prisoners and dispel the distorting imagery they imposed upon them (Gaucher, 1986). From the onset, the *JPP* has more than served this purpose. Readers generally have responded with surprise at the quality of the writing and the intelligence of the analysis. Many are swayed by the poignancy of the words. Watching this connection take place has been rewarding.

B. Gaucher
September 30, 2002

NOTES

1. In light of the political, economic, and cultural domination of Canada by the U.S.A., the extent to which the Canadian state has maintained liberal criminal justice and penal policy is surprising. The Reform Party of Canada/Canadian Alliance, the most significant opposition in the Canadian Parliament throughout the 1990s, constantly focused upon crime and punishment, and used an assortment of tawdry issues to attack the welfare state. Their issues and arguments largely mirrored the worst of American control ideology of the period. This extends from demands to bring back

capital punishment to treating ten-year-old children as adult felons. They organized a "crime victims lobby", which spearheaded their demands for draconian laws, such as (the three strikes and the Son of Sam laws) without apparent awareness of prevailing international opinion or the dismal failure of these policy options in the U.S.A. (Gaucher and Elliott, 2001). While the governing Liberal Party of Canada leaned to the right in criminal justice policy debates and needlessly broadened sanctions through legislation (e.g., homicide sentences C.C. Sec. 745, youth justice), generally the Canadian state resisted the pressure to engage in the type of punitive carceral binge the crime-control industry was successfully promoting south of our borders and across our media screens.

Provincial governments, especially the governing Conservative Party in Ontario, tinkered with public opinion through showcase moves like elimination/reduction of parole and post-integration assistance, boot camps, and superjails. The latter conveniently located in Cabinet ministers' ridings. They relied upon "truth in sentencing" ideology to legitimize savaging the remnants of liberal penal policy in Ontario. They accomplished little else.

By the end of the decade, the shift to the right was most significant and apparent in public and official discourse on social welfare and criminal justice policy. The industrialization of crime control was apparent in "rationalized" arrest, court, and prison procedures (Christie, 1999). There was also the expansion and extension of the carceral into the community through technological surveillance, and the redefinition of "problematic urban populations" as "suitable cases for treatment" by the crime-control industry (e.g., the homeless, high school students, and public demonstrators). However, while prison populations grew moderately, crime rates decreased. The increases in the federal penitentiary population were largely the product of longer, often mandatory sentences and reduced parole opportunities. The most disastrous federal initiative was the opening of seven regional women's prisons. As expected, there are now more women prisoners, and virtually none of the problems associated with Kingston P4W have been addressed and solved.

In *Visions of Social Control*, Stan Cohen (1985) identified a "continuous and intensifying master pattern" of criminal justice control and surveillance that has developed over the past two centuries in Western societies. Canadian society moved firmly if cautiously down that road in the 1990s, barely distracted by the squeals of the "wheels of injustice" grinding their way forward (Posluns, 1990).

2. Professor Stephen Richards (University of Northern Kentucky) relates that "our *New School of Convict Criminology* effort began in 1987 over dinner with ex-con Professor Emeritus John Irwin (San Francisco State University)", Dr. Jim Austin, and Professor Chuck Terry (University of Michigan Flint). Professor Jeffery Ian Ross also helped to coordinate their efforts to claim a space for the experience-grounded perspective of convict criminologists in academic and public discourse. This has been accomplished primarily through their organization of workshops and presentations at international conferences such as the American Society of Criminology (November 1999, Toronto). See Richards and Ross, eds. (forthcoming 2002), *Convict Criminology*. For an Irish example, see McKeown (2001).

3. In the 1990s, CSC created a centralized, in-house entity, LifeLine, whose role is to provide services to life-term prisoners and to assist them in re-entry into society after

years of confinement. The "in-reach" workers have primarily been individuals now serving their life sentences in the community.

4. United States Prison Marion, in southern Illinois, was opened as a replacement for Alcatraz in 1963 as the highest federal maximum-security prison in the U.S.A. In 1983 it established a penal regime of "permanent lock-down"; an attempt to seize absolute physical and psychological control over prisoners. This was to be accomplished through virtual isolation of prisoners and their manipulation via sensory-deprivation techniques (see Part IV). The Marion regime has spread across the U.S.A. There are now more than forty supermaximum prisons in the U.S.A., most of which are modelled upon U.S.P. Marion and reproduce its excesses.

5. After a number of failed attempts to establish a penal press magazine (*The Voice Inside*, 1971; *Inside Looking Out*, 1972; see Gaucher, 1989), in 1973 the women of P4W created *TightWire,* an outside-directed bimonthly. Though publication was at times sporadic, *Tightwire* was published for eighteen consecutive years, finally expiring under the repression of the 1990s. *Tightwire* represented "the penal press of the past in terms of its consistency of policy, format and quality. It was the only Canadian publication of note which maintained ties to the International Penal Press network in the 1980s. It presents a consistently critical analysis of Canadian criminal justice and corrections" (Gaucher, 1988). The commentary, poetry, fiction, and artwork that graced its pages attest to the talents and commitment of its editors and contributors. When Jo-Ann Mayhew became editor in 1985, for the first time the content became informed and framed by a politicized feminist consciousness. Gayle Horii soon joined in its production and the magazine embarked on some of its most successful years of publication. It was during this period that the problems of federally imprisoned women were taken seriously by outside women's groups and NGOs, which eventually helped to make P4W a public issue. With the active support of Claire Culhane and associates, *Tightwire* played an important part in exposing the conditions at Kingston P4W.

6. J.M. Taylor has achieved a number of university undergraduate and graduate degrees during his long incarceration. His writing has been well received nationally in the U.S.A. and he has been awarded The Nation/I.F. Stone and Robert F. Kennedy journalism awards. The combination of his own experiences with pursuing post-secondary education possibilities in prisons in Indiana and Missouri, as well as his journalistic expertise, gave him a solid base from which to engage the national discourse on educational Pell Grant support for prisoners. His contributions to the debate were noted in federal and state political discourse, and led directly to his removal to a less hospitable and accessible prison. He is currently updating and revising the second edition of *Prisoners' Guerrilla Handbook to Correspondence Programs in the United States and Canada* (1999).

REFERENCES

Abu-Jamal, Mumia. 1995. *Live from Death Row*. New York: Avon.
————. 1997. *Death Blossoms: Reflections from a Prisoner of Conscience*. Farmington, PA: The Plough Publishing House.

Al-Jamil, Hakim. 1993. "who killed mcduffie (a definitive question)". *JPP* 4(2):115–118.

Arbour, Hon. Commissioner Louise. 1996. *Commission of Inquiry into Certain Events at the Prison for Women in Kingston*. Ottawa: Public Works and Government Services Canada.

Blackstock, Harvey. 1967. *Bitter Humour.* Toronto: Burns & MacEachern.

Breytenbach, Breyten. 1984. *The True Confessions of an Albino Terrorist*. London: Faber and Faber Ltd.

Burton-Rose, Daniel, Dan Pen, and Paul Wright, eds. 1998. *The Celling of America: An Inside Look at the U.S. Prison Industry*. Monroe, Maine: Common Courage Press.

Christie, Nils. 1993. *Crime Control as Industry*. London: Routledge.

————. 1999. *Crime Control as Industry*. Revised Edition. London: Routledge.

Churchill, Ward, and J. Van der Wall, eds. 1992. *Cages of Steel: The Politics of Imprisonment in the United States*. Washington, D.C.: Maisonneuve Press.

Cohen, Stanley. 1972. *Folk Devils and Moral Panics: The Creation of the Mods and Rockers*. London: McGibbon and Kee.

————. 1985. *Visions of Social Control*. Cambridge: Polity Press.

Cohen, Stanley, and Laurie Taylor. 1972. *Psychological Survival: The Experience of Long Term Imprisonment*. London: Oxford Press.

————. 1977. *Escape Attempts: The Theory and Practice of Resistance to Everyday Life*. Harmondsworth: Penguin.

Culhane, Claire. 1979. *Barred from Prison*. Vancouver, B.C.: Pulp Press.

————. 1985. *Still Barred from Prison: Social Injustice in Canada.* Montréal: Black Rose Books.

————. 1991. *No Longer Barred from Prison*. Montréal: Black Rose Books.

Currie, Elliott. 1993. *Reckoning: Drugs, Cities and the American Future*. New York: Hill & Wang.

————. 1998. *Crime and Punishment in America*. New York: Henry Holt & Co.

Davidson, Howard. 1988. "Prisoners on Prison Abolition". *JPP* 1(1):1–4.

————, ed. 1995. *Schooling in a Total Institution*. Connecticut: Bergan & Garvey.

Davies, Ioan. 1990. *Writers in Prison*. Toronto: Between the Lines.

Debs, Eugene. 1927. *Walls and Bars*. Chicago: C.H. Kerr in cooperation with Eugene V. Debs Foundation.

Downes, David. 2001. "The *macho* penal economy: mass incarceration in the United States — a European Perspective." In Garland, ed., 2001. 51–69.

Elias, R. 1993. *Victims Still: The Political Manipulation of Crime Victims*. Newbury Park: Sage.

Finateri, Lisa, and Viviane Saleh-Hanna. 2000. "International Conference on Penal Abolition: The Birth of ICOPA". In G. West and R. Morris, eds., *The Case for Penal Abolition*. Toronto: Canadian Scholars' Press.

Foucault, Michel. 1977. *Discipline and Punish: The Birth of the Prison*. New York: Pantheon.

Franklin, H. Bruce. 1978. *The Victim as Criminal and Artist*. New York: Oxford University Press.

————. 1998. *Prison Writing in 20th Century America*. New York: Penguin Books.

Garland, David., ed. 2001. *Mass Imprisonment: Social Causes and Consequences*. London: Sage Publications Ltd.

Gaucher, Robert. 1986. "Teaching Criminology: Crime News and Crime Fiction — Offsetting the Influence of the Mass Media". In H. Bianchi and R. Van Swaanigen, eds., *Abolitionism: Towards a Non-Repressive Approach to Crime*. Amsterdam: Free University Press.

———. 1988. "The Prisoner as Ethnographer: The Journal of Prisoners on Prisons". *JPP* 1(1):49–62.

———. 1989. "The Canadian Penal Press". *JPP* 2(1):3–24.

Gaucher, Robert, and Liz Elliott. 2001. "*Sister of Sam*: The Rise and Fall of Bill C-205/220". In *The Windsor Yearbook of Access to Justice*, vol. XIX.

Glaremin, Roy. 1993. "A New Act for Prisons and Parole". *JPP* 5(1):26–32.

Goffman, Erving. 1961. *Asylums: Essays on the Social Situation of Mental Patients and Other Inmates*. New York: Doubleday.

Hall, Stuart, John Clarke, Chas. Critcher, and Tony Jefferson. 1978. *Policing the Crisis: Mugging, the State and Law and Order*. London: Macmillan.

Harris, Michael. 2002. *Con Game*. Toronto: McClelland & Stewart.

Hassine, Victor. 1996. *Life Without Parole: Living in Prison Today*. Los Angeles: Roxbury Publishing.

———. 1999. *Life Without Parole: Living in Prison Today*, 2nd ed. Los Angeles: Roxbury Publishing.

Hulsman, Luk. 1985. "Critical Criminology and the Concept of Crime". *Contemporary Crisis*, No. 10. Netherlands: Nijhoff Dordrecht.

Jackson, Michael. 1983. *Prisoners of Isolation: Solitary Confinement in Canada*. Toronto: University of Toronto Press.

Kneen, Cathleen, and Michael Posluns. 1994. *Eating Bitterness: A Vision Beyond the Prison Walls — Poems and Essays of Art Solomon*. Toronto: NC Press.

Lewis, Orlando. [1922] 1967. *The Development of American Prison Customs 1776–1845*. New Jersey: Patterson Smith.

Lowe, Mick. 1992. *One Woman Army: The Life of Claire Culhane*. Toronto: Macmillan Canada.

MacGuigan, Hon. Mark. 1977. *Report to Parliament by the Sub Committee on the Penitentiary System in Canada*. Ottawa: Supply and Services.

McKeown, Laurence. 2001. *Out of Time: Irish Republican Prisoners Long Kesh 1972–2000*. Belfast: Beyond the Pale Publications.

McNeil, Gerard, and Sharon Vance. 1978. *Cruel and Unusual*. Toronto: Deneau & Greenberg.

Mathiesen, Thomas. 1974. *The Politics of Abolition: Essays in Political Action Theory*. Oxford: Martin Robertson.

Parenti, Christian. 1999. *Lockdown America: Police and Prisons in the Age of Crisis*. New York: Verso.

Pate, Kim. 1994. "CSC and the 2 Per Cent Solution: The P4W Inquiry". *JPP* 6(2):41–61.

Pedicelli, Gabriella. 1998. *When Police Kill: Police Use of Force in Montreal and Toronto*. Montreal: Vehicule Press.

Posluns, Michael, ed. 1990. *Songs for the People: Teachings on the Natural Way — Poems and Essays of Art Solomon*. Toronto: NC Press.

Reed, Little Rock. 1993. *The American Indian in the White Man's Prisons: A Collective Statement of Native American Prisoners*. Taos, NM: Uncompromising Books.

Richards, Stephen, and Jeffery Ian Ross, eds. Forthcoming 2002. *Convict Criminology.*

Rivera, Juan. 1995. "A Nontraditional Approach to Social and Criminal Justice". In Davidson, ed. 1995. *Schooling in a Total Institution*. Connecticut: Bergan & Garvey.

Roach, Kent. 1999. *Due Process and Victims' Rights*. Toronto: University of Toronto Press.

Swackhammer, J.W. 1973. *Report of the Commission into Certain Disturbances at Kingston Penitentiary During April 1971*. Ottawa: Queen's Printer.

Taylor, Ian R. 1999. *Crime in Context: A Critical Criminology of Market Societies*. Cambridge: Polity Press.

Taylor, Jon Marc. 1999. *Prisoners' Guerrilla Handbook to Correspondence Programs in the United States and Canada*. New Brunswick, ME: Auden Reed Press.

Weiss, Robert, and Nigel South, eds. 1998. *Comparing Prison Systems: Towards a Comparative and International Penology*. Amsterdam: Gordon Breach Publishers.

PART II

WRITING AS RESISTANCE

Inside Looking Out: Writers in Prison
Bob Gaucher

The cumulative wealth of prisoners' writing over the centuries constitutes a firmly established and highly influential body of work within western literary and intellectual traditions. Ioan Davies (1990) in *Writers in Prison*, argues that the prison has served as an important symbol and metaphor throughout the recorded (text) history of Western thought, and its material realities have formed the immediate context and crucible for an influential and celebrated group of intellectuals and writers. Indeed, Davies (1990:3) states that:

> Much of the influential literature of Judeo-Christian civilization was composed under conditions of incarceration or involuntary exile. Indeed the Bible itself is a product of both prison and exile; and the Platonic dialogues, notably the *Crito*, the *Apology*, and the *Phaedo*, are centered around the trial, imprisonment and execution of Socrates. It is arguable that it is impossible to understand Occidental thought without recognizing the central significance of prison and banishment in its theoretical and literary composition.

In his broadly comprehensive and theorized account of writing from prison, Davies (1990:3) directs us to go beyond the mere recognition of the literary and intellectual significance of "writing that owes something to imprisonment" and its classification. He directs us toward theoretical issues that help us to understand "the forms that prison writing takes, its content and how the prison experience might be read". To do so we must locate these texts within their age; the political, social/cultural and intellectual context of their production, and within the confining carceral culture that frames their production and against and through which they are written. This is an analysis of prison produced text; what it carries, how its ideas have been universalized, its penetration of and integration into Western intellectual/ political and literary/cultural life, past and present. Prison culture is still characterized by an oral tradition of songs and ballads, storytelling and "dead time" conversations. The continuous written narrative (text) Davies refers to as traversing the ages, is largely provided by incarcerated intellectuals and prisoners of conscience. It is this group of writers and their text which he relies upon to ground his analyses so as to "understand how the incarcerated imagination has become part of Western ideas and literature"

(1990:7). It is within the text of the incarcerated intellectual, those he refers to as writing from the margins of both their society and the prison, that he discovers the universals of the carceral experience. While recognizing the importance of the "common criminal" prison writer "who operates directly out of a prison culture" (1990:4), as exemplified by Villon and Genet, Davies' primary interest in their work is as an entry to reading the prison itself.

Davies (1990:4) discovered that on one level "the writings merge in a collectivity of epic and self critical ur-epic where oral stories and songs become part of a folk-history of incarceration, exile and slavery".[1] For Davies, the writer's relationship to the prison, margin versus centre, informs the perspective of the text/writing and the carceral experience it assesses and portrays.

> We might argue that the nearer the writer is to the ur-epic, the less his story will be about himself and the more it will be about the folk-memory of the collectivity, while the further he is from the collectivity, the more he will see the prison as alien and the story as his own or related to another (external) collectivity. (1990:15)

The particular conjunctures and dialectical relationships of the "incarcerated imagination", the prison, and the society that imprisons, form the foundations of Davies' focus and analysis. The writing and expression that flows more directly from the centre of carceral culture has also produced a notable legacy. H. Bruce Franklin (1978, 1989, 1998), has provided the most thoroughly documented and scholarly analysis of the writings of common criminals, though his focus has been exclusively on the USA. Franklin largely denies the scope of the collective unity and universals of the occidental prison tradition that Davies proclaims, as applied to the particular history of prison writing in the USA. The specificity of the history, content and intention of American prison writing he discovered leads him to reject Davies' (1990:8) more universal "community of prisoners — across the centuries". Franklin (1998:1) argues: "But unlike the works of these individuals, modern American prison writings constitute a coherent body of literature with a unique historical significance and cultural influence".

Franklin (1978, 1989) identifies two formative traditions, the Afro-American and Euro-American, that have (dialectically) produced the extraordinary volume and variety of prison writing that is particular to the USA. In his first major work, *The Victim as Criminal and Artist* (1978), Franklin exposes the carceral roots of the broad and significant cultural contributions to US society of Afro-Americans. He identifies an oral tradition composed of the songs and poetry of slavery and penal servitude that provides an historical location for the current "great internment" and the contemporary literary expression of Afro-American prison writers. Within this unique carceral history, Afro-Americans share the circumstances, understandings and community of a people.

It is within this context that Franklin identifies the collective consciousness of Afro-Americans which frames and gives meaning and significance to their past and current penal experiences. Like Davies' concept of the ur-epic, Franklin identifies and explores an Afro-American epic that traverses the centuries. In distinguishing this tradition Franklin (1978; 1989) largely denies the "collective folk memory" or ur-epic of Euro-American writers, arguing that their work is characterized by an individualistic perspective, experience and style (i.e., autobiographical narrative). From his location of the emergence of autobiographical narratives of criminals' lives in the 16th and 17th centuries, Franklin defines this basic form of the genre as intuitive to the era of mercantile capitalism and ensuing colonialism. The singular voice of the alienated individual, acting against his people and his society. For Franklin, it is this long and often dominant form, moving through the picaresque/carnivalesque[2] to contemporary "convict fantasy fiction", that best characterizes Euro-American prison writing.

Franklin (1978, 1998) notes another style within the latter tradition, that of politically conscious prisoners, ranging from late 19th century anarchists to the socialists and Marxists of the first decades of the 20th century.[3] He (1989:133–38, 244) also identifies a "white convict" perspective emerging at the turn of the century, that adapts and reorders the dominant biographical narrative form, focussing its narratives on and against the prison and its containing society.

Franklin (1978, 1989, 1998) argues that the oral and written expression produced over the centuries from within the American gulag constitutes a highly significant (culturally) body of literature. This literature is composed of the dominant and more culturally significant collectively represented works of Afro-American prisoners and the less important, largely individualistically framed expression of Euro-American prisoners.

Franklin's focus upon literature and especially that written by "common criminals", directs him to pay scant attention to the significance of the work of Euro-American intellectuals and political prisoners, social reformers and prisoners of conscience, who play an important part in this tradition and in the framing and understanding of the prison in the containing societies. Their significant contribution to the development and definition of the collective ur-epic of the Euro-convict tradition is lost in his analysis.

The tight focus on America[4] also blinkers Franklin's analysis and distracts him from considering the unity of prison/carceral experience that interconnects the colonial empires of Britain, France and Spain. This includes the experience of transportation and penal servitude, stretching from Van Diem's Land and Devil's Island, to Canada and the USA. The domination of colonial empire, with its movements of peoples and ideas provided the context for narratives addressing this shared experience of incarceration and penal servitude. This lacuna serves to substantiate his argument concerning the lack of collective identity of Euro-American convicts as exemplified in their written text.

Similarly, though Franklin (1989:133–138) acknowledges the emergence at the end of the 19th century of a "convict" perspective (i.e., the self-identified subclass-prisoner) he does not see in it the collective ur-epic theorized by Davies (1990). It was in the 19th century that the prison became the dominant form of punishment, and therefore, it is not surprising that a prison centred culture had emerged by its end. This collective memory and consciousness embodied in the ur-epic is focussed in and on the prison, arising from the very centre of prison cultural life and custom. Much the same place where Franklin finds a wealth of song and literature produced by common criminals.

Franklin's location of the American prison as one link in an historical chain of changing forms of oppression of the Afro-American people casts the prison and prisoner in a different relationship. Here the centrality of the prison is first submerged in the continuous history of Afro-American penal repression, and secondly, the prison itself becomes a metaphor for the containing society. Now the prison is represented as "maximum security" confinement, and the containing American society within which Blacks were "conditioned to accept the inevitability of prison" (Jackson, 1972:9), minimum security. For Rubin Carter (1974:210) the USA was "a penitentiary with a flag". This framing of the prison seems to dissolve the prison walls. However, though Davies (1990) may be charged with stretching his — unity of thought shared over the centuries merging into the ur-epic of prison life — thesis, there can be little doubt that with the advent of the prison as the dominant form of discipline and punishment in the 19th century, a shared convict perspective developed. This was the great research discovery of sociologist Donald Clemmer. His study of the hidden world of the penitentiary, published as *The Prison Community* (1938) showed that behind the prison walls there existed a prisoner culture played out through primary group affiliation and informal institutional relationships. Later, Cressey (1961) and Goffinan (1961, 1964) refashion this analysis of "total institutions" arguing for the determinant role of institutional structures and organizational processes in the creation and maintenance of institutional culture and the "inmate" that inhabits it.

The specificity of the carceral experience is such one must take into account the actual prison conditions under which the expression was produced. Through much of the history of the penal oppression of Afro-Americans, the dominant carceral form (slavery, penal servitude) generated a sense of collective experience. The experience of most other convicts between 1850–1950 was constrained by prison regimes based upon close individual confinement and silent systems.[5] This produced a different response, one more directly focussed upon the carceral institution itself, as experienced through the forced solitude of the prison. With the reformation of penal custom in the late 19th century[6] and the liberating effects this had upon the prisoner and prison life, the convict perspective and prison ur-epic more clearly emerged.

Davies and Franklin provide frameworks for locating and assessing the significance of prison writing and literature. In doing so they illuminate the interconnections and specificities of societal context, the prisoner, and the prison. South African political prisoner, Breyten Breytenbach noted:

> When you are interested in prison accounts as a genre you will soon see that prisons are pretty much the same the world over. It is rather the peculiar relationship of power–repression which seems immutable, wherever you may hide. (1984:339)

*****

The relationship of a society to its penal institutions is also evident generally, in the attention given to prison writing, and specifically, in the popularity of a particular style of the genre. For example, the new international order that arose in the aftermath of the second world war significantly changed the societal context of the production of prison writing. The cold war alignment and the developing strength of anti-colonial movements produced a new roster of internationally recognized dissident intellectuals and writers imprisoned for their beliefs and work. The writing of Soviet block political prisoners and dissidents such as Koestler, Solzhenitsyn, and Djilas were celebrated in the cold war hype of the west.[7] However, under the blanket of cold war anti-Soviet ideology and McCarthyism a different type of domestic prison writing was popularized in Western Europe and North America. There the work of "common criminals" such as Jean Genet (France), Frank Norman (England), Brendan Behan (Ireland),[8] Chester Himes, Nelson Algren, Carl Chessman (USA), and Frank Anderson (Canada) predominated.

This is also apparent in the 1950s celebration of the international penal press in the USA, Canada and to a lesser extent Britain and elsewhere. For example, Tom Runyon, a 1930s bank robber serving a life (homicide) sentence in Iowa State Penitentiary, was celebrated as the editor of *Presido*[9] and as a writer. His work and biography *In For Life* (1954) was lauded for its insights into the hidden world of the prison and convict, by major newspapers such as the *New York Times* and *Chicago Tribune*[10] and by established writers like Earle Stanley Gardner.[11] The newly created Canadian penal press (1950) also received public support, and was a solid player in the international network of penal press editors and writers. Its late start meant that it was not until the 1960s that contributors like Glenn Hjalmarson (1961) with *Just Call Us Bandits* and Harvey Blackstock (1967) with *Bitter Humour* emerged as writers with a broader public audience.[12]

The first penal press magazines in Britain were produced at Feltham Borstal in 1935. The *South House Review* (later the *Scrutineer*) proclaimed that it would be the "eyes and ears of Borstal" (Maxwell, 1956). By 1960 there were 30–35 publications being produced in British prisons (Brandseth, 1972:81). The first outside directed/distributed magazine was *New Venture* (1956 or 1957) from HMP Wakefield. Like most of these publications, *New Venture* started as a prison wallsheet, which had become widespread in the 1930s. A few months later, Peter Baker (a former Conservative Member of Parliament) transformed the wallsheet at HMP Leyhill into a monthly, *New Dawn*, which gained national prominence in 1957 (Baker, 1961:181–84). The second issue of *New Dawn* included a penal exchange with *New Venture* (Wakefield) and its editor, Cecil Bertram, the convicted communist spy.

Scientist "convict" Klaus Fuchs contributed a science column (Baker, 1961:171–85). These high profile contributors provided a significant impetus for the considerable public interest in prison writing and the prison in the U.K. in the 1950s and 1960s.[13]

In the context of the emerging radical politics of the 1960s, the institutional censorship that dominated prison writing and the penal press in the past, increased.[14] The resulting conflicts led to the demise of the international penal press network and many of its outstanding publications. Within this context a new type of politically and socially conscious prison writing arose, especially and most significantly in the USA. Stan Cohen (1972:447) notes the significance of this change.

> Since the end of the fifties. ... A steady stream of new political prisoners began moving into the American jails: civil rights workers, antiwar militants, black liberation activists and articulate middle class offenders, such as students and those on drug charges. And above all, the boundary line — never very clear — between political or non-political crime, started blurring. A generation of American prisoners, especially blacks who form the majority of the prison population in many States, began thinking of themselves in ideological terms.

The reformulation of carceral identity and therefore the meaning of its prison location, as played out in the carnivalesque and comic of Genet and Norman, is revisited in this broader recasting of the 1960s. The alternative understanding of the being and identity of the "common criminal", taken for granted and celebrated by Genet and Norman,[15] is now extended to a political identity that consciously locates the convict and the prison within the constraints of imperialist ideology and practice.

In his analysis of contemporary prison writing, Franklin (1978; 1989) also comments on the new conjuncture of this period, which he later refers to as "The Movement and The Prison" (1998).

> There is no longer such a clear demarcation between the criminal prisoner–author and the law abiding citizen–reader. ...

> Now we have two overlapping groups of prison authors: the political activist thrust into prison, and the common criminal thrust into

> political activism. The distinction between the two groups tends to
> dissolve as the definition of crime, from both sides of the law,
> becomes increasingly political. (1978:242)

This process of relocation and redefinition of the convict and the prison
also occurred in Canada in the 1960s, especially amongst its over-represented
aboriginal minority.[16] In Britain, considerable agitation on prisoners' issues
took place on both sides of the prison wall (see Fitzgerald, 1977). The Irish
internment of the 1970s further established that at least in some instances
the demand for political status was undeniable.[17] The international penal
press network and its focus on penal custom and criminal justice issues
was also displaced by political solidarity and association with revolutionary,
anti-imperialist/anti-colonial struggles, nationally and internationally. The
analyses of the revolutionaries and intellectuals of these struggles, often
written from the solitary confines of the prison, confirmed and encouraged
the new temper of domestic rage and resistance that was growing outside
the prison walls.

This coming together is clearly illustrated in the lives and work of American
"common" prisoners such as Malcolm X, George Jackson and Sam Melville.
In Canada, aboriginal prisoners were involved with and informed by the
American Indian Movement from its formative stages as illustrated in the
organizing of prison Native Brotherhoods and Sisterhoods, their newsletters,
magazines and public pronouncements and their involvement in the
institutional tensions that swept through the Canadian penitentiary system in
the 1970s.

Within the prison writing genre a rich mix of perspectives and styles
mingled with the radical politics of resistance and rebellion that swept across
the West and throughout its colonial properties. In the USA, the Afro-American
collective understanding and broad location of the prisoner and the prison,
further extended by reference to international anti-colonial struggles, merged
with the perspectives and stylistic forms of the Euro-American tradition.[18]
In the prison writing of the 1960s and 1970s we see a coming together of
the traditional collective perspective of oppressed minorities (Afro-Americans,
Aboriginal Peoples), the Euro-American tradition of radical dissent and class
struggle, and the prison focussed convict (as a subclass) perspective. By
the 1960s the convict narrative with it focus on the prison had to some
extent already displaced the picaresque or carnivalesque style of the traditional
prison autobiographical narrative. It was this form which carried the new

literature into what Franklin (1998) has called the literary renaissance of American prison writing.

This coming together is exemplified in the initial appropriation of the autobiographical narrative by Malcolm X (1965), and subsequent use of this form by George Jackson (1970; 1972) and the New York Panther Twenty-One (1971) who transform it via the collective consciousness and sense of resistance and rebellion of a people. The writings of George Jackson exemplify the emerging understanding and collective spirit of resistance to racial and class oppression as played out in the realm of penal justice. Jackson carries the prison ur-epic tradition into the heart of this new account of the Amerikan gulag. Jackson's accounts address modern penal conditions: cell, isolation, repression and rebellion. In writing against and through the prison, he focuses his critique on prison culture and relationships, and in so doing reaffirms the prison ur-epic and prisoners' collective tradition of resistance and rebellion. Jackson reaffirms the universals of the carceral experience that drive prisoners. This is illustrated by the international interest and applaud his work received.

The volume, richness, and significance of prison writing during the 1960s and 1970s left an important legacy that continues to evolve in face of the changing penal conditions of the "great internment" of the past 15 years. The increase in prison populations across the West, especially in the USA[19] is also heightening public awareness and involvement, though often negatively. Censorship has increased at the institutional and societal levels: in the form of institutional restrictions on correspondence, and prohibitions on carrying on the "business" of being a writer (Franklin, 1998:14); and through national or state legislation aimed at seizing profits and therefore curtailing publication.[20] Franklin's work indicates that this trend in the USA can be traced back to attempts by the courts to muzzle imprisoned writers in the late 1960s.

> In fact, the judge who sentenced Reddy, like the judge who sentenced Imamu Amiri Baraka in 1968, explicitly cited his poetry as a reason to not lower bail. The judge claimed that the purpose of Reddy's poems was 'to mould people's minds to malicious ends'. This is literary criticism with a vengeance. (1989:243)

When the US Federal Regulation (Title 28: Section 540. 20b) constraining prison writers' relationships with the news media "was challenged in court by the *San Francisco Chronicle*, testimony revealed that it had been drafted in the 1970s specifically to ensure that federal prisoners with 'anti-establishment' views would not have access to the media" (Franklin, 1998: 15; ft19).

This trend in the USA towards censorship as part of the court sentence, and the definition of the writing, past or future, as part of the offence, has been graphically illustrated in the recent muzzling of Katherine Power and her family.[21] The attempt to pass (Son of Sam) Bill(s) C-205/C-220 in Canada (1996–1998) clearly established that the intentions of the bill's supporters was to prevent the criminalized and incarcerated from publishing by including such prohibitions within the sentence. In this instance, the precipitating moral panic and subsequent legislative response to it, was driven by the public and political involvement of the organized and punitively oriented crime victims lobby in Canada. During the considerations of this bill by the Canadian House of Commons, *the only type* of prison writing mentioned and considered by Members of Parliament and during testimony to the House Committee (supposedly) studying the matter, was "true crime" depictions of the "gory details" of "heinous criminal acts". The political utility of masking the real issues in this way was later revealed in the Canadian Senate Committee hearings, where a much broader consideration of the writing of the criminalized and incarcerated led to the rejection of the bill.[22] However, despite institutional and legislative constraints on the public availability of prison writing, the growth and development of the prison literary genre has continued worldwide.

The considerable volume of prison writing of the past thirty years is richly varied in form, style, content and intent. This wealth of writing ranges from poetry and fiction, through autobiography, ethnography, social and political analysis. Its significance has been affirmed by the growing body of academic analysis focussed upon it;[23] by "Writers in Residence" programs,[24] and creative writing classes in prison; by PEN, Koestler, and Prison Arts Foundation awards; by the continued and important role it plays in the work of political activists and their analysis,[25] and in its availability on information/ resource centre websites.[26]

Though the fringe press has been an outlet for prison writers and prisoners' causes throughout this century, especially the international anarchist ABC network, this relationship has grown and developed in the past twenty years. *Prison News Service* (1980–1996), a semi-monthly newspaper produced in Toronto by the ABC-Bulldozer Collective, had a distribution of over 10,000 copies per issue, many going "gratis" to American and Canadian prisoners. Its broad coverage of the politics of imprisonment and prisoners' accounts of the repressive actuality of criminal justice and carceral practices deems it an excellent representative of such publications.[27] Another important variety of fringe magazine, now well established, is written and edited by prisoners but produced and distributed by a group of outside supporters. *Prison Legal News* (1990–) has established itself as one of the most successful of this of this type (see Wright [Part II, this anthology]). Publications like *Prison Writing* (1992–99) in the UK, *Prison Life Magazine* (1994–1997) and the *Journal of Prisoners on Prisons* (1988–) illustrate the variety and development of this new form of prisoner publication.

In the current "radical politics" fringe press publication the strong ties between prisoners and outside political activists reestablished in the 1960s and 1970s is apparent. Their many magazines, newsletters, information bulletins and polemical tracts routinely feature the writing and art of prisoners.

*****

The absolute scope and volume of prison writing, past and present, demands some type of approach to its broad categorization. Cohen (1972:447) argues that wealth of writing emerging from US prisons by 1972 could be roughly categorized on the basis of the type of prisoner author: (1) prisoners entering the penal system for ideological offences, (2) prisoners who became politically minded in prison, (3) prisoners without political motivation. Davies (1990:4) places more emphasis upon the prison and whether or not the prisoner writes from the centre or margin of that culture and community. He alerts us to the need to understand the prison writer as more than participant observer, ethnographer, or one writing through the prison. For the prisoner is also a dialectical product and producer of the prison itself, ideologically and materially; for both the prison community and society. Therefore he categories prison writing (text) on the basis of its relationship to the ur-epic of carceral life and our desire to read the prison. He distinguishes: (1) work written by the long time criminal, (2) work written by the long time non-criminals (prisoners of conscience; and many convicted of homicide), (3) work written by short time criminals and non-criminals.

As previously noted, this sense of folk-memory and epic is also evident in Franklin's work, especially in his tracing of the carceral roots of Afro-American cultural (oral and written) expression. Franklin's categorization of contemporary prison literature, focuses upon the presence or absence of a political and collective consciousness which frames the work. He argues that the contemporary body of prison literature consists of works flowing from the collectivist Afro-American tradition and the individualistic Euro-American tradition, intertwining in one complex dialect (1989:262). Thus, this body of prison literature can be classified on the basis of: (1) prison writers who accept the collective Black definition of crime in America; (2) prison writers who see themselves primarily as victims of class oppression; (3) prison writers who, lacking a collective perspective, usually replace it with an "I did it to myself" framing of their account (1978:270).

These rough groupings of prison writers/writing allow us to give some order to the rich variety of contemporary work. They are representative of the specificities we might bring to the consideration of prisoners' accounts and their utility in other arenas of debate. From Franklin's (1989:xxiii-xxxiii) engagement in academic "cultural wars" to radical political action, the creative expression and analyses of prisoners serve as entry points and bridges to much broader philosophical, sociological, and political concerns and discourses.

In the past two decades prison populations have grown across the world (Christie, 1993; Weiss and South, 1998). In some jurisdictions, especially the USA, the rate of growth and expansion of prison populations and penal institutions has been astonishing. The prison is presently expanding into a world-wide gulag of "correctional facilities", refugee and internment compounds, prisoner of war and concentration camps. In light of the increasing utilization and centrality of the prison as a means of control and subjugation of targeted populations, the role of the writer in prison is of increasing importance. As the relations of power and repression shift so will the intent, form and content of the prison writing of the future. As a means of resistance and struggle, prisoners will continue "to map routes out of the prison" so as to expose and contest the injustices and repressions that characterize their prison and their society. In doing so they will continue the long tradition of contributing to the political, intellectual, social and cultural life of their society, and to the swirls of international discourse.

NOTES

1   Davies (1990:18) states: "By 'ur-epic' I mean the epic of the collective consciousness, not written but told. The prefix 'ur' is used because it comes from the beginning of human history".

2   In locating the roots of the tradition of "carnival" Davies (1990:10–12) notes its juxtaposition to the "solemnity of official culture" and its exteriority. I use "carnivalesque" to describe prison writing that focuses upon the prison and represents this exteriority, expressed as "laughter of all the people", "directed at all and everyone, including the carnival's participants"; "gay and triumphant, and at the same time mocking, deriding". Franklin (1989, 1998) applies the concept of the "picaresque" novel to the Euro-American tradition of "autobiographical narrative" too broadly. I rely upon its traditional usage as referring to the relating of the "adventures of rogues and villains"; often parodies of dominant social values and goals, told through mock confession or bravado success stories. With the development of forms and styles of prison writing these basic distinctions are problematized. For example, Franklin (1989) locates some contemporary fiction, such as the work of Edward Bunker (convict fantasy fiction) within the picaresque tradition.

3   Though noting their appearance over the centuries, Franklin does not consider the role and influence of the articulate, middle-class prisoner both within the prison and beyond the wall. For example, Dr. O.C. Withrow's *Shackling The Transgressor* (1933:3), written after spending two and a half years in "that horrible pit labeled K.P.", was a bombshell in Canadian society. It had a direct influence on public awareness and concern over prison conditions, and was an important influence on the creation of the Canadian Prison Association, a reform body whose initiatives led to the *Archambault Report* (1938) and subsequent major changes in prison regime and custom. See also Anderson (1997). Since the 1960s the influx of middle class drug users and occasional criminals has produced an abundance of what I call "you what?" accounts; most of which are lost in letters and or fringe publications. For an example, see Ferranti [Part IV, this anthology].

4   It is surprising Franklin largely ignores significant minorities such as First Nations, Hispanic, Canadian/French Canadian prisoner writers in America.

5   It is important to take into account the specificity of penal custom in different jurisdictions; for example the rural Southern U.S. States' reliance upon chain gangs and work camps, and the urban Northern States and Canada's reliance upon the penitentiary.

6   There is considerable commentary and analysis on the penal reform movement that commenced in the USA in the last two decades of the 19th century. In reference to its effect on prison writing, see Morris (1998) and Wright's review (Volume 10). Of major importance was the easing of restraints on prisoners' interaction and relationships produced by penal reform. Though the strict "lock step, silent system" order applied in Canadian penitentiaries until the end of World War II, its tight application was already badly eroded by the 1930s (Anderson, 1997).

7   For a discussion, see Davies (1990:6–8).

8   Though Brendan Behan was incarcerated (when a teenager) for his involvement in IRA political struggles, and this "Irish" location of the "English" borstal or prison informs

his writing, his most celebrated work is focussed upon the prison, prison culture and routine. The collectivity best represented in his work is that of prisoners.

9 *Presido* is the award winning penal press magazine started in 1934 at Iowa State Penitentiary. For a discussion see Morris (1998), especially Ch. 14.

10 Excerpts from the reviews in these newspapers are included on the dustcover of the book. The comment from the *New York Times* captures this response: "Runyon must seriously be regarded as a remarkably gifted convict observer of the passing penitentiary scene".

11 Earle Stanley Gardner was a major supporter of the penal press and often featured prison writing/writers in his column "The Court of Last Resort" in *Argosy* magazine. He started a nationwide campaign aimed at securing Runyon's release, with his piece "The Big House", in *Argosy* (April, 1955). In the early 1960s, Gardner tried to rescue the penal press (see Gardner, 1963; 1964).

12 For a short history of the Canadian penal press see Gaucher (1988).

13 Philip Priestley (1985; 1989) has done extensive research and documentation of prison writing from English prisons over the past two centuries. See also Brandseth, (1972).

14 For discussion of censorship in USA see Runyon (1959); Franklin (1989:161–62, 261; 1998:14–15); Morris (1998:147–186).

15 See for example, J. Genet, *A Thief's Journal* (1949) and *Our Lady of the Flowers* (1964) or F. Norman's *Bang To Rights* (1958). Norman's work was the basis for the B.B.C. Television comedy *Porridge*, which celebrated the wily recalcitrance of the seasoned convict.

16 The over-representation of First Nations' Peoples in Canada's penitentiaries and jails has been particularly evident in the western provinces since the late 19th century. In the 1950s, Aboriginal prisoners started to use the penal press to campaign for the creation of Native Brotherhood groups. These groups focussed upon cultural identity and education, and have been a reality in penitentiaries across the country since the late 1960s. An examination of their many newsletters and penal press magazines produced over this period indicated that the "status" Indian preceded and redefines that of prisoner. The writing of First Nations' prisoners presents the prison as a secondary level of confinement and oppression relative to the invasion of their territory and the cultural genocide of forced residential school attendance and reserves. A commonly shared conclusion is that the penitentiary has replaced the residential school as the pivotal institution in the suppression of Aboriginal culture (see Reed, 1990).

To a lesser extent this relocation and redefinition of the prison also took place amongst other Canadian prisoners as exhibited in their penal press writing and political activities. The 1970s was the most tumultuous decade in Canadian penal history (see Culhane, 1979; 1988; McNeil and Vance, 1978). During the height of the system wide disturbances in 1976; which marked the fifth year of continuous staff violence and brutality that started with the riotous opening of the control unit prison at Millhaven, Ontario in 1971; a group of politically conscious, long term "common" prisoners formed the Odyssey Group. One of their many initiatives was the establishment and observance of a National Prison Justice Day (August 10) inside and outside Canada's prisons (Gaucher, 1991). [See Part V, this anthology.]

17 In the past 30 years, Irish political prisoners in Britain and Northern Ireland have significantly added to the already rich body of political analysis, biography and literature produced by imprisoned and banished Irish nationalists. See for example: Adams (1990); South Yorkshire Writers (1991); *JPP* (1997: Vol. 7:1). MacLochlainn (1990) illustrates the continuity of these writings with Ireland's history of political resistance and struggle.

18 The USA has been a world leader in penology since the 19th century. Christie (1993) argues that within the new parameters of the "crime control industry" the USA's international leadership and influence has increased significantly. This was also the case during the exceptional conjuncture of the 1960s–70s, when the writing and analysis of USA prisoners (especially George Jackson and Angela Davis) was read by prisoners and informed their resistance, across the world.

19 Prison populations have steadily risen across the world since 1980 (see: Christie 1993; Weiss and South, 1998). The increase in the USA has been explosive growing from approximately 300,000 prisoners to the current 1,800,000. This has resulted in massive prison construction and overcrowding, both of which have major impacts on prisoner/prison culture. [See Hassine, Part IV, this anthology.]

20 See also: Morris (1998:chapters 15–18); Gaucher and Elliott (2001).

21 See Timmons (1995:15–18).

22 See Gaucher and Elliott (2001).

23 See Franklin (1989; 1998); Davies (1990); Morris (1998); Murphy and Murphy (1998).

24 The most extensive program I am aware of is in England, where the Writers in Residence in Prison is supported by the Arts Council of England and the Home Office. The Writers in Prison Network has produced numerous anthologies of the work of the writers in residence and of prisoners (see Hadaway, 1987; Hopwood, 1995).

25 For example, in the USA see Churchill and Vander Wall (1992); in England see Scraton, Sim and Skidmore (1986; 1991).

26 There is a large and growing number of websites devoted to prison and related political issues. See for example, Prison Activist Resource Center, http:// www.prisonactivist.org.

27 See for example, *North Coast X-Press.*

REFERENCES

Archambault, J. Chairman (1938) *Report of the Royal Commission To Investigate the Penal System of Canada*, Ottawa: King's Printer.

ABC. BullDozer Collective (1980–1996) *Prison News Service*, Toronto.

Adams, G. (1990) *Cage Eleven*, Dingle, Ireland: Brandon Book Publishers.

Anderson, F. (1997) *Up The Ladder: An Autobiography*, Saskatoon: Gopher Publications.

Baker, P. (1961) *Time Out of Life*, London: Heinemann.

Behan, B. (1956) *The Quare Fellow*, Dublin: Progress House Publications.

———. (1958) *Borstal Boy*, London: Hutchinson & Co.

———. (1958a) *The Hostage*, London: Methuen & Co.

Blackstock, H. (1967) *Bitter Humour*, Toronto: Burns & MacEachern.

Brandseth, G. (1972) *Created in Captivity*, London: Stoughton.

Breytenbach, B. (1985) *The True Confessions of an Albino Terrorist*, London: Farber & Farber Ltd.

Campbell, B. (Ed.) *H Block: A Selection of Poetry*, Sheffield: South Yorkshire Writers.

Carter, R. (1974) *The 16th Round: From Number 1 Contender to Number 45472*, Toronto: Macmillan Co. of Canada.

Christie, N. (1993) *Crime Control as Industry*, London: Routledge.

Churchill, W. and Vander Wall J.J. (Eds.) (1992) *Cages of Steel: The Politics of Imprisonment In The United States*, Washington, D.C.: Maisonneuve Press.

Clemmer, D. (1938) *The Prison Community*, New York: Holt, Rinehart & Winston.

Cohen, S. (1972) "Writing from Inside" *New Society*, August 31, pp. 447–449.

Cressey, D. (Ed.) (1961) *The Prison*, New York: Holt, Rinehart & Winston.

Culhane, C. (1979) *Barred From Prison*, Vancouver: Pulp Press.

——————. (1985) *Still Barred From Prison: Social Injustice in Canada*, Montréal: Black Rose Books.

Davies, I. (1990) *Writers in Prison*, Toronto: Between The Lines.

Dowd, S. (1996) *This Prison Where I Live: The PEN Author Anthology of Imprisoned Writers*, London: Cassell.

Ferranti, S. (1999) "The American Dream: Free Enterprise" *Journal of Prisoners on Prisons*, vol. 10:1 and 2.

Fitzgerald, M. (1977) *Prisoners in Revolt*, London: Penguin Books.

Franklin, H.B. (1978) *The Victim as Criminal and Artist: Literature From The American Prison*, New York: Oxford Press.

——————. (1989) *Prison Literature in America: The Victim As Criminal and Artist*, New York: Oxford Press.

——————. (Ed.) (1998) *Prison Writing In 20th-Century America*, New York: Penguin Books.

Gardner, E.S. (1955) "The Big House" *Argosy* (April).

——————. (1963) "Who Cares" *Reflector* (Pendleton).

——————. (1964) "Let's Help the Penal Press" *Reflector* (Pendleton).

Gaucher, R. and Elliott, L. (2001) "'Sister of Sam': The Rise and Fall of Bill(s) C-205/220".

Gaucher, R. (1989) "The Canadian Penal Press: A Documentation and Analysis" *Journal of Prisoners on Prisons*, 2:1, pp. 3–24.

——————. (1991) "Organizing Inside: Prison Justice Day A Non-Violent Response to Penal Repression" *Journal of Prisoners on Prisons*, 3:1/2, pp. 93–110.

——————. (1993) "Too Many Chiefs" *Journal of Prisoners on Prisons*, 4:2, pp. 135–139.

Genet, J. (1949) *Journal du Voleur*, Paris: Librairie Gallimard.

——————. (1964) *Our Lady of the Flowers*, London: A Blond.

——————. (1966) *The Miracle of the Rose*, New York: Grove Press, Translated by Bernard Frechman.

Goffman, E. (1961) *Asylums*, New York: Anchor Books.

Hadaway, T. (Ed.) (1987) *Prison Writers: An Anthology*, London: Iron Press.

Harris, J. and Ward, J. (Eds.) (1993) *Words From Within: tales & experiences of prison & prisoners*, Kingston, U.K.: Two Heads Publishing.

Hjalmarson, G. (1961) *Just Call Us Bandits*, Toronto: Longmans.

Hopwood, C. (Ed.] (1995) *Inside Out: a survivor's guide to prison*, Clwyd, Wales: Bar None Books.

Jackson, G. (1970) *Soledad Brother*, New York: Coward-McCann

————. (1972) *Blood in My Eye*, New York: Random House.

Mac Lochlainn, P. (1990) *Last Words: Letters and Statements of The Leaders Executed After The Rising at Easter 1916*, Dublin: Office of Public Works.

Malcolm X with Haley, A. (1965) *The Autobiography of Malcolm X*, New York: Grove Press.

Maxwell, R.P. (1956) *Borstal and Better*, London: Hollis and Carter.

Morris, J.M. (1998) *Jailhouse Journalism: The Fourth Estate Behind Bars*, Jefferson, N.C.: McFarland & Co. Inc.

Murphy, P. and Murphy, J. (Eds.) (1998) *Sentences and Paroles: A Prison Reader*, Vancouver: New Star Books.

New York Panther 21, (1971) *Look for Me in the Whirlwind*, New York: Random House.

Norman, F. (1958) *Bang To Rights*, London: Secker and Warbug.

Odyssey (1978–1982?) *Odyssey Magazine*, Millhaven Penitentiary: Crowbar Press.

Priestley, P. (1985) *Victorian Prison Lives: English Prison Biography 1830–1914*, London: Methuen.

————. (1989) *Jail Journeys: The English Prison Experience 1918–1990*, London: Routledge.

Ratner, R. and Cartwright, B. (1990) "Politicized Prisoners: From Class Warriors to Faded Rhetoric" *Journal of Human Justice* 2(1):75–92.

Reed L.R (1990) "Rehabilitation: Contrasting Cultural Perspectives and The Imposition of Church and State" *Journal of Prisoners on Prisons*, Vol. 2:2, pp. 3–28.

Runyon, T. (1954) *In For Life: A Convict's Story*, London: Andre Deutsch Ltd.

————. (1959) "On Being a Good Prison Editor" *Presidio*.

Scraton, P., Sim, J. and Skidmore, (1986) "Through the Barricades: Prisoner Protest and Penal Policy in Scotland" *Journal of Law and Society* Vol. 15:3.

————. (1991) *Prisons Under Protest*, Milton Keynes: Open University Press.

South Yorkshire Writers (Eds.) (1991) *H Block: A Selection of Poetry by Republican Prisoners*, Sheffield: SYW.

Stony Mountain Penitentiary (1951–1965) *Mountain Echoes*.

Taylor, J.M. (1998) "The Unity Walk" *Journal of Prisoners on Prisons*, 9:2, pp. 70–80.

Timmons, K. (1995) "Natural Born Writers: The Law's Continued Annoyance With Criminal Authors" *Georgia Law Review*, Summer.

Weiss, R. and South, N. (Eds.) (1998) *Comparing Prison Systems: Towards a Comparative and International Penology*, Amsterdam: Gordon and Breach Publishers.

Withrow, O.C.J. (1933) *Shackling The Transgressor*, Toronto: Thomas Nelson & Sons Ltd.

Writers in Prison Network (1995–) *Network Notes*, England.

Writing on the Walls: It Isn't Just Graffiti
Charles Huckelbury, Jr.

Writing is a surreal business under the best of circumstances but even more so for those of us in prison. Solely because of our status, we must overcome disadvantages free writers never face. If we write on an academic level, sharing our insights and experiences, the public assumes we are either whining or trying to advance a self-serving agenda. If we write fiction, we also face a distinctively hostile audience, conditioned to reject anything created in America's prisons while paradoxically celebrating works from men and women jailed overseas by regimes inimical to American interests. In the United States, indigenous convict writers are viewed in the same light as garden slugs encountered on the patio during a dinner party. The first instinct is to get us out of sight and keep us there, as though we have no redeeming value whatsoever. And sadly, some of us have contributed to that reaction.

Jack Abbott was a federal prisoner of some literary talent when he was discovered by Norman Mailer. Abbott eventually published *In the Belly of the Beast*, a moving collection of essays describing what it means to do hard time. He was lionized by the literati and fêted all over New York. He could have accomplished a great deal as our ambassador, but shortly after Mailer got him out of prison, he killed a waiter in an incredibly stupid altercation over using a bathroom in a Manhattan restaurant. That of course enabled a sceptical and vindictive public to point its collective finger at Abbott and say, "See? We should have left him where he was".

That identical prejudice exists from Maine to California, even without the validating crimes committed by authors given Abbott's kind of squandered opportunity. Granted, only the most morbid minds outside the forensic community would want to read the work of, say, Timothy McVeigh or Ted Bundy, but there are men and women who, like Abbott, write from cells and who do have something significant to say, either in their fiction and poetry or in their essays. Still, the philosophical framework in which their writing takes form clashes with the conventional wisdom, and it is this cognitive dissonance that produces a comprehensive rejection when potential readers learn that the author is a convict. The public immediately leaps up and screams about gratuitous concern for more prison amenities, accusing us of selfishly appropriating emotional capital better invested with their own families.

Stridency overwhelms logic, leaving us to face journalistic howitzers while armed with pop guns.

In addition to the belligerent emotional reactions to our work, we must also deal with the current legislative trend to deprive us of our intellectual properties. Many states now have laws that rigorously prevent prisoners from profiting by their crimes. These measures can include confiscation of all monies paid as a result of interviews or book or movie contracts that deal specifically with the particular crime that got us our prison sentences. Even I find it hard to argue philosophically against such measures, as restrictive and prejudicial as they appear. I can list dozens of heinous crimes for which compensation to the guilty party would be morally reprehensible, no matter how the book or movie deals might be pitched. If such lucrative contracts resulted, then my first response would be to allow seizure of those assets to be distributed amongst the victims or their families, which, of course, is the rationale driving all of these measures.

But many of these laws go beyond appropriation of assets derived from a specific crime. More draconian statutes now provide for confiscation of monies gained from the sale of any creative properties. This includes everything from magazine articles to prizes in literary contests to screen plays. Depending on the jurisdiction, no matter what you write, you might be forced to relinquish everything you gain from its sale. Your family, no matter how impoverished, would never see any of it. Most states claim that these assets go toward offsetting the expense of housing the prisoners whose money finds its way into the state's coffers. Whether you can believe legislators and members of Congress regarding fiscal responsibility is a subject for another essay. I think that instead of redistribution of wealth as the primary goal many people simply do not want to see us rise above our designated station in life. When we do, it compounds the evidence militating against the standard lie that we are worthless. Thus, to eliminate the conflict the public is swayed into passing laws that deprive of us the fundamental liberty, the freedom to create.

My point is that writing inside prison is often a lonely and discouraging experience if one writes for public approval. The problem unfortunately is that we must if we are to alter the prehistoric attitudes of today's electorate. And who amongst us does not want recognition in its own right, especially after labouring over a piece conceived and executed during the quiet hours, at 4:00 in the morning, when nearly everyone but the HBO addicts are asleep?

Just a word of acknowledgement, even in opposition, would be nice if only to let us know that someone out there is aware of what we are trying to do. Instead, we typically earn silence or hostility for our efforts.

But that does not mean we roll over and surrender. Although encouragement rarely comes, we are usually too stubborn to surrender, to accept what Blake called the "mind-forged manacles" imposed by those who do not understand and are unwilling to make the effort. We then learn to persist, to write for the sheer love of our craft, for the joy and satisfaction that using the language brings. And that is when our work begins to sing.

This dedication, however, comes with a caveat: we must guard against an unsuspecting participation in our own vilification, not in what we have done but in what we write. When we commit our thoughts to paper, we risk both pain and discovery because our best work always contains a piece of us. We in effect conspire in the condemnation if what we write does not conform to accepted ideology or worse, attacks some social or cultural icon. And, of course, it usually does; those inhabiting society's lowest stratum are always rebellious and often unrepentant.

If we do not, as Pericles urged, meet this danger with a light heart, we consequently become acutely territorial, even aggressive, about our work. We hurl down the gauntlet of righteous indignation and tell the public in no uncertain terms to go directly to hell without passing Go or collecting two hundred dollars. This repudiation of adverse public reaction turns our writing exclusively into a means of self-validation, often a strident one, an expression of the soul that defies attempts to injure or kill us spiritually. In and of itself, this transformation aids in our survival and protects us from those psychological slings and arrows we constantly endure on talk shows and C-SPAN. But to have an impact on local or national policy, we must be prepared to bend in the wind of critical response rather than categorically ignore the reasoned debate of people who disagree with or even despise us.

For prison writers, myopia is more pronounced than in the general population. We tend to reject "outside" criticism as either unfounded or uninformed, believing that anyone who has not done time cannot possibly know what it is like and therefore cannot write competently about it. We believe that only convicts can write about convicts and the conditions in which we exist. There is an element of truth in that sentiment, but such parochialism limits us even more. If we write only and about each other, then we maintain the dichotomy that currently insulates us from society and this decreases our prospects for a wider readership, something we clearly need if we are to change the antagonistic dispositions of the people who make the decisions. Even if the free world does not understand what we write or disagrees with it philosophically, we must keep our ideas and creativity fresh and continue to explore avenues for interaction if we are to make inroads against their intrinsic prejudice. That means continued writing in the face of rejection, never forgetting that we are neither the first nor the last to travel this path. Many successful authors can literally wallpaper their homes with rejection slips, and even Jack Kerouac took six long years to find a publisher for his classic *On the Road*.

In view of the customary response, even without Abbott's self-destruction, I began writing with no expectations of any approval beyond the classroom. That was challenge enough, because, as all writers know, baring your soul in your work and then offering someone else a scourge with which to beat you is an intimidating experience. As I grew, I learned to accept constructive criticism and to trust my instincts. I also learned to ignore — at least partially — the howls of protest or the venomous silence that greeted my every attempt to go public with my work. I subsequently concentrated on fiction because I believed that no one would want to read academic work from a convict. I thought my opinions would not matter "out there", and the current political climate always reminded me that I was inconsequential, less than a thorn in the lion's paw. My attempts to approach the unfettered world in essays usually did not merit the courtesy of a response, although I always enclosed return postage. It was as if my submissions had disappeared into some literary black hole reserved for the manuscripts of convicts.

Last year, for example, I wrote a descriptive, lyrical piece on the coming of fall in New England and the pageantry displayed when the hardwoods begin to turn. I submitted it to a magazine here in New Hampshire that usually features that kind of an article, but I never got so much as an acknowledgement. The same thing happened with other submissions on other topics to newspapers and magazines. Only *The Boston Globe* responded when I inquired about being a regular contributor to their Features section: they politely told me no, but at least they told me something. In perhaps the grossest insult, a literary agent in Illinois returned a query for a novel unopened because the mail room here had stamped the envelope with the prison's name as the point of origin. He wanted nothing to do with any submission by a convict, regardless that it might cost him money over the long term.

To anticipate such rudeness and overt hostility, I usually ask other prisoners to vet my work. I try to pick men who will be candid about what they read, similar to an editor's function in the real world, and not try to spare my feelings by ignoring a deficiency where it exists. This does not mean I restrict the process to English majors. To the contrary, I seek discrete levels of both education and experience, needing a gut-level response to what is on the page, especially with my fiction. When I write about "The Life", I strive for accuracy among those men who have walked the walk.

With that in mind, I must rely on others for technical points as well as literary criticism. I have been in prison for 25 consecutive years and obviously have no contemporary experience with ATMs, late-model SB automobiles, or even something as elementary as shopping. My prose accordingly can suffer from my ignorance. In one of my short stories, for example, a character changed the station on a new Porsche's radio by turning the knob. Then one of my readers reminded me that car radios are now all digitalized. It was a small mistake, but as convict writers, we cannot afford them. We must be absolutely ruthless about our own work or risk providing our most formidable critics ammunition to pick us apart. Yet in a bizarre tautology, often those hardships imposed on us by society provide us with material for what we eventually create. (The richness of the blues would not have seen the light of day had not black men and women suffered and endured.) As with the burdens enslaved peoples must bear as a result of their imprisonment, we also have a wealth of experiences that transcend those of contemporary writers. It is necessary, however, to add perspective to those experiences and to mould them into a story that someone else wants to read.

Even as a young man with less dramatic tales to relate, I had the urge. I longed to be able to write for a wide audience. I wanted to be the one to take readers where I decided they should go, to be a guide to unknown worlds and sensuous experiences beyond their own, because by serving as their guide, I also get to make the trip with them. When I write, I can leave my cell whenever I desire, and I still cheer unabashedly as favourite characters succeed and despised ones fail. In my work, if not in the physical world I endure daily, justice does exist and optimism is not a chimera. Effort counts for something, and not all bad guys wear black hats. And it all happens with no inane commercials for rodeo burgers or adult diapers. It does, however, demand both effort and discipline if readers are to respond viscerally to the characters and action the words on the page evoke in their minds.

As odd as it sounds to people who do not write, fiction writers have little control over their own characters, if indeed those characters remain the property of the man or woman who creates them. The characters and the events in which they participate often take on lives of their own, evolving in their peculiar ways and speaking dialogue that the writer should never have guessed would come out of their mouths when s/he first sat down to write. Certainly, the writer places people in specific environments and has a rough idea of where the piece should go, but the characters who populate a novel or short story become largely autonomous. It is precisely this sense of freedom that I think most prison fiction writers appreciate and attempt to cultivate in their art.

I exercised that privilege in my first fictional efforts by doing what many of us practice. I created *romans à clef*, camouflaged autobiographies, as a means of sublimating my anger and frustration, and as a means of living like a normal human being. I got back at certain guards who had shown me more than the average amount of disrespect, or else I spent time with my wife in locations I could visit only in my imagination. Since my writing took me anywhere I wanted to go, I got to choose the time and place and fill the space with characters both good and evil. I could be Everyman or Superman, and I never had to be subservient to an intellectual or physical inferior, piss in a bottle while someone watched, or locked in a cell for count. I could sit in Newton's classroom or watch one of Shakespeare's plays at the Globe. To the uninformed, this sounds like pure escapism, but the therapeutic benefits, if not the financial rewards, have been boundless. And those of us who write from inside know how critical it is to maintain our intellectual and emotional poise.

I remember a specific writing class in which maybe a dozen of us were workshopping our papers, reading them aloud for critical analysis by the other students. Something had happened while I was writing a novella; something that victimized one of the most decent and beautiful people I have ever met, a very special woman who had been kind to me when she did not have to be, at a time that became a watershed in my life. I knew who the guilty party was, and I made him the villain in this particular piece. I created a graphic scene in which he was richly rewarded — at least in my view — for his transgressions. By objective standards, it was brutal, but in our world of what goes around comes around, it was justice served. At the end of the reading, one of the other students in the hushed classroom turned to me and said softly that I had been in prison too long. I certainly agreed with him, but the catharsis that accompanied writing that piece and then reliving it as I read it for others, doubtless helped me reap psychological benefits that would have otherwise cost me dearly.

These are considerations that free writers never have to entertain. They do not live in an oppressive environment where mental sublimation is the only available remedy to stave off encroaching insanity. Yes, they can imagine themselves in specific situations and then write something to redress it, but we are compelled to live the situations before writing about them, either in fictional or nonfictional accounts. Few of today's authors have ever seen unrestricted violence or sudden death. Fewer still know what it feels like to be hunted, to have no choices in their daily lives, or to be on the wrong end of a gun, whether in the hands of a cop, soldier, or bad guy. Even Thomas Wolfe did not know what it meant never to be able to go home again. This is not to say that experience is a prerequisite for good writing, but writers write best about subjects they know. When we write about a particular event in our lives, whether cloaked in fiction or exposed as the real nitty gritty, the result carries the authority of having been there and done that.

The written word, unlike a passive medium like television, demands participation of both author and reader in a symbiosis not found elsewhere. People read about the characters we create, and their imagination brings them to life. They live lives we describe and vicariously share the actions of everyone else we choose to give them. In other words, we all think while we read (and write) and we get (or give) something in the process, a process that is a relentless quest for improvement. For me, that usually means learning to be coldly objective, specifically, knowing when to cut. As my writing professor once warned me, it can seem like infanticide, killing my own progeny as soon as it saw the light of day. Early on, I was loath to admit that anything I wrote was defective. I was as protective as a mother who has given birth to a three-headed jackass. I thought my issue was beautiful and automatically valuable, no matter how ugly it looked to anyone else. It hurt to admit I could compose junk, but it is a realization all writers must face sooner or later. All of us who write have substantial egos, but we must keep them under control if we are to perfect our work and deal with the inevitable disappointment when we are not up to the task. Yes, I said inevitable.

No matter how one approaches writing or the particular venue, do not be surprised on the days when your conceptual powers allow you to write incessantly — or especially! — on the days when nobody is home up there. The creative process is always a mysterious one, and if it sometimes seems like the sheriff has served an eviction notice on everyone who lives in your imagination, hang around. Chances are they have only stepped out for a while and will be back soon, talking and doing things that will surprise you.

Whatever genre we choose, we cannot allow our cells to become cages for our imaginations and intellects. We must hold both dear and if something smolders inside us, if we have an immense respect for the wordsmiths we have read through the years and a desire to emulate them to the extent of whatever talents we might possess, then we will take the necessary steps to make the required sacrifices. It is never easy. It takes work and dedication, but by perfecting our craft, we show the world that we are more than numbers on cheap garments, that we are human beings worthy of recognition and respect. Quality can overcome the deepest prejudice, and as convict writers, we cannot afford to put before the reading public anything less than our best efforts.

We inside have already experienced rejection by society in general, and it has not broken all of us. If writing is important, we will create something unique and worthy, even if others do not endorse us as human beings or agree with our finished product. That is where our intrinsic toughness, the ability to weather a storm and stick to a planned course of action, comes into play. We refuse to quit, to lie down and accept the defeat that is expected of us. Writers, especially convict writers, are among the most durable men and women on the face of the Earth. We have no choice, we must write, and that is why when we do succeed, the recognition — the ineluctable joy of doing something few can manage — makes all the work, all the sacrifices, that much sweeter.

Letter to Joanna
Victor Hassine

Editor's Note: Joanna was a student in an undergraduate seminar course focussed upon reading the prison through the accounts of prisoners. Victor has been a regular contributor to this course for a number of years, through his correspondence, writing, audio-tapes, and in the spring of 1999, via a live teleconference session. This piece represents his response to their collective inquiries.

D
ear Joanna:
    I am going to try and answer the questions you asked in your letter, although your questions are much more difficult than you might imagine, ["Why do you do it (write) and what sort of obstacles do you encounter ..."]. In fact, one of the reasons it has taken me so long to respond to your letter is that I have had to become fairly introspective in order to cull "the reasons" for my writing. The reality is that there are tremendous obstacles prison writers overcome to (1) find a voice, and (2) get people to listen.

You see, unlike prisoners of old, who could justifiably claim the status of "political prisoners" because of institutional racism or socioeconomic inequities or because prison conditions were so inhumane that most prisoners were actually less criminal than their jailers, I am regarded as nothing more than a common criminal. A prisoner living under relatively humane conditions considering that I have been convicted of a violent crime. Because common criminals lack the moral high ground, it is difficult for us to have our voices heard.

A society which labels and incarcerates too many of its citizens as common criminals runs the risk of making such criminals future martyrs for a revolutionary subclass of disenfranchised and dysfunctional malcontents, yet the voices of these dissidents may be considered nothing more than noise from an angry mob. Let's face facts, Al Capone, with thousands of members from his crime family, speaking out against intolerable injustices in our criminal justice system would sound trivial and disingenuous, particularly when compared to Nelson Mandela speaking out against those very same injustices. Attempting to agree on why this is true would undoubtedly cause much debate, but this sad reality cannot honestly be denied [Was it not Thoreau who said, "Who you are speaks so loudly, I can't hear what you say"?]. So there you have it, one of the greatest obstacles faced by today's prison writers is their status as common criminals because it muffles their voice in a thick atmosphere of disbelief.

While a good argument may be made that the drug laws and other social engineering laws wrongly make criminals out of the poor and addicted, solely as a means of maintaining the position of the upper classes, this debate has little value to me as a prison writer. The reality is that the tactic of labelling all of today's prison writings as products of common criminals, seems to be working, for now, and the voices of contemporary prisoners are ill-received by not only their keepers, but also by their peers.

In order that you might better understand what I am trying to say, let me tell you the story of my prison writing experience. When I first came to prison, I was a very educated man, particularly when compared to my fellow prisoners who generally were limited to a sixth-grade education. I was also different in that I did not fear or hate the bureaucrats who lorded over me. As a law school graduate, I had been trained to understand and deal with bureaucracies and bureaucrats so I was able to treat/respect my keepers as bureaucrats doing their job.

Despite my advantages, I was crippled by the shame of my incarceration which prevented me from daring to utter an objecting voice or opinion. Joanna, I cannot begin to describe how shame can cripple you and turn you deaf, dumb, and blind. For years after my incarceration, I refused visits from all but my immediate family and lawyers. I wrote no letters home and dreaded receiving mail. I felt great shame when the world outside sneaked into my prison inside, shame for being a common criminal and so I forfeited my voice, lest anyone hear it, recognize my unworthiness and hold me up to further public scrutiny. To me, social separation from society has been much more torturous than the physical conditions imposed by my exile.

So there I was in a prison that afforded me adequate shelter and food, provided me with other amenities, wallowing in shame while fearing for my life. Fear and shame dominated my day-to-day existence for the first few years of incarceration, and I thought and did little else during that time besides trying to survive and remaining anonymous.

My first "urge" to write came after I witnessed a particularly unsettling suicide attempt. One early morning (2:00 a.m.) in 1983, while I was returning to my cell from my late night shift in the prison infirmary, I saw a finger of blood growing out from between the floor and door of a neighbour's cell. What it turned out to be was a man who had savagely shredded large portions of his own body with a razor blade. Blood oozed from between strips of flesh as chunks of bleeding meat dangled from his body as if they were being peeled off of him.

Help was summoned and the bloody man was placed on a hand truck, which was normally used to haul trash, and rushed to the infirmary. As he lay on garbage, the hopeless man pleaded to be left to die as he yanked off pieces of his own flesh. Once he was removed from sight, the cell block quickly returned to normal and most of the men simply went back to sleep, indifferent to what they had just witnessed. The block guard strolled back to his post. There was not a single display of sympathy or sadness. One enterprising prisoner called the guard over and asked if he could be moved into the cell the next day because that side of the block received better television and radio reception.

I was temporarily moved beyond my fear and shame and I was possessed to write a poem about this ghastly scene of suicide and indifference. My writing was totally involuntary and I never considered what I would do with the poem. It was a bloody poem with a vivid description of what I had witnessed and it dripped with anger at a system that could/would foster such hopelessness and indifference. Surprisingly, there was also a lot of anger aimed at myself for being a silent partner to this brutality.

Months later I showed a prison volunteer my poem — I am not sure why and neither was he — and he suggested I contact the **PEN** Prison Writing Committee, which is a New York based literary organization which supports and encourages prisoners to write about their experiences. I did, but I was not yet prepared to accept a role as prison writer and I continued to live an invisible life of shame and fear. However, I did begin to read the writings of other prisoners and wished I had their courage and talent.

About a year later, I decided to give my brother a unique birthday present. I had been incarcerated for over three years by then, and in describing my prison experience, I had shared with him the rich "slang-guage" used in my prison home. I was and still am intrigued by the crude honesty prisoners use in their simple speech, as was my brother, and so I wrote a fictional account of a young man's adventures in prison-land.

I titled the story "The Adventures of Slim". I wrote it using prison jargon to describe actual events and tragedies, and I included a glossary of terms with examples of their usage. It was frightening, brutal, offensive and raunchy-funny, with comedy used to reflect moments of life within the crucible where I existed. In truth I was letting my brother and myself see the reality of my life from an emotional distance which provided us both a safe perch for observation, allowing us to laugh, uneasily, at my tragedy.

The story was a breakthrough for me because it provided a means of bearing my soul without losing any anonymity or shame. After all, my name was Victor, not Slim. The fact that my brother loved the story and constantly asked me to "Tell me what happens to Slim", encouraged me to pour my heart into my storytelling. Soon "The Adventures of Slim" was a manuscript of 35,000 words. Of course, nobody read it but my brother and I, because neither of us had developed enough courage to let our pain go public.

For many years I satisfied my urges to write by adding chapters to Slim and sharing it with my brother and we both benefited from this secret expression. I am not sure why my brother chose to remain in the shadow of this anonymity, but I remained there because the fear and shame engendered by my prison experiences had left me with little more than brutish survival instincts and a solitary existence (emotional as well as physical) to guide me.

There are many tyrannies at work in a prison; the tyrannies of institutionalization, punishment, fear, indifference, authority, self-hate, loneliness and shame. Under these tyrants, not only was I limited in my ability to express myself, but I remained in a perpetual state of anger. Almost everything I did — good or bad — had the mark of an angry man. Because of this, I recklessly threw myself into the dangerous/deadly waters of jailhouse politics and prison reform with no regard for my personal safety because deep down inside I did not care if I lived or died. Living under tyranny breeds a reckless disregard for one's own life because the future becomes the primary enemy.

This period lasted at least 10 years, and while I certainly accomplished a great deal (in terms of bringing about positive change within the prison), spiritually and emotionally I was dying because I had surrendered myself to anger which destroyed the value of any victory I might have achieved: mere conquest cannot quell an angry heart and anger never gives way to contentment or pride. So I sued the prison and won, built a synagogue and half-way house, and saved countless lives and souls, but I could not save myself from my shame and anger. These were dark times for me. Times that I thought, hoped, wanted and lived to be nothing more than a prisoner.

In the fall of 1986, I was transferred to another prison. This transfer took me far away from my friends and family. I felt as if I had been moved to a different country. This increased my anger and made me more bitter, so as soon as I set foot in my new prison home I began planning lawsuits and other challenges to the system. While my goals were noble, my motivation was not, for I first had to rise above my anger in order to bring honour to anything I endeavoured.

A month after I had arrived at my new prison (Western Penitentiary), I found myself in the midst of a prison riot. I had been in several prison riots before, but this one was the most savage and brutal (which mirrored the conditions in Western). I remember initially walking alone around the prison, as rioters destroyed everything in sight, and feeling a sense of satisfaction. As I fiendishly gloated over the prison's burning, I witnessed the most brutal and heartless savagery of my entire life.

It took witnessing this extreme display of cruelty to extinguish my own anger because I saw what this anger would one day do to me. After the riot I realized I had to rekindle the humanity within me and that there was only one way to accomplish this. I had to love someone. You see, prison had made me a deadly stern and serious man, and I avoided emotional attachments and displays the same way I avoided the thrust of a shank. You see, if I allowed myself to care about other people, I would have to care about myself and then I would ultimately be forced to deal with the demons of my own shame. Also, in prison, displays of the gentler emotions are often interpreted as weakness, which invites physical challenge. I had become more fearful of becoming like the rioters I had watched than I did of becoming a human being.

Soon after the riot I met a prison volunteer with whom I fell in love and it was from the passion of this love that I managed to regain the total range of my emotions. Only then was I able to evolve into a prison writer. Of course, my first writings were love letters and poems but what better way to regain self-expression. My love for Deborah slowly allowed me to overcome my fear and anger. I stopped being a prisoner and became a man again. That is when I was able to write about the tragedies around me because I could finally recognize them as something more than just "the way things are". The more I loved Deborah and the more she loved me, the more I wrote about my prison experiences.

It was during this period of time that I stopped hiding the things I wrote. I entered the **PEN** Prison Writing Competition and won an honourable mention for a poem I wrote. This achievement, made in absence of any anger, was a source of great pride and so I wrote even more. Soon everything I wrote I mailed to anybody I felt would be interested (friends, family members, university professors, prison volunteers and prison administrators).

In 1989, I was transferred to yet another prison, but I was no longer an angry prisoner, I did not become bitter and I simply wrote more.

In 1990, I wrote a play (*Circles of Nod*) which spoke out against the death penalty because my new prison was the "Place of Execution" for the State of Pennsylvania. This play won honourable mention in that year's **PEN** Prison Writing Competition, but more importantly, the Superintendent of my prison allowed me to stage the play in the prison. One evening, no less than 100 yards away from where the State had executed hundreds of condemned men, a dozen prisoners acted out a protest against State-sanctioned murder before 500 prisoners and community members. There was no burning, raping or rioting, there was just acting and the presentation of a point of view. It was as the audience rose to applaud the actors and the play that I realized I could never again allow myself to be held hostage by shame and fear. Now I write not because I am angry, but because I need to rejoin society as a productive human being. After all, aren't we in this thing together?

So the greatest obstacles to prison writers today are their status as common criminals, their shame, the violence and indifference in contemporary prisons, and the lack of support from the literary community (the memory of Jack Abbot has wrongly led the literary community to turn their backs on all common criminals — **PEN** American Prison Writing Committee needs to be recognized, supported and expanded).

I am not sure if this will help you, but if you have any unanswered questions, I will try to send further clarification.

Sincerely,
Victor.

N ot just anyone can be a writer. Ink slingers are a special breed that adhere to an inner calling; that voice inside their heads that drive and torment them until they capture their thoughts on paper. What is written and how it is expressed usually depends on an individual writer's personal history, experiences and interests. As a prison writer with 20 years of incarceration under my belt I naturally write what I know the most about, prison. It is my sincere hope that what you are about to read captures the true essence of prison writers, the men and women of the steel cages who push the Maximum Ink.

At the best of times prisons are a boring and depressing environment to call home. When there is excitement and action it is usually associated with turbulence, violence and death. Chronic boredom versus eternal death — how do we alleviate one while avoiding the other? Simply stated, some of us use writing as a form of escapism. Whenever we become totally engrossed in writing a story we have perpetrated a mental escape. Where we go in our minds and how long we stay there varies with each writer. We are free to take a journey and travel wherever our imagination desires. Even when prison writers attempt to expound the nuances and intricacies of their caged existence it is as if they are on the outside looking in, narrating the emotions and experiences of someone else.

Writing exercises what can easily become a stagnant thought process. Sensory deprivation and an almost total lack of stimuli are a harsh reality of prison life. Writing stimulates the brain and allows our creative juices to flow. When everything clicks just right our pleasure centres are activated. First Draft, Second Draft, revisions and rewrites. When we hold that final product in our hands a flood of endorphins is released which leaves us feeling euphoric and at peace with our inhumane habitat.

Writing is both therapeutic and rehabilitative. As we write, research and explore, our time is utilized constructively. Without our writing to sustain us we could easily fall into the common trap of tall tales, fantasies and overall criminogenic thinking. Prison obliterates the demarcation point between negative and positive. Unless we make a concerted effort to do something useful with our time, we will get sucked into the fatalistic demeanor of everyday carceral life.

As we struggle to first break the surface and then to keep our heads above the primordial soup of negativity, we gain an incredible self awareness. Through writing we explore our inner souls as only the keeper of that soul can. "Who am I? Why do I do these things? How can I change my physical actions and self destructive thought processes"? Try as they might there is not a single correctional program that can supply the answers to these questions. The truth lays buried deep within us and writing is the tool we use to peel away the layers.

Once we have stripped ourselves bare we need to rebuild and once again writing is the tool of choice. Self esteem, pride and sense of accomplishment can all be gained through the written word. Against all odds we manage to shatter the barriers of our fortified dungeons and proclaim to the world that we are alive. When we see ourselves in print particularly for the first time, it is a confirmation that we possess a very special gift. Writing offers us the chance to shine, to literally become a beacon in a world of darkness. Learning how to deal with our unforeseen notoriety in an appropriate manner is yet another step in the rebuilding process.

Writing with the intent of being published forces us to expand our knowledge base and learn marketable skills. As we target a particular readership, editor and publisher we learn to be flexible and adjust to their format. We become project orientated, set goals and have deadlines that must be met. Organizational skills are learnt out of necessity.

Somewhere along the way we discover a sense of responsibility and moral character. As writers we suddenly have the ability to influence others and assist in bringing about change. Heady stuff when you stop to think about it, especially when we are cognizant of the fact that we can stabilize or incite. The old adage 'the pen is mightier than the sword' finally makes sense to us.

Prison writers can offer a voice and platform to thousands of other prisoners who may be incapable of expressing themselves. Attempting to shatter classic stereotypes by representing our fellow prisoners in a fair, articulate and intelligent manner is an incredible responsibility. As we challenge our intellectual capabilities we must always remember to keep our blossoming egos in check. This can be difficult considering that once we have been published we become a permanent part of history with the potential to influence others long after we are gone. Ideally the messenger does not overshadow the message. Our blunders and mistakes also become part of the permanent record, never to be denied because it lays before us in black and white.

Only a small fraction of prison writers are financially compensated for their efforts. Although we are usually destitute and struggling to survive on institutional pennies, money cannot be considered a major motivating factor. Instead we see writing as a positive release of pent-up aggression, aggravation, hostility and the ever present cabin fever. Whether we get published or not, the act of expressing ourselves on paper helps to cleanse our souls and keep the demons at bay.

Although money is scarce, some of us are clearly mapping out career possibilities for the future. By building up our bio-sheets and gaining name recognition, we have greatly enhanced our possibility of employment as a writer upon our release from prison. Alternatively, other prison writers resort to stock piling their finished products until after they are paroled in order to receive a fair dollar for their hard work. This technique is used to counter the public's sentiment that prisoners should readily tell their stories without receiving a dime of remuneration.

Writing offers a visible means of tracking our growth and change. This equates into tangible evidence that bolsters our supporters, counters the critics and influences Parole Boards. This paper trail is a unique approach and grabs peoples' attention. It also beats the hell out of saying "I've changed my ways" and expecting everyone to take your word for it.

So far we have covered what can be considered the positive aspects of prison writing. It would be fantastic if that was the complete story and it ended there. It would also be totally unrealistic. Unfortunately there are no free rides in the Penitentiary and prison writers traditionally pay a heavy price.

Chronic cell searches, harassment, censorship and long term segregation are all on the agenda. Without warning, our typewriters, computers, files and resource materials are confiscated. Alternatively if they are not confiscated, we are separated from them by being thrown in the hole on trumped up charges. Two of the well worn excuses for segregation are "your life is in danger" and the all encompassing "threat to the good order of the institution". The ever popular "confidential reliable informant" clause is invoked and you have no recourse because you cannot challenge an unnamed source which in most cases does not exist.

Placing a writer in segregation is probably the most efficient form of censorship employed by corrections. Not only are we separated from our writing tools but also from our fellow prisoners whose situations are often the subject matter and catalyst of our written material. Most segregation units remain in the dark ages with draconian security measures. Ink pens are deemed a security risk and we are instead issued half a pencil and three sheets of writing paper twice a week. Any additional paper is considered to be a fire hazard. The pencils are worn down so small that they can no longer be held. Pencil sharpeners are contraband and the writer is dependent upon the guard to sharpen the pencil. Of course the writer has to wait until the guard makes his next hourly round to get the whittled down stump of a pencil back; assuming the guard brings it back at all. Long ago and far away this writer experienced several years in solitary confinement. I had become so frustrated, enraged and twisted in this horrendous environment that I actually resorted to scratching out letters in my own blood.

Penitentiary censorship takes on many forms with the common goal of suppressing and silencing us. The fact that we cannot seal outgoing mail, and that incoming correspondence is opened and read before being delivered, is the main culprit. Unless we receive notification of receipt, we constantly wonder if our stories reached their destination or sit waylaid on the Warden's desk. In some instances corrections simply refuses to post our mail citing self protective policies to support their position. Of course we have the option of filing complaints, grievances and law suits. That is if we have the time, money and have not experienced a sudden security transfer halfway across the country. As we fight the battle to be heard we are actually losing the battle of being heard. We are forced to lay silent as the wheels of injustice turn ever so slowly. By some miracle should we win in court a mere four years later, it is of no consequence to corrections. Our formerly pressing issues are no longer timely or relevant and it is not as if the Warden pays any fines or penalties out of his own pocket.

Our keepers have the ability to thoroughly dissect whatever we have written days before any prospective editor sees it for the first time. There are countless instances where phone calls are made and the standard correctional public relations campaign goes into effect. Our credibility is questioned through the most basic character assassination. "Who are you going to believe? A convicted and incarcerated felon or a dedicated public servant of 24 years?" Unless an editor has a personal relationship with the writer or has previously served prison time and knows the name of the game, the character assassination is usually sufficient. If it is not, the Corrections Public Relations Officer simply digs an inch or two deeper into the bottomless pit of resources and propaganda. If the quagmire becomes too hazardous, the considerable political clout of corrections is called upon to make reporters and editors heel.

A common problem for all prison writers is our lack of access to resource material which includes public libraries, university libraries and the internet. Complicating our already dismal access to reading material is the all encompassing correctional power to ban an endless litany of literature under the pretext of 'security'. Furthermore, interviews are practically non-existent because we cannot travel and in most cases the interviewee is denied access to us.

Over time the dedicated prison writer creates personal resources by purchasing selected books and organizing files from clipped newspaper and magazine articles. The minute our writings aggravate a high ranking corrections official or some other government bureaucrat, the files and books are deemed to be a fire hazard and confiscated.

'The Man' and His plan. He is never quite done with us and if anyone manages to get this far 'The Man' always has a few more obstacles to hurl. In many jurisdictions correctional policies state that we cannot run a business from prison unless we have specific permission from the Warden. Of course our writing for publication is deemed a business; regardless if we get paid or not. Per self protective policy, the Warden screens everything we try to get published. If a writer sells out and glorifies corrections in general and the Warden in particular, publication doors open upon the regime's propaganda machine and media connections. But if we show journalistic integrity by inscribing the truth, we are silenced and persecuted. The hate motivated 'Son of Sam Laws' round off the tools for muzzling those that would dare shed light on the government's dungeons.

Unbelievably our battles are not over yet. Next in line to take a shot at us are our fellow prisoners, the same men and women that we are trying to help. Penitentiaries contain every personality disorder known to mankind and misguided jealousies continuously surface. We have all experienced unstable and malicious individuals who bear us ill will simply because we are receiving attention that they are not. Moving along, there is the overly negative segment of the prison population that must be addressed. These characters assert psychological and physical peer pressure in support of their belief that it is taboo to openly discuss any aspect of our hidden society.

In-house conflicts may seem ridiculous to a citizen but it can mean life and death in the penitentiary. The debate over convict, prisoner and inmate is a classic example. No self righteous convict wants to be referred to as an inmate and will at times become violent to stress the point. The problem for prison journalists is that 'convict' carries an incredibly negative connotation within society, far more so than 'prisoner' and 'inmate'. The constant dilemma faced by any prison writer is how do we effectively educate and inform the public about the realities of our lives without insulting and alienating the very people we are trying to help? We become tightrope walkers, forever walking the fine line in our attempts to articulate the facts without ostracizing our fellow prisoners.

Plagiarism is a terrible crime, particularly when one incarcerated being steals the works of another. Many prisoners are habitual short cut artists and there is always a maggot or two around who will put their name on someone else's creation. The plagiarist only sees words on paper but what is really being stolen is the author's heart and soul.

Having run the gauntlet of our insane environment we still need to find an editor who believes what we write, has a format we can fit into, and is willing to deal with the negative public sentiment in regards to prisoners. The sad reality is that there is an overabundance of talented prison writers and only a handful of editors that will take a chance on us. The limited market available to us is thoroughly saturated and we are all competing for the same column space.

Finding the 'right' editor can easily turn into a disaster. Editorial liberties, the changing of just a couple of words can intentionally or unwittingly place our personal safety and indeed our lives in jeopardy. Other than the rare exceptions, magazine and newspaper editors have never experienced the realities of prison life and would not have a clue when they were placing us in harm's way. Even if they were aware, their number one priority is sales, which equates to sensationalism. Our personal well being is not on their agenda. Every prisoner who has ever been published, waited with baited breath until they saw the finished product in print.

On an extremely personal note I have a family that is humiliated every time I manage to get published. I am made to feel as if I am the family's dirtiest little secret that refuses to stay in the closet. Siblings that cringe, a mother that weeps and a father that denies my existence. "Why do you have to write these stories, Greg?" "Can't you find something else to do?" "If you insist on writing these God awful stories can't you at least use a pseudonym?" I used to send copies of my published works to my family thinking they would be proud of me, pleased that I achieved something tangible and positive. When two of my award winning stories were received as if they were disease ridden vermin, it hit me hard and brought about some noticeable changes. I no longer share anything that is published with my family. Furthermore, I now include them in my writings when the stories warrant it. Previously I had gone to great lengths to avoid mentioning my family in any manner.

Having covered the numerous negative aspects of being a prison writer you must be asking yourself why we continue to run the maze of harassment, retaliation and torment. The answer is pretty basic. After it is all said and done, we are first and foremost writers. That is what writers do, they write. The fact that we write from a steel and concrete cage instead of a lake front verandah or mountain top retreat has little to no bearing on our need to express ourselves through the written word. We are driven and compelled to write and in most cases we do not have a choice in the matter.

Cultural Struggle and a Drama Project
Mícheál Mac Giolla Ghunna

Bobby Sands once wrote:

> The jails are engineered to crush the political identity of the captured republican prisoner; to crush his/her spirit and to transform him/her into a systemised answering machine with a large criminal tag stamped by oppression upon his/her back, to be duly released onto the street, politically cured, politically barren, and permanently broken in spirit.

Republican prisoners have always steadfastly resisted this strategy, through strength of spirit and power of mind. The writings of Sands, the existence of the magazine *The Captive Voice/An Glór Gafa* (The Voice of Irish Republican Prisoners of War) and the activities of the republican community in jail bear eloquent testimony to this fact. The recent drama project in the H Blocks, leading to the creation of the play, *The Crime of Castlereagh*, is yet another illustration of the cultural resilience of republican prisoners. But there is far more to it than merely an act of resistance.

It has become almost a defining feature of political prisoners throughout the world that they engage in cultural struggle. They write, compose poetry, sing and play music, paint and carve. They utilise every form of self expression. They do so not merely because they are talented thoughtful individuals (one of the reasons leading to their imprisonment), but because they wish to give voice to the pain of their people and articulate the need for radical change to end this pain. Indeed Edward Said, the Palestinian academic, has termed this the role of the intellectual in society. Similarly the recently executed Ken Saro Wiwa described his role thus:

> For a Nigerian writer in my position ... literature has to be combative ... What is of interest to me is that my art should be able to alter the lives of a large number of people, of a whole community, of the entire country. ... It is serious, it is politics, it is economics, it's everything. And art in that instance becomes so meaningful. ...

Moreover the Italian Marxist, Antonio Gramsci, in his own *Prison Notebooks*, argues that cultural struggle is central to political change, as it concerns the creation of alternative social meanings and values which challenge the

71

dominant ideology of the ruling class. In other words, cultural struggle is about raising the political awareness of the mass population, exposing the apologists for injustice and inequality, and creating an alternative set of values and different perspectives of the world.

Irish republicans have always numbered among their ranks a high proportion of writers, poets, musicians, and artists, many of whom endured imprisonment and used those years to further their cultural activities. For others, the experience of imprisonment acted as a catalyst for their creative talents. This is particularly true of the present phase of the struggle. The dominant image is of a blanket clad Bobby Sands scribbling his poems, songs, and stories on a piece of toilet paper in a freezing and filthy cell. But others were similarly engaged in this cultural struggle. After the blanket protest, republican prisoners in Long Kesh made a sustained effort to put in place a programme of communal education based on the principles of Paulo Freire's *Pedagogy of the Oppressed*. This laid the foundation for a wide range of cultural activity from Irish language classes, poetry workshops, art and craftwork, playwriting and acting, music and song, and of course, the magazine, *An Glór Gafa*.

The Irish language activities are a classic example of the success of cultural struggle by prisoners having a wider impact on the struggle for political change. While Irish language groups had worked hard and with some success for many years to maintain and develop the language and Irish culture in general, that is to take and maintain control of our capacity to develop our own social meanings, the influx of released political prisoners into local nationalist communities in the 1980s provided a fresh impetus for this struggle. These were committed activists who had learned both Irish and the importance of cultural struggle in jail; and who now organised language classes and campaigns for cultural rights in their local areas, helped to set up and maintain Irish schools, and got involved in a wide range of other cultural activities. The effect was to increase the community's confidence in their own ability to define and express their own interests and aspirations independently. It added to the vibrancy and dynamism of a community that could sustain a broad political, social, and economic struggle over many years. This interaction of cultural and other aspects of struggle is clearly illustrated in initiatives like the West Belfast Community Festival.

It is in this context of an historical cultural struggle in the jails and its interaction with community struggle outside that the recent drama project in

Long Kesh took place. A small group of POWs came together, along with Tom Magill of the Community Arts Forum, to adapt for stage performance a trilogy of poems by Bobby Sands. Such a project offered us individual benefits such as skills development and confidence building. However, while personal development is always encouraged by the republican community in Long Kesh, it was by no means our only or even our main motivation. Rather it was a collective and conscious political act on our part to push forward the cultural struggle. In part, this is a continuation of the long history of jail cultural struggle; and the conditions that made the project possible are a result of the sacrifices and planning of those POWs who went before us. However, it is also part of what we see as the wider role of the artist: to articulate the experiences, hopes, and desires of their people. In this particular case, we wanted to tell the story of political imprisonment.

It is unashamedly a republican prisoners' version of that story, focusing on the physical and psychological torture of Castlereagh, the farcical pseudo-legal imprimatur of a Diplock court, and the brutalisation of prisoners during the blanket protest in the H Blocks. It also tells of the hidden reserves of strength within an ordinary man to resist torture, corrupt courts, and prison brutality; and of the comradeship that ultimately defeated the criminalisation policy of the British government. However, it is not a narrow, localised account of the experiences of a political prisoner. The story could easily be set in any part of the world, for it contains universal themes and experiences of imprisonment, fear, isolation, loss of family, and physical pain as well as resistance, principles, stubbornness, comradeship, and courage. There are, of course, other stories to be told — even the screws' story, and the psychological impact of the situation on them. But that is not our concern here.

The type of theatre we chose for telling the prisoners' story is also significant. Using the poetry of Bobby Sands, we organised the play on a collective basis, creating, producing, and directing as a group. In other words, rather than performing the work of someone else, we retained control and ownership of our own images, actions, and meanings. The style was surreal; thus, we created our own world with its own rules and deeper truth, rather than conforming to naturalistic conventions and the dominant version of superficial reality 'as seen on TV'. For example, which image is the truer one, the Diplock judge as a distinguished man in a red cloak, or as a pig snorting contemptuously at justice? It was also minimalist theatre; that

Festival Drama in the Blocks
Paddy O'Dowd

A s part of Féile an Phobail (the West Belfast Community Festival), republican prisoners in Long Kesh recently staged a performance of their play *The Crime of Castlereagh* an adaptation of the Bobby Sands' epic trilogy of poems, 'The Crime of Castlereagh,' 'Diplock Court,' and 'H Block Torture Mill.' It charts the experiences of a prisoner as he moves from the physical and psychological torture of Castlereagh, to the farce of a Diplock trial, to the mixture of brutality and comradeship during the blanket/no-wash protest in the H Blocks.

This production had been nine months in the making. The previous week, the cast had spent many hours rehearsing and preparing. The capacity audience, which had packed the canteen, was full of expectations. At the end of the night, no one was disappointed. Indeed, what took place over the next hour-and-a-half far exceeded anything that might have been expected. This production was excellent and must be the most thought-provoking, emotionally-charged, and energetic play ever performed in the H Blocks.

The first scene wasted no time in setting the standard for the rest of the night. The curtains opened to reveal an iron bed from beneath which emerged two black-clad ghouls in grotesque masks, filling the stage with an evil mischief. There was no room for idle props in this production, with the two figures using a towel as a noose, creating a mock gallows from the bedstead, and staging a mock hanging with both, all the while laughing menacingly.

The arrival of the prisoner (Frankie Quinn who brought great energy to a very demanding role) was swift and brutal as he was thrown onto the stage and ably assaulted by the guard or 'Watcher' (Tony Doherty who performed all his roles with a zeal). With the Watcher's departure, it soon became clear that the ghouls were the torments of the prisoner, all his fears and doubts come to life. Amid all their taunting, his loneliness and terror came across clearly, evoking a sympathy that was almost choking when the narration began:

I scratched my name but not for fame
Upon the whitened wall.

Micheál Mac Giolla Ghunna's delivery was perfect, the slow drawl carrying the feel of history and, as he was hidden from the audience's view, the walls themselves seemed to speak the words. And what better narrator of this trilogy than the walls of a H Block.

> Bobby Sands was here, I wrote with fear
> In awful shaky scrawl.

The audience had no difficulty in relating to the plight of the tormented figure on stage. The tension was razor sharp, built up with the music and sound effects of Eddie Higgins and Paddy Devenny using everything from bodhrán and whistle to kitchen utensils. Many a hair stood on not a few necks as the narration continued:

> When Christ I stared as at me glared
> The death name of Maguire.

'Maguire ... Maguire,' the ghouls echoed hauntingly (Brian Maguire died under controversial circumstances in a Castlereagh cell in May 1978).

   After exploring the psychological torment of waiting for the interrogation, the scene shifted to physical pain. A casual costume change on stage (subtle but effective) transformed the ghouls into two interrogators. Dan Kelly and Mairtin óg Meehan managed all the 'qualities' of these roles, even instilling a little humour amid the tense proceedings. Meanwhile, Johnny McCann and Marty Morris, as torturers' assistants, graphically demonstrated some of the ways they use:

> To loosen up your tongue ...
> Till a man cries for the womb
> That give him birth to this cruel earth
> And torture of that room.

The use of the sparse props throughout was superbly imaginative to which description on paper could never do service. Within this one scene, a pole was used in all manners from a torture rack to a stairway and none of it seemed out of place. To the strains of 'The Blanket Song,' the prisoner climbed to the top of that stairway, signalling his defiance in the face of the interrogators, and the end of the first scene. Thirty minutes had passed and no one was leaving their seats.

The second scene was set in a Diplock court. Its opening confronted us with the operatives: the doctor, who only diagnosed self inflicted wounds; the branchman and the prosecutor, all sharpening knives like butchers. The prisoner was dragged in by a screw, past this terrifying sight. Isolated, the prisoner was placed in:

> That dock a lonely island there
> And I a castaway,
> The sea around alive with sharks
> And hatred's livid spray.

In terms of imagery, this was unsurpassable: the re-enactment of torture, the physicalised murder of truth, the slithering snakes of witnesses, swooping prosecuting hawk, pig in wig judge, the circle of lies all done effortlessly and still with the ability to induce an emotional response from the audience. If the farce of Diplock and its central role in the conveyor belt system was ever 'captured,' this was it. The dignity of the prisoner was brought to the fore as he emerged from a repressive scrum of characters trying to bury him:

> And see that splendid sun
> That splendid sun of freedom born,
> A freedom dearly won.

The audience was even more engrossed as the curtains closed a second time.

The opening of the third and final scene brought us to the 'H Block Torture Mill.' This conveyed the horrors of the blanket/no-wash protest, as well as the strength of those who endured the physical and psychological torture while tending others' wounds and pulling a comrade back from the edge of mental breakdown. Full credit to the cast for managing to put so much into one scene without it seeming disjointed or unreal. The sight of the three blanketmen lying in the background upstage while the death and funeral of the screw/torturer took place downstage was a striking image, one for the self-righteous politics of condemnation:

> Yet! Whinging voices cried aloud,
> What did this poor man do?

He only done what madmen done
Upon the silent Jew.

The part of the POW who is losing control in face of all the brutality was a
great performance by Johnny McCann. Even the blankets around the men's
bodies were used as props to signify the claustrophobic pressure whilst the
selective use of sound effects cued us easily into the mounting degrees of
tension. The pain of imprisonment was brought out by a fine piece in which,
to the strains of 'Only Our Rivers Run Free,' one of the POWs escapes the
squalor around him and dreams of a life beyond his concrete tomb:

To dance and prance to love's romance
Is elegant and neat ...

But he is jolted back to terrible reality by his comrade's need to use the toilet
which for him is the corner of the cell:

To eat and sit where you've just shit
Is not so bloody sweet!

The tension climaxed when the POWs were dragged out one at a time by
the screws using various brutal search procedures. The cell was cleaned
and the men were returned individually and badly assaulted, signifying all
the horrors of the wing shift and the opportunism of the screws to
systematically degrade and beat the prisoners. Yet the comradeship and
unity of the blanketmen could not be broken:

And to our door we stood in scores
To conquer their black fame
For loud and high we sang our cry,
'A Nation Once Again.'

And while singing this song, the three POWs smeared the walls of their cell
again. This was no romantic struggle, this was resistance by the only means
available and a determination not to be defeated.

     For the closing of the scene and the performance, the narrator emerged
to walk among the cast reciting with conviction:

We do not wear the guilty stare
Of those who bear a crime.
Nor do we don a badge of wrong
To tramp the penal line.
So men endure this pit of sewer
For freedom of the mind.

The closing of the curtains ended an unforgettable performance, one greatly appreciated as shown by the sustained applause. This type of theatre had not been tried in the blocks before, and all involved carried it off superbly. Prisoners toughened and made cynical by long years of struggle were close to tears. With the lights turned on again, I sat in the brightness of the canteen amid the appreciative buzz of my comrades. The banner above the stage was so appropriate: 'Nor Meekly Serve My Time.' The words and imagery of Bobby Sands created under the most appalling circumstances have come a long way, from the darkest days of the blanket protest to the jail conditions that such sacrifice has achieved for us today, enabling his poetry to be brought to life by a new generation of republican prisoners. For those of us privileged to see it, this play was a proud reminder that we are part of that same noble struggle.

The History of *Prison Legal News*:
The Samizdat of the American Gulag
Paul Wright

In May, 1990, the first issue of *Prisoners' Legal News* (PLN) was published. It was hand-typed, photocopied and ten pages long. The first issue was mailed to 75 potential subscribers. The magazine's budget was $50. The first three issues were banned in all Washington State prisons; the first 18 in all Texas prisons. Since then *PLN* has published over 110 issues, grown to offset printing of 28 and 32 page issues and has around 3,000 subscribers in all 50 states. This is how it happened.

In 1987, I entered the Washington State prison system with a 304 month prison sentence and a Marxist political ideology. An oppressive and brutal state in theory was now a concrete reality.

In 1988, I met political prisoner and veteran prison activist Ed Mead while at the Washington State Reformatory (WSR) in Monroe. Ed was serving two life sentences for shooting at police during a failed bank expropriation. The bank expropriation was being carried out by members of the George Jackson Brigade (GJB), of which Ed was a member. The GJB was an anti-imperialist group composed mainly of former prisoners which carried out armed struggle in the Pacific Northwest in the middle to late 1970s. The GJB's first action had been to bomb the Washington Department of Corrections headquarters in 1975 to support striking prisoners at the Washington State Penitentiary in Walla Walla.

Ed had been imprisoned since 1976. During that period he had been involved in organizing and litigating around prison conditions. He had also published several newsletters and magazines, including: *The Chill Factor, The Abolitionist*, and *The Red Dragon*. In 1988–1989, Ed and I were jointly involved in class action prison conditions litigation and other political work. Ed's last newsletter project, *The Abolitionist*, had fallen apart over political differences he had with the other members of the editorial board.

As the 1980s ended it was readily apparent that, collectively, things were in a downhill spiral for prisoners. We were suffering serious setbacks on the legislative, judicial, political and media fronts. Prisoners and their families were the people most affected by criminal justice policies but we were also the ones with the smallest voice, if any, in deciding these policies. There was also the lack of political consciousness and awareness among the vast majority of American prisoners, like the public outside prisons.

Ed and I decided to republish *The Red Dragon* primarily as a means of raising political consciousness among social prisoners in the United States. We would model the new *Red Dragon* on the old one: a 50–60 page, quarterly magazine that was explicitly Marxist in its politics and outlook. One issue we were trying to decide was how big the hammer and sickle on the cover should be.

While a draft copy of *The Red Dragon* was put together, we never published it for distribution. The main reason was a lack of political and financial support on the outside. We lacked the money to print a big quarterly magazine and we were unable to find the volunteers outside prison willing to commit the time involved in laying out, printing and mailing a large magazine. In early 1989, I was also subjected to a retaliatory transfer to the Penitentiary at Walla Walla due to successes in the WSR overcrowding litigation and because Washington prison officials wanted to stop publication of the new *Red Dragon*. The transfer meant that Ed and I were relegated to communicating by censored mail, which made lengthy political discussions much more difficult.

We scaled back our ambitions and instead decided to publish a small, monthly newsletter. One that could grow if political support existed. Originally named *Prisoners' Legal News,* we set out with the goal of targeting activist prisoners around the country with real, timely news they could use. Our blueprint and role model was Vladimir Lenin's *What is to be Done.* Lenin advocated that revolutionaries organize around a journal or newspaper, the flow of ideas and information being crucial. All things considered, the Czarist dictatorship of the turn of the century has much in common with the American gulag at the end of the century.

With the social movements that had traditionally supported the prisoner rights struggle at a low ebb and facing setbacks of their own (i.e., the civil rights, women's liberation and anti-war movements), we saw *PLN*'s objective as one which would emphasize prisoner organizing and self reliance. Like previous political journalists who had continued publishing, carrying the torch for the next generation during the dark times of the 1920s and 1950s, we saw *PLN*'s role as being similar. From the outset, *PLN* has been an organizing tool as much as it has been an information medium. When we started we did not know things would get as bad as they have.

In 1990, I was transferred to the Clallam Day Corrections Center, a new Washington prison. At that point Ed and I had our plan of publication and had found a volunteer, Richard Mote, in Seattle, to print and mail each issue. Ed and I each typed up five pages of *PLN* in our respective cells. Columns were carefully laid out using blue pencils, graphics were applied with a glue stick. We then sent our respective pages to Richard who copied and mailed it. Ed contributed *PLN*'s start up budget of $50.

The first three issues of *PLN* were banned from all Washington prisons on spurious grounds. Ed was charged by WSR officials for allegedly violating copyright laws by writing law articles. Officials at Clallam Day ransacked my cell and confiscated my background article materials and anything that was *PLN* related. Eventually Ed's infraction was dismissed and I received my materials back. As we were on the verge of filing a federal civil rights lawsuit to challenge the censorship, the Washington DOC capitulated and allowed *PLN* into its prisons. Jim Blodgett, then the warden at the Penitentiary in Walla Walla, told me that *PLN* would never last because its politics were outmoded and prisoners too young and immature to be influenced by our ideas. The reprisals were fully expected, given prison officials historic hostility to the concept of free speech.

The biggest disaster in *PLN*'s history then struck, Richard Mote was mentally unstable. He refused to print and mail *PLN*'s second issue because he took offense to an article Ed had written calling for an end to ostracization of sex offenders. Mote took all of *PLN*'s money that contributors had sent us after receiving the first issue (about $50), the master copy for the second issue and our mailing list. For several weeks it looked like there would be no second issue of *PLN*. Fortunately, we located a second volunteer, Janie Pulsifer, who was willing to help *PLN*. Ed and I retyped the second issue of *PLN* and sent it to Janie to print and mail. We were back on track.

THE PRESSES KEEP ROLLING

Ed's partner, Carrie Catherine, had agreed to handle *PLN*'s finances and accounting, such as they were, after Mote jumped ship. This was short-lived because by August 1990, Carrie was preparing to go to China to study. The only person we knew who had a post office box and who might be able to handle *PLN*'s mail, primarily to process donations, was my father Rollin Wright. He lives in Florida and generously agreed to handle *PLN*'s mail for what Ed and I thought would be a few months at most, until we found someone in Seattle to do it.

PLN's support and circulation slowly began to grow. By January 1991, *PLN* had switched to desktop publishing. Ed and I would send our typed articles to volunteers in Seattle, Judy Bass and Carrie Roth, who retyped them and laid out each issue. Ed and I would then proof the final version before it was printed. In 1991 we obtained non profit status from the IRS in order to mail *PLN* at lower non profit postage rates. *PLN*'s circulation stabilized at around 300 subscribers. We purposely did not want to expand beyond that at that time because we lacked the infrastructure to sustain more growth. Once *PLN* had finalized its non profit status with the IRS and its mailing permits with the post office we were ready to grow.

In the summer of 1992 we did our first sample mailing to almost 1,000 prison law libraries. Since *PLN*'s reader base had grown we decided to reflect this change by changing the magazine's name to *Prison Legal News*, *PLN* was not just for prisoners anymore. We also made the editorial decision to stop calling prison officials "pigs" since we were going to solicit them for subscriptions. *PLN* was now being photocopied and mailed each month by a group of volunteers in Seattle who would meet once a month for a mailing party.

When *PLN* started out in 1990, Ed and I had decided *PLN* would be a magazine of struggle, whether in the courts or the prison yard, all would be chronicled. At a time when the prisoner movement was overcome by defeatism and demoralization we thought it important to report the struggles and victories as they occurred, to let activists know theirs was not a solitary struggle. Our local, Washington specific issue was abuses by the Indeterminate Sentencing Review Board (ISRB) a remnant from Washington's transition to determinate sentencing in the 1980s. The first several years saw *PLN* give heavy coverage to ISRB issues. Despite grumbling by prisoners affected by the ISRB, struggle around this issue failed to materialize.

Another mainstay of *PLN*'s coverage from the beginning, which has met with a better fate, is the issue of prison slave labour. This is where the interests of prisoners and free world workers intersect. If people outside prison do not think criminal justice policies affect them, by showing how prison slave labour takes their jobs and undermines their wages, *PLN* would make prisons relevant. This was helped by the fact that Washington State was, and remains a national leader in the employment of prisoner slave workers by private business. *PLN* has reported how corporations like Microsoft, Boeing, Planet Hollywood and U.S. Congressman Jack Metcalf, among others, have exploited prison slave labour. These stories were frequently picked up by other media outlets, increasing *PLN*'s exposure.

In June 1992, I was transferred back to WSR where Ed and I could collaborate on *PLN* in person for the first time since we started. In 1991 I had been infracted for reporting in the *PLN* the racist beatings of black prisoners by white prison guards at Clallam Day. Unable to generate attention to the beating themselves, my punishment for writing about it generated front page news in the *Seattle Times*. Eventually, the disciplinary charges were dropped, but not until after I had spent a month in a control unit for reporting the abuses. The presses kept rolling.

PLN BECOMES A MAGAZINE

On *PLN*'s third anniversary in May, 1993, we made the big jump. We switched to offset printing and permanently expanded our size to 16 pages. *PLN* was no longer a newsletter, now we were a magazine, bound and everything! *PLN*'s circulation was at 600 subscribers.

In October 1993, Ed was finally paroled after spending almost 18 years locked up. The ISRB, no doubt unhappy at *PLN*'s critical coverage of their activities, imposed a "no contact" order on Ed. This meant Ed could have no contact, by any means, with any prisoners. The ISRB was clear that this specifically included me and was for the purpose of preventing the publication of *PLN*. If Ed were in anyway involved in publishing *PLN* his parole would be revoked and he would be thrown back in prison, perhaps for the rest of his life.

The American Civil Liberties Union of Washington filed suit on our behalf to challenge this rule as violating our First Amendment rights to free speech. In an unpublished ruling, federal judge Bryan of Tacoma, dismissed our lawsuit, holding that it was permissible for the state to imprison someone for publishing a magazine if they were on parole. The Ninth Circuit Court of Appeals would eventually dismiss our appeal as moot when, after three years on state parole, Ed was finally discharged from ISRB custody.

In early 1994, Dan Pens became *PLN*'s new co-editor, replacing Ed. Dan had been a *PLN* supporter from the beginning, contributing articles, typing and maintaining *PLN*'s mailing list on a computer program he had custom designed for *PLN*. (This was at a time when Washington prisoners were allowed to have computers in their cells.) *PLN* also switched to an

East coast printer that offered significant savings over *PLN*'s Seattle printer. This allowed *PLN* to expand in size to 20 pages. Within a year, PLN was no longer being mailed by volunteers but by our printer.

In January, 1996, *PLN* hired its first staff person, Sandy Judd. *PLN*'s needs and circulation had grown to the point that volunteers were simply unable to do all the work that needed to be done. With some 1,600 subscribers, data entry, lay out, accounting and other tasks all required full time attention. Dan had been moved to a different prison in the summer of 1995 and could no longer maintain the mailing list as he had before. For security reasons, we were never comfortable having the mailing list inside prison where prisoncrats could get their hands on it. The downside is that data entry takes a lot of time. By 1999, Fred Markham was *PLN*'s overworked and underpaid office slave.

By May 1999, *PLN* was celebrating its ninth anniversary of continuous publishing, having published 109 issues and with approximately 3,000 subscribers in all 50 states.

PLN goes into every medium and maximum security prison in the United States as well as many of the nation's jails and minimum security prisons. *PLN*'s subscribers include judges, lawyers, prison and jail officials, journalists, concerned citizens and activists on both sides of the walls. The bulk of each issue of *PLN* is still written by prisoners. In addition to Dan and myself, we have added a number of contributing writers across the country who contribute articles and reporting to *PLN*. This includes Willie Wisely, James Quigley, Matt Clarke, Ronald Young, Darcy Matlock, Julia Lutsky, Alex Friedman, Mark Wilson, Daniel Burton Rose and Mark Cook. We have three quarterly columnists, attorney John Midgley who writes about procedural legal issues for jailhouse lawyers, political prisoner Laura Whitehorn and death row activist Mumia Abu-Jamal. For stories that require further investigation than *PLN*'s imprisoned writers can do, (e.g., phone interviews, internet searches) we can count on the support of journalists such as Jennifer Vogel, Ken Silverstein, Micah Holmquist, Daniel Burton Rose and Tara Herivel. This has allowed *PLN* to provide a wider spectrum of voices and helped us expand in size while maintaining a consistently professional magazine. One which has developed a following even among journalists for the corporate media.

In 1998, Common Courage Press published our first book, *The Celling of America: An Inside Look at the U.S. Prison Industry*. Edited by Dan,

Daniel Burton Rose and myself, the book was a *PLN* anthology. The text lays out in one place the reality and politics of the prison industrial complex. The book has received critical acclaim and helped boost *PLN*'s profile. In 1998, I also started doing a radio show on KPFA in San Francisco called "This Week Behind Bars". The show airs as part of "Flashpoints" and consists of news reports, mostly from *PLN*, about news involving the criminal justice system.

PLN does not have a hammer and sickle on its cover, but we are unique in several respects. First, *PLN* is the only uncensored, independent national magazine edited and produced by prisoners, and the longest lived. Second, we offer a class based analysis of the criminal justice system. We continue to focus on prison slave labour and the plight of class struggle political prisoners in the U.S. and around the world. Private prisons and the companies profiting from incarceration policies are frequently highlighted in *PLN*.

To date, *PLN* has remained self reliant. Despite a lot of effort on our part, *PLN* has never been able to attract much in the way of grants from foundations or other sources. *PLN* is largely funded by its subscribers with some additional funds coming from advertisers whose products/services do not conflict with our editorial mission. Book sales by *PLN* also contribute to our income.

The battles against censorship have been constant. Most censorship problems are resolved administratively. In recent years *PLN* has sued the Box Elder County jail in Utah which banned all publications; the San Juan County jail in Utah which banned publications sent via third class mail; entire State prison systems in Utah, Oregon and Washington which banned *PLN* because we were sent via third class non profit mail; the Alabama prison system which required that prisoners purchase subscriptions from their prison trust account, and the Washington DOC which banned *PLN* from sending prisoners in that State, photocopies, *PLN* clippings or subscriptions to prisoners in control units. *PLN* also sued the Michigan prison system after they decided to ban our book, *The Celling of America*, claiming the book incited riots. To date, *PLN* has won all the censorship suits it has filed.

PLN IN THE NEXT CENTURY

A question I have been asked is whether PLN has been successful. Success is a relative term. When a French journalist asked Mao Tse-Tung in the

1960s if he thought the French revolution had been successful, Mao replied that it was too soon to tell. So too with *PLN*. The prison and jail population has almost doubled, to 1.9 million, just in the time *PLN* has been publishing. By any objective standard, prison conditions and overcrowding are now worse than at any time in the past 20 years. Draconian laws criminalize more behaviour, impose harsher punishment in worse conditions of confinement than at any time in modern American history. The legal rights of prisoners are increasingly restricted by the courts. The corporate media and politicians alike thrive on a steady diet of sensationalized crime and prisoner bashing, all the while jails and prisons consume ever larger portions of government budgets.

PLN has chronicled each spiral in this downward cycle of repression and violence. We have provided a critique and analysis of the growth of the prison industrial complex and exposed the human rights abuses which are a daily reality in the American gulag at the end of the century. In that sense, I believe that *PLN* is successful. Even if we have not stopped the evils of our time, at least we struggled against them. That we have managed to publish at all under our circumstances is a remarkable success.

PLN has helped stop some of the abuses that are legion in the American gulag. We have also borne witness to what is happening and duly documented it. Recent years have seen an increase of interest and support for the prisoner rights movement and more attention being paid to prison issues by outside activists and the general public. Many of *PLN*'s criticisms of prison slave labour and other issues have even been picked up and adopted by labour groups and some elements of the corporate media.

We believe that *PLN*'s success will be measured by its usefulness to activists, journalists, citizens and lawyers who, in our day, tried to make a difference. We also hope to be useful to historians at a later date who chronicle what is hopefully a relatively brief and dark period of modern American history.

The main obstacles that *PLN* faces are those faced by all alternative media in the U.S., under funding and the corresponding inability to reach large numbers of people with our message. Without relatively large-scale funding from outside sources to do outreach work, this will continue to be a problem for the foreseeable future. The other primary obstacles *PLN* faces are prisoner illiteracy (depending on the State, between 40 percent to 80 percent of the prisoner population is functionally illiterate and thus unable to read *PLN*), and political apathy. That said, *PLN* has survived longer and published more issues than any other prisoner produced magazine in U.S. history. The need that led to *PLN*'s creation has only grown.

Despite recent changes in mail censorship policies by the Washington prison system, changes that seem designed to shut down *PLN*, we continue to publish under adverse circumstances. The mail policy changes include a ban on prisoner to prisoner correspondence, so Dan and I can no longer write each other or other prisoners, and a ban on all book and magazine clippings, limiting newspaper articles to one per envelope.

Corporate media coverage of prison issues and news tends to be abysmal, with reporters largely content to parrot press releases from prison officials. Rarely is input from prisoners sought, or if obtained, used. Since its inception *PLN* has ensured the voice of class conscious and politically aware prisoners is heard. We are heartened by the fact that prisoners in other States are starting similar publications focused on struggle in their States. This includes *Florida Prison Legal Perspectives* and *Voices Behind the Walls* in Florida and Pennsylvania, respectively.

After almost a decade of publishing, it has to be emphasized that *PLN* has always been a collective effort. Dan, Ed and I have been the editors, and the ones to bear the brunt of our captors displeasure at having truth spoken to power, but the reality is that *PLN* would have never been possible were it not for the many volunteers and supporters who have so generously donated their time, labour, skills, advice and money to *PLN*. The cause of prisoner rights has never been popular. In today's political climate, with radical chic a distant memory, it takes extraordinary courage and commitment to support *PLN*.

The volunteers without whose support *PLN* would not be here today include: Dan Axtell, Dan Tenenbaum, Allan Parmelee, Janie Pulsifer, Jim Smith, Scott Dione, Matt Esget, Cathy Wiley, Ellen Spertus, Jim McMahon, the late Michael Misrok, Sandy Judd, Rollin Wright, Bill Witherup, Fred Markham and Wesley Duran, among many others.

The lawyers that have advised *PLN* on matters as diverse as taxes and internet licensing, as well as representing *PLN* in court in censorship litigation around the country, include: Bob Cumbow, Mickey Gendler, Bob Kaplan, Joe Bringman, Dan Manville, Rhonda Brownstein and the Southern Poverty Law Center, the Washington ACLU, Alison Hardy, Marc Blackman, Brian Barnard, Mike Kipling, Frank Cuthbertson and Peter Schmidt.

The organizations that have provided financial support to *PLN* over the years, often at critical points of *PLN*'s existence, are: the Southern Poverty Law Center, the Open Society Institute, the Solidago Foundation, and Resist.

Ultimately, the people who have contributed articles and who have subscribed have made *PLN* possible today. Without all these people contributing to *PLN* , far too many to name, we would have met the fate of the vast majority of alternative, non corporate publications, we would have folded within a year.

Going into the 21st century, *PLN* will still be around for a while. Underfunded and understaffed, but still scooping the corporate media, giving a voice to the voiceless, and still going.

Revolutionary Literature = Contraband

Mumia Abu-Jamal

> The people enjoyed real freedom of thought
> The masses' rights were respected;
> The few who insisted on publishing things
> Were the only ones affected.
>
> Heinrich Heine (1797–1856)

Heine's insightful expression of state repression versus peoples 'rights', is not locked in granite, reflecting one fleeting point in time. The Germanic poet's sentiments equally apply to today's reality, specifically those in several American prisons, where an increasing number of prisoner-subscribers to the radical weekly, *Revolutionary Worker (RW)*, are being told by prison censorship bodies, and by some courts, that the *RW* will not be allowed.

The *Revolutionary Worker* is the organ of the Chicago-based Revolutionary Communist Party, U.S.A., a body which embraces a Marxist-Leninist-Maoist thought.[1] *RW* is a colorful, expressive tabloid that offers national and global news analysis from a radical slant. The cover, centerfold, and back page are often multicolored. The writing style is breezy, colloquial, attempting an open 'average Joe' tone, free of puzzling jargon. Its layout is often loose, with little use for the bars, linings and/or graphs of many American newspapers, as reflected perhaps best in the *Wall Street Journal*. *RW* graphics tend to blend with the text, as in a recent instance where a three-quarter page length photo of an American Republican Cabinet official was depicted with a reptilian forked tongue slithering out of a toothy smile. *RW* can be entertaining, as much for its offbeat writing, as its creative, provocative graphics.

RW may be the antithesis of the tight staid *Wall Street Journal*. Perhaps that is why over 500 prisoners from some thirty U.S. prisons subscribe to it.

Perhaps that is one reason why, intermittently, since late May 1985, and totally, since October 1987, *RW* has been deemed *verboten* at Huntingdon State Prison in south-central Pennsylvania.

May 13, 1985, marked the long-planned police assault against, and aerial incendiary bombing of, the Philadelphia homes and headquarters of the Black Naturalistic Move Organisation, leaving smoldering ashes of carnage and death of men, women and children behind. Scores of homes were razed by fire. Many radical and mainstream publications covered the urban holocaust, each from its own political perspective. The spectrum ranged from the conservative *U.S. News and World Report*, which decried the massive property losses, whilst opining that the fact that Philadelphia's mayor was Black was indicative that racism was not a factor in the bombing; to the *RW* which interpreted the 'Nightmare on Osage Ave.' as state terrorism launched against a Black Rebel clan and fronted by a Negro puppet politician, in hock to his very soul to the ruling class. To be sure, a number of radical, leftist papers featured remarkable coverage reflecting an extraordinary event. But, after the smoke cleared, few adopted an editorial, ongoing stance on the Move Massacre. Fewer still provided reduced rate or free subscriptions to indigent prisoners. *RW*, among others (notably the *Workers Vanguard*, organ of Spartacist League, U.S.A.), did all three.

The *U.S. News and World Report* was never censored; *RW* was censored often. At Huntingdon, *RW* papers were repeatedly seized, based upon a section of Administrative Directive 814, which prohibits publications "which advocate violence, insurrection or guerrilla warfare against the government or which create a clear and present danger within the context of the Correctional Institution" (Pennsylvania Department of Corrections Admin. Directive, Sec. IV.A.3).

Since October 1987, some thirty prisoner-subscribers at Huntingdon have been totally denied their weekly *RW*, based upon the pretext cited above. The stated purpose of the Directive 814 is to give wide latitude to inmate subscribers of publications to satisfy the educational, cultural, informational, religious, legal and philosophical needs of prisoners.

Huntingdon subscribers fall within a wide range: Black Nationalists, Prison Activists, Anarchists, Move Rebels and Socialists are among the thirty-odd individuals who routinely pass *RW* on to other interested readers.

The writer, despite prolonged *pro se* litigation in the U.S. District Court, and repeated institutional requests for a clear statement of what material was deemed offensive to censors, was never provided an answer stating what was objectionable. Repeated appeals netted *pro forma* responses, which woodenly cited the relevant rule supposedly violated, but not the material found to be objectionable, nor why.

Huntingdon Prison, located in Pennsylvania's rural, white, central counties, bears a black inmate population of over fifty percent (*Legislative Budget and Finance Committee Report*, Vol. II, June 1988:28).[2] Pennsylvania has an African-American population of about ten percent, akin to the U.S. population as a whole.

Only after the Revolutionary Communist Party (RCP) — Prisoners Revolutionary Literature Fund (PRLF), and interested civil attorneys made inquiries of government officials did a "reason" emerge for the total ban visited upon issues of *RW*. The culprit, censorship officially informed PRLF spokespersons, was a brief announcement on page two of every issue, titled "3 Main Points", authored by RCP Chair Avakian. Specifically, one point rankles censors: "The system we live under is based on exploitation — here and all over the world. It is completely worthless and no basic change for the better can come about until this system is overthrown." Here then, 'the clear and present' danger. Accordingly, *RW* has been totally banned a Huntingdon. Since September 1988, another prison has joined the *RW* ban-wagon, namely, Lewisburg Federal Prison at Lewisburg Pennsylvania. By contrast, one of America's largest prison systems, New York State, specifically allows *RW* and states as much in its media review guidelines.[3]

Recently, editors at *RW* excluded the "3 Main Points" from selected issues. Did this mean *RW* was no longer excluded? It did not. Reportedly, the September 5, 1988, issue did not feature the "3 Main Points". On September 23, 1988, subscribers were given censorship notices rejecting that issue on the identical grounds noted above, strong suggestion that the given objections are purely pretext. Is the actual basis a political distaste for a publication which unabashedly names this system as imperialistic, and exploitative? Does this degree of censorship impact upon the right wing, often racist, publications at Huntingdon?

White prisoner-subscribers here receive *White Aryan Resistance* (*WAR!*); *NAAWP News* (National Association for Advancement of White People); *Thunderbolt*; *National Vanguard* (*N.V.*), and the like, periodically and relatively hassle-free. The author has reviewed *WAR!* and *ATTACK!*, organs of the White Aryan Resistance and the National Alliance (from Arlington, Virginia), which call for "revolution" against "this corrupt system".[4] One issue of *Attack!* (No. 12, 1972) features "Revolutionary Notes — 7" which boasts of the merits and limitations of a number of small arms, from the 9mm (SW) to the .30 M1 Carbine, complete with illustrations, and descriptive texts. These articles, some 150 of them, deal with paramilitary matters, cultural enhancement of European values, and scandalous portrayals, via caricature and cartoon, of African, Indian, and Jewish peoples. Indeed, one article from a 1984 compilation describes Der Fuhrer, Adolph Hitler, as "Kind", "appealing" and even "maudlin"! These materials are free from censorship. Radical materials which criticize the U.S. Empire are freely and routinely censored.

White prisoners may subscribe to fascist-oriented materials, which deify Hitler, belittle (or praise) the World War II Holocaust of millions of Jews, Gypsies, Communists, and others, and liken Jews to stereotypical shylocks, and Africans to servile Sambos, without significant comparative censorship, as afflicts *RW*. Perhaps more significantly, literature of this type supports psychic and racial barriers between prisoners, and inhibits development of any degree of political/ideological unity amongst prisoners vis-à-vis the administrators. As in the "free world", racism is a valuable tool of division which rulers use to manipulate the ruled.

Pornography, soft and hard-core, also circulates quite freely here. Prisoners routinely receive and circulate materials depicting a provocative panoply ranging from male/female penile-vagina sex, penile-anal sex, and oral sex; to homosexual oral, anal and digital sex; to human/bestial sex. In a state where conjugal visits have never been allowed, and where the very notion of penitentiary was initially conceived and implemented under strong Quaker influence,[5] prisoners may fantasize to one's hearts content about myriad sexual couplings, but no more. Presently, eight States and a number of countries, Canada, European and Third World, provide conjugal visits. In the State where America's Constitution was molded, written and ratified, and where the Pennsylvania Constitution specifically grants broad press freedoms,[6] the *RW* stands victim to a state-initiated total ban at Huntingdon. As the Move Rebels of Philadelphia were excepted from the expansive guarantees of the United States/Pennsylvania constitutions as reflected by the May 13, 1985, police bombing so too, the Free Press Rights boasted in both Constitutions, apparently does not apply to *RW*. Add another log to the fire.[7]

Prisoner-subscribers to the Black Nationalist Monthly, *Burning Spear*, published by the Oakland, California-based African Peoples Socialist Party, face a similar ban at Huntingdon, but the *Spear* is not banned by other state prison media bodies.[8] The *Spear* offers news and analysis on political, social and cultural issues affecting the global Black community. The *Spear* too is banned. Appeals to prison administrators have resulted in as little specific responses, as in the case of *RW* censorship appeals.

What of court challenges to this wave of censorship? The federal courts, having been duly Reaganized, offer poor prospects for a *pro se* prisoner-litigant, who pits his meager resources and research tools against the computerised, professional arsenal of government counsel.

The naming of conservatives to the Federal Bench during the Reagan Administration leaves the majority of the bench with an ideological bent of "deference" to the executive branch, with little appreciation of individual and/or prisoners' rights, as preserved in the Bill of Rights. This bodes ill for the impoverished, the imprisoned, powerless, who dare to believe the lofty rhetoric that resonates within the Constitution, or more importantly, try to apply it.[9]

As the issues raised here address far more than the narrow question of "prisoner's rights", but rather impinge upon the First Amendment rights of publishers of alternative and radical publications, it is the publishers who must join in the struggle with prisoner-subscribers, to liberate the minds of men from the mental shackles of an exploitative, oppressive system. There is no safe middle ground.

Until publishers recognize their principled, interwoven interests with those who read, and thus consume their product, the corporate major media will, by portraying crucial censorship issues in terms yet another "prisoner's rights" case, marginalize and obfuscate its impact and import.

Poet Heine's insightful observation, cited in this article's opening, bears reflection. He shows, in poetic clarity, how an increasingly repressive state camouflages its acts, with grandiose, glorious and utterly hypocritical words.

Incredibly, it would be easier for prisoners at Huntingdon to receive an edition of Barricada from Managua (I know a subscriber here of the Sandinista's English edition), than to get a copy of Chicago's *RW*. There's the pity. As with every assault on folk's rights by this system resistance must be the response. This article is one form. How you, the reader, may opt to respond may be another.

"The worst kind of tyranny is that over the mind."

                                                                                          Anonymous

A people can never acquiesce to the State's imposition of mental contraband.

NOTES

1. Although at first glance such a tripartite grouping (i.e. Marx — Lenin — Mao Tse-Tung) may appear somewhat unorthodox, the Revolutionary Communist Party/U.S.A. is of the view that Mao Tse-Tung thought, or the political philosophical view of the late chairman, have enriched Marxist theory, and further, that the present pro-western regime in Beijing is deeply revisionist.
2. The *Legislative Budget and Financial Committee Report* places Black inmates at fifty-two percent of Huntingdon's population; the statewide figures for the Black inmate population is fifty-seven percent. These figures count Hispanics as "whites", so the statistics are conservative.
3. See New York Directive 4572. Sec. II.H.6., which states, in part, "... publications such as *Revolutionary Worker* shall generally be approved".
4. See "Why Revolution?" *Attack!* No. 6, 1971.
5. The world's first "penitentiary" was opened in Pennsylvania in 1790 as the Walnut Street Jail, based upon "penitence". This "Philadelphia System" was copied globally (Takagi, 1980).
6. The United States Constitution, Amendment One and the Pennsylvania Constitution, First Article, both promise free press rights; the latter in Article II, Section 7 notes, "The free communication of thoughts and opinions is one of the invaluable rights of man" (See *Pennsylvania Declaration of Rights and Constitution*).
7. Both a state and federal grand jury declined to indict any officials involved in the May 13th Move Massacre; nine Move people presently serve 100 year sentences for allegedly killing a cop in 1978, despite admitted knowledge of their innocence.
8. A notarized affidavit of a *Spear* subscriber showing that *Spear* is not censored at another prison accompanied this article (ed.).
9. On May 15, 1989, a predominately Reagan-appointed majority of the United States Supreme Court held prison officials needed "greater flexibility" in determining which publications to censor. *Abbot v. Thornburgh* makes it easier for federal prison wardens to exclude critical, and predominately leftist material.

REFERENCES

Heine, H. (1982) *The Complete Poems of Heinrich Heine*. Boston: Suhrkamp/Insel Publishers.

Takagi, P. (1980) "The Walnut Street Jail: A Penal Reform to Centralize the Power of the State". In T. Platt and P. Takagi (Eds.) *Punishment and Penal Discipline*. San Francisco: Crime and Social Justice Associates.

The Resurrection of the "Dangerous Classes"

Jon Marc Taylor

R ecently, *The Nation* columnist, Alexander Cockburn (1994A), resurrected the socially archaic phrase the "dangerous classes" as a comprehensive term dusted off and used to describe the focus of the hardening "fascist" attitudes of some towards immigrants, toward the desperately struggling welfare dependent poor, and toward, in many cases, the resultant criminal. Ironically, at nearly the same time, conservative columnist George Will (1994), writing for *Newsweek*, noted that "Fascism flourishes as a doctrine of vengeance ..." and is a philosophy favoring "... the visceral over the cerebral". Concomitantly, Dr. Jeffery S. Adler (1994), associate professor of history and criminology at the University of Florida, explored not only the American origins of the term "dangerous classes", but also the birth of the concept of deviance in the United States and the policies enacted to combat the then newly "publicly" identified social threat. These definitions and prescriptions today sound all-too-familiar in the debate over immigration policy, welfare reform and criminal justice legislation.

The development of the concept of the dangerous classes extends back nearly two hundred years, originating after the social disarray of the Napoleonic Wars in Britain and continental Europe (Gaucher, 1987). The first use of the phrase "dangerous classes" was by Miss Mary Carpenter, a well-known English writer on criminal matters in 1851. She noted those branded (literally) by imprisonment or "... if the mark has not yet been visibly set upon them, are notoriously living by plunder — who unblushingly acknowledge that they can gain more for the support of themselves and their parents by stealing than by work ... form the dangerous classes" (Carpenter, 1851). Then in 1859, the *Oxford English Dictionary* encoded the term in the official lexicon of that society (Tobias, 1967).

Adler (1994:34) explains that between 1850 and 1880 Americans 'discovered' the "dangerous classes". Newspapers, paradoxically, borrowed the phrase from the French and molded it to fit American conditions. The New York City Draft Riots of 1863 (in response to the life-threatening conditions and economic hardships imposed by the Union's newly enacted conscription law that also allowed the wealthy to "buy" stand-ins) gave impetus to the concept of this class that the era's experts explained was composed mainly of immigrants and tramps. The apparently (from the perspective of the monied class) irrational, unfocused, and wide spread violent destruction of property and random assaults on by-standers and authority figures (over 100 people died during the five-day riot) "... haunted intellectuals and reformers for years to come" (Adler, 1994:35). The great national railroad strike of 1877 (caused by draconian management, repeated wage cuts, dangerous working conditions, and little job security) rekindled the memories of the Draft Riots and reinforced in the country's conscience the existence of the dangerous classes. By 1882, the term "dangerous class" was in wide use in the United States.

The mainstream exponents of this new theory claimed that large numbers of immigrants formed this class, but they disagreed about why this was so. The rationales ranged from immigrants being wretches kicked out of their own societies, to the traumatic experience of immigration, to the separation from their old community mores compounded by the influence of the evils of the big city. A social worker of the time wrote of immigrants that "... they go to pieces and become drunken, vagrant, criminal, diseased and suppliant" (Hunter, 1904). From the bourgeois viewpoint, those who avoided work were believed to have rejected the bonds of society and scorned the established social order. Edward Devine (1994) of Columbia University observed that "... the mere act of obtaining gainful employment indicated that a person sought to participate in orderly society". Such gainful participation, however, was hard to find and hold onto for many due to the perpetual economic dislocations (i.e. recessions and depressions) resulting from the evolving and self-obsolescing unrestrained capitalistic industrialization of the late 19th and early 20th centuries. Moreover, for the foreign born and colored, discrimination such as "No Irish Need Apply" and "Whites Only" employment policies, and blatant labor exploitation, such as the Chinese building the Union Pacific Railroad, was rampant and socially acceptable.

The resulting domestic social controls imposed on the dangerous class focussed on the tramp and the vagrant, or, in other words, on surplus and/ or undisciplined labor. Policies championed by the papers of the time are exemplified by the New York Times (1877) editorializing that the "... tramp is at war in a lazy kind of way with society and rejoices at being able to prey upon it". To combat the purportedly dangerous social deviants, legislatures approved anti-tramping statutes. Between 1876 and 1893, 21 states enacted tramping laws. City and county officials also passed vagrancy laws and tightened disorderly conduct and pauper statutes. As Adler (1994:40) notes, "... the hysteria surrounding the dangerous class profoundly affected the criminal justice system". Public officials anxious to visibly address this problem resorted to older practices. Some of these efforts included auctioning arrested tramps off for six-month terms to the highest bidder, posting rewards for the apprehension of beggars, and giving officials bounties for tramp arrests. Some states mandated solitary confinement and others even re-imposed whipping. Altogether, Gaucher (1982) reports that in the northern United States from 1800 onward, the criminalized population were largely composed of immigrants and blacks, the mainstays of surplus labour.

These reactionary practices included the expansion of police powers to "... preserve the social order over the need to protect individual liberty" (Adler, 1994:41), even to the point of arresting "dangerous characters" before the commission of any crime. Thus, police forces employed a "trawling" strategy in attempts to snare as many tramps at one time as possible. The *Tampa Morning Tribune* editorialized that it was "... better that two innocent ones be arrested than one guilty creature should escape" (City Brieflets, 1895). These law enforcement tactics were backed up by reformers who argued that the dangerous classes needed to be controlled through immigration restrictions, more aggressive child saving efforts (orphanages), vice suppression (blue laws and censorship), and temperance legislation (prohibition and drug laws). Officials also increasingly made poor relief more punitive. Worrying that such would sustain or even promote expansion of the dangerous class, reformers strove to separate the "worthy poor" from the "unworthy". Thus, workhouses replaced soup kitchens and strict ordinances controlled "indiscriminate giving". Experts even cautioned city officials to halt the practice of allowing the homeless to shelter in municipal buildings' basements during inclement weather.

All of this action and effort by the criminal justice system to control the "dangerous classes" was, as Gaucher (1987:169) comments, to "... mask the needs of capital — needs such as surplus labour, a stable social order and a disciplined workforce — particularly in times of high unemployment". By shifting the focus of the problem from economic manipulation and exploitation to law enforcement, social capital is spent on symptoms instead of invested in treating the causes. Thomas Mathiesen (1974), in *The Politics of Abolition*, proposes that imprisonment fulfils four critical social functions integral to bourgeois legitimation activities: the expurgatory function (removing the incarcerated from social participation); the power-draining function (reducing if not eliminating the socio-economic influence of the incarcerated); the diverting function (the shifting of attention from the society to the individual); and the symbolic function (that action has been taken and progress made in combating social disorder). Thus the dangerous classes were controlled by legislatures essentially outlawing unemployed poverty, truncheon wielding cops pummelling the out of work, and the chain gang performing labor that society did not then have to pay for — at least not directly.

If we fast forward one hundred years, the tune may have changed but the lyrics are resoundingly similar. For example, many of the proposals for welfare reform, sound suspiciously familiar. The GOP plan would cap the alleged spending growth in six major means tested programs ranging from Aid to Families with Dependent Children to Supplemental Security Income, while ending support after two years. As Republican Representative John Myers (IN) explains, "... our current welfare system penalizes the working poor and rewards the indolent". Proposals for reform range from fingerprinting welfare recipients before allowing them to receive assistance (*New York Times*, 1994) to denying aid to non-naturalized immigrants (Hudson, 1995) and any new unwed mothers under the age of 21 (*Tribune Media Services*, 1994), to Norplant insertions conditional for social benefits (Cockburn, 1994B). And, who could forget, the Speaker of the House, Newt Gingrich's call to mandate orphanages for the children of the unemployed poor. All measures designed to combat, as Representative E. Clay Shaw (R-FL) ludicrously claims, "... abuses by teenagers who have babies simply to receive more benefits" (Dunham, 1994).

Other efforts to combat the newly rediscovered dangerous class include cracking down on indiscriminate giving to the homeless. In San Francisco, Food Not Bombs volunteers have been arrested 720 times for giving homeless people sandwiches. Keith McHenry, a founder of the group, has been arrested 92 times, and now instead of misdemeanor permit violations (you have to have a myriad of permits to give food to the homeless in the city by the bay), he is being charged with felony assault (Cockburn, 1994C). If convicted three times, McHenry faces life imprisonment without possibility of parole under the golden state's recently adopted "three strikes, you're out" legislation — another measure to combat and control the dangerous class. Cockburn (1994C:18) observes "... that the way many cities and states are confronting social misery is to criminalize poverty".

The criminal justice system plays a major part today as it did a century ago in thwarting the dangerous class. The Omnibus Crime Bill of 1994 requires the Attorney General to study ways in which anti-loitering laws can be used to fight crime and to prepare a model act for states to implement (ACLU, 1994). More disturbing, though, is the "anti-gang" provision, which penalizes any group of two or more people who, either individually or as a group, commit two defined crimes within ten years. This provision defines as "gangs" any group "... that exhibit at least five of the following characteristics: formal membership with required initiation or rules for members; a recognized leader; common clothing, language, tattoos, turf where the group is known; and a group name" (Bryan, 1993).

The fact that aggressive and ambitious prosecutors have historically expanded legislation's parameters far beyond the lawmakers' initial intent (just look at the scope of RICO prosecutions) does not mean that they would use the anti-gang provision's vague and general criteria to violate the constitutional guarantee of due process. Under these guidelines, however, the Kansas City Chiefs football franchise, or any sports, fraternal or social organization for that matter, could find its entire organization under arrest if two members were arrested, for let's say, felony drunk driving (we won't suggest cocaine possession). Don't laugh: formal membership with rules for members (team players and NFL game Rule Book); recognized leader (coach Shottenheimer and quarterback Steve Bond); common clothing, languages and tattoos (red and white jersey with arrowhead symbol, "hut-hut-hut", and would a red and yellow Band-Aid horizontally placed across the bridge of one's nose count as a tattoo?); turf where the group is known (Arrowhead Stadium); and a group name (the Kansas City Chiefs). Then again, such mainstream, power-connected organizations like the Chiefs, Shriners and Jaycees, really would have nothing to fear, but would groups like the Nation of Islam, the Black Panther Party; the United Farm Workers Union or even the National Organization of Women feel as secure?

Already in Los Angeles County more than 105,000 young black men are considered "gang members" and listed in the GREAT (Gang Reporting, Evaluation and Tracking System) computer file (*L.A. Times*, 1992). Nearly half of those listed, however, have no previous arrest record, but instead were so tagged because they were identified in block, even neighborhood sweeps conducted by the police and sheriff departments' gang task forces. Shades of the 19th century and Depression Era "tramp trawling"! These individuals were literally in the wrong place at the wrong time — though it's hard to imagine why being in one's neighborhood is the wrong place — and

now face possible federal prosecution if any other "gang member" they are
match with in a computer record search is accused of two or more crimes.
Moreover, the labelling ceaselessly continues. In Compton, California, there
are more names in police gang files than young males in the city (Cockburn,
1994C). And once a gang member, always a gang member as far as the
police are concerned (GAO/T-GGD-92-52 at 16).

The Senate crime bill's anti-gang provision allocates $100 million for
additional U.S. attorneys, new mandatory minimum sentences, and the
lengthening of already long sentences; allows serious juvenile drug offenses
to be considered the same as serious adult felonies; and allows juveniles to
be tried as adults (ACLU, 1994). With the vast majority of identified gang
membership composed of minorities and/or immigrants (93 percent of Denver
Police gang listings are for example, of Black or Hispanic origins), the ACLU
comments that these statistics indicate that race, class, neighborhood and
clothes not conduct, often characterize a person as a gang member. In
hundred-year-old terminology, vis-à-vis members of the dangerous class it
is better for social order "that two innocent ones be arrested than one guilty
creature should escape".

In keeping with the retrograde stratagems and theorems to deal with this
once again newly identified social threat, some states, like Washington and
three others, have imposed "civil commitment" (indefinite incarceration)
programs for some offenders *after* they have completed their prison terms,
because of what they "might do" in the future (Wright, 1995), while other
states, like Alabama and Arizona, have re-instituted chain gangs (Leland and
Smith, 1995). Even more outrageous, the Mississippi legislature is considering
bringing back corporal punishment to its prisons (Nossiter, 1994). So today
one might not be guilty of any crime, except that of being labelled among the
dangerous classes, arrested anyway, be whipped while in the joint, and then
held after the end of your bit because of what you might do in the future —
all for the good of social order, of course.

The myth of the dangerous class a century ago slowly faded into obscurity
as reformers began to understand the influence of social structural forces.
These second generation social experts began instead to focus on the
economic and environmental roots of social problems. Slowly more refined,
though, really no less accusatory, explanations such as race ("Coloreds"),
intelligence (imbecility), economics (poverty) and social conditions
(alcoholism) were seen as causes of social deviance. A "class", as such,

was no longer openly labelled. Adler (1994:46) explains, and recent commentators remind us "the idea of a dangerous class has proved more resilient than the label". As Rothman (1994) has observed, the underclass, from which the dangerous class predominantly originates, has served as the scapegoat for deteriorating social conditions, instead of being defined as the victims of the deterioration itself.

As the economy expanded and the Progressive Era produced more equitable living standards and governmental protections, and as the expansion of the social safety net through the New Deal and War on Poverty programs softened the structural inequities inherent in capitalism, the dangerous class became nearly extinct in the social conscience. However, as the economic conditions of the post-industrial/information-service era become leaner, meaner and starker (not "kinder and gentler") for more and more of the population, social deviance in the guise of family dysfunction, drug abuse, and crime seems to grow.

As structural and social forces made the label of dangerous classes politically incorrect after the turn of the century, changes in these same forces are now coming full circle. America's working poor, those earning less than $14,764 a year for a family of four, have risen in numbers a shocking fifty percent in the last decade and now compose 15 percent of the national population according to the latest Department of Commerce figures (*St. Louis Post-Dispatch*, 1994). All the while, the IRS now calculates low income as a single taxpayer earning less than $23,500 (Librach, 1994). Yet as the poor grow in number, the federal government allocates less than two-thirds of the budget in constant dollars (now approximately one percent or $14 billion) for welfare than it allocated in 1970 (Bernstein, 1994A). According to the Washington based Center on Budget and Policy Priorities, subsidized housing program allocations — adjusted for inflation — have been cut by 62%, employment and training by 59%, community-development block grants by 29%, energy assistance by 54%, and legal services by 29% (Foust, 1994). As adjusted wages have stayed flat or declined since the 1970s (Stanglin, 1995), the gap between rich and poor is now at Depression Era dimensions (Bernstein, 1994B).

Political commentator William Greider (1991), writing for *Rolling Stone*, comments on the bankrupt strategy emanating from Washington, labelling it as "scapegoating". This he explains, is a way to change the subject from what is really hurting people and panders to an impulse that is ingrained in American politics and canonized by Machiavelli. As Greider (1991) writes,

"... whenever things are going badly, whenever people are losing their jobs and social decline is visible, it's easier to blame the troubles on minority segments who seem to be getting more than their share".

The modern version of the tramp and vagrant are the homeless, the panhandlers, and those who "will work for food". The present day dangerous class equivalents are those isolated and alienated souls left behind in our headlong quest for the elusive American dream and are concentrated in the inner cities — primarily people of color, people of other languages and cultures, and the expanding number of people suffering from poverty. "Whether or not the dangerous class existed in industrial America", Adler concludes (1994:45), "the idea of such a class encouraged middle-class Americans to view the poor as a threat to society and persuaded policy makers to rely on the criminal justice system to address the effects of poverty".

Sociologists Emile Durkheim and Kai T. Erikson (1966) postulate that society *needs* crime (as defined by the powers that be) to tighten bonds of cultural solidarity and thus have developed institutions whose purpose (even if unannounced) are to maintain a steady supply of deviants. Jeffrey Reiman (1984), in *The Rich Get Richer and the Poor Get Prison*, advances what he calls the Pyrrhic Defeat Theory, in which he believes the failure of the criminal justice system, and in essence the socio-political structure itself, to reduce crime, serves the interests of the rich and powerful in the United States by fulfilling a controlling function to mop up the messy and potentially destabilizing by-product of capitalism, surplus labor and poverty. Reiman (1984:39) notes "The fact is that the label 'crime' is not used in America to name all or the worst actions that cause misery and suffering to Americans. It is primarily reserved for the dangerous actions of the poor".

Today it is the policy makers who have persuaded the bourgeoisie that the resurrected dangerous class exists and threatens their diminishing standards of living. From highly publicized, though rarely documented, cases of welfare fraud and dependency, (one-third of all adults leave the assistance rolls within two years) (Bernstein, 1994A), to the myth of exploding crime rates (overall per capita property and violent crime rates are lower today than in 1973), (*Corrections Compendium*, 1993), the single preferred solution is to continue reducing social programs while generously providing for the poor in federal spending for new prison construction. This conservative (dare one say neo-Fascist) ideology mirrors that of the British ruling class of a century and a half ago, as illustrated in *A Just Measure of Pain*:

> The persistent support for the penitentiary is inexplicable so long as
> we assume that its appeal rested on its functional capacity to control
> crime. Instead, its support rested on a larger social need. It had
> appeal because the reformers succeeded in presenting it as a response,
> not merely to crime, but to the social crisis of a period, and as part
> of a larger strategy of political, social and legal reform designed to
> re-establish order on a new foundation. As a result, while criticized
> for its functional shortcomings, the penitentiary continued to
> command support because it was seen as an element of a larger
> vision of order that by the 1840's commanded the reflexive assent
> of the propertied and powerful. (Ignatieff, 1978:210)

The dangerous class, though, has never left us. In fact, they have always
been with us, existing under varying chameleon like labels. They are not,
however, the tramp and the homeless or the immigrant and the unwed mother,
but rather they are the policy wonks and law makers who, in the parlance of
the street, "make book" on the inequities perpetuated by unrepentant
capitalism, overt and covert racism, and cultural xenophobia. Cockburn
·"called money" when he labelled such perpetrators fascists, for their "rap"
today differs little from the rhetoric of the past. Or as Adler (1994:46)
summarizes, "... popular and even scholarly descriptions of the modern
urban underclass often bear striking similarities to late nineteenth century
descriptions of the 'dangerous class'". As Gaucher (1982) pointed out fifteen
years ago, "... rather than accepting the ruling class and its petit-bourgeois
ideologues' depiction of the working class as degenerate, one must come to
terms with the fact that it is 'lower class' life and social relations that are
under attack in a most general way".

The right, led by the Gingrich, continues to redefine America in more
and more exclusive and down right mean terms. *Wall Street Journal* editor
David Frumm (1994), in his new book *Dead Right*, observes that the
republican philosophy is moving toward a new kind of isolationist
"nationalism". He foresees an aggressive GOP bashing immigrants, decrying
affirmative action, and more vengeful in military and criminal justice spending.
To be forthright then in their intentions, they, as well, should openly resurrect
the term of the dangerous class. At least then we will all be using the same
terminology, if viewing it from different perspectives. This would be better
and more honest than using the current round of code words for classicism
and racism, such as criminal and gang member, welfare cheat and unwed
mother, and illegal alien and foreigner.

All we need now is for Rush Limbaugh to slap his desk and in the same breath lament the predations of feminazis and the dangerous class, as he plops his oversized and underworked rump into his overstuffed and overworked chair — all to the sycophantic applause of a largely white ("I've got mine"), conservative ("and I'm going to keep it"), applause-metered studio audience.

REFERENCES

ACLU (1994). "ACLU Analysis of Major Civil Liberties Abuses in Senate Crime Bill (HR3355)". (January 7).

Adler, J. (1994). "The Dynamite, Wreckage, and Scum in our Cities: the social construction of deviance in industrial America". *Justice Quarterly*, V. 11, N. 1 (March):33–49.

Bernstein, A. (1994A). "Why Clinton's Workforce Won't Work", *Business Week*, (March 7):92.

———. (1994B). "Why America Needs Unions But not the Kind it has now".

Business Week (May 23):70–82.

Bryan (1993). *Congressional Record-Senate*, November 9:S15400.

Carpenter, M. (1851). *Reformatory Schools for the Children of the Perishing and Dangerous Classes, and for Juvenile Offenders*, vii–98.

"City Brieflets" (1895). *Tampa Morning Tribune* (August 1).

Cockburn, A. (1994A). "Beat the Devil: Peretz and Black Mothers", *The Nation* (April 25):548.

Cockburn, A. (1994B). "Beat the Devil: Norplant and the Social Cleansers, Part II", *The Nation* (July 25/August I):116–117.

———. (1994C). "Beat the Devil: Cut out His Heart, In San Francisco", *The Nation* (July 4):7–8.

———. (1994D). "Throw the Bum Out", *The Nation* (September 26):301. *Corrections Compendium* (1993). "Crime Fell More Than 5 Percent Last Year, Reaching a 20-year Low" (December):18.

Devine, E. (1994). "On the Subject of Crime" *Survey* 31 (January 3):417–418.

Dunham, R. (1994). "Welfare Reform from a Mom Who's Been There ", *Business Week* (June 27): 29.

Erikson, K. (1966). *Wayward Puritans*, NY: John Wiley & Sons.

Foust, D. (1994). "America's War on Poverty Has Been Going Broke", *Business Week* (August 1):20.

Frumm, D. (1994). *Dead Right*, NY: Basic Books.

GAO/T-GGD-92-52, at 16. *Information on the L.A. County Sheriff's Department Gang Reporting, Evaluation and Tracking System.*

Gaucher, R. (1982). *Class and State in Lower and Upper Canada 1760 to 1873: Groundwork for the Analysis of Criminal Justice in Pre-Confederation Canada.* Unpublished Ph.D. dissertation. University of Sheffield, England.

————. (1987). "Canadian Civil Society, the Canadian State, and Criminal Justice Institutions: Theoretical Considerations", In Ratner, R. and McMullan, J. (eds.) *State Control: Criminal Justice Politics in Canada*, U.B.C. Press

Greider, W. (1991). "The Politics of Diversion: Blame It On the Blacks, *Rolling Stone*. (September 5):32, 33, 96.

Hudson, R. (1995). "Ashcroft, Other Conservative Senators Offer Welfare Plan: It'd Mandate Work, Reward Volunteering", *St. Louis Post-Dispatch* (July 21).

Hunter, R. (1904). *Poverty*, NY: Harper and Row.

Ignatieff, M. (1987). *A Just Measure of Pain*, London: MacMillan.

L.A. Times (1992). "Sheriff's Gang Tracking System Needs Safeguards, GAO Says". (June 29).

Leland, J. and Smith, V. (1995). "Back on the Chain Gang," *Newsweek*. (May 15):58.

Librach. P. (1994). "Who is Rich? IRS Answer May Ruin Your Day," *St. Louis Post-Dispatch* (April 7).

Mathiesen, T. (1974). *The Politics of Abolition*, Oslo: Martin Robinson.

Myers, J. (1994). "The GOP's Welfare Reform Alternative," *Indianapolis Star* (June 28).

New York Times (1877). "Vilest of the Vile" (January 7):5.

————. (1993). "2 out of 3 Young Black Men in Denver are on a Police List of Gang Suspects" (December 11):A8.

————. (1994). "Welfare crackdown puts spotlight on fingerprint systems" (May 31).

Nossiter, A. (1994). "Making Hard Time Harder, States Cut TV and Sports", *New York Times National* (September 17).

Reiman, J. (1984). *The Rich Get Richer and the Poor Get Prison*, NY: MacMillan Publishing Co.

Rothman (1994). "The Crime and Punishment", *The New York Review* (February 17).

Stanglin, D., et al. (1995). "Washington Whispers: Labor Pains", *U.S. News & World Report* (March 13):21.

St. Louis Post-Dispatch (1994). "Working Their Way into Poverty" (April 4).

Tobias, J. (1967). *Crime and Industrial Society in the Nineteenth Century*, London: Batsford.

Tribune Media Services (1994), "Teen moms are the new welfare reform targets" (May 12).

Vermeulen, M. (1994). "What People Earn", *Parade Magazine* (June 26):4–5.

Will, G. (1994). "Fascism's Second Spring", *Newsweek* (May 2):72.

Wright, P. (1995). "WA Civil Commitment Sham", *Prison Legal News* (May):17–18.

Three Strikes Racks 'em Up
Paul Wright

Editor's Note: Reprinted with kind permission from Prison Legal News, *Volume 5, Number 6, 1994.*

In November of 1993 voters in Washington state passed Initiative 593 which mandates life without parole for defendants convicted of one of 42 qualifying felonies for the third time. The first attempt, in 1992, failed to get the necessary 182,000 voters' signatures for the initiative to qualify for the ballot. It appeared that the 1993 effort would meet the same fate until within the last few weeks before the July deadline by which initiatives must be filed with the secretary of state with the required signatures, the National Rifle Association (NRA) pumped $90,000 into the campaign (out of a total $170,000 raised). This allowed for a massive direct mailing to citizens across the state as well as paying professional companies to gather signatures.

Washington voters passed Initiative 593 "Three Strikes You're Out" by a three to one margin. Since then California has passed a similar measure, about 30 states are considering some form of it and it is the centerpiece of Clinton's vaunted "anti-crime bill". The proponents of three strikes claim it will keep "career criminals" off the streets and in prison. Within what passes for mainstream American politics today no one is seriously opposed to such measures (it should be noted that the American Correctional Association [ACA] and the Judicial Conference of the United States, which represents federal judges, have gone on record opposing three strikes legislation). The only dispute is how wide the net should be cast, i.e., all third time felons or just "violent ones", life without parole or at least 25 years without parole. This is hardly a debate.

Little noticed by the mainstream media are other effects these laws have had. The Washington three strikes law eliminated good time or other time reductions for several offenses, including murder, rape, and robbery. It also forbids placing wide categories of prisoners in any kind of work release, home detention, or similar type of facility. The California law requires sentences be served consecutively, restricts good time credits for California prisoners and limits prosecutors' ability to strike prior felonies in reaching plea bargains.

It seems that no one has pointed out that these laws have already been tried in the past. Until 1984, Washington had a "habitual offender" statute which mandated a life sentence for a defendant convicted of a felony for the third time. Most states have some version of this law on the books. Its main purpose is to avoid trials whereby defendants will plea bargain to other charges in exchange for prosecutors agreeing not to "bitch" them. Occasionally the media reports the hapless defendant, usually in Texas, who gets a life sentence for stealing a carton of cigarettes after being charged as a "habitual criminal".

Just who are these "career criminals" that are the focus of "three strikes" legislation? Fred Markham once told me that prisoners reminded him of the Wizard of Oz. The Wizard said he was not a bad man just a bad wizard. Likewise, the vast majority of prisoners are not bad men, just bad criminals. Anyone who has done time in prison will tell you that they are not filled with rocket scientists. Most of the people in prison are not evil nor professional criminals, they tend to be poor people with emotional, drug or alcohol problems who are caught doing something stupid. The "professional career criminal" tends to be a media myth, unless we count savings and loan bankers, fortune 500 companies. ...

About nine hours after California's three strikes law went into effect on March 7, 1994, Charles Bentely was arrested in Los Angeles and charged with the crime that could send him to prison for 25 years without parole: a 50 cent robbery. Donnell Dorsey, 37, is also looking at this third strike, for sitting in a stolen truck. The California law also doubles presumptive sentences for second time offenders.

In March 1994, Samuel Page became the first person in the U.S. convicted and sentenced under a "three strikes" law. He pleaded guilty in Seattle. In total, by mid-1994, about 15 people in Washington state, mainly armed robbers and sex offenders, have been charged with a qualifying third strike. According to the latest report by the Washington Sentencing Guidelines Commission, in fiscal year 1993, there were 204 defendants who would have qualified as three strikes defendants had the statute been in effect at the time (the law took effect December 2, 1993).

On April 15, 1994, Larry Fisher, 35, was convicted of his third strike in Snohomish county Superior court in Washington. He will be sent to prison for the rest of his life. Fisher was convicted of putting his finger in his pocket pretending it was a gun and robbing a sandwich shop of $151. An hour later police arrested him at a bar a block away while he was drinking a beer. Fisher's two prior strikes involved stealing $360 from his grandfather in 1986 and then robbing a pizza parlour of $100. All told the take from Fisher's criminal career totals $611; he has never harmed anyone.

How much will society pay to protect itself from this $611 loss? On average it costs $54,209 to build one prison bed space, and $20,000–$30,000 per year to house one prisoner. The costs are higher if financing and related costs are factored into the equation. If Larry Fisher lives to be age 70, the total cost will be approximately one million dollars. Is society really getting its money's worth?

Using the Sentencing Commission's figures as a base to assume that 200 defendants a year will be third striked in Washington state alone, allows us to calculate a need for that many prison beds a year. Because they will never get out this will continue to grow; within ten years they will occupy at least 2,000 prison beds. The average prison in Washington holds about 800 prisoners. At the same time that Washington voters passed I-593 they passed I-601 which limited the ability of the legislature and governor to raise taxes. All tax increases are now tied to population growth and must be approved by voters. This will present something of a contradiction in coming years; voters want to lock everyone up for the rest of their lives but do they want to pay for it? More importantly, can they pay for it? Stagnant economic growth (itself a leading cause of crime) results in a smaller tax base from which to pay for more prisons.

There is a lot wrong with these three strikes laws. Aside from the fact that only poor people will bear their brunt there is the matter of proportionality. Everyone has heard the term "an eye for an eye". The original meaning of this was that punishment should be proportionate to the offense. If someone's cow wandered into your pasture this meant your village did not destroy the village of the cow's owner. Does stealing $151 merit life in prison? Is 50 cents worth 25 years?

There are already numerous laws which mandate life without parole for certain first time or repeat offenses. The federal Armed Career Criminal Act, passed in 1988, mandates 25 years without parole for a three time felon found in possession (not using mind you, just possession) of a firearm. Michigan and the federal government also mandate life without parole for possession of more than 650 grams of heroin or cocaine for a first time offender. The only other offense in Washington state which carries a life without parole penalty is aggravated murder.

When the laws make no distinction in punishment between killing five people, having a gun, having 650 grams of drugs or stealing $151 there is something wrong. Washington and California police have reported that since the 'three strikes' laws went into effect suspects have become more violent in resisting arrest. A suspect knowing that if convicted for a $151 robbery he will spend his life in prison has, quite literally, nothing to lose if he has to kill a few people to avoid arrest. The result of this, I suspect, will eventually be the broadening of the death penalty. Seattle Police Sgt Eric Barden was quoted in the *New York Times* saying "It now looks like some of these three strike cases might try to get away or shoot their way out. Believe me, that's not lost on us. We're thinking about it".

It is perverse logic where the proponents of these type of laws cite with approval the increasing numbers of people receiving such sentences, be it life without parole or the death penalty, claiming they are a deterrent. If such laws were effective the numbers would decline. Neither the mainstream media nor the politicians have any interest in using logic or common sense in formulating public policy. All these laws will achieve are an increasing number of poor people in prison, more violence, more state repression and eventually, greater use of the death penalty.

No laws will be passed making corruption by public officials, endangering public health by corporations, a "three strikes" offense. In 1989 the Federal Sentencing Guidelines Commission was going to increase the penalties and punishment for corporations convicted of crimes, including making its executives criminally liable. Corporate America promptly lobbied the Commission and Congress and these amendments never materialized. Unfortunately, poor people affected by three strikes laws don't command a voice that Congress or the media will listen to: the rich get richer, the poor get prison.

Karl Marx wrote that history repeats itself, first as tragedy, then as farce. In 19th century England people were hanged for offenses like pick pocketing and poaching. In this country many mandatory minimum sentences were repealed in the 1960s and 1970s as people realized they did not work and their only effect was to destroy what chances prisoners had to rebuild a life. Unfortunately, this repetition of history will not be farcical for those swept up by baseball slogans masquerading as social policy.

These three strikes laws give the impression that most defendants had a chance to hit the ball the first few times. In reality, by the time most defendants step into a courtroom for the first time they already have a couple of strikes against them: their class, alcohol and/or drug problems, illiteracy, joblessness, poverty and oftentimes their race or a history of abuse. They've been striking out a long time before they got up to the plate.

Assuming a three strikes defendant has been to prison twice before he gets his third strike it would seem that its only fair to receive a decent chance to get a hit or a home run. Instead, most prisoners go back to the same neighborhoods with the same poverty, joblessness, illiteracy and other problems with which they left, compounded by the brutalization and dehumanization inherent in the American prison experience of the 20th century. Right now legislators and DOC's are endeavoring to "make prisons tougher" by eliminating what token vocational and rehabilitational programs now exist. Combined with idleness, overcrowding, endemic violence etc., a self fulfilling prophecy is being created: more third strikers. It's hard to get any wood on the ball under these conditions.

Will things get any better? Georgia's governor is proposing "two strikes you're out". California governor Pete Wilson, hot on the heels of signing "three strikes" into law declared that California needs a "one strike" law for child molesters, arsonists and rapists. He called for a mandatory death penalty for murders committed during drive-by shootings or carjackings. It won't be long now before they dispense with the wimpy one strike stuff and just go for the death penalty.

Slaves of the State
Paul Wright

Editor's Note: Reprinted with kind permission from Prison Legal News, *Volume 5, Number 5, 1994:14-15.*

Many people have the mistaken impression that slavery was outlawed or abolished in the United States after the civil war by the passage of the 13th amendment. Unfortunately, that was not the case. The 13th amendment reads: "Neither slavery nor involuntary servitude, *except as punishment for crimes whereof the party shall have been duly convicted,* shall exist within the United States, or any place subject to their jurisdiction". The effect of the 13th amendment was not to abolish slavery but to limit it to those who had been convicted of a crime.

The reality was made apparent in the aftermath of the civil war when large numbers of newly freed black slaves found themselves "duly convicted" of crimes and in state prisons where, once again, they laboured without pay. Until the last 20 years it was common practice for state prisons to "rent" prison labor out to private contractors in a modern form of chattel slavery. This situation led the Virginia Supreme Court to remark in an 1871 case, *Ruffin* v. *Commonwealth,* that prisoners were "slaves of the state". All that has changed since then is that the state is less honest about its slave holding practices.

Until the 1930's most state and federal prisons were largely self sufficient, producing most of the goods and food they consumed and even produced for sale a surplus of food and some industrial products. In many states prisoners even served as armed guards (until the mid-1970s the state of Arkansas held some 3,000 prisoners with only 27 civilian employees) and many other functions which required minimal investment by the state. Prison self sufficiency and excess production for profit largely ended during the mid-1930s when the U.S. was in the midst of the depression and both unions and manufacturers complained about competing against prison made products on the open market. In most manufactured products the labor cost is the most expensive component. Cut the labor cost and the resulting profit margin increases. With a prison labor force working at no cost the state and federal prisons could easily compete against any private manufacturer and workers. One of the laws passed was the Ashhurst-Summers Act which prohibited the transport in interstate commerce of prison made goods unless the prisoners were paid at least minimum wage.

Prison labor did not start to become a major issue again until the 1980s. Until then most prison produced goods were either for use within the prison system or sale to other state agencies, license plates being the most famous example. This began to change when the U.S.'s massive prison building and incarceration binge began to gather steam. In a 1986 study designed to reduce the cost to the government of its prison policies, former Supreme Court Justice Warren Burger issued the call for transforming prisons into "factories with fences". In essence, prisons should once again become self sustaining, even profit producing entities requiring minimal financial input from the state. The "factories with fences" proponents seek to turn the clock back to the time when prisoners were merely slaves of the state.

While some think that slavery, i.e., unpaid, forced labor, offers enormous profit potential for the slave owner, there are historical reasons slavery is no longer the dominant mode of economic production. First, the slave owner has a capital investment in his slave, regardless of whether the slave is working or producing profit he must be fed and housed in minimal conditions, to ensure the slave's value as a labor producer remains. With the rise of industrial capitalism in the 18th and 19th century capitalists discovered that capitalism has its boom and bust cycles characterized by over-production. Thus idle slaves would become a drain on the owner's finance because they would still require feeding and housing, regardless of whether they were working. However if the slave was "free" he could be employed at low wages and then laid off when not producing profit for the employer. The wage slave was free to starve, free to be homeless, etc., with no consequences for the owner.

Another reason slavery was inefficient compared to wage slavery was that the slaves would occasionally revolt, destroying the means of production and killing the slave owner. More common and less dramatic were the acts of sabotage and destruction that made machinery with its attendant capital investment, impractical for use by slaves. So by the middle of the 19th century wage slaves employing machines could outproduce, at greater profit for the factory owner, chattel slaves using less easily damaged more primitive machinery.

The problem slave owners of old faced was what to do with non-producing slaves. Today's slave owners (i.e., the state), face the opposite problem of having idle slaves who must be fed, clothed and housed whether or not they produce anything of value. The current thinking argues that any potential profit produced by prison slaves is better than none.

Some of the proponents of prison slavery try to disguise it as a "rehabilitation" or "vocational" program designed to give prisoners job skills or a trade which can be used upon their release. This is not the case. First, almost without exception, the jobs available in prison industries are labor intensive, menial low-skill jobs which tend to be performed by exploited workers in three places: third world dictatorships, by illegal immigrants in the U.S., or by prisoners. Clothes and textile manufacturing is the biggest and most obvious example of this. Second, because the jobs don't exist in the first place, the job skills acquired are hardly useful. Does anyone expect a released prisoner to go to Guatemala or El Salvador to get a job sewing clothes for the U.S. market at a dollar a day? Third, if it's rehabilitational then why not pay the prisoner at least minimum wage for his/her work? Fourth, it ignores the reality that the U.S. has at least 8 or 9 million unemployed workers at any given time, many of them highly skilled, who cannot find jobs that pay a meaningful wage to support themselves. So-called "job retraining" programs are a failure because all the training in the world won't create jobs with decent wages. In pursuit of higher profits (i.e., lower salaries) U.S. and multinational corporations have transferred virtually all labor intensive production jobs to Third World countries. If prisoners are going to be exploited as slave labor it should be called what it is.

The U.S. has little problem condemning the export of prison made goods from China. What makes this rank hypocrisy is the fact that the same criticisms levelled by the U.S. government against Chinese prison made goods can be levelled at U.S. prison made goods. According to a March 18, 1994, story in the *Seattle Times*, prison made goods from California and Oregon are being exported for retail sales. In a supreme irony, the California DOC is marketing its clothing lines in Asia competing against the sweatshops of Indonesia, Hong Kong, Thailand and of course, the Chinese. The "Prison Blues" brand of clothes, made by prisoners in the Oregon DOC, has a projected sales of over $1.2 million in export revenues. U.S. State department officials were quoted saying they wished prison made goods were not exported by state DOC's because it is being raised as an issue by other governments, namely the Chinese, which have cited U.S. practices in response to criticisms. For their part the Chinese have announced a ban on the export of prison made goods while the U.S. is stepping up such exports.

The California prisoners making clothes for export are paid between 35 cents and $1 an hour. The Oregon prisoners are paid between $6 to $8 an hour but have to pay back up to 80% of that to cover the cost of their captivity. As they are employed by a DOC owned company this is essentially an accounting exercise where the prisoners' real wages are between $1.20 to $1.80 an hour. Still competitive with the wages paid to illegal immigrant sweatshop workers here in the U.S. and wages paid to garment workers in the Far East and Central America.

Fred Nichols, the administrator of Unigroup, the Oregon DOC prison industries, was quoted saying: "We want them to work in the same environment as on the outside' ..." in terms of hiring interviews and such. Yet obviously this does not include the right to collective bargaining and union representation which are, of course, common to the labor process outside prisons and would teach important rehabilitational values such as collective dispute resolution, and the principle of a fair wage for work.)

Companion articles to this one detail conditions in the federal prison system's Unicor Washington state industries. While the particulars may change, the trend continues towards increased exploitation of prison slave labor. Some states, especially those in the south such as Texas, Arkansas and Louisiana still have unpaid prisoners laboring in fields supervised by armed guards on horseback, with no pretense of "rehabilitation" or "job training". In those states the labor is mandatory, refusal to work brings harsh punishment and increases prison sentences served.

In 1977 the Supreme Court decided *Jones* v. *North Carolina Prisoner's Labor Union* which removed the notion that the courts will offer any protection for the idea of prisoner union organizing. In the past, *Prison Legal News* has reported on efforts and court cases to seek a minimum wage for prison laborers. For the most part such efforts through the courts have been unsuccessful with courts bending over backwards to read exemptions (which are not written) into the federal *Fair Labor and Standards Act* (FLSA). Still, the litigation should continue to chip away on that front.

On the political front we must expose prison slavery for what it is and at the same time seek collective bargaining for safe working conditions, fair pay, etc. It took workers in this country nearly 160 years to obtain this in 1934 and it has since been whittled away. So it will be neither easy nor quick. The problem that slave owners of old faced is still faced by modern slavers, namely resistance by the slaves. To the extent that private business run slave operations in prisons, there is the massive state subsidy that they receive and for state run enterprises there are the hidden costs. Under guise of "security" go the enormous expenses associated with guards, checkpoints, controls, etc., that are otherwise not present with wage slaves on the outside. The occasional mutiny by irate slaves with concomitant loss of production, capital investment in machinery, etc. is likely to occur and deter private ventures.

In Washington the state offers a lot of incentives for private businesses to employ prison slaves. Class I venture industries pay no rent, electricity, water or similar costs. They are exempt from state and federal workplace safety standards, pay no medical, unemployment or vacation/sick leave to slaves who have no right to collective organizing or bargaining. In a case like this we are seeing welfare capitalism where private business is getting a handout from the state at taxpayer expense. One which, I suspect, will largely swallow the profit paid back to the state under guise of taxes, room and board, etc., by the prisoner. To the extent that prison slaves are forced to pay state and federal taxes there arises the question, linked to the right to vote, of taxation without representation. If forced to pay taxes like any other citizen under guise of rehabilitative or vocational employment, then why not the right to vote given other taxpayers?

Workers on the outside should also be aware of the consequences that prison slave labor has for their jobs. Ironically, as unemployment on the outside increases, crime and the concomitant incarceration rates increase. It may be that before too long people can only find menial labor intensive production jobs in prisons or third world countries where people labor under similar conditions. The factory with fences meets the prison without walls.

A Non-Traditional Approach to a Curriculum for Prisoners in New York State

Juan Rivera

THE DIRECT RELATIONSHIP

The need for a non-traditional approach to education in the New York State prison system derives from what a group of innovative prisoners calls the 'direct relationship' between the sixty-two prisons in New York and the specific communities where prisoners come from. A curriculum reflecting the reforms requested by New York's Commissioner of Education are needed, but for prisoners the curriculum must include an additional dimension. It must include a non-traditional, community-specific approach that takes the community into account and links the needs of the community with those of the offender. After all, those needs brought most of the offenders to prison in the first place.

Why a non-traditional approach, and what does it mean? To answer this we must first define a traditional approach. From our perspective this is a curriculum which is Eurocentric, white, and middle-class. It is taught to a variety of ethnic groups on the false assumption that anyone is able to fit into this society. In contrast, a non-traditional curriculum recognizes Latino and Afrocentric perspectives. It acknowledges the poor and the reality that we are not allowed to fit into Eurocentric society. Fundamental differences between cultures must be considered and understood in all curriculum initiatives, since they concern every aspect of our lives.

Why should prisoners in New York demand such a non-traditional curriculum? They want it because it reveals the direct relationship — that is, although Blacks and Latinos together represent less than twenty-five percent of the total general population in New York, they comprise 82.3 percent of the State's total prison population,[1] with the Latino population the fastest growing segment in the State's prison system. Furthermore, the direct relationship reveals that seventy percent or more of the prisoners come from New York City (Correctional Association, New York and New York State Coalition for Criminal Justice, 1990:7). Perhaps more important it recognizes that eighteen specific assembly districts in New York City contribute seventy percent of the prisoners, which leads to our next question: What is occurring in those eighteen assembly districts that is not occurring in the other 132 districts in New York State?

120

There are 'crime generative factors,' commonly known as family breakdown, poor health care, substandard housing, under-education, high unemployment, drugs, discrimination, prison, etc., that are prevalent in those assembly districts and are the root cause of our problems. Without question these 'crime generative factors' are the reasons why such a disproportionate number of Latinos and Blacks are in prison. Consequently, these root causes must be understood from a Latino and Afrocentric perspective.

Our analysis is not a unique one with respect to socio-economic conditions, but it is one that seeks a solution from the perspective of those most affected by the ever-increasing incarceration rate and a recidivism rate which, according to the Department of Correctional Services, was at 39.5 percent in 1988 (1988:8–9). Since approximately ninety-five percent of the prison population when released return to the communities from which they come, and since four out of ten of these people will return to prison, this suggests that released offenders returning to their communities are contributing to the higher percentage of the overall crime rate in these districts.

TRADITIONAL VERSUS NON-TRADITIONAL

There is a popular assumption that while people are in prison something is being done to address the problems that caused them to come to prison. However, the traditional methods that are used do not work for the majority of prisoners, who today are either Latino or Black, because the traditional methods do not take into account the institutional failures and 'crime generative factors' that exist in our communities. The traditional methods imply that the fault rests solely with the offenders: that they commit their crimes because there is something wrong with them (i.e., that they are inherently evil). Conversely, the non-traditional approach claims that there are socio-economic conditions, in addition to the individual's behavior, that cause a person to commit a crime. We say that these factors cannot be overlooked and in fact should be addressed by providing a non-traditional course in basic civic and community politics. Instead of rehabilitation, we like to call this an empowerment process which allows individuals to transform themselves from what they were to what they can become. In place of the helplessness poor people often feel, a sense of control over their future is instilled in them and this empowerment works to transform a criminal mentality into a progressive and law-abiding one by permitting the ex-offender insight into failing institutions in their own communities.

In addition, African and Latin American history classes should be established and attached to all educational institutions, including the General Education Diploma (G.E.D) educational program. At the Green Haven Correctional Facility we have observed that prisoners who attended both the Black and Latin American history classes acquired a G.E.D. diploma and went on to enroll in the Dutchess or Marist College with greater success than those who did not attend either class. Although we have not conducted an empirical analysis of the success rate of students who take these classes, we believe the classes capture the interest of students and stimulate their learning ability. Moreover, these classes serve to instill a natural sense of self-worth which cannot be inculcated through a Eurocentric approach. For the Italian, Irish, and other Europeans, the Anglo-Saxon model might be a normal and suitable standard of achievement; however, the African descendant needs an African frame of reference and the same is true for the Hispanic.

MODEL CLASSES

In order to release from prison people who have been educated with a new vision of themselves, and of the purpose and direction their lives should take from that point onwards, we have created two classes which we think can serve as models for other prison education programs and which address the responsibilities we have to ourselves and our communities.

Addressing these responsibilities is essential if we are to survive as individual ethnic groups and simultaneously thrive as American citizens. These classes take into consideration three principal characteristics of the prisoner which the state's traditional approach does not address: (1) the crime generative attitudes of the prisoner and their origins, (2) the ethnic status and identity of the prisoner, and (3) a sense of community. Let us examine these from the perspective of those who have lived in prison.

The first characteristic, the crime generative attitudes of the prisoner, are created by the socio-economic conditions which exist in the community. These are the attitudes which lead one to believe that, "You must make it in this society by being tough and mean, or by any way you can." Thus, a disrespect for the laws of American society arises. This happens when a distinct people experiences segregation, injustice, inferior education, and the force of police as the slave patrols (Williams and Murphy, 1990:3–5).

This happens when people are deprived of community control, political control, and economic independence (i.e., they lack repatriation) (Blauner, 1990:111).

The longing to fit the traditional European model often leads to self-hatred because we fail to 'fit in' and this places our community members on a collision course with the 'white man's law.' We seek compensation for our failures by acquiring symbols of success, money, and material possessions, which for most of us can only be gained illegally and often in the form of ethnic crime. Hence, we develop the attitude that illegal activity is all right.

Ethnicity then is central to the problem of crime, and understanding ethnicity in this way must become part of a prison curriculum. The study of ethnic status and identity helps prisoners to deal with the reality of their ethnic status in American society, which is that of second-class citizens. More positively, it identifies the role of ethnic groups in American history. This develops the positive self-esteem needed to advance past the stereotypes and stigmas created for us by others. An understanding of ethnic status also challenges the feeling of powerlessness which keeps us from doing something about our present conditions.

The final characteristic, the sense of community, must also have a place in prison education programs. Having a sense of community empowers prisoners because it links them with groups in the community and teaches them how their community operates. We learn from an historical perspective about the development of community concepts, including community concepts of social control which take into consideration the impact of crime generative factors on community empowerment movements. All of these factors afford the prisoner insight into how s/he fits in the community, thereby instilling in ourselves concern for the community and the people in it. The prisoner learns to see how people are struggling as a community to survive.

The classes are designed to develop a well rounded person with some basic knowledge, ranging from the meaning of ethnocentricity to what is liberation theology. We recommend these classes be scheduled for a period of six months. Throughout the course outside speakers should participate and provide insight to related issues. We also encourage grass-roots groups from the community to assist us in improving what we have developed so far, for we sternly believe that there are no prison problems, only community problems which we bring with us to prison. And since it is the community's survival that is at stake, their input is most essential.

PURGING STAGES

Equally important is the need to help prisoners deal with negative influences which have been embedded in their personalities. Hence, we advocate self-development purging stages which help to create a new Hispanic or Black person through (1) emotional purging; (2) educational purging; and (3) social purging.

The first purging stage addresses emotions such as racism, sexism, hate, vanity, and desires. We also examine the negative and positive practices of machismo. Educational purging attempts to eliminate the effects of mis-education, the result of skewed demographics, all-white American history, and traditional (i.e., Eurocentric) learning. Emphasis is placed on re-education by acknowledging our own history and non-traditional knowledge. We find that the social purging stage is the most important part of the process by which we come to understand why we are who we are and how we got that way. It addresses both those aspects of our social perspective that need revamping and changing in our minds and the way we conceptualize our own reality. This is where we begin to breach the stereotypes and stigmas that society creates for us, which are the major restrictive constructs, the subliminal underpinnings of our psycho-social problems.

A theory which supports the purging stage is the labeling perspective. We must be in a position to choose between positive and negative role models, but this cannot be done until we are in a position to identify and understand these role models. For example, C.H. Cooley's (1983) theory the 'looking glass self' suggests just how important it is to understand the labeling process and its detrimental effects on the individual's self-image and the image of the entire community. The labeling process is executed through the traditional educational system. Both the labels and the labeling process are made to appear real/natural by the media. We must understand this process and its dangerous effects so we can begin to redefine our own reality and make concerted efforts towards changing conditions in our communities. In this way, we can become a life-giving component instead of an element which destroys those very communities in which we live and die.

CONCLUSION

We as prisoners are making an honest effort at reconciling ourselves with those communities we helped to destroy. We realize that we harmed not only ourselves but the community as well. With these classes we hope to open prisoners' eyes, to give new meaning to our lives, and to allow us to see ourselves as part of the community.

We do not have all the answers, nor do we pretend to have them. Nevertheless, we have begun something meaningful which can become a turning point in this destructive process taking place today. Also, we realize that much of the community hesitates to accept us, and we understand these feelings. Thus, we have formulated a five-step reconciliation process entailing recognition, responsibility, reconstruction, reconciliation, and redemption. It attempts to bring together the community and prisoners for the purpose of creating non-traditional approaches to the problems of crime and criminal justice. Prisoners must recognize that they have committed wrongs against their communities so that reconciliation with communities can begin and meaningful working relationships can be developed amongst themselves as participants in the workshops.

Here at the Fishkill Correctional Facility, we are attempting to formulate another class similar to the ones we created at the Green Haven Correctional Facility. We call these model classes the *"Conciencia* and Resurrection" study groups. *Conciencia*, in Spanish translates "to be in a state of consciousness." The class attempts to address our problems from a Latinocentric perspective. Likewise, the Resurrection study group instructs from an Afrocentric perspective.

We encourage anyone who is interested and able to assist us in enhancing these classes and our curriculum, and/or anyone who wants more information concerning the classes to contact us in writing. *CONCIENCIA*!

NOTES

1. Ethnic distribution of inmates under custody in New York State Correctional Facilities as of June 4, 1990.

2023-06-01

REFERENCES

Blauner, R. 1990. 'The Internal Colonialism,' V.N. Parillo, ed., *Strangers To These Shores, Race and Ethnic Relations in the United States*. 3rd ed. Boston: Houghton Mifflin.

Cooley, C.H. 1983. *Human Nature and the Social Order*. New Brunswick, NJ: Transaction Books.

Correctional Association of New York and New York State Coalition for Criminal Justice. 1990. 'Underlying Social and Economic Factors.' *Imprisoned Generation*. New York: Correctional Association of New York (September).

Department of Correctional Services. 1988. 'Increasing Parole Success.' *Today*, 1(9): 8-9.

Williams, H., and P.V. Murphy. 1990. *The Evolving Strategy of Police: A Minority View*. Washington, D.C.: The National Institute of Justice, U.S. Department of Justice.

In the Shadow of the Thirteenth Amendment

James Morse

In the wake of the 1992 riot in Los Angeles, *The New York Times* published an editorial entitled "Young Black Men", which rejects the prevalent presumption that young men of color are "inherently criminal", as their overwhelming numbers in the state prison system suggests. In an immediate reply to this editorial, dated May 7, 1992, an executive of the Federation of Welfare Agencies laments the fact that the criminal justice system in New York, as elsewhere, is the only institution that eagerly welcomes young Black and Latino males. The author then mentions one of the most dreaded consequences of imprisonment: scarcity of available resources to aid ex-offenders re-entering free society — a traditional disincentive to a law-abiding lifestyle.

Responding to another editorial of November 29, 1992, entitled "The Inmate Riddle and Its Moral", a professor of sociology and criminology at John Jay College, refers to the "consistent findings" of direct ties between street crime and the brutal realities of life in the urban slums. Also, under the bold caption "Children of Prisoners Face Grim Inheritance", another response in *The New York Times* Editorial/Letters section affirms the fact that a child with a parent in prison possesses five times the likelihood of becoming a prisoner too. Clearly, like welfare, imprisonment possesses intergenerational ramifications.

Responding to this predicament, a group of New York State prisoners, dubbed "inmate scholars", have developed a revealing perspective called "The Nontraditional Approach To Criminal Justice". In part, it uncovers a direct political relationship, a "symbiosis", between a minority specific state prison population and a few low income urban enclaves in New York City. The nontraditionalists espouse that ex-offenders returning to these select enclaves should somehow arrive there as upstanding, crusading reformers, potential leaders in their blighted communities. Since most prisoners are eventually released from prison, this continues to be an aim worth pursuing. To accomplish this goal, the nontraditionaists would, for instance, mandate that community service become an element of parole conditions. According to one source, they even propose a model prison to be solely administered by prisoners — no doubt a type of penal utopia.

Most importantly, the nontraditionalists have formed an organization called the Community Justice Institute to lobby their outlook in Albany and, undoubtedly, to educate the denizens of the select enclaves regarding their traditional relationship to the state's prison system.

Because the problem of state prisons in New York combines two of the most volatile domestic issues in contemporary America — crime and race — no one can fault the nontraditionalists for treading lightly, tentatively even, during these ultra-conservative times. Apparently wishing to establish an outlook that would coexist with the fashionably narrow view concerning an ever expanding minority specific prison system, the nontraditionalists have opted to focus primarily upon the geo-political aspects of the current criminal justice operation in New York City.

Also, due to the current popularity among minority prisoners of criminal justice conspiracy theories — which tend to be rawly blunt and accusative — prisoner strategists seeking to build widely based support coalitions may find it politically correct to steer clear of potentially controversial issues such as race, but at the risk of diluting the moral force of their strategies. Nonetheless, because a perpetually expanding minority based prison system is pushing free society closer to the brink of certain disaster, a bold interpretation of the facts is urgently required. At the risk of alienating moderate advocates of penal reform in the short term, a bold interpretation of the facts — many of which are hidden — has the superior advantage of producing more suitable solutions that are likely to become increasingly fitting as the present crisis progresses and intensifies, as it is certain to do.

As stale as last week's headlines is the fact that, though males of African descent comprise only six percent of the nation's general population, they are forty-seven percent of the national male prison population. According to recent reports,[1] in New York, one of every four young males of color is under some form of criminal justice supervision, as if born in the shadow of the Thirteenth Amendment to the United States Constitution, and thereby verifying all of the superstitious portents that the number thirteen signifies. This ominous shadow of crime and punishment casts a permanent shade upon a few select, prisoner specific enclaves in New York City that are characterized by intense poverty, drug-induced violent crime, substandard housing, and de facto segregated public school systems. Together these enclaves comprise the eighteen assembly districts — out of New York's 150 — that seventy-five percent of all state prisoners originate from and return to when released from confinement. These enclaves are located in

Harlem, Brownsville, East New York, Bedford-Stuyvesant, Lower East Side, South Bronx, and Jamaica.

Importantly, these urban sectors are not "neighborhoods" in the traditionally middle-class sense of socially stable, economically viable residential areas. Owing largely to the polarizing effect of conservative economics during the Reagan–Bush debacle — whereby the rich became super-rich and the poor became super-poor — these sectors are principally pockets of extremely low income and dependency, exhibiting a constant and rapid turnover of residents that establishes social instability as the prevailing norm. Promoting this social instability, and characterizing these enclaves as prisoner specific, is the perpetual outflow and influx of myriads of individuals to and from the state's prison system. According to current estimates, each year, 26,000 individuals are admitted to state prisons and 23,000 are released, and the prisoner specific enclaves are the locus of three-quarters of this traffic.

In a 1990 report, published by a quasi-official agency, the Federation of Protestant Welfare Agencies (FPWA), it is disclosed that persons of color are pre-eminently arrestable and convictable due to an almost exclusive concentration of police anti-drug operations within these select urban enclaves, which has contributed to the swell of a minority-based prison system during the past few years. The report highlights the contradiction in law enforcement operations whereby white, middle-class persons are acknowledged as being far more active in the sale and use of illicit drugs than ghettoites, but much less likely to be apprehended, not to mention imprisoned when they are. According to the report, what differentiates the middle-class from the ghetto-class for law enforcement officials is that within the blighted urban enclaves, drug activity is more visible, and drug-induced violent crime is more prevalent. This official rationalization of selective prosecution of enclaved minorities seems to suggest that if only the poor were middle-class, notwithstanding drug use and sales, they too would be virtually immune to arrest and conviction.

After documenting evidence that the end result of criminal justice in New York is basically a segregated penal apparatus — from which whites are systemically excluded — the authors of the report coyly disclaim a conclusive finding of unfairness to minorities in sentencing practices "without researching the actual offenses and criminal histories" of imprisoned offenders (FWPA, 1990). This disappointing inconclusiveness unfortunately represents the traditional rub, the classical blind spot in advocate/underpeople relations wherein well-meaning advocates sometimes are unable to stand in the shoes of underpeople and perceive the essential picture, not because advocates are insincerely motivated, but rather because the outsider typically experiences the problem differently from the people at the bottom of the heap. Also, the role of advocacy may be complicated by the necessity of listening to the clash of opposing voices, which often places the advocate between the why and wherefore, the pro and the con, literally speaking. Frequently, the underpeople themselves even fail to grasp the essential picture. And, having waived the right to speak up, underpeople are mute or whisper.

Thus, what urgently needs to be said, loud and clear, is that regardless of why or wherefore, when the criminal justice process results in a basically segregated penal system — in a society wherein racial segregation is unlawful — then the result itself is criminally unjust. Put another way, "each tree is known by its own fruit". Therefore, it would certainly be unusual for a person to stand in an apple orchard and surmise: "*Yes*, it looks like an apple, smells like an apple, and even tastes like an apple, *but* I first must research the origin of the tree before I can be conclusive". Actually, disrobed of euphemisms, the "correctional facility" emerges as a segregated entity that is no less denigrating a process than a segregated lunch counter, a mandate to sit in the back of the bus, or the "separate but equal" disquality of life legalized by *Plessy* v. *Ferguson* [163 U.S. 537 (1896)]. No matter how it comes about, regardless of how well it is hidden from public view, segregation is the visual representation of broken promises. And for the person of color, the penal totalitarian setting is necessarily experienced as a retrogression in American race relations, exclusive of crime and punishment, which fosters the socially divisive presumption that criminal justice is race specific and, in the historical sense, business-as-usual.

It is no coincidence that the Jim Crow prison system emerges as a teeming incubator for cultural myths and racial stereotypes. Owing to the customary configurations of a mainly all-white staff of overpeople ruling a prison population of mainly all-minority underpeople, in rural upstate New York, the old, enduring images of the black slave/white master archetype spring readily to life from the mildewed, worm-eaten chronicles of yesteryear. Nothing more accurately defines the dominant images, themes, and self-concepts of persons within a social setting than the argot they utilize, which unveils the realities that such expressions identify. Though not of recent vintage in the prisoner lexicon, the word "nigger" is a tellingly prevalent argot expression, used frequently by young prisoners of color and Latinos[2] to describe themselves and their peers. In the minority-based prison system, the historical definition of "nigger" has become so institutionalized that it readily anticipates the persons cast into the setting. For young Blacks and Latinos, "nigger" appropriately embodies a stereotype and worldview imposed by separate and unequal life opportunities before, during, and after imprisonment. Thus, these young men too are troubled by conflict and ambivalence: "*Yes*, I violated the law, *but* must I be denigrated as a consequence, with little likelihood of recovery?"

This is the pain that spawns all of the so-called criminal justice conspiracy theories indigenous to the segregated penal setting. While the prisoners of the current generation are, on the whole, not as politically sophisticated as their forerunners, it is true that one need not be a weatherman — or a prisoner scholar — to tell which way the wind is blowing. Environmentally speaking, no one need ever utter the word "nigger" — the setting itself speaks loud and clear. For, as a rule of thumb, white males get the breaks in life, and "niggers" get imprisoned.

Let us turn aside momentarily to briefly examine one of the formative social institutions of which the average young prisoner of color is an alumnus. The public school system throughout the network of New York City's prisoner specific enclaves and the state penal system possess numerous characteristics in common. Both are traditionally segregated with a preponderance of Black and Latino youth as clients. Because the enclave school and the prison always service more persons than they are designed to, overcrowding — the familiar practice of "packin' 'em in there" — gives both these social institutions the appearance of being perpetually pregnant, but without great expectations. Consequently, fiscal resources are stretched to the point where "programs" are eliminated or they qualitatively decline. Since the staffs of the enclave school and the prison alike are overwhelmingly white, the problem of absent or ineffective role models for minority males is standardized. Minorities in both social institutions typically complain of staff insensitivity, which in the segregated prison setting has evolved into open hostility. In a large number of enclave public schools, the metal detector and the security guard are as standard as they are in the prisons. As a result, in both social institutions, "academic freedom" becomes the handmaiden to "security" concerns. Regardless of the why or wherefore of segregated social institutions, the result is uniformly inferior and damaging.

It is widely acknowledged that segregated social institutions in a free society are self-defeating because they tend to normalize the abnormal, imposing a kind of caste status and outlook upon the segregated. For the average young prisoner of color — who has gone from one segregated social institution to the other — the enclave public school and the prison complement each other in producing diminishing prospects for entry into the mainstream of American society. Even the average alumnus of the enclave public school, who has not been to prison, is likely to remain enclave-bound for life, while the average ex-offender returns to the enclave with increasing possibilities of ending up prison-bound for life. To one degree or another, the political purpose of the enclave is to keep racial expendables conveniently out of sight and out of the way.

Emblematic of the fashionably narrow view of a minority based prison system is the public apathy concerning the extent to which New York's penal apparatus has been transformed into an entrenched representation of "the color line" predicted to be "the problem of the twentieth century": solidification of the "two societies, one black, one white — separate and unequal", forewarned by the Kerner Commission twenty-eight years ago. What is broadly viewed and experienced by the public, especially by minorities, is the telltale effect of this racial fault line in the social landscape, which ascribes to all persons of color a moral differential that imputes an automatic mistrust and suspicion that is all too familiar. The males are viewed as potentially violent, and the females, regardless of rank or standing are viewed as quintessential seductresses. The concrete basis of this perceptual distortion is the present minority-based prison system, which inevitably casts a very, very long shadow. In the unavoidable terms of social relativity, not even affluent persons of color can completely evade the omnipresent shadow of the Jim Crow prison system; relentlessly, it follows them to the suburbs, to the boardroom, to the first class vacation abroad. In spite of material acquisitions, individual acceptance, and professional distractions, the shadow is always there, looming like a "friendly reminder". And the inescapable truth is that the more the segregated prison system expands, the longer the shadow becomes.

Unlike the rare middle-class offender whose fall into prison renders "rehabilitation" — the future restoration of prior status [New York Penal Law, Article 1, Section, 1.05, Subdivision 6.] — a viable possibility, the young prisoner of color arrives from the enclave to the prison gate in bad shape. And unless he is a die-hard fatalist, during his "vacation" from the lethal pitfalls of the urban ghetto, he usually envisions something better than restoration to his prior status. For his biographical profile is the standard underclass testimonial: he was raised by a single parent in or near the prisoner specific enclave, became maladjusted to the shocks of poverty and the routine incidents of racial discrimination, dropped out of the segregated public school system to become under-unemployable — the traditional stepping stones to the perils of street-life, the quick/slick dollar, crime and, ultimately, the Jim Crow prison system, beckoning with open arms. Because the prisoner of color usually possesses some degree of willingness to better his future prospects (and because he usually desires to get out of prison), he invests his time and energy in the rehabilitation fantasy mandated by the Penal Law, in the guise of "inmate programs". In this manner, he is subtly indoctrinated into believing that he, exclusive of all other factors, is the sole problem in his life, and that inmate programs — in the segregated prison — will miraculously render him invincible to all of the external influences and criminogenic factors that made him a prime candidate for prison in the first place. Meanwhile, back in the prisoner specific enclave — for which the young prisoner of color is inescapably earmarked — overall conditions are further deteriorating, and recidivistic activity is booming at the rate of forty-seven percent.

Concomitant with the process of being "restored to prior status" — the young prisoner of color is the object of an operational concept also mandated by the Penal Law called "deterrence", whereby the prison sentence is supposedly executed to forewarn other potential offenders. This is the case despite the fact that within the prisoner specific enclave, where the perpetual going to and coming from prison is a cultural norm, deterrence competes very poorly against inducements to "get paid" and incitements to rebel. In fact, in the enclave, where existential reversals are institutionalized in a manner that the middle-class mentality cannot fathom, deterrence regularly produces the opposite result: the more individuals imprisoned, the more criminogenic the prisoner specific enclave becomes. Therefore, though deterrence, as a judicial practice, is far less effective than say a beneficial education leading to the assurance of gainful employment, an examination of deterrence's most active principle — the "principle of less eligibility" — reveals the reasons for its abiding appeal, even as it produces the very results that it claims to prevent.

The principle of less eligibility was popularized in England by a utilitarian philosopher, Jeremy Bentham, as the foundation for the then new concept of the penitentiary. Simply, convicts were deemed less eligible to enjoy the same privileges of citizenship and standard of living possessed by the noncriminalized. It was theorized that in order for the *poor* to be sufficiently deterred from crime, prison conditions had to be worse than the living conditions of the poorest in society. Otherwise the prisons would be perceived as attractive. As applied to the young prisoner of color, in particular (who was born less eligible), the principle of less eligibility enjoys a wide and enthusiastic usage on both sides of the prison wall. For example, in one New York prison, a degree program in social work was abruptly terminated on the grounds that prisoners, from an "ethical" standpoint, are less eligible to become social work professionals. Actually, it was feared that prisoners, by virtue of their "peculiar" status, would necessarily "degrade" the profession of social work — a precept that has its basis in New York Correctional Law.

Generally, and in a manner that prompted one perceptive observer to remark that "mistrust is the mother of recidivism", the young prisoner of color is deemed indelibly less eligible to be trustworthy, even if the offense committed occurred ten, fifteen, twenty years ago — officially, the offense remains fresh, as if it occurred yesterday. Importantly, although the majority of young prisoners could be positively induced through a system of escalating rewards to alter their behavior pattern, the principle of less eligibility demands an unwavering dosage of mistrust and suspicion to achieve "deterrence", which accounts in large part for the neurotic tone of prison operations, and a high recidivism rate. Once released from prison and restored to the prisoner specific enclave, the ex-offender is less eligible to reside in a community that is not infested with drugs and violent crime; less eligible to obtain gainful employment because, while in prison, he was less eligible to obtain job training related to the current job market. In short, for the young prisoner of color, a four-year prison sentence all but guarantees a lifetime of social disability.

Back amid the teeming temptations of life in the enclave, the young ex-offender of color realizes that his bulging portfolio of prison program certificates does not amount to a hill of beans in the real world — even to display them invites the familiar mistrust and suspicion. Thus, he feels that he has been duped, lied to, especially if he left prison expecting to be welcomed with open arms. Demoralized and angry, he lapses into his old ways, thereby becoming just another criminogenic factor in the confines of the prisoner specific enclave. Once he recidivates, which is very likely, he is then pre-eminently less eligible to escape the draconian mandatory sentencing statutes that, once applied, trigger the same denigrating cycle once more. This penological rope-a-dope is carried out in the name of "public safety" [Penal Law, Article 1, Section 1.05, Subdivision 6.]. Hence, it is estimated by the nontraditionalists that, annually, less eligibly restored ex-offenders will be responsible for 11,000 new offenses — many of them violent in nature, which coincides with the findings of the National Research Council that persons of color are far more likely to become victims of crime than whites.

Speaking from experience, the root cause of the vast majority of the current violence within the prisoner specific enclave is externally generated by the influx of illicit drugs. What better target for the consumption of drugs and alcohol than the minority "expendables" permanently confined to the misery of the enclave? The citizens of affluence who ultimately reap the great wealth from the enclave drug traffic remain safely beyond the reach of law enforcement officials. The real "drug czars" do not build mansions in the South Bronx or East New York, but in more genteel environs. Curiously powerless to halt this violence inducing influx of illicit drugs, law enforcement officials take the easy way out by declaring a "war on drugs", and invading the prisoner specific enclaves. Yet, for all the casualties and prisoners of war, this strange campaign does little except inject fresh blood into the market. For every single street-level drug dealer imprisoned, at least two new ones appear to fill the empty slot. In fact, it is not at all unusual for street-level drug dealers to work with the police and inform on each other in order to corner a bigger share of the street market for themselves: so much for deterrence. After all, every "war" has its quislings. After successive campaigns, the prisoner specific enclave begins to resemble an underdeveloped third world country. For in addition to the initial drug epidemic, and the ensuing "war on drugs", the enclave is also the locus of a perpetual crime wave.

One of the most common offenses for which the enclave bound youth of color is imprisoned is robbery. The drug habit demands instant and constant tribute, and when all else fails, the compulsion for relief leaps all prior bounds of personal limits, and a robbery ensues. On the average, each kilo of crack cocaine sold in the prisoner specific enclave is guaranteed to generate at least eighty robberies — two robberies per ounce, which is a conservative estimate. Typically, along the rough road to the prison house, the robber himself has been a target of the drug epidemic, a casualty of the "war on drugs", and a victim of the crime wave too. In fact, the most enduring rationale for succumbing to drug abuse initially is: "Since I have to put up with all of this crap, I may as well use drugs too"! But once the young inmate of color is packed tightly into the cellblock, he alone is stamped as the principal social malefactor, a violent threat to "public safety". Meanwhile, back in the enclave, that same kilo of crack cocaine is now generating one hundred robberies, not to mention its quota of homicides, assaults, burglaries, and other assorted miseries. Consequently, even law-abiding persons begin to wonder if the so-called "war on drugs" is just a war on people; the most vulnerable, people of color.

Light years away from reality, what the prison official sees as a socially useful operation — inept "inmate programs" that, in most cases lead nowhere except back to square one — the young prisoner of color experiences as business-as-usual, this time aimed merely to occupy his attention while confined. During quiet moments, the underperson-in-the-cell hangs his head between his hands and wonders, "How much longer"? Ultimately, the answer is: Not long! From the lofty heights of their hands-off points of view, what the "tough-on-crime" proponents are unable to perceive is how every essentially unjust situation necessarily generates an incipient moral dynamic to annul it, to make it right. Typically, this incipient moral dynamic is very quiet and difficult to pin-point. Seemingly nonexistent, it is like the proverbial seed that is haphazardly thrown upon the ground and forgotten about, only to leap forth in a blooming excitation. Because the young prisoner of color is actually a real human being, he too is subject to this moral dynamic and is thereby amenable to the expiating force of imprisonment, which is officially unacknowledged but equally unconquerable.

Simply stated, in the segregated prison system; whether the prison sentence is just, unjust, or too long, whether the instrument of pain is the cage, the room, or the dormitory; the vast majority of prisoners feel the bite of confinement, experience suffering, and are thereby uplifted and empowered. Although this moral dynamic is too often nullified by the process of less eligibility, it is not for nothing that prisoners suffer and die in prison. Like all bitter harvests, this one also must be reaped in time. Characteristically, when the young prisoner of color becomes fully conscious of, and motivated by the expiating force of punishment, he is likely to utter something unusual like, "The life-snatchers have me, but they won't get my children"! Hence, the young prisoner of color entertains vivid dreams of returning to the enclave, not as a ready recidivist who is less eligibly restored, but as a person empowered to serve as a positive role-model for troubled youth. But to the fawning patrons of business-as-usual, and to the iron-clad proponents of "more is better" (i.e., more prisons, more time) — to whom it is politically incorrect to acknowledge that the young prisoner of color is amenable to expiating forces — such talk of becoming a shepherd in the enclave is so much discordant idealism. For, as a rule, once the young prisoner's destiny has been imposed, it must not be altered — he must be less eligibly restored, no matter what.

Thus, when the prison official urges that the addict robber or addict burglar[3] is much too violent to be less eligibly restored in the foreseeable future, the public yields to the misbelief that the prisoner can only be subdued by the cell, the gun tower, or the Special Housing Unit. In the majority of cases, this is an official self-serving exaggeration. Anyone who has lived in a maximum security prison for any length of time — especially one wherein violence is institutionalized — observes that violence for the mere sake of violence is manifested by only a small percentage of prisoners. When all is said and done, the only force that prevents the majority of prisoners from destroying the prison and each other (as in a prison riot) is nothing more than their individual choices not to do so. This moral choice — which prison staff do not acknowledge, but bet their lives on each working day — is largely due to the expiating force of punishment, of suffering, evidenced by the fact that many prisoners turn to religion and education while confined. Once removed from the influences of the enclave's criminogenic factors, plucked out of the man-made concentration of recidivism — which prisoners humorously refer to as "being rescued" — the average young prisoner of color appeals to his higher self and becomes more human, in the existential sense. As one prison official sardonically remarked, the prisoner now desires meals and dental appointments.

A further affirmation of this truth is that each business day of the year prisoners are transported from state prisons throughout the state to county courthouses to stand in judgement for new Penal Law offenses committed while in prison. Newly committed offenses range in magnitude from possession of illicit drugs to homicide, which proves that there are opportunities in prison to be lawless. Again, in the end (and for many, many prisoners with eternal life sentences, this is the end) if the majority of prisoners were truly inherently violent, criminal and untrustworthy, the prisons would be ungovernable. Hence it is inevitable that as the young prisoner of color arrives at a clearer understanding of his assignment in relation to the prisoner specific enclave, and as the denizens of the prisoner specific enclave more clearly understand their assignment in relation to the segregated prison, Jim Crowism will reap diminishing returns. After all, from a historical perspective, how long can a good thing last?

The apologists for the penal status quo — feigning astonishment at the very existence of a segregated prison system — instinctively counter that the criminal justice system selects its clients according to criteria other than race, and that the resulting disproportions of minority prisoners is merely "demographically coincidental". "Demography" is the new code word used to deflect the fact that segregation is the culmination of past discrimination. Only when pressed by the weight of the evidence will it be reluctantly conceded that the criminal justice apparatus customarily removes offenders from the de facto[4] segregated enclave, thereby creating a de jure segregated prison system, only to less eligibly restore the ex-offender to the enclave — three distinct movements that suggest intent and design. It is precisely because the de facto form of segregation is continuously the precondition for the de jure form and vice versa, that the state's minority-based penal system is the most egregious violation of both state and federal guarantees of "equal protection of the laws" [New York State Constitution, Article 1 Section II. United States Constitution, Amendment XIV, Section 1.]. Throughout this denigrating process, the prevailing official presumption is that segregation, and the inevitable discrimination that accompanies it, is quite normal to minorities.

Even when social malpractices are widely acknowledged, they may be traditionalized to the extent of being accepted as "lesser evils" which is itself a very traditional political ploy calculated to appeal to the fears and insecurities of the populace. The "lesser evil" formula cleverly pays tribute to virtue by exaggerating the imminence of vice. Hence, the business-as-usual proposition that the de jure segregated prison system can only be eliminated at the risk of more crime in the streets. This formulated artifice incorporates the same degree of conflict and ambivalence of purpose exhibited in justifying the prototypical injustice: "*Yes*, slavery is morally wrong, *but* what about the cotton"? However, as long as the "lesser evil" rationale flies with the public, its proponents will be amenable to a limited degree of compromise and cosmetic changes that do not threaten the continuation of the malpractice. Therefore, the establishment of a prisoner administrated prison, for instance, is really not so far-fetched because it would actually validate the practice of penal segregation.

Typically, the moment that the swell of minority prisoners began attracting critical attention and alarm, the practice of the "lesser evil" began to be propagated as an outright "positive good". We now read testimonials about the "benefits of an unwelcome trend" — of what an economic boost prison expansion is to upstate rural communities. Townships avidly compete for new prisons to be erected in their locales, and town supervisors rhapsodize about "recession proof" and "environmentally safe" prisons. Business-as-usual patrons may even be seen on local television extolling the virtues of prison expansion for all of the jobs it creates, all of which is an insulting irony to prisoners of color who are destined to remain historically under-unemployable, especially in New York City where the ratio of black/white joblessness is nearly three to one.

In order to clearly understand how joblessness and penal segregation have become the twin towers of contemporary racism, it is necessary to briefly re-examine its source. From 1619, when the first Africans set foot on North American soil, until the present time, people of color have been the continuous objects of adverse labor relations. During the first constitutional convention in 1787, the course of adverse labor relations was firmly set when the free states of the North acceded to the demands of the Southern slavers in three well known respects: a provision to count a slave as three-fifths of a person for the purpose of sending Southern representatives to the lower house and to the electoral college; a clause to force the federal government from prohibiting the importation of slaves for twenty years; a clause to mandate the return of slaves who had escaped to free states. Although these constitutional provisions [Article I, Section 1 and II; Article IV, Section II] were eventually amended, the rising degree of penal segregation bears a curious relationship to the Thirteenth Amendment and the constitution remains a pro-slavery document.

This curious relationship between penal segregation and the Thirteenth Amendment can be traced to the final months of the American civil war when Northerners outlawed the chattel slavery of African Americans, but modified the practice for other usages, as if this traditional form of adverse labor possessed a residual appeal. The Thirteenth Amendment, ratified in

December 1865, formally introduced penal slavery and involuntary servitude as punishment applicable to all individuals "duly" convicted of criminal offenses. Surprisingly, lawmakers believed that legislative action alone would transmute an uncivilized practice into a socially useful one. Currently, over one half of American states have similar provisions in their constitutions authorizing a penal form of slavery and involuntary servitude for individuals convicted of criminal offenses. State constitutions that do not explicitly authorize this form of punishment provide for de facto penal bondage systems that ultimately conform to the spirit of, and are authorized by, the Thirteenth Amendment.

Although the constitution of New York State does not *explicitly* authorize penal slavery and involuntary servitude, a historical reading of the applicable state laws reveals that penal bondage is in fact the end result of imprisonment. Significantly, Article II, Section 3, of the state constitution mandates disfranchisement of voting privileges for individuals convicted of "infamous crime". Since it is principally persons of color who are imprisoned for such crimes in New York, this disfranchisement code, in its effect, bears a historical resemblance to the Northern "black laws" of the antebellum period that were used to render people of color political nonentities in free society. Also, the New York Correction Law either completely arrogates, or severely limits, all personal freedoms guaranteed by the Bill of Rights, such as the right to privacy, and to be free from arbitrary searches and seizures. The young prisoner of color is thus rendered a total penal bondsman of the state government, the polar opposite of the individual at liberty to come and go as one chooses; to exercise autonomy over one's person; to freely associate with individuals of one's choice; and, most importantly, *to freely profit from one's labor*.

Historically, an involuntary servant is a person of color who is forced to perform menial labor, either without payment or for a meager pittance. A slave is a person of color who possesses no political rights, and who is owned as property by another individual or entity, such as a company or a state. It is in both of these senses that prisoners of color have traditionally referred to themselves as "state property" — a self-evident acknowledgement of the old substance in the new practice. That the white prisoners in prison rarely, if ever, refer to themselves as "state property" is due to the fact that, having no historical references to themselves as property, imprisonment to white prisoners (and to the overwhelmingly white staff) is received and experienced in an altogether different existential realm.

Regarding the pivotal question of labor, Article VII, Section 171, of the Correctional Law of New York affirms penal bondage as the foundation of New York's de jure segregated prison system. Not only may prisoners be compelled to labor ("other than Sundays", as in the antebellum situation), but other enactments in the same article specifically prohibit a prisoner's labor and time (read lifetime) from being contracted out to private individuals and entities. Also, the penal labor and time of prisoners may not be disposed of on the free market to compete with the labor and time of free persons. By law, any product of prisoner labor or time — mainly license plates and office furniture — may only be marketed by prison industries to other agencies within the state government.

Thus, in effect, Article VII guarantees that the average prisoner of color leaves the prison poorer than the day he arrived, which is why many ex-offenders "throw a brick" ["throw a brick at the penitentiary"; i.e., commit a crime] within the first few hours of being released. Other enactments in Article VII [Section 187 and 200] provide that prisoners "may" be compensated for their labor, and for participation in academic and vocational programs. Hence, the median daily pay for a prisoner is about seventy cents — an extremely meager "incentive" even by prison standards. The result is that in many prisons, services that are supposed to be free — laundry, haircut, legal assistance, et cetera — come with a price tag. Every prison has a brisk underground economy, literally speaking, a black market. In a setting where the strong customarily prevail over the weak, protection rackets are not uncommon. Since basic daily survival in prison requires much more than the state provides, most prisoners rely upon the largesse of their families to supplement the prison diet and to dress warmly, a situation that prison staff have long regarded with sour resentment and a growing appetite.

Knowing from observation that the average prisoner struggles to make ends meet, and that he never is paid enough to support "dependent relatives" as Section 189 so grandly provides for, prison officials nonetheless propagate the self-serving deception that they provide all the basics for survival. This fiction has solidified into an official worldview that is then used as the basis of court decisions, [*Sanchez et al.* v. *Coughlin, et al* (Sullivan Co. Sup. Ct. 1992)] which then provides prison officials with a legal basis to view all incoming aid from families as surplus and fair game for seizure. With the recent prison building binge having stretched fiscal resources to the limit, prison officials have not only devised schemes to take back the few dollars per month provided to prisoners as an incentive, but also have deployed shrewd stratagems to hold prisoners financially hostage to their families, who are mostly the enclaved poor.

Even many indigent prisoners who relied upon court appointed lawyers arrive in prison owing the court system a one hundred and fifty-two dollar surcharge for each felony conviction. Prison officials then become the debt collectors, and the prisoner's account is docked — sometimes for years — until the debt is paid. Articles such as laundry bags and knit caps that were formerly provided to prisoners are now sold in the prison commissary. If a prisoner receives a misbehavior report and fails to prevail during the ensuing administrative hearing, his account is then docked for a five dollar "surcharge" [*Born Allah* v. *Coughlin* (S. Ct. Ulster C. 1992)]. Even freedom now comes at a cost in that, once the ex-offender is less eligibly restored to the enclave, he must then pay a thirty dollar per month fee for parole supervision.

By far, the most sinister plot devised to keep the young prisoner of color poor and pointed backwards is the newly imposed twenty-five dollar application fee for the General Equivalency Diploma examination. Although a New York Department of Education regulation exempts prisoners from this fee [8 N.Y.C.C.R., Section 100 (i)(ii)(c)] a recent court ruling [*Sanchez,* Ibid.] affirms the right of prison officials to override the Department of Education regulation and impose the fee. At a time when the American Council on Education reports that "minority students are far less likely to finish high school than white students", the imposition of this fee requirement upon a prison population that is ninety-five percent minority clearly functions as a discouragement and a prohibition to obtaining a G.E.D. Not surprisingly, the court in the *Sanchez* case ruled that since the fee requirement is applied to all prisoners, there are no grounds upon which to allege racial discrimination! Here is a very good example of how prison officials and the state courts exploit the presence of a few white prisoners to deny the reality of de jure segregation. Like the other curious relationships discussed above, this educational stumbling block is aptly reminiscent of the antebellum prohibition against teaching a slave to read and write, for an educated penal slave is a contradiction in terms, and a potential problem.

Essentially, from the standpoint of political economy, the young prisoner of color is still "pickin' cotton" and remains a complete stranger to the product of his labor and time. Importantly, within the contemporary penal economy, there and is no such thing as an "idle" prisoner. Although the prisoner's labor and time is of no value to him, even if he did nothing except sleep and eat, he is thereby producing value for his keepers. By merely being a prisoner he renders valuable the labor and time of his masters (prison employees collectively). To the prisoner of color, this value is alien and hostile because it is no sooner produced than it turns against him, threatening his very existence. Thus, the more value the young prisoner of color produces, the more impoverished he necessarily becomes; the more license plates he manufactures, the more he contributes to his own economical plight. For within the global economy of the real world, the young prisoner of color is conditioned to be dependent.

The Article VII prohibitions that render the prisoner's labor and time of no value to him highlights the historical antagonisms between free and slave labor that crystallized into the Free Soil politics of the 1840s. The Free Soil Party held its first convention in Buffalo, New York, in August 1847. Under the banner "Free Speech, Free Labor, Free Men", this party opposed the expansion of chattel slave labor into unsettled territories such as Kansas and Nebraska. It was this protracted, heated discord between the free enterprise industrial capitalism of the North and the slave agricultural economy of the South that eventually erupted into the civil war. Free Soilers, like contemporary labor unions and business interests, insisted that slave labor and its products depressed the free enterprise economy through the unfair competition of cheap, unfree labor. Thus, in keeping with free market principles, the solution, then and now, is to bar slave labor and its products from the free market. As a result, prisoner labor — which is preponderantly black labor — is wanting of even reformative value because it is economically inferior, a deformity traditionally despised by free labor.

This festering problem of adverse labor relations reveals the segregated prison system as a towering monument of the work-related stereotypes that have traditionally undermined the economic well being of African Americans, particularly the males. It was during the antebellum struggle between the free labor economy of the North and the slave economy of the South that white labor became indelibly typed as superior and black labor typed as inferior, which accorded with the standard perception of black personhood generally.

In the public view, white free labor was more efficient because it was voluntary, whereas black slave labor was inefficiently driven by the whip —

hence, the origin of the tenacious myths of the black worker as "shiftless", "lazy", and "unproductive". This stereotype became institutionalized to the extent that labor associated with blacks was viewed as dishonorable, and even despised by poor whites as "degrading". While the abolition of chattel slavery was essential for the liberation of free labor, it still has not liberated people of color from an exclusionary labor market. The rise of penal segregation in contemporary America is the highest, most resistantly fortified expression of adverse labor relations since antebellum slavery. What has evolved is an intergenerational ethic of under-unemployability that establishes a direct relationship between joblessness and a de jure segregated prison system, wherein all of the traditional stereotypes achieve full force.

It is a generally accepted truism that social evils, like personal ones, possess their own seeds of disaster. The most telling factor that has set the current practice of penal segregation upon the same collision course as its antebellum predecessor is the "more is better" phenomenon; that is, the inherent tendency of institutional slavery and involuntary servitude to rapidly proliferate and expand. For example, in 1982 there were thirty-eight state prisons and eleven years later there are over sixty-two prisons. Likewise, in 1983, New York State prisons housed 28,499 inmates, a total that increased to 63,000 by 1993. With each new prison built, the original penal segregation became more pronounced and institutionalized. Rather than wisely investing fiscal resources to address the social problems of racial discrimination, poverty, and crime concentrated in the prisoner specific enclaves — which includes a mere twelve percent of New York's general population — elected officials, goaded by personal vanity and the violent rhetoric of the war on drugs, chose instead to invest billions of dollars in the expansion of a segregated prison system that is visibly a memorial to Jefferson Davis, J.E.B. Stuart, Stonewall Jackson, and Robert E. Lee. The revenue used for prison expansion was provided by the Urban Development Corporation, a bond issuing authority established by Governor Rockefeller as a memorial to Dr. Martin Luther King, Jr. The original purpose of U.D.C. was to build housing for the poor.

Determined to "pack 'em in there", but fiscally restrained from building even more prisons, there is now a movement afoot in the state legislature to house two prisoners in a little cage that is far too small for one prisoner. Basically, "double bunking", as this proposal is called, is but a cunning manoeuver aimed at expanding penal segregation internally rather than externally. Against all of the weight of historical evidence to the contrary, slavery and involuntary servitude is again accepted as a positive good, and "mo' better" again appears to be reasonable and logical, especially to the patrons of business-as-usual who seek the immediate gratifications of the paycheck. In fact, the minority based prison system has become so central to the upstate rural economy that the mere mention of decreasing the prison population triggers an instant protest from union representatives, replete with picket lines in front of the prisons. Ominously, the potential for history to repeat itself is striking.

In truth, "mo' better" is *not* better but worse because ultimately a free society will be judged by its record of producing life-giving values — be they material or social — as opposed to the negative, alienating values generated by penal bondage and segregation. Any government that squanders its fiscal resources by making "war" on its most excluded, vulnerable, and poorest citizens in effect makes war against itself by creating its own internal enemies. An expansive Jim Crow prison system is never a life-giving value to free society because a segregated entity — regardless of why or wherefore — is a superseding icon of injustice, and a monument of shame that casts a very long shadow of contention and unrest across the whole social landscape.

Having presented detailed proofs of how penal slavery and involuntary servitude is the legal basis of New York's de jure segregated penal system and, having demonstrated the direct relationship between the current practice and its antebellum prototype, it is sufficiently clear that a truly "nontraditional" approach to criminal justice in New York must necessarily address the problem of prisons within the broader context of racial justice, which is presently a dominant theme within the greater society.

Over one hundred years ago, when New York's prison population was predominantly white, the New York Prison Commission reported that,

> Protracted incarceration destroys the better faculties of the soul. ... Most men who have been confined for long terms are distinguished by a stupor of both the moral and intellectual facilities. ... Reformation is then out of the question. [quoted in CANY and NYSCCJ, 1990]

These compelling observations spurred the initiatives called the "Irish system", consisting of computation of prison sentences, and tickets of leave to reduce the length of confinement as a reward for good behavior. A parole system was the next initiative in this decarceration plan, which was supplemented further by legislative action allowing for a one-third deduction off of minimum sentences. These powerful measures, fortified with post-release services, were not implemented to reduce overcrowding or expenditures but to avert the proliferation and expansion of a bad practice that although still in its infant stage, was clearly and predictably antithetical to public safety. The fact that the current incarceration rate for whites in New York is relatively low is evidence that decarceration initiatives are very effective, when tailored to the social needs of the prison population.

That the one-third deduction off of minimum sentences was repealed by the legislature in 1970 [Correction Law, Article 9, (Section 230)], just when minority prisoners were becoming the overwhelming majority, is another curious coincidence. The result, however, has been the permanent ruination of myriads of good persons who deserved a break in life, and could have been enabled to take advantage of good opportunities which they were forced to miss. As opposed to negative incentives, which are abundant, a decent opportunity to advance is so rare in the lives of young men of color that, once missed it is usually gone forever. Presently, in the segregated prison system, the same person who deserves a break, a chance to be out for that once in a lifetime encounter with opportunity, remains locked-down and at the mercy of a different kind of prisoner who looks forward to nothing more than the next recreation period in the yard, the next episode of the daily soap opera on television, the next conflict with the staff and other prisoners.

For decades, it has been axiomatic among prison officials that, as in free society, it is only the minority of prisoners who routinely trouble the waters of the prison order, thereby precipitating one thousand and one petty restrictions throughout the prison. Within the resulting tyranny, the prisoner who is diligently attempting to do something positive with the remnant of life left to him ends up suffering the same fate as the prisoner who is wholly indifferent and generally a loose cannon. Thus, in a cruel reversal of normal proprieties, the prisoner who consistently walks a straight line becomes a mere anonymous figure who is regularly taken for granted, or draws the bizarre suspicion of officialdom for not acting like "a real inmate". In this manner, all attention is focused upon a few prisoners who typify what staff persons expect from prisoners. These few prisoners often fare better in the negative scheme of things owing to the inducements they receive to behave.

As it is presently constituted, the prison system — tied as it is to the dead carcass of the prisoner specific enclaves — rarely leads to anything except the certainty of ruination.

That there should be a one-third deduction off of minimum sentences for prisoners who are opportunity-ready and *merit* an early release from penal segregation has been a foregone conclusion for years. However, the current resistance to this just policy in the state legislature by double-bunking advocate lawmakers, who would no doubt expand penal bondage to eternity, is a sure sign that certain legislators are determined to keep the segregated prison system on the collision course to the bitter end. This is exactly why a genuine nontraditional approach to criminal justice must disseminate the ugly truth and enlighten citizens of New York — in prison and in free society — concerning the necessity of focusing attention and resources upon the issues in front of the problem, where the focus belongs. Criminal justice and penal bondage have evolved to the point where it cannot reform itself. What Thomas Jefferson observed about the South in 1820, is quite fitting for New York in 1993: it has "the wolf by the ears and cannot let go".

Now that bondage and segregation have reunited into the most pristine and potent form of racism, it is unquestionable that, *to the degree* that slavery/ involuntary servitude is legally practicable, African Americans — and other minorities such as Latinos, will necessarily preponderate in penal bondage. This is true because within the context of American history the recessive tendencies of racism, according to its inherent logic, always aim to reestablish the original injustice, and the de jure segregated prison system it is. Thus, as a long-term strategy, a nontraditional approach to criminal justice must aim to repeal the exception clause of the Thirteenth Amendment to eliminate forever the enduring relationship between people of color and the institution of bondage, in any form. Once the exception clause is repealed, the Thirteenth Amendment will then read

> Neither slavery nor involuntary servitude shall exist within the United States, or any place subject to their jurisdiction.

Until Americans are convinced that penal bondage, with its flagrantly racist characteristics, is inconsistent with the inclusive aims of a democratic society, people of color in New York and their allies must employ short-term, viable solutions to prevent the ruination of future generations of minorities, who are definitely earmarked for penal bondage. One viable solution is a radical affirmative action initiative (not another "program") to exclude African and Latino Americans from being disproportionately "selected" for penal bondage, and thus proportionately included in the opportunities to be real Americans too. Such an affirmative action initiative will have to be based upon a quota system that would limit the imprisonment of minorities to the percentage of their representation in New York's total population. If persons of color represent, say, fifteen per cent of the general population, then they should represent no more than that percentage within the state prison population. There is no other method of forcing state government officials — who exhibit a process addiction to imprisoning minorities for social control — to remove their fiscal resources from the back of social problems that lead directly to penal bondage and re-deploy such resources to the front of these problems, where they will be most effective.

In a number of Supreme Court decisions, like *Brown* v. *Board of Education* [349 U.S. 294 (1955)], the legal principle has been well established that the government has an obligation to remove all of what one Justice in 1883 described as the "badges and incidents" of slavery. Such "badges and incidents" include the long history of joblessness in New York City that has been the scourge of minorities for generations, leading to economic inequalities directly responsible for the advent of prisoner specific enclaves, with their substandard housing, abject poverty, and de facto segregated public school systems. Now, having failed so spectacularly in removing these "badges and incidents" of slavery, it is as if the state government has announced, "If you can't beat 'em, join 'em", and erected the most ironclad badge and incident of slavery of them all, the Jim Crow prison system! In the *Brown* decision, the Court noted that de jure segregation has the greater negative impact because it gives to segregation the official seal of approval. Thus, a radical affirmative action plan is urgently needed to eliminate this present effect of past discrimination. And if a de jure segregated penal system, that sucks the life-blood from a mere twelve per cent of the population, does not qualify as a present effect of past discrimination, then the narrow view has progressed to total blindness.

Once such a quota system is in place, and it is clear that the old skin game does not work anymore, it won't take long for fiscal resources and manpower to encircle the social problems directly related to segregated penal bondage. Fortunately it is not as if the site of these social problems is scattered all over creation. No, the worst of these social ills are highly concentrated in only a few prisoner specific enclaves within a mere eighteen assembly districts. By being so conveniently concentrated, these locales seem to be begging for help. Once law enforcement is emancipated from the never-winning "war on drugs", and the politics thereof, then maybe it can figure out a way to keep the drugs out of the entire state? No! Only out of the seven targeted enclaves in only eighteen assembly districts, for starters! This penal quota system would also save many lives and lots of money by freeing resources for "drug treatment", which every official and his brother is always talking about. Now there would be less talk and more action. And best of all, once the penal quota system is implemented, minority males in New York, especially, would not be born in the shadow of the Thirteenth Amendment anymore.

But, as sure as daybreak, and as predicable as nightfall, the first thing that Mr. "Business-as-usual" will say to Mr. "Mo' Better" is: "What about my paycheck"?! Sooner or later, one way or the other, Mr. "Business-as-usual" will arrive at the understanding that his "labor" for the segregated penal system produces value, "yes, but" value of a socially negative and alienating type. For if it is the goal of social institutions to produce positive, life-giving values, then it must be conceded that when the young prisoner of color, who was born less eligibly, is lesser eligibly restored to the prisoner specific enclave with very little except a forty-seven per cent certainty of becoming just another criminogenic factor, then it is very likely that if Mr. "Business-as-usual" is more productively re-deployed to the front of the problem too, his labour would then be more creative.

As for Brother "Mo' Better"; as perennial residents of the prisoner specific enclaves and the segregated prison systems "of this world" we understand, and much mo' better than you, that many of us need to be imprisoned, but not excessively, and without the penal bondage, please — it smacks too much of the antebellum thing. That the Auburn State Prison was in existence for forty-five years before the Thirteenth Amendment was ratified is proof that an individual can be properly locked-down without being subject to the legalities of penal bondage, which people of color very rarely recover from, if at all, even when it is applied in small dosages.

As for the well-meaning nontraditionalists who would establish prisons administered solely by prisoners themselves? No matter who administers the segregated prison system in New York, we do not want our children in them, thank you anyway.

NOTES

1   See: Correctional Association of New York and New York State Coalition for Criminal Justice (1990): and Federation of Protestant Welfare Agencies (1990).
2   Together Blacks and Latinos comprise ninety-five percent of the state prison population. Both ethnic groups usually originate from and return to the same prisoner specific enclaves.
3   Penal Law, Section 70.02, Subdivision b, classifies Burglary in the Second Degree as a violent felony.
4   De facto segregation is due mainly to residential patterns, while the de jure form is government imposed/influenced.

REFERENCES

Correctional Association of New York and New York State Coalition for Criminal Justice. 1990. *Imprisoned Genderation: Young Men Under Criminal Justice Custody in New York.* New York.
Federation of Protestant Welfare Agencies. 1990. *Cause for Alarm: The Condition of Black and Latino Males in New York City.* New York.
New York Times. May 1992. "Editorial: Young Black Men".
———. Nov. 1992. "Editorial: Children of Prisoners Face Grim Inheritance".
———. Nov 29, 1992. "Editorial: The Inmate Riddle and Its Moral".

Corrections Is a Male Enterprise

Jo-Ann Mayhew

The initial motivation for this article occurred on Prison Justice Day, August 10th, 1987. I had given it an ironic title taken from the Carson Commission Report, *Corrections Is A Human Enterprise*. I am no longer satisfied with the title or much that I wrote. I still live confined within the fortress structure of the Prison for Women in Kingston, Ontario, Canada. It remains a limestone monument to social failure. The structure effectively incarcerates women from across the entire country. The concrete walls, cement cells, and barred windows represent a rigidity of social thinking, perpetuated, obstinate blindness to suffering in the interest of serving the economic needs of the Kingston community. I have been told that Kingston ranks as one of the prettiest cities in Canada. To my mind it is a city whose vitality has been fed by the blood and pain of prisoners.

George Jackson in *Soledad Brothers* (1970) says that words written by prisoners for readers on the outside must proceed obliquely; otherwise, those writing them need only to take words covered in blood, spit, and sperm and fling them on paper. These are the dangerous words, the ones padlocked inside. So are the stories of the women contained behind the walls of this prison.

I have told the story slant ways. I am editor of the prison magazine because I am a well socialized, middle-class white woman, conditioned and educated to master the placating word. I am also mistress of an idealistic love for one dead man, two living children, the Atlantic Ocean and a country called Canada. It is not a grandiose social view but it is my own and the anger I feel at having this view of living torn from me is intense.

I grew up in southern Ontario when the city of Cambridge was still called Galt. I walked through the piles of leaves on Main Street to Central School with the lines of a memorized poem playing in my head — "Where we go to school each day, Indian children used to play." I knew Indians were people of the past. I had collected the artifacts of their lives in the summer fields. Almost forty years later I have found the daughters of these forgotten, wished away Indian people within the walls of this prison. Mostly they have been transported from the Prairie provinces but I have also met Cree Native from northern Ontario as well as une femme du Montagnaise from Sept-Isles. Not only do these women suffer the normal pain and hardship of imprisonment far, far from their homes, they must also endure the upheaval and chaos of adjusting to alien white culture, both its standards and language nuances. Their own culture is far from dead within them; many have been taught in traditional ways. They share these with us. I have attended Pow Wow with them, a celebration of living. They have taught me to bead and stitch moccasins. I have heard their elders speak and have smelled the smoke of burning sweet grass. These women do not relate well to the words of our psychologists nor do they respond well to mind altering drugs. As the pressures of a long period of incarceration mount, they seek relief by slashing their own bodies. They cut their arms and they cut their throats. The walls and floors are covered in their blood. The psychiatrist told me such blood letting was a euphoric relief. I told him it was sick, an abnormal response to abnormal pain. Prison does not sustain the middle-class values of my southern Ontario childhood. It has altered my narrow idealistic view of Canadian society.

I was transported from Nova Scotia to the Prison for Women in October, 1985. I had been convicted of second degree murder following the shooting death of my husband in May of the same year. It was a drunken tragic end to over twenty years of partnership. I was sentenced to life in prison. I had been held in a forensic unit in a mental hospital for months before my trial. After the conviction, I was taken to the Halifax County Correctional Centre and placed in a cell to await transportation east. There are no facilities in the Maritimes for women serving Federal sentences. After several weeks in the cells and one final visit with my two daughters, I was driven several hundred miles to Dorchester prison en route to Kingston. I had never been arrested before and the prospect of what lay ahead was terrifying. I arrived at Dorchester only to be informed that there had been an error in my paperwork. I was not scheduled to depart until the following week. I was returned to the cells at Halifax. Some days later I was awakened at about 4:30 a.m., driven again to Dorchester, placed in shackles, a body belt and handcuffs, for the flight to Kingston.

Unlike my Native Sisters, I had a personal case history that included the services of several psychiatrists. I believe my sanity was fragmented and that only forty years of "respectable" behaviour gave me the ability to achieve an acceptable standard of stability. Within myself I was being torn apart by the loss of my best friend, knowing I was responsible for his death. I was in agony with concern and worry for two daughters left behind in the turmoil of unresolved grief and family affairs. I had not been allowed to attend my husband's funeral; I was allowed only a brief six minute phone call to my daughters. I was very confused and disoriented. The thin veneer of my behaviour cracked when I was moved from a Range to the Wing for "medical reasons" and I had to cope with new bath fixtures!

Shortly after this, it was suggested that I might benefit from a trip to the "treatment centre" across the street at Kingston Penitentiary. I agreed, wondering if some raging maniac was truly lodged within me. I spent the winter of 1986 at KP. The treatment unit was under reconstruction and little activity was possible. I was given industrial ear baffles on my first day. These were a curious contrast to the type of verbal therapy I had anticipated. I strongly suspect that only survivors of concentration camps have ever had to deal with personal tragedy in such bizarre surroundings. Jack-hammers pounded at old concrete walls as new ones were erected making the women's unit smaller and smaller. I felt I was living out some tortured Poe-like vision.

Once a day I was permitted to go out to a small twenty by fifty foot yard. It was surrounded by a tall Steelco fence ... and another taller wire fence mounted with razor edged barbed wire ... surrounded by the outer concrete wall of Kingston Penitentiary. Above, guards watched me from the guard towers. I walked through the snow and ice knowing where I was but finding disbelief equally plausible. This was the only refuge from insanity offered by the system to distressed women. It seemed more like a grim tale of Siberia than that of *Chatelaine* Canada.

I save only a few memories of those months in Kingston Penitentiary. One is of a daily, warm, friendly smile of encouragement from one of the male prisoners who served the breakfast line. I knew no man had come to this place by an easy route, yet this fellow traveller was strong enough to offer hope as well as food. Another memory is as harsh and bitter as the chill that leaked through the old windows of our unit. I had the company of a young woman. She too had been sentenced to life in prison and was rebelling against this circumstance. She had slashed her arms repeatedly and had finally turned to self-starvation in protest. The therapeutic response to her actions was to have the staff remove her clothes, issue summer weight pajamas, and place her under lights in an observation cell. She was held in this condition for ten days. On one occasion the nurse outside her cell remarked, "I wish I was wearing my fur coat."

I returned to the Prison for Women a little saner and a little wiser. To call a situation that resembles the setting for gothic horror a "treatment centre for women" is the construct of insensitive or sheer brutish planning.

Who is responsible or irresponsible? Nameless, faceless bureaucrats without the imagination to visualize their mothers, wives, or daughters condemned to these conditions? Or are there more sinister overtones? Are convicted women treated with uncaring contempt for contravening the myths of true womanhood, found failing as women because of human error? The gross inequities facing women incarcerated by the Correctional System of Canada are too extreme to be explained by mere bureaucratic oversight.

Largely unknown to the public and virtually ignored by Government, the Prison for Women continues to exist in an outrageously expensive, mind boggling time warp of confusion. It is common to have new arrivals seriously wonder if they have been institutionalized in a mental hospital by mistake and equally common to hear statements such as "I feel like I am on a different planet" or "I feel like Alice after she fell down the rabbit's arse hole."

The confusion of prisoners is well matched by that of visiting officials. Somewhere along the path of historic non-development, a stereotypical compensation was offered to female offenders to fill vast discrepancies with a larger male system. By the questionable virtue of these compensations, women are allowed to wear civvies and purchase cosmetics. The result is a hundred perky-looking women awash in cheek blush and eye shadow, going nowhere. However, to the casual eye on the quick tour, we do look fine and immeasurably more presentable than our male counterparts in basic green.

Given our society's priorities on appearances, it is not too difficult to understand how hard it has been to get any senior administrators to look beneath these superficial trappings to the far deeper problems and confusions that lurk below. However these have become blatantly obvious to many of us inside, and I, along with other sisters, feel it is past time to break through the deplorable compounded confusion that has surrounded women imprisoned in this country.

Most of the confusion comes from the basic nature of the Correctional Services itself. Even now, as it is (once again) under review, Canada's correctional system is described as segmented, fractionalized, and criticized for lack of co-ordination and consistency. Yet the analysis behind these observations is directed at only the larger body of institutions, all male. The Prison for Women is less than an aside to the entire reform. This is less amazing when it is recognized that this is not a new instance of neglect but merely a repeat of similar "oversights" throughout the years of so-called prison reform in this country.

The Prison for Women was opened in January 1934. It was constructed from a design used to build Kingston Penitentiary in the 1830s. This means that women of the 1980's are incarcerated in circumstances planned when rules of silence were in force and relief of monotony from long cell hours was being reduced by permitting the use of crayons and jigsaw puzzles. Today we prisoners dubiously benefit by attempting to fit these same turn-of-the-century, seven by ten foot cells with an extensive array of allowable personal effects. The result is the harshly archaic two-tiered A range filled with the conflicting needs of some attempting to up-grade their education without desks or bookshelves and others trying to relax in a bedlam of noise created by stereos and/or televisions. Likewise, the fire hazard of library and academic material as well as the quantity of clothing now allowed prisoners was never given serious consideration. We female prisoners are still locked in by the bolting action of a main wheel in addition to individual cell levers that need manual operation from the outside. Truthfully, the thought of fire in this prison is too terrifying to dwell on.

As early as 1938, the Archambault Commission reported on the appalling conditions at the Prison for Women and urged that it should be closed. This has been reiterated by commission after commission report. Indeed, these recommendations have been given serious consideration by many public officials as well as concerned citizens, but not one has been acted upon. Since my arrival in 1985, I have been told that more up-to-date programs and improvements have not been implemented because this prison is closing. This excuse has finally worn too thin. The emperor of the Correctional Service of Canada will have to find new clothes. Judging from the past, awaiting future developments at the Prison for Women will allow ample time to survey the non-productive results of prison reform.

New terminology does little to change the substance of prison living. A most recent example at this prison was a total re-classification of the prison population during the winter of 1988. Significant attention has been drawn to the fact that female prisoners were designated much higher security risk classifications than their male counterparts. In the past, probably almost half of the population was considered maximum. In response to this unwarranted discrepancy, new security labels were affixed and the majority of the population were re-classified as medium, with almost twenty-five per cent being considered minimum. However, not one living regulation has been modified to allow more prisoners responsibility and institutional freedom.

The living reality has not been changed by an inch, but the new figures will look impressive on yet another, another and another sheet of paper. To administrators and to most of you outside reading this, that is what prisons and prisoners are about: facts, figures, numbers, surveys, statistics, and paper. A thousand times more care and attention is given to these details than is ever awarded the individual inside the system.

This article was returned to me for rewriting. There were crisp editorial notes pointing out that as I traced the historical patterns of the main body of the Correctional service, noting the easement of living for male prisoners provided by constructing more moderate living circumstances in the guise of new prisons, I appeared to be supportive of prison reform in that direction. I do not think that the building of more prisons is any step to reform. However, I doubt that most readers will find it credible that since the 1950s a system of Corrections was devised for this entire country without one ounce of planning put into effect for women. Yet that is the truth of the situation. This article is being written from the upper tier of A range, that portion of the Prison for Women that was declared unfit in 1938! As I have stated once before, I am serving a life sentence and the most progression I can look forward to is a return to a Wing unit, an old army barrack located down three flights of stairs. No man is expected to serve a life sentence with such a total lack of expectations. There are no carrots or sticks for women, just larger, unremitting portions of boredom.

I do not suggest that a parallel system of Corrections be implemented for women. The establishment has rationalized inequality by justifying its position with economics. It is too expensive to provide the same services to women as are provided to men. Most have accepted this explanation and walked on. I do not. I do not believe that the mere handful of women involved in the "cystem" justifies the overwhelming abuse. What does explain the reluctance to face these abuses is the function of paternalistic capitalism at its worst.

The women inside these walls are very real, human, mainly conservative, and often depressingly dependent. Their problems are not bizarre or complicated. In the main, over eighty per cent are addicted to drugs and/or alcohol. Their crimes were committed while under the influence or while obtaining these substances. An equally high percentage are victims of incest, rape, and/or battering. The likelihood of these traumas contributing in part to addiction is very high. In the Fall of 1987, over fifty per cent were below grade nine literacy levels and it is the exceptional few who have marketable work skills beyond the lowest status of employment.

It is not hard nor too complicated to understand. These women need someone to believe in them until they can come to believe in themselves. Addiction is no longer a vague mystery. Much help can be found in both psychological and physiological treatment. Education can be upgraded and job training situations are within development potential, if (the saddest and most futile word in our language) the political will exists. The needs of female prisoners are no different than the needs of many Canadian women. The severity of the particular situation may vary, the lack of family or associate support may vary, but the basic needs are similar. These are not being met in most Canadian communities for the majority of women and it is most unlikely that the current Government (1988) will make any enlightened move on behalf of female offenders while continuing to remain unmoved by the voices of women still free in society.

Another unspoken truth about prisons in Canada is that they are Big Business. Nowhere is that more evident than in the city of Kingston. The economic welfare of many individuals employed by the Correctional Service as well as that of the merchants of the area is a direct result of employment by prisons. Thousands of marginally trained, relatively uneducated men and women receive high salaries for maintaining the human zoos in this region. To have one prison closed would pose a grave economic threat to the entire population. It is likely that provocative situations would be deliberately created to promote the image of "violent" prisoners and enhance the need for these fortress structures to restrain the violence of those within. A study by Doob and Roberts makes it clear that the Canadian public already perceive violence associated with offenders in this country at over seventy per cent of its real occurrence (Doob and Roberts, 1983). It is far easier for those wearing uniforms of law and order to destroy the credibility of prisoners than for us within the confines of the "system" to be heard and our reality acknowledged.

The reality within the Prison for Women is that life is hard, sometimes brutal; living barely adequate and programming in all areas marginal. Yet, even these limited facilities are light years ahead of the almost-non-existent facilities housing women left in the provincial prisons. Far less provision has been made for meeting their needs. They are frequently housed in a prison within a male institution and denied access to the ordinary facilities such as gym, library, chapel, or small work opportunities (e.g., kitchen or laundry). Their time is passed in tedious, unproductive minutes. As Jessica Mitford (1974) says in *Kind and Usual Punishment*, "The lives of women in prison are not the worst but they are lives of planned, unrelieved inactivity and boredom, a pervasive sense of helplessness and frustration engulfing not only the inmates but their keepers, themselves prisoners."

Boredom, blood, tears, futility, that is what prison is all about. How uncanny that this description echoes words often spoken of life in the trenches of war. It seems that the same sort of approach to dealing with problems through violence is applied in both small and large situations. I do not believe our planet can survive another global war and I do not think my country can continue to solve its social problems through building more prisons.

My position is supported by others. I owe a debt of gratitude for the insight being provided by the Church Council on Justice and Corrections. In 1986, this organisation began presenting a new language as a basis for approaching not just reform but the transformation of the justice system. Originally called the language of reconciliation, it has continued to expand and incorporate the broad social thinking of many legal minds. In 1987, in a brief review of the Law Reform Commission, the Council has suggested a model of accountability be established:

> Accountability means confronting offenders with the harm they have done and providing them with the opportunity to repair the damages and reassure the community. This does not mean that accountability is soft on an offender. It might be harder for the burglar to hear of the long term trauma of the victims than to simply do time. (Law Reform Commission Update, 1987)

These individuals see that the wasteful process of scapegoating and punishment must stop. It will require a much deeper process of truth telling and calling to account on a personal level. To begin rebuilding, we must stop fooling ourselves about the true nature of human violence. If we can take one first step to implementing alternatives to prison for women, approach re-integration with communities, and spend funds on community resource development rather than more prison construction, we will pave the way for a better social future. At this moment the Canadian Government is giving serious consideration to building another prison for women in British Columbia (See *The Whig Standard*, Friday, December 18, 1987:2). I have been told this 1990 model still contains barred cells. These will stand as monuments to failure in the century ahead. These new cages will be filled with women, sisters and daughters of the future.

The women now behind the walls of the Prison for Women in Kingston have been called "too few to count." I disagree. Alterations will come about in the system. If the real needs of these few women are honestly addressed, we can be counted upon to make a significant contribution to the larger body of Corrections. I have long loved the potential vigour of this country. It is time to tap that vitality and move beyond patriarchal policies that have sustained these prisons and the limited vision they represent.

Editor's Note: Kingston Prison for Women was eventually closed and replaced by seven regional facilities for women prisoners. As Mayhew suggests, most of the problems associated with Kingston P4W have been reproduced in these "new" prisons.

REFERENCES

Doob, A.N. and Roberts, J.V. (1983), *An Analysis of The Public's View of Sentencing*. Department of Justice.

Jackson, G. (1970), *Soledad Brothers: Letters of George Jackson*. Bantam Books.

Law Reform Commission (1987), *Update*.

Mitford, J. (1974), *Kind and Usual Punishment: The Prison Business*. Vintage Books.

N ative people lead the kkkountry in statistical categories such as unemployment, alcoholism, infant mortality and early death rates from violence and criminally-related activities. According to a study by Trent University, Native people in the criminal justice "cystem" are more likely to be "gated" under *The Dangerous Offenders Act*, Bills C-67 and C-68, and therefore are deemed the most dangerous and most violent offenders in Canada. This is also true for Native women.

Native women, however, face quadruple standards of discrimination when entering the prison cystem: (1) because we are women; (2) we are Native; (3) we are poor; and (4) we do not usually possess an education necessarily equivalent to the status quo.

PROFILE: Ms. Cree is eighteen years old, a single parent with two children. She lived in the city of _____, where the offence took place. She was convicted of manslaughter and sentenced to four years. Her parents are deceased. She has two sisters and two brothers. Ms. Cree was a housewife whose sole income was social assistance.

Ms. Cree entered the institution with a grade four level of education. She quit school due to problems in her foster home. Ms. Cree has not been involved in an education upgrading program. She has been offered a job cleaning yet has refused this placement. She also feels the school supervisor does not treat her or other Native students properly. As a result she will not work anywhere in the institution.

Ms. Cree was first arrested at the age of sixteen for uttering and forging documents. She was put on one year's probation which she completed successfully. The subject displays no responsibility for her criminal involvement. The subject clearly has a drug and alcohol problem. Her institutional participation is limited to Native Sisterhood. The writer strongly suggests that Ms. Cree remain a maximum security inmate. The writer is not in support of community release at this time. Day parole denied. Full parole denied. Escorted temporary absence denied for one year. Ms. Cree was involved with a would-be serious incident with a number of her friends on May 1, 198_ when security staff were proceeding to dispel an incident in another part of the building. As a result of Ms. Cree not being able to remain charge-free for any length of time, her cavalier attitude, her activities and friendships with many known drug dealers in the institution, it is the writer's opinion that Ms. Cree meets the #2 and #3 criteria under Bill C67-68.

Ms. Cree is a danger to society, to herself and the staff members of the institution. Ms. Cree is being referred under Bill C-67-68. Ms. Cree's sentence expires January, 199_. Next case management review scheduled December, 198_.

This is a fictional profile, but it closely resembles a perceived reality on the part of the bureaucracy who assess the Native woman as she enters prison. Those who do so come from an opposite life-experience. The average case management person is Caucasian, married, has one or two children, may have a university degree, is from a middle class background with no comparable experiences to those of a Native woman.

Obviously there are going to be some very profound difficulties that the Native woman will have in making adjustments within the institution and in serving out her sentence. Almost every Sister I have talked to has told me they were raised in foster homes, sent to juvenile detention centres, were victims of sexual abuse, were victims of rape. And, finally entering Prison for Women, we have all become victims of bureaucracy because we do not have the right colour of skin, the right kind of education, the right kind of social skills and the right kind of principles to get out of here.

Most often criminal defense lawyers in conjunction with crown prosecutors and judges agree that a guilty plea with a lengthy sentence will correct past lifestyles, our way of thinking, and make us into law-abiding "citizens". It is an absurd, phucking joke to think that the criminal just-us, cystem with their residential care, treatment, programming, counselling and mental health programs are specifically designed programs to meet the needs of Native women when we have never had an equal footing in the case management strategic planning sessions that take place. The bureaucracy and paper pushing outweighs the importance of listening to what the Native woman says she needs.

Usually the woman in the cage is too busy *surviving* the new rules, new regulations of daily life in La-La land to even consider what the future holds after she is finished her sentence.

When we come to prison, we need to adjust to greater and greater violence in our lives. We adjust to increasingly deadly conditions, and come to accept them as "natural". We adjust to having freedoms stolen away from us, to having fewer and fewer choices, less and less voice in the decisions that affect our lives. We come to believe that making $4.20 a day and the things we can buy with it are the most important life goals. We have adjusted to deafening silence because it is now mandatory to wear headphones. We have adjusted to the deafening noises and screams coming from segregation when our Sister has just been stripped of her clothes and maced in the face. We have adjusted to the deadening entertainment of bingo games that give out prized bags of taco chips and we hear glees of happiness at this score because some pathetic individual hasn't tasted taco chips since 1979. We have adjusted to the lack of conversation because some days there is absolutely nothing of significance or meaning to a few cheap words. We have adjusted to dreaming of our futures. We have adjusted to divorcing ourselves from our relationships with our husbands. We keep adapting to new and ever more dangerous conditions and ideas in the name of survival.

We forget how life once was, how blue the sky is, how good food tasted. We forget because the changes are gradual and unannounced. No one can forewarn us of what lays ahead. If we could imagine ourselves taking pleasure in a slave job like cleaning floors over and over again, day after day, year after year, and see ourselves as fanatical psycho's when our freshly waxed floor gets a scratch on it and ruins our entire day, we would recoil with horror and shame because our minds and values become as twisted and irrational as those that impose these conditions upon our lives. We become so phucking numb from the incredible b/sh we are exposed to: trying to see a case management officer to get a call to our children is a major event. It is no wonder that so many of us cut our throats, lacerate our bodies, hang ourselves. It is no wonder that we need to identify our pain onto our physical bodies because our whole lives have been filled with incredible pain and traumatizing experiences — psychic pain, physical pain, spiritual pain.

When you ask a Native woman why she was placed in a foster home she'll likely tell you it was because Children's "Aid" arrested her because her parents didn't send her to school regularly. When you ask a Native woman where she was sexually abused, she'll likely respond it took place in the foster homes. When you ask a Native woman why she finally killed somebody she'll tell you she was a battered wife and she lost control of her sense when she was taking another beating. She didn't mean to kill her husband, her lover, her friend, she was just so spun out after each licking she lived through — she just was so spun out.

I am your typical Native woman and one who has survived the criminal Just-Us Cystem. When I think about the time in prisons, I often wonder how I maintained my sanity. I never conformed in my heart or in my mind but my body danced. I learned how to cope with lies. I believe justice does not exist for Native people. The battle of will is to see through the wall, to see through the screws and their power plays — their bureaucratic games of power and pleasure.

I learned there is a certain degree of hypocrisy in the groups that represent women in prison. The money and efforts that go into "services" is a mere band-aid effort in conspiracy with the criminal-just-us-cystem. The money and efforts would be better directed at commuting the families of the incarcerated women to the prisons. The time that is spent on conducting study upon study is wasted time because statistics stay the same, the pain stays the same, the faces of the women change but the stories are identical. I entered Prison for Women as a young, poorly educated, Native woman. I will soon be released with similar characteristics but you can add another deficiency. After seven years I am now an *ANGRY*, young, poor, uneducated, Native woman!!!!

Signed in the blood of My Sisters

Prison for Women's Invisible Minority

Melissa Stewart

I would like to begin by telling you about how I came to be a prisoner at the P4W. Here is how my life unfolded, from being sane, joyful, community spirited, and relatively calm, to living a nightmare.

I remember the very first time I met Gordon. He was immaculately dressed, his hair neatly combed. He was wearing a suit, with a perfectly knotted tie. Everything was in place. He was big and powerful and moved purposefully. I thought he was the most handsome, suave, debonair man I had ever met. He was very polite and seemed totally taken with me. I was selling real estate at the time. He told me he wanted to buy a small piece of land near the ocean, on which to build a cottage. He kept telephoning me with excuses to have dinner with me, and the like.

Two weeks later we were living together common-law. What started off as a honeymoon became the worst nightmare of my life. Gordon was a violent alcoholic, as were his father and brothers. I never really knew his family very well, except the one time Gordon and his father landed in detox centres at the same time. His younger brother committed suicide about three years before Gordon died.

My whole life was centred around keeping this man "happy." During those years of knowing him and living with him, I felt certain I could "save" him. He criticized me constantly, and I developed feelings of inadequacy and insecurity. I did not feel that I was capable of doing anything right. During this time I was living in limbo, trying to fight off depression.

The physical beatings started right after we were legally married. I wore heavy make-up to cover the contusions and bruises inflicted at various times. He would play one cruel game in which he would put a plastic bag over my head while we were having sexual intercourse and strangle me, saying he wanted me to have a stronger orgasm. He would strangle me to the point where I would almost pass out.

Prior to the physical assaults on me, Gordon would always tell me I was "cruising for a bruising." I wish I could go back and undo the pain of the past. I lived in constant fear. I believe he was a psychopath who liked to inflict pain. He put welts all over my back by beating me with a leather strap. On other occasions he kicked me and cracked my ribs and collarbone. My kidneys were bruised from his beatings.

Gordon began threatening both my daughter and me, stating that he would kill her. About this time he began making sexual advances towards her. He was drinking a lot and taking cocaine and valium. I was at rock bottom.

On another occasion he held a loaded handgun to my head and pulled the trigger. The firing pin jammed in the gun, saving my life. I called the police. He was charged with the careless discharge of a firearm. They seized his guns and when he went to court he was prohibited from having any firearms for five years.

On the day that Gordon died, he had just been released from jail where he had served two months for assaulting me. This was his second charge of assault against me. On the day that he died, he came after me with a knife. I was asleep in bed when suddenly he was standing over me and holding the knife to my throat. He abducted me at knife point after ordering me to get dressed. We left the apartment and drove around in the car. That day, I told him I was never going to live with him again as man and wife. And that day, he raped me. He performed oral sex on me. He put his penis on my face, then in my mouth. I choked and gagged. I was so frightened. He started striking me on the head. There was no safe place. I could not get away. I was trapped.

After the years of battering, verbal abuse, sexual abuse, alcohol and drug abuse, I finally recognized that my life was on the line. Everything was unmanageable. My relationship with my children had deteriorated. I had been mentally and emotionally denying the torture I had lived through.

I did not mean to kill Gordon. I only wanted to get away from him. When he was standing behind the car urinating, I sensed that it was my only chance to get away. I slid over under the driver's wheel, turned on the ignition very quickly and put the car in gear. But I put it in the wrong gear; I put it in reverse instead of forward. I backed the car over him, and I left the area at a very high speed. I just wanted to get out of there. We were on a logging road in the woods. I very much regret what happened on that day. I believe my survival can only be credited to luck.

The R.C.M.P.'s Lower Sackville department charged me with first degree murder. At my preliminary hearing, the judge threw the charge out, saying there was not enough evidence to support a first degree murder charge. He had me stand trial on second degree murder instead.

The trial only focussed on that one day in our lives. No mention was made of any battering or sexual abuse in our relationship. My defence lawyer should have brought that up. Only the rape was discussed. There was courtroom testimony about my pubic hair and Gordon's seminal fluid analysis. I felt nauseated with shame.

I pled "not guilty" all through my trial. When I was found guilty of manslaughter by the jury, the judge said his reason for sending me to the federal prison was, "deterrence to the public."

After sentencing, I was taken to the Halifax County Correctional Centre. After spending three months there, I was taken from my cell in that dirty rat and bug infested hole at 4:00 a.m., with no prior warning, in shackles and handcuffs. I arrived by van at Springhill Institution around 6:30 a.m. There I was fingerprinted, had my mug shot taken and was listed as a number, before being taken to Moncton N.B. to fly in an RC.M.P. airplane along with some male prisoners to Kingston, Ontario. All prisoners were designated to different prisons in the Kingston area.

The ride in the airplane was turbulent, but worst of all I was seated next to a very large, odorous, garrulous man, who continually leered at me. His flesh sprawled onto my chair and seat and he kept leaning against me. It was my first close encounter with a man since my husband died. I found this very uncomfortable and completely unnerving, and I thought it insensitive on the part of the R.C.M.P. to seat a battered woman next to such an aggressive man. We arrived in Kingston and were taken in different vans to local area prisons. I was taken to the Prison For Women (P4W).

My first impression of the P4W was its dungeon-like appearance. There was a stench of urine and cigarette smoke in the air. I was admitted into the basement area of the prison, along with two other female prisoners. By this time it was around 8:00 p.m.

The walls inside the P4W were grey and ugly, with paint peeling off the bars. Everything was steel and concrete. I was asked routine questions on admittance such as whether I had any enemies amongst the other prisoners. This would influence the decision on where to put me. Most prisoners are placed on "A" Range for the first three months, for assessment, unless they are in need of protective custody or are mentally ill.

After the questions, a nurse was called and a body cavity search was performed on me and the other two women. It was a terrifying and humiliating experience.

"A" Range in the P4W resembled a zoo. There are 50 cells, six by nine feet each in size, in two tiers, with a small sink, toilet, single cot, and a steel dresser in each. I was put in the upper cell level. By this time I was totally exhausted from the 16 hour trip. The noise level was incredible, with clanging, banging, screaming, and cursing. Some curious prisoners were peering at me inside my cell, wondering who the new "fish" was and whether I would fit into the prison sub-culture. Paired uniformed guards patrol "A" Range every hour.

My first months in the P4W caused me severe emotional deprivation, fear, pain and panic as I began to come to terms with where I was and how I would survive. I suffered multiple crises: being away from my family, the loss of relationships, social isolation, social stigmatization, economical losses, the loss of home and goods, and feelings of unworthiness. My self-hate grew into the thought of suicide. I entered into an agonizing, dark aloneness. I felt emotionally shredded. I was completely numb and my mind was blank. I had no sense of time passing. It helped me to block the pain. I was like this for three months.

LIFE AT THE P4W

Upon entering prison, each prisoner is assigned a case management officer who collects all information pertaining to the prisoner from the police, court and sentencing reports and the judge's recommendations. When this information is correlated, the case management officer classifies the prisoner. In the fourth month after my classification I was moved to the wing area of the prison. Usually the more quiet prisoners reside there, along with some protective custody cases. Fifty women are caged on the two wings. Lately, with the increase in women prisoners, double-bunking has occurred.

Women prisoners in the P4W do not receive natural light and fresh air. They are housed in dismal surroundings, with a lack of privacy. It is a maximum security prison, caging three security levels of prisoners. Intrusive security measures are in force daily. Prisoners have little access to adequate health, education and professional services. There is also a lack of women-centred and culturally sensitive programs.

The contraband system is very common in the P4W, with commodities such as drugs, alcohol, contraband appliances, clothing, institutional privileges, contraband food and canteen items. Sometimes, suicide seems like the only alternative for a prisoner if she owes money to one of the range's leaders. The prisoners' code keeps women from talking too much.

A typical day in prison begins when you are awakened at 6:00 a.m. In one hour, each woman is to shower, dress, make her bed, tidy up her cell, and be ready to go to the common dining room to eat breakfast by 7:00 a.m. Breakfast consists of "juice," cereal or toast, coffee or tea, sometimes a piece of fruit. On Sundays, prisoners are served bacon and eggs and pancakes for breakfast.

During the day, some women are assigned work duties within the prison and go to work at 8:00 a.m. Some attend a program to upgrade their education to the Grade 10 level. Others might play cards if they have purchased their own deck, or do nothing. The work day finishes at 3:00 p.m. The gym is also open one hour per day for those who wish to exercise.

Lunchtime is from 12:00 noon to 1:00 p.m. It consists of soup, a sandwich, a dessert, and tea, coffee or "juice." Meals are adequate. Dinner takes place between 5:00 p.m. and 6:00 p.m. Each section of the prison eats separately. The wing area, which houses 50 women, eats first, then "B" Range. Women in segregation are served meals in their cells. In the punitive area of segregation women are served what looks like a large overcooked hamburger, made of questionable ingredients. Liquids are controlled and are given at the discretion of the guards.

Most prison programs focus on counteracting aggressiveness, anger and volatility. As such, the programs treat women as offenders rather than as victims. The prison system is not interested in fostering assertiveness. An assertive prisoner is a potential nuisance to prison authorities, who are mostly concerned with keeping "the good order of the institution," rather than viewing prisoners as future citizens.

The answer to the suicides of Native women in the P4W (as well as the suicides of two Anglo-Saxon women) by administrative staff was to ban some Native programs and suspend some Native social workers from entering the P4W. The other measure they took was to increase the ratio of guards/prisoners to 78/96.

These degrading conditions and the lack of constructive activity can lead to suicidal thoughts and attempted suicides. Suicide is a mechanism to escape the brutal conditions. Rather than receive appropriate treatment/counselling, the suicidal prisoner will be placed in the new secure segregation units.

In response to the April 1994 riot, brought to public attention by the CBC television program *The Fifth Estate,* this new higher security segregation was ready in April 1995 at a cost of $475,000 to the taxpayers. Prison officials thought this would be the answer to "those unruly women." It consists of 10 cells located across from the kitchen area, in the basement of the prison. The cells have steel doors in place of bars. Each cell is monitored 24 hours a day by individual TV cameras. The beds are welded to the walls. This new segregation unit has a smaller closed outdoor pen for exercise. One of the cells can even accommodate a handicapped person. Why would someone in a wheel-chair need to be put in segregation? A reason given by acting prison warden Maureen Blackler was, "There are a few women that are violent and are dangerous to others, they pose a risk to both staff and inmates."

BATTERED WOMEN AND PEER COUNSELLING AT THE P4W

I soon realized that there were a number of women who were in prison for an act committed in self-defence. These were battered women. These women numbered 25 to 30 (a group which included me), were of all different ages and came from very different educational, cultural and ethnic backgrounds. Despite these differences, almost all of them had been victims of physical, psychological or sexual abuse both as children, and then later from their spouses. Eventually, this abuse led to the crimes that brought them their federal sentences: often the killing of the abusers. These desperate acts stood in stark contrast to the women's usually meek, self-effacing personalities.

Many of the P4W's repeat offenders, who are familiar with the prison culture, have developed skills to cope with its harsh environment. Battered women prisoners are horrified by their first encounter with incarceration. The stress of their abuse and their subsequent removal from mainstream society are compounded by their sense of shame and alienation within the prison population.

Within the overburdened federal prison system, these shy and reclusive individuals can become invisible. They sometimes go months between meetings with their case management officers and often find their most basic rights neglected. Women of faith miss out on passes to attend church and in the most extreme cases, prisoners do not receive their allocations of clothing or even feminine hygiene products.

As a result, the combined emotional and practical needs of battered women prisoners are urgent. However, until I became a member of the prison's Peer Support Team in 1992 and first became aware that we made up a distinctive category of prisoner, there were no programs through which these women could take recourse.

The first P4W Peer Support Team was formed in May 1990, after two years of suicides in which time four Native women hanged themselves. There were eight suicides in total from 1988 to 1996 in the P4W, when again on February 21, 1996, another young woman, Brenda D., was found hanged in her cell.

Prison psychologist Julie Darke and social worker Jan Heney began the first P4W Peer Support Team. Heney had done a study on self-injurious behaviour at the P4W and discovered there existed amongst the women prisoners an informal network of counselling and support. She recommended that a team be formed and formal training started. The first class of five prisoner/counsellors graduated in May 1992. These women could be available to help other women in crises; thus began a team of women prisoners ready and willing to help others. It gave me the opportunity to help other women; something positive which came out of something so overwhelmingly negative.

Peer Support Team members have many of the same experiences as the people who use their services. However, peer support counsellors' own access to many resources is limited. As well, confidentiality is difficult since service users and counsellors live in the same close quarters among the very same people. While correctional staff still have more resources at their disposal than peer counsellors, many prisoners are more comfortable dealing with peer counsellors as they often feel they are in an adversarial relationship with correctional staff.

In the absence of programs specifically designed for battered women, many relied heavily on peer-support counselling to help them cope. Sometimes a woman would call three or four times in one week. Realizing that the peer-support program could not effectively meet this sort of demand, I approached the administration and suggested that a battered women's support group be formed. Nothing happened. Then Dr. Heather McLean of the psychology department wrote a letter in praise of the proposal, and permission was granted. Under the supervision of chaplain John Hess, we held our first meeting in April 1993.

Together, members formulated the criteria for admission to the group. They decided that each member must be the survivor of abuse, that she must support the group's vision of itself which is founded on a "hope to heal in a non-healing environment," that she must respect fellow members' rights to confidentiality, and she must be in prison for a crime committed in self-defence.

We also established group guidelines, drawing heavily from the Quaker-sponsored Alternatives to Violence Project, which has offered workshops in the prison since 1992. These guidelines include looking for and affirming one another's good points, volunteering oneself only, committing oneself to non-violence, and being willing to take risks and possibly to suffer, if necessary, in order to maintain that non-violent stance. We recognized that non-violence is not passivity, submissiveness, or martyrdom. Members also have the right not to participate in an activity. The aim of these guidelines is to establish a "principled space" in which members can encounter the most positive aspects of themselves and each other.

Soon the Battered Women's Support Group (BWSG) grew into a positive force in the P4W. Membership in the group was voluntary, as was attendance. Members were permitted to drop out at any time if they needed to, then return as their circumstances permitted. Instead of being referred to the group by staff, prisoners learned of the group by word of mouth and attended entirely of their own volition.

Meetings were informal. Members sat in a circle for presentations, which were then followed by question and answer sessions. However, some evenings were reserved for talking things out and struggling with the emotions stirred by the talk. Vital to the group's success was the commitment of volunteers from outside the prison. These volunteers visited from as far as Toronto and came from a mixed-bag of backgrounds. As founder of the BWSG in The P4W, I was invited by the previous warden to attend group meetings as a community volunteer, when I left the prison on day parole in July 1994. This was something close to my heart, so attendance at meetings was something I enjoyed. The group had always functioned as a collective, and made its decisions accordingly. Over the three years we had been meeting, the group had evolved into a cohesive entity. I marvelled at the level of trust that had developed, and at the feeling of camaraderie we had built up.

The dedicated community volunteers attending the battered women's support group included Jo-Ann Connolly, a Kingston lawyer and currently chairperson of the Canadian Association of Elizabeth Fry Societies Battered Women's Defense Committee. We also worked with Queen's University Law Professor, Sheila Noona, who originally did the ground work for a legal process which would permit women incarcerated for defending themselves against abusive partners to have an "en bloc" review of their cases. Sheila has offered insights into how the battered women's syndrome could affect reintegration into a small community because of the nature of the offense and the complex relationship between victim and offender in small, often isolated communities. The communities themselves are often unwilling to accept prisoners back after release from prison. Today, Sheila continues to be a support to many group members.

Toronto broadcaster Sian Cansfield commuted weekly to show her solidarity with the women and gave them a voice on her radio program. She did a one hour show just before Christmas 1994, and discussed issues surrounding abuse survivors and how the group members were dealing with their pain and separation from family members during the festive season. The broadcast resulted in Christmas gifts being donated to group members.

Sandra Dean, a local interior designer, has offered constructive suggestions on dressing and speaking in ways that increase a woman's chances of being treated with dignity and consideration. She did a presentation on colours and the right choices of wardrobe, as well as proper etiquette.

Addictions counsellor Carol Bielby brought in three of the Boston Terrier pups she breeds. She talked about the love and devotion a dog can offer, and the respect and affection they deserve in return. The direct emotional connection between the women and those six-week-old pups was intensely moving. Some group members had lost touch with their feelings, and the puppies provided a way to emotionally connect again. In prison, women are not encouraged to express their feelings. And all of the feelings associated with addictions, along with the unique and serious emotional experiences these women have endured, can be so overwhelming. Only a pet could bring these feelings to the fore.

Healer Bonita Currier helped some of the women release residual feelings from childhood sexual abuse, and Salvation Army Major Carol Barkhouse brought in entertaining and instructive videos. Some of these topics dealt with same-sex relationships, addictions, group dynamics, family violence, as well as comedies.

Supplementing the steady contributions from our six stalwart volunteers were presentations from various guest speakers, including:

- Dr. Mary Pearson, on diet, exercise, and wellness
- Shiatsu therapist Beth Morris, teaching massage techniques
- Criminal lawyer Josh Zambrowsky, on the impact of Bill C45 on women prisoners
- George Best (who counsels battering men), on the connections between early childhood conditioning, gender roles and male violence
- Four University of Ottawa criminologists: Sylvie Frigon and Christa Armitage, on the legal use of the battered women's syndrome; and Ashley Turner and Irene Sernowski, on the value of keeping a journal (along with gifts of a notebook and pen for each group member)
- Kingston Interval House staffers Terri Fleming and Pamela Needham, on power and control issues in relation to domestic violence and the importance of equality in partnerships
- Drama workshop facilitator Susan Raponi, of the Salvation Armies in Toronto, leading illuminating role plays

Two gatherings were particularly outstanding. One was the Christmas party — with "imported" home-made foods, portable piano keyboard to accompany carols and, best of all, carefully selected gifts for each member of the group. As much as the gifts themselves, the women appreciated the fact that they had been specially purchased by people from the outside who just wanted to express their support and affection. The gifts came at a time when, for the first time in years, parcels from home were not being permitted into the institution because of concerns about contraband.

The other important gathering was the National Day of Awareness, held in the gymnasium on August 30, 1994, and attended by representatives from North American Native societies, local community and church groups, the various levels of government. Group members told their personal stories. Film producer Barbara Doran then showed her film *When Women Kill*, which kicked off a panel discussion. Journalist June Callwood spoke, as did federal justice committee chairman Warren Allmand. Also in attendance was Member of Parliament, Peter Milliken. This gathering was attended by over 110 guests. Substantial donations of money were sent by retired Supreme Court Justice Bertha Wilson and the Kenora Sexual Assault Centre. Despite the resounding success of this event, prison authorities ruled out the possibility of such gatherings in the future. As a concession, they let us use the gymnasium for a bingo on March 22, 1995, to which no outsiders were invited.

Later, in response to the fall-out from the Commission of Inquiry Into Certain Events at the Prison for Women (1995) chaired by Madame Justice Arbour, corrections department officials took over the operation of the Battered Women's Support Group and began to regulate it as a prison program. Prisoners must now attend the group for six weeks, at the end of which time they receive certificates of completion. All meetings are chaired by a guard instead of having a member facilitate. Instead of sharing their feelings when they are ready, participants are told when to express themselves. These conditions violate the original goal of the group which was to provide a "safe space" in which abuse survivors could share their experiences and work to heal themselves. The presence of the guard can be intimidating for many members, while the six week certificate of completion trivializes the emotional pain with which survivors of long-term abuse must wrestle.

The good news is that as of September 3, 1996, after I relayed these concerns to corrections officials, I have been assured the group can go back to its original mandate, without the presence of the guard. Once more I will attend the group to help members draw up a new constitution, as well as arrange to have a different group member volunteer to facilitate the next meeting. This will give members a chance to hone their organizational skills and to feel more comfortable in the limelight. This is especially crucial now, as the Correctional Service of Canada is gearing up to relocate the P4W's population to five new regional facilities across the country. Prisoners have no choice about where they will go and, in many cases, the move will separate women from their partners of long-standing. The turmoil and pain this process poses for prisoners is exacerbated by a lack of information about the relocation process. There seems to be little information about the move available to many Corrections employees, and what information exists is not filtering down to the prisoners. This has created an atmosphere of fear, suspicion and tension. Prisoners will need ongoing support as they adjust to their new environments.

After the fall-out from the P4W inquiry, access to the prison by outside groups in 1996 has been increasingly restricted. Currently, only three community volunteers are allowed to attend the Battered Women's Support Group: Sandra Dean, Jo-Ann Connolly and me.

A news release from the Department of Justice in Ottawa, October 4, 1995 stated:

> The Solicitor General of Canada, Herb Gray, and the Minister of Justice and Attorney General of Canada, Allan Rock, today announced the appointment of the Honourable Lynn Ratushny, a judge of the Ontario Court of Justice (Provincial Division), to lead a review of cases involving women convicted of killing their abusive partners, spouses, or guardians.

When I spoke with Judge Ratushny on August 13, 1996, she told me there were 98 cases submitted for review. The "in custody" applications total 63; 35 cases are not in custody. She states that she has dealt thoroughly and fairly with 45 cases, and has contacted the women involved. Some of these files have been looked at, because she is dealing with the women in custody first. There are still 15 women in custody, whose cases need to be reviewed.

Upon leaving the P4W in July 1994, I began developing my vision of having an agency run by and for prisoners, enlarging upon the peer support team model I had learned in the P4W. With the help of important community leaders and since its incorporation in April of 1995, Project Another Chance Inc. has, with the support of the Trillium Foundation, made great strides towards establishing a conduit to the community for women in prison and female parolees. We now have 75 committed volunteers, many of whom have received intensive crisis response and suicide intervention training, as well as orientation on Native women's issues. The "Right-On Line," a crisis phone line for women prisoners and parolees, has been in official operation since December 1995.I have been taking calls on restricted hours since May 1995 and already the response from service users is very positive. After a great deal of organization and training, we are beginning to see the results of the very necessary service we provide. We have made a specific mandate to seek the cooperation of prison administrators across the country in order to allow prisoners, who have increasingly restricted telephone access to the outside, to use our services.

Operated by a tiny staff and over 40 professionally-trained volunteers (including several ex-prisoners), the Right-On Line offers quiet, non-judgmental support, suicide intervention, referrals to prison and community resources and strives to establish a community link for women in conflict with the law. Parolees who call the Right-On Line can tap into practical information on resume-writing, conquering addictions and finding affordable products and services, as well as building a supportive network of friends and advisors.

The P4W has always been and continues to be a living nightmare, designed and operated as a maximum security prison. This is inappropriate and harmful to federally sentenced women. They struggle with geographical and cultural dislocation, and have little or no contact with their children, families and communities.

When leaving prison, you are usually told a day or so ahead of time that you will be released. This gives the prisoner time to pack up her belongings, clean up her cell, say their farewells and prepare herself for the outside. It is quite disorienting and overwhelming when you know you will be released. Some women panic at this stage and are unsure if they can "make it" outside.

The dehumanizing aspects of incarceration cause prisoners to become more angry and bitter. They lose faith in the "system," and while imprisoned they are essentially schooled in the commission of crime. Those released are less able to function as responsible, caring citizens.

Prisons represent a temporary warehouse where goods will eventually come out. But what if these goods are then more spoiled? We have prisons because we have come to believe in them, even though they do represent only a small proportion of the criminalized. Prisons represent that end of the system where we put the most readily detected, the most readily prosecuted, and the most readily forgotten about.

The Prize of the Poor
Steven King Ainsworth

The epitome of power is the right to kill, to kill under the colour of law. "The decisive means of politics is violence" (Genovese, 1972, p. 25), and capital punishment is the graphic use of that violence.

At the close of 1997, the United States had executed 431 human beings in the Modern Era (1976–present) of capital punishment. If the rate of executions continue unabated, as they did in 1997, the United States will execute its 500th human being before the close of 1998. The argument over whether Texas should execute Karla Faye Tucker, who would be only the second woman executed in the Modern Era, and the first woman executed in Texas since 1863, is simply the latest controversy. Karla Faye Tucker was denied clemency and executed by Texas on February 3, 1998.

The debate over the viability of death as punishment has continued since the time of Hammurabi (1792–1750 B.C.), who first codified capital punishment in the ancient laws of the Amorites. Sectarian and secular rulers freely employed capital punishment to control and punish those they ruled throughout history. The Spanish Conquistadores following in the wake of Columbus, as well as the early English settlers, brought capital punishment to America and used it frequently, under the guise of God's will. The Ruling Council of Jamestown probably hung the first white man (1609) on the eastern seaboard just months after landing on the American shore.

The death penalty was the punishment of choice for a myriad of crimes: adultery, sodomy, theft, murder, rape, witchcraft, assault, robbery, infanticide and others, in colonial America. Even religious dissenters [Quakers] were subject to death by the authorities of Massachusetts Bay Colony (Friedman, 1993, p. 42). These early Christian colonies seemed to rely on the Old Testament scriptures as their authority to kill, in ignorance of Christ's law of mercy proclaimed in the Sermon on the Mount. Favourite passages from Genesis (9:6), Leviticus (24:17), Exodus (21:23–25) and Deuteronomy (19:19–21) were often heralded as the Biblical right to kill. [Similar arguments rage on today as the 'Christians' of America struggle to justify their support for capital punishment]. At the same time the 'Benefit of Clergy' often saved a condemned person from execution (Schwarz, p. 128; Friedman, p. 43). Early 17th century records indicate that the Puritans of Massachusetts enacted death penalty statutes based on the Mosaic (Old Testament) model for "blasphemy, bestiality, conspiracy, rebellion, cursing a parent and ravishing a maid," (Rantoul, 1836). Capital punishment was freely applied to control slaves in early Virginia; special courts [segregated] of oyer and terminer (Tate, p. 93–96) were set up to deal with crimes committed by slaves, including capital crimes. There is even evidence that an attempt to speed up executions, such as the recent *Anti-Terrorism and Effective Death Penalty Act* of 1996 has a legal forbearer in *The 1692 Act for more Speedy Prosecution of Slaves Committing Capital Crimes* (Hening, p. 102–103; Billings, 1981, p. 577). Capital punishment has long been the prize of the poor and minority in America (Ainsworth, 1997).

The American record for mass execution was carried out by military tribunal on December 26, 1862, at the behest of Abraham Lincoln, who ordered the hanging of 39 Lakotas Souix at Mankato, Minnesota (Fingle, 1992, p. 347–351). The use of capital punishment to put down dissent (or rebellion) has a long history in America. It was utilized in controlling and ending a rebellion of poor whites and slaves in 1676 known as 'Bacon's Rebellion' (Zinn, 1992, p. 90–94), and again in 1786 to quell 'Shay's Rebellion' (Zinn, 1992, p. 167). Throughout pre-Civil War America, capital punishment was employed to control the poor white, Indian and slave populations, culminating in the hanging of the abolitionist John Brown in 1859 (Sutler, p. 6–9).

Throughout the period between 1609 and the Civil War (1861–65), the use of capital punishment as a criminal sanction became limited to fewer and fewer crimes, although it was still in force and mostly the province of the poor, ill-educated and racial minority. It was never abolished despite the early abolition efforts of people such as Dr. Benjamin Rush (1745–1813), who published the first proposal to abolish capital punishment in 1787 (O'Sullivan, p. 104–105). Rush following in the footsteps of Beccaria (Wormer, 1949, p. 225) advised the Founding Fathers that "the power over human life is the sole prerogative of Him who gave it. Human laws, therefore, rise in rebellion against this prerogative, when they transfer to human hands" (Rush, 1787). This early movement to abolish capital punishment did have some effect in the United States by the mid-19th century. A hundred years after Beccaria's Treatise (Beccaria, 1764) against the death penalty, the movement for abolition had borne fruit; capital punishment was abolished in Michigan (1847), Rhode Island (1852), and Wisconsin (1853).

The Civil War quashed this early effort, but matters, at least from an accused citizen's perspective, did improve after the Civil War, through the expanded rights granted U.S. citizens of the several states by the Civil War Amendments (1868) to our Constitution, and subsequent Federal Court decisions (Bedau, 1997, p. 183) which at least gave some civil rights protection to those being tried for capital crimes, or so it appeared.

Although the Fourteenth Amendment required the States to abide by the Fifth Amendment's due process provision and guaranteed equal protection of the laws, both of these requirements "slippery open-ended concepts" (Friedman, 1993, p. 298) and their application may be questionable in at least two capital cases [and many more] of the early 20th century; Nicola Sacco and Bartholomew Vanzetti (executed in 1927) (Zinn, 1992, 367), and the legal machinations surrounding the Ethel and Julius Rosenberg's trial, appeal and execution in 1953 (Zinn 1992, 424–428).

The Eighth Amendment's provision forbidding cruel and unusual punishment also came into play in the litigation war waged against capital punishment. Public sentiment for "limbing" [as in the 'Life and Limb provision of the Fifth Amendment] waned early on (Schwarz, p. 145), and the last vestige of this particular 'cruel and unusual' punishment (castration) survived into the late antebellum period (Genovese, 1972, p. 34). It has since been replaced in the modern era by chemical means. However, since the Civil War, hanging, firing squad, electrocution and lethal gas were all employed as methods of execution and all were challenged to no avail (Bedau, 1997, p. 183). These methods were joined by lethal injection in the modern era and all five methods have been used in the present decade, all of which have been held to be constitutional by the U.S. Supreme Court, although some questions are still unanswered as to lethal gas.

The horrors of World War II seemed to bring a new sense to the populace concerning the value of human life, and in the post-World War II era public sentiment seemed to turn from its former bloodthirst. The new prosperity and educational opportunities in the 1950s and 1960s, as well as a strong civil rights movement, brought a new sensitivity to race and individual rights into the debate concerning criminal justice and capital punishment. Consequently, the pendulum of punishment swung from the brutality and harshness of the pre-World War II era to a more humane system of rehabilitation after the war.

This movement may have reached its zenith with the *Furman* (*Furman* v. *Georgia*, 1972, p. 238) decision in 1972. Racism, oppression of the poor, due process, equal justice, cruel and unusual punishment and public sentiment were all addressed in the *Furman* decision opinion(s). Justice Brennan's opinion in *Furman* brought a new test to determine what was cruel and unusual punishment as forbidden by the Eighth Amendment. The principles of Brennan's test were cumulative:

> ... if a punishment is unusually severe, if there is a strong possibility that it is inflicted arbitrarily, if it is substantially rejected by contemporary society, and if there is no reason to believe that it serves any penal purpose more effectively then some less severe punishment, then the continued infliction of that punishment violates the command of the clause ... (Bedau, 1997, p. 190).

The *Furman* court had found a way to conquer the troublesome 'and' in the clause. While judicial homicide certainly was not unusual in the U.S., no one can argue that killing a viable human being is not cruel! The new test in Brennan's opinion found that all of its principles were being violated by Georgia's statutes [and by inference by all jurisdictions then employing capital punishment] in their application of capital punishment.

The immediate effect of *Furman* was to *abrogate* the power to kill of the state and federal governments. The *Furman* relief was short lived. While it and the debate leading up to it forestalled any actual executions from taking place for a decade (1967–1977), the immediate response in the following *months* by various legislative bodies soon circumvented the holdings in *Furman* and new and improved (umph!) death penalty statutes were enacted. *Furman* came up short, as it *did not* rule out the possibility of there being a constitutionally protected right to kill that could be employed by the powers that be.

Supposedly, these new statutes were in response to a new public vigour for the death penalty, possibly as a backlash to the 1960's liberalism, reaction to the urban riots of the era, the political assassinations and world-wide publicity surrounding the Manson Murders of 1969. Who knows? The public perception of crime (Hall, 1996, p. 545), as distorted by politicians clamouring for a reinstatement of their political means of violence, and the fear fanned by the media prohibited the nation from taking a breath and giving capital punishment a closer look. Crime statistics indicate the murder rate per 100,000 was 9.4 in 1973, rose to a high of 10.2 in 1980, and was 9.2 in 1992, a total fluctuation of 0.8 percent. One might question the public's perception of its need to kill its fellow citizens.

Furman also had some impact on the number of crimes that are punishable by death. While the issue is not completely settled, I do not believe any has been put to death in the modern era (1976–present) for a crime in which some sort of homicide was not involved. In the wake of *Furman*, the court ruled death was "grossly disproportionate and excessive" (*Coker* v. *Georgia*, 1977) for the crime of rape. There are statutes in some jurisdictions providing capital punishment for non-homicide crimes that have yet to be challenged, and California gubernatorial candidate, Al Checchi, was advocating the death penalty for serial rapists and child molesters in his 1997–98 television campaign ads. It remains to be seen what the Rehnquist Court or a subsequent court will do with this issue.

The *Gregg* decision [428 U.S. 153] in 1976, reinstated capital punishment in the U.S. by approving the procedural changes in their capital crime statutes. Georgia had, in the eyes of a majority (7–2) of the Supreme Court, met constitutional muster and could once again kill under the colour of law. Ostensibly, these new procedures met the evolving standards of decency within U.S. society.

Other states and the federal government joined Georgia in pushing the trundel to the killing ground. However, a companion case to *Gregg* eliminated mandatory death sentences (*Woodson* v. *North Carolina*), and the *Gregg* court opted to recognize that "one of the most important functions any jury can perform ... a selection [between life in prison and death in a capital case] is to maintain a link between contemporary community values and the penal system" (Bedau, 1997, p. 199), and this became the new norm in death penalty cases. The jury either actually chooses the punishment or recommends it. I might note here that while in California the trial judge can reduce a jury *verdict* of death to life without parole (LWOP), he/she cannot elevate a LWOP verdict to death. This is not the case in some jurisdictions where the jury *recommends* a sentence. In several of the southeastern states, a recommendation of life by a jury has been elevated by the trial judge to death, a procedure the Rehnquist Court has ruled constitutional. To me, this is a sinister use of power and a slap to the jury system!

The new and improved *Gregg* procedures actually gave capital defendants more issues to appeal and acted in part to lengthen the appeal process. Both *Furman* and *Gregg* did away with most general challenges to capital punishment, and the majority of challenges today are limited to individual case issues. In my opinion, only the words have changed from pre-*Furman* to post-*Gregg* and in actual application of the death penalty, it remains the province of the minority and the prize of the poor. Neither *Furman* nor *Gregg* addressed the issue of who is charged with a capital offense. This diabolical choice is made by a county prosecutor in most jurisdictions, an elected official, who may pick and choose those accused for capital prosecution. A choice that may be, and often is, based on his/her political aspirations and bias.

> Capital crimes are so political that winning becomes far more important for the average District Attorney, we are not talking about being competitive, we're talking about winning at all costs. Deliberately deceiving the Court, withholding favourable evidence, arguing things they know are not true, harassing defence witnesses, concealing deals they make with their witnesses, winning means a death sentence ... (Le Boeuf, 1998, p. 58).

The ability of the defendant to defend himself/herself, the race, gender or wealth and position of the victim, the county locale, and the race of the defendant more often decide who is capitally prosecuted than the nature of the offence. This seems contradictory to the tenet that *the obligation of the prosecution is to accomplish justice, not just get a conviction.*

The last post-Gregg attempt to address the race issue that has been inherent in the use of capital punishment from the beginning, was dealt with by the Rehnquist Court surreptitiously. They chose to ignore the fact that the petitioner *McClesky* (*McClesky* v. *Kemp*, 1987) had shown "a discrepancy that appears to correlate with race" (Friedman, 1993, p. 319) in Georgia's application of sentencing, but he (*McClesky*) failed to prove that race had any bearing on his own trial, conviction and condemnation (*McClesky* was black and the victim was white). Had the Court recognized the racism in *McClesky*, its ruling would have seriously impaired the power to judicially kill in the U.S., if not eliminating capital punishment entirely.

Ironically, Justice Blackmun, who participated in all three cases [*Furman*, *Gregg* and *McClesky*], voting in the minority in *Furman*, and with the majority in *Gregg* and *McClesky*, as well as Justice Powell, who took part in the latter two cases, voting in the majority in both, had, after twenty plus years on the high bench, changed their minds about the constitutionality of capital punishment. Blackmun, just before retiring, declared capital punishment a failure, unconstitutional, and that he "would no longer tinker with the machinery of death" (*Callins* v. *Collins*, 1996). In a biography of Powell, after his retirement, he said that the only vote he regretted and would change if he could was his vote in *McClesky* in 1987, a case decided by a 5–4 majority. Changes of mind and heart certainly did not aid the 431 human beings executed from 1977 through 1997.

While Justice Brennan points out in Furman that an executed person has "lost their right to have rights" (Bedau, 1997, p. 191), and Bedau makes reference to the "Universal Declaration of Human Rights" (1948) (ibid, p. 191), in which the right to life is recognized as the most basic human right of all, the United States has consistently ignored the fact, that all rights stem from the right to life. As long as it exercises its power to commit judicial homicide, all human rights in the United States are hollow and at risk.

REFERENCES

Ainsworth, S. (1997). "Relic of the Past," *Frontiers of Justice, Vol. 1. The Death Penalty.* Blunswick, ME: Biddle Pub. W.

Angle, R. and Miers, E. (1992). *The Tragic Years: A Documentary History of the American Civil War.* New York: DeCapo Press.

Beccaria, C. (1764). *An Essay on Crimes and Punishment.* Philadelphia: H. Nicklin.

Bedau, H.A. (1997). *The Death Penalty in America.* New York: Oxford University Press.

Billings, W.M. (Nov. 1981). "Pleadings, Procedure and Practice: The Meaning of Due Process of Law in Seventeenth-Century Virginia." *Journal of Southern History,* XLVII.

Callins v. *Collins* (1996).

Coker v. Georgia (1977) 433 U.S. 584.

Friedman, L.M. (1993). *Crime and Punishment in American History.* New York: Basic Books.

Furman v. *Georgia* (1972) 408 U.S. 238.

Genovese, E. (1972). *Roll, Jordan Roll: The World the Slaves Made.* New York: Vintage Books.

Hall, K. (1996). *American Legal History.* New York: Oxford University Press.

Hening, W.W. (1619–1792). *Statutes at Large,* Vol. III. Philadelphia and New York.

Le Boeuf, D. (Jan. 19, 1998). "Loyola Resource Center," *Time Magazine.*

McClesky v. *Kemp* (1987) 481 U.S. 281.

O'Sullivan. *Report in Favor of the Abolition of the Punishment of Death by Law* (N10)

Rantoul, Jr., R. (Feb. 22, 1836) "Report Relating to Capital Punishment." Commonwealth Of Massachusetts, House Doc. No. 32.

Rush, B. (1787). *An Inquiry into the Effects of Public Punishment Upon Criminals and Upon Societies.* Philadelphia: Joseph James.

Schwarz, P.J. *Forging the Shackles: The Development of Virginia's Criminal Code for Slaves.*

Sutler, B.B. "The Hanging of John Brown," *American Heritage,* No. 2.

Tate, Thad W. (1965) *The Negro in Eighteenth Century Williamsburg*. Williamsburg, Va.:
    University Press of Virginia.
Woodson v. *North Carolina* (1976) 428 U.S. 281.
Wormer, R.A. (1949). *The Law: The Story of Lawmakers and the Law we have Lived by
    from Earliest Times to the Present Day*. New York: Simon and Shuster.
Zinn, H. (1992). *A People's History of the United States: 1492–Present*. New York:
    Harper-Collins.

Bureaubabble and the Beep
Amy Friedman

PART ONE

L
ike few Canadians, I followed the press coverage of the Arbour Commission hearings held in Kingston, Ontario, an Enquiry commissioned in 1995 by Canada's Solicitor General on the tail of the C.B.C.'s *The Fifth Estate*'s televised airing of portions of a videotape taken in April 1994 at the Prison for Women in Kingston. To those who believe that Canada is a most humane nation but are unfamiliar with Canadian prisons, the sight of sleeping women prisoners, bound in chains, being stripped of their clothing and pulled from bedless cells by "Darth Vadar" suited, armed, male guards was sickening. This could not have happened in Canada seemed the general consensus. But those of us who know Canadian prisons, from the inside, were not shocked. To us these actions were mild in comparison to what we know goes on inside segregation cells in prisons throughout this country. The Commissioner of the Correctional Service of Canada (CSC) called the event an "aberration," but the aberration is, in truth, the fact that the public even saw the brutal strip search and that an Enquiry into such an occurrence, the first of its kind, was ever called.

Unlike most Canadians, I attended some of the Enquiry sessions and there observed closely the way in which Commission lawyer, Patricia Jackson, and the prisoners' lawyers, attempted to extract from CSC officials their thinking in not only calling for and condoning such a procedure but in covering up the fact that they had done so for nine months afterwards. Ultimately, given mountains of evidence revealing numerous illegal acts on the part of members of CSC — the stripping of women by men being just one — some officials did admit that it was probable that the Service had acted illegally. But officials prevaricated. Well, they argued, no one but CSC officials and staff know what happened before the Emergency Response Team was sent into those segregation cells. Madame Justice Louise Arbour, the presiding judge, presented her recommendations to the Solicitor General based on Enquiry findings in late March 1996. However, because so few journalists were covering the Enquiry itself — seemingly having lost interest once the more titillating aspects of the show drew to a close in September — it is unlikely many members of the public will ever hear another word on the subject of the P4W Enquiry, and thereby, few will ever understand the way in which CSC in truth metes out "justice" in our prisons.

I have a personal stake in Madame Justice Arbour's findings. Four years ago I married a man who has been, since 1985, serving a federal prison sentence, also in Kingston. My husband and I met when I entered a prison as a journalist. I had long lived near this city that houses eight of Canada's federal prisons, but I knew little about them, media coverage having focussed primarily on high profile cases. For five years previous to my first visit to prison I had written a weekly column for *The Whig-Standard*, the highly-respected Kingston daily. In April 1992, I was a columnist of some renown, and Joyceville Penitentiary administrators rolled out the red carpet when I entered. I met dozens of staff, administrators and prisoners, among them a man who was then Chairman of the Inmate Committee. The Committee was, then, politically active, the Chairman vocal about administrators' illegal acts; acts resulting in grave consequences for prisoners and, by extension, the public. After this man and I had talked to each other for just under two weeks, the red carpet was suddenly jerked from beneath my feet. CSC officials directed the publisher of *The Whig* to censor me. The publisher complied, forbidding me to write about the prisons, instructing my editor to carefully scrutinize each column I wrote. One month later, when I wrote a column about a former junior high school teacher's abuse of power, the publisher warned me that I was, "treading too close to the line." Two weeks after that, a new editor cut my column to twice monthly. Three months later the column was abruptly cancelled. I was, at the same time, removed from my position as editor and writer of a feature I had created for the paper, which had been syndicated to eight other papers. I no longer had work in my hometown.

I sought work elsewhere. I tried, briefly, to tell the publisher and other journalists about the administrative cover up in the works at Joyceville, but no one listened. And besides, by then I had begun to understand that I would never be able to write truthfully about the institutions which employ so many of Kingston's denizens. I applied to become a personal visitor of the Chairman of the Inmate Committee. I was approved after the standard "investigation." He and I fell in love with each other, and meanwhile we spoke openly to each other about illegal and demonstrably harmful acts. He and other Committee members continued to challenge administrators with paperwork and in meetings about many of their more heinous acts. He and I decided to marry. During the months following our application to marry, prison officials consistently "lost" those papers which required the warden's signature. These were "discovered" very suddenly, five days before our scheduled wedding, one hour after my husband had been transferred out of that medium security prison to a maximum security in what is known in the Service as an Emergency Involuntary Transfer.

We should not have been surprised. Over the weeks preceding the transfer, several prisoners released from segregation had told my husband-to-be that a member of the prison's oligarchy had approached them with offers of transfers to minimum security if they would tell him something damning about my husband. My husband's Case Management Officer warned him to get off the Committee if he was serious about his marriage. He did not have time to heed warnings. Five days before our wedding, officials shipped him off to a maximum security institution far from our home. There we did, ultimately marry. Since that time, nearly every decision taken in my husband's case has been based on the allegation which prompted transfer. "One Informed source" (who we learned was a prisoner who was a diagnosed paranoid schizophrenic, had been taken off his medication, and owed thousands of dollars to other prisoners for drug debts) informed the prison's Internal Preventative Security Officers (IPSO, the prison's secret police) that my husband and another prisoner, also transferred, were "conspiring" to "seriously injure" a third prisoner. Five days after officials at Regional Headquarters rubber stamped the transfer, the alleged victim-to-be, a friend of my husband's and a relation of one of the IPSO officers, wrote an affidavit stating that there was no animosity between himself and my husband; ten days after that the "one credible source" recanted his story in another affidavit. A year later we learned that the informant had, in fact, never even mentioned my husband's name to IPSO officers. To cover their tracks, IPSO officers searched for more "proof." Two months after my husband had been removed from the Institution, a "second credible informant" surfaced; the next month, astonishingly, a "third credible informant" appeared. A third inmate was offered a transfer to a minimum security if he would add his name to the list; he refused and sat in segregation for two months, after which he was transferred to a prison in British Columbia. The transfer prevailed and the wholly invented story about my husband enabled officials to label my husband dangerous and to ensure additional punishment. Beyond that, "news" of our marriage and "news" of my husband's alleged "conspiracy" were published anonymously in Frank Magazine, though there the conspiracy turned into "conspiracy to murder." No one at the magazine ever contacted me to check facts——most of which, including my husband's sentence, were wrong. No matter. Apparently a lot of people read the "news." My husband's security ratings escalated to the highest levels possible, the invention remained on file, represented as truth, and my husband sat in his cell in maximum security for nine months while we fought for an investigation. I, meanwhile, struggled to find work, emotionally distraught by the bumpy landing I had taken when the red carpet was pulled away.

My husband and I have, for three and one half years, tried to redress in all legal ways available to us, the unlawful acts committed against us. Redress has been impossible. Few people believe a word either my husband or I say, and that includes many of my former colleagues. Meanwhile, nearly everyone who works for the Service, and everyone who does not, believes the word of Service employees, particularly those who choose to speak against us, or against most any prisoner.

As a result of my experience, I am acutely aware of and distressed by the absolute power of CSC and by its vividly apparent goal: to protect not the public, as mandate proclaims, but to protect itself in whatever manner possible, no matter the cost, in both dollars and lives. I am made aware daily of the fact that the Service, at nearly every juncture, disregards policy and law in its treatment of prisoners, and in its treatment of their families, and in the use of "informants." The privileges granted informants in return for their stories (true or false), puts the public at risk, for the ability to spin a yarn in exchange for favours does not a reformed criminal make. Though I have long shied away from the term "victim," I know that my husband and I are but two of thousands of victims of unimpeded abuse of power, victims of the way in which suspicion, rumour, and innuendo guide the manner in which the Service determines, in its recommendations to the National Parole Board, who will be set free and who will not.

PART TWO

My husband and I have friends and family. We had become especially close to Claire Culhane, one of the few stalwart prisoners' rights activists who has, in her four books and more than twenty years of outspoken activism, tried to make the public aware of the heinous abuses by "the system," and the way in which the evil running rampant in our prisons harms us all. Our family survives, but sometimes only barely. We have written to every official, including MPs of every political stripe, to two Solicitor Generals and to their critics. We have submitted grievances and have hired lawyers. In nearly every instance our attempts to redress wrongs have been met by the Service's stonewalling and protection of its own. It is stonewalling, lies, innuendo, and threat which often hobble me. The abuse of power, when employed behind closed doors, will destroy whomever it must.

When CSC's unlawful acts are made evident, as they have been at the P4W Enquiry, Service officials must rationalize these. It did not startle me to hear officials at the Enquiry explaining away their actions in exasperated tones. The public, they reasoned, could not begin to comprehend how dangerous these women are, how at risk his staff was at that prison, and by extension, the public is. Innuendoes focussed on portraits of dangerous women with violent records and untamed impulses. Officials claimed that these women had engaged in unceasing violent attacks on guards for four days prior to the strip search and justified the womens' subsequent eight months in segregation. Journalists and readers swallowed whole the story officials told, despite the images we saw on screen. On video we watched small women, chained and stripped naked, manhandled by club wielders. We were told that these women had, prior to this search, thrown urine at guards and lit fires, though no one had explained how these women managed to do this while locked in segregation cells emptied of all belongings. On screen we saw that none of the women resisted when the Emergency Response Team entered their cells. Some were asleep. And still, letters to the editor which followed the public airing commended guards for their bravery and courage in handling such a life-threatening job.

I do not know any of the women prisoners personally, but I do know that implications, innuendoes and lies told to my publisher about me and about my husband resulted in the publisher's swallowing whole the notion that what I might write would be not only untrue but might be dangerous. At first the publisher seemed concerned that I could love a "con" (whom he has never met or talked to). Later I came to be perceived as a possible Bonnie to my husband's Clyde. Unfortunately, we have no videotape of our own actions taken prior to allegations levelled against us. The Service's word sufficed. If a prison official said we had done something wrong, in the absence of proof (beyond our word) to the contrary, it must be true.

Prisoners and their families are nearly always portrayed as capable of any and all criminal acts, and not to be believed, unless of course it is other prisoners or prisoners' family members against whom we allege transgressions. For instance, the former Police Chief of Kingston went so far as to state in a letter to *The Whig-Standard* that one explanation for Kingston's crime rate was the influx of prisoners' families into this community (as if we move here to bring heavy arsenal and criminal intent rather than to maintain contact with our partners and to offer love, stability and hope). Although such slander, had it issued from any disempowered source, might well have resulted in criminal charges under Canada's new Hate Law, not one word of dissent met Chief Rice's letter. In 1993, the Assistant Deputy Commissioner of the Correctional Service in Ontario gave a speech in which she explained that when she was a warden, the prison's visiting room broke her heart; for there, she said, she saw the children who would be the next generation of prisoners. Members of her audience sighed dejectedly at this thought. No one pointed out that the statistics do not bear out her beliefs or that she had just labelled our children and all prisoners' parents. Those who do not sigh, instead lock their doors and shudder when they hear we are near. If our children do let others know where their fathers or mothers reside, they are on occasion forbidden to visit "the good people's" homes, and so, they often keep their parents' whereabouts a secret, protecting themselves from castigation. Nonetheless, the trauma they experience is never attributed to society's rejection and labelling. When sympathy is given a prisoner's spouse or parent, we are assumed to be unlovable wretches whose only hope of finding love sent us to prison or whose parental failures sent our children there. Those wives I have seen appear on daytime talk shows enliven this caricature. Why, after all, would Rolanda wish to interview a calm-voiced, intelligent and deeply loved prisoner's wife?

The despoiling of our images has been effective. With no credibility and almost no political support, we have few avenues left for addressing abuse committed against us. We can, of course, go to court, but few can afford the lawyers' fees necessary for mounting a case against a system with its plethora of "file material" (sometimes wholly invented) and the Service's stable of lawyers. Besides, on those few occasions when a prisoner or family member has taken a case to court (where secret IPSO sources must be revealed) and has been awarded compensation for crimes committed against him or her, vocal critics make political hay: "Look!" they cry, "its only the criminals who are protected! What about the victims!?" "Those prisoners are spoiled!" Crimes committed against us are considered, simply, our due.

Those crimes include the petty, such as the theft of prisoners' personal belongings (a daily occurrence) and disregard for policy and mandate. But they include heinous crimes as well. Consider, for example, that in October 1993, a black prisoner named Robert Gentles died in Kingston Penitentiary after six guards visited his cell. Whatever those six guards did inside that cell was not videotaped, though prisoners in the cellblock alleged wrongdoing by guards. Those prisoners were, of course, deemed incredible because they are prisoners, though in my husband's case, as in thousands of others, the word of one prisoner sufficed as proof enough to proffer devastating punishment. Prisoners are, all the time, punished on the "word" of other prisoners whose words are set in stone in IPSO files. Because informant prisoners' identities are cloaked by IPSO confidentiality, we seldom know what their privileges might be, but we know that any stories told about us will be believed, if necessary. On the other hand, prisoners' allegations against guards are deemed irrelevant as Robert Gentles' mother pursued justice. The Attorney General of Ontario refused to press charges in the death of her son. When a coroner who is not employed by either CSC or the Attorney General's office found the cause of death to be asphyxiation, a Justice of the Peace did find cause for pressing charges; it seemed the guards might have their day in court. The Attorney General dropped the charges. Mrs. Gentles presses on, though most of us suspect that she has no hope of finding justice.

PART THREE

As Carmelita Gentles has discovered, the public's argument against pursuing allegations — even of murder — against the Service, goes like this: "Prisoners have committed crimes. That's why they are in prison, and there they deserve whatever punishment the Service deems appropriate." And, further, because we are their loved ones, we too are suspect at all times, deserving of whatever we get. One small example might help illustrate.

In March of 1995, my husband was a prisoner at Collins Bay Institution, a medium security institution. While there, the Institution introduced a new machine known as an Ion Scanner. It appeared in the entryway one day, without warning or explanation. That day I came to visit my husband as I do regularly and frequently. Members of the community and employees of the Service who know me and my husband well are well aware of the fact that neither of us indulge in either alcohol or drug use. Despite our "clean" record (the exception being the "suspicions" lacing my husband's IPSO file), every prisoners' visitor is required by policy to submit for "inspection" all of our belongings. Items we are allowed to bring into visiting rooms include I.D.'s, change, diapers and, sometimes, depending on the Institution's whim, letters and photographs. That day in March I handed over an envelope containing both a manuscript my husband and I were working on and a letter his son had written to him. The routine had heretofore been this: I would take the envelope into the vestibule outside the visiting room. There I would place it in a mailbox where guards would extract it, check for "contraband," and finding none, deliver it at some later time to my husband in his cell.

The ion scanner added a new hoop. I was instructed to hand over the envelope to the guard manning the contraption which looked benignly enough like a microwave. The guard placed the envelope inside the machine's belly where it was electronically scanned. A beep sounded. The guard withdrew the envelope, and, pen poised, she asked for my name.

"For what?" I asked her.

"I have to record this."

"What are you recording?"

"I can't give you that information, ma'am. I'm required to record all information received."

"What information did you receive?"

"You beeped. That means you tested positive."

"Tested positive for what? How? And who gets this so-called information?"

"We haven't yet devised our policy on that."

I persisted. I asked what the guard was writing down for inclusion in my file, or in my husband's, or in both of ours, for I knew from past experience that sooner or later this "information," however false or misrepresented, might come back to haunt us. The guard persisted in her refusals. She informed me that if I wished I could take the matter up with the warden. No, she would not contact the warden. "There are people in line behind you," she said, and then she handed me the envelope to take inside. "But," she warned me, "once policy is established, a beep might result in your losing visiting privileges or in a strip search. A beep might necessitate police laying criminal charges on you if we do find contraband."

I am well aware of the fact that because I visit a prisoner in prison, everything I carry, say and do is at all times subject to search, scrutiny, recording and to interpretation as to meaning or implication by any and every CSC employee. My husband and I have been accused of all manner of "inappropriate" behaviour, though no charges have stemmed from any of the innumerable "suspicions" which lace our files. These suspicions include the belief by some that my husband and I sometimes argue; that he might, one day in the future, commit an illegal act; that we might write something damning about "the system"; that we might have behaved sexually prior to our marriage; that my husband's changes might be "superficial." A young officer recently asked us to explain an argument we had three years ago in what is called a "Private Family Visit." Nearly all of our personal information has been made available to any and all members of the Service who wish to avail themselves of my husband's file. Our telephone and visiting room conversations are subject to electronic eavesdropping, and again to interpretation. Our letters and manuscripts cannot, by law, be read by Correctional Service officers, but two years ago our "privilege" to write a novel together was withdrawn after a guard "chanced" to read one of our manuscripts. He thought our book was inappropriate. We were writing a thriller. Two weeks later, after the exchange of many phone calls and letters, our "privilege" was reinstated. We requested a letter stating precisely what we were permitted to write and how we were to exchange manuscripts. That letter never surfaced, despite four further requests.

And now this "beep" from this electronic nose. The machine, I learned, measures in nanograms (billioneths of a gram) for traces of cocaine, heroin, amphetamines and marijuana. I had and have still no idea how many nanograms my envelope recorded which prompted the machine's hideous squawk and the recording in a secret file (so secret that I was refused a copy or even knowledge of its contents). I do know that my envelope had, prior to that day, passed through both U.S. and Canadian postal services, through U.S. Customs, through my postmistress's hands and, too, because I had used the same envelope prior to that day, it had passed through the Institution, through many guards' hands, and possibly many prisoners' hands as well. I was, that day, permitted to give the envelope to my husband.

National Headquarters later informed me that the Ion Scanner is used, frequently, by U.S. Customs. I learned, later still, that researchers have found that more than 65% of U.S. currency tested by the ion scanner measures positive for illegal substances. I also heard that when a Service official visited Collins Bay Institution, his $50.00 bill beeped. I doubt very much that either his name or this information were recorded anywhere, and as I understand it from people witnessing this "test," observers laughed to think that a man of means and circumstance might ever indulge in any form of substance abuse — or even shake the hand of someone who had.

Over a period of several weeks, I sought, with the help of the John Howard Society, more information pertaining to my beep. The Institution informed us that at some point in the future those individuals bringing in items which tested positive in some measure (as yet undetermined) would or could be denied visits with their incarcerated loved ones. As the guard had told me, it was possible that we would lose visits altogether, or that we could be charged, and that we most certainly would be asked to submit to a body and cavity search if we tested positive.

Over the ensuing months I often stood in line awaiting "testing" while watching guards and other "Official Visitors" enter and leave the Institution, without scrutiny. In most cases these individuals carried some kind of bag. In one case a guard entered carrying a duffle bag, and as we waited impatiently in line, he waltzed inside. "Isn't it possible," I said to the guard doing the testing, "that some individuals other than prisoners' visitors might smuggle contraband inside? In a duffle bag, for instance?"

"He's staff," she laughed, "Why would staff bring in contraband?"

I politely suggested that financial gain was the goal of those who traffick in drugs and that even those individuals who are not prisoners sometimes seek such ill-begotten gains.

"You're paranoid," she said.

I watched one elderly father who spoke little English break down in tears after his I.D. beeped and he was sent away without seeing his son. I listened as family members pleaded with guards to let them know what this machine was saying about them. On occasion I asked about the way in which the testers sometimes neglected to change their gloves, or to clear the desk on which a tainted item had just lain. I was deemed a troublemaker, a label given to all those who challenge the system in any regard and to many who simply ask rational questions. Consider, for example, the case of Dr. Bob Bater, who, on viewing the P4W strip search asked what the Institution could have been thinking in ordering such a horrendous act. In return for his question, he was forced to resign from the Citizens Advisory Committee, a group designed to serve as "liaison" between the community and the prisons, but a group that is forbidden by policy to "advocate" for prisoners in any regard.

For the first several months, the women who were assigned by the warden to take responsibility for the Ion Scanner testing were polite and even, on occasion, outspoken in their compassion for us. However, the guard's union protested the warden's decision to place only certain individuals at this post, and thereafter, on occasion, a less-than-pleasant guard greeted us. Some guards are, frankly, less equipped than are others to meet and greet the public, which contrary to popular opinion and to portraits painted, we prisoners' visitors are.

"I don't do drugs!" became the cry heard most often in that vestibule after the sound of the beep, even though we all were well aware of the fact that few would listen to or believe anything we might say in our own defense. Sometimes a woman we all knew would test positive and cry out for help; to our despair and shame, we sometimes turned away from her. Association (that is with others alleged to have committed an offense) is punishable crime in prison, and if we spoke with her, we could, by suspicion, be considered "associates." We grew more and more depressed.

PART FOUR

Ultimately, in efforts to unearth my secret file as it pertained to the beep on the Collins Bay Institution Ion Scanner, CSC officials informed me and the John Howard Society that on the day that I beeped, they had not yet determined "levels," and that, therefore, the "information" collected about me and my envelope had been destroyed. I sought written confirmation of this destruction of records but never received such, though three John Howard Society representatives were told the same thing. We were also promised answers to our questions: how were these tests being conducted? on whom would the experiment's findings render judgment and what would the judgment be? what were the levels considered too high? and what punishment would follow? The Service never did provide this information. Warren Allmand, the single MP who did attempt to aid me in my quest for information, wrote to me to say that the Solicitor General had advised him that the machine's purpose was to help to stem the flood of drugs into the Institution.

I contact the Civil Liberties Association as it seemed clear that the civil liberties of prisoners' visitors were being violated. Despite numerous calls, faxes and letters sent to the Association, I received no response of any kind.

And meanwhile, other prisoners' visitors and I would often wait up to forty-five minutes to enter the building for our two hour and forty-five minute visits, now reduced to less than two. We were told that staff and/or other visitors were also tested, but only once in eight months, in five visits weekly, did I observe such an occurrence. A volunteer teacher's wallet beeped. "I don't do drugs," she cried. "How can this be happening." I've never ever done drugs!" Some wives lost their visits for a day. A few women lost their private family visits when their suitcases beeped. Some women were strip searched, and then — when nothing was found — they were granted their visits. Our denials of wrongdoing met with smug disinterest and the continuing recording of "information." I suppose in some cases charges were laid, and I suppose too that in some cases some individuals were stymied in real attempts to smuggle in contraband.

Nine months later, I learned one end to which my beep was to be employed. My husband had by then been transferred to minimum security institution. One day his new Case Management Officer — a thorough and apparently fair man whose primary interest seems to be keeping me from writing him letters ("it makes so much more work" he told me) — informed my husband that in reading through his file he had come upon an Incident Report written in early March. (Any and all staff can provide for any and every prisoner's file Incident Reports which are not necessarily shared with the prisoner). My husband's Incident Report alleged that in March 1995 an (unnamed) visitor tested positive for traces of cocaine and when informed of this fact by the officer challenged the officer's findings. My husband's new Case Management Officer said he thought the report must be referring to Amy. He smiled knowingly, for by that time he knew that I was someone who would likely challenge, and he half-believed me when I told him the facts, though it was obvious a shade of suspicion remained in his mind. "This is what we mean," I said to him, "when we talk to you about the innuendoes and suspicions — meaningless misrepresentations that are used against us to increase punishment."

"Oh, c'mon," he said, "you're overreacting." And then he stipulated that my husband's Correctional Plan include regular urinalysis tests (costly affairs). And besides the newest implication now embedded in my husband's file, we know that if necessary, some day in the future, an overzealous official might infer from this little "beep" that my husband had a visitor who was bringing him drugs as late as March 1995, an "inference" that would be useful if and when the Service chooses to produce another "credible inmate source" with a story about my husband and drugs.

My husband's new Case Management Officer calmly told us to "put the past behind us." Their past, not my husband's, that is. If I have learned anything over the past four years, it is this: challenging the system is a most heinous and punishable offense. It is a fact made clear at the Arbour Commission hearings to anyone who listens with an eye and an ear for the truth. At that hearing, the Deputy Commissioner grew red, then white, at the lawyer's questions as to whether he believed his "investigative" staff might have prepared an investigative report about the strip search (a report which neglected even to mention that male guards had stripped women prisoners) in an effort to please their bosses. The Deputy Commissioner waxed indignant. He talked about how easily the Service would be "found out" were anyone to willfully lie. When Jackson pushed, asking how they might be found out, he said that, for instance, all prisoners have, at all times, access to the public.

This statement was so painful and demonstrably false to me that I ran at once to one of the only two reporters covering those final days of the Enquiry. After all, one aspect of the Enquiry has to do with the established fact that the P4W women were denied access even to their lawyers for ·seven days after they were locked in segregation cells, and to the fact that in order to release the tape to the public, one of the women had to take the matter to court. The statement was personally painful to me because it had been this same man — the Deputy Commissioner — whose letter to the publisher of *The Whig Standard* called for my censorship and resulted in my losing my job.

"There," I said to the reporter who had once been a colleague of mine at *The Whig*, "That's the gist of it all. If all prisoners at all times have access to the public, why was I censored?"

The reporter looked suspiciously at me. "I never understood what happened back then."

"What happened was this. I spoke to the man who is now my husband. One official told me I was not permitted to speak to him, but I continued to talk to him. And then the Deputy Commissioner wrote to the publisher and informed him that I had behaved inappropriately and was, therefore, denied access to any of the prisons."

"Why did you speak to him after they told you not to?" the reporter asked.

I felt bereft. "Look," I said, "you're covering this Enquiry. If I tell you that you can interview anyone you wish here today, but you cannot speak to the Deputy Commissioner, what will you do?"

"I won't speak to the Deputy Commissioner," he said flatly.

"You won't ask why you can't speak to him?"

"Well, yeah," he wavered. "I'd ask."

"And if I told you, you couldn't speak to him because he's dangerous?"

He shrugged, and I — too wracked by emotion to walk this man down the logical path — left the room. It felt hopeless, for I had already listened to the testimony of the woman who had led the "internal investigation" into the "P4W incident." Listening to her, I experienced a terrifying deja vu. This "investigator" (promoted days after the finalization of her report) was the same woman who three years earlier had been the Deputy Warden at Joyceville Institution, the woman who approved my husband's transfer and supplied this same Deputy Commissioner with whatever lies she found necessary during the course of the same kind of specious in-house investigation into my husband's emergency involuntary transfer.

Later I learned that even if I had been able to encourage *The Whig* reporter to understand that statements are not facts, particularly when those statements issue from individuals who have discredited themselves in later testimony, it would not have mattered. On that last day of the Enquiry testimony — before final arguments and recommendations — *The Whig* ended its "prison beat." From mid-December on, coverage of prisons in Kingston at least will be done on an ad hoc basis only.

During cross examination of Correctional Service officers, much evidence of illegal acts and cover up of those illegal acts was made available to those few members of the public who attended, and to the only two reporters who covered the event to its near conclusion. *The Whig* reporter reported as fact that the women prisoners had staged a "riot" prior to the strip search, despite the fact that proof of this depends upon the veracity of the officials' word, and many of these same officials have been shown to have lied about other salient facts. The reporters fell victim to the images and stories about all prisoners that have been branded on the public's mind.

Each time I realize that so many otherwise intelligent, educated and reasonable human beings are so easily convinced that all men and women in prison, and nearly all of their families and friends, are incredible, criminal to the core, never to be believed, I grow more frightened and sad. It is certainly true that there are many members of the Service who lawfully and in some cases humanely attempt to protect all members of society, including prisoners and their friends and families. It is certainly true that there are prisoners and family members of prisoners who do engage in illegal activities, just as it is true that some individuals in the community at large do so, even if undetected and unpunished. It is also true that thousands of prisoners and their family members, and the public as well face horrors in a thousand different ways because a few members of the Service choose to abuse their unchecked power.

Prisoners and their families seldom speak out or challenge openly. When we do, we are sometimes severely punished. We are frightened of a press and a public which has labelled us so thoroughly, and we know that the prison officials hold the keys to our very lives. Our fear has allowed us to permit the deceptions and misperceptions about us to go on. We can only hope that Madame Justice Arbour has begun to see that internal investigations and the dependence for such on suspicions, lies, innuendo, rumour and implication, will not only harm prisoners and their families, but will harm us all.

ADDENDA

On March 31, 1996, Madame Justice Arbour issued her 300-page findings. She found the Correctional Service to be systemically unlawful and adjudged the culture of the system to have no regard for the law or for human rights. The Commissioner resigned. A clone has been assigned to take his place.

S ince the early 1970s, thousands of women have trekked to jails for
visits, week in, week out, year in, year out. With their partners serving
lengthy sentences, they have had to struggle on their own, often in
dire circumstances. Here is one woman's story, but it is typical of many.

Marie (not her real name) was still a teenager when she was married in
1973. Within a few years, her husband was arrested and she was left to raise
a young daughter by herself for the next six years. Her husband's release
heralded but a brief period of married life together; two years later, he was
arrested again and sentenced to an even longer term of imprisonment. Marie
was then pregnant with her second child. By the time of his eventual release,
they will be twenty years married; fourteen of these, Marie will have spent
on her own.

With courage and honesty, Marie speaks of her life — the loneliness and
doubts, the hardship and struggle to keep her family together. She talks
candidly of the strains in the relationship with her husband, and of the
unrealistic expectations imposed by people in the republican and the wider
community. Marie's experience reflects the reality for many partners of
prisoners.

*How did your life change after your husband's arrest, both the first and
second time?*

The first time he went into prison in 1977, I thought my whole world had
fallen in; it was like a death. I was in mourning for a long time. I had to listen
to his family going on about 'our poor Sean' but what about me? I had my
daughter Orla to bring up, no money, and I was running up every week to
see him. At times I used to say, 'I wish I was dead, I can't handle it,' but I
always put on a front, it was really hard. Then I had to be both a mother and
father to my daughter and try to explain to her why her father was in jail. I
just never thought he'd end up in prison, I'd just blocked it out of my mind.

If my daughter was sick, I had to sit up with her and make all the
decisions too. I felt very lonely many a night and I was on my own, and to
me, both our families didn't understand one bit how I felt; I was doing time
just as much as my husband but they would say to me, 'You have your
freedom.' Oh I used to hate him and them at times! Then there were nights

when you felt like having sex. You had to put that to the back of your mind, but I know I must have been hard to stick as I felt I was missing out on a lot of things my personality would change. Then I got a wee job and it made life a bit easier but I still had to put up parcels, clothe him, and put money in for his tuckshop.

The second time, he was arrested in 1985. It was hard, but not as hard to accept, as always in the back of my mind I knew he could land in jail again. I knew I had to be strong as I was pregnant again and on my own. The two years he was out he was my husband, lover, and best friend all rolled into one, and it was hard to take in that he was away. Still, I had days when I didn't care about him. I would say to myself, 'That's it, I'm not going to see him any more, I don't care what the families say.' The first time around you would stay by your husband and even your mother would say things like, 'you have to stick by him,' now I wouldn't listen and if I wanted to leave him I would and nobody would stop me. They still don't know what it's like. 'Good old Marie, she stuck by her husband' but it was a fighting battle I know I've overcome as the years have gone by.

It is hard to explain how I felt when I went into hospital to have Liam, our second child. It was great when it was over. Me and the baby was perfect, but then I used to see the other women's husbands or boyfriends in visiting and I'd have mixed feelings — I'd love and hate my husband at the same time. I didn't stay long in hospital, I asked to get out early. When I walked into my house, there was nobody there, only Orla; my sister was with me and I just felt like screaming out of me, 'Will someone help me!' Oh they all helped, but still didn't understand the lonely feelings I had and I felt as if no one cared. I know it was my fault, I never would say anything; maybe if I had, they might have understood a bit more.

I always had to get someone to look after the baby when I was going up on visits. Thank God this time around I was near his mother and she watched the child all the time. I can't thank her enough. It got to the stage for a while that I didn't want to go up to the prison, but I never said. I had to get up very early those mornings, about 6:30, get Liam ready and in a good mood, then take him down to his granny's. But then I'd an older child too, I had to think of her. Although she was a great help too, she was like a wee mother to the baby, I don't know how I would've managed without her.

It took me a long time to get used to him out of the house. Every day around teatime, he would have come in for his dinner, and if I heard the door open around that time I would say to myself, 'That's Sean,' and if I was making the dinner, I would forget and put a plate out for him. Sometimes out in the kitchen, I would look at the clock, if it was the time he used to come home I used to have tears in my eyes knowing he wasn't coming. It hurt very bad.

How did jail affect your relationship? Did/does it cause problems?

It does cause problems and you have to work at the relationship. When I was younger, going up to see him the first time he was in, I took it for granted — we were married and I didn't need to work at the relationship. Then later on, when I got the wee job in the bar, I noticed things were changing between us, he would ask more questions like, 'Does anyone tap on you? Do you miss sex a lot?' At the time I just said, 'No' to keep him happy, not that anyone did tap me up anyway but I did miss sex now and again. If any fella in the bar had said to me, 'You're looking well tonight, Marie,' I wouldn't have told my husband as I knew he would've taken it the wrong way; but, it made me feel good all the same, it made me feel I was a woman. At the time, I felt I was put under pressure and he didn't trust me enough. Anyway, even if I had wanted to, how could I get up to much? All his friends either drank or worked in the bar (a republican bar) so if I'd put a foot wrong he'd have been told right away. It used to get on my nerves that, their eyes were always on you. Sometimes on the visits, we'd be talking and he'd tell me he'd never be in jail again, that he loved me. Most times I believed him; other times I'd say to myself that he's just saying all that to keep me coming up to see him. In those days, we couldn't talk to each other very openly; we were still close and I knew he was worth waiting for but, yes, sometimes he did take me for granted. I always held back too in my letters if I was down, I never told him. I remember one time someone on the bus going to the jail talking about some other girl. She was saying the girl's husband had told her own husband, 'My wife's always moaning about something and is always down.' Guess what the person says? 'Do you not think her poor husband, locked up and all, has enough on his plate? She shouldn't be telling him things like that.' That stuck in my head, that's the way it was with some people.

The second time, I knew what to look out for and I wasn't going to be taken in by him. Now don't get me wrong: he didn't hold me down and I didn't run up to jail because I felt sorry for him. I wanted our marriage to last and I love him. But I noticed myself he'd changed and was thinking of me more and he trusted me more too, I think. As the years rolled by, we started to talk more and more openly with one another and the relationship between us was blooming. I felt great. Now a few times we'd talk about sex. Yes, I do miss sex, but he knows I'm not going to run out and try and pick someone up — no way! There's times months would go by without me even thinking about sex, then maybe something on the TV would make you think about it and I would say to myself, 'Is Sean worth all this? I have to go without a lot of things.' It is a fighting battle at times but thank God I've got to a stage where it doesn't bother me any more. Oh I think about sex still now and again, but I don't question myself any more. I can wait till he comes home.

With the kids you have to work and try and build a good relationship with them and their father. I would talk to them all the time, when they were young, about their father and still do with Liam, the youngest one. I'd buy wee presents and say, 'They're from your daddy.' I remember saying to Liam, 'That's your daddy, say hello when you see him and give him a big kiss.' Sometimes, there were problems when they were up on visits, maybe not taking him on enough and I'd be saying things like, 'That's the way kids go on.' But sometimes, I knew he'd be hurt if they didn't want to sit on his knee or give him a kiss, children don't understand those things. Nowadays, they're bigger and it's far easier, they all get on great. To me, we had to work on everything through the years to get the way we are now in our relationship. I hope I don't upset Sean in some of the things I say here, but I know we are very close now and it feels wonderful.

What do prisoners or people in your community expect of a prisoner's wife? Does this extend to her behaviour?

Well, I'm not really sure how to answer that but I'll start with the prisoners. I think that a prisoner takes his wife or his family for granted at times. They listen to what he says but he mightn't listen too much to what they are saying to him at times. Say there's a march coming up, you would have to go 'cause that's what he wants you to do. It's expected of you. Now I'm not saying I go just because of that, I go because I want to go as well. A prisoner's wife is supposed to go up every week to see her husband and stand by him; we're supposed to hold the family together and have no social life, we're supposed to be strong.

Now the second bit of that question is nearly the same as the first. It's like if you go out to a bar you are allowed to drink but not to get drunk, or if you go up to dance everyone is looking at you. I remember when I worked in the bar, I would only dance with fellas who were friends of my husband so people wouldn't talk. If you did go out with a few friends and were enjoying yourself, people would look at you. You're supposed to sit there nice and quiet and not make any noise. Every time you'd move you'd see the eyes following you. Do people think that a prisoner's wife is only out for one thing, sex, just because her husband is in jail! We have rights too. We are just like other wives who go out for the night to enjoy themselves; but, because you're married to an IRA man, his friends and everyone else expect too much. As I said before, you stand by your husband, go up and visit him, and yet you're not supposed to show any feelings that it's getting to you. At times, I feel mad, they wouldn't even ask how you are keeping, it's always, 'How is he?' At times, I would say, 'Sure, he's a well-kept man.'

I know both families look at me at times and say I'm a great mother and all that, but I'm supposed to be like that. I wondered at times if I were ever to say that I'm not going up to see him any more, what they'd say then. I think it would hurt them very bad. But as I said before, I've changed too; I don't let anyone stop me from doing what I want to do. After all, it's my life not theirs. Before, if anything happened with the children or if one of our parents were sick, it was all, 'Don't tell Sean, it'll upset him.' Big deal! It upsets me as well! They would say that he's no one to turn to, but they forget: who have I to turn to? Sure, hardly anyone visits me, so I've to bottle up my feelings.

Do you think that you're treated/viewed as a prisoner's wife or as a person in your own right? Does this change in different circumstances?

I think I get treated mostly in my own right; but, then I don't be out and about very much to meet different people. Right enough, I noticed when I started training again with my friend Anne last year and we went down to the leisure centre and we met these other girls who knew Anne. Well, they must have heard me saying to Anne that I was up seeing Sean (they never asked me or I'd have been proud to tell them) so they found out that Sean was inside, and when they talked to me there was pity in their voices. So it does change in different circumstances. If you're in company and you're talking away, you'd see their faces change when I mention Sean's in jail. To tell you the truth it doesn't bother me.

What I notice too is if there's any bother in the families or if somebody wanted to find out something, they would come and ask me could I help. They'd think, because Sean's inside, that I could do something. Then you get the people who look upon you as if you're a god. 'Look at her, isn't she great, she's a prisoner's wife.' I know too that some people, even those I know, would look at my kids to see if I dress them nice. They think, just because Sean's not here, I should be down and out, that's why I make it my business to keep the kids and the house nice. I know myself there are other prisoners' wives who just can't manage it all but they would do their best.

To me, I'm the same person I was before Sean went inside again but some people look at you and make excuses just 'cause he's in jail. What I mean is, say I don't wash my hair and run up the town for something, well someone would see you and say, 'Sure, her man's inside.' A girl I know said, 'You've lost a lot of weight,' but I was always thin. Or if I get my hair cut they'd say, 'You're looking great.' All I did is get my hair cut. So what I'm trying to say is people make excuses 'cause your husband is in jail. It's the way they must expect you to be, sorta down and out.

Earlier you said you felt that you'd missed out on a lot of things, that it changed your personality. In what ways and why do you think it changed you?

Well, it boils down to jealousy. Even with our Orla and her fella I'd see them really happy together, sitting on the sofa holding hands and all lovey dovey, and I'd be a bit cranky and get on to her now and again. It's just that I feel that we've missed out on a lot: us growing up together, being able to hold hands, or make love whenever we'd want to. Our life seems to be put on hold all the time. Times I was mad at him on the visits, we'd be kissing and we still couldn't be at ease. That's a few years back. Now it's better because I can handle it better and I can understand my own feelings more too.

When I did work in the bar, I'd see a lot of couples having a good time and I'd wish I could too. But, I knew I couldn't as after all, I was married to Sean and wanted our marriage to work. Don't get me wrong: it wasn't always easy and maybe for a few seconds I'd say to myself, 'To hell with him, I'm going out to enjoy myself' and I'd hate him at the time. It was always a fighting battle between me and my conscience. I'd see a fella looking at me and maybe I'd even flirt a bit but in my mind, that was all. It just made me feel good. Even now there's a bar we go to and I always try to look my best, even a bit sexy as there's no harm in that. But, I think I must have a sign on the back of my head that says, 'Look and Don't Touch' as no one (and I mean no one) would try or ever has tried to tap me up.

What I do miss very much is Sean sitting beside me, just his arms around me, holding me tight, making me feel I'm wanted — that's what hurts most. Thank God I don't think I'm as bad now, you get used to not having sex. But one thing I have noticed about myself is that I've got hard on the outside, you build a wall around yourself so you can't get hurt. I dare say, I've given people the wrong impression of myself in the past. I think that's when my personality changed. Sometimes you hate to see others just so happy but I've come a long way now, as people would say, 'She's a big girl now.' That's true. I'm a big girl now and I can understand myself better.

Your life has been a battle. Why did you keep going and not give up?

The way I look at it is the day I married Sean, I had a small battle on my hands. What I mean is Sean was on the run, I was having a baby, and we'd no money, no nothing. It wasn't a good start, but I was happy. I think both our parents had their doubts if the marriage would last. Then Orla came along and there was me trying to be a mother, a wife, and a housekeeper as well but it didn't bother me. It was something you had to do. Looking back now it was a battle to survive. Then, as I said before. Sean being inside was a battle on its own — keeping a family going and together, going up on visits, and keeping a good relationship between us. Then there was the battle because you were cut off from sex. You'd be fighting against your own conscience asking, 'Is he worth it?' And there was showing both parents I can do this, keep my family together and try and manage on the money I had. I think if I had a wee bit more money, life would be a bit better.

As for keeping going, I kept going because I had to and I wanted to. I wanted to keep my family together but the big thing was did I love Sean enough to go through all these years waiting on him. The answer is yes, I did love him, and as the years were passing, that love was growing. Then Sean was never a bad person. He was always good to me and Orla and he was a good husband, father, and lover. What I mean is he cared for me and took my feelings in as well. I know we've had our ups and down but who hasn't had? So if I was having any doubts, they would last for a few seconds only as all the good points would come back into my head.

When we were just married, I noticed Sean was out looking for a job or anything to make things easier and everything he did was for me and Orla. In my eyes he seemed so strong. I kept going because I didn't want to throw everything we had out the window. Let me tell you, I thought of giving up a few times. I was just that mad at him leaving me a second time; then too I was scared myself. I didn't know if I could wait it out or not. It's like an illness. At the start, you're a bit ill, then in the middle it gets worse, and now I feel stronger and it's getting better. Does that make any sense?

If the roles were reversed, you in jail and your husband outside, would the marriage have lasted?

No I don't think so. Men want sex more, it's more, it's more important to them, and I think Sean would be the same after a while. Ach, I think he'd try his best but it wouldn't last and he'd give in. Then too, people would say, 'Sure, it's only natural as his wife's in jail,' but if it was me or any prisoner's wife, they'd be going out and running you down as no good. That's the way people are. They make excuses for a man flying his kite, but if a woman does it, she's a tramp and no good. It's not right but I don't think it'll ever really change. But it's just not right anyway.

Finally, what are your hopes for the future?

Well, just to be happy. What I mean is I would be daydreaming, having a picture of us sitting in the living room just watching TV but we're all there. Sean out working, coming in home, although I know rightly he might not get a job, but just knowing we are happy, and to be loved. What I miss most too is we mightn't have any more children. Christmas is great having the children around. I know we've both missed out. Sean not being to see the kids growing up or opening their presents on Christmas morning or their birthdays. But that is all behind us and I believe him this time that me and the kids come first. To tell you the truth, I can't wait. I don't really look into the future too much. The way I feel now is I'm just waiting for Sean to come home, that's my future.

PART IV

IN THE HANDS OF THE STATE

The American Dream: Free Enterprise
Seth M. Ferranti

The prison industry is booming. New institutions are being built like crazy, incarceration costs are increasing, and prison guard unions are gaining political clout. The overwhelming attitude is 'lock them up and throw away the key'. If this trend continues, one day you might either work in a prison or reside in one. Currently more than 1.8 million people are locked up in the United States, and I am one of them.

*****

"Hey, is your mom here?"

"No way, dude. She won't be home 'til 4 p.m."

"OK. Wait here," I say as I run out to my beat-up Subaru and grab my duffel bag. Paranoia creeps into my mind as I sling the bag over my shoulder and enter the split-level home my friend's family resides in. The house is nestled comfortably in the heart of suburbia. What a perfect cover, I think. Reconvening in my partner's room, I unzip the duffel bag and remove the contents.

"Damn, dude. How much you got?" he asks.

"Twenty pounds, man. Now get the triple-beam and the bong. We have to break this up before your mom gets home." We weigh the marijuana out in ounces, then place the measures in ziplock sandwich bags from the kitchen for easy transfer to sell to our friends, and their friends.

"Hey, call up Chris and John. Tell them to come over." As my partner-in-crime dials the phone, I fill up the water bong and hit it hard, anticipating the money coming my way. A few minutes later the doorbell rings and Chris shuffles up the stairs.

"What's up, man?" he inquires with a smile. As smoke slowly slips from my mouth, I say, "Free enterprise, dude."

*****

At 6:27 in the morning of October 2, 1993, the cops bust into my hotel room, Berretta nine millimetre pointed at my face. I was scared — past scared. I was in shock. I was handcuffed and taken to Jail. I WAS GOING TO JAIL.

I could not believe it. I was in a county jail. I was from the suburbs. What was I doing in jail with a plastic mattress, no pillow, no sheets, no nothing? I was in an orange jumpsuit with K-Mart special slip-on shoes. I lay on the plastic mattress and stared at the stainless steel toilet and sink. The walls of my cell closed in.

I remember crying in disbelief, in frustration. How could they put me here? I am not a criminal. I just sold marijuana. I am a businessman. Free enterprise, right! I WAS IN JAIL.

To the guards I was not even a person, was not even human. I was just another number. They did not care that I did not like the food. They did not care that I did not have any sheets or toilet paper, or that I only had one pair of underwear and no socks, or that I wanted to take a shower. They did not want to hear it. But this was only the beginning.

*****

"You don't think that cop saw the joint."

"I don't know? Just keep driving," I tell my girlfriend as I look back towards the police cruiser we passed on the entrance ramp.

"Just drive real safe-like real legal-like," I say. She puts the joint in the ashtray and moves to the slow lane, keeping the car moving at a steady, 65.

"What's the speed limit here? 55 or what? I'm doing 65."

"I don't know. He's right behind us. Just be cool. We're OK." The cop flashes his lights and momentarily we are gripped with panic but the cruiser switches to the fast lane and rockets past us.

"Damn," my girlfriend says as she grabs the joint out of the ashtray and lights it.

"Give me that," I say, snatching it and taking a long, hard toke. I look at the bag in the back seat which has 25 pounds of pot in it and say to myself, "That was close, too close."

*****

I was brought before the judge. My chubby lawyer asked me if I felt lucky. What does luck have to do with it, I thought? The prosecutor went on and on about how I was a machine-gun toting, skinhead, LSD-marijuana freak, who corrupted society and deserved to go to prison for life.

My lawyer told the judge how I was a drug-addicted, mixed up kid who fell in with the wrong crowd, but really was a good person at heart who wanted to change for the better. Neither the prosecutor nor my lawyer was right, but at this point I do not think it really mattered.

The judge listened to all this while trying not to fall asleep. Finally he says, "304 months." Three hundred and four months, I think, that is not bad. Wait. How long is 304 months? It clicked, 25 years, for selling pot and LSD? I could not believe it. I WAS GOING TO PRISON.

They handcuffed me and put me in leg irons. They pointed Mossberg 12 gauge riot guns at my face and put me on a bus with other similarly shackled prisoners. I noticed there were not many white people and no one struck me as a suburbanite.

The bus went to an airport that was surrounded by a fence with razor wire; nothing as simple as barbed wire here. They put me on a DC-8 plane waving M-16 rifles in my face to make sure I did not get out of line (in my leg irons and handcuffs). The plane took off. I was at 40,000 feet in a DC-8 with handcuffs and leg irons — welcome to Con-Air. "What happens if the plane crashes?" I thought. "What happens if I have to go to the bathroom?" No emergency exits were marked. There were no oxygen masks, flotation devices or barf bags, and the guard-flight attendants were not serving drinks.

If this was not enough, I got special treatment: the Black Box. This apparatus fits between your wrists holding the handcuffs in place so no movement is possible. A chain is wrapped around your waist and secured to the black box and your handcuffs. It was very uncomfortable. Try to eat in this set-up. I did, but not very successfully. We were graced with the Con-Air meal, a cheese sandwich, which the guard-flight attendant threw at us.

We finally set down and they loaded on prisoners from the prison before they took us new recruits off. I had only been in county jail up to this point and I was not impressed with the occupants, but these guys from the prison were another story. Huge, mean-looking blacks, muscle-bound, tattoo-imprinted Latinos, and white guys that looked like Thor. The lot getting on the plane were what I envisioned prisoners looking like — and me, a 22-year-old-kid from the suburbs was being taken to live with these Charles Manson wanna-be's.

*****

"Come here."

"Where?"

"Back here to my room."

"Why?" she asks. "Are you trying to get me alone?"

"Yes," I responded as I lead her into my room and lock the door.

"Why'd you lock the door? I'm not having sex with you, yet. I mean, I hardly know you." I laugh nervously and tilt my head at her, smiling.

"What's the most money you have ever seen?"

"What does that matter? I mean, I don't even know," she replies as she looks at me quizzically. I open my closet and get out a shoebox and throw it at her.

"Open it up. Go ahead."

She glances at me furtively and opens the shoebox. Astonished, she looks up and asks, "How much is it?"

"Sixteen grand last time I counted. Let's count it again."

We count out the money, placing the 20s, 50s, and 100s in their appropriate piles in bunches of $1,000. She handles the money like a banker.

"Where'd you get this?" she asks. I tell her it does not matter as I push the money aside and kiss her.

*****

Federal Correctional Institution. My new home for the next 20 years. I had a lot to learn. I had mucho to adjust to. Talk about culture shock. I was a spoiled rich kid. This was hell. I WAS IN HELL.

Imagine living in your bathroom except that there is no tub or shower. There is a bunkbed instead. A metal bunkbed with a dinky mattress and, if you are lucky, a pillow. All your belongings fit in a 3 inch by 2 inch foot locker. You can go to the store once a week to buy what you need. Only once a week. The store does not offer much. Junk food, gray sweatsuits, toothpaste. No pizza, no Slurpees, no Big Macs, no Nintendo, no CDs, no nothing.

You can buy a radio, but you are in the middle of nowhere, so no radio stations. The guards treat you like cattle, not human beings. They justify taking the cookie from you that you brought from the chow hall by saying they are just doing their job. You cannot accomplish anything productive because policy dictates this and policy dictates that. If you have a problem you better deal with it yourself because the prison officials will say they are here to help you, but when you ask for help, they will direct you to so and so, who will direct you to so and so, whose policy is not to help.

When I lay in my cell at night listening to my cellie snore, I wonder to myself, "What was I thinking?! What have I done to myself?"

*****

"Look dude, this has all been great. I mean free drugs, money, and the like, but it can't last forever. Anyhow, I gotta go back to school in the Fall. So, like, what are you gonna do?"

"I don't know, man," I say, "maybe move a couple more loads or something, you know?"

"Check it out dude, you should get a real job for awhile. Everybody knows about you. You're high profile, dude. You've been moving a lot of weed and acid. Chill out for a while man."

"No way, dude, this is like my life, man. I'm pursuing the American Dream. Free Enterprise, you know? I'm a businessman, dude."

"I know, dude, but look. You could get busted or something. You gotta stop, chill out for at least a little bit. Buy a new car or something. Take a vacation. If you keep going, you're gonna get caught."

"No chance, dude. A couple more times and I'm out. Only stupid people get busted anyhow; I'll never get caught."

*****

I was trying to pursue the American Dream. I thought I could set my own rules. Thomas Jefferson did. Jerry Garcia did. Why couldn't I? I was a businessman. Free enterprise, capitalism, you know? Buy a product, sell it, and count the money all the way to the bank.

But it is not like that. The politicians have enacted strict drug laws to save the country from itself. When I was growing up, I thought America was the land of opportunity, the land of the free. But it is not. You play by the rules or you do not play at all for long.

Runaway Prison or Mr. Smith Goes to Harrisburg
Victor Hassine

P rison overcrowding is the screeching raven of catastrophic change, a change so profound it transforms the very structure and operation of an entire prison system, not just individual prisons. This mutation in turn gives rise to the formation of a renegade bureaucracy with a singular goal of maintaining its own uncertain existence.

To better illustrate the nature and extent of the change prison overcrowding promises, consider the following analogy.

Imagine you're standing on the boarding platform of a train station waiting for your train. As you stand waiting, you take for granted that the train will come to take you to your destination. Experience has led you to rely on the train as an efficient means of mass transit.

Your train finally arrives. You board one of its cars and take your seat among a carload of other commuters. As the train travels you can feel it moving faster than usual. This does not alarm you, but you stop reading your newspaper, take a look at your watch and then peer out one of the train's fixed glass windows. You notice the countryside whizzing past you at an alarming rate. Suddenly you observe the train speed past your station stop.

Now you are alarmed, but a voice over the loudspeaker apologizes for the inconvenience, assures everyone everything is under control and promises the train will stop at the next station. You are now annoyed as you anticipate being late for work. The train continues to accelerate.

Soon, you watch as the train speeds past yet another station stop and you begin to realize that something is seriously wrong. You get out of your seat to find a conductor or anyone in authority and you get caught in a crush of passengers who have decided to do the same thing. You hear the voice over the loudspeaker, but because of all the confusion you can't make out what it is saying. In any event, you no longer trust the announcements. The train continues to accelerate.

The crowd, the uncertainty and the noise causes panic and it is at this point that the train has changed from a vehicle of mass transit to a machine that does nothing more than generate fear, panic and anger among the passengers who now must face an uncertain future.

As the panic and confusion persists, you and your fellow passengers eventually become accustomed to this life on the edge and desperation sets in. No one cares anymore about jobs, schedules or the future. Everyone is thinking about right now and how they are going to survive the madness. Every human intuition has surrendered to the primitive instincts of "survival of the fittest". The passengers are no longer passengers and the train is no longer a train.

Now imagine yourself the train engineer. You were the first to realize the train's acceleration problem. Because you are a trained expert you felt certain you could fix any mechanical problem you discovered. You radio the home office and inform them of the problem. You then pull out your repair manual and go about trying to fix the engine. As you attempt to make repairs, the train continues to accelerate and refuses to respond to any of your efforts. At this point you begin to worry.

As you work feverishly to return the train to normal operation, you begin to hear the passengers banging on the door that separates the engine room from the passenger cars. The frustration of your failed efforts, the loud high-pitched hum of the uncooperative engine and the panicked cries of the passengers combine to unnerve you. You angrily take a moment to bark over the loudspeaker, "Everything is under control, passengers please remain in your seats". But the banging and screams intensify as the train continues to accelerate. You need help but you know you're not going to get any.

As you relentlessly try to fix the engine, you realize the longer you are unable to stop the train's acceleration, the more problems you are forced to fix. Weaknesses in design and construction of the train has caused additional mechanical failures. You find yourself reacting to a multitude of new emergencies which gives you little or no opportunity to address the original acceleration problem. You are convinced that unless this acceleration is stopped, there will likely be some catastrophe in the form of a collision or derailment.

It is at this point that you are no longer a trained professional making sure train schedules are kept or that the train engine itself is operating properly. You have become a reactionary crisis-control manager who no longer cares about where the train is headed. Your sole function has become to avert a catastrophe. Meanwhile, the train continues its acceleration.

Now imagine yourself another commuter waiting for his train. You're standing on the loading platform and all of a sudden you watch and feel your train speed past you. You manage to spy some passengers banging on the window of the passing train. You notice some of the passengers are holding up signs which you can't make out because the train is moving too fast.

This causes you some concern until you hear an authoritative voice over a loudspeaker apologize for the inconvenience and announce everything is under control. You are instructed to wait for the next train which will arrive shortly to take you to your destination.

Though annoyed, you are a bit relieved that you will be able to reach your destination, albeit late. It never occurs to you that once you board the next train the same thing that happened to the sign-waving passengers you just saw could happen to you.

In July of 1981, as I entered the Pennsylvania State Correctional Institution at Graterford (SCIG) for the first time, I became like the man who boarded the runaway train.

When I first entered SCIG, I expected to find myself in a rigid, structured environment designed to deter and punish. I hoped to discover that prisoners were, in fact, being coddled in prison as the papers and TV reported so often. In any event, I believed everything was under control and that my prison home had a definite purpose and end. However, within the first few weeks I realized something was very wrong. Fights were breaking out everywhere, the sale of drugs and contraband was rampant and it seemed as if everyone was carrying a weapon.

After only three months I watched a man in the cell across from mine catch on fire in his cell. The solid steel door of his cell was locked but I could see him through the fixed glass window at the top of his cell door. His muffled screams for help and his banging on the steel door could be heard as smoke squeezed out of some narrow openings in his cell. It took some time for the guards to isolate and respond to his cries. As the smouldering man was finally carried out of his cell, I remember telling myself, "I had better never need any help in this prison".

About 30 days later, with the image of the burning man still on my mind, the prison was locked down while prisoners with pistols and shotguns had a shootout with State Police in a botched escape attempt turned hostage taking. As the drama played out over the next few days — I stayed in my cell watching heavily armed State Policemen rushing past, back and forth. "My God, how did these guys get guns?" I asked myself, and that is when the panic set it.

In the months and years following the hostage crisis at SCIG, things got more violent, more uncontrolled and a lot more crowded. I was in such a continuous state of panic that I stopped being scared and became desperate.

I lived every moment as if it were my last and I began to believe I would never survive. I watched as prisoners beat and stabbed other prisoners and guards alike. I also watched as guards beat prisoners. I watched as gangs of prisoners robbed and stole with impunity while staff smuggled in contraband for sale on the black market. Rapes were common as were sexual contacts between prisoners and staff members. Then there were no less than three riots in a 12-month period, all precipitated by electrical failures which caused blackouts on the housing blocks at times when all cells were unlocked.

Like the passenger on the runaway train, I had entered a system which had changed into a relentless generator of despair, corruption, and violence. I had become a "moment dweller" with no thought of a future.

In 1984, I filed a conditions of confinement suit in Federal District Court for the Eastern District of Pennsylvania, *HASSINE* v. *JEFFES*, 896, F.2d 169 (3rd Cr. 1988). It was my way of banging at the window and screaming for help. But like the all too common nightmare scene in a low budget "B" horror movie, no one around could near my loud cries for help.

Prisoners, experts, guards, the warden, and even the Commissioner of Corrections Glen Jeffes testified at the trial. The judge listened intently, but nevertheless in the end all he heard was the Department of Corrections' (DOC) claim that everything was under control and that they would spend $40,000,000 in capital improvements. Like the runaway train's engineer, the DOC felt it could fix the machine, all the while ignoring the hapless sounds of the passengers banging on the engine room's door. The judge accepted the DOC's promise to repair and ruled in their favor. In the summer of 1986, three months after the trial, I was transferred across the state to SCI Pittsburgh (SCIP).

SCI-Pittsburgh was one of the first Pennsylvania state prisons to begin double celling prisoners in 1983. My suit at SCIG delayed double celling in that institution until 1988, so when I arrived SCIP was in fact more crowded than SCIG. Also, Commissioner Jeffes had caused to be constructed a 500-cell Federal style housing unit right on the grounds of the existing SCIP main yard. The plan was to move all the prisoners into the new units and then tear down the old housing units to make room for a new yard. Unfortunately, the DOC never did tear down the old cell blocks, so 2,100 men lived in space designed for 1,000 and there was now no exercise yard.

Violence and despair were a way of life at SCIP, and corruption had become institutionalized. My first day at SCIP I witnessed a Lieutenant beat a prisoner over the head with a blackjack right in the middle of the cell block. Thirty days later there was a riot at SCIP. The auditorium was set on fire, two guards were seriously hurt and many prisoners were beaten and/or raped. I witnessed many atrocities which demonstrated to me that human beings can very easily revert to prehistoric savagery. I realized that my transfer to SCIP never took me off the runaway train, it just moved me to a different passenger car. After the riot, things only got worse at SCIP. In 1987, I filed another conditions of confinement suit, *TILLERY* v. *OWENS*, 907 F 2d 418 (3rd. Cir. 1990).

At the *Tillery* trial in 1989, there was testimony from more prisoners, experts, another warden and the new Commissioner of Corrections, David Owens. Conditions at SCIP were so extreme that the judge found living conditions at SCIP violated the constitutional ban against cruel and unusual punishment. Nevertheless, the DOC continued to claim that everything was under control. The judge appointed a master to oversee court mandated repairs, which totalled more than $70,000,000.

In January of 1989, the random violence of SCIP hit me. I was mysteriously assaulted and nearly killed by another prisoner. I was hospitalized for three months and then transferred to yet another institution — SCI-Camp Hill (SCICH). SCICH was the jewel in the DOC's crown. It was a fenced institution that loomed adjacent to the main offices of the DOC. In fact, one of the upper story conference rooms in the DOC had a large picture window which overlooked all of SCICH. If the DOC was in fact a train, then SCICH was the first class car that lay directly behind the engine.

It was during my first day at SCICH that I met Richard C. Smith who was then the Deputy Superintendent of Operations for SCICH. He was the youngest man in Pennsylvanian history to be appointed to the position of Deputy Superintendent. A ruddy, stocky man, he worked his way up through the ranks, starting as a Correctional Officer I at SCIP in 1977. His meteoric rise to power promised him the possibility of a commissionership sometime in the future.

I spoke, in depth, several times with Deputy Smith and he never hesitated to tell me he neither liked me nor wanted me in his prison. He told me I was just a manipulative inmate crying wolf for attention or sympathy.

He assured me he ran a tight ship and he did not want me to start any trouble. He rejected my claims that it was the conditions and not me that had cost the DOC so much money in repairs, and he certainly did not want to hear my claims that the prison system was out of control.

Mr. Smith transferred me to SCI-Rockview (SCIR) in August of 1989, unwittingly sparing me the consequences of one of the greatest catastrophes ever to hit the Pennsylvania DOC.

SCIR is a medium/minimum security prison which was considered at the time the Allenwood of the Pennsylvanian state prison system. So as I lay in my cell still recovering from my serious injury and adjusting to my most recent transfer, I began to think about all the prisons I'd been in and all the prison managers I'd met who, like Mr. Smith, had portrayed me as the problem. I knew that until Mr. Smith and men like Mr. Smith acknowledged that there was a serious problem with the functioning of their prisons they would never be motivated to find solutions capable of fixing the problems.

Like the engineer in my example, Mr. Smith was so caught up in the day-to-day crisis management of his overcrowded prison that he could not (or would not) see the underlying problem. His passengers (prisoners) no longer meant that much to him, because the runaway prison left him no time to consider them as anything other than a nuisance.

I began to think nobody in the DOC would ever acknowledge the truth about the runaway prison system, that is until Mr. Smith went to Harrisburg.

1989 proved a particularly disastrous year for the Pennsylvania DOC. In March of that year, a small riot broke out at SCIR, then in October a small riot broke out at SCI Huntingdon (Pennsylvania's most secure prison at the time). Then on October 25, a little more than a month after Mr. Smith transferred me, SCICH had the largest and most costly riot in Pennsylvania's history. SCICH housed about 3,000 men at the time and for four days the prisoners controlled the whole institution. Hundreds of angry and desperate prisoners burned down buildings and destroyed property. Many prisoners and guards were savagely beaten and raped. In the aftermath of the riot the prison was almost completely destroyed before the Pennsylvania State Police managed to regain control. The lead car of the runaway train had derailed and Mr. Smith was in charge.

Shortly after the riot, Mr. Smith was fired, bringing his promising career to an abrupt end. On February 21, 1990, the Pennsylvania Senate Judiciary Committee conducted an open hearing to investigate "Recent incidents at Pennsylvania State Correctional Institutions". Mr. Smith was asked to give sworn testimony at the hearing.

In a diatribe lasting some 162 pages, Mr. Smith attempted to explain why the riot was not his fault and why his firing was not fair. Instead, Mr. Smith, for the first time ever, gave an insider's view of what was really happening in the DOC as overcrowding caused the prison system to race out of control. Mr. Smith became the Joe Valachi of the Pennsylvania DOC as he graphically and methodically outlined incident after incident of corruption, violence, drug dealing and incompetence by his former DOC bosses, co-workers and subordinates. These shocking and sometimes horrifying accounts gave outsiders a real understanding of how overcrowding changes each and every aspect of a prison system. However, one should never forget that if Mr. Smith had not been fired, he would have continued to keep his secrets in accordance with some mafia-like vow of silence. He only decided to share his experience with the public after he felt he had been jilted.

It remains to be seen how the SCICH riots and Mr. Smith's testimony will impact on the future development of the Pennsylvania DOC. I am certain that if more people examine Mr. Smith's "Tell All", problems could then be identified and proper repairs made. Unfortunately, as it stands today, I am still a passenger on a runaway train. Whatever you do, don't listen to those reassuring voices on the loudspeaker, instead listen to Mr. Smith. He knows the real deal.

On Being a Nigger
Charles Huckelbury, Jr.

> In the folds of this European civilization I was born and shall die,
> imprisoned, conditioned, depressed, exalted, and inspired. Integrally
> a part of it and yet, much more significant, one of its rejected parts.
>   W.E.B. DuBois in *Dusk of Dawn*

Notwithstanding recent attempts to depict race as an artificial construct of governing bodies, I consider myself white. Fifty years ago, I was born into an upper middle-class family that traces its roots to northern European immigrants who entered this country not long after the Mayflower landed at Plymouth. I did not question in my formative years and do not question now the gifts endowed by nature and the abilities honed by nurture that have enabled those of European descent effectively to decide, for better or worse, the fate of the planet on which we live. I came of age in the sixties and enjoyed the privileges and perks (usually assumed as my right) that included an education at excellent universities and exposure to art and culture that extolled European civilization above all others. Before the ravages of five decades took their toll, my hair was light brown leaning to red. My eyes are blue, and my skin freckles in the sun, indicating that my particular phenotype is far more comfortable in colder climates where melanin is not required to shield the body from intense ultraviolet radiation. And yet, in society's eyes, I am a nigger.

Imagine if you will, the shock of this discovery, flying in the face of everything I had come to believe and defying the logical extension of what I saw as a European progression that had lasted relatively uninterrupted for over two millennia. During the turbulent sixties, I had managed to remain aloof, refusing to acknowledge the claims of racial and ethnic minorities of being victimized by society in general. I believed that any man or woman could do whatever his or her talents dictated. Meritocracy and the Jeffersonian ideal of an intellectual aristocracy appealed to me; ability and opportunity were the twin pillars on which my philosophy rested. If life was a metaphorical foot race, then everyone certainly deserved an equal place on the starting line, but never did I presume that everyone would or should finish in the same position.

Of course, my peers were all white, and although I recognized certain disparities in abilities, I never questioned the freedom for all of us to expand to our personal limits. I projected this same assumption onto people of colour, refusing to listen to their cries against a racist society that denied them even the most fundamental opportunities for self-improvement. I believed that they simply lacked substance or else preferred subsistence living as social parasites. I pointed to obvious success stories like Ralph Bunche and Thurgood Marshall — it would be Colin Powell and Clarence Thomas today — to demonstrate the rewards discipline, intellect, and motivation brought, never believing that a man or woman would permit anyone to dictate what happened to him or her and their children.

I do not remember the first time I either heard or used the word "nigger" and obviously do not recall the context of either incident. Both doubtless referred to blacks in general, since during the fifties, the more reactionary elements of society used the term inclusively instead of preferentially, some even going so far as to use the n-word as an ethnic umbrella, under which "every" person of colour was gathered. I had heard blacks refer to each other as niggers, and in my naiveté, I could not understand the hostility when a white person dared use the same epithet. Never could I grasp the magnitude of the insult. Indifferent to historical precedent and the stigma slavery had stamped on the soul of every African descendant brought forcibly to this country, I blithely passed on the periphery of the black population, content with my own existence and wholly unconcerned about 10 percent of the nation that remained disenfranchised.

In 1974 all that changed when I was sentenced to life in prison. I quickly discovered that skin colour does not confer nigger status; one's position in society does and is imposed by the prevailing power structure, that is, society itself.[1] As a student of history, albeit one with an incomplete education, I soon discovered the parallels between slavery and incarceration, and the environment in which I found myself clearly demonstrated that I had been relegated to the status of nigger. White, black, red, yellow, or brown, "every" convict was a nigger, with our rights circumscribed by both our confinement and the law of the land. Like *Dred Scott*, I was property, not of any individual, but of the state and its monolithic prison system, and were I to escape and make my way north via some latter-day underground railroad, I could be returned at the discretion of the owners, that is, the State of Florida. Whereas the United States Constitution counted male slaves as three-fifths of a person for demographic purposes, convicts did not rate that high; we were, and are non-persons, niggers in the most authentic sense of the word and consigned to the social oblivion historically enforced by every court in the country.

In 1896, for example, the United States Supreme Court ruled in *Plessy* v. *Ferguson* that separate facilities for races were legal and just. I discovered the same attitudes and applications in prison, at least with respect to separation. We were segregated not by race but by our refusal to obey the law, yet unlike the aftermath of the *Plessy* decision, no effort was exerted to make our position ostensibly equal to those outside. No one cared about such rudimentary things as food, clothing, or education, and society assumed that we could survive on less than they. Indeed, many expressed outrage that we had what few comforts we did and publicly stated that we should be flogged and fed fish heads and rice twice a day. More moderate suggestions, including ones concerning education, were met with pre-*Brown* v. *Board of Education* rhetoric, the polemics usually taking the form: "Why educate the bastards? They're no good anyway and too stupid to learn." I began to hear Old Massa's voice loud and clear.

Our loved ones suffered along with us, required to commute to and from the prison on the weekends in a generally futile effort to keep the family together. Given the long sentences most of us had, no tactic could have preserved such a union where the husband or father would be absent for twenty to thirty years — and often permanently. As it was in the days when the men, women, and even children were sold separately, convicts watched as their wives, sons, and daughters left them forever. After all, niggers did not need families; we were not "normal" and therefore could claim no societal obligation to maintain our nuclear families. We had no civil rights, and our human rights were constantly in question. Like the Spaniards in the New World, society needed a reminder that their niggers also possessed souls, but we had no Lás Casas to plead our case.

Whatever label one puts on it, incarceration "is" a form of slavery, or at the very least, indentured servitude, and manifests a blatant teleological philosophy. No concern is ever given to the propriety of the act itself; only the end result is important. And for convicts, that end result is the total, coercive humiliation of a human being, breaking him psychologically and constantly reminding him that he is less than his fellows, that he is in fact a nigger.

We are transformed into second-class citizens, if in fact citizens we still are. Guards are the functional equivalent of overseers, the crackers of the plantation, and have "carte blanche" to treat us in whatever manner they choose. They beat us and kill us with impunity. We are required to shine their shoes or boots, serve their food, or fetch and carry. We must defer to their every whim and often pay for rebellion with our lives. Lord Acton's observation on the corruptive ability of absolute power found its proof in the antebellum South, and its modern affirmation stalks the corridors of today's prisons. Niggers we are and niggers we will remain in society's eyes and in the eyes of those it appoints to keep us in our places.

And yet, and yet ... the pendulum does swing. Slaves were freed by the Thirteenth Amendment, protected by the Fourteenth, and enfranchised by the Fifteenth. Society at that time, at least part of it, recognized that even its niggers had never abrogated their rights, even when they were held in physical and psychological chains, deprived of their families, kept illiterate, and reduced to the status of chattel; they had had those rights, basic human rights that Jefferson recognized, ripped from them as soon as they were placed in chains. Efforts to redress those wrongs led eventually to the giant strides made by the Civil Rights Movement of the sixties, although resistance was concerted and often brutal. Blacks ceased being niggers, at least in more enlightened discussions, not because society's opinion had changed — it had not — but largely because they were now seen as political fodder whose bloc votes could be courted and won by the most patronizing office seekers. But at least publicly they were recognized as human beings worthy of consideration.

Compare these advances with those articulated by the United States Supreme Court under Chief Justice Earl Warren. Beginning in 1961, prisoners' rights became a "cause célèbre," attracting activists of every strip and resulting in several landmark opinions (*Miranda* and its progeny) that police and prosecutors continue to criticize. No longer could we be beaten until we confessed to whatever crime the police were having difficulty solving, and we could request and receive legal counsel as soon as custodial restraint was instituted. Moreover, conditions in many prisons were so deplorable and the lack of "due process" so egregious that the federal courts had no choice but to intervene to eliminate gross Eighth Amendment violations. Like the Black community before it, the convict community began to achieve titular recognition as a group of human beings worthy of fundamental rights. Indeed, the Court eventually decreed in *Furman* v. *Georgia* (1972) that States could no longer kill us arbitrarily and capriciously. We had come a long way, baby.

Now, however, we are suffering the effects of a uniform retrenchment at all levels. Gone is the acceptance that we are also human beings, unquestionably flawed but humans nonetheless. And like Blacks before us, we have become a political football, only this time the politicians make no effort to hid the animosity in their public faces; without the franchise, we do not count except as beasts of burden to bear the victors' spoils.

In every election, one issue leaps to the forefront and becomes the linchpin of the campaign. In the late sixties and early seventies, it was the war in Vietnam and civil unrest at home. In the mid-seventies, Nixon gave the Democrats the ammunition they needed to regain the White House, but Jimmy Carter fell victim to an orchestrated economic attack by OPEC that raised gasoline prices and produced the infamous — and erroneous — malaise he is accused of describing in those affected chats. In the eighties, along came Ronald Reagan and his confrontational tactics with the "evil empire." But accompanying these obvious issues was a more subtle effort to shift public opinion regarding crime and punishment, until in the last two decades of the twentieth century, when the country is at peace (except for intermittent excursions to validate the Monroe Doctrine, kidnap heads of state, or protect oil-rich proxies), when a strong economy and low unemployment guarantee prosperity for most, and when no other external or internal threat looms, crime and criminals became the hot button in successive campaigns for local, regional, and national races.

Yes, we are it; society's niggers are always good for a vote on one end of the political spectrum or the other. No one wants to be perceived as soft on crime, and with monsters like Ted Bundy, Jeffrey Dahmer, John Wayne Gacy, and others constantly making headlines, support for more repressive laws and confinement is easy to find, especially when public servants convince the body politic that niggers neither deserve nor require a millisecond's consideration. If, as Emerson observed, a foolish consistency is the hobgoblin of small minds, then the attitude cultivated and maintained by society toward its prisoners clearly demonstrates the limited imaginations of a people responsible for increasing the prison population to over one million men and women, executing mental defectives and minors, and raising paramilitary police tactics to an art form.

This is not to say that, like the Black community and their enslaved forebears, we are blameless. Most assuredly we are not, and I make no attempt either to argue with detainment for criminal behaviour for society's protection or to claim kinship with a people whose only offense was to be chained and transported by force to this country. Unlike expatriate Africans, we are active participants in our own confinement. But culpability is not the issue; society's insistence on creating a permanent underclass and the philosophical posture that denies our fundamental humanity are, and the members of that underclass — niggers — have no chance to rise above the station society has selected for us. Indeed, it is society's intent to keep us there, just as slaves were kept in their place by brute force and repressive legislation. Like the plantation owners in the antebellum South, the majority of Americans today do not discriminate, if you will pardon the irony. Slaves were seen as all of a piece; unworthy of inclusion on equal terms into the family of man. Today's convicts are likewise deprived of any preferential assessment: all of us are scum, all are irremediable, all are equally despicable.

One factor, however, escapes most analyses when treatment of, or attitudes toward convicts is discussed. Whereas for 350 years, slaves had no logical reason to expect manumission, our eventual freedom is guaranteed in over 90 percent of cases. Treating humans like niggers is always morally reprehensible, but from a utilitarian position, it hardly matters as long as that status remains invariant. If a society never intends to free those it holds in captivity, then treatment is irrelevant, and one's keepers can exercise their will without restraint.

The obvious concomitant to perpetual captivity is the ability of the captors to break their prisoners' spirit and convince them that they are in fact niggers deserving of their fate. This has historically proven difficult. Alabama's chain gangs and the new supermax prisons to the contrary, it is futile to attempt to break the human spirit by force alone. We are simply too resilient and in some cases, far too stubborn. Surprises, of course, do occur, as in Nat Turner's short-lived rebellion, John Brown's futile raid on the federal arsenal at Harper's Ferry, and the insurrection at Attica, to cite but a few of the more notorious examples.

But, and the but is monumentally significant; if one's keepers have no choice but to release their charges after a specified time, then it does not take a giant leap of logic to understand that their attitudes should reflect that awareness. Perhaps a society can impose nigger status on those it loathes, and in some instances, make that label stick. What happens, however, when that nigger gains his freedom and during the course of internalizing his status, comes to understand that a perpetual state of war exists between him and society who sees him as a nigger? What happens when he begins to act like the nigger society tells him he is?

A prisoner made the observation some years ago that ex-convicts have only three options upon release: we can reintegrate into society and become productive, contributing members; we can become public wards and strain a struggling system already on the brink of collapse; or we can resume the role of predators. The first option represents the most beneficial, both from society's and the ex-convicts' perspectives, and it makes the most sense. The second evolves from hopelessness and an anomic loss of self, derived from the indoctrination that convinces the susceptible mind that he is unworthy and therefore need not try to change his status. But the third is the creation of anger and a gutwrenching, mindbending need to pay somebody — anybody — back for the years of being treated like a, yes, like a nigger.

Last year, a journalist examined the maximum-security unit at Pelican Bay (California) and interviewed some of the men inside, one of whom was frighteningly candid. He said that things had been done to him inside that no slave, no animal should have to endure. This individual was ending his sentence; no parole, no supervision of any kind, and he made the point that he could go wherever he wanted, do whatever he decided, and he was mad enough (and bad enough) to get the job done. This is the unavoidable result when society creates niggers by permanently subjugating a race or class of people, keeping its collective foot on the necks of those it tries to hold down, and never letting them up either to breathe freely or even to catch a glimpse of blue sky instead of the dirt in front of their faces.

Niggers of any colour eventually get angry, and in my twenty-two consecutive years in prison, I have seen scores of them. Most are long-term prisoners who will have two or sometimes three decades of prison behind them when they are released, and they are mad. They are mad like you would not believe. Their families are gone; they are largely unemployable; and the vast majority are psychologically unstable. I stress here that these people are going to be released because they have done their time — you cannot stop them. They will be living in your neighbourhoods and shopping in the stores where you, your wives, your sisters, and your children shop. Think about it: mad niggers everywhere you go but without the identifying skin colour that would have previously warned you when you thought all niggers were black. The scenario scares me, it should terrify the average citizen.

But you answer, we have police to protect us from such predators. That is certainly true, but the very nature of crime and random violence precludes its prevention, and like it or not, it does not take a lot of creativity to avoid the police long enough to commit a crime. The role of the police is after all, apprehension. They catch us *after* we have committed whatever offense it is that we have chosen to perpetrate, which means that no one is safe from someone harbouring a grudge that has festered for twenty or thirty years. I repeat: no one is safe. Examine the conventional wisdom: niggers are crazy. We do not care who we hurt in the process of getting what we want. If that is the case, then why persist in legitimizing a system that creates niggers in an assembly-line process, turning them out year after year like so many new models of automobiles with built-in engineering defects: accelerators jammed at full throttle with no steering?

Some primitive societies believe that knowing a person's name confers an advantage on the one knowing, and thus names are kept secret. So it is with convicts. I know my name, even if society sees me as a nigger and even refers to me as such. If society agrees about the definition of a nigger, that distinction is society's alone. Most men and women do not see themselves in that role, no matter how often they hear the term applied to them. They retain their distinct, personal identities, even if they have to submerge them to survive, and society should be thankful that they preserve that degree of autonomy instead of acting according to the model urged on them.

Call me Ishmael or what you will, I refuse to be anyone's nigger, because, whether society realizes it or not, its niggers are dangerous people when pushed, and I have more important things to do than ponder revenge. That is, unfortunately, not a universal sentiment behind the walls and fences communities have erected to contain their prisoners. Those men and women whom society has discarded — its niggers — will, like Frankenstein's monster, one day turn on their creator, not behind the walls where society will be able to ignore the consequences but out there in the street. For those of you who have forgotten, Mary Shelley's novel was subtitled "A Modern Prometheus," but unlike the legend, the fire this time will consume rather than console.

NOTES

1. For an excellent discussion of this phenomenon, I recommend Paulo Freire's (1989) *Pedagogy of the Oppressed.* New York: The Continuum Publishing Company.

Rehabilitation: Contrasting Cultural Perspectives and the Imposition of Church and State

Little Rock Reed

As observed by Dr. White, Administrator of Psychology Services for the North Central Region of the United States Federal Bureau of Prisons, in the Beginning, and indeed throughout Judeo-Christian history, the desire for retribution has

> characterized society's response to criminal behavior. The imposition
> of mutilation, torture, or even death was universally accepted as
> appropriate punishment for a wide range of social transgressions.
> The roots of this philosophy were inextricably entwined in our Judeo-
> Christian tradition and reinforced by years of biblical teaching which
> stressed the notion of an eye for an eye and a tooth for a tooth.
> However, by the beginning of the 18th century the more humane
> practice of imprisonment slowly began to replace branding, corporal
> punishment, and execution as the preferred method of dealing with
> lawbreakers. Under this new doctrine punishment actually served
> two purposes: to exact society's retribution and to deter the offender
> as well as others who may consider committing future crimes.
> Finally, the early 19th century saw the forerunner of the modern day
> prison system with the development of the Walnut Street Jail, a
> uniquely American creation designed to not only punish and deter,
> but to rehabilitate offenders by making them penitent (the
> penitentiary) for their actions by forced solitude and biblical reflection.
> (White, 1989:31)

As I shall demonstrate in the forthcoming discussion, this forced biblical reflection continues as a matter of American correctional policy, though the force is employed in very subtle forms so that the policy-makers and "rehabilitators" may, as they steadfastly do, contend that their rules and procedures do not violate the establishment of religion clause of the First Amendment to the United States Constitution by forcing Judeo-Christianity upon the prisoners of America. This forced Judeo-Christianity comes under the guise of "rehabilitative" programs which prisoners are required to participate in. Thus, in examining the contrasting cultural perspectives on rehabilitation from a Native American standpoint — which is the primary aim of this paper — the imposition of Church and State inherent in the

231

government-sanctioned "rehabilitative" programs quite inevitably becomes a fundamental aspect of the discussion.

Many of the existing policies and practices relating to the rehabilitation of prisoners in the various prison systems of North America are in fact producing results which are the opposite of the rehabilitative objectives which purportedly underlie the implementation and maintenance of those policies and practices. This can be attributed, in great part, to the administrators', counselors', and treatment personnel's general lack of knowledge and understanding of the contrasting values, attitudes, customs, and life experiences of a great many of those for whom the existing "rehabilitation" programs have been established.

The implementation and maintenance of Alcoholics Anonymous (AA) and Narcotics Anonymous (NA) programs in most prisons, and the unequivocal sanction placed in them by the legislatures, prison administrators, and parole authorities are a case in point. In most states and in the Federal Bureau of Prisons, for example, prisoners are given a reduction in the time required for parole eligibility or discharge dates and/or are given special privileges or lower security status for their faithful participation in AA and/ or NA.[1] These types of policies serve to corrupt the incentive of many prisoners to participate in the programs, effectually transforming the nature of the programs from rehabilitative to mere shortcuts to freedom. Indeed, at least one prisoner in this prison has disclosed to the author that he has never been involved with alcohol or drugs, but he is a faithful participant in both AA *and* NA because of the good-time credit he receives. It is common knowledge among most prisoners that these programs — due to their high standing with the parole authorities — are, as so adequately stated by one prisoner who is a veteran of these programs,

> a complete farce, man. They're a joke, because the majority of the men who are there, including myself, are only there because we were told by the parole board or the classification committee that we should get into the programs. You've got a few guys in there who are sincere, but this just makes it hard for them 'cause they're intimidated by the fact that the majority of us think the whole thing is a crock. ... This causes the sincere ones to clam up and not really get anything out of the programs because they're uncomfortable around [those of] us who are only there for parole or good-time

reasons, or so we won't have to wait as long to be transferred to a minimum-security joint. ...

In many prison systems, the parole boards have such confidence in the AA and NA programs that they require prisoners to participate in them as a prerequisite to parole consideration even when there is nothing in the prisoner's record to indicate any involvement with alcohol or drugs other than the prisoner's own admission upon entering the prison system (when filling out questionnaires) that s/he has experimented with drugs or alcohol at some point in her or his life. Once such an admission is made, it is, as standard procedure, used against the prisoner so long as the prisoner refuses to participate in the AA and/or NA programs after having been directed to participate in them.[2] In the view of the parole board in Ohio, for example, all evidence the prisoner might submit which indicates that s/he has no affiliation with alcohol or drugs is deemed irrelevant and is given absolutely no consideration by the parole board.[3] The prisoner's failure to participate in AA or NA after having been recommended by the parole board or prison classification committee to get involved is automatically taken to indicate that the prisoner is uncooperative and incorrigible.

It is worth noting that AA has had a great rate of failure on a global scale. According to Carson, Butcher and Coleman:

> AA ... does not keep records or case histories. ... The generally acknowledged success of [AA] is based primarily on anecdotal information rather than objective study of treatment outcomes. One recent study, ... however, included an AA treatment in their extensive comparative study of treatments of alcoholics. The [AA] treatment method had very high dropout rates compared to other therapies. Apparently many alcoholics are unable to accept the "quasi-religious" quality of the sessions and the group testimonial format that is so much a part of the AA program. The individuals who were assigned to the AA program subsequently encountered more life difficulties and drank more than the other treatment groups. (Carson et al., 1988:383)

Assuming that AA isn't the failure it appears to be, let's take a look at this program from an Indian point of view to see if one needs to be "incorrigible" to reject it. This author certainly cannot speak for all Indians, but I think the voice of the great majority of the Native population will ring through in this discussion of how and why AA concepts, philosophies, and principles are inapplicable to Indians in general. This presentation is in no way intended to offend those individuals who agree with the concepts of AA or to attack the program itself. Indeed, the concepts are excellent for people from many different walks of life. I simply intend to show that AA is *not* the "universal" therapeutic program it is claimed to be, and that coerced participation in the program as a prerequisite to having one's liberty restored is morally, ethically, and legally wrong.

A passage from *Alcoholics Anonymous* (1976:62):

> Selfishness — self-centeredness! That, we think, is the root of our troubles. Driven by a hundred forms of fear, self-delusion, self-seeking and self-pity, we step on the toes of our fellows and they retaliate. Sometimes they hurt us, seemingly without provocation, but we invariably find that at some time in the past we have made decisions based on self which later placed us in a position to be hurt.
>   So our troubles, we think, are basically of our own making ...

Anyone with even the slightest knowledge of the historical and contemporary realities facing Native Americans will agree that this particular point does not reflect those realities.

Step Two of the Twelve Steps of AA requires the belief that a Power greater than ourselves, and *only* a power greater than ourselves, may restore us to *sanity*. To adopt this belief is to make an admission of *insanity*, which is pretty hard for most Indians to accept and understandably so. Assuming that we *are* willing to accept it, this Step contradicts the concept (cited above) that "our troubles ... are basically of our own making." If we and we alone are capable of bringing about our own troubles without any external influences how does it logically follow that we are absolutely incapable of restoring our alleged lost sanity — i.e., correcting the sum of our troubles — without a complete dependence upon an external power? This idea is ludicrous to most Indians; not because we lack a dependence upon or belief in external powers, but simply because there are such gross inconsistencies between these two concepts, concepts that must be adopted in order to fit into the AA program. Are non-Indians not also aware of these inconsistencies?

I would like to illustrate the totally unrealistic nature of this proposal for Indian people. As part of the AA program we list persons, institutions, and principles that we are angry at or consider enemies. We go to our enemies

> in a helpful and forgiving spirit, confessing our former ill feeling and expressing our regret. Under no circumstances do we criticize ... or argue. Simply we tell them that we can never get over our drinking until we have done our utmost to straighten out the past. We are there to sweep off our side of the street, realizing that nothing worthwhile can be accomplished until we do so, never trying to tell him what he should do. His faults are not discussed. We stick to our own. If our manner is calm, frank and open, we will be gratified with the results. In nine cases out of ten the unexpected happens. Sometimes [our enemy] admits his own fault, so feuds of years' standing melt away in an hour ... (ibid.:77–78)

When shown this passage from the AA book, one of my Choctaw friends exclaimed "Oh good! Finally a solution to the 'Indian problem'! But where do you think we should all go first, to the Bureau of Indian Affairs (BIA) headquarters or to the White House?!'" But before I could respond, another brother broke in: "Do you really think that if we go to them in a helpful and forgiving spirit and take the blame for everything and say we're sorry they will begin to honor perhaps nine treaties out of ten?" No response was necessary.

It is a rule of AA that the individual must remain free of anger. *Under no circumstances* is anger to be expressed, and if ever anyone offends the individual, he or she, is simply to say, "This man [or government or agency or mineral company?] is sick. How can I be helpful to him [it]? God save me from being angry. Thy will be done" (ibid.:67). If we do not have the "strength" and "courage" to do this, and if instead we express any anger, according to the philosophy of AA it is because we are selfish and dishonest. On the contrary, some people (including Indians) feel that the expression of anger can be pretty healthy at times, not to mention it being consistent with human nature. On the other hand, to uncompromisingly suppress one's

anger as a matter of rule — regardless of the justification for the anger or
the circumstances from which it arises — can lead to an accumulation of
frustrations that can prove to be quite unhealthy; especially in light of 1) the
discriminatory actions that Indians are faced with day after day in the course
of non-Indian custom, and 2) the stressful situations that are so commonplace
in the prison environment where the potential for violence is magnified, and
often encouraged by the administrators and guards.[4] One must also wonder
if such strict adherence to this rule may not enhance the probability of one's
development of a passive-aggressive personality disorder.[5]

According to the concepts of AA,

> Resentment is the "number one" offender. It destroys more
> alcoholics than anything else. From it stem all forms of spiritual
> disease, for we have not only been mentally and physically ill, we
> have been spiritually sick ... (ibid.:64)

When hearing such language, one cannot help but wonder if it has ever
occurred to the founders and proponents of AA that some people drink not
because they are "insane," "mentally ill," or "spiritually sick," but because
they are trying to numb the pain caused by the fact that they are religiously,
politically, socially, culturally and economically oppressed by an alien
government and people who are imposing their religious, political, social,
cultural and economic values and laws on them without their willful consent
and in direct violation of the majority of the human rights and fundamental
freedoms that appear in the various international human rights instruments.
To this end, it is the view of many prisoners (regardless of race or ethnicity)
that the AA and NA programs are no more than social control mechanisms
— that is, mediums through which the ruling class effectively subdues the
discontent of the lower classes and underprivileged by having their attention
diverted from the true sources of their problems (poverty, unemployment,
despair, etc.). "What other reasons can there be," poses one black prisoner
from the Cleveland slums,

> for them to force us into programs that are known to be failures in
> the treatment of substance abuse? Not only are we being forced
> into these programs here, but every day the underprivileged are
> being ordered by the courts to participate in the same programs in

the free world if they wish to stay out of prison. The programs are failures, so why? I believe the answer is because the programs aren't really failures at all — they are highly effective at controlling the lower classes. That must be why the government sanctions them as they do. ...

I want to examine another aspect of the AA/NA format, the very principle of anonymity itself from which these programs have taken their names. Anonymity denies to an individual the social and cultural identity which research has indicated is essential to the successful treatment of Native Americans with substance-abuse problems. As was stated by Grobsmith:

... Indian people for the last century have been lost. When their religion and languages and cultures were taken away from them in the period of forced assimilation on the part of the U.S. government, Indian people's knowledge of their own ways was largely disappearing.

Because of the introduction of alcohol, the lack of a strong economic base [and] tremendous unemployment, the situation has become very, very drastic and very depressing; drug use at an early age and so on. Indian people have, I believe, lost themselves.

The return to Native religion — and there are other sources that document this, and I'm not the only person who's observed this — indicate that this return to [their traditional native] spirituality helps them in ways that other kinds of programs do not, by giving them something strong to identify with that is Indian, giving them pride. ...

Indian people are not comfortable in AA. They're not comfortable in a large rehabilitation program that's not basically Indian, because many of them are embarrassed or ashamed to admit their problems and their dependence on alcohol with people who are not going to understand them, and who may have prejudice against them.

And AA is an approach that requires an attitude of an admission of guilt. You get up, and you give self confessions. You admit guilt and shame. It is not suitable to the Indian culture. It is not effective. AA is notorious ... [for its] great rate of failure with Native Americans; and this is nationwide. (Grobsmith, 1987:281–84)

In wrapping up the discussion on AA and NA, it is also worth noting that these programs unquestionably qualify as "associations" (see *Black's Law Dictionary*), and that Article 20(2) of the Universal Declaration of Human Rights states that "no one may be compelled to belong to an association." It appears, therefore, that all policies and practices that demand the participation of prisoners in these programs as a prerequisite to the restoration of their liberty or as a stipulation in their parole programs are in need of an overhaul. Not only do such policies and practices violate the above-cited right, when the individual who is coerced into the programs holds cultural, social, political or religious values or beliefs that are in conflict with those propounded by the programs, such policies and practices may violate most, if not all, of the rights guaranteed by the following:

From the *Universal Declaration of Human Rights* of the United Nations,

> *Article 18*: Everyone has the right to freedom of thought, conscience, and religion; this right includes freedom ... either alone or in community with others and in public or private, to manifest his religion or belief in teaching, practice, worship and observance. [The freedom of manifestation is impaired when conflicting beliefs are imposed on the individual.]

> *Article 22*: Everyone is entitled to realization ... of the ... social and cultural rights indispensable for his dignity and the free development of his personality.

From the United Nations' *International Covenant on Civil and Political Rights*,

> *Article 26*: All persons are equal before the law and are entitled without any discrimination to the equal protection of the law. In this respect, the law shall prohibit any discrimination and guarantee to all persons equal and effective protection against discrimination on any ground such as race, colour, language, religion, political or other opinion, national or social origin, property, birth or other status.

And the First Amendment to the United States Constitution declares that no law shall be made which respects an establishment of religion or which prohibits the free exercise thereof. As used in constitutional provisions forbidding the establishment of religion, the term "religion" means a particular system of faith and belief in the existence of a superior being or beings exercising power over human beings by volition; man's submission to mandates, precepts, rules of conduct, etc., imposed by supernatural or superior beings; these concepts shared, recognized and practiced by a particular church, denomination, association, group or sect. According to the legal definitions of "religion" as promulgated by the United States Supreme Court in numerous decisions, AA and NA are in fact religions. When I suggested this to a social worker here in the Southern Ohio Correctional Facility and emphasized that these programs are "Christian-oriented," he and his fellows became very perturbed and summoned me into an office where I suppose they expected to intimidate me. They confronted me with my "accusations" that these programs are Christian-oriented, and what followed only served to illustrate that they indeed are. They insisted that these programs have absolutely no connection with religion and are suitable for *everyone* regardless of ethnic or religious affiliation, *including atheists*. This is absurd since an atheist rejects all religious belief and denies the existence of any god. When I stated this to these social workers, they told me that *I* was being unreasonable and "copping out" for not wanting to participate in the programs. They insisted that the AA program doesn't really have anything to do with religion because the individual participant is to consider this "God" to be in whatever form or manifestation with which the individual is comfortable, i.e., "God as you understand Him." This "God," they assured me, can take the form of a tree, a group of friends, the Great Spirit, or anything at all — "as we understand Him." Regardless of what image this "God" takes, however, the fact remains that it is a religious symbol; a superior being with supernatural powers; a superior being that sets standards of conduct for us to live by and believe in, and which happen to be standards of conduct which clash with the standards of conduct *my* god has set for *me* to live by and believe in. These social workers, or anyone, may conjure up all the abstract theories they wish in an attempt to make someone believe that the "God" in these programs is not really the religious kind. The abstractions do not and cannot eliminate the supernatural quality that makes it religious. According to the dominant society's own standards and rationalizations that we Native Americans are so familiar with, the AA and NA programs are either religious in nature or are superstitious in nature — take your pick. And it should also be noted that the AA meetings here, as well as in other prisons, which these social workers and prison officials insist are in no way related to religion, conclude with the Lord's Prayer. Amen.

And in returning to some additional Rights guaranteed by the United States Constitution, we must not overlook the Fifth or the Thirteenth Amendments:

> *Amendment Five*: No one shall be ... deprived of ... liberty ... without due process of law. [Please see my note following Amendment Thirteen below.]

> *Amendment Thirteen*: [N]o ... involuntary servitude, except as punishment for crime whereof the party shall have been duly convicted, shall exist in the United States. ...[6]

In addition to the laws listed above, many other similar laws and administrative regulations are violated when programs such as AA and NA are imposed on prisoners against their will. Such practices and policies are a direct offense against the inherent dignity of the human being and are clearly demonstrative of the policy-makers' and enforcers' intolerance of and contempt for the pluralism and self-determination that are claimed to be held in such high regard in those societies that are allegedly "democratic."

It should also be noted that this imposition of AA and NA is discriminatory. *Black's Law Dictionary* (1979) defines discrimination as such:

> In constitutional law, the effect of a statute or established practice which confers particular privileges on a class arbitrarily selected from a large number of persons, all of whom stand in the same relation to the privileges granted and between whom and those not favored no reasonable distinction can be found. Unfair treatment or denial of normal privileges to persons because of their race, age, nationality or religion. A failure to treat all persons equally where no reasonable distinction can be found between those favored and those not favored.

It logically follows that the effect of a statute or established practice which gives "good time" credits or any privileges (e.g., trustee status or the option to transfer to less security) only to those prisoners whose beliefs correlate with the AA/NA programs — or to those who are willing to sit through the programs in violation of their beliefs — is discrimination and constitutes a violation of the equal protection of the law. In order to adhere to the International Bill of Human Rights and corresponding American constitutional law, it is necessary to neutralize such statutes and practices so that the privileges presently granted by participating in these programs will become available to all prisoners. For example, if a state statute or regulation credits good-time to prisoners who participate in AA or NA, then such good-time must also be credited to Indian prisoners who participate in programs such as the Red Road Approach to Recovery, or the United Native Alcohol Program, which I will discuss in greater depth in a moment.

I am emphasizing substance abuse treatment because it is time for some concrete measures to be taken to alleviate the problem. Alcohol-abuse has long been recognized by social scientists as "the foremost medical and social problem" among contemporary Indian populations (see Beauvais and La Boueff, 1985; Grobsmith, 1989a; Hall, 1986; Mail and McDonald, 1981; Pedigo, 1983; Price, 1975; Snake et al., 1977; Task Force Eleven, 1976; Weibel-Orlando, 1984; Weibel-Orlando, 1987). It has been well-documented that Indian youth suicide, which is double that of the national population, is alcohol-related (French, 1982; Grobsmith, 1989a; Rosenstiel, 1989; Shore et al., 1972; Weibel-Orlando, 1984); that the leading causes of death among the American Indian population are attributed to alcohol use (Grobsmith, 1989a; Indian Health Service, 1989); and that almost all arrests of Indians are alcohol-related, including juvenile arrests (Grobsmith, 1989a; Grobsmith, 1989b; Lex, 1985; Mail and McDonald, 1981; Weibel-Orlando, 1984). According to Grobsmith's studies, 91 to 100 percent of Indian crimes are alcohol or drug related (1989b). As stated by Dale Smith, a former spokesman for the Tribe of Five Feathers, the Indian cultural/spiritual group at the Lompoc Federal Prison in California, "if we have, say 50 guys, 49 of them are here because of alcohol problems" (Thornton, 1984). And as observed by an Idaho/Montana prisoner who expresses the general feeling among Indian people: "I feel that [with regard to] our Native people, the percentage who are in prison on alcohol and drug related crimes [is] 99 ... if not 100 [percent]. Alcohol has been the most destructive factor to our people since the day we were introduced to it."[7] And a former president of the Native American Council at the Southern New Mexico Correctional Facility, Harvey Snow, has stated that "of our twenty members, 19 of us are [in for] alcohol or drug related [offenses]."

And the problem is not going to be alleviated through the use of "rehabilitation" programs that fail to take cultural factors into account, as observations and research have clearly shown. The failure of non-Indian programs to successfully treat Indian substance-abuse problems has been well-documented (Grobsmith, 1987; Heath et al., 1981; Kline and Roberts, 1973; Native American Rights Fund, 1978; Pedigo, 1983; Stevens; 1981, Weibel-Oriando, 1989). Despite these observations, most substance-abuse intervention programs offered to Indians (including those on the reservations) are generally designed by non-Indians and are "based on Western schools of thought that have little to do with Indian values and beliefs" (Beauvais and La Boueff, 1985; Butterfield, 1989; Stevens, 1981). "Increasingly, evaluators, treatment personnel, and potential clients deplore the Anglo cultural bias of existing alcoholism intervention programs and call for the integration of more traditional [Indian] forms of healing practices into programs with ... Native American clients" (Weibel-Oriando, 1987:264).

Over a five-year period, the Alcohol and Drug Study Group of the American Anthropological Association visited and observed over 40 Indian alcoholism recovery homes as well as traditional Indian healers in California, South Dakota, New Mexico, Arizona and Oklahoma. The alcoholism treatment programs were categorized across a range of six different types running on a continuum from what can be described as culture-sensitive to assimilative. They had found that "Indian alcoholism programs with the highest rates of sustained client sobriety are those that integrate a variety of [traditional Indian] spiritual elements and activities into their treatment strategies" and suggested further that "involving the concept of sacred separation as a viable ethnic stance and abstinence as one of its demonstrable forms may be a culturally appropriate intervention strategy and the effective *first step* toward sustained sobriety for contemporary American Indians ..." (Weibel-Oriando, 1985:219–23, my emphasis).

Harvey Snow sent me the Twelve Steps in the Native Way which were given to the brothers in the Southern New Mexico Correctional Facility by a medicine man who spends some time with them. The distinctions between these steps and those of AA are very pronounced. Table 1 (p. 244) compares five of the twelve AA steps with five of the twelve steps the Native Way, "Sobriety Through the Sacred Pipe."

In studies conducted by Westermeyer and Neider, they found that "those [Indians] ... engaging in more traditional Indian activities ... tended to have better outcomes a decade later. It appears that more intense contact with one's own culture ... favors a better outcome among Indian alcoholics" (1984:183).

The importance of cultural differences must be recognized in any program that is to be successful with Native Americans (Bowechop, 1970; Guajardo, n.d.; Jilek and Jilek-Aall, 1972; Jilek-Aall, 1974; Miller n.d.; Pedigo, 1983; Task Force Eleven, 1976; Topper, 1976; Weibel-Orlando, 1987). The programs must be based on Native values (Alday, 1971; Grobsmith, 1987; Jilek and Jilek-Aall, 1972; Jilek, 1974; Reed, 1989; Topper, 1976; Underhill, 1951). Native American involvement and staffing are essential to the success of substance-abuse treatment programs for Indians (Ferguson, 1976; Leon, 1968; Native American Rights Fund, 1978; Pedigo, 1983; Provincial Native Action Committee, 1974; Shore, 1974; Task Force Eleven, 1976; Turner, 1977). Where such involvement and staffing are not feasible, it is imperative that any non-Indian attempting to counsel effectively (whether or not such counselling is related to substance-abuse), should have some knowledge of the historical and contemporary realities facing Native Americans and the differences in Indian and Anglo values (Guajardo, n.d.). As Guajardo pointed out, "what is a positive value for the Anglo (e.g., being outgoing, competitive) can be a negative value for the American Indian. Calling values 'positive' or 'negative' is always relative to those who espouse [them]," and to approach any type of counselling or therapy from the" "'Textbook' ... [which] emphasizes white middle-class values, is both improper for, and antagonistic to, the Native American client" (ibid.:3). Guajardo, in citing Richardson (1973), listed examples of the contrast between Indian and Anglo values as shown in Table 2 (page 243).

In returning to the discussion of substance abuse, the most effective approach to the problems among Native Americans is simply that of refamiliarizing them with the traditional values of their culture, and strengthening those cultural values and norms (Albaugh and Anderson, 1974; Pedigo, 1983), for as was observed by Lex (1987:298), "the erosion of traditional behaviors [and values of Indians] accompanies drinking problems." As stated by Dale Smith, founder of the United Native Alcohol Program (UNAP) at Lompoc, "we try to say to them, 'Hey, the pipe is good, and the pipe is strong' . ... The difference [between our philosophy and that of Alcoholics Anonymous] is that they dwell on the negative aspects of alcohol,

Table 1: Comparison of Anglo and Native AA Steps

	Anglo AA Step	The Native Step
Step 2	We come to believe that a Power greater than ourselves can restore us to sanity.	We come to believe that the Power of the Pipe is greater than ourselves and can restore us to our Culture and Heritage.
Step 5	We admit to God, to Ourselves, and to another human being, the exact nature of our wrongs.	We acknowledge to the Great Spirit, to ourselves, and to the Native American Brotherhood, our struggles against the tide and its manifest destiny.
Step 6	We are entirely ready to have God remove all these defects of character.	Be entirely ready for the Great Spirit to remove all the defects of an alien culture.
Step 8	Make a list of all persons we have harmed and become willing to make amends to them all.	Make a list of all the harm that has come to our people from Demon Alcohol, and become willing to make amends to them all.
Step 11	Seek through prayer and meditation to improve our conscious contact with God as we understand Him, praying only for knowledge of His will for us and the power to carry that out.	Seek through prayer and meditation to improve our conscious contact with the Equality and Brotherhood of all Mother Earth's children and the Great Balancing Harmony of the Total Universe.[8]

while we prefer to accentuate the strength of our traditional ways" (Thornton, 1984). We asked Dale if he would share some additional insights about UNAP. His response follows:

Table 2: Comparison of Anglo and Native American Values

Native American	Anglo American
Uncritical attitude	Critical Attitude
Cooperation	Competition
Sharing	Ownership
Humble	Outgoing if not arrogant
Happiness	Success
Honor elders	No respect for elders
Silence	Verbalism
Tribal values	Individualism
Simplicity	Complexity and sophistication
Tradition	Innovation
Spiritual values	Material values
Learning from elders	Learning in schools
Few rules	Multiplicity of laws
Mysticism	Empiricism
Smallness	Bigness
Natural medicine	Synthetic medicine
Unity of animal kingdom with humanity	Separateness of animal kingdom from humanity
Accept others as they are	Change or proselytize others

What is UNAP?

Dale: UNAP is a substance abuse rehabilitation and prevention program. It is designed specifically for Native Americans. UNAP employs traditional Indian spiritualism and culture as well as up-to-date behavior modification techniques applied in a traditional Indian context.

UNAP breaks with conventional rehabilitation programs in many areas. For instance, UNAP does not treat alcohol or substances as problems. Those are simply symptoms of the real problems which are deeper underlying turmoils.

Additionally, the program focus of UNAP differs from the conventional in that it chooses to focus on the positive nature and spiritual strengths of mankind rather than on negative case histories. Focusing on guilt complexes and personal shortcomings is not a practice of UNAP.

The ultimate goal of the UNAP project is to repair and rebuild the damage of substance abuse, prevent abuse from occurring, and to provide a lasting sense of direction through encouragement, support and instruction in the Native spiritual practices of regional tribes. Suggestions on uses of work and leisure time, an important aspect of program aftercare, are also provided in the UNAP program.

When and how did UNAP start?
Dale: The UNAP concept was conceived in 1978. Research and development, as well as a large degree of self-education on my part, continued for five more years until in 1984 the first draft of the UNAP program was completed.

I participated in AA back in those days, but somehow could not bring myself to say the standard AA greeting, which is, "Hello, my name is _____ and I am an alcoholic." I always felt that in the context of that greeting, the phrase was unnecessarily demeaning and demoralizing. It was like being asked to slap myself in the face then follow that with a few psychological kicks in the butt for my past indiscretions. I said, "no way, buddy!" Besides, what was AA giving me?

I still had difficulty understanding how the AA concept applied to me. And it didn't help that I didn't believe in the Christian concept of God. Eventually it became a real problem for me to sit and listen to other people's testimonials about their loss of things I never had, like big brick homes and high society girlfriends, and to hear of their salvation through religious concepts which were alien to me.

Finally, I listed the problems conventional rehabilitation programs failed to address for Native people. I spoke to many different Indians about substance abuse and listened with an Indian ear for the deeper meanings within the stories I heard. And after more than four years of studying the problems, I put together UNAP and offered it as an alternative solution.

Where is/was UNAP developed?
Dale: UNAP was first introduced at the federal prison at Lompoc, California. The very first sessions were conducted for the Tribe of Five Feathers, the Indian prisoners group there.

Like an underground movement UNAP traveled through the federal system. It surfaced at facilities in Phoenix, Arizona; Lewisburg, Pennsylvania; Terre Haute, Indiana; and it remains active at Lompoc.

It's unfortunate, but for the most part, federal administrators uniformly resisted the development of UNAP. Their spoken reasons ultimately revert to security concerns. However, even a streamlined UNAP proposal which addresses every conceivable security consideration meets with resistance. So, one must presume that other motives for the resistance exist.

Outside the institutional setting, UNAP has been made available to several organizations and tribes. The Sho-Ban tribes in Idaho and Fort Peck tribes in Montana are among the list. Additionally, the Indian Center in Kansas City and a clinical psychologist of Indian descent at Berkeley use concepts taken from the UNAP program.

Your vision for UNAP?
Dale: The UNAP concept is such that it projects its own future. The Medicine Wheel which is an integral part of UNAP tells the story.

As the outer circle of the wheel is symbolic of the cycle of life in our universe, I see UNAP as having limitless potential. It has the potential of reaching people from all age groups and all nationalities, if not directly then by proximity to those it does touch.

And as the cross intersects within the wheel, UNAP has the potential to draw people together. I see Indian people one day looking at each other as one nation, regardless of tribal or political affiliation and regardless of historical animosities, because it is my belief that we Indian people, and all indigenous people of the world, will see a day in the future when our unity will be the only thing that stands between us and the final holocaust.

My vision for UNAP? In a word, it is HOPE.

And Dale certainly isn't alone. Other people with the same vision have been pushing to see the implementation of similar programs throughout

North America. The Red Road Approach to Sobriety, another culturally specific program developed by Gene Thin Elk, another Sioux, is an example. The Red Road Approach program is now being used in prisons in several states, as well as by various Indian tribes and centers. It is unfortunate, however, that these programs are being met with resistance not only by most prison administrators but by funding agencies upon whom the Indian people must rely for assistance in keeping the programs alive in Indian communities.

On the discussion of substance abuse in the first volume of the *Operations Guide Manual for the Cheyenne River Swift Bird Project*, the Native American Rights Fund clarified what is probably the most important distinction between Native American and Anglo attitudes and approaches toward the problem:

> ... [We] have made a special effort *not* to compartmentalize substance abuse problems. The problems of alcohol and drug abuse are not singular problems that can be identified and isolated out of the total life context of the [individual]. Other social, medical, spiritual and personal problems have not been adequately addressed in non-Indian correctional facilities. [We must be] careful not to disassociate these problems from the total context of the [individual's] life. Indian culture and tradition are not a distinct aspect of Indian life but form an integral set of qualities which pervade daily life. In the same way, the problems that exist for Indians cannot be addressed as isolated problems, but must be viewed in the cultural context as an integral part of the larger whole.
>
> Substance abuse programming [must be] developed from this integrated cultural perspective ... (Native American Rights Fund, 1978:31)

To this end, *all* approaches to counselling at the Swift Bird Project, whether substance-abuse related or not, were designed from this integrated cultural perspective and within the framework of traditional Indian concepts and methods of handling antisocial behavior:

... The project integrates acceptable concepts from the field of counselling with the use of traditional Indian values and practices.

The primary goal of the counselling program is to meet the personal needs of the individual resident at Swift Bird and upon release and re-entry to his home community. Traditional Indian approaches combined with [acceptable] non-Indian approaches form the basis for a successful program. In conjunction with basic counselling techniques this approach has the potential for an effective and comprehensive counselling program for [Indians].

Counselling is conducted on both an individual and group basis. The total approach to counselling allows cultural flexibility and adaptability to accommodate the cultural beliefs and experiences of residents.

Important objectives of the program include:
1. Assisting the resident in developing and maintaining a positive self-image and sense of self-worth.
2. Assisting the resident in developing his psychological functioning, aptitude, interests, interactions, and personal goals.
3. Enabling the resident to identify his immediate and long-term goals.
4. Identifying and affirming strengths, achievements, and successes for building fulfillment of self and fulfillment of significant others.

The traditional Indian approach to counselling [differs from] current non-Indian counselling practices ... in the way ... services are delivered. Traditional Indian counselling is an ongoing process which is not characterized by sessions or meetings. Traditional counselling services are delivered informally, by providing positive models and examples, and by integrating supports and models into all aspects of daily life. Native American practitioners (medicine men) are essential to the counselling program ... (ibid.:28–9)

It becomes evident, then, that the development of traditional Indian components to the greatest extent possible within the prison setting would (and has) served to enhance the rehabilitation of individuals.

As Larry McCook, Associate Director of the Native American Prisoners Rehabilitation Project, has pointed out with respect to the white man's theft of Indian things and labelling them white man's "discoveries," the principles of Gestalt psychology and other types of contemporary psychology have been employed by Native American tribes since time immemorial (McCook, 1989). The ideas underlying Gestalt psychology have been absorbed and continue to have a significant impact on psychology (Saccuzzo, 1987:15).[9] Carson et al. (1988) have pointed out that various comparative sociocultural studies of the incidence of psychological disorders have indicated significant contrasts between those in the United States and those in Native tribal populations. For example, while major depression is rampant in the mainstream United States, it is almost non-existent among Native tribal peoples until their cultures are disrupted by Anglo influence (ibid.: 303–4). It seems probable that this is as it is, at least in great part, because the same ideas that are the core of Gestalt psychology are in fact integral concepts held within the religions and cultures of tribal peoples; whereas, in the mainstream U.S.A. these holistic concepts are generally ignored if not intentionally rejected.[10]

For example, while such things as the interpretation of dreams are often thought to be ridiculous, this Gestalt technique used to increase self-awareness and self-acceptance has been practiced by Native people for thousands of years. As a matter of fact, fundamental aspects of Gestalt therapy can be found in all the major individual and organizational functions of Native American cultures and religions. The vision quest, the sun dance, the pipe ceremony, the medicine wheel, the sweat bath — all are essentially Gestalt. And the definition of Gestalt Psychology is merely one way of defining the fabric of traditional Native American philosophy.[11]

The purification ceremony of the sweat lodge and its associated practices is a critical ritual that is virtually universal among Native American tribes throughout North America. To Indian people, the sweat lodge has long been a center for spiritual, physical and psychological healing and strength, and is seen as a fundamental rehabilitative tool:

> ... It has become a major means of spiritual support for many young people. Its rehabilitative effects on troubled young men is particularly evident. ... It is frequently used to combat the effects of alienation, such as alcoholism and other destructive, anti-social behavior ... (Walker, 1985:32–2)

The positive rehabilitative effects of the sweat lodge have been well documented (Hall, 1986; Hanson, 1983; Johnson, 1988; Navajo Nation, 1989; Nebraska Parole Board member, personal correspondence, 1989; Reed, 1989; Seven, 1988; Specktor, 1983; Spotted Eagle, 1983). Prior to the March 1989 decision by the federal court in Utah, Lee Bergen, staff attorney with the Navajo Department of Justice, pointed out that "Utah's ban on the sweat lodge ... effectively destroys the only successful rehabilitative tool available to [Indian] inmates" (Sisco, 1989). Statistics compiled by the Navajo Corrections Project, which serves the rehabilitative and religious needs of prisoners in at least 36 state and federal institutions, indicate recidivism rates of 7 percent for prisoners involved in sweat ceremonies as opposed to a national average of 30-to-50 percent.

The Native American Church and its associated practices have been described as the most successful Indian alcoholism program of all (Bergman, 1971; Pascarosa, 1976; Roy et al., 1970; Underhill, 1951; Wagner, 1975; Weibel-Orlando, 1989). "Most Indian people working in alcoholism programs say, usually away from the funding agency, that the most successful Indian alcoholism program is the Native American Church" (Stevens, 1981:141).

In the mid-70s, when the people involved in the Seattle Indian Alcoholism Program recognized that over 90 percent of the Indians in jails and prisons are there for alcohol-related offenses, they set up culture-specific programs in Washington's four major prisons. Within four years after these programs were established, the proportion of Indian prisoners in the state's prisons had dropped from 5% to 3.5% (Walker, 1981). While this decline in the Indian population (of nearly 1/3) cannot be claimed as the direct result of the implementation of the programs in Washington's prisons, that possibility must not be ruled out, especially when these statistics correlate with other research cited in this paper. And as observed by Seven:

> For prison officials, the [purification ceremony of the sweat] lodge and other religious programs are ways to reduce the high rate at which released inmates commit crimes.
> Robert Lynn, religious program manager for the Department of Corrections, says inmates in Oregon's prisons who were actively involved in religious programs over several years in the late seventies had a recidivism rate of 5% compared with the national rate of close to 75% at the time ... (1988)

With statistics like these, the relevance of and need for spiritual/cultural programs for Indian prisoners can hardly be refuted. In fact, it would seem that such statistics would encourage prison officials and administrators to actively seek the development of such programs with the tax dollars they are currently wasting in their attempts to defend the suppression of the religious practices which would be accommodated through the programs. As was stated by Hoffstettor in Scott:

> It has been my experience based on twenty years of juvenile and adult correctional work, both as a clinical psychologist and program administrator that ... the more an inmate is involved in his own rehabilitation process the more effective will be the outcome. (1973:140)

We Indians think that's pretty sound logic. How can a prison official or administrator know what rehabilitation process will be effective for *any* prisoner when the values and beliefs held within the cultural context of the prisoner are contrary to those of the culture to which the prison official belongs? It is impossible unless the official is willing to sit down with the prisoner in an attempt to bridge that cultural gap. Repeated displays of insensitivity and indifference to the laws and to the basic human needs of the prisoners by prison officials such as those who force Indians into programs that propagate philosophies, values, principles and beliefs that clash with those of the Indians serve only to enhance the alienation of the Indians and make them more bitter and resentful toward the society those prison officials represent. In other words, such practices not only fail to rehabilitate, but to the contrary, they serve to increase conflict (and undoubtedly the criminal recidivism rates). Consider what must run through the minds of many prisoners who are continually faced with these ethnocentric displays and attitudes. Better yet, consider what would reasonably run through your own mind under the same circumstances. Perhaps something to the effect of, "the officials themselves have no regard for my human dignity or for the laws they have made — so why should I?"

CONCLUSION

It is worth noting that while we are focusing primarily on the contrasting cultural perspectives on rehabilitation of Native Americans, the fundamental concept involved — the concept of giving consideration to historical, ethnic, cultural, socioeconomic factors etc., in approaching rehabilitation techniques, rather than taking the textbook approach which emphasizes middle-class Anglo values — is also applicable to substance-abusers and prisoners of other cultural and ethnic minorities. If prison administrators throughout the country were to apply this concept to their approaches in the treatment of prisoners, there would undoubtedly be an overwhelming reduction in recidivism since the majority of prisoners in the country are members of cultural and ethnic minorities rather than the Judeo-Christian group upon whose ethos the contemporary American prison systems are admittedly based. Grobsmith (1989b:17) has summed it up well:

> ... [Many] correctional system[s] make no pretense of offering real therapeutic rehabilitation. Overcrowded and underfunded, they do not consider themselves ... rehabilitation center[s] but ... place[s] to house inmates and secure their isolation from society and protect the public for a time. One cannot help but wonder, however, whether investment in better therapy and the prospect of reduced recidivism rates might be more cost effective by paying for therapy now and helping the inmate NOT to return again. ...

In conclusion, I want to point out that all of this has tremendous significance not only to Indian prisoners, but to the entire Native American population and as Dale Smith would say, "all age groups and nationalities, if not directly then by proximity to those it does touch."

According to the Indian Health Service (IHS), "75% of all Indian families have at least one alcoholic member, and ... nearly 100% have been affected in some way by alcoholism" (Butterfield, 1989). Meanwhile, the IHS has primary responsibility for funding tribal substance abuse programs, yet the IHS doesn't seem to want to provide funds for programs that are culturally sensitive. In light of the evidence I have presented here that our own programs are the answer to our problems, and that the non-Indian programs are not, we wonder why that is?

*****

Hey Dale. A lot of social scientists have wasted billions of dollars over the years trying to answer the question, "Why do Indians drink?" I personally know a lot of Indians who drink because of the poverty conditions imposed on our people while these social scientists waste all that money that could be used for real solutions rather than abstract contemplations and rhetoric. But of course, I'm not an expert (I don't tote a Ph.D.) so my opinion doesn't count for much. Also, some folks think I'm just too hostile to be listened to. So let me ask you, Brother. You've talked with thousands of Indians and listened with an Indian ear for the real causes. Why do you think Indians drink?

Dale: This is a good question. Why do Indians drink? Try to follow me.

Indians of modern times are born with a "soul wound." From the first moment of life we begin learning to understand Tunkasila's purpose for us. Indians are the guardians of Ena — Mother Earth. Tunkasila gave us logic and separated us from our animal relations. With logic we are capable of helping to regulate corporal activities on earth as a means of protecting the natural balances.

Look around. We have failed our mission. Moreover, as we grow toward adulthood we consciously and sub-consciously assume the suffering of all our ancestors.

The Trail of Tears, Sand Creek and Wounded Knee, the Nez Perce run for Canada. These events. The thought of them brings tears to my eyes, for the pain of our people, and for the shame mankind deserves for committing such atrocities.

Those are the cause aspects of the Indian soul wound. The soul wound is the cause of spiritual imbalance. Spiritual imbalance is the cause of substance abuse.

Those are the problems. The solution is to achieve spiritual balance and a clear understanding of our unique Indian psychological patterns. Indians have got to be damn smart to survive in this world today! Some assimilate, and if they find peace in that, I say that's great. But the ones who either don't want to assimilate or who have tried and found no spiritual peace in it, those are the people I am here to help find their way home.

Thank you, Dale.

NOTES

1. "Good-time" is a term used to indicate a reduction in actual time that must be served by the prisoner. For example, many states automatically give good-time credit to prisoners when they enter the prison system, and this good-time will only be taken away if the prisoner violates prison rules. For instance, in some states, if a prisoner is sentenced to five years, he will only have to serve an actual three years because he is automatically given two years good-time credit. On the other hand, in some states (such as Indiana) when good-time credit is taken away for rule infractions, it can be regained for faithful participation in AA or NA. Other states have different kinds of good-time laws and regulations. Ohio's House-Bill 261 is a good example. It offers good-time to prisoners for their faithful participation in "programs" — AA and NA are the *only* programs this good-time law is applied to in the Southern Ohio Correctional Facility (SOCF), and it is probably the same way at the other Ohio prisons. When this law was passed and the prisoners found out it would become effective, it was a mad race to the sign-up line! Coincidentally, because of the limited capacity for participants in these programs, there are far more people on the waiting lists than there are in the programs, and the wait runs into the years (unless the policies and practices have changed since the turn of the year when I last checked).
2. For example, this morning one of my friends saw the parole board for the first time in sixteen years. He hasn't had a drink in sixteen years and claims that he's never been an alcoholic. His work evaluations have been above average the whole time he's been in prison, but the parole board has taken it upon itself to evaluate him as needing treatment because he has a "serious disruption of functioning" as a result of an alleged "frequent abuse" of alcohol.
3. My own parole was denied on the sole basis of my refusal to get into AA or NA. It was denied despite the fact that a substantial portion of this paper was submitted to the parole board verifying that the AA and NA programs propagate values and beliefs that clash with my own, that I do not use alcohol or drugs, and that those programs as they are implemented in this prison are almost completely without rehabilitative value. The members of the parole board decided that despite the evidence, they believe I have a "severe" drug and alcohol problem which renders me unable to function in my daily affairs. When you finish reading this paper, *you* decide who's functioning properly and who isn't.
4. Many prison officials tend to deal with isolated incidents of misconduct of prisoners by establishing policies or practices that inflict punishment on the whole prisoner population. There may be a stabbing one day; for the rest of the week the warden might let the prisoners know he is upset about it by locking down the whole prisoner population. If the stabbing involves possible racial conflict (i.e., white stabs black, or vice versa), tensions are going to rise between the races involved. Regardless of whether there are racial undertones or overtones, this collective type of punishment creates tension between prisoners and staff, and between the prisoners who have not "caused" the collective punishment and those who have. What leads to violence if not tension?

    There are many other ways the prison administrators and guards encourage violence. The prison guards here at SOCF wear coats (and often gloves and ear muffs) in the hallways, the cell blocks, and the chow hall in the winters. They do this to keep warm while the prisoners are cold and miserable. They open the windows in the chow hall to "encourage" us to eat fast and to discourage us from sneaking through the line for a second helping of food. They often pile us into the chow hall by the hundreds, so that if we want to eat we must pay for our meals by standing in the literally freezing chow hall food line for up to forty-five minutes. We have no long-sleeved shirts. We have no jackets or coats. This is a form of corporal punishment for simply being in prison. Our complaints about this type of treatment fall on deaf ears. Some guards laugh in our faces (is this not encouraging violence?). Some guards express sympathy but say there is nothing they can do about it.

In many prisons, "white power," very racist anti-color publications that promote violence against minorities (all non-whites) are permitted into the prisons without any screening, while in those same prisons, pro-black, *non*-violent publications are prohibited as a blanket policy regardless of content (Abu-Jamal, 1989). Is this not the encouragement of violence? These are only a few examples of how prison administrators and guards encourage violence. Any prisoner who isn't scared to speak out about the encouragement of violence on the part of the administrators and guards can give you examples all day long. It is unfortunate that the great majority of prisoners are scared to speak out until *after* they are released from prison and, of course, off parole. It is also unfortunate that by *that* time the ex-convict would rather just forget the whole ordeal, so the conditions persist.

5. A passive-aggressive personality disorder is characterized by never confronting a problem situation directly. Individuals with this disorder "typically express their hostility in indirect ways, such as procrastination, pouting, 'forgetting,' or being obstructionistic, stubborn or intentionally inefficient" (Carson, 1988:233), such as the janitor who is angry at his boss and expresses it by smiling and saying "yes sir" when ordered to sweep the floor a second time, and then sneakily "putting one over" on the boss by intentionally leaving dirt on the floor where the boss *won't* see it. Before having ever made my acquaintance, the psychologist in this prison diagnosed me (for the parole board) as having this disorder on the basis of my responses to the 550-item Minnesota Multiphasic Personality Inventory (MMPI), an examination which is absolutely inapplicable to Native Americans (I am prepared to meet any scholar's challenge to this claim), and which all Ohio prisoners are required to take if they wish to see the parole board. After having become acquainted with me, the psychologist admitted (but only to me) that had he known anything of my background he would never have diagnosed me as he did. Nevertheless, because he is a blind conformist, I remain officially classified as a "passive-aggressive personality disorder." Ha ha. Who knows, maybe if I'm lucky I can advance to paranoid schizophrenia for my next parole hearing. "Alcoholic," "drug addict." I'm doing pretty well!

6. The refusal of a prisoner either to participate in AA or NA or similar programs, or to agree to accept a stipulation requiring such participation upon release in order to secure his/her liberty, is not a crime. If his or her liberty is delayed or denied on the basis of such refusal, the delay or denial constitutes involuntary servitude without due process of the law since the question of his or her original crime is no longer at issue.

7. This was relayed to the author in personal correspondence from Jim Spurlocks, who at that time (mid-August 1989) was in Orofino, Idaho state prison. At that time he had

a petition for a writ of habeas corpus pending in the Idaho State Court because he was being required to obtain "treatment for chemical dependency" as a prerequisite to being considered for parole while there was *absolutely no type of chemical dependency treatment available* at the Orofino prison and none of the Idaho officials or parole board were responsive to his repeated pleas to either have such programming established or to have him transferred to a facility that could provide the treatment that was being demanded of him by the parole board. Jim has since been transferred to the Montana Department of Corrections where he can obtain the treatment demanded of him, but it is worth noting that it took the Idaho Department officials two years to finally heed his cries (which were joined by concerned supporters on the outside) and those two years alone cost the tax payers from $50 to $80 thousand. Jim's situation was not unique. He is just another Indian in prison. Oh, and what for? Not for a crime, by the way. He is there for drinking in violation of parole stipulations after having served time for any crime he may have committed in the past. No new offense. No new crime — only for drinking. They are *your* tax dollars.

8. It should be noted that these Twelve Steps in the Native Way were contrived strictly as an *alternative* for Indians in prisons where AA is "encouraged" by prison officials who at the same time resist the development of substance abuse programs that are suitable for Indians.

9. Gestalt Psychology is defined as "the school of thought that emphasize[s] the importance of studying the whole — that the properties of the parts depend on their relation to the whole" (Saccuzzo, 1987:14).

10. This failure of the mainstream U.S.A. to acknowledge holistic concepts (realities) can be seen by turning to the medical model's view of criminality as a "'sickness' which could be treated, and the offender as a person who, once treated, could be returned to the community cured of his *social* disease" (White, 1989:31) (emphasis added). To face the holistic reality of the situation, one must begin by acknowledging the possibility that social diseases are manifested by the societies in which they manifest, rather than isolating the "sickness" from that society in an attempt to examine it. As noted by Pedigo (1983:274), "the holistic [Gestalt] value system necessary for tribal existence cannot regulate behavior where daily life is controlled by a society with an isolationistic value system." And I note that prior to the disruption of our tribal cultures by Anglo influence, we had no need of prisons.

11. It should be understood that I am not suggesting that Gestalt Psychology as applied in the contemporary field is suitable for Indians, because it is not. Definitionally (see note 9 above) and theoretically, Gestalt Psychology suggests a holistic approach to analysis; however, the application of Gestalt therapeutic techniques can hardly be said to exemplify holism. For example, the Gestalt therapist places emphasis on the immediate present — the here and now — while consciously rejecting both past and future. This cannot be done in the application of a truly holistic-oriented theory or philosophy, for "*the properties of the part* [which is the present] *depend on their relation to the whole* [which includes both past and future]." If we ignore the past or neglect the future in our present, then we ultimately neglect our present responsibility for recognizing our relationship with the past and the future. It is this very negligence inherent in the dominant society's value system which causes much distress to Indian people. For example, consider the rejection of the future consequences of raping and

poisoning the earth for a present dollar bill. When our grandchildren have been robbed of their inheritance of a healthy environment to live in as a result of our present negligence and irresponsibility, and when they go to seek help for their distress, will the Gestalt therapist have an adequate solution in striving to have our grandchildren block out their past (our present), upon which their well-being (our future) depends?

REFERENCES

Abu-Jamal, Mumia (1989) "Revolutionary Literature = Contraband." *Journal of Prisoners on Prisons*, 2 (1):25–30.

Albaugh, B. and Anderson, P.O. (1974) "Peyote in the Treatment of Alcoholism among American Indians." *American Journal of Psychiatry*, 131:1247–1250.

Alcoholics Anonymous (1976) *Alcoholics Anonymous*, 3rd edition. New York: Alcoholics Anonymous World Services, Inc.

Alday, R.K. (1971) "Alcoholism versus the Southwest American Indian." *Selected Papers of the 22nd Annual Meeting*, Washington, D.C.: North American Association of Alcoholism Programs.

Beauvais, F. and La Boueff, S. (1985) "Drug and Alcohol Abuse Intervention in American Indian Communities." *International Journal of the Addictions*, 20 (1):139–171.

Bergman. R.L. (1971) "Navajo Peyote Use: Its Apparent Safety." *American Journal of Psychiatry*, 128 (6):695–99.

Bowechop, S. (1970) "The Drunken Indian." Unpublished senior thesis. School of Social Work, University of Washington.

Butterfield, N. (1989) "Sobriety Movement in Indian Country." *News From Indian Country: The Journal*, 3 (10):25.

Carson, R.C., Butcher, J.N. and Coleman, J.C. (1988) *Abnormal Psychology and Modern Life*, eighth edition, Glenview: Foreman and Co.

Ferguson, M.F. (1976) "Stake Theory as an Explanatory Device in Navajo Alcoholism Response." *Human Organization*, 35:66–75.

French, L. and Hornbuckle, J. (1982) "Indian Alcoholism." *Indians and Criminal Justice*.

Grobsmith, E.S. (1989a) "The Relationship Between Substance Abuse and Crime Among Native Americans in the Nebraska Department of Corrections." *Human Organization*.

———. (1989b) "The Revolving Door: Parole, Recidivism and Treatment Issues among Incarcerated Native Americans, Parolees and Ex-Offenders." *Plains Anthropologist*.

———. (1987) Testimony in the case of *Perry Wounded Shield* v. *Frank 0. Gunter*, Civil No. 85-L-459, U.S. District Court for the District of Nebraska, Lincoln.

Guajardo, E.A. (n.d.) "Cultural Differences and Counseling with Minorities: Native Americans, Black, Hispanics and Asian Americans." Paper prepared for the United States Air Force, Albuquerque.

Hall, R. (1986) "Alcohol Treatment in American Indian Populations: An Indigenous Treatment Modality Compared with Traditional Approaches." *Alcohol and Culture: Comparative Perspectives from Europe and America*.

Hanson, A.V. (1983) "Film Documents Indian Religious Ceremonies in Prisons." *Minnesota Daily — University of Minnesota*, Friday, August 5.

Heath, D.B., Waddell, J.C. and Trapper, M.D. (eds.) (1981) *Cultural Factors in Alcohol Research and Treatment of Drinking Problems*, New Brunswick: Rutgers Ctr. Alcohol.

Jilek, W.G. (1974) "Indian Healing Power: Indigenous Therapeutic Practices in the Pacific Northwest." *Psychiatric Annals*, 4(11):13–21.

Jilek, W.G. and Jilek-Aall, L. (1972) "Transcultural Psychotherapy with Salish Indians." *Transcultural Psychiatric Research Review*, 9 (1):58–62.

Jilek-Aall, L. (1974) "Psychosocial Aspects of Drinking among Coast Salish Indians." *Canadian Psychiatric Association Journal*, 19 (4):357–361.

Johnson, L.T. (1988) "Healing Spirits: Indian Spiritual Counselor Helps Inmates Regain Traditions." *The Sunday Herald*, September 11.

Kline. J.A. and Roberts, D.C. (1973) "A Residential Alcohol Treatment Program for American Indians. " *Quarterly Journal of Studies on Alcoholism*, 34:860–868.

Leon, R.L. (1968) "Some Implications for a Preventive Program for American Indians." *American Journal of Psychiatry*, 125:232–236.

Lex, B.W. (1985) "Alcohol Problems in Special Populations." *The Diagnosis and Treatment of Alcoholism*, 2nd edition. New York: McGraw-Hill Book Co.

——. (1987) "Review of Alcohol Problems in Ethnic Minority Groups" *Journal of Consulting and Clinical Psychology*, 55 (3):293–300.

Mail, P.D. and McDonald, D.R. (1981) *Tulapai to Tokay: A Bibliography of Alcohol Use and Abuse among Native Americans of North America*, New Haven, CT: HRAF Press.

McCook, L. (1989) "Whatever We Do Will Have Great Impact on Lives to Come." *The American Indian in the White Man's Prisons: A Story of Genocide*, (In press).

Miller, M. and Ostendorf, D. (n.d.) "Indian Mental Health Programs." Paper prepared by the Tribal Guidance Center, White Mountain Apache Reservation.

Native American Rights Fund (1978) *Operations Guide Manual for the Cheyenne River Swift Bird Project*, Prepared for the Cheyenne River Sioux Tribe.

Navajo Nation (1989) *Amicus Curiae Brief in Support of Plaintiff's Motion for Summary Judgment in the case of George Roybal et al* v. *Gary W. DeLand, et al.*, Civil No. C-87-0208A, U.S. District Court for the District of Utah, Central Division, Salt Lake City.

Pascarona, P., Futterman, S. and Halsweig, M. (1976) "Observations of Alcoholics in the Peyote Ritual: A Pilot Study." *Annals of the New York Academy of Sciences*, 273:518–24.

Pedigo J. (1983) "Finding the 'Meaning' of Native American Substance Abuse: Implications for Community Prevention." *The Personnel and Guidance Journal*, January:273–77.

Price, J.A. (1983) "Applied Analysis of North American Indian Drinking Patterns." *Human Organization*, 34:17–26.

Provincial Native Action Committee (1974) "Native Alcoholism Programs." Unpublished report of the Provincial Native Action Committee. Edmonton, Alberta.

Reed, L.R. (1989) "The American Indian in the White Man's Prisons: A Story of Genocide." *Humanity and Society*, 13 (4):403–420.

Richardson, E.H. (1973) "The Problems of the Indian in the Affluent Society." Paper presented at Indian Health Meeting (Region E), Rapid City, SD.

Rosenstiel, A. (1989) "Suicide and Native American Adolescents." *Native Affairs*, Spring.

Roy, C., Choudhuri, A. and Irvine, D. (1970) "The Prevalence of Mental Disorders Among Saskatchewan Indians." *Journal of Cross-Cultural* Psychology, 1:383–392.

Saccuzzo, D.P. (1987) *Psychology: From Research to Applications*, Boston: Allyn and Bacon, Inc.

Scott, T.M. and Scott, K.L. (1973) *Criminal Rehabilitation ... Within and Without the Walls: With Contributions from Experts Within the Field*, Springfield: C.C. Thomas.

Seven, R. (1988) "Ritual of Rebirth: Sweat Lodge Reaffirms Indian Inmates' Heritage." *The Seattle Times/Seattle Post Intelligencer*, January 24.

Shore, J.H. (1974) "Psychiatric Epidemology among American Indians." *Psychiatric Annals*, 4 (11):56–66.

Sisco, C. (1989) "Judge Favors Indians' Sweat Lodge: Its Status is Like Prison Chapel's." *Salt Lake Tribune*, Friday, March 17.

Snake, R., Hawkins, G. and La Boueff, S. (1977) *Report on Alcohol and Drug Abuse Task Force Eleven: Alcohol and Drug Abuse*, Final Report to the American Indian Policy Review Commission, Washington, D.C.: Author.

Specktor, M. (1983) "'Spirit' Looks at Indian Inmates' Religious Rites." *St. Paul Dispatch*, Thursday, May 12.

Spotted Eagle, C. (1983) *The Great Spirit Within the Hole*, A 60-Minute documentary film produced by Spotted Eagle Productions: Minneapolis.

Stevens, S.M. (1981) "Alcohol and World View: A Study of Passamaquoddy Alcohol Use." *Cultural Factors in Alcohol Research and Treatment of Drinking Problems*, New Brunswick: Rutgers Ctr. Alcohol.

Task Force Eleven: Alcohol and Drug Abuse (1976) *Report on Alcohol and Drug Abuse*, Washington, D.C.: American Indian Policy Review Commission.

Thornton, D. (1984) "Indian Inmates Fight for Rights." *Talking Leaf*, August.

Topper, M.D. (1976) "The Cultural Approach, Verbal Plans and Alcohol Research." *Cross-Cultural Approaches to the Study of Alcohol*, M.H. Everett et al (eds.) Mouton: The Hague.

Turner, E.J. (1977) Unpublished testimony prepared for hearings by the State House Institutions Subcommittee on Alcoholism and Drug Abuse.

Underhill, R.M. (1951) "Religion among American Indians." *Annals of the American Academy of Political and Social Sciences*, 311:127–136.

United Nations (n.d.) *Human Rights: Selected Standards*, London: Amnesty International.

Wagner, R.M. (1975) "Some Pragmatic Aspects of Navajo Peyotism." *Plains Anthropologist*, 20:197–205.

Walker, D.E. (1985) A Declaration Concerning the American Indian Sweat Bath and American Indian Religion. Prepared for the Native American Rights Fund for use in *Sample* v. *Campoy, et al.*, Civ. No. 5-85-0208-LKK.

Walker, R.D. (1981) "Treatment Strategies in an Urban Indian Alcoholism Program." *Cultural Factors in Alcohol Research and Treatment of Drinking Problems*, D.B. Heath et al (eds.) New Brunswick: Rutgers Ctr. Alcohol.

Weibel-Orlando, J. (1989) "Hooked on Healing: Anthropologists, Alcohol and Intervention." *Human Organization*, 48(1).

————. (1987) "Culture-Specific Treatment Modalities: Assessing Client-to- Treatment Fit in Indian Alcoholism Programs." *Alcoholism Treatment and Prevention*, M. Cox (ed.) New York: Academic Press.

————. (1985) "Indians, Ethnicity and Alcohol: Contrasting Perspectives On the Ethnic Self and Alcohol Use or Non-Use." *The American Experience with Alcohol: Contrasting Cultural Perspectives*, L. Bennett and G. Ames (eds.) New York: Plenum.

————. (1984) "Substance Abuse among American Indian Youth: A Continuing Crisis." *Journal of Drug Issues*, Spring:313–335.

Westermeyer, J. and Neider, J. (1984) "Predicting Treatment Outcome After Ten Years among American Indian Alcoholics." *Alcoholism: Clinical and Experimental Research*, 8(2):179–184.

White, T.W. (1989) "Corrections: Out of Balance" *Federal Probation*, December:31–35.

A Clockwork Grey
Stephen Reid

T hirty years ago, in simpler times, I was sent to the penitentiary. They gave me a haircut, stitched a number above my breast pocket, and tossed me in a cell on the fish range. My biggest worry, besides my sentence, was whether I would ever get the right-sized boots.

It is the year 2000, and I am back in prison. No haircut, I have to memorize my number, and my biggest worry is whether I will get the right criminogenic index rating. The fish range is now called an Assessment Centre. They have painted murals on the concrete and renamed guards correctional officers. Prisoners have become inmates or even residents, we wear street clothes instead of blues, and there are more behaviour modification programs in here than bars.

The key to understanding the new paradigm in our prisons may lie in the corporate logo: the CSC, Correctional Service of Canada — it works both forward and backward, in both official languages. My eleven-year-old, on her first visit, saw the word "Corrections" on the ubiquitous signage, and said, "I think it should be 'Mistakes,' Dad."

My Regional Reception Assessment Centre Handbook informs me I will be here for ten to fourteen weeks, during which time I will be evaluated, assessed, analyzed, tested, probed, and profiled. A team of IPOs, C02s, psychologists and unit managers will collect, collate, graph, and interpret the data. They will determine risk factors, crime cycles, pen placement, treatment programs and how much fibre I will need in my diet. It could be argued, and convincingly, that this is the evolution of penology.

Three decades ago this system was called the Canadian Penitentiary Service, and it was not forward-looking, or working in anyone's language, so a handful of determined federal bureaucrats began to study some of the European models. They adapted them so well that Canada has become a world leader in penology. Other countries now come here to study us, even, belatedly, some Americans. The United States has gone through a twenty-five-year "devolution" and its prisons are experiencing an unprecedented level of inhumanity and brutality. The Clockwork Grey of the new CSC seems a small price to pay to preserve our country's humanity. That said, this is an evolution with an absurd edge.

Designing programs and implementing them are the two solitudes of CSC. To order someone into therapy is often to subvert the purpose.

Willingness is the key to change — you have to want it to get it. So there exists a jumping-through-hoops mentality by prisoners, and an air of resignation on the part of the staff. But in fairness, the percentage of prisoners who genuinely wish to change, and the caliber of instructors willing to help them, is much higher than the skeptics would have us believe.

My Regional Reception Assessment Centre Handbook is a humourless text, but as I read the earnest descriptions of available programs I cannot help but wonder. The Violent Offender Program? Would Billy the Kid have emerged nine months later as Billy the Inner Child? Anger Management? Could Vinnie (Mad Dog) Coll have become Vinnie (Assertive Dog) Coll? Would Bonnie and Clyde, made to enroll in Skills for a Healthy Relationship, have come to terms with their co-dependency and been granted a conjugal visit? Pushed into taking Cognitive Skills, Machine-Gun Kelly would soon identify his trigger thoughts. Ma Barker, in her seventh week of Family Violence Circle, might have reached the stunning conclusion she had been a life-long enabler.

I am ahead of myself. Before anyone reaches their inner child or enabling self, they have to take tests. Lots of tests. It is tests that drive the modern personal correctional plan.

My favourite so far has been the 560-odd questionnaire called the Minnesota Multi-Phasic Personality Index. Never mind that it has been proved culturally-biased and hopelessly-flawed, the centerfold of my "critical needs assessment" will be determined by such questions as, "Have you ever wanted to be a girl?" Think of the possibilities. Had the question been, "Have you ever wanted to be a woman?" I might have answered differently. But a girl? Did they mean a child, or a "grrrl," or is "girl" what they still call a woman in Minnesota? Think, think. If I were a "grrrl" I could have a conjugal visit with myself. No, better play it safe and mark False.

Next question, "Do you love your mother? Or if she's dead, did you?" You do not stop loving someone just because they are dead, but my mother is alive and I love her very much so I mark True.

"Do you believe you are being controlled by an unseen force?" Does this mean subliminal advertising and the all-pervasive consumer culture? I glance at the woman administering the test—she is staring back with the look of someone who thinks more along the lines of "Did Satan order you to rob that bank?" I circle False.

I am most intrigued with, "If you were a reporter, would you like to report on the theatre?" At first, this seems McCarthyesque, as in, "Would you like to keep an eye on those socialist homosexual so-called actors?" Of course it could also mean if you were a reporter would you not prefer to report on child poverty or political corruption? In other words, something substantial. But, I like the theatre! Besides, if it is good theatre it deals with child poverty and political corruption. Stop thinking, just answer the question. Okay, True. I will be a pansy art critic. At least I did not say I wanted to be a girl, even if I did.

"Would you like to be a florist?" No, no, no. Read my lips. Give me some questions on hockey here, or how about them Blue Jays, eh? I handed in my test, unfinished. I figured if I did not have a personality they would assign me one.

Next came the real pick of the litter, the Psychopathy Checklist Revised. It determines, unequivocally, whether you are a psychopath or not. I remember John Gray, our John Gray, the playwright, not the Venus and Mars guy, interviewing the author of this test. John used the doctor's own statistics to extrapolate the fact that there had to be, at minimum, 40,000 psychopaths living in British Columbia. With a couple of hundred locked away in prisons, that still left 39,800-odd psychos at large. The good doctor reassured John these were people who put their psychopathy to good use. They lived productive, well-adjusted lives as surgeons, CEOs and ambulance drivers.

The light bulb went on. The CSC does not have to go through all these gyrations to reprogram anyone, they just have to find every prisoner the right job.

Psychos become CEOs. Bookmakers could work for the 6/49 Lotto Corp. The government weenies currently running SportsAction are rank amateurs compared with real bookmakers. The action would double in three months.

Small-time drug dealers could be issued white smocks and put behind the pharmacy counter. Dispensing fees are ten times the mark-up on an eightball of cocaine. A B&E artist would slip like a crowbar into the home security business. In custom-protecting your home he could charge you more for alarm systems than what he could steal from your house, anyway.

The weight pit crews, all pumped up and tattooed down, could be recruited for *World Wrestling Federation Raw*. They would take wrestling to new levels, and earn as much as $10,000 a night, just for being themselves. Even those criminals too corrupt or too incorrigible to be anything else could hang out a shingle and practice law. The worst that could happen is nobody would notice.

But the CSC is not an employment agency. Its self-determined mandate is to reconcile the twin pillars of punishment and rehabilitation, a difficult enough task without the public, political, and media scorn. It takes a certain brand of courage — some would call foolhardy, some would call moral — to continue to pursue a humanitarian vision of corrections, but to abandon course now would surely be a "Mistakes."

In simpler times, on that fish range thirty years ago, I was celled with a young man, one of the last to get the paddle. One of his memories, besides the scars on his skin, was of being bound at the ankles and wrists and having a hood pulled over his head. He was the last of a dozen men that day, and he remembers the hood, the inside, being slick with the mucous and spittle and blood from the broken lips of those who went before him.

I have spent years in U.S. prisons, and more years here inside. I have observed the public mood in this country. I know the CSC vision is all that stands between me and a black hood filled with the blood and the fear of my fellow prisoners.

A Decade of Diesel Therapy in the Floriduh Gulag
Gerald Niles

INTRODUCTION

In 1979, in the Wapello County Jail in Ottumwa, Iowa, prisoners were allowed to sit and visit with family and friends in a normal manner. Suddenly, plexiglass barriers were installed, with a telephone receiver on each side. The prisoner stood on one side of the plexiglass while visitors peered through the other side. The prisoner could speak with one visitor at a time on the receiver, hardly conducive to family visits. I wrote the local newspaper editor in an attempt to publicize this ridiculous situation. My intent was that prisoners would know that their plight had been publicized, people in the community would realize the way their taxes dollars were being wasted, and jailers would know that their implemented abnormality was exposed and that no one was pleased with their actions. Or so I hoped.

In the winter of 1998–99, construction of a new jail in Ottumwa was frozen like the ice, because the public finally balked at the further expenditure of public funds. Possibly my letter to the editor two decades earlier sowed the seeds of this current public indignation in the farming State of Iowa. Certainly my letter started a chain of events in which I am still enveloped. In the past decade I have been subjected to a tour of the Floriduh gulag via "diesel therapy". This retaliatory ploy by prison officials relies upon multiple transfers to quell prisoners' resistance. My response is to publicized this carceral practice as played out in Floriduh.

*****

For me, a primary means of resistance to mistreatment or abusive conditions has been litigation; sometimes in the courts and often via the prison system's own grievance procedures. Prison officials do not like having their gregarious conduct corrected by captives. A typical and unlawful response is to transfer the prisoner in retaliation. For every prison transfer there is an official reason which rarely reflects the real reason. I will stick to the "truth". I am no fiction writer.

A current denizen of any of the "joints" named herein will quickly observe changes that have occurred since I was there. Some places like the Leon County Jail in Tallahasse, Florida (circa 1990) do not even exist anymore. It had to be shut down. Furthermore, turnovers of populations, construction or logistic overhauls can give a prison a facelift overnight.

In 1990, the jail in Tallahasse contained the "Bundy Slammer". During my 11 months in that jail, a few months were spent in that "slammer". On visiting day, I could look out the little window in the door at the butts of visitors to the cell block across the hall. One day, a young lady broke into tears upon learning that she stood next to the cell which had held the ghostly Bundy. A deputy provided solace. "There, there, he's dead now ..."

The day came for my commitment to the "floriduh department of corruption". For six weeks there was processing at the North Florida Reception Centre (NFRC) Main Unit. Each prisoner was administered a battery of mental, physical, and psychological tests, so prisoncrats could formulate ideas concerning the type of creatures that were now in their custody. In 1991, NFRC guards routinely beat prisoners. Countless times I saw a prisoner handcuffed and then pounced on by a gang of guards, before being dragged across the compound. Docility Training! A beating might be meted out for not having a top shirt button buttoned, for not looking straight ahead when commanded to, for "stealing" four packs of sugar from one's breakfast tray, or innumerable petty offenses. The terror lay in not knowing what they would decide to define as an infraction. During head count, prisoners had to sit for hours on their bunks, never daring to flinch, or else! Days were spent in the yard, under the sun, evenings in open dorms where TV viewers faced directly into the shower room. Of course any grievance there would be construed as a "request for a beating".

In the summer of 1991, with a group of other captives I was crammed onto a Bluebird Bus refitted for prison transport; a big cage on wheels. If you are lucky enough to sit next to one of the eight windows (in order to breathe), you can stare through heavy mesh as obscured swamps and pine trees fly by. After an overnight stay in the South Florida Reception Centre at Miami, we wearily rolled out to be deposited in the "sweet kamp" at Avon Park. I spent nearly two years there, watching snitches have foot races to see who could tell first and child molesters brag about it being "their camp". They were safe there, and could only molest each other, having no other options. The "sweet kamps" are supposed to be considered privileged locales, and any dissent is most unwelcome. Eventually I was doomed to dungeon Hardee, because my grievances never sat well with prisoncrats at Avon Park. Prison officials at Avon Park were determined to enforce the pettiest rules. However, when a prisoner utilized grievance procedures and filed civil suits to compel them to follow their own policies, the gestapo reeled off the reprisals.[1] I never let them run things unchecked. No one could call me a happy camper. I could never be happy in prison.

In dungeon Hardee "plenty" of legal action was necessary; we contested property seizures to beatings. Litigation in this prison led to the turnover of the entire administration. It was precisely "because I brought legal action" that I was shipped to DeSoto, a fragile regime. After only five weeks (my request for an inter-State transfer to Iowa was supposedly denied), I was on the Bluebird again. DeSoto was another a "sweet kamp" and would tolerate no complaints. After a few days back at SFRC Miami, I was taken back to NFRC Lake Butler. There I was given the opportunity to observe guards beat up several prisoners — always one at a time, of course.

In the summer of 1994, at midnight, I met TRANSCOR, a private prison transportation corporation. In vans, shackled hand and foot, for the next five days and nights we dropped prisoners off and picked prisoners up at jails and prisons in Florida, Georgia, South Carolina, North Carolina, Tennessee, Kentucky, Illinois, and finally Iowa. There were no overnight stays for rest. Meals were the cheapest possible fare from fast food outlets. When we dropped a guy at the jail in Iowa City, I overheard the TRANSCOR guards discuss going to Wisconsin and Minnesota before my destination, which I knew to be the Iowa Medical and Classification Centre, two miles from where we sat. It took considerable persuasion to convince the guards of this. They would not believe it until verified by local jailers and the personnel at Burger King.

By this time, aggressive litigation had become a bad habit. Iowa prisoncrats, being no different than any other species of guards, reacted with no less than nine bogus disciplinary reports. "The first and most serious charge is rioting ..." began the judge. "What does that mean?" I interrupted. Reading from the Department of Corrections' own definition, the judge began, "Three or more ..." I interrupted again. "Because I am the only person charged and because I am only one person, this charge is as invalid as the other eight". The judge agreed, found me not guilty of three charges and dismissed the other six.

So in typical "sore loser" fashion, the gestapo changed my confinement status to "administrative", which can be based upon any reason or none at all. Soon I learnt of their plan. The worst prison in Iowa was better than the best prison in Floriduh, so the worst thing they could do to me was to send me back. So they did, via TRANSCOR, with overnight stays in jails in Jamestown, North Dakota; Dodge, Wisconsin; and Ashland, Tennessee. The Jamestown jail was small and new. TRANSCOR guards made us leave our smokes in the van, telling us that it was a non-smoking institution. We were surprised to walk into the little cellblock and see ashtrays on the tables. In Minnesota we picked up a crack addict who became sick from withdrawal, so he was dropped off in a hospital in Dodge, while we spent the night in a local jail. There were more bodies than beds, so half of us bedded down on the floor. Our next stop, Ashland City, Tennessee, is the dirtiest jail I have ever seen. The walls were smeared with faeces and maggots. Though we had no clean clothes we wanted to shower. In the shower, sewage seeped out of the drain, so in the end it was more sanitary not to bathe. The whole trip took five days. It was not easy eating fast food in full shackles, and we were too cramped and weary to even appreciate the scenery; especially that provided by the jails and prisons at which we stopped.

In the mid-August heat, I was deposited back at the North Florida Reception for further classification. I remained there for 100 days, during which I wrote two accounts of "Iron Fists Striking", for *Prison News Service*. These articles described the increasing frenzy with which guards were ganging up on individual prisoners; chaining, kicking, dragging and stomping them. Some devil had robbed those poor guards of their consciences, and to this day I wonder whatever came around for them.

Just in time for Christmas 1994, I was shipped to Baker prison. It was cold in the cells, there was no heat. So I joined in a civil suit against the prison. They reacted with a half dozen bogus infractions, and when I still refused to drop the lawsuit they shipped me to Columbia prison. The Floriduh DOC had recently rewritten its policy for long-term solitary confinement and begun their construction blitz of new Control Model units. The new policy made assigning prisoners to these units much easier. Based upon the bogus disciplinary reports from Baker prison, I qualified for 13 months in the control unit at Columbia.

After five months, Columbia changed the unit's regime, and as a result I was transferred with a group of others to the control unit at Taylor. After a month in Taylor, I won release from the control unit by having the Baker prison disciplinary reports invalidated by an outside court. I was in open population in Taylor for only ten days, when guards threatened to put their boots on my throat for asking a question during orientation. I was immediately locked up for being a threat to security. Three weeks later I was shipped down the road to Cross City prison, where kinfolks of the Taylor guards were employed. The first day in Cross City, a guard came to me and threatened to carry out what his brother in Taylor had started. More kinfolk joined the fray with assorted threats. In Dixie County, Florida, always beware of the incestuous _____ Clan, who must breed faster than rabbits.

I reported the Cross City assault to the Warden and was locked up at once for being a threat to security; as if you could not guess by now. After a few weeks in a cell with the paedophilic son of a prison guard, I was shipped to Gulf prison. Ten months in Gulf brought umpteen bogus infraction charges, and when I beat all of those, the guards planted a knife in my cell. I was found guilty of possession and spent 60 days in the "box". They committed battery against me a few times, once while Warden Henry Alford watched. I considered every dirty work they meted out to be their admission of defeat. My litigious actions increased.

On June 17, 1997, I was shipped to the new super maximum Control Model Unit at Santa Rosa prison. Although the "shank" charges served to justify my transfer to Santa Rosa, the conviction had already been reversed on appeal. Therefore, the Santa Rosa officials kept me on indefinite confinement status, each week assuring me that they would hold the necessary hearing the next week. After three months I tired of the game and sued. About the same time, I was moved to attend the federal jury trial in the Baker prison "heat" suit. The jury ruled that it was okay for Floriduh prisoners to freeze in their cells. I pondered this in light of my summer of baking in Santa Rosa's hotbox. Later, a State Judge ordered Santa Rosa officials to hold a Control Model review hearing or release me to the open population.

Upon return to Santa Rosa I was released to the open prison population. So that regime and I rock 'n' rolled on litigation and the inevitable assaults by guards that followed. I litigated to get yard time, a laundry operation, a library, usurious canteen prices reduced, and a myriad of other claims. When the threats by guards came, I reported it to prison officials and they did nothing. So I went to outside law enforcement agencies for relief. Rather than act against their own assaultive guards, I was shipped to Marion prison to take a drug treatment program.

At Marion I was able to establish that I had never used alcohol or drugs, therefore invalidating their justification for the transfer. They were unhappy at my refusal to participate because it meant the loss of per enrollment federal funding. They really sell the program hard; for example, the participants are rewarded with the best prison jobs. The incredible part is that the programming consists of nothing more than the gruesome behaviour modification tactics well known to all of us here. So they did their worst and sent me back to Santa Rosa prison. The trip was pretty much a waste of nine weeks. I caught two colds and they were hot!

After four months back at Santa Rosa they asked if I wanted to go to DOC cooking school at Quincy prison. I said "no thanks". So they sent me anyway. Sitting here now pondering the various cells, bunks, and "holes" (CMs) in 17 prisons I have visited at least once for an overnight stay, I suspect that my travels through the Floriduh gulag have not come to an end. I guess they have 50 more jails and prisons I may yet visit during my life sentence. Then I will be able to say "Now I have seen them all"!

Editor's Note: The next correspondence we received from Gerald Niles was dated November 19, 1999. He wrote:

> *Finally Quincy got rid of me. There are three prisons in this Hamilton complex. Things are going okay. By that I mean Resistance is progressive. I have been getting back into advocacy here.*

Since then, Gerald has continued his travels.

NOTES

1. For an elaboration of the revenge tactic schematics of the Floriduh penal staff, see: Niles, G. "Submission, Subservience, Model Inmates and the Fear Factor: Observations from a Sweet Kamp down Florida Way", *JPP*, 1993, vol. 4:2, 111–114; Gaucher, B. "Editor's Introduction", *JPP*, 1993, vol. 5:1, 2–3.

Monochromes from over a Prison's Edge
Victor Hassine

GOOD OLD CHEROKEE

Wgghen was the last time you gave any thought to going crazy, living crazy or dying crazy? Chances are, you have never thought of these things at all, insanity being something that happens to other people. That was pretty much how I thought about it, that is, until I landed in prison. Even after I had been in prison for sometime, I never considered my mental health at risk, as I had focused all my attention and efforts on keeping myself physically intact. Only after having overcome the physical level of prison survival did I discover the next more challenging issue, that of maintaining sanity. This part of the American prison experience involves overcoming the effects of a forced and steady march toward insanity.

Most convicts ultimately avoid the final destruction of this involuntary journey, *but* the journey itself leaves scars on those prisoners fortunate enough to survive the physical dangers, only to be thrust into a continuous struggle to keep all of one's wits. As I reflect upon this harsh reality of contemporary prisons, I find it odd that any nation which, on the one hand, applauds the mental achievements of its people, operates a criminal justice system designed, in the end, to drive every citizen who is confined in prison crazy.

My first encounter with prison induced insanity came when I first met Cherokee, who, at the time, was Graterford's most esteemed prisoner. As I was beginning my life sentence in 1981, Cherokee had already served more than 40 years of his. Sometime during this extraordinarily long period of incarceration, the staff at Graterford had ceased seeing him as a prisoner and had, in their eyes, elevated him to something akin to a mascot. To the other prisoners he was not a convict, but a part of the prison like the bricks and mortar. Mascot or fixture, neither seems a fitting way to treat another human being who was doing nothing more than what the State demanded of him.

The first time I met Cherokee, he was swinging the upper half of his body up and out of a large stuffed prison trash can. He had been scavenging in the refuse and was now surfacing with a handful of treasure. It just so happened at the same time I was standing directly in front of him with only the dirty container between us. Having lived in New York, the sight of a man mining in garbage was hardly shocking, and I do not believe I paid him much attention but, I guess, in Cherokee's mind I was paying attention.

This old man with his hands gripping a load of garbage instantly produced a genuine smile that was overflowing with sincerity. He quickly placed his valuables into a large plastic bag that was made to stand at his side by the collection of junk that had been stacked in its enclosure. I then found myself engaged in a conversation.

"Why hello. You must be a new fellow. My name's Cherokee," he said.

Cherokee stood over six feet tall and sported a pot belly which pushed forcefully against his tight and dirty prison uniform. His hair was a dingy yellow and white, which had the appearance of straw standing up and being blown away from the head that hopelessly anchored it. His teeth matched the colour of his hair and were fully displayed by his smile. Despite this unappetizing appearance, the friendliness and gentility he exuded, obliged a courteous response.

"My name is Victor," is all I could think to say.

His puffy cheeks swelled almost breaking out of his round face as his lips spread wider to extend the smile. "You don't get many Victors in here," he said melodiously, the voice matching the smile. "You look like such a nice young fellow. You don't look like you belong in here." At this point he had made me a friend for life.

Cherokee looked down at his bag of junk which seemed as dishevelled and well fed as he. Then he said, "You'd be surprised how much good stuff I find around here, like cups and shoes and socks. Why, once I found me a pretty good coat. Wasn't nothing wrong with it. I gave it to another young fellow who didn't have one to wear." Then he chuckled, "You young folks today seem to like to throw things away."

I wanted to say something but I did not know what so I just nodded and he continued to speak. "I give a lot of stuff away to anyone who needs it. You know how fellows can get down on their luck. So if you got anything you want to throw out, you be sure to let old Cherokee know. And you don't have to worry about me, I'm okay. Everybody knows me. Just ask anyone about Cherokee."

After saying this, he picked up his bag and began to lumber off in the direction of another trash can which was also overflowing with garbage. After taking a few steps, he stopped, turned around and said, "Oh, did I tell you I collect stamps? If you get any, I hope you'll give them to me. I'll stop around your cell." With that, the man and his garbage moved on.

Throughout my stay at Graterford, I often saw Cherokee. Usually he was digging his way into a trash can or dumpster, but sometimes he would stop by my cell and ask if I had any stamps he could have. I would give him all the cancelled stamps from the letters I had received, and this seemed to make him very happy. Once in a while I offered him some cigarettes, candy or coffee, but he refused to accept anything as if I had insulted him simply by making an offer. What I ended up doing was putting some commissary items in a brown bag, then when he would come by my cell I would give him the bag to "throw out for me." He would always take the bag and never say a word. His smile was all that needed to be said.

There was no doubt that Cherokee had lost his senses and might not have even been aware that he was in prison. But it was not Cherokee's odd behaviour which made him noteworthy, it was the way the prison administration treated him. Cherokee stood out in a prison world of misfits because his keepers wanted him to stand out.

Cherokee was allowed free run of the prison to forage anywhere at anytime. The only requirement being to return to his cell for the 9:00 p.m. count. He needed no pass to get anywhere in the prison and his cell was only locked at 9:00 p.m. He could eat anything he wanted from the kitchen and staff members would often give him candybars and snacks purchased from a prison vending machine. It was unlikely that any prisoner would say an unkind word or in any way threaten Cherokee because if the guards did not get-him, the prisoners certainly would. This treatment of a prisoner in a maximum security prison is extraordinary.

At first I did not give much thought to the special treatment Cherokee was receiving, after all he had spent an un-Godly amount of time in Graterford and his seniority had entitled him to some consideration. Besides, he was a harmless old man who was kind, likeable and not likely to escape even if all of the prison walls were to come tumbling down. The sad reality was that Cherokee's home was Graterford.

Before long, I became suspicious of the institution's altruism toward Cherokee, which began when I met other men who had served as much, if not more time in prison than Cherokee. The institution chose to treat these men as they would any other prisoner. There were no special privileges. Naturally, I wondered why Cherokee had been singled out by the prison administration to receive the benefit of their kindness.

The prison administration's motives became more apparent once I realized that tolerance of Cherokee's odd behaviour was not really a form of kindness or humanitarianism. If prison managers wanted to do the decent thing by Cherokee, they should have sent him to a better prison or helped him to get a commutation of his sentence so he could be committed to a nursing home. All these things were possible. Even if they were not, the least that should have been done was to provide Cherokee with adequate mental health care. Somehow, to allow this harmless old man to live out his life bobbing for goodies-in-prison trash cans does not reflect kindness or decency, but, is in fact, degradation and humiliation, regardless whether Cherokee had the sense to know it or not."

This understanding led to the realization that Cherokee's privileges were not primarily meant to benefit him. These measures were calculated to advance a prison interest, displaying the administration's vision of the model prisoner.

The prison system had invested over 40 years to hammer, bend, fold, shape and, in the end, rehabilitate Cherokee. In their eyes, they had achieved their purpose. The old convict was obedient, functional, low maintenance, harmless, completely dependent and not likely to injure another human being. What more could a prison want? It made no difference that in the process of rehabilitating Cherokee and making him the perfect prisoner, he had become mad. But Cherokee had to be punished for his crime, and forfeiting his sanity was a small price to pay for achieving Graterford's version of redemption.

So what passed for kindness was actually inducements for others to conform to the lifestyle of the model prisoner. Certainly, staff members had grown a fondness for Cherokee and their relationship to him contained an element of affection, but in a prison, fondness always stands a distant second to control. Cherokee was a poor, helpless and unwitting pawn in a prison's endless scheme to control its prisoners.

Understandably, it is difficult for anyone who has not felt the pinch of prison shackles to believe that an American governmental bureaucracy would knowingly induce human beings to abandon their senses and become mindless dependents reduced to searching for their piece of the American Dream somewhere in the dirty darkness of a prison trash can. But, if you were the warden of an overcrowded prison plagued with violence, corruption, drugs, disease and perpetual lack of resources, Cherokee's fat and smiling face, fresh out of a trash can to respectfully greet you might secretly tempt you to pray that every one of your prisoner charges would somehow become as respectful, obedient and well-behaved as Cherokee.

I Think I'm Going Crazy

It is always getting harder to find time alone in a prison's general population. Overcrowding has seen to that. So whenever I find an opportunity to be by myself, I exploit it. I remember one hot summer day in 1988 when the heat was so oppressive that few prisoners bothered to venture out into the small area of dirt and dust shamelessly designated as the prison recreation yard.

In the early 1980s, some prisonocrat had developed an ingenious plan to renovate Pennsylvania's oldest penitentiary in use by building a new 500-cell, 1,000-bed housing unit within its walls. More specifically, the plan called for three phases. The first phase called for building the new housing units in the main recreation yard of Pittsburgh Penitentiary which was also known as Western. The second phase called for shutting down the old housing units at Western and converting them to a massive counselling and work complex. The third and final phase called for the demolition of the existing work and counselling building and the construction of a larger recreation yard and field house.

By early 1988, the first phase of the plan was completed and Western had lost its recreation yard and gained 500 new cells. Unfortunately, funding for phases two and three had dried up and the oldest functioning prison in the state now held twice as many prisoners. Western had become the most densely populated prison in the state.

There I was that hot summer day looking for some privacy in a walkway running between the various housing units that the prison administrators of Western had designated "the main yard". This yard had no grass, no space and no room to exercise. All that remained was a long, crooked concrete walk flanked on both sides by parallel strips of dirt which had a few bleachers intermittently placed wherever they could fit.

Finding any unoccupied space under these circumstances was usually impossible. But this day, because of the stifling heat and burning sun, the yard was completely empty, so I hurried to a remote spot and sat on one of the scorching bleachers. This was a small price to pay for privacy. I closed my eyes and forgot the discomfort as I slowly drifted off into myself.

Before I had a chance to fully appreciate my solitude, I felt a tap on my shoulder accompanied by a voice. "Victor, I need to talk with you," the voice said with urgency.

Normally, I would have ignored the voice until it moved away. But I recognized the voice as belonging to one of the more respected and honourable men in the prison. I had known this man at Graterford before I had been transferred to Western Penitentiary. He was a prison gangster who did not take a lot of nonsense from anyone. But he was also a fair and reasonable man who only challenged those who tried to interfere with his space. His name was Kareem. While I numbered him as one of my friends, I nevertheless made it a point to stay out of his way. Realizing it was Kareem and recognizing the urgency in his voice, my eyes immediately sprung open as my thoughts were instantly refocused on the moment and I felt danger was near.

"What's going on, Kareem?" I asked fully alert and expecting to learn there was trouble on the way.

Kareem must have detected my concern so he adjusted his voice. "No, it ain't nothing like that, there ain't no trouble. I just need to talk with you about something personal," he said.

My body was still racing with the adrenalin his initial statement had produced. I was too aroused and anticipating to be able to do anything else but listen to what he had to say. Soon Kareem was sitting next to me on the bleachers. We were the only two men foolish enough to brave the yard. The sun had chased the other 2,300 prisoners indoors.

"What can I do for you?" I asked a little annoyed but nevertheless interested. Kareem was not the sort to waste anyone's time.

"I'm going crazy, Victor, I'm losing my shit," he blurted out as his eyes hawkishly searched our surroundings.

"What do you mean?" I asked surprised and uncertain about the nature and direction of this conversation.

Kareem's dark brown eyes were soon on me, wide and piercing as he explained, "I've been hearing voices. I know they're not real, but I hear them anyway."

What was I to do? I was sitting in a prison yard burning under a hot sun and listening to a man tell me he was hearing voices. Prison life has taught me to be prepared for anything, and so I collected my thoughts as I slowly leaned back to rest against an upper row of bleachers. Then I calmly asked, "What do these voices say?"

Kareem must have detected my look of resignation because he immediately relaxed and allowed his muscles to uncoil. "They tell me to do stupid stuff. You wouldn't believe it. I don't do any of them. I just hear the voices," he said.

My curiosity had been peaked and I realized I had the opportunity to talk to a man who was on the verge of some mental breakdown. For some reason, the mechanics leading to this breakdown interested me. "Yeah, prison will make a man hear voices. It's a shame what they do to a man in here."

"Isn't that the truth?" he answered, sounding relieved that I understood his problem. "I've seen lots of old heads lost their shit but I never thought it would happen to me."

"Well, maybe it's just a temporary thing and will go away. You're a strong man. You can beat this," I suggested with confidence.

"No, man, I don't think so. I can feel myself flipping in and out. I tried to fight it a couple of times but my mind just keeps snapping — I'm just going crazy," he chuckled.

Hearing him laugh about his predicament encouraged me to get personal. "What do you think brought this on?" I asked.

"Nobody in my family's crazy — it has to be this prison. The time is getting to me. I've been doing this bit for a long time," he said.

Kareem had served over 20 years of a life sentence and his prison escapades made commutation less than a remote possibility. For a minute I reasoned that maybe he was a drug abuser whose mind just suddenly surrendered to his addiction. Almost as if Kareem knew my thoughts he said, "All my life I've avoided drinking and doing drugs because I'd seen what it did to other people. Now look at me anyway," he said in disgust.

"I don't know what to tell you, Kareem. Sane or insane, these people want their time out of you. You're going to have to fight this thing," I told him.

"You know, I've done a lot of time in the hole. When I started my bit I didn't care nothing about going to the hole, but these last few times, they were real rough," Kareem said as if ignoring what I had just said to him.

"What happened in the hole?" I asked.

"Nothing this last time," he answered, "but just being down there with these guards messing with you and all that time alone. I think I started slipping while I was in the hole," he announced.

"Did you hear these voices in the hole?" I asked.

"No. I just started hearing these voices. When I was in the hole, I didn't hear nothing. I'm not good with reading so I just sat in my cell sleeping and thinking," he explained.

"You think the hole made you crazy?" I asked.

Kareem thought for a moment. "No. I don't think it was the hole alone, I think it's everything put together. You know, doing time ain't no joke," he answered.

"No it isn't," I agreed.

"And you know what is the most amazing thing about all this?" Kareem asked with the animation of a little child who was eager to share a secret. "The way it just kind of crept up on me. One minute I was normal and then the next minute I was bugging out in my cell talking to myself. I didn't know going crazy could snatch me from behind like that," he confessed.

There was then a long silence between us as if neither of us knew the other was there. Both of us had a lot to think about.

"You're doing a life bit too, aren't you?" Kareem asked.

"Yeah, I got eight in and that's killing me. I can imagine how you feel," I answered.

"No you can't and you really don't want to," he cautioned firmly. "Don't you worry about any of these motherfuckers messing with you. You just make sure you hold on to your mind. Don't let these people sneak up behind you and snatch your shit," he said as he reached out with his hand and made like he was grabbing at something in the air.

"Nobody deserves to be treated like that. They might as well have killed me," were Kareem's last words as he got up and left me alone on the bleacher. Suddenly I didn't feel much like being alone. I realized I would never forget my conversation with Kareem.

It Happens All the Time

Tony was my neighbour when I was at Graterford. I met him the first day I entered general population. He was a tall rectangular man who cast an imposing shadow into my cell. His thick black, well-trimmed beard with matching neatly-groomed hair gave his block of a body a crown of sophistication. "If you need to know anything about this joint, just ask me. My name's Tony and I live a few cells down," I remember him telling me as I was sorting through my belongings.

There was much I needed to know about my new home and Tony was more than willing to instruct me. He had read about my case in the paper and knew I had knowledge of the law, this is what motivated him to be as helpful to me as possible. Nothing is free in prison, and the price for Tony's friendship was my help with some criminal cases he was appealing. You see, Tony was a jailhouse lawyer. Every morning he hung a paper sign up in front of his cell announcing, "LEGAL AID."

His cell was arranged as much as possible, considering its location, like a small office. The steel desk mounted on one side of his cell had all the necessary office supplies and adornments including a manual typewriter. Alongside his desk was a makeshift chair, assembled out of stacked boxes and old newspapers. The chair stood alongside the entrance to his cell so a client didn't have to enter too far into his home in order to conduct business. On a shelf above his desk and peppered throughout his cell were big thick law books which completed the statement he was trying to make.

Tony was admittedly no legal wizard, and when asked what he did for a living he would proudly and without hesitation announce, "I rob banks." Tony explained helping people out with their legal work kept him busy and his cell filled with commissary. He was doing 15 to 30 years so he had plenty of time to occupy.

Tony was an intelligent and a well-disciplined man, so he had managed to teach himself enough about the law to recognize legal issues and fill out appeal forms. However, he lacked the ability to properly litigate an appeal to its end. In most cases, he would read a man's transcripts, fill out an appropriated appeal form and have the court appoint a real attorney for his client. For these services he would charge what he felt the man could afford; some cigarettes purchased in the commissary to a couple hundred dollars.

Tony functioned as effectively as any legal secretary I had ever known and he provided a needed service. Many men at Graterford were illiterate and the only way for them to begin the process of appealing their convictions was by using the services of a jailhouse lawyer. The reality is that most collateral appeals filed on behalf of prisoners are the product of jailhouse lawyers — a poor man's last hope for justice.

As you can imagine, there are some jailhouse lawyers who are honest and qualified and others who are con-men hoping to jilt prisoners out of money and worse yet, ruin their chances on appeal. Like the streets, the caveat "Buyer Beware" holds true in prison as well.

To his credit, Tony was a reliable man who made up in enthusiasm what he lacked in legal knowledge. Often I would refer minor cases, like parole violations and guilty pleas, to his able office. This spared me a lot of nuisance cases and made Tony very happy. Once I became his neighbour, his clientele doubled and he gained a few pounds from all the commissary cakes and candies he was eating.

Every morning before I went about my business, I would stop at Tony's cell, sit on his clients' chair and be treated to a hot cup of instant coffee and some commissary pastry. Tony and I would then chat for a half hour or more about legal issues, the prison and anything else on our minds at the time. It was always a good way to start off a morning. One afternoon while I was working at my assigned prison job as a janitor in the infirmary, I was asked by one of the nurses to escort her to the special needs unit. This unit was a small caged-in portion of the infirmary where the seriously mentally ill were housed. It was a dark and bleak place where men resembling zombies would spend their day sitting or pacing and waiting for their meals or medications to be served. These men were not allowed outdoors for exercise and some had spent years inside this forgotten limbo. ·

Female nurses liked to take a prisoner janitor with them when they made their rounds in that ward, because it made them feel safer. In turn, janitors liked to make these rounds, despite the unit's depressing conditions, because it gave them an opportunity to flirt with a woman. After all, men will be men.

As instructed, I gladly carried a tray of medication, complete with little paper cups filled with water, behind the nurse as we headed toward the special needs unit, also called D-Rear. The guard assigned to D-Rear unlocked a wire mesh gate and allowed us entry into the dark, dirty and foul-smelling unit.

Ghoulishly assembled around a large table were about twenty men eagerly waiting for the nurse to hand them their medicine. Men of all colours, sizes and shapes stared with wide-eyed expectation for the nurse to call out their name. Whenever a prisoner was called, he would slowly shuffle over to the nurse who would hand him his medication. Then I would give the man a cup of water, he would take his medication and move away somewhere into the darkness to wait for the drugs to take him away.

It was such a sad sight. I could not wait to get out of there. I did not want to be reminded that places like this existed. When the nurse finished calling all the names on her list, she told me to follow her to a patient who was not able to walk. Reluctantly, I trailed the nurse deeper into the bowels of D-Rear. Somewhere in a far corner of a common area sat a lone man obscured by shadows. Everyone else was slowly walking a tedious circle around the ward getting some recreation for the day. Here, it was too dark for me to be able to identify the man.

Looking away at the ceiling as the nurse gave the man his medication, I heard myself being asked to bring some water. I walked over and reached out with a small cup of water only to be shocked by the sight of Tony sitting motionless with drool oozing from his mouth.

"Tony, that can't be you," I called out in complete astonishment. I had had my usual morning coffee and chat with the man less than eight hours earlier. "This must be some kind of mistake," I told myself.

The nurse saw my alarm as I attempted to awaken Tony. "He can't hear you, Victor. He's on too much medication. Is he a friend of yours?" she asked with genuine concern.

I wanted to tell her about Tony, what a smart guy he was, the little office he had in the cell, and the way he never took advantage of people, but I could not. All I could do was stare at this shell of a man who sat silently in front of me. "Yes, he is," was all I could say.

The nurse gently swung me around with her arm and began to herd me out of the unit, but while my body turned my eyes remained on Tony.

"Look, there's nothing you can do for him. He's really out there right now," the nurse comforted as we finally exited D-Rear.

"What happened?" I finally thought to ask.

"No one really knows. I got a call to report to the block to pick up a prisoner and take him to the infirmary. When I got there, your friend was laying on the bed in his cell mumbling gibberish and repeating that he couldn't do the time. He wasn't violent or anything. He was pretty much like you saw him. Do you know if he got some bad news about anything?" she asked.

"No," I immediately answered, despite the fact that I had no way of knowing. "What's going to happen to him? What can I do?" I asked in a delayed panic.

"Calm down, Victor. There's nothing you can do. The doctors will treat him. And soon he'll be back out in population. He'll probably have to stay on some kind of medication. There's lots of guys who go through this and they come around eventually. It happens all the time," the nurse told me and then walked away.

In 1983 I filed a class action lawsuit against Graterford and the Department of Corrections challenging, among other things, the conditions in D-Rear. A Federal judge, after inspecting D-Rear, declared it an unfit place for human beings. Shortly thereafter, the D-Rear was discontinued and a licensed mental health group operated an independent special needs unit inside Graterford.

When the new mental health unit finally went into operation, I said a little prayer for my friend Tony and all the others.

Fast Walk

"Why do you think so many people become insane after being in prison a while?" I asked while I tried to keep up with my exercise partner's pace as we fast walked around the yard.

"You're writing some more stuff?" he asked as he quickened his stride.

"Yeah," I huffed. "I wanted to do something on madness, like what it is about prison that drives people crazy."

"Why do you say prison drives people insane? My experience is that a lot of people come into prison half crazy already," he said, his voice without a hint of physical effort. I thought to myself that if he didn't slow down I might not be able to finish this discussion.

"What do you mean?" I asked trying hard to ease my breathing.

"Well, most guys coming into prison have some kind of drug addiction or alcohol addiction. They've lived hard on the streets and by the time they come to prison, their madness just catches up with them," he answered slowing just a bit.

"So you think drugs cause all the insanity we see in here?" I asked with a little disbelief.

"No. It's not only drugs and alcohol, but it's mostly that these guys are just weak individuals who crack under stress. It just so happened that they got the stress in prison so these weak people lose their mind," he clarified.

"So prison does have a part in driving men insane because of the stress?" I countered.

"No. Listen to what I say. These people are weak individuals and while the stress from prison might have taken them over the edge, it really could have happened anywhere. If they were out on the streets walking somewhere, the job stress might have driven them crazy. If you're weak in prison, you'll go crazy in here," he explained picking up the pace once more.

"I don't know if buy that. I mean I've seen some pretty tough guys go crazy in here," I countered, my disbelief giving me the extra strength to keep up.

"How tough could a person be if he went crazy? When I first came to prison over twenty years ago, one of my old heads told me that prison will be either build a man's character or break him down to a fool. Those were the truest words I've ever heard. If a man isn't strong enough to deal with prison, it will crush him," he explained.

"But then what you're saying is prison drives people crazy — but it's only weak people or people who are partially crazy already."

"Well, I'm not sure I'd put it like that, but yes, prison don't make you crazy, your weakness does," he tried to explain.

At this point I was pretty confused and I was not sure whether it was because I was out of breath or because I was not sure if he actually did agree with me. I stopped walking and watched as he continued to speed walk down the track. He never said a word. I decided to get a drink of water from the fountain.

As I caught my breath I thought about what he had said. Certainly, some of it was true, but I think he placed too high a standard on human beings. Certainly, there were conditions that could drive the strongest man crazy — and in my thinking, prison fostered those conditions.

By the time I reached the fountain I began to wonder if prison had made him a little crazy and I knew that he thought the same about me.

TOMORROW'S MODEL PRISONER

While the prison in the past dispensed justice by testing the extent of human physical endurance, a more enlightened modern society required prison managers to develop a less physical means of punishing law breakers, one which would leave the body unbruised and intact. But this enlightenment did not require a humane limit to punishment, but only sought to bring about a change in the way punishment was dispensed.

In response to this enlightenment, prison managers relied less on punishing the body and more on punishing the mind. Gone were nightsticks, leather straps, whips, chains and unrestrained acts of brutality and cruelty. In came psychologists, counsellors, medication, electric shock and solitary confinement. Behavioural modification, à la B.F. Skinner, became the new bible of prison salvation and redemption. Prisons became Skinner boxes complete with mazes, bells, whistles, carrots and the occasional stick.

As behaviouralism swept through the criminal justice community, rehabilitation became a glorious end as prison managers hoped to find utopia in the promise of behavioural science. After all, if Skinner could teach a chicken to play Tic-Tac-Toe, then certainly prisons could teach human beings how to be law-abiding citizens. Unfortunately, humans proved to be less responsive to conditioning than were chickens and laboratory rats.

Thus, rehabilitation was foolishly tied to a mistaken belief that people could be conditioned into conformity, regardless of their own desires. This doomed arranged marriage of the ideal of human rehabilitation and the stern "science" of behaviouralism was, in my opinion, the cause of the criminal justice system's current state of ruin and absence of meaningful purpose.

This unfortunate state of affairs has been motivated by the assumption that the shortcomings of behaviouralism has proved that rehabilitation is not possible. The ends of rehabilitation should stand independent of whatever failed means might be employed. Therefore, abandonment of behaviourism should not have included the rejection of a belief in human rehabilitation. But it did.

The criminal justice system has placed itself in a holding pattern until such time as another model can rise up out of the ashes of discarded behaviouralism and once again provide some meaningful purpose to achieve. This state of limbo has left prison managers with only a single strategy adopted by default: warehousing and controlling prisoners.

The rise in the use of super max prisons, "no perk" prisons, solitary confinement cells and mind-altering drugs clearly reveals the end product envisioned by prison managers. They are limited to creating prisoners who have suffered punishment and become obedient under supervision. The question of whether that convict can or cannot be rehabilitated is no longer a consideration. However, since concerns over humane treatment still prevail, prisons have been forced to rely on medicine and psychology to punish and control its multitude of unredeemable prisoners without breaking the skin.

Unfortunately, because psychological and chemical inducements leave no visible scars or physical damage, prison managers are able to inflict more punishment on their wards, in the form of psychological and emotional distress, than they were in the past when using physical force. Since mental and emotional pain and suffering have not been determined to be legitimate grounds for complaint by prisoners, prisons have not been inclined to develop some means of controlling the amount of pain and suffering they might inflict.

I am not suggesting that some plot or conspiracy exists aimed at mind control and psychological servitude, I simply believe that a lack of purpose has led the criminal justice community to focus entirely on the management and economics of the system to the exclusion of any notions of rehabilitation. A person entering prison today will find himself required to do nothing more than obey all of the volumes of rules. The ends of this prison machine being limited to ensuring obedience and conformity.

Convicts have always been subject to the nightmare of becoming "stir crazy." This condition is a natural byproduct of institutionalization. Contemporary prison management has accelerated this process by venturing into the business of applied psychology and psychiatric medication to induce population conformity. This abandonment of rehabilitation has left every prisoner in danger of becoming nothing more than a bitter prisoner. Whether being a bitter prisoner ultimately proves to be a form of insanity, society will have to make that determination at some point in the future.

Until then, I will be left to remember Cherokee, Kareem and Tony and pray for the realization that human beings are redeemable so I may be spared the fate of becoming tomorrow's model prisoner.

WOMEN PRISONERS

Suicide: The Challenges Faced by Female Federal Prisoners
Melissa Stewart and P. Durnford

Prisons can be a breeding ground for the feelings that lead to thoughts of suicide. Historically, there has been little or no support for prisoners, both in terms of suicide intervention, and in helping fellow prisoners cope with the aftermath of a suicide or a suicide attempt. This article will detail the unique needs of female prisoners, with a focus on the current environment of fear and uncertainty. Both the events leading up to the Arbour Commission and the effects of the dispersal of female prisoners to institutions across the country, with no regard to the relationships these women have built over the years, have created a potentially disastrous situation. The recent programs implemented to help these women survive the prison experience will be outlined.

According to Ramsey et al. (1987), Canada's federal prisons have an average rate of completed suicide of 125 per 100,000. This is more than eight times the rate in the general population. The average rate of self-mutilation is more than twice the estimated rate in the overall population of Canada. Adjusting for age and sex, prisoners complete suicide almost four times more often than people in the general population. While data about the frequency of self-mutilation in similar age and sex groups are not available, these behaviours occur at least three times as often in females. "Although specific control studies have not been done, it is probable that all types of suicidal behaviours occur in inmates of Canadian prisons at a markedly higher rate than might be expected if such persons were not incarcerated" (Ramsey, et al., 1987:3).

Between 1988 and 1990, six women hanged themselves at the Kingston Prison for Women (P4W). There is no information available concerning the number of attempted suicides, nor of self-mutilation (slashing or carving) both of which are common. In these years there were a total of 31 suicides completed by federal prisoners in Canada. Thus, the women accounted for over 22 percent of the total federal prisoner population who committed suicide. What factors are contributing to this problem and what can be done to address it?

Theoretically, it has been suggested (Gilligan, 1982; Miller, 1976) that the reasons for suicidal behaviour in women are different from those of men. Typically it has been thought that the fact that women complete suicide at a lower rate than men, while attempting it more often, is a result of the fact that women tend to be more hysterical and impulsive, and use attempted suicide in a manipulative way. This is an attitude rooted in the male paradigm of aggressive behaviour.

However, there is a body of work (Weissman, 1974; Rosenthal, 1981; Bancroft, et al., 1979; Simons and Murphy, 1985; Lester and Lester, 1971) that suggests that women's suicide can be better understood by the "self-in-relation". There are many interrelated aspects including empathy, connectedness and mutuality which is central to a woman's experience. Kaplan (1984) has suggested that within the proposed framework, a better understanding of why women attempt suicide more often may be gained. The key elements of this framework are vulnerability-to-loss, the inhibition of anger, the inhibition of assertiveness, and a sense of low self-esteem. As will be shown, these elements are overwhelmingly present in many female federal prisoners, along with other risk factors such as addiction problems. These factors are exacerbated rather than helped, by the institutional setting and practices.

The number of female federal prisoner suicides is a statistic not readily available. Since the number of female prisoners is so low, statistics in general are included with the men. Admittedly, such a small group would likely show wide variations over the years, but including them with the men disguises many problems and differences in prisoner characteristics. The Correctional Service of Canada (CSC) seems not to know how to deal with this small group of women. This is reflected in the application of treatment programs and disciplinary procedures.

Because no one seemed to know who these women were, apart from age, offense, length of sentence, addictions (if self-identified) and education level, the Task Force on Federally Sentenced Women undertook a survey (the first of its kind) from August to November, 1989. At the time of the survey, 203 women were in custody serving federal sentences: 125 of them at P4W; 78 women were being held in provincial institutions, usually on Exchange of Service agreements; 15 women either refused to participate or were on temporary absences.

The majority of women serving sentences of five or more years were held at P4W. Prisoners ranged in age from 19 to 75 years of age, and two-thirds had children. At P4W, 58 percent had children, 48 percent of them had at least one child less than 16 years old, and 24 percent of them had at least one child less than five years of age. However, only 30 percent of women of P4W had any visits from family and/or friends.

Three-quarters of the women had, at some stage in their lives, been addicted to alcohol or drugs. Of these women, all but 17 had some current problem with addiction. The Aboriginal women tended to have severe problems[1]: 71 percent said that substance abuse was a major factor in committing their current offense and those committed previously; 40 said they had committed an offense to support a drug habit; and drug-related offenses were the reason for the presence of 49 of the women. Physical abuse was suffered by 68 percent of all the women (a few noted occasional childhood discipline). This abuse skyrocketed among aboriginal women, of whom 90 percent said they had been physically abused, often severely and over a lengthy period. Sixty-one percent had suffered sexual abuse, as opposed to 53 percent in the overall female prisoner population. Twenty percent said they had slashed, cut, or attempted suicide during their present sentence, and 53 had done so at some point in their lives. Thus the situation of Aboriginal women among the general female federally incarcerated population is in some sense similar to that of women as a minority within the greater population of federally sentenced prisoners, which compounds their problems.

The institutions have also been described as being "awash with drugs." One prisoner commented, "It's easier to stay off drugs on the street than on the inside" (Solicitor General of Canada, 1991). "Home brew" is also available. The study ignores the problems of mental illness and emotional abuse the women may have suffered.

Thus there is a small population of women, many suffering from the effects of years of various kinds of abuse, and struggling with addictions problems in a situation where temptation is everywhere. Now add to this the institutional environment and the effects of isolation from family and friends.

> The prison is an old-fashioned, dysfunctional labyrinth of claustrophobic and inadequate spaces holding 142 prisoners of all security levels, minimum through maximum. It has been described as "unfit for bears." It is inadequate for living, working, eating, programming, recreation, and administration. Spaces are insufficient,

poorly ventilated, and noisy ... the prison grounds are surrounded
by an enormous wall, which in the male system, is used by maximum
security institutions only, and in many other aspects the building
has the characteristics of a maximum security institution.
(Commission of Inquiry into Certain Events at the Prison for Women
in Kingston, 1996:9)

Study after study has been done on the correctional system and/or the
Prison for Women. Every major inquiry has commented on the prison, some
very unfavourably. It has been generally agreed for years that the prison is
unsuitable for women, and that in fact it amounts to a form of discrimination
against female prisoners.[2] Indeed, just four years after the prison was opened,
Archambault (1938) recommended closure of the prison. In 1978, Solicitor
General Jean-Jacques Blais announced that within a year, the prison would
be closed. It was not. Instead, in the early 1980s, $1.4 million was spent
building an 18 foot concrete wall around the prison.

There seemed to be little political will to make changes until *Creating
Choices: The Report of the Task Force on Federally Sentenced Women* (1990)
was released. The majority of the Task Force members were women, many
of them Aboriginal.

The task force reiterated the findings of previous governmental and
non-governmental reports on the Prison for Women: that it was
over-secure; erroneously based on a male model of corrections;
that women prisoners were geographically dislocated and isolated
from their families; that the programs did not meet the needs of
prisoners serving a life sentence, or Francophone or Aboriginal
women; and that there were few community or institutional links.
(Commission of Inquiry into Certain Events at the Prison for Women
in Kingston, 1996:23)

It was finally announced that the prison would be closed in 1994 and five
regional institutions would be built with a cottage-like setting. One of these
would be a Healing Lodge for Aboriginal women. Two of the institutions
have opened and have had some major problems duly reported by the media.[3]
The current deadline for the closure of P4W is March 1997. *[Ed's Note: It
did not close until 2001.]*

The women feel a lot of trepidation about the move, are uncertain if they want to be moved, and uncertain where they might be sent. They face the possibility of being separated from their friends and in some instances their partners.

Another issue, besides the physical surroundings, is that only 30 percent of women at P4W receive visits from family or friends. Women housed in provincial institutions tend to receive more visits, however difficulties remain. CSC makes some attempt to place prisoners serving shorter sentences in their home provinces, but because of the size of the country, this does little to alleviate the isolation. Of particular concern is the separation of mothers and their children. Many times contact can only be maintained through telephone calls and letters; most times economic circumstances prohibit travel of any real distance.

"Since 1985, four studies have been commissioned by the Canadian government to examine the impact of separation on women and their families, the social costs of incarceration, mothers and the possibility of institutional nurseries. But no action [has] ever been taken to address the critical problems" (Solicitor General of Canada, 1991). In the meantime mothers suffer a devastating loss and often lose touch with their children, who are cared for by relatives if lucky, or bounced from foster home to foster home if not. Those mothers fortunate enough to maintain physical contact with their children often do so in uncomfortable conditions. Few prisons are set up to accommodate children. Often they must make do in a common visiting room, for a couple of hours at a time. P4W does have two bungalows, but they are primarily used for conjugal visits.

It has happened that prisoners have not been told about a death in the family until considerable time has passed. In addition, even if the woman is notified in time, it may not be economically feasible for her to attend the funeral. There are no counsellors available to help her deal with her grief except the prison psychologist. Although about half of the prisoners[4] view the psychologist favourably, the rest are distrustful. In any case, since the opening of the new prisons the Department of Psychology has been gradually eroded. Currently they have very little time to do counselling. Instead, they must concentrate on the assessment of prisoners upon their admission to prison. This erosion of psychological services has occurred despite an increase in the prison population to 151 from a low of 95.

Rules and their enforcement also cause tension. Many women perceive that the rules are arbitrary and applied randomly. Women's behaviour in prison tends to differ from that of men (it tends to be more verbally abusive), and, "in many countries there are suggestions that many disciplinary charges in women's prisons relate to very trivial behaviour for which men would not be charged" (Solicitor General of Canada, 1991). The rules are thought to be petty, inconsistent and unfair. This leads to tension and anger, and prisoners have suggested that clearer outlines and less discretion in the laying of charges would be more acceptable to them.

Prisoners feel that their rights are not respected, and, as revealed in the *Commission of Inquiry into Certain Events at the Prison for Women in Kingston* (the Arbour Report), this is often in fact the case. Many prisoners are denied their legal rights while in segregation, to the point of denying them phone calls to their lawyers. These rights are spelled out in Correctional Service policies and Commissioner's Directives. Custodial staff, however, seem to view these as privileges rather than rights: to be given or denied as a form of reward for good behaviour, or as a means of coercion to elicit particular behaviour from prisoners.

The grievance procedure is very bureaucratic, unwieldy and frustrating for prisoners as well. Lengthy delays and pat responses are common. The Arbour Report found that,

> Particularly at the appellate level, both Regional and National, responsibility for the disposition of grievances is often given to people with neither the knowledge nor the means of acquiring it and worse, with no real authority to remedy the problem should they be prepared to acknowledge its existence. ... At present, it would seem that the admission of error is perceived as an admission of defeat by the Correctional Service. In that climate, no internal method of dispute resolution will succeed. (*Commission of Inquiry into Certain Events at the Prison for Women in Kingston*, 1996:162)

This aggravates the feelings of anger and despair felt by the prisoners. Whether she has a valid concern or not, she feels powerless and that no one will listen to her.

There is also an informal hierarchy in the prison where prisoners with little power can be particularly vulnerable. Also, there is an underground economy that operates within the walls, and prisoners may find themselves in debt without the means to repay. (This is particularly true of drug debts.) Prisoners may be raped, beaten, or threatened with death by other prisoners.

They are sometimes murdered. Some of the guards may turn a blind eye to this activity making the prisoners again feel powerless and despairing. 'Ratting' (informing on other prisoners) is the worst thing a prisoner can do within this informal structure, so often the prisoners have no choice but to bear with it.

Prisoners also tend to form attachments to one another, given the lack of other emotional supports. They may invest a great deal of emotion in these relationships, and for many such a relationship is the first of its kind. If the relationship is in trouble, the women feel intense despair. Once the relationship ends, a woman must deal with living in close quarters with her former lover, and watch new relationships form. This can be very difficult.

Treatment programs for addictions and anger management are available, but they have primarily been developed in the context of a male model, because of the small population of female prisoners. Alcoholics Anonymous and Narcotics Anonymous are viewed with some hostility, particularly by Aboriginal women, because of their Christian basis. Also, there is some evidence that AA and NA do not work well (Chiauzzi and Liljegren, 1993). This may be particularly true for women because of the effects of labelling ("alcoholic" = "bad mother"), the confrontational approach taken (non-acceptance of a label implies denial of the problem), and the call for "God" to intervene (the alcoholic cannot control herself, and must ask for help; it also continues the dependence of the woman on others). Also the existence of a male God may be distasteful to some women.

The problem of treatment programs being designed for (and by) men, but being applied to women, is pervasive. Female federal prisoners have very different life experiences than do men, as well as different histories of offending. These programs may not be suitable for this very reason. Yet, the small numbers of federally incarcerated women do not make it economically feasible to research and design specific treatment programs.

The prison is obligated to educate the women to the Grade 10 level, but this depends on the willingness of the particular prisoner. Vocational training and work programs are primarily geared towards prison maintenance, and are traditional "women's work" in nature, such as laundry, beauty parlour, and clerical work. These are limited in nature, and do little to allow the prisoner to escape the cycle of poverty once released.

These women have suffered estrangement from their families, isolation, and perhaps losses because of relationships on the inside; they are not free to express their anger and have it validated for fear of punishment. They cannot assert themselves, and if they try to "right" perceived injustices through the grievance procedure, they are brushed off. Many women have very low self-esteem stemming from years of physical and emotional abuse. They are imprisoned in bleak surroundings, most times at a level of security not warranted by their histories (*Commission of Inquiry into Certain Events at the Prison for Women in Kingston,* 1996). It is not surprising that so many women resort to self-mutilation or suicide. It is perhaps surprising that so many of them survive the experience.

"During the latter part of 1979 and the early 1980s the number of suicides and self-inflicted injuries among inmates in Canada's federal prisons rose sharply" (Ramsey et al., 1987). In response to this, CSC commissioned a study to examine these behaviours. They made a number of recommendations, dealing with implementing new policies and specialized staff training. This treatment model was developed in Calgary and demonstrated in three Atlantic institutions of varying security levels. Since female federal prisoners not at P4W are primary housed in provincial institutions elsewhere, this study did not include them, nor were their concerns considered separately from those of the men (Ramsey et al., 1987). From the subsequent rash of suicides at P4W, it seems evident that if staff there did in fact receive this training, it proved ineffective. This is another example of non-applicability of male-based models to female populations.

If a prisoner at P4W slashes or attempts suicide, she is placed in segregation, her clothes are removed, and she is given a paper gown. This is a long-standing practice. The environment in the segregation unit is punitive. The bars are painted black (in fact after the events leading to the Arbour report the cells were fitted with metal treadplate, making them dimmer and more cage-like). There is a cot, a sink, and a toilet. Until recently, the electrical wiring was so inadequate that prisoners could not have a radio or television, in direct contradiction of CSC directives concerning segregation.

Prisoners feel that, "[w]omen cannot shut out the pain of their neighbours, and each incident threatens to become a contagious epidemic" (Kershaw and Lasovich, 1991). After the suicide of Marlene Moore in 1988, an outside consultant was brought in. Jan Heney, who had had success treating women outside of prison, stated bluntly that,

...long-standing prison practices and policies had fostered the kind of tension and desperation that provoked self-mutilation; more than that, the institution's manner of responding to women who slash was likely to escalate rather than reduce the rate of self-mutilation and suicide among prisoners.

She recommended an immediate end to the use of segregation for women who slash, saying that isolation increases rather than decreases suicidal tendencies (Kershaw and Lasovich, 1991).

However, the involuntary segregation of suicidal prisoners continues. The segregation unit is so feared and hated by the prisoners who are in such desperate need of human contact, that many women who slash sew themselves up rather than seek medical attention. This leads to a great deal of scarring.

If a prisoner does complete suicide, the lights are turned off in her cell for 24 hours "as a show of respect." Since the lights in the prison are normally on continuously, this is a grim reminder to the women that one of their group could not make it. These women are friends, lovers, enemies: all know one another. This can lead to a rash of suicide attempts. On November 25, 1988, a prisoner attempted to commit suicide. Before dawn there were two more suicide attempts, and one week later Marlene Moore was dead (Kershaw and Lasovich, 1991).

In 1990, a Peer Support Team was initiated by two members of the Psychology Department, in response to the rash of suicides, attempts, and slashings. This program, while successful in its way, has inherent limitations. The Peer Support counsellor (a specially trained prisoner), while often sharing the same experience(s), has little or no access to other resources. Confidentiality is also difficult because of the close living quarters. Corrections staff have access to more resources but the prisoners often feel they are in an adversarial relationship with them.

A Battered Women's Support Group was also started at the Prison for Women in 1994. This group helps women deal with their histories of abuse and attempts to give them a sense of empowerment, and to help them break out of the cycle of dependency. However, in 1995 this was made an official program by the Prison for Women and chaired by a guard. The women spend six weeks being urged to speak whether they want to or not, after which they 'graduate' with a certificate. Attempts are being made to restore the group to its original collective format. There is also an attempt being made to establish a Grief and Bereavement group inside the prison in order to help prisoners deal with their losses.

The Elizabeth Fry Society can also be of help to prisoners, but again, many prisoners are distrustful of their close relationship with CSC.

The need was seen for a non-judgmental, independent agency which would counsel prisoners in crisis and provide community resource information and emotional support. In 1994 Project Another Chance Inc. (PAC) was formed with a grant from the Trillium Foundation. PAC's mandate is to aid female federal prisoners and parolees in distress and to aid their transition into the community. The lines are staffed by volunteers with many backgrounds, including ex-prisoners and those who have struggled with addictions problems. Most volunteers have received extensive training in crisis management, addictions, and awareness of native issues. PAC is also investigating the development of a women's treatment centre, for addictions problems, parallel to those existing for men. No treatment for addictions is currently available for female ex-prisoners.

Thus far, the response has been encouraging. Particularly for prisoners with no contact with family or friends, having a person they can call on to express frustration, anxiety, find information about legal matters, or simply to chat, is a welcome change. PAC has managed to avert several would-be suicide attempts, and contacted one institution on behalf of a prisoner when she was asking to be put into segregation for fear she would self-injure. She was finally put into the enhanced unit and is fine.

One concern for PAC, with the dispersal of female prisoners to the new regional prisons, is that CSC is resisting the continuation of the current practice of allowing prisoners access to PAC's crisis line. Instead, one Warden had determined that she will use the services of the Canadian Mental Health Association (CMHA). While the CMHA provides a valuable service, PAC maintains ongoing contact with a number of prisoners who will be moved, and who are suffering some anxiety about it. One would think that any means available to reduce the tension in the new facilities would be welcomed, in light of the problems encountered with the transition so far.

Women prisoners are likely to remain a small proportion of the total number of prisoners. Their backgrounds necessitate innovative treatments and strategies in order to successfully integrate them into their communities upon their release.

NOTES

1. Aboriginal women have been recognised to have a particular set of problems, namely:
   - Aboriginal women are over-represented in the prison population of Canada
   - They are quite distinct culturally, linguistically, and socially from the broader prison population of federally sentenced women
   - They have significantly different personal and social histories
   - They have significantly different offending histories
   - The dispersion of Aboriginal communities across the country is a special burden to them

   The holistic approach to healing and reintegration into the community is at odds with the cultures and philosophies of conventional prison environments (Commission of Inquiry into Certain Events at the Prison For Women, 1996:218).
2. Female federal prisoners have been treated as if they were an afterthought of the CSC. In fact, the undue hardship they must face in dislocation from their families was the subject of a court challenge (based on a Charter of Rights argument) (Commission of Inquiry into Certain Events at the Prison For Women, 1996:246). This was overturned on appeal, but without the opening of the regional institutions this would no doubt have been the subject of further challenges.
3. In Edmonton, there was a multiple escape (3 women), a suicide, self-mutilations and an attack on staff in the first 5 months. "Uncaged Women," *Sunday Sun*, April 28, 1996. "Escapee Caught in Edmonton," *The Toronto Star*, May 1996.
4. This remark stems from conversations held between Project Another Chance staff and volunteers and the prisoners themselves, in an informal survey.

REFERENCES

Bancroft, J. et al. (1979)."The Reasons People Give For Taking Overdoses: A Further Inquiry," *British Journal of Medical Psychology*, 52(4), pp. 353–365.

Bettridge, Brenda (1987). "The 'Self-in-Relation': Understanding Suicidal Behaviour in Women," *Canadian Women Studies*, 8(4), pp. 58–60.

Chiauzzi, Emil J. and Steven Liljegren (1993)."Taboo Topics in Addictions Treatments," *Journal of Substance Abuse*, 10, pp. 303–316.

Commission of Inquiry into Certain Events at the Prison For Women in Kingston (1996). The Honourable Louise Arbour, Commissioner. Public Works and Government Services, Canada.

Ekstedt, John W. and Curt T. Griffiths (1984). *Corrections in Canada: Policy and Practice*. Toronto: Butterworth & Co.

Gilligan, C. (1982). *In a Different Voice*. Cambridge: Harvard University Press.

Holey and Arboleda-Florez (1988). "Hypernomia and Self-Destructiveness in Penal Settings," *International Journal of Law and Psychiatry*, 11, pp. 167–178.

Kaplan, A.G. (1984). "The 'Self-in-Relation': Implications for Depression in Women," *Work in Progress*, no. 14, Wellesley, Mass: Stone Centre Working Paper Services.

Kershaw, Anne and Mary Lasovich (1991). *Rock-A-Bye Baby: A Death Behind Bars*. Toronto: McClelland & Stewart Inc.

Lester, G. and D. Lester (1971). *Suicide — The Gamble with Death*. Englewood Cliffs: Prentice Hall.

Miller, J.B. (1976). *Towards a New Psychology of Women*. Boston: Beacon Press.

Ramsay, R. and C. Bagley (1985). "The Prevalence of Suicidal Behaviours, Attitudes and Associated Experiences in an Urban Population," *Journal of Suicide and Life Threatening Behaviour*, 15(2) pp. 151–167.

Ramsey, R.F. et al. (1987). "Suicide Prevention in the High-Risk Prison Population," *Canadian Journal of Criminology*, 29(3), pp. 295–307.

Rosenthal, M.J. (1981). "Sexual Differences in the Suicidal Behaviour of Young People," *Adolescent Psychiatry*, 9, pp. 422–442.

Shaw, Margaret (1990). *Survey of Federally Sentenced Women: Report to the Task Force on Federally Sentenced Women on the Prison Survey*. Ottawa: Solicitor General Canada.

Simons, R. and P. Murphy (1985). "Sex Differences in the Causes of Adolescent Suicide Ideation," *Journal of Youth and Adolescence*, 14(5), pp. 423–433.

Solicitor General of Canada (1991). *The Female Federal Offender: Report on a Preliminary Study*. Ottawa: Solicitor General Canada.

Statistics Canada (1980–1995). *Correctional Services in Canada*. Canadian Centre for Justice Studies.

———. (1971–1979). *Correctional Institutions Statistics*. Ministry of Industry, Trade and Commerce.

Task Force on Federally Sentenced Women (1990). *Creating Choices: The Report of the Task Force on Federally Sentenced Women*. Ottawa: Solicitor General Canada.

Weissman, M. (1974). "The Epidemology of Suicide Attempts, 1960–1971," *Archives of General Psychiatry*, 30, pp. 737–746.

Whitehead, P. et al. (1973). "Measuring the incidence of Self-injury: Some Methodological And Design consideration," *American Journal of Orthopsychiatry*, 43, pp. 142–148.

The Bear and Me
Jo-Ann Mayhew

Grief is too present in my life. I have to start writing this story or die. I am not sure how I will die. Several possibilities come to mind but none with any guarantee of success. I have been finding it increasingly easy to locate the carotid artery in my neck. Seems simple, I will only need the blade from my pink BIC and a few moments of resolute determination. But then I see the face of Marie. She lay on the cold gray cement outside my cell. From behind grim bars I stood a frozen watch as the blood oozed from the gory slashes on her neck. She did not die. Marie was put in steel shackles. She bled a lot until a nurse could be found. Trusting her death to a BIC did not work.

Hanging, from what I hear, is messy and despite determination, death not a given. Johnny's long-lingering coma is grim witness to this fact. I suppose none of us survive long without some sense of hope. For those entombed behind tonnes of concrete and steel of the Kingston Prison for Women (P4W), the most fragile fragment of hope is incredibly precious. Johnny's fragment dissolved. She was a warrior woman who decided to hang-to-death but failed. For months she was held by the cruel threads of a mindless coma until death finally came. I do not trust hanging. But Johnny is also connected to Pat Bear and hence to my story.

The first time I saw Pat, or her feet, was at the Regional Treatment Centre (RTC). She was wrapped in a blue blanket sitting on a ledge in front of an ice covered window. From under the blanket peaked two of the tiniest feet I have ever seen on an adult. They were so small they looked as if they belonged to a child rather than a young woman. Could have been size three but I suspect they were even smaller than that. I had been in my cell when she arrived. Now I had a chance to find out who this new person was. I said, "Hi, I'm Jo-Ann. How come they sent you over to these dungeons?" She smiled sort of shyly and said, "I'm Pat Bear. I guess they just got tired of me over there." I sure liked her smile and I just blurted out, "I bet they sent you here because your feet are too small to walk up and down all those tunnels and stairs at P4W. You came here to give your feet a rest!" Well that just set Pat off laughing and laughing. She was laughing so hard she could barely talk but she finally gasped, "Jo-Ann, you're a comical woman." This short conversation set the tone for happy and comfortable familiarity.

When I asked Bear where she was from, she replied, "Out West." Since we were in Kingston I asked her, "Do you mean west like from Toronto?" "Oh, no! I've never been to Toronto! I mean west. West like the prairies." I sort of remembered some stuff about the prairies from distant days of school geography but I was totally ignorant of the fact that while Pat's distance from her geographic home could be measured in miles, the distance from her cultural roots was immeasurably further. Probably because of our mutual loneliness we came to a meeting of hearts rather than minds. Simply by accident, I had stumbled upon a fundamental most dear to Cree social life, humour.

It was a good thing that we could warm our hearts with each other's company. For at the RTC the only treatment was January's freezing weather whining through the ancient windows of Kingston Penitentiary. I recall a female guard commenting that she wished she had worn her fur coat into work. This comment was made as she stood outside the cell of a woman left naked except for a house blanket type of nightie. The grim offense for which this woman, Lisa, was being punished was that she was refusing to eat. Treatment also included the drilling of jack hammers as cement blocks and bars were rearranged to accommodate more female prisoners. We were the ones who had broken down at P4W. We were transferred across the street to old Kingston Penitentiary (KP). I seriously wondered how the Correctional Service treated more critically distressed women.

At that time KP was notorious for housing Canada's worst sex offenders. I am not sure what disturbed me more; the drilling noise making cells smaller and smaller or the thought of being a female hostage in a prison of 400 men. I did not understand how deeply Pat was affected by being separated from her Cree society but I know these experiences were separating me from any sense of social decency existing in Canada. I do not know how far Pat shared the grim projections of my mind but she sure shared the same chilling temperatures and the same numbing noise.

When we were let out of cells to socialize on our concrete doorstep, I always greeted Bear with a little gasp of surprised astonishment and say, "Wow, you STILL have those tiny feet; they haven't grown at all!" Since they really did fit rather well with the rest of her compact body, Bear was constantly amused at my astonishment. Her laugh at my foolishness was a chuckle that suited her equally well. She would usually grin and tell me I was just being silly.

However, one day to her "stop being silly comment," she added the threat, "or I'm going to get you!" And there she stood armed with a chunky square of thickly iced chocolate cake. This rare treat had appeared on our supper trays. One thing, for sure, was the guys serving the food line always tried to give us something special like the biggest pieces or an extra bit of fruit. They seemed to really feel for our isolation.

Well! There stood Pat with a wicked, lively grin on her face dabbing her fingers into the gooey icing. Before I had time to really take in the scene she had plunked a huge gob of icing smack on my nose. This was a declaration of war! Clutching my blanket, I whipped in and out of my cell for my chocolate treasure. I totally forgot my plan to save it for a night time munchie. Yelling back, "I'll get you," I ran after Pat who was running for a hideout in the mildewed shower room. Suddenly she stopped, turned, gave a whoop and lunged at me with two sticky black cake covered hands. Laughing and screaming in return, I broke off a chunk of cake and threw it at her. My pitch caught her square in the forehead. Pat now came to a full halt. One mucky hand went up and she slowly pulled the chunk off her face and stuffed it in her mouth. She was laughing so hard she nearly choked. I laughed with her until my sides were aching. What a sight we must have made. The guards had come onto the unit after hearing our yelps but they looked more stunned than angry at the sight of our light-hearted cake fight exploding within the confines of a maximum security prison.

As I look back and consider not only the nightmare quality of our surroundings but also a span of twenty years between our ages the amount of playful laughter we shared was truly amazing. And there was also the matter of cultural difference. Bear was a young native woman from the prairies. I was an eastern white. Somehow our spirits were joyfully joined in small ways and we eased each other's time at the RTC.

Neither of us stayed there a long time. Only a couple of months. In the way of women serving federal sentences a few months is not a remarkable amount of time. We both returned to P4W where over months and years our paths crossed but never intertwined so intensely. I would see Pat hanging out with Johnny from time to time and I was glad she had another pal. But I knew that a special bond had been formed between the two of us and it was easily recognized by others; probably because we continued to laugh so easily when we ran into each other.

I guess I became more stable or appeared to be so. Pat did less well in keeping up appearances. It seems to me she became a victim to competing ideologies. One month she would meet with visiting Native Elders and they would encourage her to use traditional healing medicines like smudging with Sweetgrass or Sage and going to a Sweat Lodge when this was occasionally possible. The next month Pat would see a white male psychiatrist who would give her his medicine bundle of anti-psychotic pills. She found no relief in this cross-over of treatments. I have been told that in former days, Pat had had a problem with solvent sniffing. She now seemed to return to this behaviour in some attempt at alleviating her turmoil. Her situation was fairly common knowledge but no more effective action seems to have been taken on her behalf.

One day the guards called me to talk to Pat. She did not want to leave her cell and was very upset. This time we could not laugh. Pat was about to be set free. She felt terribly dislocated and unwanted. She had nowhere to go. I could not console her. The guards just took her away to the harsh isolation of segregation, for her own protection. Shortly thereafter, the doors of P4W finally opened to Bear. She was turned out to Kingston and after a few days hung herself to death in a city park.

I was walking down a prison tunnel when I overheard guards talking about her death. My reaction was, at first, disbelief. Then, the next day I saw a very brief mention of her name in *The Whig Standard*, Kingston's daily paper. I felt incredibly helpless, wishing I could have done more and left knowing so little. Pat died outside the prison walls so no one from the prison acknowledged any responsibility for her death. I was never to know what became of her body or where she was laid to rest. But I do know I have continued to carry her in my heart.

It was not that long after Bear's death that Johnny attempted to suicide. Actually this became an era for a large number of suicides at P4W. I managed to survive through seven years inside but in attempting to live I feel I am joined by spirits of sisters who have chosen a different path. The power of their examples has moved the once remote thought of a suicidal death into the range of common place. For me it is a good thing that the echoes of Bear's happy laughter still linger in my soul.

One Prison, One Death, One Mass Coverup
Dawnya Ferdinandsen

INMATE KILLS HERSELF AT ORW

A twenty-year-old inmate died Friday after she hung herself at the Ohio Reformatory for Women.

Carol Bell, 20, from Greene County, was found hanging from a bed sheet in the cell at 9 P.M. by a corrections officer doing a routine count of prisoners. Bell was alone in the cell at the time.

Bell was serving a 16–50 year sentence on a conviction for aggravated robbery, attempted murder, and kidnapping stemming from an incident in the Dayton area in 1996. She and two accomplices allegedly stabbed a cab driver and took his money.

Bell was 16 at the time.

In March of 1999 she had an additional four years added onto her sentence for attempted escape from the ORW.

She would not have been eligible for parole until 2010.

Attempts to revive Bell were unsuccessful. She was pronounced dead at the scene.

The Ohio State Highway Patrol, which handles incidents on state grounds, was called to the scene to investigate.[1]

*****

Carol Ann Bell was sixteen when she arrived at the Ohio Reformatory for Women. She came in very young and afraid, and knew no one in a population of over 1,800 women. At her age and faced with a sentence of sixteen to fifty years, she felt like she was surely going to die here and inevitably she did just that.

Carol Ann had suicidal problems when she arrived here in 1996. In March of 1997 she attempted to hang herself while in lock-up and was placed on watch for a mere day or so before being told she would be all right. In August 1998, Carol Ann attempted to escape, managing to get over the first perimeter fence before being caught by prison officers. Upon seeing her attempt to escape, a captain took a 357 magnum from a perimeter officer and threatened to shoot her, Carol Ann informed the captain repeatedly that she did not care and that she had nothing to live for. She was then placed immediately in a lock-up area (ARN-4) on suicide watch for over two weeks with no psychiatric evaluations, rushed through institutional hearings and returned to lock-up for another sixty days. She then told officers that she heard voices telling her to kill herself, and was placed back in the Residential Treatment Unit (RTU) from October to December. During this time she was heavily medicated, raced through Union County and given an additional four years for an attempted escape.

The day before she was placed back in the lockup area she slit her wrist; this was brushed off and she was placed back in lock-up with a slit wrist. A captain continuously informed Carol Ann, at eighteen years of age, that he would personally see to it that she did three to five years in her cell for her escape attempt. This taunting caused her to go back on suicide watch, where several male officers allegedly asked her to expose herself to them or they would ensure that she did years in the hole.

Carol Ann was then released into general population in September 1999, and sent directly to a maximum security cottage, housing the most notorious women in the state of Ohio. She was nineteen years old when sent there, after thirteen months of solitary confinement and no adjustment program back into population. Carol Ann was scared of these women, since prior to her escape attempt she was housed with only young offenders in a segregated housing unit. While in the maximum housing unit, some women stole things from her, threatened and bullied her, and used her for her $10 a month state pay.

Her unit continually informed her that she would be getting her blue shirt (close status) to no avail. This was just one more act of cruelty, since while her institutional record scored to decrease her security the institution would not. Two weeks before her death she was informed by a prison official that she would have to wait for another nine months. If I could only explain what state of mind that put her in, her whole outlook on her time here, then you could begin to understand why she should have been placed in a better housing unit, one with less violent offenders, along with better programming opportunities. This is all Carol Ann wanted and the institution knew it. The fact remains that she earned it, her points called for a decrease. She was trying to get through cosmetology school and had completed numerous groups as a way to better herself.

Needless to say, Carol Ann snapped. She said repeatedly that she could not do another year with maximum security women. Two weeks later, she hanged herself in her single-woman cell. During those last two weeks of her life she had repeatedly tried to find help through our residential treatment unit program and through the outpatient psychiatrist. Carol Ann burned her left forearm several times with a lit cigarette from her wrist to her elbow. The burns were as deep as the tip of your finger. When she went for help she was informed by our psychiatric staff that that was "normal" behaviour for her and that she should return to her cottage. Carol Ann had never burnt herself before.

At 3:30 P.M. on the day of her death, Carol Ann informed an officer that she needed a psychiatrist because she could not handle her feelings. The officer told her, "You'll be okay. Go to your room and sleep it off." After the 4:00 P.M. count, Carol Ann was asked if she wanted to go to dinner. She said, "no." She was never checked again by staff until her lifeless body was found at 8:55 P.M. by another officer. Many prisoners had told the officers that Carol Ann was very upset and that they should check on her. One prisoner informed them that Carol Ann was banging on her locked door for help, but they brushed her off for the last time. Carol Ann covered the window of her door at 6:30 P.M.; the officers never checked on her from 5:30 P.M. on. Carol Ann died around 7:40 P.M. and was not found until 8:55 P.M., and only then because it was an institutional count time.

This means that she slit her wrists, tore a bedsheet up, strung it up to her window latch, climbed up to the window sill while her wrists bled, made a noose and tightened it around her neck, and leaped to end her tragically young life. Had continuous rounds been made, like the maximum security post orders state for officers to do, her window being covered would have been discovered and she would never had the time to slit her wrists and hang herself.

Now the institution wants to point the blame at her relationship, saying that she hanged herself because she and her girlfriend broke up earlier that day. Staff has held meetings with other prisoners (juveniles, mentally ill, and maximum prisoners) telling them that the suicide is a result of Carol Ann's relationship. The bottom line to them is that suicide is no one's fault. However, institutional negligence in meeting responsibilities is in question here. The meetings have consisted of slanderous remarks, along with ludicrous comments by staff about her family, friends and her intimate partner, suggesting that had we known better we would have seen this coming, and pointing the finger at her only means of support. They are trying to take the focus off themselves, the only ones who had the keys and degrees to save her.

Carol Ann was a child pushed through the cracks and forgotten. Please do not let her be forgotten now. I know that people in society will say that she was just a convict, but she too is one of God's children and only God has the right to judge her. The-system-that-vowed to rehabilitate-her-is-the very-system that in the end destroyed her life? The true story of Carol Ann Bell needs to be told to ensure that a tragedy like this never happens again. If you need any further information and feel compelled to be Carol Ann's voice, please contact her mother, Jane Ann Zertuche at 308 Trunk Drive, Dayton, Ohio 45431, or call (937) 254-6891.

POSTSCRIPT

Since the death of Carol Ann Bell, her other friends and I have been harassed; our mail stopped, opened and read; and outgoing mail has never left the institution. The contents of these envelopes were Carol Ann's story, and the institution does not want to release it to the public. The amount of cover-up here makes it evident that this was not an unforeseen suicide. The entire case needs to be investigated thoroughly.

NOTES

1. Source of article unknown; submitted by author.

MARIONIZATION

Breaking Men's Minds: Behavior Control and Human Experimentation at the Federal Prison in Marion, Illinois

Eddie Griffin

> _Having spent a total of two and a half years in this experimental behavior laboratory-type fortress, I have witnessed atrocities that are on the same par as Pinochet's concentration camps in Chile and that of Hitler's Auschwitz. (Victor Bono, Marion Captive)

Throughout the state and federal prison systems, there are circulating stories and hearsay about the Marion, Illinois Federal Prison. These tales weave their way through the grapevine and, over a period of time and distance, become mystique and legendary, especially among young prisoners making their unfortunate debut into the system. For example, in 1972 at Terre Haute Federal Prison, it was not uncommon to hear young prisoners unfold myths about an 'underground prison' called Marion, where those who entered would never see the sun again until their release. Others would claim the Control Unit at Marion was underground, and whoever was placed there would spend the rest of their sentence in it. No one really knew for sure because, up until then, no prisoner returned to Terre Haute from Marion. Real or unreal, a dread grew up around the myths. Whatever existed behind the walls of Marion generated apprehension of a legal form of assassination.

Prison officials at other institutions cultivate and exploit these fears by threatening to send certain resistive prisoners to Marion. A man is told to conform to the institution, or he will be sent to Marion to have his behavior 'corrected.' The thought of being 'corrected' by unknown means has a chilling effect on the senses, and it tends to sterilize any resistance which might exist in prison populations. Evidently, Marion was a control mechanism for the entire prison system — a penal cesspool where other institutions discarded their waste.

I was one of the so-called 'incorrigibles' who had come into conflict with Terre Haute officials, and I was threatened with being sent to Marion. After receiving an injury in the prison machine shop, where I narrowly missed losing a finger, I was patched up, administered a painkiller, and then sent back to work. Soon afterwards, there was almost a repeat of the same accident, so I decided to quit my work in the machine shop. I was immediately locked up in segregation for refusing to work, and for eight months, I continuously refused to work until I was guaranteed a job change. But the administration declared that they would use me wherever they needed me. Prisoners do not control their institution. My insistence about the work hazard led to my being shipped to Marion, no doubt to have my obstinate behavior corrected.

A BEHAVIOR MODIFICATION LABORATORY

Upon first glance, Marion differed radically in its appearance from what one would believe from the horrid myths. The ominous sword of Damocles over the prison system appeared to be no threat. But the human eye can be deceived by what is contracted on the phenomenal level. A vague but bleak sensation invades a man's being when he passes through the grill doors into the prison's interior. Each electronically controlled grill seems to alienate him more and more from his freedom — even the hope of freedom. A sense of finality, of being buried alive is raised to the supra-level of his consciousness. He tries to suppress it, but the clanging of each door leaves an indelible imprint on his psyche. This is the first evidence that Marion is more than a physical star-chamber. It is a modern behavior modification laboratory.

Behavior modification at Marion consists of a manifold of four techniques: (1) Dr. Edgar H. Schein's brainwashing methodology; (2) Skinnerian operant conditioning; (3) Dr. Levinson's sensory-deprivation-design (i.e. Control Unit); and (4) chemotherapy and drug therapy. And, as I will point out, the use of these techniques, the way they are disguised behind pseudonyms and under the philosophical rhetoric of *correction*, and even their *modus operandi*, violate the *Nuremberg Code*, the *United Nations' Standard Minimum Rules for the Treatment of Prisoners*, the *Universal Declaration of Human Rights*, the *International Covenant on Civil and Political Rights*, the Department of Health, Education and Welfare policy on human experimentation, and the First, Sixth and Eighth Amendments to the *United States Constitution*.

The constructs of the prison are somewhat peculiar. Some not-so-outstanding features do not make the least economical sense, and are often totally out of physiological order. But these features, when viewed from a psychological angle, begin to take on new meaning. For example, the prison is minced into small sections and subsections, divided by a system of electronic and mechanical grills further reinforced by a number of strategically locked steel doors. Conceivably, the population can be sectioned off quickly in times of uprising. But even for the sake of security, the prison is laced with too many doors. Every few feet a prisoner is confronted by one. So he must await permission to enter or exit at almost every stop. A man becomes peeved. But this is augmented by the constant clanging that bombards his brain so many times a day until his nervous system becomes knotted. The persistent reverberation tends to resurrect and reinforce the same sensation, the damp bleak feeling that originally introduced the individual into the Marion environment. It is no coincidence. This system is designed with conscious intent.

Every evening the 'control movement' starts. The loud speakers, which are scattered around the prison, resonate the signal: 'The movement is on. You have ten minutes to make your move.' The interior grill doors are opened, but the latitude and limits of a man's mobility are sharply defined, narrowly constricted. His motion, the fluidity of his life, is compressed between time locks. There is a sense of urgency to do what prisoners usually do — nothing. It is just a matter of time before the last remnants of a prisoner's illusion become obliterated.

At the end of the ten-minute limit, the speakers blare out: 'The movement is over. Clear the corridor.' The proceedings stop. Twenty minutes later the routine is repeated, and so on, until a man's psyche becomes conditioned to the movement/non-movement regimentation, and his nerves jingle with the rhythmic orchestration of steel clanging steel. In prisoners' words, it is 'part of the program' — part of the systematic process of reinforcing the unconditional fact of a prisoner's existence that he has no control over the regulation and orientation of his own being. In behavioral psychology, this condition is called 'learned helplessness' — a derivative of Skinnerian operant conditioning (commonly called 'learning techniques'). In essence, a prisoner is taught to be helpless, dependent on his overseer. He is taught to accept without question the overseer's power to control him. This rebels against human consciousness, so some prisoners seek means of resistance. Others try to circumnavigate the omnipotent force via escape.

But the omnipotent is also omnipresent. Nothing escapes Marion's elaborate network of 'eyes.' Between television monitors, prisoner spies, collaborators, and prison officials, every crevice of the prison is overlaid by a constant watch. Front-line officers, specially trained in the cold, calculated art of observation, watch prisoners' movements with a particular meticulousness, scrutinizing little details in behavior patterns, then recording them in the Log Book. This aid provides the staff with a means to manipulate certain individuals' behavior. It is feasible to calculate a prisoner's level of sensitivity from the information, so his vulnerability can be tested with a degree of precision. Some behavior modification experts call these tests 'stress-assessment.' Prisoners call it harassment. In some cases, selected prisoners are singled out for one or several of these 'differential-treatment' tactics. A prisoner could have his mail turned back or 'accidentally' mutilated. He could become the object of regular searches, or even his visitors could be strip searched. These and more tactics are consistent with those propagated by one Dr. Edgar H. Schein.

A HISTORY OF THIS BEHAVIOR MODIFICATION LABORATORY

At a Washington, DC conference in 1962, organized for the Federal Bureau of Prisons (BOP) by the National Institutes of Mental Health, Schein presented his ideas on brainwashing. Addressing the topic of 'Man against Man: Brainwashing,' he stated:

> In order to produce marked changes of behavior and/or attitude, it is necessary to weaken, undermine or remove the supports to the old patterns of behavior and the old attitudes. Because most of these supports are the face-to-face confirmation of present behavior and attitudes, which are provided by those with whom close emotional ties exist, it is often necessary to break those emotional ties. This can be done either by removing the individual physically and preventing any communication with those whom he cares about, or by proving to him that those whom he respects aren't worthy of it and, indeed, should be actively mistrusted. (quoted in Chorover 1979)

Dr. Schein then provided the group with a list of specific examples:

1. Physical removal of prisoners from areas sufficiently isolated to effectively break or seriously weaken close emotional ties.

2. Segregation-of-all-natural-leaders.

3. Use-of-cooperative-prisoners-as-leaders.

4. Prohibition of group activities not in line with brainwashing objectives.

5. Spying on prisoners and reporting back private material.

6. Tricking men into written statements which are then showed to others.

7. Exploitation of opportunists and informers.

8. Convincing-prisoners-that-they-can-trust-no-one.

9. Treating those who are willing to collaborate in far more lenient ways than those who are not.

10. Punishing those who show uncooperative attitudes.

11. Systematic withholding of mail.

12. Preventing contact with anyone non-sympathetic to the method of treatment and regimen of the captive populace.

13. Disorganization of all group standards among prisoners.

14. Building a group conviction among the prisoners that they have been abandoned by and totally isolated from their social order.

15. Undermining-of-all-emotional-supports.

16. Preventing prisoners from writing home or to friends in the community regarding the conditions of their confinement.

17. Making available and permitting access to only those publications and books that contain materials which are neutral to or supportive of the desired new attitudes.

18. Placing individuals into new and ambiguous situations for which the standards are kept deliberately unclear and then putting pressure on him to conform to what is desired in order to win favor and a reprieve from the pressure.

19. Placing individuals whose willpower has been severely weakened or eroded into a living situation with several others who are more advanced in their thought-reform whose job it is to further undermine the individual's emotional supports.

20. Using techniques of character invalidation, i.e., humiliations, revilement, shouting, to induce feelings of guilt, fear, and suggestibility; coupled with sleeplessness, an exacting prison regimen and periodic interrogational interviews.

21. Meeting all insincere attempts to comply with cellmates' pressures with renewed hostility.

22. Renewed pointing out to the prisoner by cellmates of where he has in the past, or is in the present, not been living up to his own standards or values.

23. Rewarding of submission and subserviency to the attitudes encompassing the brainwashing objective with a lifting of pressure and acceptance as a human being.

24. Providing social and emotional supports which reinforce the new attitudes. (ibid.)

And, of course, following Schein's address, then-director of the BOP, James V. Bennett, encouraged the administrators and wardens throughout the federal prison system to put Schein's techniques into practice. 'We can manipulate our environment and culture. We can perhaps undertake some of the techniques Dr. Schein discussed. ... There's a lot of research to do. Do it as individuals. Do it as groups and let us know the results' (ibid.).

That was in 1962. Since then the results have been compiled and evaluated many times over, and all but one of Schein's suggested techniques have been left intact at Marion — along with the addition of several new features.

A BOP policy statement (October 31,1967) sanctions, after a test period, experimentation on prisoners when the benefit from the experiments are 'clear in terms of the mission and collateral objectives of the Bureau of Prisons' and for 'the advancement of knowledge.' In other words, prisoners are expected to feel inspired at the thought of 'advancing knowledge' to benefit science and corrections. But what prisoner knows that s/he is aiding the development of behavior modification techniques to be used in controlling and manipulating not only other prisoners, but also segments of the public? Besides other things, s/he is denied knowledge of what s/he is involved in — or rather forced into. The truth of behavior modification is that it is applied to prisoners secretly, and sometimes remotely (via manipulation of the environment).

EXPERIMENTATION IN ACTION

At Marion, these techniques are applied for punitive purposes, and only one subsection of the prison population is allowed any relief. First, a man's emotional and family ties are broken by removing him to the remote area of southern Illinois and by enforcing a rule whereby he can not correspond with community people within a fifty-mile radius. Sometimes the rule slackens, but when the prisoner's correspondence expresses ideological perspectives, it is enforced more strictly. Families of prisoners who move into the area are often discriminated against and harassed by government agencies. Visitors complain of being intimidated by prison officials, especially when the visits are inter-racial. On three occasions, for example, a man's wife, who had traveled from Puerto Rico, was stripped and searched. This caused great concern among prisoners, because it could happen to any one of their wives, mothers, or children. Another tactic to break a prisoner down is to punish him by removing family and friends from his visiting list,[1] or by placing him on restrictive visits. These types of visits are conducted in an isolated, partitioned booth by telephone. Such restrictions often discourage families from visiting, especially when they have to travel long distances. Officially, close family ties are encouraged; practically, they are being severed. And more often than not, a man's family is looked upon and treated with the same disdain reserved for a 'criminal.'

Another method of separating prisoners from friends and outside supporters is the two-faced campaign waged by the prison administration. On the one side, prisoners are told they have been totally rejected by society, and that even those who 'pretend' to be interested in them are 'only using prisoners for their own selfish benefit.' By this a prisoner is supposed to believe that he was never a part of a community or of society in general, that his ties among the people were never legitimate, and that their interest in him is a fraud. On the other side, a brutish, bestial, and 'sociopathic' image of prisoners is presented to the public. The horror image further alienates the people from the captive, and it sometimes causes a family to fear their own loved ones. This further isolates the prisoner and makes him more dependent on the prison authorities.

But discernment of this sophisticated system may be far beyond a prisoner's imagination, or even his comprehension. It is impossible for him to retain his sense of being, his human worth, and dignity having been reduced in the eyesight of humanity to the level of an amoeba and placed under a microscope. He can not understand why he feels the strange sensation of being watched; why it seems that 'eyes' follow him around everywhere. He fears his sanity is in jeopardy, that paranoia is taking hold of him. It shows: the tension in his face, the wide-eyed apprehensive stares, and spastic body movements. Among the general prison population, paranoia tends to spread like wildfire — from man to man. Everyone knows that the paranoid person is a walking state of danger. His mood throws everyone else out of equilibrium. The small world cannot contain the imbalance. A general alarm is sent out in hopes that someone can reach the individual before the disequilibrium ends with disaster. Sometimes the alarm is successful, sometimes not. In any case, the induced state of paranoia is a primary cause of the violence which has occurred throughout Marion's history.

The pervasive 'eyes' at Marion are not without the complement of 'ears.' Besides officers eavesdropping and the inside spies trying to collect enough intelligence to make parole, there are also listening devices out of view. Loudspeakers, for example, are also receivers, capable of picking up loose conversations in the hallways, cellblocks, and mess hall. Recently a strange device, that someone called a parabolic mike, was found. It is hard to figure out exactly how many more such devices are scattered around the prison, embedded in the wall or situated behind cells. The administration is known for collecting an enormous amount of information on prisoners, some of which could only be gathered from such eavesdropping methods. Sometimes a prisoner is confronted with the information in order to arouse suspicion about the people he has talked with. At other times the information is kept secret among officials, and traps are set.

Most sacred of all is a person's ideas. There is a standing rule among the prisoners: Never let the enemy know what you are thinking. At Marion, a man is labeled by his ideas, and his 'differential treatment' is plotted accordingly. Thus, if a man's expressed ideas are at variance with the ideas and perception of the prison administration, behavior modification is used on him to reconcile the difference.

What life boils down to is an essay of psychological warfare. An unsuspecting, or a prisoner unable to adjust and readjust psychologically and develop adequate defense mechanisms, can be taken off stride and wind up as another one of Marion's statistics. Prison officials and employees come well prepared, well trained, and well aware of the fact that a war is being waged behind the walls.

BEHAVIOR MODIFICATION AND THE MISUSE OF THERAPY TECHNIQUES

There is a small elite group in the prison population that is looked upon by the administration with great favor, because the group shares the same basic ideals with the administration. The group's members see the prison authority as a 'parent.' They think of themselves as 'residents' rather than as prisoners or captives — because to change the word is to change the reality. And they believe the program in which they are being trained will make them 'qualified therapeutic technicians' and help them secure a change in residency.

At Marion, this program is called Asklepieion — which literally means 'nothing.' The prisoners call the group 'groders' or 'groder's gorillas,' named after the psychologist who implemented Dr. Schein's brainwashing program. The 'groders' live in a special cellblock that, by prison standards, is plush. They are allowed luxuries and privileges which regular prisoners can not receive. However, they are convinced that they 'earn' these things because they are trying to do something to 'better themselves.' Generally, they look on other convicts with contempt. When confronted with evidence that they are a brainwash group, they reject the proof and accuse other prisoners of being envious.

But the reality speaks for itself. The program employs a number of noted therapeutic techniques; e.g., transactional analysis, Synanon attack therapy, psychodrama, primal therapy, and encounter group marathon sensitivity sessions. The administration's favorite is transactional analysis (TA). Essentially, TA propagates the theory that people communicate on three different levels: parent, child, and adult. These become character roles. It is up to the corresponding party to figure out which role the first party is playing, then communicate with the person on the proper counter-part level.

What this technique actually does is create an artificial dichotomy between people, each straining to fit into the proper character role. Thus, communication becomes artificial, stilted, and utterly meaningless in its content. Everyone sounds like a pseudo-intellectual. Ultimately, it propagates the idea that the authorities always fit the role of 'parent,' and the prisoners must submit to the role of a 'child.' Although some 'groders' pretend this practice is a fakeout on 'the man,' it still is a real social practice. Changing the words to describe it *does not* change the reality.

Other techniques include Dr. Schein's 'character invalidation.' These techniques are incorporated under the auspices of 'game sessions' (Synanon attack therapy) and 'marathons' (encounter group sensitivity sessions). In 'game sessions,' members of the group accuse a person of playing games, not being truthful with the group, lying, and so forth, or the person is accused of some misdeed or shortcoming. Before he is allowed a chance to explain (which is considered as only more lying), he is relentlessly barraged by dirty-name calling until he confesses or 'owns up' to his shortcomings. He is then accused of making the group go through a lot of trouble in having to pry the truth out of him. So, for this crime, he is forced to apologize.

'Marathons' are all-night versions of literally the same, except that they include local community people who come into the prison to be 'trained' in the techniques. After so many hours of being verbally attacked and denied sleep, a person 'owns up' to anything and accepts everything he is told. After being humiliated, he is encouraged to cry. The group then shows its compassion by hugging him and telling him that they love him.

These techniques exploit the basic weaknesses in human (aggregative) nature, especially those weaknesses produced by an alienating society, i.e., the need to be loved, cared about, accepted by other people, and the need to be free. In turn, they are transmuted into 'submission and subserviency,' the type of behavior conducive to the prison officials' goal of control and manipulation. The 'groders' will not resist or complain. Nor will they go on a strike to seek redress of prisoners' grievances. They are alienated from their environment, and their emotional inter-dependency welds and insulates them into a crippled cohesion (of the weak bearing the weak). They are not permitted to discuss these techniques outside the group, because one of the preconditions for admittance is a bond to secrecy. Yet almost anyone can spot a 'groder' because the light has gone out of his eyes. He literally wears the look of humiliation.

Some years ago, the prison population wanted to do the 'groders' bodily harm because they allowed themselves to be used as guinea pigs, and because the techniques they helped to develop would be used on other prisoners and people in the outside world. In their lust for freedom, 'groders' would help to sell out an entire generation. Today, they are generally looked upon as mental enemies. So prisoners just leave them alone. Meanwhile, the brainwashing programs are still finding their way into communities in the outside world — under a number of pseudonyms other than Asklepieion. And the 'groders' still have hopes of joining these programs when they are sufficiently spread. They will become 'therapeutic technicians.' This is what Dr. Groder laid out in his 'master plan,' utilizing prisoners as couriers of the techniques into the community. It is also what former warder Ralph Aron meant when he testified at the 1975 *Bono* v. *Saxbe* trial that 'the purpose of the Marion control unit is to control revolutionary attitudes in the prison system and in the society at large.'

What the 'groders' fail to realize is that, even as 'therapists,' they will remain under observation long after their release from prison — under what is euphemistically called 'post-release follow-through.' And what Dr. Groder fails to realize is that by camouflaging Dr. Schein's techniques under pseudonyms, whereby prisoners who volunteer for the program cannot recognize its real meaning and objectives, extensive violations of the *Nuremberg Code* have taken and are taking place. Even the implication of freedom as inducement for volunteers is considered a means of coercion by the Code's standards. The first principle in the Code proclaims:

> [V]oluntary consent of the human subject is absolutely essential. This means that the person involved should have legal capacity to give consent; should be situated as to be able to exercise free power of choice, without the intervention of any element of force, fraud, deceit, duress, over-reaching or other ulterior form of constraint or coercion; and should have sufficient knowledge and comprehension of the elements of the subject matter involved as to enable him to make an understanding and enlightened decision. ... Before an acceptance of an affirmative decision by the experimental subject, there should be made known to him the nature, duration and purpose of the experiment.

There is much that is not explained or accounted for at Marion. Prisoners are left to discover it all on their own, via studying the prison and the prison system's history. In light of most of the surprise discoveries one makes when learning this history, it should come as no surprise that some aspects at Marion are at variance with the *Nuremberg Code*.

CHEMOTHERAPY: THE MISUSE OF DRUGS

Chemotherapy is administered four times daily at Marion. The loudspeaker announces: 'Control medication in the hospital ... pill line.' Valium, librium, thorazine and other 'chemical billy-clubs' are handed out like gumdrops. Sometimes the drugs mysteriously make their way into the food. For example, the strange month of December 1974, recorded five unrelated, inexplicable stabbings. During the same time, eight prisoners suffered from hallucinations in the 'hole' and had to be treated (with thorazine injections). Drugs are often prescribed for minor ailments and are often suggested to prisoners as a panacea for all the psychological ill-effects of incarceration. Some drugs such as prolixin make prisoners want to commit suicide. Some attempt it; some succeed.[2]

THE END OF THE LINE: THE LONG-TERM CONTROL UNIT

Segregation is the punitive aspect of the behavior modification program. It is euphemistically referred to as 'aversive conditioning.' In short, prisoners are conditioned to avoid solitary confinement, and to avoid it requires some degree of conformity and cooperation. But the 'hole' remains open for what prison authorities and Dr. Schein call 'natural leaders.' These prisoners can be pulled from population on 'investigation' and held in solitary confinement until the so-called investigation is over. During the whole ordeal, the prisoner is not told what the inquiry is about — unless he is finally charged with an infraction of the rules. If the Marion authorities think that the behavior modification techniques will eventually work on the prisoner, he is sent to short-term segregation. If not, they use the last legal weapon in the federal prison system: the long-term control unit.

The long-term control unit is the 'end of the line' in the federal prison system. Since there is no place lower in all of society, it is the end of the line for society also. Just as the threat of imprisonment controls society, so is Marion the control mechanism for the prison system; ultimately, the long-term control unit controls Marion. Prisoners in the unit can feel the heaviness of this burden, knowing that it is a long way back to the top.

Usually a prisoner does not know specifically why he has been sent to the control unit, other than that his ideological beliefs or his personal attitude toward prison authority is somehow 'wrong.' And he usually does not know how long he will be in the control unit. A prisoner is told he is being placed on thirty-day observation, and that he has the right to appeal the decision if he wishes. Until recently, most prisoners simply waived the appeal because they were given the impression that they would be getting out soon. One particular prisoner was told by the Control Unit Committee that he would be getting out of the control unit after the observation period because they 'needed the room.' Later he was given an indefinite period in the unit — that is the case with most prisoners.

In the control unit, a prisoner only does two things: recreate and shower. Only one range of men (18 out of 72) is allowed to work. Although everyone recognizes that the work is exploitative, it is generally considered a privilege. The rest of the control unit prisoners spend 23½ hours a day locked in their cells. According to what state the man's mind is in, he may read or write. He sees the Control Unit Committee for about thirty seconds once a month to receive a decision on his 'adjustment rating.' He may see a case worker to get papers notarized, the counselor to get an administrative remedy (complaint) form, and a phone call authorization (on a 'maybe' basis). He may see the educational supervisor for books. Other than that, he deteriorates.

The cell itself contains a flat steel slab jutting from the wall. Overlaying the slab is a one-inch piece of foam wrapped in coarse plastic. This is supposed to be a bed. Yet it cuts so deeply into the body when one lays on it, that the body literally reeks with pain. After a few days, you are totally numb. Feelings become indistinct, emotions unpredictable. The monotony makes thoughts hard to separate and capsulate. The eyes grow weary of the scene, and shadows appear around the periphery, causing sudden reflexive action. Essentially, the content of a man's mind is the only means to defend his sanity.

Besides these methods of torture (and they are torture), there is also extreme cold conditioning in the winter, and a lack of ventilation in the summer. Hot and cold water manipulation is carried out in the showers. Shock waves are administered to the brain when guards bang a rubber mallet against the steel bars. Then there is outright brutality, usually in the form of beatings. The suicide rate in the Control Unit is five times the rate in the general population at Marion.

At the root of the Control Unit's behavior modification program, though, is indefinite confinement. This is perhaps the most difficult aspect of the Control Unit to communicate to the public. Yet a testament to this policy was a man named 'Red' Hayes. After thirteen years in solitary confinement (nearly six in the control unit), he became the 'boogie man' of the prison system — the living/dying example of what can happen to any prisoner. The more he deteriorated in his own skeleton, the more prisoners could expect to wane in his likeness. He died in the unit in August 1977.

In essence, the Unit is a Death Row for the living. And the silent implications of behavior modification speak their sharpest and clearest ultimatum: *conform or die!*

> In several instances [the control unit] has been used to silence prison critics. It has been used to silence religious leaders. It has been used to silence economic and philosophical dissidents. (Judge James Foreman, U.S. District Court, St. Louis)

NOTES

1   As an example, the co-editor of [Volume 4:2] of the *Journal* [Little Rock Reed] has had family and friends removed from his visiting list at the Southern Ohio Correctional Facility (which follows the Marion model) without any notice, so that family and friends have been denied entrance into the prison after traveling hundreds of miles to visit. On each occasion that this has occurred, the prison officials claimed that they had no idea how it could have happened. Certain names just jumped off the visiting list and scampered their way out of the double-locked filing cabinet all by themselves. Complaints to Warden Arthur Tate (who spent his last paid vacation touring Marion, Illinois, and found it 'highly impressive') fell on deaf ears. He refused to even acknowledge receipt of the complaints, thereby fully endorsing such illegal treatment as legitimate [Editor].
2   It is of more than passing interest that the U.S. Supreme Court ruled on February 27, 1990, that prison officials may administer any kind of powerful, mind-altering drugs they wish to any prisoner whose behavior they feel is undesirable. The decision as to whom these powerful, mind-altering drugs may be administered is left to the absolute discretion of prison officials, and no outside review is allowed, so long as the prison psychiatrist (whose employer is the warden) states that it is in the prisoner's best interest [Editor].

REFERENCES

Chorover, S.L. 1979. *From Genesis to Genocide: The Meaning of Human Nature and the Power of Behavior Control.* Cambridge: MIT Press.

Female Political Prisoners and Anti-Imperialist Struggles
Susan Rosenberg

Dear Editors,

Greetings of solidarity.

Thank you for asking me to write for your newsletter. You ask are there political prisoners in the U.S. prisons, and you ask me to write about my own experiences. Definitely the answer to the first is YES. There are over 150 political prisoners in U.S. prisons. We are in almost every federal prison in the country and spread throughout different State prison systems. I define a political prisoner as someone whose beliefs or actions have put them into direct conflict with the U.S. government, or someone who has been targeted by the government because of his/her beliefs and actions. While this is a somewhat generic description, it complies with international legal definitions. The other grouping of people who are in prison who are political are the prisoners of war from the Puerto Rican and New Afrikan/African-American liberation movements. These are individuals who make that claim under international law in pursuit of the recognition of their national liberation struggles for self-determination. The political prisoners and POW's in the U.S. who have struggled for human rights and social liberation — people who come from movements that range from the anti-imperialist left to the Native American struggle for sovereignty have all been treated by the government as political dissidents, but have been denied the dignity of recognition as political prisoners. Rather, we have been criminalized or wrongly defined as 'terrorists'. We have been repressed to the maximum.

The criminal justice system has been subverted into the main counter-insurgency mechanism of the state to "bury us alive." The government denies that the laws are applied for their political agenda; they deny that sentence length and manipulation of parole release are applied to the maximum depending on the content of the political beliefs of the prisoners; they deny that we are designated to spend years in isolation/control units *because* we are political. A case in point: Donald Bray bombed ten abortion clinics, three of which had people on the premises, none with warning calls. He was released after serving forty-six months. Tim Blunk and myself were convicted of weapons possession (not use) and were sentenced to fifty-eight years with recommendations of no parole. At our sentencing the judge told us we would have plenty of time to read *The God That Failed*. We are now entering our sixth year in prison. This sentence was the longest ever given for this particular offense. If one is from the right it shakes down one way and if one is from the left it shakes down differently. This is simply unjust.

If I can change here ...

Picture: An underground basement containing sixteen cells painted all white, with no natural light. Wire mesh covering all windows making a view out impossible. No sound from outside. Eleven large rotating surveillance cameras. Electronic gates controlled from a command center in another building. Constant surveillance and controlled movement supervised by specially trained prison guards. Infrequent family visits. Two ten-minute phone calls a week that are later listened to, recorded, transcribed, analyzed and forwarded to other law enforcement agencies for analysis. Sexual intimidation and constant harassment by male guards. Never more than five women in this place. A psychological prison (torture center) in Uruguay? A scene from the film 'A Clockwork Orange'? No. The U.S. Federal Bureau of Prisons (BOP) High Security Unit (HSU) at the women's federal correctional institution in Lexington, Kentucky, which opened in October 1986.

The HSU was officially shut down on August 15, 1988. During the almost two years it was operational, it held three women political prisoners: Alejandrina Torres (a Puerto Rican Independentista and Prisoner of War); Silvia Baraldini (an Italian national and anti-imperialist convicted of participating in the 1979 prison liberation of Black Liberation Army member Assata Shakur); and myself, Susan Rosenberg (a North American anti-imperialist convicted of weapons possession). Two other social prisoners — Debra Brown (currently on death row in Ohio) and Sylvia Brown (currently at the Marianna maximum security women's unit) were also subjected to the experiment. The administration unofficially informed the political women that we could only be considered for transfer into general population if we would renounce our political affiliations and beliefs. At the same time, the two social prisoners were told that if they did not associate with the political women their stay in the HSU would be considerably shortened. None of the political women were placed in the HSU for disciplinary infractions committed while in prison.

The HSU came to symbolize the U.S. government's hypocrisy: while it claimed that it had no political prisoners in its prisons, the HSU was the first explicitly political prison. It was the subject of militant opposition initiated by the Puerto Rican Independence Movement, an opposition which included groups ranging from social justice-oriented church groups to radical women's and lesbian groups. The HSU was condemned by Amnesty International as 'small group isolation', an internationally recognized form of psychological torture — and it was closed officially by a court ruling from the legal challenge in *Baraldini* v. *Thornburgh*. Judge Barrington Parker concluded in his decision, "It is one thing to place persons under greater security because they have escape histories and pose special greater risks to our correctional institutions. But consigning anyone to a high security unit for past political associations they will never shed unless forced to renounce them is a dangerous mission for this country's prison system to continue". *On September 8, 1989, the U.S, Court of Appeals in Washington D.C. overturned the Parker decision.*

The appeals court held that the government is free to use the political beliefs and association of prisoners as a basis for treating us more harshly and placing us in maximum security conditions. Further, the appeals court ruling means that no court can question or dispute the prison's decisions, even if those decisions explicitly involve the prisoner's politics or political identity.

This legal decision gives official sanction to the BOP to place political prisoners into control units. A control unit is a prison block within a prison. There is no movement in the units, and they are designed to break the prisoner through sensory deprivation and control. The control unit is the U.S. equivalent of the West German or British 'dead wings' or 'white cells'. The appeals court ruling will also affect Marion penitentiary for men, where prisoners have been locked in their cells twenty-three hours a day for over five years. Marion has also been condemned by Amnesty International, and it is also used as a control unit for political prisoners and prisoners of war. While Marion is supposedly a punishment facility, a growing number of political prisoners have been designated there directly from trial. The new Lexington legal decision allows the BOP to build more control units and to carry out this 'mission' against the government's political opposition. All the government has to do is label someone a 'terrorist' or a 'security risk' and they can be subject to the most repressive prison conditions and human rights violations.

The BOP never acknowledged the condemnation of the conditions at the HSU. They continued to maintain that the conditions were 'humane'. They never complied with the original court order enjoining them to transfer any of us into general population. Instead, they built a new 'maximum security' unit for women inside the men's federal prison in Marianna, Florida. The 'mission' of BOP at Lexington will be carried on in a slightly more palatable form at Marianna. This 'mission' is one part of the overall program of the BOP to increase control, regimentation, and repression against all women in prison.

Since 1980, a growing number of women have been arrested and given long sentences for political activities against the government, including Puerto Rican, Black/New Afrikan and North American revolutionaries. Now that the transfer of political prisoners to the Marianna prison has been approved by the appeals court decision, it is just a matter of time before some, if not all, are sent there.

What happened as a result of the Lexington experiment is that the definition of 'general population' for 'maximum security' women underwent a drastic change. Restrictions increased ten-fold, and any semblance of parity between women and men is gone. Just as the Marion lockdown pulls the whole prison system towards greater repression, so too does the Lexington experiment.

After five years in U.S. prisons and jails, over three and a half of which I have spent in either solitary confinement or small-group isolation, I have reached the conclusion that in order to secure our human rights we must actively struggle for our political identities and commitments. To do otherwise is to succumb to the war of attrition being waged by the government against all of us. This 'war' being the length of our lives versus the government's counter-insurgency strategy of live burials through life sentences and isolation. In this conflict of political prisoner versus government we are no different than our counterparts around the world. I have also concluded that because the U.S. government is faced with a contradiction between its democratic facade and its own need to utilize a permanent state of repression, the abuses and violations against prisoners is subject to pressure, more through political and social action than through the courts.

Venceremos,
Susan Rosenberg[1]

Editor's Note: Article reprinted with the kind permission of the editorial staff at The Critical Criminologist.

NOTES

1   Susan Rosenberg is also a Resistance Conspiracy Case defendant. The Resistance Conspiracy Case is a conspiracy trial against six long-time political activists charged in conspiring to "Change, protest, and influence U.S. foreign and domestic policies through violent and illegal means." The indictment includes four bombings of U.S. government and military installations where property was damaged but no injuries occurred. One of the acts charged is the bombing of the U.S. Capitol after the U.S. invasion of Grenada in 1983. This political show trial is expected to begin in the spring of 1990.

USP Marion's Version of Orwell's *1984* and Beyond
Ronald Del Raine

Editor's Note: This essay is a consolidation and revision of the author's two previous essays, "The Marion Experience," which took First Place in the 1975–76 PEN prison writer's essay contest, and "The Marion Experience — Revisited," which received an Honorable Mention in PEN's 1988–89 essay contest.

When one has [a maximum security or control] unit, one uses it. When I came here, our Bridgewater Unit had 80 to 100 youngsters who were considered the most dangerous in the state. We have closed that unit and we haven't missed it a great deal. As long as we had it, it was full. If we were to build one that would hold 300 vicious youngsters tomorrow, within six months it would be filled with 300 vicious youngsters that were suddenly discovered within our system. So I would suggest to be aware of that. (Dr. Jerome B. Miller, former Commissioner of the Massachusetts Department of Youth Services)

In my first essay, written in the 'hole' in Lewisburg federal prison after being transferred from Marion, I draw an analogy between the newly inaugurated Marion prison program and those utilized by the omnipotent, shadowy agents of government as depicted by Franz Kafka in *The Trial*. The analogy was based upon personal experience: my enduring twenty-eight months of the new program during 1972–1974.

The Marion procedures were enacted in the former segregation unit (the 'hole') which was now labeled the Long Term Control Unit (new program, new name). They began as newly arrived convicts disembarked from the transfer bus and were lodged in segregation for a few days as a matter of normal procedure. They then expected to be released into the general population, unless they had been charged with a rule violation. However, normalcy no longer prevailed at Marion.

Instead of being released, many unfortunates were summarily sentenced to indefinite terms in the Control Unit for no discernible reason. When their protestations of 'You must have me mixed up with someone else,' were not answered, and they then inquired, 'What did I do wrong?' some were told, 'We don't want you in *our* population!' Since this is a difficult 'accusation' to refute, they then remained in the Long Term Control Unit. And if any doubt exists that 'Long Term' does not refer to the length of their felony sentences but defines the length of their stay in lock-up, consider that one prisoner spent five years there, while many were there three or four years.[1]

Perhaps this new policy of arbitrarily selecting random victims for their 'program' was the Bureau of Prisons' (BOP) equivalent of 'preventive detention' and 'no knock' legislation. Just as the passage of the Omnibus Crime Control and Safe Streets Act of 1968 purportedly made the streets safe for honest citizens, so too the federal prisoncrats may claim they are making their penitentiary tiers safe for prisoners (or for guards). However, the Omnibus Bill was enacted by Congress, while the BOP enacted its policy *sub rosa*. This surreptitious convict control plan, choosing as if by lot, young, old, short-term, long-term, violent, non-violent, first-timers, and recidivists, certainly is not designed to benefit the victims; however, the more zealous, persistent practitioners of the policy often benefit by a Washington, DC headquarters assignment. A blind subservient acceptance of orders — of such stuff are promotions made. Ever onward, ever upward, climb the ladder of success; never mind whose bodies are used as rungs.

As the Marion Inmate Disciplinary Committee officials dispense terms of endless years in segregation for reasons so nebulous and evanescent as to defy articulation, their demeanor certainly does not betray any guilt, apprehension, or doubt. Rather, they seem quite righteous, smug, and virtuous in the performance of their duties. Since their actions are inexplicable by rational standards, what psychological factors could explain their conduct? Or, how are they themselves persuaded that they are correct, that they are making just decisions, that they are taking appropriate actions?

One factor influencing their mental make-up is the effect upon them of the free-will philosophical school of thought. This ideology states that people have complete untrammeled freedom of choice when they make a decision; they deliberately choose to do good or evil, right or wrong. In utilizing this belief, such influences as the person's past environment, heredity, psychoses, neurosis, culture, panic reactions, economic conditions, and the exigencies of the moment are negated. (An apt analogy is Voltaire's description of a fly landing on a horse-drawn carriage and proclaiming, 'Oh! Look at *me*! *I'm* pushing the carriage!' or something to that effect.) Authoritarian, disciplinarian-type personalities who are attracted to prison careers will, almost without exception, believe in free-will. They conclude that all convicts are in prison because they deliberately, and with malice, chose to commit an evil act. Accordingly, there should follow punishment. And this the Marion (and other) administrators are prepared to apply endlessly.

Another prevailing attitude among the vast majority of prison personnel is that convicts have it too soft, that conditions are too luxurious, and that a return to the 'good old days' is in order. Considerable resentment of bleeding-heart liberals who have introduced penal reform with its attendant amelioration of the convicts' condition into *their* prisons is evident. Therefore, when an opportunity arises to increase the population of the Long Term Control Unit, and other similar control units, with convicts who have exercised their free-will and chose evil, and who, beyond any doubt, are already being pampered, then the prison administrators need not wrestle with any moral dilemmas as to the convicts' guilt or innocence. The decision is clear — lock 'em up!

In addition to these influences, the administrators are also subject to, or perhaps victimized by, an all-pervasive subtle propagandistic tactic which was detailed in *The New Republic* years ago. Briefly, this technique of peacefully persuading people to follow your dictates consists of first, convincing them that they live in the freest country in the world, that this is indeed the best of all possible worlds (and for those inclined to believe it, that this present world is not important, but the life after death is). Most people thoroughly imbued with this belief will then tend to passively accept whatever conditions prevail in their society and they condemn those 'criminal types' who rebel. Since the structure of society is organized so that it functions, at least theoretically, in a perfect, or nearly perfect, manner, then any who rebel within the system — or against the system — must obviously be culpable. One advantage of governing people by this tactic is that no such crude, expensive instruments such as guns, clubs, or force are required. Such people are self-policing. Such a tactic is effective without being offensive — and thus efficient.

Closely allied with this 'best of all possible worlds' influence is the related effect of the 'best of all possible prison systems' influence. The BOP has long been regarded as the paradigm for the world. When state penologists seek a model to emulate, it is toward the BOP that they turn. Experts from foreign countries tour this system seeking advice and counsel on how best to direct and administer prisons in their own lands. One director even wrote a book on the history of the BOP. Some prominent bureau officials, past and present, testify before various committees as 'experts' — parroting the usual stereotyped penological pronouncements. (However, the testimony of a genuine expert, Dr. Richard R. Korn, professor of criminology at Berkeley, would befit the federal system when he aptly states of the correctional process: 'The sickness is in charge of the treatment ... We are not the doctors, we are the disease.') So the administrators at Marion (and other prisons that follow the model) have the psychological assurance of knowing they are performing their duties within, and sanctioned by, the world's most respected penal system.

When the members of the prison disciplinary tribunal exercise their prerogatives of office and sentence innocent, unsuspecting prisoners — who have not even been accused of any transgressions — to indefinite terms in Control Unit, are they absolutely convinced they are morally correct? Probably not. The average person finds it difficult to completely discard all his moral precepts, especially if they were integrated into his personality while he was still young. Perhaps the administrator retains a vestige of conscience, or a faint fundamental belief in the innocence of the innocent. He knows he should not put innocent people into segregation — yet he does. He will then be impelled to find a rationalization to justify his decisions to himself, his colleagues, and his underlings. But this situation leads to a contradiction, or a cognitive dissonance, which results in a psychological condition of stress. The average individual will then try to resolve that dissonance/stress by sustaining, often subliminally, that element of the contradiction to which he has the most intense attraction, and will change that element to which he has the least intense attachment. In this case, the idea of the innocent not being punished constitutes the least intense attraction and is suppressed. By emphasizing the idea that convicts exercised their free-wills and chose evil, that the convicts have it too soft, that the convicts live in the best of all possible worlds, and that, as an upper-echelon member of the BOP (or other such prison), his policy must be correct, then he is stressing that element of the contradiction to which he has the most intense attraction. This tends to reduce or eliminate the dissonance, which then leads to a sense of relief.

In the renowned *1984*, George Orwell, in a percipient analysis of similar mental phenomena, labeled the process of simultaneously recognizing and not recognizing a fact as *doublethink*; he said that it requires a splitting of intelligence. If the term 'Marion Administrator' is substituted for 'Party Intellectual' and the 'BOP' is substituted for 'Ingsoc' in the following passage from *1984*, then Orwell could very well have been describing Marion:

Doublethink means the power of holding two contradictory beliefs in one's mind simultaneously, and accepting both of them. The Party Intellectual knows in which direction his memories must be altered: he therefore knows that he is playing tricks with reality; but by the exercise of *doublethink* he also satisfies himself that reality is not violated. The process has to be conscious, or it would not be carried out with sufficient precision, but it also has to be unconscious, or it would bring with it a feeling of falsity and hence of guilt.

Doublethink lies at the very heart of 'Ingsoc,' since the essential act of the Party is to use conscious deception while retaining the firmness of purpose that goes with complete honesty. To tell deliberate lies while genuinely believing in them, to forget any fact which has become inconvenient, and then, when it becomes necessary again, to draw it back from oblivion for just so long as it is needed, to deny the existence of objective reality and all the while to take account of the reality which one denies — all this is indispensably necessary. Even in using the word *doublethink* it is necessary to exercise *doublethink*. (Orwell, 1949:175–6)

As fitting as this classic passage is, perhaps only Erich Fromm's statement in the 'Afterword' of the same book better describes the administrative minds of Marion: '... [I]n a successful manipulation of the mind the person is no longer saying the opposite of what he thinks, but he thinks the opposite of what is true.'

Then what is the attitude of the average guard as he performs his duty of insuring that the occupants of the Control Unit are indeed controlled for a 'Long Term?' He will usually accept whatever conditions or orders his superiors have determined he shall accept. His years of turning keys, like a well oiled automaton, have merely reinforced his conditioned reflex response to perform and not to question. His milieu has not been such as to whet intellectual curiosity, so lemming-like, he does not question official policy that classifies the human merchandise stored in the concrete cubicle as deserving of its punishment or that his function is to keep it there. So keep it there he does.

Also to be considered is the fact that the Long Term Control Unit (and other such administrative and punitive control units in different prisons) exists; that is, it has been built. It must exist for a purpose, why not utilize it? Even the name (Long Term Control Unit) suggests that a prisoner should not be locked up in it for a short term. So the psychological redolence of the very title reinforces the 'lock 'em up' attitude.

My own Marion experiences are illustrative of the workings of these administrative and psychological processes. In 1972, I was starting my fourth year on a 199-year federal prison sentence at Leavenworth, Kansas, for a bungled 1967 bank robbery 'shoot out.' J. Edgar Hoover and Myrl Alexander, director of the BOP, had conducted an acrimonious public debate about our case, that, at the very least, caused my name to be placed on the penitentiaries 'hot list' (i.e., those given special scrutiny and frequently, special treatment). On April 7, 1972, I was locked up in segregation for 'agitating for a work strike.' Never mind that I was working every day in the shoe factory at the time of the strike. I worked because I thought it stupid to begin a strike for the institution of Latin movies, foods, cultural programs, and for the observance of Mexican holidays; additionally, nothing untoward had happened recently to cause a strike (unlike two other recent work stoppages). Some of us believed that any action involving and benefiting only one ethnic group merely furthered our master's 'divide and conquer' tactics.[2]

Of course, any convict knows that one can not work during a strike while urging others to stop working. Even the most silly, stir-simple stumble-bum understands this contradiction. Nevertheless, when I protested my innocence to the lieutenant who locked me up, he assured me that I could explain it to the Disciplinary Committee the next day. Instead, I was trundled into a prison bus and deposited in the 'hole' at the Medical Center for Federal Prisoners in Springfield, Missouri, for six weeks.

The next stop on my odyssey was the segregation cell block at Marion, Illinois (H-Unit — later entitled the Long Term Control Unit), where I spent the next twenty-eight months. Joining me in lock-up were three 'ringleaders' from Leavenworth who did not report to work and who had been given a special transfer to Springfield, but in a few weeks they were all released into general population, while I was given a variety of patently fabricated excuses for remaining in segregation. I now have twenty-five different official and written reasons for my stay in *durance vile*, including, for example, (1) my original conviction which resulted in my prison term; (2) an incident which occurred in county jail; (3) a felony in another state for which I had never been charged or even questioned about; (4) what I might do; (5) various prison disciplinary charges for which I had long ago served my sentences; (6) being involved in 'devious' plots, the nature of which I could never discover; (7) if a lawsuit were filed because of me, they were liable; (8) *ad infinitum, ad nauseam.*

In a few months, those three 'ringleaders' were back in lock-up again, along with others, for another strike. Then a few days later, during a heat wave, a few lads on an upper tier started a minor disturbance, breaking some cell lights and hollering. In response, the 'goon squad' wheeled in 'Big Bertha,' pumped out tear gas on all four tiers and took *everything* from everybody, except our shorts. Because of a .38 bullet hole in my neck, which hit the spinal column, sleeping on the concrete was painful; so, I saved paper milk cartons for a bed, but the 'hacks' took them also.

In 1973, the People's Law Office in Chicago, with the assistance of the National Prison Project of the American Civil Liberties Union (ACLU), filed a class action lawsuit for those segregated as a result of the strike, but Judge James M. Foreman, a recent Nixon appointee, perhaps determined not to 'coddle criminals' denied relief. (See *Adams* v. *Carlson*, 352 F.Supp. 982 [E.D. IL 1973]). When the case was remanded back to him with directives from the Seventh Circuit Court of Appeals, he ordered that the prison disciplinary committee give new hearings to the men who had been in segregation. A prison lieutenant investigated the charges against the men and submitted written reports which were used as evidence to *again* convict them. Excerpts from his reports stated:

> ... Obviously a report would not have been written if the officer had not believed that the incident would happen. [Investigative report, Leon Bates.]

> ... Facts true until proven false. [Investigate report, Chester James.]

> ... As per the reporting officer, Miranda must have been agitating, otherwise there would have been no reason to write a report. [Investigative report, Raphael Miranda.]

Three of his reports even exonerated the prisoners:

> ... Officer Killman verified that [Hallman] reported to work on 7-25-72, the date of the offense ...

... Officer[s] Hill and Pringle verified that Warren had worked on 7-25-72, the date of the charge...

... Officer Roman stated that Patmore did report to work but he was ordered back to his cell for the count...

One portion of the Memorandum filed by the prisoners' lawyers stated:

Inmate Bates was even told by the guard who allegedly wrote his incident report that he in fact never filled out such a report and if called before the Committee would testify as to that: yet Bates was denied the right to call him as a witness.

However, since the Court of Appeals had stated that sixteen months segregation for a work strike was disproportionate punishment, the judge was forced to order thirty-six prisoners released into general population, in spite of BOP frantic last minute legal protestations filed with the court, swearing that, in effect, riot, ruin, and revolution would surely ensue if these dangerous desperadoes were allowed to mingle with the other prisoners. But of course, all was peaceful and quiet when they were finally released.

Since my own entreaties for release had been consciously ignored, I finally decided to execute a desperate, or perhaps deranged, plan, one that would not endear me to my masters, but held a faint hope of relief. I filed a petition for a writ of *habeas corpus*, asking for release from segregation. In addition to the legal argument, I included the following philosophical oratory hoping to soften the cold judicial heart:

As an *obiter dictum*, I can only quote Socrates in this peroration:

For of old, I have had many accusers, who have accused me falsely to you during many years. ... Hardest of all, I do not know and cannot tell the names of my accusers ... and therefore I must simply fight with shadows in my own defense and argue when there is no one who answers.

Notwithstanding the fact that the federal *habeas corpus* statute (28 U.S.C. 2243) states that 'a court judge or justice entertaining an application for a writ of *habeas corpus* shall forthwith award the writ or issue an order directing the respondent to show cause why the writ should not be granted' and that 'it shall be returned within three days unless for good cause additional time, not exceeding twenty days, is allowed,' and that the 'court shall summarily hear and determine the facts, and dispose of the matter as law and justice require,' and omitting the fact that I filed two petitions for a writ of *mandamus* in a vain attempt to compel the court to comply with the requirements of this law, a year and two months elapsed before I was given an evidentiary hearing. At this hearing, a Marion administrator testified that an unknown informer told an unknown guard who wrote an unknown report (at least all unknown to me), that I had agitated for a strike in Leavenworth. Actually, this informer, guard, and report were so unknown that four years and several different prisons later, when I requested that my prison file be searched under the new Freedom of Information Act for signs of a disciplinary report, a memo, a document, or any reason for my twenty-eight months in segregation, my requests were returned to me with notations indicating that the reasons were still *unknown*.

Five months after the hearing, the good judge rendered his decision, and my legal education proceeded apace as I was forced to assimilate the unpalatable fact that these laws (*habeas corpus* and *mandamus*), while perhaps applicable to some, do not apply to me and certain others similarly situated. It stated in part:

> It appears that Petitioner is in administrative segregation, rather than punitive segregation imposed pursuant to any specific rule infraction. [Yet the thirty-six prisoners ordered to be released lived alongside me in identical cells and were accorded identical treatment] ...
>
> The Court feels that it would not be proper to order that Del Raine be released to the prison's general population, since some prison officials have already concluded that if he were in the general population he would present a threat to prison officials, other inmates or himself. The Court will not order the Respondents to do an act which would endanger lives at the institution.

Strange! One might conclude from this judicial reasoning that I am Jack the Ripper reincarnated, incarcerated. Completely ignored is the fact that I have never even been accused of harming or attempting to harm anyone during my many years in prison.

But there was yet hope. The court ordered that I be given a due process hearing to determine if I should be continued in 'administrative segregation' (the use of this euphemistic label is a favorite legal tactic to avoid deciding certain cases on their merits). But in order to justify my two years in the 'hole' — which is approximately the amount of time one spends locked up after killing another convict — some rule infraction needs to be recorded — and the more serious it is, the better the government's case will appear.

Lacking any bodies to use as evidence, but determined to perform their duly allotted role in the charade with what 'evidence' they had, they issued me an Incident Report, stating in part, "The last Mental Health Evaluation made by our staff psychologist recommended that should [Del Raine] be returned to our population he would be a threat to himself or others or to the orderly function (sic) of the institution.' The decision of the three committee members was that I should remain in segregation. However, their wishes were nullified when the General Counsel for the BOP granted my appeal in the newly inaugurated administrative remedy procedure, and I was released into population at Lewisburg prison after twenty-eight months in segregation.

But in 1986, only a dozen years later, the U.S. Attorney sent me another copy of the Incident Report as part of his motion to dismiss my case, which stated:

> The last Mental Health Evaluation made by our staff Psychologist recommended that should [Del Raine] be returned to our population he would *not* be a threat to himself or others or to the orderly function (sic) of this institution. (my emphasis)

So much for the integrity of the BOP Disciplinary Committee. Thomas Jefferson aptly described such judicial proceedings as 'Twistification of the Law.'

But *voila*, the U.S. Attorney also attached to his motion to dismiss (perhaps not realizing its significance) a bonanza, i.e., a Memorandum dated April 7, 1972 (the date I was locked up), stamped 'F.O.I. EXEMPT,' (Freedom of Information Exempt) which informed me — after fourteen years — why I was locked up.

In one of my *pro se* appeal briefs to the Court of Appeals, submitted in conjunction with my court-appointed attorney's brief, I commented as follows: [Note: In order to fully express my analysis of the Memorandum, I have chosen to utilize a non-judicial, satirical style of expression.]

It is noteworthy that I'm not even mentioned in the first five paragraphs of the Memorandum since I was so inconsiderate to the furtherance of the 'conspiracy' as not to go to the yard, thus depriving the author of observable 'evidence' of my guilt. But not to worry, he recoups lost ground in paragraphs six and seven.

In paragraph two, chief suspect Welge didn't just go to the yard and talk to people as all others did; no, that's too mundane. Instead, he made 'voice contacts' with 150 others (not conversation, chit-chat, or greetings, but the more sinister, conspiratorial 'voice contacts'). Of course, he didn't just stand around in the yard, he 'stationed himself' (just as 007 James Bond does before plunging into another exciting adventure).

In paragraph three, corroboration of the 'conspiracy' is further shrewdly noted by the ever vigilant author, the BOP counterpart to Sherlock Holmes. Since one of the first 'contacts' chief suspect Welge makes is with possible suspect Hopwood, then he is a key member of the conspiracy. And then what does Hopwood do? *Aha!* Of course. He 'stations himself' on the ventilator (others may sit or lie down on the ventilator, but he 'stations himself'). Very incriminating. Then after thirty minutes he's in the southwest corner of the yard (hardly the actions of any innocent person). Instead of just looking around, or even just glancing about, he 'keeps close surveillance' with the prime perpetrator (*à la* Gang Busters).

In paragraph four, McCracken, a new protagonist, joins the plot. After walking around the track (undoubtedly on a scouting mission for enemy agents), he makes for the rendezvous, the apex of operations — the ventilator — where he confers with Hopwood. Of course, his 'close surveillance' and 'occasional contact' with Welge does not go unobserved. (Now, the average reader might not be able to trace McCracken's link to mastermind Del Raine from these activities, but using arcane inductive modes of deduction — known only to a chosen few — our Sherlock could immediately perceive the guilty link.)

In paragraph five, the plot thickens: arch villain Bodenbach, 'stationed' as a 'point man' (the author missed his chance in not using this particular prison parlance), would 'signal' Welge and his 150 'contacts' when the guards walked up (just as John le Carre might have written it). (Of course, a skeptic, a realist, might ask why Welge and his 'contacts' couldn't see the uniformed guards walking up to overhear their 'plotting.' But perhaps they were suddenly struck blind by occult forces and needed the signals.) (However, that would raise the question how they could see Bodenbach's signals. But never mind. Any author who has concocted such science fiction as this can surely invent further phantasmagoria buzz words to further his fable. Also, it's best for the purpose of this fiction to ignore the well-known fact that Bodenbach is a certified lunatic, an informer who is frequently being knocked on the head, and on one occasion, even stuffed into a garbage can.)

In paragraphs six and seven, all the tenuous threads of the criminal conspiracy are unraveled for all the world to see. With such scientific, conclusive proof of my evil machinations ('exercising' and 'talking in a quiet manner') officially documented, the only recourse open for me is confession of my crime. Yes, indeed, I am guilty! I did exercise with, and talk to, McCracken, a friend of mine. As for suspects Welge and Bodenbach, sorry, I don't know them, although Bodenbach's activities were known to many. With a report such as this written against me for 'talking in a quiet manner,' I wonder what might have been written had the author overheard our many vociferous disagreements — perhaps I would have been charged with 'inciting to riot.'

Paragraph six states, 'there is an obvious chain of conspiracy here starting with Del Raine, McCracken. ...' Based upon any rational analysis of this Memorandum, I suggest if one must ferret out a conspirator, then the author be given prime consideration as the conspirator. Or, perhaps one should properly consider this report as belonging to the realm of comic book literature, i.e., not to worry good folks, this surreptitious, sinister convict conspiracy has been unmasked by Peerless Fearless Fosdick, operating under deep disguise in this case as a Leavenworth Senior Officer Specialist ...

In the appeal brief, I then described BOP reasoning as follows:

• Everyone is suspect.
• He who is doing something suspicious is suspect.
• Most suspicious is he who is not seen doing something suspicious.
• Every suspect can become an accused.

- Suspicion is sufficient grounds for arrest.
- The arrest of a suspect is sufficient and conclusive proof of his guilt.

The Court of Appeals then reversed and remanded my case back to the district court for the second time; in 1990, it was again reversed and remanded.

Charles Dickens' *Bleak House*, recently shown on television as one of the Masterpiece Theater series, portrayed the litigants in *Jarndyce* v. *Jarndyce* contesting the disposition of an estate. But the case endlessly dragged on for so many years that the court costs consumed all the value of the property: the heirs were left with nothing. As with the interminable *Jarndyce* lawsuit, the dispensation of justice (or is it just-us?) seems to proceed rather slowly in my case.

Then what are the results of such prison policies and practices? What of the human merchandise stored endlessly in the concrete cubicles? After the shock, amazement and disbelief begin to wane, certain general behavior patterns begin to emerge. Some prisoners adopt the attitudes and actions most completely acceptable to the administration. They become *inmates*, cringing sycophants always absolutely in agreement — with every utterance of the staff; they continuously reassure them of their willingness to please with a servile smile. Some few become so blatantly obsequious that they nauseate the normal convicts. They seem oblivious — or perhaps *are* oblivious — to the titters and smirks of the guards who know they have reduced this particular prisoner specimen to the slavish state they desire. However, if they reinforce their fawning with a few choice nuggets of information, they may then be labeled 'rehabilitated.' Even release may then become possible.

Others of a more defiant nature protest their resentment of 'life in lock' by vehement vocalizations. If their vociferousness becomes too annoying, the 'goon squad,' armed with the usual array of equipment (pick-ax handles, tear gas, helmets with visors, shields, and the like) will soon silence them. This type of convict is quickly labeled as a desperado (incorrigible), and his actions are recorded as evidence of the necessity for his preventive detention.

A few unfortunates seem never to acquire the foggiest notion of how they arrived at their present dilemma or what course of action might possibly release them, so they just stagnate in their cells and endure; some, who can not read, literally lie on their beds year after year enduring. This category accounts for many who are shipped to the Medical Center as psychotic.

Another group well understands the situation they are trapped in, but also the Hobson's choice they face: they can not debase themselves by fawning upon their keepers; informing violates their moral code. They realize that provoking the 'goon squad' merely results in bumps and bruises. Litigation is a chimera never yet successful without an attorney. Since all alternatives are futile, nothing is left but to endure.

However, some in this group, realizing that the official charge against them is weak or non-existent, try not to provide any reason which could be used to justify continued segregation. They hope that, by maintaining a stoic silence, they might get out. But they are yet to be undone. All staff members entering the Control Unit are required to record all comments, requests, or actions that could be construed as derogatory or critical of the administration. And, of course, anything the unwary occupants write, such as letters to their family or friends, can be used as *prima facie* evidence against them. But even the most vigilant prisoner, who has the experience and self-discipline to be constantly alert, will, in all probability, relax and make a candid remark critical of his captors. And that does it: this is now recorded as proof of his 'bad attitude' and used as factual evidence documenting the reason he is locked up in the Long Term Control Unit. Law and Order in Action. I say their 'Law' is out of 'Order'!

One of the first final victims of their program was a friend of mine. He was a bemedaled veteran of World War II, about 5'9" tall, weighing approximately 140 pounds. After being arbitrarily singled out as a participant in a work strike, locked up for over a year, denied judicial relief as usual, he became despondent. After a verbal dispute one morning, the 'goon squad,' seven or eight strong, arrayed in their battle gear, swarmed into his cell, beat him, then dragged him to a special isolation or 'boxcar' cell. The manager of the Control Unit was informed by two guards, and even a prisoner, that he was sick, that he was acting very strange: the manager said he was faking. A day or so later he was found dead — standing on air. A.E. Housemen inimitably pictured the scene when he wrote, 'A neck God made for other use, then strangling in a string.'

Then another friend of mine was shipped to the Medical Center, given various unknown chemical concoctions,[3] and sent to a county jail where he also began acting quite peculiar. Shortly thereafter, he was found dead — his neck in a noose.

Then two others in the Unit took themselves off the count: gave themselves a back door parole in a box — via the noose! To us involved in it, the Marion experience began to resemble Hitler's 'final solution.'

Then how did these deaths affect our keepers? Only what might be expected: a deep resentment of these trouble-making convicts causing us all this trouble (or, the victims of oppression are regarded as the cause of oppression). Rabindranath Tagore, the Indian poet, understood this attitude when he wrote, 'Power takes as ingratitude the writhing of its victims.'

Then, perhaps, the Marion prisoner in the Long Term Control Unit, along with Kafka's protagonist in *The Trial*, knows the same futility, despair, and impotent rage of experiencing a nameless accuser, reciting a nameless charge, before a nameless authority, condemning him to endless imprisonment. Thus it would seem that the question is still valid in the BOP 1900 years after Juvenal asked it, 'But who will watch the keepers themselves?'

My Marion experience of 1972–74 was wretched, but upon my return in 1980, the Marion experience revisited has been even more intolerable. In the late 1970s, the BOP hierarchy had convened a conference and prepared contingency plans to lock Marion down — 'if and when.' The 'if and when' arrived in 1980 when another extended work strike occurred. The industry was then relocated; other work assignments necessary to keep the prison in operation were given to the guards, with idleness for all prisoners resulting. Time on the yard was drastically curtailed, and all cell blocks ate separately (with the result that we sometimes ate breakfast at 2:00 p.m.). With this new routine, assaults became more frequent; more lads tried to escape; the staff became more vindictive, e.g., several guards in the Long Term Control Unit urinated in a bucket and threw it on several individuals; when complaints were lodged, a minor internal investigation ensued, and I believe the guards were admonished not to do it again.

Then on October 27, 1983, while two lads were serving many endless, monotonous, mind-numbing years in the Long Term Control Unit on different tiers, they were charged with killing two guards and stabbing two others after coming out of their handcuffs. Shortly afterwards, the entire prison was converted into a Control Unit.

Attorneys from the Marion Prisoners' Rights Project, Donna Kolb, Jim Roberts, Jacqueline Abel, Martha-Easter Wells, and others, tried to gain access to the prison, but they were denied admittance until they obtained a court order. In June 1984, with the help of the People's Law Office in

Chicago, and Nancy Morgan of Seattle, Washington, they filed a class-action lawsuit for us, stating in part:

> Plaintiffs move the court for an injunction restraining the defendants from beating, torturing, and abusing plaintiffs; from using illegal rectal searches and unwarranted strip searches as a means of humiliating and terrorizing plaintiffs; and from denying plaintiffs reasonable communication with free persons. Plaintiffs request that the court enter specific orders designed to end both brutality which is planned, or condoned by defendant administrators as a means of control; and brutality which is directed against prisoners by individual guards, acting alone. In support of this motion, plaintiffs state as follows:

> 56 In retaliation for the killing of two guards ... defendants launched a comprehensive attack against prisoners throughout the prison. At least fifty prisoners were seriously beaten ... [90 by August 1984.]

> 58 Defendant administrators used guards from throughout the federal system to assist in the reprisals against prisoners. Defendants knowingly selected guards from the riot teams of other prisons and permitted them to conduct the searches and beatings in riot gear, including helmets with face masks, without any identifying name tags.

> 59 In the course of the prison-wide search, defendants stole and destroyed prisoners' authorized property. Many family pictures and religious articles were destroyed or defaced on the spot. Religious articles and legal materials, some of them irreplaceable, and other items were removed, ostensibly to the property room, and then reported to have disappeared. [Truckloads of our property were buried on the adjacent prison camp after earth-moving equipment dug holes for it. Al Garza's radio — with his name stamped on it — (along with *at least* one other radio) was given to a white collar criminal at the camp who was too frightened to testify for us at the court hearings. I lost 5½ boxes (canned goods size) of legal materials, all addresses, pictures, etc.]

12 ... Defendants have opened and read his [Edgar Hevle] legal
   mail and systematically withheld and interrupted his personal
   mail. In November 1983, he was removed from his cell by
   unidentified guards in riot gear, and taken to segregation with
   hands cuffed behind his back. In the hallway he was severely
   beaten with fists, feet and clubs, and his head was repeatedly
   run into walls and metal doors. Defendant administrators Carlson
   [Director, BOP], Miller [Warden], and Ralston [Regional
   Director] saw this beating.

17 [Geovani Montey de la Cruz] is a Cuban ... [He] speaks only
   Spanish ... During the prison-wide search in November 1983,
   defendants wantonly smashed his painting of Saint Lazarus.
   [Kept as part of his Santeria religion.] In December 1983,
   defendants charged him with destruction of property (a plastic
   cup), beat him severely, and placed him in a cell in segregation
   after injecting him with an unknown drug which caused him to
   remain unconscious for two days.

20–21 Garvin Dale White [and Jeremiah Geaney were] ... assaulted
   by defendants, subjected to illegal X-rays and an illegal forced
   rectal search, and confined to a cell [without water] for four
   days handcuffed behind [their backs] and wearing only
   underwear. (The cuffs were not removed so they could use the
   toilet. This was done because their X-rays were 'cloudy.' No
   contraband was found on or in them.]

25 On June 20,1984, the beating and torture of prisoner Henry B.
   Johnson. Mr. Johnson was beaten and tortured by four
   lieutenants and chained to a bed in metal handcuffs and leg
   irons for 35 hours.

28 In June and July 1984, the repeated beating and torture of
   prisoners Tomas Hernandez Santos and Jose Santiago Tanco.
   These prisoners, who speak only Spanish, were refusing to eat.
   Defendants force-fed them twice a day from approximately
   June 1, three days after they stopped eating, until their transfer
   to Springfield on June 13th. For at least one week in early July,
   they were beaten daily by guards including at least one lieutenant.
   From July 1 through July 13, defendants did not lubricate the

tubes which were pushed down the prisoners' noses twice a
day for the forced feeding.[4]

Three individuals testified for us as expert witnesses, and also submitted
affidavits, after touring the prison. One was Craig Haney, associate professor
of psychology at the University of California, Santa Cruz. Professor Haney
specializes in the effects of confinement on institutionalized persons, he has
served as a consultant to the U.S. Department of Justice, and he has worked
with prison systems in New Mexico, Texas, and California. He testified:

> The penitentiary's use of collective punishment has held large
> numbers of prisoners responsible for actions in which they clearly
> played no part. Indeed, the entire institution has been converted
> into a massive Control Unit all in response to the actions of a very
> few. It is difficult for prisoners to perceive either the wisdom or the
> justice in this lesson. I share their reaction.

Frank Rundle, a psychiatrist specializing in medical and psychiatric problems
in prisons stated:

> I make this affidavit with an anxious sense of urgency and foreboding
> ... so that the matter may be brought to the Court's attention at the
> earliest moment possible. ... Since October 27, 1983, the prison
> has been in near total lockdown status with most of the population
> being held under security conditions of a degree I have seen nowhere
> else in ten years of visiting prisons around the United States.
>
> In my opinion, the psychological effect upon most inmates is
> to generate a sustained state of smoldering rage, resentment and
> bitterness and a preoccupation with thoughts of violent revenge.
> An enormous pressure cooker of human emotions has been created
> and unless the pressure is reduced, staff and inmates alike will taste
> the poisonous stew made up of mutual suspicion and distrust, fear,
> hatred and vengefulness.

Joseph G. Cannon, associate professor in administration of justice at the
University of Missouri–St. Louis, and former director of corrections in
Kentucky and Maryland testified:

> I have worked in and around prisons and jails for the greater part of
> my life (now in my 60th year) and I have never seen procedures so
> extreme and so seemingly designed to degrade and aggravate the
> prisoners.

On August 15, 1985, Magistrate Meyers denied all twenty-nine issues
raised by the prisoners, except that those chained hand and feet to the metal
rungs embedded in the new concrete beds should be checked more
frequently. All prisoners' testimony was declared non-credible, except for
one inmate turncoat who testified for the government after they broke his
nose and finger (the magistrate even declared that if he was not an expert
witness, he did not know who was). All the guards' testimony was declared
credible, except for David Hale's, who admitted beating prisoners (of course,
he is now an ex-guard).[5] Then the magistrate finished his decision — and
our hopes for relief — with this diatribe:

> USP Marion is USP Marion. It houses the most vicious,
> unmanageable, and manipulative inmates in our penal system today
> and perhaps in the history of the penal system in the United
> States. ...
>   It is abhorrent that correctional staff and officers have been
> subjected to so many vicious and unjustified attacks on their integrity.
> Such exploitation is an abuse of the judicial process.
>   Finally, the Court is of the firm conviction that this litigation
> was conceived by a small group of hard-core inmates who are bent
> on disruption of the prison system in general and of USP-Marion in
> particular. These inmates will spare no effort, means or tactics to
> accomplish their final objective: the control of USP-Marion. This
> Court will not be an accomplice to such an endeavor.

Chief Judge Foreman approved these findings in *Bruscino* v. *Carlson,* 654
F.Supp. 609 (S.D. 111. 1987). On July 22, 1988, the court of appeals upheld
the district court's ruling. So much for the much vaunted due process of
law in America.

Upon consideration of the events transpiring in this program, could
Edward S. Herman's comment be analogous, when he stated in *Covert
Action Information Bulletin,* #26, at page 33:

This is the ultimate Orwellism: Those who terrorize the most are able to take the puny responses of their victims and use them to justify their own future excesses.

Or would Noam Chomsky's depiction of this scenario in the same issue be more fitting:

Alexander the Great captured a pirate and asked him, 'How he dare to molest the sea?' The pirate replied, 'How dare you molest the whole world? Because I do it with a little ship only, I am called a thief; you do it with a great navy and are called an Emperor.'

Some years ago a Kansas City newspaper printed a letter of mine in which I decried, in effect, two escaped Oklahoma convicts who had embarked on a mad murder spree. But perhaps I was too critical. If someone were to escape from here now (virtually impossible, of course) and begin a retaliatory campaign of mass murder, robbery, arson, sabotage, and terror, I would have to ask whether it were not merely an expression of W.H. Auden's truism: 'Those to whom evil is done, do evil in return.'

NOTES

1 'Red' Hayes, who had apparently been designated as the new Birdman of Alcatraz (perhaps to serve as a warning example to others), could not equal the Birdman's forty or so years in the 'hole' — he became ill and then psychotic, dying after only thirteen or so years of lock-up, thus depriving the BOP of its prime paradigm.

2 My judgment that it was a foolish tactic to launch a strike for the benefit of only one ethnic group was later verified when a lawsuit was filed for Chicanos only. See *Gonzales* v. *Richardson*, 455 — F. 2D — 953.

3 It is of more than passing interest that the U.S. Supreme Court ruled on February 27, 1990, that prison officials may administer any kind of powerful, mind-altering drugs they wish to any prisoner whose behavior they feel is undesirable. The decision as to whom these powerful, mind-altering drugs may be administered is left to the absolute discretion of the prison officials. No outside review is allowed so long as the prison psychiatrist (who is employed by the prison officials) states that it is in the prisoner's best interest.

4 The same tube pulled out of one's nose would then be inserted into the other's nose — without cleaning. When Jose was suddenly flown here from Puerto Rico, he had a gold chain intertwined through the skin on his chest, as part of his Santeria beliefs. The prisoncrats told him that no pagan African religions were allowed and to remove it. When he refused, the 'goon squad' clubbed him down and ripped it out. When he later

replaced it with thread, they beat him again and tore that out. After I filed a petition for a writ of *habeas corpus* on his behalf, the court appointed an attorney to represent him. The lawyer interviewed one guard, who naturally denied all wrong-doing, so the good lawyer recommended that the case be dismissed, and so it was. In prison, this all too familiar type of attorney is called a 'dump truck.' Nor was this an isolated instance. After the 1983 anti-Marion nationwide propaganda campaign began, local attorneys were afraid to represent those incarcerated there. One lawyer (to my knowledge) even returned a fee rather than take a Marion 'untouchable's' case.

5   In their zeal to fabricate an even stronger case against us, and especially to incriminate the attorneys who volunteered to help us, an Assistant U.S. Attorney (AUSA), upon information and belief, was overheard by an 'outside' lawyer (not one of our volunteers) and reported for suborning perjury from a prisoner. As a result, the AUSA was transferred. When none of these efforts persuaded our volunteers to cease and desist, an attorney's office door was pried open and *one* convict's file was stolen (the only one still at Marion who was accused of involvement in the guards' deaths). Shortly thereafter, she left the state. But COINTELPRO (the government's program of burglarizing political dissidents' residences) has been declared to be discontinued — right?

REFERENCES

Orwell, G. 1949. *1984*. New York: Harcourt, Brace and Jovanovich.

It's a Form of Warfare:
A Description of Pelican Bay State Prison
John H. Morris III

The bus ride from Folsom State Prison to Pelican Bay State Prison is breathtakingly beautiful. You pass through Clear Lake with its raised boat houses, wander up Highway 101 through towering redwoods and alongside the Eel River until you reach Eureka and the Pacific Ocean. You stare, mesmerized, at crashing waves on glorious California beaches and at pretty women in shorts and miniskirts enjoying this warm May day. You cannot get enough of the sights, sounds, and smells; then you reach Smith River and the prison.

At first glance, there is nothing remarkable. It is just like all the other new California prisons (Ione, Corcoran, Tehachapi, etc.) built in the mid 1980s. That perception changes as you are escorted off your bus by two baton-wielding correctional officers, down a long enclosed hallway to your new home.

California's newest prison, Pelican Bay, is also touted as its most secure and innovative, technologically speaking. It is home to the supposedly strongest 'hole' in the United States. The Security Housing Unit (or S.H.U.) is literally and figuratively a world unto itself.

There are two facilities, called C and O. Each facility is divided into ten units. The units are subdivided into six pods. These pods contain eight two-man cells. Not all the pods are double-celled, although they will be shortly as the S.H.U. fills. Each pod has a 'yard' with approximately 200 square feet of space, with twenty-foot walls. There is no exercise equipment. Nothing but you and a camera mounted behind thick steel mesh that covers the 'open sky' portion of the yard. Each prisoner is allowed an hour and a half of yard each day. There is one shower per tier. You are given ten minutes to shower and shave (without a mirror) and return to your cell.

The doors, run pneumatically, are opened and closed by a guard in a centrally located booth in each unit. Since the guard controls the doors and all traffic s/he is called 'control.' This guard has a rifle, usually a 9mm semi-automatic assault type. All prisoners are strip searched and handcuffed before a door is opened to allow you to go to or from the yard, the law library, the doctor or dentist, and elsewhere. Each prisoner is escorted by two guards carrying their nightclubs at all times.

Visiting is via phone and behind a thick plexiglass partition only. There are no contact visits or conjugal visits ('family visits') for S.H.U. prisoners, as the rest of the state's prisoners enjoy. Even the law library is caged. Working behind glass are the free-person-law-librarian and his/her guard. You knock on the window and your order is filled. Books cannot be checked out. The library, which is only a law library, is understaffed and the collection is not up to even the simplified standards for a S.H.U.

Personal clothing that belongs to the prisoner is limited to the basics: running shoes, t-shirts, socks, shorts and thermal underwear (all white). All other clothing is 'state issue' and consists of a mustard yellow jumpsuit which ties instead of zips or snaps (for metal control), white socks, t-shirts, shorts and so forth. Items such as deodorant, shampoo and soap are either what you brought from your sending institution or what you purchased here at the canteen. The toiletries are placed in bags or paper container after being removed from their original wrappings. Deodorant is taken out of its plastic housing. Things evaporate or dry up quickly, or go stale in the case of cookies or chips. Coffee, tea and Koolaid are sold, but no tobacco items. There is no smoking in S.H.U., no 'dip' or 'chew' either, no matches. Staff routinely smokes or 'dips' in front of you, but I haven't been able to smoke since I arrived, nor will I.

You are forced to send any other personal property home. If you are unlucky enough to be alone, you can either donate your property or destroy it. You cannot have your property set aside for you when (hopefully) you reach a 'mainline' prison after your S.H.U. stay is up. There are no rules which allow this practice and it only applies to S.H.U. prisoners. So you send all your personal belongings home; stuff it has taken you years to accumulate: your photos (you can only keep fifteen), books, tapes, headphones, levis, sweatshirts, pants, all the stuff which over the last ten years has made doing twenty-one to life bearable.

Mail comes every day except Sunday. It often takes nine days or more to reach you even from close by. It is either the Post Office's routing or the delay is here; you cannot find out which.

The former Governor of California, George Duekmejian, and the Director of the California Department of Corrections, James Rowland, both claimed that this new S.H.U. is only for California's worst prisoners, but you know that this is patently untrue. It is home to whomever a warden or program administrator wishes to send here. Although the majority of prisoners are here for either violent acts inside prison or for gang membership, gang association or both, there are many prisoners who are not here for these reasons. Some are drug users/dealers inside the prison, some are merely the unfortunate ones who have run afoul of some officer or staff member and were shipped up here.

The criteria for being housed here are specific, but not always followed. Like all prisons, there are prisoners who simply 'fall through the cracks' in the rules, and there are ones who get shipped 'just because.' Either way, the prisoners here are placed in S.H.U. for either a set term (e.g., fifteen months) or 'indeterminate.' Indeterminate is supposedly designed to control the gangs, gang associates, and anyone the Department of Corrections deems dangerous. It is to keep anyone named 'indeterminate' from ever going to a mainline prison until he breaks and 'debriefs.' Debriefing is a euphemism for 'snitching.' Until the prisoner debriefs and tells on himself and his comrades, he is here for 'life' or until he is deemed 'okay' by a judgment which is entirely arbitrary.

The whole set-up is designed to cause mental, physical and emotional stress. First off, the prison is located in a remote corner of the state near the Oregon border. Most of the prisoners are from the southern section of California, like Los Angeles and San Diego. This means that visitors must travel more than a thousand miles to get to the prison. Most prisoners and their families are poor. Travel costs present a hardship for these families. That is why visitors are rare.

The isolation goes on even inside the prison. Contact with staff is kept to a minimum and what occurs is formal. You cannot see out from your cell as in other prisons. The 'sky' in the yard is your one source of 'outside.' Even your senses are kept dulled. Colours when used are muted, mostly just white, off-white and grey. Although the food is outstanding in taste and warmth, the menu is unaltered and soon becomes predictable. These things taken separately mean little or nothing but when placed together they take on an altogether sinister form.[1]

Television is an example. To those few who are lucky enough to own a personal television, the situation is bizarre. The speaker wires are cut to facilitate the use of earphones because headphones are prohibited. Even though the region surrounding the prison uses local cable television or satellite broadcast, this prison points its dish at (of all places) Denver, Colorado. Satellite dishes are not taxed according to where they are pointed; therefore, there is no fiscal advantage to the prison for tuning-in Denver. Denver is at least 1500 miles and a couple of time zones away. Even the guards cannot explain it. I suggest that the reason is to isolate us from local events. Again, by itself this is nothing, but along with the grey walls, the limited personal property and similar restrictions (e.g., you are given one book a week to read) the intent seems quite clear. Most people simply 'zone out' on Denver television or become exercise freaks or both.

Even the cells are eerie. There are no mirrors. The only time you can see yourself is on the little knob in the shower. You shave on your knees looking at the 1 inch reflection. There is very little for you to control in your cell. The light switch is a silver bump and no one seems to knows how it works. You have, of course, the usual sink/toilet combination to play in. Since showers are every other day, 'bird baths' are the order of the day. There is a weird, overly cemented table/desk/seat arrangement which is uncomfortable at best, and a couple of cement bunks. The lower bunk has a couple of 'lockers' or shelves which are very poorly designed. They are so deep that anything pushed back is almost beyond salvage and requires a pole or whatever to drag, push or pull it out. Though the cells are more than eighty square feet, with or without a 'cellie' (cell mate) they quickly shrink when you are inside them for twenty-two hours a day.

It is a physical and psychological form of warfare being carried out against you. No one could honestly say it is by accident that all these things 'just happened' at once. This is done to break you, to punish you, to ruin you. After spending years in here, what comes out will not be quite 'right.' But, of course, the California Department of Corrections has that solved. When or if you are released from S.H.U. you are sent to Pelican Bay's mainline. They have a semi-lockdown type of 'step' program there. If you screw up (an entirely arbitrary decision by some staff member who may have taken a disliking to you) you return to S.H.U.; if not, you are sent to another equally strict prison.

I lay there in my bunk thinking. Fairly soon, with all of California's prison building, this state will surpass all of the country's prison systems for sheer volume and will pass Russia's also.[2] This is the thought that passes through your head as you lie thinking in your Pelican Bay Security Housing Unit bunk; this and a few stray ones of beautiful redwoods, pretty women in shorts and miniskirts, and northern California beaches with big Pacific waves rolling in.

NOTES

1. James McConnell writing in *Psychology Today* notes, "I believe the day has come when we can combine sensory deprivation with drugs, hypnosis and astute manipulation of reward and punishment to gain absolute control over an individual's behavior. It should then be possible to achieve a very rapid and highly effective type of positive brainwashing that would allow us to make dramatic changes in a person's behavior and personality" (McConnell, April 1970:14).
2. The American Civil Liberties Union reports that the incarceration rate in the United States is the highest in the world. For "every 100,000 Americans 426 live behind bars. In South Africa, 333 of every 100,000 are in prison; in the Soviet Union, 268; Great Britain 97; Spain, 76; the Netherlands, 40.

    Perhaps even more shocking is the finding that Black males in the United States are imprisoned at a rate of four times that of Black males in South Africa: 3,109 per 100,000 compared to 729 per 100,000" [Ed. Note. Elvin 1991:1].

REFERENCES

Elvin, J. (Winter 1991) "U.S. Now Leads World in Rate of Incarceration." *The National Prison Project Journal*, 6 (1):1–2.

McConnell, J.V. (April 1970) "Criminals Can Be Brainwashed — Now." *Psychology Today*.

CAPITAL PUNISHMENT / STATE MURDER

Mephistophelean Volition
Steven King Ainsworth

O h, how cruel and diabolical we can be in our efforts to judicially murder individuals we have deemed beyond the pale!

In the spring of 1992, just prior to California's stepping into the position of being a killer state with the gas chamber execution of Robert Alton Harris after a quarter of a century hiatus, a civil rights class action suit was filed on behalf of all condemned inmates in California challenging the constitutionality of execution by lethal gas [*Fierro* v. *Gomez*, 790 F. Supp.966 (N.D.CAL.1992)].

In California, executions in the gas chamber are performed by lowering one pound of sodium cyanide pellets wrapped in cheese cloth into a mixture of sulfuric acid and distilled water. The chemical reaction will produce hydrogen cyanide gas, the same gas known by its trade name Zyklon used by the Nazis to exterminate over a million men and women at Auschwitz-Birkenau.

Unfortunately, after some questionable rulings and conflicts between the 9th Circuit Court of Appeals and the United States Supreme Court[1], the following bit of macabre occurred:

> At 3:49 A.M., Harris walked into the gas chamber. Two minutes later, as the sulfuric acid was being pumped into the vat below Harris, Judge Pregerson telephoned the gas chamber, informing prison officials of the stay of execution. Harris, of course, could not understand the reason for delay. At 3:58 A.M., the sulfuric acid was drained from the vat. At 4:01 A.M., Harris was taken from the gas chamber. While Harris had been strapped in the chamber, the Attorney General's office had sought an order from the United States Supreme Court vacating his stay of execution. In a one-paragraph motion to the Supreme Court, the Attorney General's office had typed "Mr. Harris is presently in the gas chamber". That sentence was crossed out by hand. The Attorney General's facsimile machine

stamped the time of the correspondence to the Supreme Court at 4:06 A.M., minutes after Harris had been removed from the gas chamber.

At 5:45 A.M., the stay was lifted by a 7–2 vote in the U.S. Supreme Court and Robert Alton Harris was rushed back into the gas chamber and executed.

The last-ditch attempt to save Harris was unsuccessful, but the class action lawsuit challenging the method of execution survived, and as a result the California legislature quickly passed a law, which the governor immediately signed, giving a condemned human being the option of choosing the method of his or her execution; lethal gas or lethal injection. If the condemned refuses to choose, they would be executed by lethal gas. [California Penal Code: Section 3604][2]

I questioned the validity of this latest legislative move in a letter to the *San Francisco Daily Journal* in early January of 1993:

So the good people of California offer death by injection thinking it to be a more humane method, or was it to avoid the civil suit aimed at the gas chamber? Is it to make the whole process easier? To make killing less cruel? Having been in the ... system most of my adult life and seeing firsthand some of the ineptness of these civil servants, I can well imagine the mess they will make of death by injection.[3]

This latter observation is aptly illustrated in the recent execution by lethal injection of a man in Illinois:

As he was wheeled into the chamber, he made no eye contact. Almost his last sight of this world was an exit sign over the door. At 12:04 A.M. the order was given to push the two buttons which were to release the lethal "juice" into the veins. As the poison began to work — a deadly cocktail of sodium pentathol, pancuronium bromide and potassium chloride — there was a reflex jerk of his head, followed by a loud snort. For three minutes, his puggish, wide open eyes bulged in their sockets. His flabby belly heaved in and out. Then, as if in a surreal black pantomime, an official stepped calmly forward and closed the theatre-like curtain. What had happened, it seems, is that the Illinois State death machine had malfunctioned. A technician had to replace the tubing because some of the poison had "gelled". When the curtains reopened, John had turned purple and was still twitching. Instead of taking ten minutes to execute him, it took nearly 20. He was finally pronounced dead at 12:58 A.M.[4]

With both of these executions in mind, many men and women on death rows across the nation, in states where an option of method is proffered, no doubt ponder this Mephistophelean volition and further agonize over their fate. It is human nature to fight death, especially a premeditated one, a death well planned in advance, a death not fought in a physical sense but one that is contested in a judicial arena. Even the matter of choice has been contested. To date, most courts have adopted this view:

> Individual reactions to the various methods of execution and the right to choose vary greatly. In some cases, a person may be so appalled by the thought of physically hanging by the neck [shot in the heart, choking on lethal gas or strapped into an electric chair and fried] that the option of death by lethal injection is welcome. To others, the idea of lying strapped upon a gurney awaiting the lethal poison to seep into one's veins at an unknown time may be equally abhorrent. These individuals embrace the idea of choosing the method of their death as a way to avoid their own private terrors. But to a third type of individual, the choice itself is cruel. As they await the day of their death, they are faced not only with the terror of death itself but also with the terror of making the wrong choice on how to die. These individuals do not embrace the idea of choice; they dread its requirement that they take an active part in their own demise. [*State* v. *Rupe* (WASH. 1984) 683 P.2d.571]

Judicial resolution of this matter may well be beyond a court's ability. A court, not being actually faced with a fatal choice itself, must speculate whether removing the choice is to impose a cruel method of execution or retaining the choice imposes cruel psychological pressure on the condemned, or if in fact requiring an individual to actively participate in his or her own killing is in itself cruel and unusual.

The catch-22 is, how do you present evidence to support any of these contentions? The evidence can only come from the condemned. California provides that the choice must be made in writing not more than 10 days after being served with a notification of an execution date being set [California Code of Regulations, Title 15, Section 3349 (A,B,C,D)], which means from 20 to 60 days from actual execution. Psychological evidence can be gathered prior to that on the matter of being faced with choice and whether or not to choose at all. After the choice is made, psychological evidence can be gathered as to the impact of the choice upon the condemned.

However, many obstacles must be overcome. First and foremost is the condemned's willingness to talk about what obviously is a most private matter at a most inopportune time. A court would have to order the state to allow access to the condemned by independent psychologists to evaluate the issue at a time when prison officials are most concerned with security. Examination at this point on a matter that may well prohibit an execution would be contrary to the goals of the state and their own psychiatric evaluations that are prerequisite to an execution.

Some evidence might be gathered in the years prior to a condemned human being's actually being faced with the choice. But such evidence may be tainted with beliefs that judicial relief will be granted long before a choice has to be made, that a stay of execution is imminent or that actual innocence is at issue and the condemned refuses to contemplate any outcome other than total exoneration.

What is the answer? It is my view that giving a condemned human being a choice about how he or she wishes to be exterminated is cruel. Requiring a condemned person to actively participate in his or her own state-sanctioned killing is cruel and unusual. Finally, if the State cannot make up its mind how it wishes to extinguish the lives of those it has condemned to death, then it should not be doing the killing at all.

NOTES

1. *Gomez* v. *U.S. DIST. CT.*, 112 S.Ct. 1652; *Gomez* v. *U.S. DIST. CT.*, N0.92-70237, 1992 U.S.APP. LEXIS 7735; *Vasquez* v. *Harris*, 112 S.Ct. 1713(1992).
2. "Thoughts on the Cause of the Present Discontents: The Death Penalty Case of Robert Alton Harris", Chas. Sevilla and M. Laurence, CACJ Forum Vol. 20 No. 1 (1993) FN:130.

S unday, March 13, 1994, at 12:35 p.m., exactly 35 hours and 26 minutes before my scheduled, state-sanctioned murder, the "Death Row Escort Squad" arrived at my cell, saying "It's time ByrdDog". "Strip", said one. A number of men stood in front of my cell, nervously watching as I shed my clothing, perhaps for the last "strip-search" of my life. After going through the usual routine of "lift em, and spread em", I got dressed, backed up to the cell door, and was handcuffed.

While this was going on, an eerie silence had settled over the entire cellblock. There was none of the usual boisterous yelling, laughter, loud radios or tv's playing. Nothing. Complete silence. Then as I backed out of my cell and started on that long walk, the cellblock erupted into a cacophonous uproar — "Stay Strong", "Good Luck" the voices yelled out to me. As I bid them farewell, I vowed "I'll represent us ALL well, no matter what happens, Stay Strong"!! Meaning that I would not grovel and whine, as some involved in the process would like to see.

Along the way, as I walked down the long main corridor loud voices raised in solidarity and encouragement greeted me as I passed each cellblock. The shouts from the cellblocks caused my escorts, and the numerous guards that lined the corridor, to become alarmed. The fear and terror of the past riot still fresh in their memories. In an effort to make me speed up the leisure pace I had assumed, meeting each and every eye along the way, they started walking faster. I maintained my stride, and soon they slowed down, resigned to the pace I had set.

Upon arriving in J-1 Super-Max, I was once again strip-searched and my regular death row clothing were exchanged for death house clothing. "Odd", I thought to myself, "what effect does what one is wearing have on the fact of one's impending death"?!

The atmosphere of the Death House was smothering, suffocating as if there were a shortage of oxygen. Everyone moved as if in slow motion. Their every move seeming to have been thoroughly rehearsed, learned, robot-like professionalism, as now, for the first time in over thirty years, they (the elite Death Squad) had been called upon to commit murder in the name of the State of Ohio. In some of their eyes I saw fear, concern, and revulsion. In others, sadistic glee. Looking at each one of them with steady, unblinking eyes, I sized them up individually.

Shortly after entering the death cell proper, my attorneys arrived to inform me as to the current state of my situation. We discussed this at great length, and I felt confident that everything possible was being done to halt the insidious plot to murder me that had been set into motion by the State of Ohio.

After enjoying the time spent with my lawyers, I immediately contacted my woman, and later, other family members on the phone that had been provided. I attempted as best I could to assuage their worries and fears. With each one I tried to explain the situation, based on my knowledge and information provided me by my lawyers. This was very difficult, given the fact that they all were well aware of the appeal process, and knew this latest attempt by the State of Ohio to murder me was simply a political move, and not based upon law. I still wanted to calm their fears, give them strength, and assure them all that everything was under control, and that my lawyers were on top of everything, every move the state was trying to make.

For the most part, I remained in constant contact with my woman and family by phone, and was permitted to have a couple of short visits with my lovely woman, engaging in spirited conversation with some of the people who had come down from the Ohio Public Defenders Office, and was truly touched by them.

There were periods when time seemed to stand still, then suddenly speed up. I was offered food, but refused to eat, fearing that it may have been "doctored up" with drugs to make me less resistant and responsive. This refusal was not based on some unreasonable paranoia, but on years of incarceration. I know first hand just how devious prison officials can be, and I wasn't about to take any chances! The whirlwind of activity continued around me, and as night approached, there was no thought of sleep in my mind. Throughout the night I was on the phone talking to people I haven't heard from in years. Everyone expressing their support, love, concern, and pledging their assistance.

Monday morning, March 14, 1994, was indeed a "Blue Monday" for us all as we learned of the apparent, unprecedented and mean spirited tactics being employed by the "honourable" Carl Rubin, the judge assigned to my case. It seems that even though he had my writ of habeas corpus and motion for the stay of execution before him since March 7th, he decided to wait until the "eleventh hour" before making a ruling, knowing full well that the situation was critical, and time was of the essence. An example of the insidious plot he had hatched in his muddled mind began when he instructed two of my attorneys to meet in his chambers at noon. At the conclusion of the meeting he informed my attorneys that he would deny my motion for a stay of execution, and that he would issue his ruling at approximately 3 p.m. Nine hours before my scheduled execution! He made this ruling with full knowledge that it was legally wrong, but in keeping with his own "personal" feelings about the length of time my appeal was taking. As he stated on one occasion, "There comes a time when all of this must come to an end". Now he had appointed himself the Supreme litigator, usurping the power of the United States Supreme Court, as well as that of his own District Court. Had it not been for the tireless efforts of my attorneys, who fought gallantly, he may well have succeeded. Through their efforts, an emergency panel of the Sixth Circuit Court convened and issued a stay of execution around 6:30 p.m.

Not to be outdone, Ohio Governor George V. Voinavitch personally contacted his friend Ohio Attorney General Lee Fisher to form a pack and they went to the United States Supreme Court, asking them to dissolve the stay of execution, and order my murder to occur as scheduled. This move was purely political, both having political aspirations with elections coming up this year, knowing how profitable it was to jump on the "Kill us quick" bandwagon.

After the U.S. Supreme Court in its entirety had been convened, they declined to lift the stay of execution at approximately 11:30 p.m. Everyone breathed a great sigh of relief, including, I might add, the correctional officers that had been present during the whole ordeal. Around 12:20 a.m. Tuesday morning I was again escorted, however, this time, back to Death Row. Again the corridors were filled with loud cheers and good wishes, but it was when I arrived back on the "row" that I received the most thunderous ovations. Everyone had been following the events closely as they unfolded over the tv and radio, and were all aware that I was coming back.

In the aftermath of Judge Carl Rubins' machinations with my case, he was removed from further involvement. This indicates and validates my previously held suspicions that he was overtly prejudicial towards me and my case, all death row prisoners, and was losing his judicial temperament. To him, the bench from which he's suppose to make decisions based upon law, had instead become a soapbox, which he had claimed to orate his personal convictions! For those that are chomping at the bit for my death, complaining about the length of time my appeal was taking, it doesn't matter whether I'm innocent or not. All they want is to have their blood lust sated. Nothing else matters. Damn Justice, "Give Us The Body" they cry.

Many people have written and asked what it's like being on Death Row, being sent to the death house, and coming within thirty minutes of being murdered by the State? Why I refused to eat my "last meal", and why I chose the electric chair instead of lethal injection? I will try to answer these questions based on my experiences, as I'm sure it differs from some others that have been as fortunate as myself. To walk into the very Jaws of The Beast, and walk out again. Sadly this has not been the case for many throughout this country that are similarly situated.

Being on Death Row, in and of itself, is a form of death. The environment sucks the life from you, and the passing of a single day at times can be but the blink of an eye, or as long as a heartbreaking life. Then there's the drudgery, the soul wrenching monotony of staring at the same steel and concrete, the same people, ad nauseam. Being taken to the death house is, in a way, a relief. Finally one is afforded the opportunity to confront one's killers, who cowardly hide behind the mask of shamelessness. To look into their eyes, smell their raw fear, and feel one's own strength being pitted against the ultimate sanction, Death.

As for the so-called last meal, and my refusal to eat it and other meals? As I said earlier, years of conditioned paranoia, coupled with the exigencies of events going on around me, eating was the furthest thing from my mind.

I chose the electric chair because I refuse to give any credence to the State's attempt to contrive a rationale for its murders, by offering a lethal injection as a "more humane" form of murder. If they were going to kill me, I was intent upon making it as ghastly as possible for all that bore witness to it.

What went through my mind during those thirty-six hours, were thoughts of my woman, people that I care about and love, and what my death would do to them. I was hoping for the best, and expecting the worst. Those thirty-six hours were devoted to the ones that I care about and love. I had to keep my wits about myself, because as I saw it, it was on me to give the ones I love and care about strength. I had to maintain courage in the face of adversity, so that the burdens of the ones I care about and love would not be overbearing. Their love and support had sustained me all this time, and it was my turn to show and give them strength.

There is a plague in this country that is being controlled and manipulated by politicians, judges, prosecutors, police, professional victims, and victims' rights groups. Until society faces what's really going on in this country and starts wanting real answers for what's going on in our streets, a number of innocent people are going to be put to death, or imprisoned for the rest of their lives. This attitude of lock them up and kill them is not the answer. Who do you think are going to be the ones filling our Death Rows, prisons and jails? Open your eyes before it's too late. The future of this society is at stake. YOU the PEOPLE must take off your blindfolds and look at the real problems, dealing with them rather than sweeping them under the rug with a quick fix that has never worked. Crime is nothing new, the way it is dealt with is a reflection of the society we live in. The reflection I see is a holocaust against the poor and less fortunate.

To all the Brothers and Sisters, mothers and fathers who are on Death Rows, in jails and prisons throughout this country, or struggling to get through the day to put food on the table, Stay Strong and don't give up. Stop turning on each other and stand United against the oppressors and raise your voices in Unity!

Commemorative Celebration
in Honor of Ronald Keith Allridge
James V. Allridge III

With an execution date being set a day before my birthday, 1995 proved to be a very stressing year for me. For those of you who have known me for a while, you know that the hardest thing that I've had to deal with that past year was the execution of my own brother, Ronald Keith Allridge. He was executed by the State of Texas on June 8, 1995.

Ronnie will most likely be remembered by most for the many negative aspects of his life, but not to me. I will remember him as a loving, sensitive, caring, intelligent and quietly reserved person. He loved to read and gather knowledge on all levels. He was a storehouse of erroneous information and would have done well on any quiz show like *Jeopardy*!

He will be remembered by those remaining on Death Row and those in the abolition movement as one of the first not to willingly walk to his death. He refused to voluntarily come out of the Death Watch Cell and made them come in and physically carry him out. He felt by doing so, he would show them to be exactly what they are — murderers going to get their victim.

The administration proved just how cold-hearted they could be when they asked me to help talk him out of the cell. They attempted to use my desire to see my brother one more time as a bargaining tool to defuse the situation and to quietly lead him to his death. My last words to him were, "Do what you have to do."

I think Beatrice speaks of the disdain of this act best when she wrote to me, "... What they did by [trying] to get you to talk Ronnie out of the cell is the very worst thing they could have done. This is pure torture in my eyes. It is very wrong for them to do. They put Ronnie and you in a dilemma. In a situation that has no solution. You knew that you could see him again if you went, that you wanted to go, but if you went, this would mean that you would help to get him to the execution. Someone who asks this from a brother is the most detestable person in the world. ... They are allowed to confine you, to keep you in prison, to take away from you a certain freedom, but they are certainly not allowed to torture you."

Ronnie wrote his "Final Thoughts," what proved to be two days before his death. I would like to publish them, in full, for the first time since his murder. I want you all to have a somewhat personal glimpse of the love that he had for those that were involved in his life.

Final Thoughts
by Ronald K. Allridge

As I sit here, about to face my "punishment," I can't help but to wonder what it all means. Will it affect anyone besides me and my family? Will it stop someone else from doing what they are about to do? Will it deter crime? Or, will it just make someone more determined not to be apprehended?

I have been on Texas' Death Row for over nine years now and I have learned quite a few things. One of them is that the violent crime rate in Texas hasn't had a significant decrease in the last ten years, but Texas has executed more people than any other state. Even though Texas has been in the forefront with the amount of executions they've carried out, they are still overwhelmed by crime. Even though they continue to execute people at an alarming rate, they are constantly opening up prisons instead of shutting them down! Why is it so hard for people to understand that, "lockin' 'em up and throwin' away the key" is not the answer? Why can't they realize that capital punishment doesn't deter violent criminal acts? Why do they say they are concerned about the futures of their children when they continue to spend more money on prisons than they do on schools? Haven't they realized that its cheaper to send someone to college than it is to prison? It would definitely be more beneficial to society and the economy to have them with a college degree than a set of parole papers.

I don't know the answer to the world's problems or even all of mine. But I do know that this country is faced with a very dismal future if it continues to journey down this road. It leads nowhere. It didn't lead anywhere in times past and it will lead nowhere in the future. As I said, I don't have an answer to the problems that society faces, but I have solved one problem for myself. That's my fear of dying.

When I was issued my last execution date, I faced that day with an overwhelming dread and a paralysing fear. The mere thought of it terrified me, even though I tried to put up a brave front for my family's sake. Fortunately, I do not have that problem this time. As I face this execution date — assigned to me for June 8, 1995 — I have no fear of what lies ahead. I know I do not know what will come after, but I do not fear it. I realize that it is not so much the dying as it is "the fear of." I believe that human beings generally have a fear of death that makes them miss out on a lot of life. They need to conquer that fear before they will ever be able to sincerely feel the most enjoyment out of what they experience in this existence. This is just my opinion, but I believe it to be pretty close to the truth. Anyway, I have conquered that fear now and I have done it just in time. I did it myself, but only because of the help and love given me by the people that mean the most to me. Hopefully, they will hold my memories dear, and cherish their thoughts of me forever.

I want to pay a special tribute to: **James Vernon Allridge, Jr.**, my Dad. He has always been there when I really needed him. Through the good and the bad times he has literally been there, and I know he will continue to be. If I could I would change a few things about our relationship and the way things went growing up, but I would never change the fact that I had someone who was always there. I know whenever I needed someone to turn to, Dad would be there. He might not have done everything right, but he wasn't far from it. He will definitely always be special to me. Thanks Dad, for being you.

Otharee Moss Allridge, my Mom. She really is a special person and means more to me than life. I would have done anything to make her happy because she has always tried her best to do that for me. I have no regrets at all about her being the person that gave me life. That most precious gift has allowed me to experience all the joy, happiness, learning and loving that I have been through over the years and I want to thank her for that more than anything else. We have not always agreed, but we've never argued. And I know the way she feels for me is experienced by only a select few human beings. She has truly made life worth living and I apologize sincerely for any and all hurt or pain that I've caused her. Thank you Mom, for keeping me close to your heart.

Ah, and my daughter. She has truly been a joy to me. I know we have never been with each other in "the world," but my thoughts of her have kept her with me everyday. As I looked into her eyes yesterday and saw the love there that she has for me, this just gave me a feeling that I can't even describe. To know that she could still love me after all the moments she's missed with me just tears my heart. It really makes me wonder what our life would have been like had I been where I was supposed to be. What joys could we have experienced together? What future would we have now? I guess these things you don't consider when you are being selfish. Hopefully someone will learn from my experience and realize that, "what you have is more important than what you might get." I just want my daughter, **NaDine**

Michelle Allridge, to know that I have always loved her. She has always had a place in my heart, even before she was who she is now. Daddy loves you Baby!

To my brother, **James**. I want to thank you for all that you have been. I really have enjoyed and appreciated having your support throughout my life, but especially over the last 10 years. I sincerely wish I could have kept you from this fate, but I was probably too selfish at the time to realize just what I was causing. So, I have tried to make amends by showing you love, devotion and respect, and hopefully this is what you'll remember me for the most. I know I've told you that I love you but those are mere words that I can utter. The true depth of my feelings for you I don't think could ever fully be expressed with mere words. But I want you to know that I do love you, cherish you and will always respect you. I can't imagine a better person to have as a brother and I will always hold your memory dear to me. I don't know what you will experience after I am gone, but I want you to keep your head up, to be strong and always think of me with a smile. Don't be sad for me because I'll be somewhere better. I love you Weinerhead!

To my son, **Darius**. Even though I wasn't responsible for your birth, I still have always felt as if you were my son. I know I did some things wrong, but I never meant to cause you any harm. Hopefully you can remember me and the times we shared with fondness and decide that I wasn't such a bad person after all. You take care of yourself and your little brother and sister because both of them need you much.

To my brothers: **Darren, Lamont,** and **Stan**. I really appreciate all of you keeping me in your hearts. I know I've been away from you more than I've been with you, but you still managed to love me regardless of that fact. It just makes me proud to realize that I have such fine young men as members of my family. Hopefully, our spirits will cross paths again and the next time we'll appreciate it more than we did this time. I wish you to know also that I never meant to cause you any pain, things just worked out that way. I just want you to be strong for each other and always take into account each other's feelings. Its when we forget about others' feelings that things seem to turn out wrong. And remember, "I Will Always Love You."

I wish to send a special thanks to my "big sister," **Peggy**. I know she didn't have to let me into her heart, but she did. I hope to meet her one day again so I can let her know just how much she means to me. May you have a bright and beautiful future filled with nothing but wonderful experiences.

I wish to send a special thanks also to my Great Aunt, **Robbie Moore**. She has provided me with her love and support, and also, a beautiful daughter who is my "big sister." They know that I will always love them and I know they will keep me in their hearts for now and ever.

I wish to thank my attorneys, **Don, Bruce**, and **Steve**, for really trying to save my life. They knew it would be an uphill battle all the way but they fought the good fight. It's just too hard for a few people to try and fight a whole state. But knowing they couldn't win didn't stop them from giving their best efforts. To all of them, I wish to say, I sincerely thank you.

I have to thank my "little sisters," **Mookie** and **Ines**, for coming into my life and giving me their devotion, trust and love. I really needed them at that particular time, just as I need them now. I hope they continue to have happiness and I want them to know that I will keep them inside of me always.

I wish to send a special thanks to my "wife" because she has meant a lot to me, especially in the last few months. I know we didn't have a formal relationship, but it meant more to me than any I've had. I wish her continued success and happiness in life and I send my love to her and **Junaid**. I don't know how she'll feel about me leaving her like this but I know it isn't easy for me. Damn, I love you woman and I just know that we will meet again. A love like ours just has to be repeated. I freely love you, **Shontia Lahon "Kittit-Kittie" Harris-Allridge**!! May you have a bright and beautiful future.

I have countless others that I have on my mind and in my heart. If I were to try and mention them all, I know I wouldn't have enough time left. But I know they will feel me thinking of them and I wish them to think of me. As I embark on this journey, I want only to say that it has been a learning experience. Everything didn't turn out right, but everything didn't turn out wrong either. I hope I have left behind something that will give someone pause or put a smile on their face.

To everyone that means anything at all to me: MUCH PEACE AND LOVE!

*****

I won't try to paint a perfect picture and say that Ronnie was an angel, filled with love and compassion for his fellow human being. That would be far from the truth — simply, a lie. But he was capable of love and had a great deal of love for many. I miss the love that he showed for me daily.

It is my hope that his death and the many others before him were not in vain. Texas has slacked up on executions, only because of current pending litigation in the courts. I'm sure they would have been executed if the State of Texas and Governor Bush had their way.

June 8, 1997, will be the second anniversary of Ronnie's execution. I am asking that everyone who reads this to light a candle in remembrance of him on this day, or do something to further the abolition of the death penalty. Write a letter to the Governor, help circulate a petition or phone or fax a letter to President Clinton.

Not to diminish the pain and suffering of the victim's family and survivors, but there are always two sides to every story and I know only too well of the pain and suffering of the executed's family. My mother speaks of how she misses Ronnie each time she comes to visit and when she writes. My father tells me how he goes out to the cemetery and just sits and talks to Ronnie when things are troubling his mind. But the thing they don't tell me is how painful it must be for them each time they come to visit me and not see Ronnie there next to me after 8 years of visits. They don't tell me how painful it was for them to have one son executed by the State (with their three youngest sons witnessing the execution) in June of 1995 and then, only a few months later, have the other son come within 5 days of being executed. I have a very strong family and I admire them for their strength and courage.

Ronnie wrote the title poem for my recently released chapbook, *Deadly Executioner*. He also has several other poems included in the book. The book is dedicated to the numerous men that have been executed by the State of Texas since the reinstatement of the death penalty here in the United States. The book has been received very well so far and I would like everyone to get a copy or two, to pass along to a friend.

PART V

RESISTANCE STRATEGIES FOR SURVIVAL

Sunday, Bloody Sunday
John Perotti

On Easter Sunday (April 11, 1993) at the Southern Ohio Correctional Facility (SOFC) located in Lucasville, Ohio, the years of oppression exploded into a full-blown riot. For all familiar with the treatment and conditions there, it was known to be long overdue. Brutality, racism, murder, and inhumane treatment have been documented with the state and federal courts as well as with Amnesty International and other human rights organizations — yet the prisoncrats just kept tightening the screws.

Years of whitewashing by the state legislative watchdog committee (Correctional Institution Inspection Committee, CIIC) didn't help. The CIIC in 1990 called for a full-scale investigation into conditions at Lucasville that they turned into a political fiasco by creating an 800 member Aryan Brotherhood (AB) and focusing on that aspect, saying the AB controlled gambling, drugs, and prostitution inside the prison. No mention was made of the other factions, and the fallacy about the AB just caused younger prisoners to want to start one or join. Governor Celeste called for a full-scale investigation by the State Highway Patrol after the FBI, SHP [State Highway Patrol] and CIIC had just investigated allegations of two black prisoners being killed by white guards for touching a white nurse. All the SHP did was twist and turn their investigation to cover for the guards' and prisoncrats' illegal activities. SHP also called for more security; the hiring of additional guards and putting the prison on semi-lockdown. This created the increase in tension and oppression that led to the events of the Bloody Easter Sunday riot. The failure of the courts and legislature to provide relief from the oppressive conditions, coupled with the constant harassment of prisoners who tried to use legal avenues to address the everyday constitutional violations left only one option — revolution. Judges, politicians, and even prisoncrats pay lip service to the public about how prisoners should and are encouraged to use the courts and grievance system to air complaints and violations. In reality, they bog down prisoner cases for years, dismissing 90% of them without a trial, then retaliate with long-term isolation in control units — cell and body searches for harassment purposes and the thousands of other ways they harass us.

The years of frustration came to a head when forced/mandatory TB testing was done after the state had put active TB carriers in areas of the prisons where it could spread — refusing to isolate them properly. When gorilla tactics were used by prisoncrats to enforce this mandatory testing, prisoners rebelled. What started as a spontaneous event turned into a takeover of all of L Side, the taking of eight guards hostage, and the killing of nine prisoners and one guard before the takeover was over. The prisoners were liberated and some of those who refused to participate were beaten and some were killed. The takeover/riot began at approximately 2:45 P.M. on Easter Sunday and didn't end until the last hostages were released unharmed and the prisoners surrendered on national TV eleven days later. The negotiated surrender was made possible when Niki Schwartz, a civil rights attorney from Cleveland, Ohio, was called in to assist and advise the prisoners involved. It is still rumoured, and unofficially confirmed by some prisoners involved, that there is a much larger body count of prisoners killed, but the state is covering it up. Right now the Ohio Department of Justice is calling the shots at the prison.

Approximately 330 to 340 prisoners, who were on the recreation yard when the riot began, remained there until approximately 3:30 A.M. when over 200 guards, dressed in riot gear, entered the yard. They herded the prisoners into the gym, stripped them naked, and threw all their belongings into a community pile (this property hasn't been recovered to this day). Handcuffed behind their backs, prisoners then marched naked down K Corridor while female and male guards made comments about their nudity and manhood. They were then locked up, five to ten prisoners in a cell. It took more than four hours before the handcuffs were removed. Prisoners remained in these conditions for four days: five to ten in a cell, no medical attention, no anything except for a couple of cold-cut sandwiches a day until they were moved to one-man cells. One prisoner, Dennis Weaver, who had a history of litigations but who was a non-participant, was killed while on K side. The way he died has not been confirmed to this writer.

During the riot and negotiations, the Department of Corrections spokesperson repeatedly treated the incident as a joke. This was the same tactic used when the four Brothers took control of JL supermax back in 1985, and it is a common tactic used by the state. It backfired this time, leading to the execution of a guard, Robert Villandinghams.

The prisoners hung sheets out the windows telling the media that the state wasn't playing fair. The state's response was to move the media away from L Block so they could neither see nor hear the prisoners. After Villandinghams' body was dumped from a window, the state started taking the prisoners seriously. During all this, rumours abounded: it was reported from unnamed sources that there were seventeen to fifty bodies stacked in the L Side gym and to this day there are confirmed reports of more prisoners killed at the beginning of the riot than the DRC is reporting. I'm told that the Justice Department is calling the shots now and a cover-up (at least to the media) is being done *vis-à-vis* body counts.

Demands were issued to the DRC at the start; the different factions inside the prison worked together after the initial takeover. While the media reported there was dissension amongst prisoners, it was, in fact, at a minimum. One of the problems is forced integration. The reason the state is able to maintain the fallacy about an Aryan Brotherhood is because those prisoners who don't want to be forced into integrated celling have to say that they're racists in order to obtain a 'Green Card.' Such a card is a tag in a prisoner's file saying it is against his religion or philosophy to cell with another race. Those who have done time know that a lot of Black/White cells are homosexuals and their Man, and this has been a stigma against integrated cells (see *White* v. *Morris* consent decree). It is even recognized by leading jurists that integration by court order is no longer effective. Integration in prison should be by choice due to the volatile environment.

Demands that the state agreed to consider were:

1. Follow all administrative rules and regulations.
2. Administrative discipline and criminal proceedings will be fairly and impartially administered without bias against any specific individuals or groups.
3. All injured parties will receive prompt medical care and follow-up.
4. The surrender will be witnessed by religious leaders and news media.
5. The unit management system will be reviewed with attempts to improve in areas requiring change.
6. SOCF will contact the federal court to review the *White* v. *Morris* consent decree that requires integrated celling.
7. All close-security inmates have already been transferred from K side, and L side close-security inmates will be immediately evaluated for transfer.
8. Procedures will be implemented to thoroughly review prisoners' files pertaining to early release matters and changes will be made where warranted.
9. 600 inmates transferred to relieve overcrowding.

10. Current policies regarding inappropriate supervision will be rigidly enforced.
11. Medical staffing levels will be reviewed to ensure compliance with ACA standards for medical care.
12. Attempts will be made to expedite and improve work and program opportunities.
13. The DRC will work to evaluate and improve work and program opportunities.
14. There will be no retaliatory actions taken toward any prisoner or group of prisoners or their property.
15. A complete review of all correctional facility mail and visit policies will be undertaken.
16. Transfers from the correctional facility are coordinated through the Bureau of Classification. Efforts will be increased to ensure prompt transfers of those prisoners who meet eligibility requirements.
17. Efforts will be undertaken to upgrade the channels of communication between employees and prisoners involving quality of life issues.
18. The complete commissary pricing system will be reviewed.
19. The DRC will consult the Department of Health regarding any further TB testing.
20. The FBI will monitor processing and ensure that civil rights will be upheld.
21. The DRC will consider case by case the interstate transfer of any prisoner if the DRC feels that there is a reasonable basis to believe that they would be unable to provide a secure environment for that prisoner. Any prisoner denied transfer will be reviewed by the Federal Bureau of Prisons.

On Monday April 12, 1993, the bodies of six prisoners were placed on the yard for the DRC to pick up. They had been beaten and hanged. All were older prisoners, some who refused to participate in the riot, some who were snitches. On Tuesday, prisoners had dismantled windows and went from L Side to K side and got prisoners in K-8 to destroy their cells. Back in the AC Blocks, prisoners tore out their cell lights and wiring, beat on their cell doors, and started fires with all state-issue property. This was not shown on TV. On Wednesday the 13th, a helicopter manned by the Ohio National Guard and Northern Assistant Regional Director Joe McNeil had engine failure and crashed outside the prison, injuring those inside, while another officer broke his leg trying to rescue those inside the helicopter. Governor Voinavitch ordered 500 National Guard to surround the prison, replacing the Ohio State Highway Patrol. Water, food, and prescription medication were delivered to the prisoners. All water, electricity, and food had been cut off since the beginning of the takeover. In exchange for the release of a hostage, the prisoners were given airtime on TV. A prisoner identified as 'Inmate George' (later a private investigator called the media telling them that 'Inmate George' was George Skaizes, a former client who she believed to be innocent of the murder for which he was imprisoned) told the public that all prisoners of all races joined together in unity during the takeover to show the public the oppressive conditions they were living under and that they were all willing to die if their demands were not met. They called for the firing of Warden 'King Arthur' Tate. Guard, Darrold R. Clark, was released as a result of the broadcast. George also apologized to Villandinghams' family for his death, saying it was sad but necessary. He also told the family of another hostage, Bobby Ratcliffe, that he was all right and would be home soon. The hostages were well treated and guarded by the Muslims and White Brothers.

On Friday the 16th, prisoner Abdul Samad Mulin and guard James Demons were permitted out on the yard where an impromptu press table was erected and two state negotiators sat allowing media coverage of the event. Abdul Samad called upon the Muslims of the world to monitor the situation and to retaliate if any of the Brothers were killed by the state. He then went on to voice the complaints of the Muslims regarding the SOCF refusal to allow their prayer garb and other issues pertaining to the customs of Islam. It was obvious that they were given a limited time to voice these issues. He also stated that the mandatory TB testing violated their religious tenets and had sparked the incident, and told how the Security Point Classification systems and transfers were unfair. Guard, James Demons, was garbed in a Muslim robe and stated that he felt the incident could have been prevented and that shutting the water and power off jeopardized the hostages lives. He also said that the prisoners killed were not killed by the Muslims and were killed for being snitches. He was then led off the yard and none of his fellow pigs clapped or cheered for his release. He would later tell the media that he acted like he embraced Islam merely to save his own life and that he resented the way the situation was handled as Villandinghams' life could have been saved if the state would have taken matters seriously.

When Niki Schwartz was brought in, things got going more smoothly. On April 21, 1993, eleven days after the riot started, the negotiated settlement of the 21 points (listed above) were accepted and the surrender of the prisoners on national television began. Prisoners were shipped to MANCI, Trumball, Lebanon, Lorain, and Chilicothe.

The fact remains that Ohio's prisons arc operating at 200% overcapacity and the conditions are so bad that the same situation is liable to happen at any of these prisons. The public attitude that supports stiff sentences and more prisons does not deal with the root problems of crime. As long as there is racism, unemployment, sexism, poverty, drug use, and inadequate community resources for children and young adults, the crime rate will continue to escalate. President Clinton's plans for the criminal injustice system involve more funding to hire more police which will lead to more arrests and imprisonments, all of which translates into more overcrowding. One issue that the Brothers at Lucasville didn't touch on, or the state wouldn't let out, is the fact that the Adult Parole Authority isn't paroling enough prisoners who merit parole and the Governor refuses to exercise his authority of emergency releases of prisoners in overcrowding situations. The parole board members have ultimate power over prisoners and often exercise it arbitrarily and capriciously, though there is an Ohio Criminal Sentencing Commission ready to issue a report to require mandatory sentences, but also more community alternatives to prison. The sentencing structure in Ohio is ridiculous. Some prisoners are serving sentences in excess of 100 years for offenses that in other states would get two or three years flat. It has been proven that the longer the incarceration the more detrimental the effect. But prisons are industries nowadays, employing people in rural areas and creating an enormous job pool, so penalties get increased to maintain the business.

What is the answer? Obviously, rioting isn't the best way to bring about change due to the violence that goes with it. However, when men are treated like animals with no alternative means of getting justice, rioting is the only avenue left to focus the public eye on what is happening in our prisons. Now, hopefully, committees will be formed to bring about positive change. It's up to those in the progressive community to make this happen. I would urge those attorneys, legislators, and civil rights groups to join together and try to organize committees to make the state address all these prisoners' issues so there's not another blood bath. Those involved need your support more than ever to fend off the multitude of forthcoming criminal charges as well as retaliation by the state. Remember we are in here for you and you are out there for us. Solidarity.

The Unity Walk
Jon Marc Taylor

In the fall of 1991, at the maximum security Indiana State Reformatory (ISR), a series of events culminated in an unprecedented display of solidarity by the prisoner population. This, in turn, was followed by an unprecedented wave of repression by the Department of Corrections (DOC). Years in the making, days in the protest, and months in the punishment, the actions of the fall and winter of that year have consumed seasons of contemplation comprehending all that transpired.

To understand the forces that created the event, we must look ten years into the past from those halcyon days. At the beginning of the 1980s, ISR was largely populated by men sentenced to indeterminate terms.[1] The turnover of the population was slow but constant. The parole board and its flickering flame of hope a distinct presence in their lives. The way one did time then was to establish a pattern of aggressive rebelliousness early in one's term, followed by a gradual mellowing out towards the years of parole eligibility. That way one could demonstrate "rehabilitation" or "a maturing mindset" to the Parole Board. Depending where one was along the continuum of his sentence, the individual's reaction to any particular situation could be generally ascertained. The joint, while occasionally manifesting individual violence, possessed a stable and predictable air.

As those under indeterminate sentences were gradually replaced by those with determinate sentences, the relative quality of life began to change. Men with essentially longer sentences and less to lose[2] responded to the maddening frustration of doing time in the same aggressive, antisocial ways that landed most of them in the penitentiary in the first place. Coupled with understaffing, violent encounters between prisoners, and between prisoners and staff, increased.

As the environment became more unstable and unpredictable, various factions of the staff formed clandestine extra-judicial units (i.e., "guard gangs"). Organized beatings with wooden ball-bearing tipped riot batons, of men in lockup units, became routine orchestrations. Prisoners were strapped naked to metal bed frames in open-windowed, unheated isolation cells in the dead of winter for hours on end. Brutal drenchings by firehoses were common experiences for those unlucky enough to be thrown into the hole.

In a period of two years, in the early 1980s, a series of major prisoner clashes took place between housing unit groups,[3] with custody staff at times joining the fray, armed with their own previously stashed shanks, on the side of their housing unit's prisoner faction. Symbolizing the near-anarchy of the period, one cell house had "Dodge City" scrawled above the doorway.[4] After these mini-riots the institution would be locked down for a few days and the involved units a few weeks, undergoing thorough shakedowns.

The situation grew so out of control; sparked by the intense beating of a prisoner activist,[5] a handful of his followers conducted a running battle, attacking previously selected officers and those that unluckily happened to get in the way. Eventually seven officers were stabbed, three taken hostage, and a cell house with approximately one-hundred offenders was seized. The DOC reacted with an inadequately trained emergency response unit hastily assembled from other prisons across the state. After 12 hours, with death threats from both sides and on-site negotiations with state legislators, the hostages were released unharmed and the standoff ended peacefully.[6] The result was a one-month lock down for the entire reformatory, and a ninety-day lock down for the housing unit involved.[7]

Both sides had been scared by the near multiple-death event. Several sociological factors changed, affecting the milieu of the penitentiary. While security policies and procedures were tightened, draconian abuses were curtailed. In the latter half of the decade, personal appliances ranging from crock pots to radios and eventually televisions, were sold on the commissary, improving the quality of life in the spartan, cold water tap cells.

Overall, the staff, with a few notable exceptions, seemed to adopt a live and let live philosophy and did not go out of their way to hassle the prisoners. A measure of respect, and fear of the violent potential of each side, had been realized. This mediated the need for displays of extreme machismo, reducing tensions and the flow of testosterone. During this period, because of the reduction in parole-induced turnovers as more and more men were sentenced to determinate terms, the population began to age. The average age rose from mid-twenties at the beginning of the decade to early-thirties by the end. With the parole of almost all those serving indeterminate sentences, and the lower turnover in the population, a period of peaceful stabilization seemed to exist.

In 1988, post-secondary education became a no-cost program opportunity.[8] Enrollment grew from 30 full-time students in 1987 to 150 by 1990, or 15 percent of the main line population. The ISR–Ball State University college extension program was the largest single prisoner assignment/employer in any of the state's prisons.

Fights were not altogether uncommon, while serious blood spilling was. Disturbances involving more than a few men were random and isolated. In a sense, the population had matured. They remembered the turmoil and horrors earlier in the decade, seeing no value in returning to those times.

By the turn of the decade however, the environment had already begun to change. Young bloods; teenagers and young adults from harder times and meaner streets began to arrive. The beginning of a new generation gap developed: R & B met Rap; album rock clashed with acid head-bangers. The young bloods came from a different America than the older convicts had. Life was starker and tougher on the streets. Crack, even worse poverty, and the widely held perception of the futility of the situation ever improving had devastated a generation of young men who quite readily expected to die before they turned 30. These prisoners were even more poorly educated than the previous generation, their understanding of others less, and their desire to comprehend a situation beyond their own limited perspective nearly non-existent.

The newer prisoners were also more angry and antagonistic towards the powers that were. Assaults on staff (though still relatively rare) and even more so between prisoners increased. A few rotten apples in uniform geeked the hot heads, creating minor dramas for no other reason than they had the power to do so. More unsettling was the amount of time the new fish were bringing with them. These boys, and they largely were boys, were routinely laden down with 60, 90, 120, even 200 year bits. Essentially they had no future beyond the walls, with nothing to lose by lashing out to kill momentary anger, boredom, or frustration. The stability of the old ways was disrupted and an air of uncertainty settled over the prison.

In the fall of 1991, a virulent rumour of the impending shipment of all the reformatory's lockup unit prisoners to the state's new maximum restraint unit[9] spread throughout the population. The young bloods, with many of their cohort in the lockup unit,[10] seeking drama in their lives and angry at the perceived unfairness of the mass transfer, wanted to riot, take hostages, and "burn the mother fucker down"!

The older convicts, who had survived the turmoil and mass violence of the mid-1980s, suspected such an action would play into the hands of the DOC, and moreover change nothing for the better. It was known that the DOC had quietly, though not secretly, invested considerable effort in revamping their emergency response strategies and units. A repeat of the

"February Takeover" of years past, it was feared, would result in a bloodbath — predominantly prisoner blood.[11]

As in most penal settings a substantial number of the older prisoners were respected, and had measurable influence with the younger offenders. Many of these penitentiary role models were by now also college students or even graduates of the liberal arts associate and baccalaureate degree programs. Knowing the destructive and ultimately futile action of riot, these men began to persuade the hot heads to cool their agitation, seeking a different means of response to their anger.

Inspired by readings from Thoreau's *Civil Disobedience*, as well as the tactics and the effect of Ghandi and King, a handful of college students reasoned a unique (at least for the penitentiary) though potent response. Beginning on a Friday in late October, taking place only during the first of the evening's three sequential recreation lines and toward the end of the recreation period, men of all races and creeds commenced their demonstration. Approximately 300 men stopped their various personal activities and quietly, with dignity, assembled on their own volition and marched in rough formation around the large drill ground, completing the circuit by shaking hands and embracing each other. Then, without threat or rancour towards the guards, they quietly returned to their previous pursuits.

The custody staff naturally grew nervous over the unprecedented and apparently organized peaceful behaviour. Even more unsettling, as the men returned to their housing units, barely a word was said during the usually raucous line movement. The convicts were as nervous and unsure of the "screws" reactions, as the guards were of the prisoners'. With the superintendent out of the state for the weekend, the shift captain ordered the cautionary locking down of the participating units; the rest of the institution remained on regular schedule.

If the reasoning behind the partial lock down order was to dissuade any further demonstrations, the failure of that strategy became apparent the next evening. During the first recreation line on Saturday,[12] towards the end of the period, the men, more than the usual number who went to recreation, repeated the now-called "unity walk" around the drill ground. Returning to their housing units, the same silence permeated the air. In accordance with the previous day's decision, the shift captain ordered these units locked down along with the first two. On Sunday evening, the same events transpired, with nearly every resident of the last two non-locked down housing units participating in the units' walk.[13]

By Monday morning, the superintendent returned to the prison to find it
locked down. Not for violent altercations, but rather because the prisoners
had walked in peaceful unit formations around the drill ground during the
assigned recreation periods. Technically not a single DOC rule had been
violated. The prisoners had issued no threats, demands, or continued any
other action. Other than what informants might have told the administration,
no official or organized explanation of what exactly the demonstration was
in reference to was communicated. By lunch on Monday, the superintendent
lifted the lock down, and the reformatory returned to its normal schedule.

At lunch on Tuesday however, the entire camp was once again locked
down. This time it was to last for seven long, hard, punishing months. It
was to become, at the time, the longest continuous lock down in the history
of the prison and entire Indiana Department of Corrections. Only later, would
we learn, that the punitive lock down was ordered by the DOC commissioner
of the period.[14]

The official reason for the lock down was initially to investigate the
peaceful demonstration. For two weeks, nothing happened. The population
was confined to their cells and dorms, allowed no visits or phone calls, and
fed three brown bag meals a day. Then the most exhaustive shakedown of
the reformatory in 15 years was conducted. The month-long search
culminated in a media dog and pony show by the DOC dramatically displaying
some 50 "weapons" confiscated during the shakedown of the prison. Part
of the problem with this "cache of confiscated weapons" was that a third of
them were not weapons at all, but rather tattoo guns, scissors taken from
teachers' desks, and screwdrivers removed from housing units' maintenance
lockers. Another problem with the haul was that a third of the weapons had
been confiscated months if not years before the massive shakedown occurred.
Thus, after four weeks of the most extensive search of the 1,500-man
maximum security prison in anyone's memory all the DOC had to truthfully
show for their efforts was an odd assortment of 15 to 20 shanks, pipes and
razors. Reality be damned, the shakedown had become the reason for the
lock down and the confiscated items visual justification for the cessation of
all prisoner activities

As the Thanksgiving holiday came and went, and the penitentiary was
still locked down, the DOC declared the continued action was "for the
protection of the staff and offenders". Protection from what was never
explained, much less questioned by the docile media. After the passing of

the Christmas holiday season with no visits, phone calls, or canteen purchases, with the prisoners continuing to eat brown bag meals, the new year commenced with yet another rationale for the lock down.

The action was now to allow the administration to "identify and isolate prison predators". Why these predators were not identified during the previous two and a half months was not asked or explained. Nor was it questioned how the alleged predators could be identified at this juncture in time when no contact between offenders had been possible for the previous weeks. All the media did was dutifully report the DOC pabulum and dropped the story until the next press release.

Even a superficial check of the state's main newspaper would have revealed some incongruities with the prison predator myth. Between 1984–1989, not a single employee had been killed in the state's prisons. Moreover, less than a week before the lock down, the governor's press emphatically stated that "our incidence (of injuries in prison) is much below the national average. We do not have unusual problems". These statistics indicate that in a period in which levels of violence in prisons has decreased (by half) nationally, rates in Indiana were still "below the national average". What they reveal is a period of relative docility and peacefulness.

By mid-February, half of a 300-cell unit had been caged off into a separate unit and filled with questionably identified "predators". Many of those so tagged were the very same college educated older convicts who had averted a potentially bloody, costly and violent riot with their persuasive reasoning for the unity walk. All the while the hot headed young bloods that agitated for anarchy were left in the general population. If the administration's intelligence network could identify the peaceful organizers, they could also assuredly know of the agitators.

As winter bloomed into spring, the punishing lock down continued. By now the media had completely abdicated any pretense in reporting on the story. Thousands of letters from the prisoners and their families had been sent to the papers, as well as hundreds of phone calls by concerned outsiders to television stations questioning the lock down and lack of coverage. All to no avail.

During the lock down, with only 12 percent of the state's penal population, the reformatory had experienced six illness and suicide related deaths.[15] When compared to 1989's total of seven male deaths from all causes in the entire Indiana Department of Corrections, the reformatory was only one death shy in a seven month period of equalling all the deaths occurring in the state just three years before. All of which was information not reported by the Fourth Estate.

The first of June began with tentative easing of the lock down, as one hot meal a day was served in the chow hall. By the middle of the month, the lock down had been lifted and the shell shocked survivors emerged from their concrete caves and brick caverns into the light of day and fresh air, returning to their industry jobs, vocational and educational classes, and sparse therapeutic programs. Psychologically numbed by the overwhelming repressiveness of the punitive lock down, the population was in no mind to rebel further. The consensus of prisoners was that "we walked the drill ground and shook hands, and they locked us down for seven months. Hell, if we riot, they'll just walk down the ranges and execute us".

Interestingly, whether actually planned or not, the transfer of the lock up unit offenders never occurred.

*****

In retrospect it is amazing how much we accomplished. Not so much in what the unity walk prevented the DOC from doing, but in that the effort forced the DOC to overreact. Clearly if their intention had been to transfer the lockup unit offenders to the super maximum prison or elsewhere, they could have done so during the lock down with total impunity from reaction.

No, what the men of the reformatory accomplished was to terrify the DOC into gross overreaction to a situation for which they had no established contingency plan. Administration officials had never imagined that a majority of the diverse population could organize and carry out a continuous peaceful demonstration of their disquietude with the impending transfers. The DOC's efforts since the 1985 takeover hostage situation had been to refine their emergency response (SWAT-type) unit to react to violent situations. Nowhere in their arsenal was there a weapon to deal with a peaceful mass demonstration. As such tactics brought the British Empire to its knees in India, the unity walk caught the DOC without a plan.

The assessment of the success or failure of the unity walk depends on how encompassing a goal one projects for the action.

The effort was both a success and failure from the viewpoint of the prisoners. It was a success in that the unity walk was organized and carried out for three continuous days. To be fair, the unity walk was a failure in that nothing was accomplished to change conditions, with a seven-month lock down endured by the men, and by extension their families and friends. The sense of power from the unification of purpose permeated the population. For the first time the men felt they had some control, some say in the way their environment was run. They not only chose to be defiant, but chose a creative act that befuddled the powers that minutely controlled their lives. Such a feeling, however fleeting, was exhilarating.

Elements that contributed to the success of the unity walk were the critical mass of the experienced intelligentsia, no visible leadership, and simplicity of action chosen. Perhaps the most important element in the success of the unity walk as an alternative to rioting, was the older penitentiary experienced, liberal arts educated convicts who crafted and advocated for the demonstration chosen. These men, no more than 30, with an active central core of half a dozen, used their convict reputations to garner respect of the youngbloods, searched and debated their "collective educational experience" to craft an alternative effort, and utilized a mixture of street rap and speech communication skills to advance their alternative action.

By composing a loose collective to form an alternative to riot, no visible leadership was created. Spread throughout the housing units, the intelligentsia (for lack of a more definitive term) met, debated and resolved a synthesis of ideas at recreation, meals, and work assignments. Without a centralized plan, other than to avert a riot, this constantly merging and diverging group, developed by consensus the idea of the unity walk. By not establishing a hierarchical leadership, it became much more difficult for the administration to take preventative action by isolating the "leadership". Such a designation of individuals was too elusive to determine.

The action chosen of forming a totally participatory, loose formation during the recreation period to walk around the drill ground was a plan of genius given the circumstances and limitations of the situation. Since each housing unit group sent to recreation would be the only units participating at a given time, the need for wider coordination was not required. This also simplified the organization of the march within the unit, with only a few persuasive individuals in each unit needed to start forming the action.

By choosing the end of the recreation period to walk, when most of the unit had completed whatever activities in which they participated, the greatest number of idle individuals could be persuaded by motive, reason, or peer pressure to participate.

These elements of a loosely formed core group of experienced, reasoning individuals, forming no visible leadership, choosing an easily enacted demonstration were critical to the success of the action. What is still debated was the lack of a manifesto of goals or demands. Should a collective list of desired changes or grievances have been presented to the administration? Perhaps so if any long-term change was the goal. By doing so, however, a vulnerable leadership would have bean exposed to isolation if not retaliation.

With the only discussed goal being to avert riot while making a noticeable demonstration, the unity walk succeeded beyond the dreams of those orchestrating the action.

Finally, the success of the unity walk can be gauged by the reaction of the DOC. The initial befuddlement of the custody staff as to what was transpiring is understandable. The action taken by the population occurred without forewarning, transpired during recreation, and was followed by a reduced level of activity during line movement. The "rolling lock down" too is understandable as a precautionary measure until an ascertaining of the situation was made. The prolonged lock down, however, was not predictable given past actions, nor was it justifiable, especially with the constantly changing litany of "reasons" for the lock down.

The purpose of the continued lock down was to break the "spirit" of the population, to destroy the feeling of emancipatory power that the peaceful unified action had given the men. To this extent, the Department of Corrections succeeded. To the extent the prisoners of the Indiana State Reformatory shook to its foundation the administrative complacence of the DOC, the men succeeded beyond their wildest expectations.

NOTES

1. In 1978, Indiana adopted a determinate sentencing penal code, dictating a range of set terms for offenses. The "goodtime" provisions in the code provided day for day, or more euphemistically called "two-for-one," time credits. Thus, for example, barring major disciplinary violations, an offender sentenced to a 20-year term would serve 10 years irrespective of "rehabilitation" efforts or lack of them, or "nature and circumstances of offense." The Parole Board gradually evolved into the Clemency Board. Clemency, the only earlier release mechanism currently available, was a joke with less than one percent, and later under a democrat governor zero percent, of those applying receiving a commutation.
2. When the legislature adopted the determinate sentencing scheme, the term lengths for various offenses remained basically the same as before. With the two-for-one goodtime formula, however, prisoners served half the numerical value of their imprisoned terms,

instead of the previous usual one-third of sentence under the indeterminate structure. Sentences for the same offenses were longer and without the possibility of good behavior paroles, thus that controlling safety mechanism no longer positively influenced behavior.

3. "Groups" is the appropriate term since, although superficially similar to, the organized and highly antagonistic gang culture of the "crips" and "bloods", that phenomena had yet to be imported to the prison to any significant extent.

4. Within this unit one could easily find two or three breweries, cat houses, gambling dens, tattoo parlours, and shooting galleries, a dozen stores and hot sandwich shops, out of the various 300 one-man cells.

5. Or gang leader depending on your perspective. His exact words shouted down the hallway were: "Go ahead and do your thing brothers, they are beating me to death".

6. The event was a national story covered by the networks, making the cover of a newsweekly, which labeled the Indiana State Reformatory the most violent prison in America. In actuality, while a dangerous place, the Reformatory was no more violent, and in some cases less so, than other prisons across the country. But media hype sells the sizzle of a story rather than the reality of the situation.

7. Several years later, various correctional officers were convicted of federal civil rights violations, and officially credited with causing the riot.

8. In 1987, an prisoner class action lawsuit resulted in prisoners being declared eligible to receive state-funded higher education grants. Coupled with federal higher education (Pell) grants, post-secondary education enrollment became a fully subsidized opportunity.

9. The Maximum Restraint Unit (MRU) at Westfield, Indiana, is only the second prison in the United States, other than California's notorious Pelican Bay facility to be "condemned" by Amnesty International. During this period, in protest of the extreme conditions of MRU, two prisoners cut off fingers and attempted to mail them to U.S. Senators. Thus the fear of unwarranted transfer to the MRU added intensity to the concern over this issue.

10. Approximately 100 prisoners.

11. Some months after this period, at a new prison, a mile from the 70 year-old Indiana State Reformatory, a staff member was taken hostage by a shank wielding prisoner. Within hours, the prisoner was negotiated to a position where he was killed by a strategically placed sniper, affirming the efficiency and lethality of the DOC's emergency response unit.

12. The reason the first line was chosen was that at this time of the year, the large drill ground was closed for the later second and third recreation lines due to the season's early darkness. To give all the units equitable access to the large drill ground and its facilities, the three recreation lines, composed of two housing units each, were rotated everyday. Thus once every three days a housing unit's residents had access during first line to the large drill ground.

13. On most occasions, only about half of a unit's residents would attend every recreation.

14. Ironically, this information came to light when the DOC commissioner received an award from some correctional association for the long lock downs he instituted first at the reformatory and then at the state prison.

15. There were four reported suicide attempts in addition to the successful suicide.

Organizing Inside: Prison Justice Day (August 10th), A Non-Violent Response to Penal Repression

Bob Gaucher

In the summer of 1991, Prison Justice Day was observed for the sixteenth consecutive year in Canada. Originating in the cauldron of violence and repression that characterized Millhaven Penitentiary in the mid-1970s, National Prison Justice Day is the product of prisoners' organized political action. It is a day of remembrance, a memorial day for those who have died in prison. It is also a day on which prisoners stand together in a show of solidarity and present their concerns and demands.

In this essay, I will provide a history of the Odyssey Group and their initiative, National Prison Justice Day. In doing so, I will also address the political struggles of prisoners and their significance. The political consciousness and struggles of Canadian prisoners has been either denied or ignored by Canadian criminologists and social scientists.[1] The slow, grinding struggles characteristic of the process of advancing prisoners' rights have also led some prisoners to devalue their political struggles as pointless or unproductive. However, in the tradition of the penal press, prisoners continue to reach outside the walls to educate and radicalize the public *vis-à-vis* the nature of criminal justice and penal oppression. Contemporary groups such as "Infinity Lifers" (1986–1991) at Collins Bay Penitentiary and "The Justice Group" (1987–1991) at Stony Mountain Penitentiary, represent this tradition. The success of the Odyssey Group's Prison Justice Day initiative exemplifies the outside directed nature of prisoner politics and the ability of prisoners to effect change. It should give strength to prisoners and their outside supporters and encouragement in their struggles for rights and against penal oppression. In addition, I will illustrate how the penal press provides an entry into the discourse and analysis of Canadian prisoners. A major lacuna in Canadian social science and historiography is the perspective and position of the criminalized underclass and carceral population. The penal press is the only comprehensive body of writing which allows us to access this "history from below." If those in control seriously started to take into account the discourse of prisoners, instead of being driven by entrepreneurial desire or the spirit of managerial manipulation and panic, prison life might be less a matter of survival, and we as a society might discover reasons to reduce our reliance on criminal justice and criminalization to address social conflict and inequality.

The Odyssey Group 1976–82

To understand this prison group it is necessary first to examine the context of violent repression which gave it birth. The reform urge of the 1950s — with its emphasis on bringing prisoners' initiatives in line with the provision of vocational training and education — gave way to the new individual and individualizing treatment ideology of the 1960s. Though Canada's federal prisoners had initially supported the post war reforms, by the late 1950s they were rejecting them as superficial window dressing created for public consumption.[2] The new treatment programs of the 1960s (e.g., group therapy) were actively opposed by both prisoners and custodial staff. Internal strife and competition over the control of institutions mounted: senior management, custodial staff and treatment staff; custodial staff and prisoners; and treatment staff and prisoners all squared off. Of major significance was the unionization of penitentiary staff within the Public Service Alliance of Canada in 1968, and the subsequent surge of power and control of frontline custodial officers. The events of the 1960s lay the ground for a decade (i.e., 1970s) of penal repression and prison disturbances unparalleled in Canadian history. The decade opened with one of the worst prison riots on record. The Kingston penitentiary riot (1971) set the stage for the *noir* nightmare regime of the new Millhaven prison, opened in its aftermath.[3] It is no small, nor laudable achievement but Millhaven became legendary for the overt brutality of its regime in the first five years of operation. It is in this context that we must situate the creation of the Odyssey Group.

The Odyssey Group was formed in 1976, and was modelled upon one of the first prisoner groups in that institution, The Quarter Century Group, also created by long-term prisoners (*Odyssey Newsletter*, 1979, 1:6:23–25). A constitution was drawn up by the first executive committee, consisting of Howie Brown (chairperson), Leonard Olbey (vice-chairperson), and Chip Tracy (secretary-treasurer), and ratified by its membership on September 21, 1976. The group's constitution was formally recognized by Millhaven's administration on August 30, 1977 (Ibid.) The constitution presents a clear frame of reference as to the:

Purpose and Concept of Odyssey
1. We shall aid in the preparation of proposals and presentations concerning all facets of prison programs and rehabilitation.

2. We shall [make] constructive suggestions on all types of reform, and establish a liaison with the Law Reform Commission of Canada.
3. We shall ask professional advice, by invitation, as an aid to the group. The group may consider and implement any program it deems beneficial to its development and well being.
4. Odyssey shall contact interested citizens, (professional, student, laymen, etc.) in the society to establish dialogue and programs of rehabilitative value (Ibid.).

Despite the rhetoric directed at the prison's administration via the stated goals of its constitution, Odyssey was clearly a prisoners' rights group.[4] In light of the history of overt repression and violence at Millhaven and the political consciousness of Odyssey's members, the group was opposed to violence and dedicated to using non-violent means to effect change. They wanted

> ... to bring to the attention of the public what we, the members of the Odyssey Group and other contributing authors, believe to be gross injustices perpetrated by the Canadian Correctional Service, Canada's Justice System and all other services related to the corrections field. ...
>
> The Odyssey Group is a group of long-time prisoners who feel that the justice system in Canada can be changed by non-violent means. It is our purpose to do all in our power to bring about those changes (*Odyssey Newsletter*, 1980, 1:9:1).

Their strategy was to prepare briefs and analytical statements on prison conditions and justice issues, and to publicize them through group meetings with outsiders and through widespread distribution of their newsletter.[5]

The group consisted of fifteen inside members; prisoners were accepted into the group by application and ballot (i.e., membership approval). This total matched the number of outside guests allowed to attend a meeting. The executive was elected bi-annually. After the leadership period of the initial executive (approximately two years), the executive committee constantly changed within a six-month to one-year period. In part, this was a strategy to protect members from harassment, and in part, the result of the transfer of members to other prisons. Odyssey met weekly from September 1976 to

October 1982. It attracted a wide variety of guests and was in contact with numerous outside organizations, individuals and members of the mass media. Two groups' involvement and support stand out. The Ottawa Civil Liberties Association provided up to ten outside members and regularly attended meetings from February 1978 until mid-1980. Ray Sunstrum and Liz Elliott were prominent in co-ordinating this support.[6] Later, in 1980, sociology students from Queen's University under the co-ordination of Professor Laureen Snider provided strong support.

The groups' success in involving and influencing outside groups and individuals was considerable. For example, their brief on Special Handling Units (SHUs) and the use of segregation was used by the Church Council on Justice and Corrections in their lobbying efforts to stop this practice. A feature article on Odyssey in *Centerfold* states:

> Talking in terms the Government can understand, the Odyssey Group acts within due processes of law. Briefs, hearings and management efficiency studies are prepared and circulated. ... If the Odyssey Group's work is measured in terms of response from officials, they could indeed be said to be effective. The chairman of the group, Howard Brown and the editor of *Odyssey Magazine*, George Watson, have both been shipped out ("Millhaven Prisoners Write for Active Reform" [Aug./Sept., 1979]; see also *Tarpaper*, 1979:18–30).

Noted guests who became strong supporters of Odyssey initiatives included prison rights activist Claire Culhane, who visited the group for the first time on October 23, 1979 (*Odyssey Newsletter*, 1979:56).

ODYSSEY NEWSLETTER

The principal vehicle for their public education activities was their newsletter whose expressed purpose was "that the Millhaven Prisoners' voice will be heard" (*Odyssey Newsletter*, 1978:2). Its aim was to "inform the prison population and the people in the society of our thoughts, goals and accomplishments" (*Odyssey Newsletter*, 1979:24):

> Public apathy can only be combatted through education. Hopefully this newsletter will serve that purpose. (*Odyssey Newsletter*, 1980:1)

The first issue of this bi-monthly was published in August 1978.[7] Over the next four years thirteen additional issues were published. The first six were published on schedule, but typically, administrative censorship and obstruction subsequently lead to a more sporadic output and smaller publications.[8] Through its newsletter we can trace the development of Odyssey and its extension outside the walls, as well as the group's eventual demise. It reached its peak audience of 500 plus subscribers with the June/July 1979 issue which focused on two of the group's primary concerns, Special Handling Units (SHUs)/administrative segregation and Prison Justice Day (*Odyssey Newsletter*, 1979, 1:6:4).

The Odyssey Newsletter was initially edited by the group's original chairperson, Howie Brown, and George Watson. Brown was transferred from Millhaven after the first issue and George Watson remained editor for the first year before he was transferred. Watson exemplifies the type of politicized prisoner whose writing appears in the Canadian penal press through the latter part of the 1970s and the 1980s. In all there were eight editors and fifty-five contributors, including men and women from other penitentiaries. Much of the writing and analysis in this publication is highly politicized, going beyond the liberal consensus version of prison critique and penal reform, locating the 'prison problem' within the exploitative and oppressive context of the dominant capitalist order. Major issues addressed included: SHUs; the concept of 'dangerousness' and administrative segregation; prison violence, suicide and death; the power and control of custodial staff and their union; involuntary transfers; mandatory supervision and parole; the double standard of 'social justice' in Canada; the absurdity of rehabilitation in prison, especially maximum security prisons like Millhaven; and most prominently, prisoners' rights.

A constant theme in the first eight issues is Prison Justice Day, an Odyssey Group initiative that has become a national tradition inside and outside Canada's penitentiaries.

PRISON JUSTICE DAY — AUGUST 10ᵀᴴ

Prison Justice Day (PJD) originated in Millhaven Penitentiary on August 10, 1975, when the prisoners of that institution commemorated the first anniversary of the death of Eddie Nalon, who committed suicide while in solitary confinement in Millhaven's SHU. This first observance took the form of a hunger strike and day of mourning. Another fast by six prisoners in Millhaven's SHU also began that day and lasted for eighteen days (Rye, 1979:4–6). By the following summer (1976) it had become an established memorial day; a day in which "prisoners pay tribute to the prisoners who have died in this country's prisons" (*Odyssey Newsletter*, 1979:8). It also came to represent the demand for prisoners' rights, and was soon observed inside and outside Canada's penitentiaries. In the *Odyssey Newsletter*'s (1978–79:16) farewell to Howie Brown, the initiation of PJD is largely attributed to him, although in a conversation with Rick Rye of *Tarpaper* (Rye, 1979:2–6), Brown credited Jack McNeil as co-founder. Brown's involvement stemmed in part from the fact that he was in the SHU at the time of Nalon's death. In 1978, after spending eight years in maximum security prisons in central Canada, much of it at Millhaven and in solitary confinement, Brown was transferred across the country to a maximum security prison in British Columbia. This and the numerous other involuntary transfers used by the Canadian Penitentiary Service to breakup Odyssey and prisoner solidarity at Millhaven inadvertently led to the expansion of this and other prisoner rights activities at that time.

Solidarity with the Millhaven prisoners' initiative was immediately forthcoming. The first formally defined PJD, August 10, 1976, generated support both inside and outside Canada's federal penitentiaries.

> The prisoners of Millhaven from here on in will be known as the '100%ers' for that is what we gave on August 10th to the remembrance of our brothers .... 100% support and respect. We congratulate our brothers and sisters in other prisons who supported our "one-day hunger fast" by their show of UNITY and compassion. Our support is growing and it can only continue to grow as long as we continue to struggle without faltering. ... To the citizens who supported us and did so much to organize Prison Justice Day, our sincere and heartfelt thanks. (*The Millhaven Momentum*, August, 1976:22)

Tightwire (May/June 1977: 28) reported 98% support for 1976 at Kingston Prison for Women, and the penal press throughout the country reported observances in their areas. While trying to play down the day, penal authorities provided testimony to the widespread support:

A spokesperson for the Canadian Penitentiary Service made it known
that the hunger strike of those lodging in federal penitentiaries had
no effect in the Maritimes and Western provinces, while prisoners
in Quebec, Ontario and B.C. seemed to have followed the strike in
95% of cases. (*Le Devoir*, August 11, 1976 quoted in Brisson,
1983:2)

In Quebec, the Prisoners' Rights Committee of Montréal and the Human
Rights League publicized the prisoners' appeals and its members also observed
a day of fasting. In B.C., a coalition of prisoners' rights and feminist groups
organized 24-hour vigils outside Okalla prison and British Columbia
Penitentiary.

By August 10, 1977, inside support for PJD had spread to penitentiaries
across the country, particularly in the large maximum security institutions.
A spokesperson for the Canadian Penitentiary Service revealed that over
3000 members (1/3 of the federal prison population) had taken part (Ibid.),
although the penal press reported greater support, including the maritime
and prairie regions. However, not all federal prison populations yet supported
the initiative, in part, because of the learned caution of survival, and in part,
because of institutional penalties. Through the exhortations of prisoner
activists and penal press writers this soon changed (e.g., see Smith, 1977:1).
By 1979, virtually all federal maximum security prisons were solidly
represented and the proportion of federal prisoners taking part continued to
grow through 1981. This was paralleled by growing national recognition
and support outside the prison walls. Claire Culhane's Prisoners' Rights
Group of Vancouver, Marrianne Roy and the Prisoners' Rights Group of
Montréal, and the Civil Liberties Association of Ottawa continued to provide
publicity and organize major events in their areas, while smaller demonstrations
of support sprang up in other cities. The Law Union organized Toronto's
first public demonstration of support in 1978, and laid the basis for the
tradition in that city. Increasingly, outside support took the form of vigils
and demonstrations outside prisons, including press conferences and the
presentation of briefs outlining prisoners' concerns and demands.

THE MEANING OF PRISON JUSTICE DAY

Together with Eddie Nalon, the Landers brothers came to symbolize the
political nature and particular focus of PJD. In "A Comrade is Dead"

(*Millhaven Momentum*, 1976: 8–9), Howie Brown eulogized Bobby Landers as a leader of prisoners' struggles against oppression and for their rights. As a prisoner who had survived numerous attempts to 'break' him by using physical and psychological violence, Landers' death from a heart attack in Millhaven's SHU (resulting from a lack of medical attention) came to epitomize the focus of PJD. In reporting the inquest into Landers' death in *The Toronto Star*, N. Van Rijn states:

> He entered Millhaven May 1, and on the morning of May 21, he was found on the floor of his cell, dead. He was in a segregation cell, designed to keep troublesome prisoners away from other inmates, because the prison director suspected him of pressing for prisoners' rights. (Van Rijn, Sept. 28, 1976, quoted in *The Communicator* 1976:26–28)[9]

Van Rijn notes that in the previous year a coroner's inquest into the death of another prisoner had recommended the installation of an emergency call alarm system in the SHU. Such a system could have saved Bobby Landers' life. His death and subsequent PJD agitation forced CPS to install such a system.

Prison deaths continued unabated, and proper medical attention and diagnosis continued to be a focal point of prisoners' concerns. The January/February 1978 issue of *Tightwire* (46) printed a poem by a nineteen year old prisoner Isabella Fay Ogima, followed by the reprint of a newspaper report of her death. According to an editorial in the March/April 1978 issue of *Tightwire*, Ogima died of acute hepatic failure and the editor charged that lack of proper medical diagnosis and treatment was the determining factor in her death. For prisoners, prison deaths symbolize their tenuous hold on life and their vulnerability to the vagaries of institutional control. Throughout its history, prison deaths have remained the central focus of this memorial day. The list of casualties continues to grow reflecting the poor quality of medical attention; the desperation of prisoners, especially in solitary confinement, who take their own lives; and the brutal repressive consequences of fulfilling custodial goals. In 1977, Glen Landers was shot to death trying to scale Millhaven's fences in an escape attempt, and ten years later, Sandy Alexander Fitzpatrick was shot and killed by a tower guard at that institution. Peter Collins writes that:

Many men and women have died under what's known to be suspicious circumstances. ... There have been many deaths, before and after Eddie Nalon's. More recent is the sad circumstances surrounding Alexander (Sandy) Fitzpatrick. Sandy was shot to death on October 14th, 1987, by a Correctional Officer at Millhaven Penitentiary.

Sandy was shot to death by a prison guard armed with an AR-15 assault rifle. A rifle that has a top firing rate of 650 rounds per minute. The Correctional Service of Canada equip these "high velocity" .223 caliber rifles with a "dum-dum" projectile, a form of ammunition that is designed to expand at a rapid rate upon entry. When this death dealing bullet entered Sandy's body, it tore his chest cavity to shreds ensuring [sic] death.

It is more than a passing point of interest that this type of ammunition is outlawed by the U.N. for use in war. It is also illegal for hunting animals in Canada.

Every year on August 10th, we remember Eddie, and now Sandy, among the many men and women that have died while in (and at) the hands of the Correctional Services of Canada and for all the men and women that have died in or at the hands of other countries' prison services. (*The Partisan*, July/August, 1988)

As Howie Brown writes on the occasion of PJD:

We do not intend to ever forget his [Eddie Nalon] dying, just like we do not intend to forget all of the other deaths that have taken place. That is what August 10th is all about. Remembering our friends, our comrades, our brothers and sisters who have died in prison ... (*Odyssey Newsletter*, 1978:3)

The focus and demands of PJD have gone beyond memorials to those who have died and address the conditions that produce prison deaths, especially SHUs and solitary confinement. *The Odyssey Newsletter* (1979:1) provides a list of demands that is indicative of this extension today:

PRISON JUSTICE DAY, AUGUST 10TH, 1979, FOR THE END TO SENSELESS DEATHS IN PRISONS, IN SUPPORT OF HUMAN RIGHTS FOR PRISONERS.

TO ATTAIN:

THE RIGHT TO MEANINGFUL WORK WITH FAIR WAGES,
THE RIGHT TO USEFUL EDUCATION AND TRAINING,
THE RIGHT TO PROPER MEDICAL ATTENTION,
THE RIGHT TO FREEDOM OF SPEECH AND RELIGION,
THE RIGHT TO FREE AND ADEQUATE LEGAL SERVICES,
THE RIGHT TO INDEPENDENT REVIEW OF ALL PRISON
   DECISION MAKING AND CONDITIONS,
THE RIGHT TO VOTE,[10]
THE RIGHT TO FORM A UNION,
THE RIGHT TO ADEQUATE WORK AND FIRE SAFETY
   STANDARDS,
THE RIGHT TO OPEN VISITS AND CORRESPONDENCE,
THE RIGHT TO NATURAL JUSTICE AND DUE PROCESS.

These demands have not changed substantially over the years (e.g., see *Cemetery Road*, August 1983). In his column "Imaginary or Real," Myles Sartor captures the underlying meaning of PJD for many prisoners:

> When trying to find the meaning of Prisoner's Justice Day we must seek beyond the symbol and find out what it represents. Prisoner's Justice Day presents on one level an act of solidarity, on another level it represents a period of remembrance in which past injustices within prisons become the focus of attention for a single day. On a higher level the most important aspect of Prisoner's Justice Day is that it symbolizes *a way of life*.
>   This means that within our caged existence we must continually be aware of the constant struggle for survival ... (Sartor, 1983:3)

Above all, the original Odyssey Group initiative has transcended itself.

> An idea had been born. An idea can't be put in solitary, tear gas doesn't faze it, a rubber truncheon swings right through an idea — missing everything. Besides, this particular idea had already broken out of prison and was running around the countryside knocking on doors, waking folks up. Lights were coming on all over the place. Wardens whispered worriedly, the prisoners were on to something. They refused all enticements, ignored all threats. They had seized

their freedom simply by not participating in their imprisonment
("A Lesson in Freedom," 1986:2)

NATIONAL PRISON JUSTICE DAY

As with most long-term political struggles, support for PJD has at times
faltered. However, continuing deaths and incidents of overt repression have
served to re-energize both inside and outside support. For example, the
post-hostage taking brutality at Archambault penitentiary in 1982 (see
Gosselin, 1982; Amnesty International, 1983), the waves of Native prisoners'
suicides at Saskatchewan Penitentiary, the shooting death of Sandy Fitzpatrick
at Millhaven (1987), and the continuing high suicide rates at Kingston Prison
for Women (P4W) have served to bolster prisoner support in those institutions
and regions. When prisoner support has waned, the urgings of politicized
prisoners such as Gayle Horii (see Horii, 1988) and outside prison activists,
like Claire Culhane in Vancouver and Jean-Claude Bernheim in Montreal,
have stiffened the resolve and carried the day. In her letter to the editor of
The Partisan, Claire Culhane writes:

> Out this way, we didn't rate media coverage but we did our thing.
> A Rock Against Prisons concert on the Saturday at a people's park
> in downtown Vancouver and on the Sunday, a Cavalcade ... to nine
> prisons to parade our variety of placards, such as REMEMBER
> OUR DEAD ... END SOLITARY CONFINEMENT NOW ... NO
> MORE CAGES ... and so on.
>   While some prisoners are writing to deplore the lack of support
> shown N.P.J.D. in their particular joint, what really matters is that
> IT HAS BEEN HAPPENING FOR THIRTEEN YEARS AND IT IS
> STILL HAPPENING — as it will continue to happen somewhere if
> not everywhere for the next thirteen times 13 years ... and THAT'S
> WHAT COUNTS. (*The Partisan*, Nov/Dec. 1988)

And the support continues. For example, Eugene Turnbull in "The Editor's
Desk" (*The Partisan*, Sept/Oct. 1988:1) notes massive support in the Ontario
region in 1988; 100% in Millhaven, Collins Bay and Joyceville, and 80% in
P4W and Warkworth.

   Outside support has also been maintained, with the Prisoners' Rights
Groups of Vancouver and Montreal leading the way. By 1981, the Prisoners'

Rights Office of Montreal had garnered the support of twenty popular, union and political groups in Quebec (Bisson, 1983:5). In 1983 they reported that they had extended PJD internationally, receiving support and publicity from the Paris radio station *Frequence Libre*.

> Various demonstrations were to take place in France to mark August 10. In Paris, on August 9, *Frequence Libre* broadcast an evening devoted to the commemoration day with the participation of Jean-Claude Bernheim of the PRO, the secretary for prison affairs of the International Human Rights Federation. Outside Lille prison the Committee For Action in Support of Prisoners' Demands laid a wreath and observed a minute of silence in memory of all prisoners who had died in prison. (Ibid.:7)

At the tenth anniversary memorial in Vancouver (1986), the developing international attention was evident with messages of solidarity arriving from the U.S.A., Australia, Holland, England and Scotland (*Kent Times*, 1986:3).

CONCLUSION

In examining PJD as the most outstanding of the numerous accomplishments of the Odyssey Group, I am struck by the impossibility of what they achieved. Even CSC has finally capitulated. After years of harassment of those prisoners who took part in PJD, including the loss of privileges and 'good' time for the general prison participants, and segregation and kidnapping (i.e., involuntary transfers) for the leadership, in 1988 the senior management committee of CSC decided to eliminate the practice of issuing 'performance notices', although those who refused to work were still docked a day's pay (*Tightwire*, 1988:15). Some members of Odyssey are on the street and doing well, some are still doing time. Prison violence and prisoners' deaths continue. Last month (March 1991), ten women in the segregation unit of Kingston Prison for Women engaged in a hunger strike in response to the suicides of six Native prisoners in the past eighteen months and the institution's repression of the prison population's grief and anger.

> Aboriginal women inside the prison have endured not only the violence and oppression a patriarchal society forces on women, but also the genocidal campaigns of our white supremacist state in

its attempts to conquer the Indigenous peoples of Turtle Island. The resistance of Feb. 6 (1991) was a response among the Native women and their sisters inside the walls to the death just days before of their sister and the racist and vile attempts of the prisoncrats to blame the death on Native women and on the Native services which elders provide. (*Through The Walls*, "Press Release", March 6, 1991)

Last week (March 1991) two men at Saskatchewan Penitentiary were shot to death by guards during a hostage taking standoff. The C.B.C. national news coverage of this 'event' showed the 'triumphant' prison guards responsible for the deaths sharing high-fives in the prison yard in the immediate aftermath of the killings. Certainly George Jackson's view of prison employees remains valid for Canada's gulags as attested to by the shooting death of Sandy Fitzpatrick in 1989, and the recent killings at Saskatchewan penitentiary.

Anyone who can pass the civil service examination today can kill me tomorrow. Anyone who passed the civil service examination yesterday can kill me today with complete immunity. (Jackson, 1971:6)

Although prison disturbances and violent reactions to overt and life threatening repression still occur, Odyssey provided a new model for politicized non-violent responses to the degradation and destruction of prison life. National Prison Justice Day epitomizes this new politicized way of thinking. By commemorating PJD, the struggles and sacrifices of those who came before are recognized. The Odyssey Group's success in creating this national forum for public education on criminal justice and corrections issues also provides encouragement and strength to those who engage in prison-focused struggles both inside and outside the walls. In an interview for *Kent Times* with Jack McCann and Bobby Paul on PJD, Steve Reid provides a sense of the meaning of those past struggles and their accomplishments.

KT: As a survivor of long years in solitary — as chronicled in *Prisoners of Isolation* — how do you look back on those times of heavy prison-prisoner confrontations?

JM: Guys don't realize the fury, the anger, the bitterness. The pain that a lot of guys put out to achieve some change, I mean we were hurt. We were hurt.

KT: So August 10ᵗʰ symbolizes the cost of achieving change?

JM: Exactly. I remember the cost.

BP: The hole. There's a good example right there. Now you can smoke. You get your meals. Look how many years were spent on bread and water. Not too long ago neither. That's something that came about because of the guys who were sacrificed. The guys who died, the other guys who spent years in solitary being labelled ringleaders. The younger guys don't realize it, they [the Canadian Penitentiary Service] or nobody didn't just come along and say "hey, we better change this." It was changed because it was brought to people's attention with blood, literally with blood. Then they changed it. (*Kent Times*, 1986:17)

The types of political activities in which the Odyssey Group, PJD, and prisoners' public education have engaged remain major means of effecting such changes.

Dedicated to the memory of Billy Asham, who died in The Hole in Saskatchewan Penitentiary in 1971.

NOTES

1. See for example R.S. Ratner and B. Cartwright (1990). Their argument denigrates prisoner politics and in doing so represents many of the problems associated with a variety of academic criminology and social science discourses which deny political credibility to prisoners' struggles. For a broader discussion see Gaucher (1988). For an analysis of the Canadian Penal Press see Gaucher (1989).
2. See for example *The Telescope* (1955–59) or *Transition* (1955–59) for prisoners' critiques of the faulty promises of the new post-war prison reform movement.
3. In the aftermath of the Kingston Penitentiary riot (1971), prisoners transferred to the newly opened Millhaven Penitentiary were forced to run a gauntlet upon entering the institution, and were then subjected to years of violent repression. See J.W. Swackhammer (1973); MacGuigan (1976); G. McNeil and S. Vance (1978).
4. See *Quarter Century News* (1973–74).
5. For a clear statement of this, see R. Van Bree 1979:7–9.
6. See for example *Odyssey Newsletter* 1978, (5):42–43.

7. A penal press convention dating from this time is the creation of magazines that commence or recommence publication with an August issue commemorating Prison Justice Day. See for example *Cemetery Road* (1983); *Kent Times* (1986) 1:1; *The Partisan* (1988).

8. For a discussion of this specific problem, see *Odyssey Newsletter* 1979:4. For a general discussion of the censorship and obstruction of the Newsletter, see 1978:63; 1979:26, 2–6; 1981:32-4; 1982:13. These are dominant themes throughout the history of the penal press.

9. Also see R.K. Yellowbird, "Death!! Suicide or Public Execution" in *Millhaven Momentum* (1976:34–38), which extends this political connection in a discussion of a series of deaths at Saskatchewan Penitentiary.

10. A recent decision (January 1991) of the Canadian Federal Court recognized prisoners' right to vote in federal elections. This decision has been appealed by the Justice Department. [*Editor's Note: The Supreme Court of Canada is currently considering this issue: August 2002.*]

REFERENCES

"A Lesson in Freedom" (1986) *Kent Times*, 1 (1):2.

Amnesty International (1983) *Report on Allegations of Ill-Treatment of Prisoners at Archambault Institution, Canada, Québec*. U.S.A.: A.I. Publications.

Bisson, M. (1983) "August 10: Prisoner Solidarity Day," *Prisoners Rights Committee of Montréal*. (Photocopy).

Brown, H. (1976) "A Comrade is Dead", *Millhaven Momentum*, 2:8–9.

Centerfold (August–September 1979) "Millhaven Prisoners Write for Active Reform."

Gaucher, R. (1988) "The Prisoner as Ethnographer" *The Journal of Prisoners on Prisons* 1(1):49–62.

———. (1989) "The Canadian Penal Press" *The Journal of Prisoners on Prisons* 2(1):3–24.

Gosselin, L. (1982) *Prisons in Canada*. Montréal: Black Rose.

Horii, G.K. (1988) "Misplaced Misgivings" *Tightwire*, XXII:3.

Jackson. G. (1972) *Blood in My Eye*. New York: Bantam Books.

MacGuigan, M. (1977) *Report to Parliament by the Sub Committee on the Penitentiary System in Canada*. Ottawa: Supply and Services.

McNeil, G. with Vance, S. (1978) *Cruel and Unusual*. Canada: Deneau and Greenberg.

Ratner, R.S. and Cartwright, B. (1990) "Politicized Prisoners: From Class Warriors to Faded Rhetoric," *Journal of Human Justice* 2(1):75–92.

Rye, R. (1979) "Prison Justice Day," *Tarpaper*, 10(1):2–6.

Sartor, M. (1983) "Imaginary or Real?" *Out of Bounds*, 16:3.

Smith, L.R. (Aug., 1977) "Editorial" *Off The Wall*, 1.

Swackhammer, J.W. (1973) *Report of the Commission into Certain Disturbances at Kingston Penitentiary During April 1971*. Ottawa: Queen's Printer.

Van Bree, R. (1979) "Message from The Odyssey Chairman," *Odyssey Newsletter*, 1:7.

Van Rijn, N., (Sept. 28, 1976) "How a Millhaven Inmate Died in Solitary" *The Communicator* 1976, 4, 26–28.

Yellowbird, R.K., (1976) "Death!! Suicide or Public Execution," *Millhaven Momentum*, 2:34–38.

Penal Press Publications

Cemetery Road, Kent Institution, 1983:2, (1982?, 1985?)
The Communicator, Springhill Penitentiary, New Brunswick, 1977, vol. 5.
Kent Times, Kent Institution, British Columbia, 1986, 1:1
Millhaven Momentum, Millhaven Penitentiary, Ontario. 1976:2.
Off the Wall, Saskatchewan Penitentiary, 1977, August.
Odyssey Newsletter, (1978–82), Millhaven Penitentiary, Ontario. 1978: 1:l; 1978: 1.2; 1978–79: 1:3; 1979: 14, 1:5, 1:6, 1:7; 1980: 1:9; 1981: 1:10; 1982: 1:12.
Out of Bounds, (1980-89), Williamshead Institution. British Columbia, 1983:16.
The Partisan, (1988–89), Millhaven Penitentiary, Ontario. 1988: Sept.–Oct.; Nov.–Dec.
Quarter Century News, (1973–74), Millhaven Penitentiary, Ontario.
Tarpaper, Matsqui Institution, British Columbia, 1978: 8:4; 1979: 10:1.
Tightwire, Kingston Prison for Women, Ontario, 1977: III.3; 1978: 4:1, 4:2; 1988: XXII:3.
The Telescope, Kingston Penitentiary, Ontario, 1951–63.
Transition, British Columbia Penitentiary, 1951–63.
Through the Walls, "Press Release — March 6", 1991.

Remembering Prison Justice Day
Robert Brydon

K evin and I met while incarcerated within the confines of Drumheller Penitentiary. We worked in the same shop and lived in the same unit so it was natural that we became friends. This friendship was not instrumental or shallow in substance, but rather one of closeness like brothers share. The biggest fear we had in common was that of dying inside.

After our release, Kevin called me at the half-way house to tell me that he was in the Calgary lock-up and would I come to see him. Without hesitation, I went. I arrived at the police station and met his mother and sister. After introductions and a few moments of idle conversation, I left, promising to return later. It was then that Kevin and I spoke to each other in that silent, universal language that only those who have suffered greatly can speak. His look told of the terror to come, our common fear of dying inside, and the degradation he must suffer. His eyes pleaded with me not to leave, but I did. I live with that look to this day, almost ten years later.

I returned to visit Kevin that same day, only to discover he had been transferred back to the penitentiary at Drumheller. From further inquiries, I learned that the authorities either could not or did want to deal with him so he was transferred again to Edmonton Maximum Institution. I heard later that Kevin was placed in solitary confinement — for reasons unknown — and he 'committed suicide,' all this because of a parole violation on a couple of years sentence for a crime against property. He was not charged with an offence when his parole was suspended. He was incarcerated for a technical violation of his parole condition. What an ungodly form of justice he received.

Thoughts of Kevin and others who met the same form of justice give rise to reflections on Prison Justice Day, August 10: what it meant to me then and what it means now.

At first, August 10 was nothing more than a day of protest for me. It was a day to shut down the prison for twenty-four hours and stay in the cell and fast. Each of us who remained in his cell was not credited with three days remission, which meant already 'overworked' classification officers had even more paperwork to do. I could also vent pent-up anger and frustration on those who did not join the protest. For me Prison Justice Day was nothing more than that.

On August 10, 1988, I was at a minimum security prison camp just outside Stony Mountain Penitentiary in Manitoba. We planned our usual fast and work stoppage, and included a memorial service for the evening at the prison gravesite.

As we gathered for the half-mile walk, I looked in the direction of the gravesite. The adage, 'out of sight, out of mind' certainly applied. The gravesite was tucked away in a far corner of the prison property. Unless you knew it was there, you would not know about it.

As I began to walk, there was a gentle rain. I became engulfed with unfamiliar emotions as my capacity to feel returned, overtaking strong defense mechanisms ingrained over years of incarceration. I began to feel sorrow, the pain of prisoners lost, the loss of Kevin. Names, faces all came into focus, as did the deprivation of simple basic aspects of life I no longer knew. Most important, for me, the true meaning of Prison Justice Day became clear. It did not matter what others did or did not do. This was my day to grieve the way I wanted to, remembering those who died naturally or unnaturally while inside. The tears came, the rain increased; in the words of a dear friend, "God knows our suffering, and is crying with us."

I was appalled upon reaching the gravesite. It was littered with small identification plaques (about eight by ten inches) placed on the grass. These plaques had numbers on them identifying the persons beneath. As in life, so in death, the prisoner is denied even the most basic dignity. These plaques signify always that a person who dies inside will remain nothing more than a number on a small plaque on the ground. I became angry. Prison Justice Day now had spiritual meaning.

I was released to Ottawa the following year. As August 10 approached, I was contacted by Jocelyn, the wife of a prisoner serving a twenty-five year minimum life sentence. Together we organised a memorial service on Parliament Hill. People from all over the country were invited. A group from Montréal, people from Kingston, and as far away as Saskatchewan were there. Some of the men and staff from the local John Howard Society half-way house were there, too. And there was the mother of a prisoner from British Columbia who had died while inside.

Alice, this prisoner's mother, and I introduced ourselves. It was with great surprise, then total anguish when she said to me, "You were my son Kevin's only friend." As these words sunk in, it all came back to me; the lost look I saw in Kevin's eyes, his unspoken fear, the indignities, the inhumanity, the deprivation, the hatred.

I conducted the service on that day amid bursts of tears and sobbing. Somehow I managed to get through it although I do not know how. Throughout the next two days, tears filled my eyes, the anguish was that deep. Even as I write these words, tears come for I think of the hardships we all suffer on the inside, but equally important, the hardships and suffering we go through once released to the outside.

Alice and I talked after the service. We cried together and even managed a small bit of laughter. We both needed that service to lay Kevin to rest in our minds. But we laid to rest more than Kevin. Many of the ghosts have now disappeared. I left a lot of crap on Parliament Hill that day.

Shortly after August 10, 1989, I set down a goal for myself. A goal of continued freedom. Only by remaining in the community can I become a stronger individual and in some small way give meaning to the deaths that occur inside. Without doing this, I would most certainly be sucked into the hungry jowls of the justice system, digested and passed through it into a shallow grave like so many others.

I would end up in a gravesite
on some prison property
with a numbered plaque on my grave
viewing the walls of an archaic penal institution
that symbolizes a system
which literally thrives on pain.

Remembering Women in the Struggle
Mary McArdle

As women, we are often reminded that our contribution to the struggle has gone largely unnoticed and unrecorded. We were delighted therefore that the theme for Prisoner's Day 1995 was to be 'Women in the Struggle' and we were honoured to be able to make our own contribution to the events. I, along with Mary Ellen Campbell, had the privilege of attending to represent women POWs. The event attracted ex-prisoners from all parts of the country including Bronwyn McGahan from Tyrone, the most recently released woman POW from Maghaberry jail [Northern Ireland]. Also present for the occasion were Donna Maguire and Póilín Uí Chatháin, both of whom were recently released from jails in Germany.

The day began with a volleyball match between Armagh and Maghaberry, an enjoyable event for both the players and the spectators. The winning trophy, in memory of Rosaleen Russell, a tireless worker on behalf of women's rights who died earlier in the year, was presented to the Maghaberry women who were victorious on the day.

At lunchtime, Tar Anall, the new drop-in centre for ex-POWs and their families, was officially opened. Maura McCrory gave a short speech after which Pam Kane and Briege Norney unveiled the opening plaque. Maura outlined the importance of Tar Anall and invited everyone to avail of its services. Briege then spoke of the plight of prisoners in English jails and the hardships endured by their families.

After the formalities were dispensed with, those who had gathered for the opening mingled informally before moving next door into the Felons' Club which hosted a variety of prison-related exhibitions. Among these exhibitions was a photographic display representing the various roles women have played throughout the war. Cell-like structures had also been created to show different phases of prison struggle with detailed information provided on each particular chapter. The traditional array of POW handicrafts were also on display. One poignant aspect of the exhibition was the display which included personal letters belonging to Tom Williams as well as newspaper cuttings about his case and trial. Also included in this display was the shirt Tom wore on the day of his arrest.

A quilt made by Irish Women's groups, which was taken to the UN Women's Conference in Beijing, was also featured. The theme of this quilt was 'Women's Rights are Human Rights' and the woman POWs in

Maghaberry had contributed a panel to it. A massive poster expressing solidarity with the Basque prisoners seemed particularly appropriate with a large Basque delegation in attendance.

A video entitled 'What Did You Do in the War, Mammy?' which documented the experiences of republican women through several decades, was one of the highlights of the day. Full credit for this excellent production goes to the Falls Women's Centre for their hard work and persistence which, despite this being their first venture into the world of film making, produced this high-quality documentary. Narrated by Caral Ní Chulainn, the video was a clear testimony to the changing role of women in the republican struggle and had Eileen Brady, a long-time activist, lamenting the fact that she was not nineteen again.

After the showing of the video, several women shared a panel and spoke of their experiences of imprisonment, which included internment, the no-wash protest and hunger strikes in Armagh, the opening of Maghaberry jail, and the present-day conditions faced by women POWs. Pamela Kane talked of her experiences in Mountjoy and Limerick jails, outlining the hardships and isolation associated with being the only female IRA prisoner in the twenty-six counties. There then followed a question and answer session, chaired by Una Gillespie, that raised many pertinent questions in relation to women's struggle.

The evening function proved to be a moving event. A statement, paying tribute to the sacrifice of the women who had given their lives during the struggle, was read out on behalf of the women POWs in Maghaberry. It further acknowledged the roles that women have played over the years and called on this potential to be utilised in all future initiatives.

Presentations were then made to Louise McManus, Anne O'Sullivan, and Lily Fennell for their selfless work on behalf of the republican movement. Other presentations were made to ex-prisoners Bronwyn McGahan, Pamela Kane, Póilín Uí Chatháin, and Donna Maguire. Madge McConville and Greta Nolan, both of whom were arrested with Tom Williams, were presented with framed pictures in recognition of long years of dedication to the republican cause. Madge and Greta then unveiled a cross in memory of the dead volunteers and presented it to Liam Shannon who accepted it on behalf of the Felons' Club.

A colour party led by a lone piper then entered the hall, their flags lowered as a mark of respect, and a minute's silence was observed. The sombre mood that had descended upon the proceedings created a fitting atmosphere for the presentation ceremony for the families of our fallen women comrades. The family of each volunteer was presented with a plaque that contained a small photograph of their loved one. I was touched by the dignity and courage of the families whose grief, despite the passing of time, is still so apparent.

Finally the day was at an end. It had been a long day and after months of research, hard work, and effort it was, despite its sadder moments, a day that republican women could be proud of. What we, as POWs, had wanted most of all was to ensure that the role of women in our struggle was not forgotten. We especially wanted to honour our comrades who died for Irish freedom and to offer our support to their families. We sincerely hope that we achieved that.

Presentations were made to the families of the following comrades who have died:

Patrica Black
Margaret Mcardle
Maura Drumm
Rosemary Bleakley
Ann Parker
Annmarie Pettigrew
Mairead Farrell
Bridie Dolan
Dorothy Maguire
Maura Meehan
Eileen Mackin
Laura Crawford
Catherine Mc Gartland
Sheena Campbell
Ethel Lynch
Julie Dougan
Bridie Quinn
Pauline Kane
Vivienne Fitzsimmons

Birth of the Blanket Protest
Ned Flynn

Editor's Note: Ned Flynn, from Andersonstown in West Belfast, was nineteen years of age in 1976 when he was sentenced and became the second man to enter the historic blanket protest in the H blocks. As we commemorate the twentieth anniversary of the beginning of that campaign, he reflects on how the protest started.

Twenty years ago, Britain's three-pronged strategy to break the republican struggle was in full swing, i.e., normalization, Ulsterisation, and criminalisation. Normalisation involved the British Government portraying the conflict to the international community as one which was well under control, with a degree of normality now evident. Ulsterisation involved the six-county sectarian militias of the Royal Ulster Constabulary (RUC) and Ulster Defence Regiment (UDR) taking primary control of security, with the British army now playing a secondary back-up role. Criminalisation was a media-orientated policy, overseen by Northern Ireland Office (NI0) officials, that portrayed the republican struggle as acts of criminals, with terms such as 'mafia-type gangsters,' 'godfathers,' 'racketeers,' and 'drug barons' being circulated daily by the media. Furthermore, the struggle was represented as sectarian and this portrayal was fuelled by British military intelligence who organised Loyalist death squads and even recruited a Military Reaction Force (MRF) within the nationalist community, mercenaries who were ordered to carry out attacks on nationalists and attribute them to loyalists. To reinforce criminalisation, Britain declared that any republican prisoner captured after March 1, 1976, would be classified as a criminal rather than a POW, and as such, would be treated accordingly.

To enhance the success of their three-pronged strategy, the British Government set up a conveyor belt system to remove political opponents and community activists from the streets. It was a quasi-legal alternative to the use of internment without trial which was ended in December 1975 due to international and human rights pressure. The conveyor belt system began in Castlereagh RUC interrogation center where people perceived as a threat to the state were tortured to extract a false confession. This was later confirmed to Amnesty International by none other than the resident physician, Dr. Irwin. After a long period on remand, the victim was then brought before a Diplock, non-jury court where a single judge appointed by the

British Government would blatantly reject the medical evidence of torture and convict on the word of the RUC interrogator. The end result was the victim being dispatched to the H blocks of Long Kesh to serve out his or her sentence.

Like so many other young men and women who entered the jail system in 1976, I was incapable of articulating Britain's cleverly-designed strategy but, as time would tell, the contribution of the men in the H blocks and the women in Armagh jail was to prove crucial in turning Britain's three-pronged strategy on its head and reviving republican morale within the nationalist six counties. However, the cost in terms of sacrifice was high indeed. In the summer of 1976, Crumlin Road jail was overflowing due to the RUC's systematic round up of nationalists. The talk on everyone's lips, besides their own impending 'trial,' was what lay ahead of us when we ended up in the H blocks of Long Kesh. No republican POW incarcerated after the 1st of March had been sentenced yet so we didn't know how Britain was going to enforce their criminalisation policy. While the fear of the unknown was playing on everyone's mind, we were sure of one thing: we were republican POWs, and irrespective of the consequences which lay ahead, there was no way we were going to let the British Government demonise us or our struggle.

In October 1976, three weeks after Kieran Nugent, the first man sentenced, entered the H blocks, I was sentenced to three years imprisonment. I found myself in the unenviable position of travelling to the H blocks of Long Kesh in a 'meat wagon' (an armoured lorry) with five loyalist prisoners. While the loyalists were generally chit-chatting amongst themselves on the journey up, I was overburdened with the sense of being all alone, wrapped up in my own thoughts, wondering what the impending welcoming party held for me.

On entering A and B wing of H1, which housed ordinary criminals, I told the screws there was no way would I wear the prison uniform or conform to prison rules because I was a republican POW. At this they laughed and told me in a threatening manner that I would change my mind very shortly. From that moment onward, the screws tried every conceivable method the British Government could conjure up to try and dehumanise us into submitting to their criminalisation policy. They moved me to C and D wing H1 which was not in use. I was put into a bare cell, given a blanket to cover myself, and then the screws left without giving me any food or a mattress to lie on. I was in need of a friendly voice to give me some reassurance, so I got up to the door and called out to Kieran Nugent thinking he would be somewhere in these two wings; but, all I heard was my own echo resounding up and down the corridor. I was on my own.

Over the next number of days, the screws kept up the psychological pressure, informing me at every opportunity that I was on my own as Nugent had put the uniform on; but after a few weeks, I found out he was in a cell in A and B wing. As the days went by, I began to lose all track of time as well as weight because they were just giving me the bare minimum to keep me going. However, when they saw that this and the isolation was having no effect, they switched tactics.

I was taken to the punishment block within the camp where I was charged and sentenced to 14 days loss of remission, 14 days loss of privileges, and three days solitary confinement, which was a bit ironic since I had been in solitary confinement since I entered the blocks and would remain so for the rest of my sentence. The real reason for my move to the punishment block became apparent when a number of screws came into my cell and gave me a beating. All I could do was curl up into a ball and wait until it was over. Undoubtedly, this was one of the lowest points of my time in jail; I was on my own, isolated from my family, friends, and comrades, and the screws took great delight in informing me that much of the same and more was to come.

From what seemed like an eternity of complete isolation, but which in effect was only about three weeks, I was moved to A and B wing H1 where six of my comrades, sentenced a few days beforehand, joined Kieran Nugent and myself on what was now called the blanket protest. After my ordeal over the previous three weeks or so, I can only describe the joy of hearing a friendly voice as akin to somebody giving me a million dollars. Sadly the luxury of spending time with my comrades, even if the conversation was conducted between walls, was short-lived. Two days later I was on the move again.

The NIO was obviously desperate to fragment our unity from the inception of the blanket protest and they thought this was best done by singling out the younger members of the protest for specialised treatment in order that the blanket protest would crumble. Therefore myself, Kieran Nugent, and Paul McEnarney, all under 21, were moved to H2; me to D wing, Paul to C, and Kieran to B. Once again the administration were hoping that isolation from our comrades would sap our will to continue the blanket protest, and that us breaking would have a domino effect on the rest of our comrades.

Isolation was only one part of their strategy. Inhuman and degrading treatment as well as mental and physical torture were all methods designed to cause the collapse of the protest. Initially, what little food they gave us was brought to the cell by ordinary criminals, but after a week or so, they said if I was not fed, I had to leave the cell naked and go to get it. On the one side of the wing, there were ordinary criminals, on the other side, the cells were all empty except for the one I occupied, so in order to get my food, I had to go naked into a canteen full of men. The screws took great pleasure in making lewd remarks about certain parts of my anatomy and they encouraged the criminals to do likewise. At every available opportunity, they paraded us like cattle. For example, every fortnight they forced us to go out to the circle (the central area of the block) naked so that the doctor could examine us and declare us fit to be punished. Picture the scene: on a freezing December morning a naked blanket man forced to stand for thirty minutes in front of seventy criminals and numerous screws; he is blue with cold and shivering from head to foot, yet this so called member of the medical profession declares him fit for anything. The NIO would go to any lengths in order to try and degrade us into capitulating and accepting their criminal status. For example, they told us we would be deprived of going to Mass unless we went naked or wore the prison uniform and so it was, that rather than miss the sacraments, we went to Mass naked on Sunday.

As well as the humiliating and degrading treatment, we also had to contend with the physical abuse and the constant threat of it which was worse than the actual beatings. One screw in particular was given a free hand to do as he wished to the blanket men and no one was left unscathed. Any young lad coming onto the blanket was put through a gruesome ordeal. He was always brought up to H2 at 5:00 pm when all the screws were in the circle, and when he declared he was going on the blanket, many of the screws joined in on stripping him naked and beating him senseless.

The deprivation was all encompassing. We were locked up 24 hours a day, put into a bare cell at 8:30 each morning, and moved into a cell with a bed in it at 8:30 that night. We had no books, radios, tobacco, writing material, or anything of that nature; all of these things were confiscated when we went on the blanket. By Christmas 1976, I had been in the H blocks three months. I did not even know if the outside world knew I existed because I had not seen any of my family as the screws would not let us take visits unless we wore the prison uniform. Our only statutory entitlement was

Deconstructing "Criminalisation": The Politics of Collective Education in the H-Blocks

Jacqueline Dana and Seán McMonagle

For people involved in liberation struggles, it is not enough to commit oneself to the ideal of freedom; instead one must break from the structures put into place by the oppressor government and society. One of the crucial steps in gaining freedom is forming a system of self-education where the ideas of a revolutionary movement can be developed, tested through discussion and passed on to others within the movement. In the case of the Irish Republican movement, a good deal of this education takes place within the confines of prison, amongst political prisoners.

Brazilian educator Paulo Freire proposed that oppressed peoples wishing to be free must first learn not to perceive of themselves as ignorant outsiders with an inferior culture to that of the dominating class. According to Freire all people possess knowledge about their own freedom. This is where education comes to the forefront of the struggle. Friere (1989) argues in *Pedagogy of the Oppressed*,

> No pedagogy which is truly liberating can remain distant from the oppressed by treating them as unfortunates and by presenting for their emulation models from their oppressors. The oppressed must be their own example in the struggle for their redemption. (Friere, 1989:39)

One of the problems with some populist-type movements is that the leaders often belong to the upper class, members of the "educated" elite which invariably possess, in Freire's judgement, "a lack of confidence in the people's ability to think, to want, and to know" (Friere, 1989:46). In this way oppression never is addressed head on, and substantive changes never come about, for the leaders second-guess the people's needs (while rarely taking actions that would drastically alter the status quo).

The oppressed instead must come to realize their responsibility for their own liberation, and accept their ability to transform their own situation themselves. In the end revolutionary change can only come through dialogue, not from what Freire calls "libertarian propaganda." Education then must take on a new form — instead of indoctrination is also must take on the form of dialogue where everyone's experiences and knowledge are considered and explored. Students become not receptacles for knowledge but "critical co-investigators" working together with their "teacher" to learn new truths about their situation. As Freire puts it, within such a system "no one teaches, nor is anyone self-taught. Men teach each other, mediated by the world" (Friere, 1989:67–68).

Freire's concept of non-hierarchical, dialogue-based education can be applied to the system begun by prisoners within the prisons of Northern Ireland, particularly within the H-Blocks at Long Kesh. From a desire to share and enjoy their native Irish culture as well as from their need to learn more about the political struggle, incarcerated Irish Republicans developed an educational strategy to combat the pervasiveness of the English world view. Education, in fact, became a focal point in the battles against Britain that would be staged within prison walls.

When large numbers of Irish Nationalists and Republicans were arrested and interned beginning in 1971, the new prisoners made a determined effort to share whatever knowledge they possessed of their traditional Irish culture with the rest of the internees. In Long Kesh internment camp, alongside the IRA military drills, weapons classes and strategy discussions that were a priority at the time, the few POWs who knew Irish Gaelic or had a knowledge of history or other subjects became teachers, sharing their knowledge with the others within the freedom of the "cages" where there was little interference from guards or restriction of movement.

This process changed dramatically with the introduction of the new prison system, in place after 1976. Following the recommendations of Lord Diplock, officials built a new prison with traditional cells, and in tandem began a policy of "criminalisation." Henceforth, instead of internment without trial, and subsequent prisoner-of-war status and treatment, political prisoners were sent to Her Majesty's Prison Maze, known popularly as the H-Blocks. Here they were expected to wear a prisoner uniform and be restricted to individual cells, relinquishing all elements of their inherent political status.

The British government was not prepared for the level of resistance to criminalisation that would come with the new policy. Newly convicted Irish Republicans refused to wear a uniform and thereby accept the British attempt to depoliticize their motivations, and this meant in turn that they had no options other than to replace the detested uniform — their only clothing option — with blankets wrapped around themselves. Because they did not "conform" to prison rules, they were denied free association and many other "privileges" granted to conforming prisoners. Unfortunately, this meant the end to the formal prisoner taught classes in language, history and politics that had existed within the cages of the internment camp.

However, the "blanket protest" as it became known, along with the subsequent "dirty" and "no-wash" protests, did not bring an end to political education on the part of the prisoners. Because they were on protest, Republican prisoners could not sit together and have classes. Instead of admitting defeat, the prisoners discovered that they could still educate one another, but now by shouting to their neighbours through doors, out windows or along water pipes. In this way a slow process was established where all men in a wing could share information by repeating it along the line until everyone was included. As former Republican political prisoner Felim O'Hagan explained, such a process had a great "levelling" effect on the prisoners (O'Hagan and McKeown, 1991:7). Individual status amongst the prisoners was effectively negated by a lack of interaction, forcing them to acknowledge themselves as equals. Without the availability of books, classrooms or even anything but the crudest of writing materials, each man became equally responsible for contributing his own knowledge to the best of his ability. Those who had become fluent in Irish while in the internment camp, for example, now were able to bring their knowledge to the corridors of the H-Blocks.

After five years of prison protest and hunger strikes, in 1980 and 1981, the British government unofficially began to grant many of the Republican prisoners' demands, including 24-hour association in the wings and access to study materials. As a result, the prisoners now are able to organize themselves in a communal society, where everything is shared as equally as possible, including the general maintenance of the wings, food received in parcels, postage stamps, and the use of the television and other items. For these men, living as political prisoners means the 'community' always comes before personal gain.

Living in this way teaches the men how to interact on an equal level. Regardless of one's position outside, in the H-Blocks no one is considered more or less important than another, and each man is obligated to contribute to the best of his abilities. In turn, this system affected the formation of the prisoners' own educational system. The communal lifestyle encouraged the prisoners as a whole not to return to a hierarchical educational system where one person alone would be the teacher and authority. The prisoners instead arrange classes and debates in such a way that they incorporate everyone who wishes to participate, holding each person accountable for doing a fair amount of reading and then interpreting the ideas and leading discussions, and appointing only a facilitator to keep things on track. In this way they become actively involved in the pursuit of knowledge instead of simply being passive recipients.

In order to understand the prisoners' educational program, it is helpful to examine some of the classes that the prisoners commonly organize for themselves in the Republican wings of the H-Blocks. Each wing sponsors many different subjects pertinent to the interests of the prisoners, including historical analysis, political ideologies, jail history and Irish language. Each *rang*, as a class is called in Irish, usually is led by two men who ensure that all avenues and sides of any given topic are explored. These leaders facilitate the discussion by posing questions to the others and make sure that there is adequate debate on all subjects.

The first *rang* new prisoners participate in, and the only one required of those considering themselves political prisoners, is "Jail History." The class covers the history of Republican prisoners in Long Kesh, from the time of the blanket protest and hunger strikes to the present day. Those in the political wings make this class compulsory because it examines the importance of the struggle inside the H-Blocks, helping to define what being an Irish Republican POW is all about. In this class, men discuss the prisoners' successful struggle for *de facto* political status and better living conditions for all Republicans held in prison in Northern Ireland. From others who experienced the early days of the prison regime they learn how the prisoners in Long Kesh and elsewhere achieved the unofficial political status that they enjoy now through both physical resistance and determined protests.

As a result of the jail history classes Republican activists learn they can continue the struggle even while incarcerated. Whether on the outside a prisoner was an active IRA volunteer or simply a civilian who sold the political newspaper *An Phoblacht/The Republican News*, there is a role for him within the prison — he learns not to become complacent and accept his fate at the hands of the British government. All POWs discover that because of the Republican educational program no one is useless, and that being in prison does not mean that the British government has defeated them. Their work just takes on a different form and operates within a different context.

Other classes address the prisoners' political involvement from a theoretical viewpoint. A frequent class is the politics or ideology *rang*, which is commonly made up of about eight men who examine different ideologies such as capitalism, socialism, liberalism and fascism. The men read up on one of the ideologies each week and debate positive and negative aspects of the topic. In this way they have a better grasp on different methods of government and economic systems, making it easier to consider the ramifications of those which the Republican movement espouses. After a group completes a basic introductory *rang* in ideologies, some of the men may elect to go deeper into these issues, choosing to have a more intensive capitalism versus socialism *rang*, where they can debate the specific merits and flaws to each system.

Continuing from the days of internment are the abundant Irish language classes. In the early days of the H-Blocks, when men were on the blanket protest, future hunger striker Bobby Sands was one of the main people to encourage the use of Irish in the wings. Having become fluent himself while in the cages of the internment camp, he began teaching the others Irish "out the doors." This entailed shouting the lessons up and down the wing, and the "students," if lucky enough to have a bit of graphite and toilet paper, would write the words down. Others would write the lessons on the walls if possible or try to commit the lesson to memory. In this way Sands and other Irish speakers began the classes, with the focus on general phrases about day-to-day activities.

Quickly, the study of Irish became a crucial part of the POWs resistance to the prison regime. Since most prison officials did not understand Irish, the prisoners took advantage of this, and much of the Irish spoken conveyed information about the prison and the guards to other prisoners. When they realized the effectiveness and popularity of this system, Sands and others began teaching the language in earnest, helping the men build up a much larger vocabulary so they could engage in conversations. It was generally acknowledged among Republican prisoners that if they wanted to know what was happening then they would have no choice but to learn Irish.

With the end of the protests, prisoners set up a formal educational program for Irish. As it operates today, those with good Irish organize a number of courses for different levels of learners. Those with a moderate knowledge of Irish might teach a *bun rang*, or beginner's course, while those prisoners holding *gold fainni* and considered fluent take the advanced *rangs*. In the beginners' class the prisoners tackle easy vocabulary that allows them to express ordinary actions that take place on the wings. The higher level classes use textbooks, but these books are left up to the discretion of whoever facilitates the class. In all Irish classes, everyone is encouraged to test each other. The "teacher" is there to facilitate and guide the *rang*, but ultimately everyone is responsible to himself and for each other.

Another class, one known as "Historical Analysis," is perhaps the most important to the Republicans, for in many ways participating in this group helps solidify their own ideas on the struggle and helps form their dynamic ideology. Functioning as a discussion and debate circle more than a "class," Historical Analysis allows POWs to explore the history behind incidents in the period 1966–1986, such as the civil rights marches, the fall of Stormont, internment, the hunger strikes and Bloody Sunday. The class has a certain amount of pre-planned structure. A draft outline of contemporary Irish history was written down by one of the POWs, and it is this draft that the prisoners use as a starting point. In the draft, each chapter outlines an important event and asks questions for the class to tackle. For example, the first chapter considers the Northern Ireland government in the years 1966–69, with the problems created by the conflict between civil rights marches and Stormont, and poses the question, "Was the state reformable?"

A section of the Historical Analysis class would have about eight men participating, and each week two of the men would take turns covering one of the chapters in the outline and assigning reading to the others. The week's leaders draw up a number of points to discuss, as well as formulate questions to ask the others as a way to initiate discussion. The group then examines the topic from all sides, trying to determine what happened, why the event happened the way it did, and engaging in debate to decide if the Republican movement could have done anything differently and what lessons can be learned from the event. In this way British, Loyalist and IRA actions are all held up to equal scrutiny. Sometimes the group will agree with the ideas in the drafted history, but often they see new aspects of the event that had not been considered before. Furthermore, as an important dimension to this process, often at least one of the men in the wing may have been a participant or witness to the event discussed and can share his experiences with the others, bringing an emotional and human side to the otherwise academic discussions.

Besides the classes, on each wing there is the Sinn Féin Cumann, a gathering of some of the more politically active men on the wing. This group sponsors at least one discussion a month on a variety of current events and issues important to the men as a whole. Some recent topics include the recent IRA cease-fire, the Downing Street Declaration, issues of crime and punishment in the community, sectarianism, and the role of the Irish language and culture in the struggle. Overall, those involved in the Cumann work through issues affecting the Republican community as a whole, both inside and outside of prison, and it would be these men that members of Sinn Féin consult for a representative selection of the feelings and ideas of the prisoners. And once out of prison, many Cumann leaders become more actively involved in the political side of the movement, some even becoming Sinn Féin candidates in elections.

Seen together, these classes and debates open up a dialogue between the prisoners where all who choose to do so can take an active role in the education and political development of the wing. No one needs to sit and receive information handed down by experts removed from the scene of the struggle — instead, everyone becomes both teacher and student. And information and knowledge is not static and pre-determined, but instead is constantly updated and developed through the combination of everyone's experience and analysis.

As a result, the education that takes place in the H-Block empowers the prisoners to work for the end to their own oppression. Although many of them attend the prison administration's classes to A and O Level exams and work within the prison's Open University system to get university credits, the prisoners' political education, that which refines their knowledge of the struggle and their own place within it, occurs in the wings, unofficial but very much alive. As long as they continue to explore their own culture and history and debate the ramifications of events outside, the Republican prisoners resist the criminal label the British government tries to attach to them. Ultimately the "educational programme" in the H-Blocks helps Republican prisoners remain actively involved in the movement, and in some ways even contributes to the movement as a whole, for it is the men in the H-Blocks — the prisoners — who have the leisure time to read and debate topics fully. These men come to terms with what it means to be an Irish Republican activist in today's political climate, and they also come to a serious understanding about what the struggle has meant to the people of Northern Ireland for the last twenty-five years.

Sweet Grass in the Iron House
Danny Homer

A chronological history of Native spirituality is nothing more than an exercise in futility. Unlike Christianity which has well defined roots that can be traced, Native spirituality has been in existence from time immemorial, or so legends say. This spirituality exists today and will continue to flourish as time goes by. What is new is the emergence of Native spirituality in federal and provincial prisons.

Because prison officials have not seen or heard of Native spirituality before, they feel threatened and in many cases attempt to suppress its practice. This is not at all foreign to the Indians. Modern history has shown time and time again that the government of Canada has not completely accepted Native people. In fact, it was not until the 1950s that Natives have had the right to practice their religion freely in open society.

The white man knows little about Native religion because Indians cherish unto themselves the gifts that the Creator has given them. Many believe that their spiritual beliefs are just that ... theirs alone. For example:

> our traditional teachings are ours and can never be shared with other races and nationalities. This is what was given to us by Sonkaitison, our Creator, for the Onkwehonwe. (North American Indian Travelling College, 1984:iv)

But just because the beliefs are not widely known is no reason for repression. All it comes down to is the Indian people are attempting to regain a strong hold on part of their culture.

A systematic shattering of Indian identity has occurred in the past. But, as prophesied through legend and stories, when the situation looked the bleakest the Indian people would come together. There are numerous methods used to accomplish the splitting of a people and the most effective continue to be used today.

Many Natives, after being separated from their people, end up in prisons with little or no knowledge of their culture. Thus, some elders have brought the culture to the prisons in an attempt to reclaim their people. It is interesting to note that their efforts have ignited debates among Natives. Some have argued that these prisoners have left the people (i.e., the reserves, bands, etc.) by choice, so why give them anything? It is also argued that spirituality cannot flourish in prison because jails are representative of evil forces; the trueness of the circle cannot be acquired because the prison is a square iron house. However, spirituality has emerged in the prisons because Natives are Natives, whether or not they are in jail.

Those who favour the efforts of these elders argue that since Natives have been taken away from their people (by the Children's Aid Societies, for example) and have not had opportunities to learn about their culture and heritage, they must be taught the traditional ways. And even more it has been argued that true Indians care for their brothers and sisters, so who is anyone to deny to them the knowledge of the Creator?

Native spirituality is a life-long, total commitment to the will of our Creator. Spirituality is not something that can be turned on or off. It keeps the individual in touch with the Native community and in touch with the Native tradition. It serves as a means of survival in the foreign-environment of prisons; the prison experience is altered as a result of the commitment.

Indians have their own beliefs as to the origins of humanity, laws, and morals. The centre of Native beliefs revolves around honouring the Creator, his helpers (spirits) and that which was created. In its most simple form, nature is a beauty to behold. Natives have become one with nature; therefore, it is reasonable to assume that they know what they are doing when they use what nature has provided for their means of worship.

White people are not used to these worshipping rituals. Out of their ignorance and fear they have desecrated the sacred paraphernalia that is used in the ceremonies. Many prison officials (guards and administrative personnel alike) who do not know how to relate to these sacred objects show disrespect, contempt and ignorance about their use. This leads to one of the frustrations that Natives have to endure while incarcerated.

For example, sweetgrass, a grass that is used in the purification ceremony, is the most commonly known object used in prisons by Indians. Guards know it, have smelt the grass after it has been burnt, and yet in some prisons the sweetgrass is not allowed. Excuses have come up from nowhere to justify its ban. The most common one is that sweetgrass poses a fire hazard. Poor ventilation in the cells is another favorite excuse.

It is known from the beginning that hardships such as these will have to be endured. It is not without warning that the persecutions unfold before many Natives. Shock and bewilderment greet the Native once s/he leaves the reserve for the first time. The white society has become so 'convenient' that almost anything can be bought. The pace of life is accelerated in the eyes of the first-time viewer. Rules of society, which may be taken for granted by many, are confusing and foreign to many Natives. An encroachment and breach of these rules will land many Natives in a yet stranger society, prison.

Although a report of the Standing Committee on Justice noted that '[s]ince the early-1980s, the rate of growth in the Native proportion of inmates in federal institutions has exceeded the rate of growth of the inmate population as-a-whole'(Government of Canada, 1988:211), two of the most avoided and unanswered questions are: why are so many Natives in jails and prisons, and why are the numbers increasing at this rate.

But even while s/he endures such ridicule, the spiritually-aware Native person has supports to rely upon. The Creator has provided leaning posts to make the spiritual path a little easier to walk. Because the prison climate is such that its internal functions divide along cultural lines, Native brotherhoods and sisterhoods have formed, and these groups help to lessen the blow of the prison experience.

In Canadian prisons, social functions include brotherhoods and sisterhoods, although not all prisons recognize these groups as valid and permit them to exist. When they are permitted, they exist only as a means of socialization, not the progressive and innovative class that can be achieved through good leadership. Prison officials are content to sit back and have them function as a whitewash in the bureaucratic system. However, for the offender the groups allow an 'easing' of the frustration of doing time.

For the most part these groups create unity among their members. Personal burdens and responsibilities become shared experience. This unity allows the newly incarcerated Native a sense of belonging and identity. How far one gets into the spiritual aspects of the brotherhoods and sisterhoods depends on one's own judgment. Counsellors and elders are available for those needing assistance.

Brotherhoods and sisterhoods also have their drawbacks and failures. In general, the groups have what can be considered reliable volunteers; however, the occasional member has succumbed to the pressures of the prison administration and left once honorable intentions in the dust. As in other segments of society, deceitfulness and selfishness exists everywhere. A few 'stings' and the groups become wary of whom they accept as counsellors. In the majority of cases, the prisoners are able to weed out those that do not belong, and the prisoners can rely on the brotherhood or sisterhood members for spiritual and emotional development. These groups have genuine interests in honour and its meaning, and shine as examples of the planting of the seeds of truth.

The struggle to have what may appear to be considerable spiritual support has not been an easy one. Resistance by the authorities has been relentless. It has been partially penetrated by the persistence and diligence of Native spokespersons, elders and ex-offenders. Were it not for individuals like these, the foundation of spiritual awareness would be dealt a severe blow.

As a person grows spiritually, one's perspective of the world takes on a different meaning. The individual comes to understand what is happening around her/him and is able to adapt to and change the environment. S/he is also able to change the environment by her/his experience which in turn is able to change the prison experience. S/he can deal with the persecution of the authorities with an understanding of why the oppression is taking place. S/he knows strength from what is set before her/him and at times can feel the strength which was also experienced by the forefathers. The individual thus grows in maturity and is able to take on responsibilities customary for any mature person. The prison experience then becomes the fate of the prisoner herself/himself; for just as responsibility is accepted for spiritual growth, so will the opportunity be gained to choose one's own path.

REFERENCES

Government of Canada (1988) *Taking Responsibility: Report of the Standing Committee on Justice*. Ottawa: Supply and Services.
North American Indian Travelling College (1984) *Traditional Teaching*. Cornwall Island.

PART VI

TALKING BACK: COUNTER-INSCRIBING THE PRISON INDUSTRIAL COMPLEX

"Victims' Rights" As a Stalkinghorse for State Repression
Paul Wright

How the ruling class defines and punishes "crime" goes a long way towards demonstrating whose class interests are being served by the criminal justice system. The criminal justice system in the United States is used as a tool of social control to ensure that dangerous classes of people, primarily the poor, are kept disorganized, disoriented and otherwise incapable of mounting any serious, organized challenge to the political and economic status quo (D. Burton-Rose, D. Pens and P. Wright, 1998).

A key component of this strategy is to first define crime so that the poor are overly included and the wealthy and powerful are largely excluded and weeded out of the arrest, prosecution, conviction and imprisonment cycle. For an excellent discussion of this process, see J. Reiman (1978), *The Rich Get Richer, The Poor Get Prison*.

The flip, and equally important side of this process lies in defining who is a victim and who is not. At different levels some victims are defined as "worthy", others are not. Recent years have seen increased activity by victims' rights groups as well as legislatures who loudly claim concern for the victims of crime. While more questions than answers exist on this complex issue, to date, "victims' rights" has been used primarily to expand state power and repression in a manner that police and prosecutors would otherwise have been unable to do directly (Elias, 1993).

The first step lies in defining who "the victim" is. An illustrative example are the steps being taken to add a victims' rights amendment to the U.S. constitution. This amendment would require that prosecutors notify victims of any court hearings involving the defendant, give victims an opportunity to speak at sentencings, be consulted about plea agreements, et cetera. This amendment is due to be voted on by the U.S. Senate in the near future. A key change made after the bill was introduced was to define the term "victim" to include only the victims of violent crime. The victims of economic and property crime are excluded from coverage by this amendment. Since more people are victimized by economic and property crime than violent crime, apparently that victim majority is not worthy of protection.[1]

The thousands of people bilked out of their life savings by the likes of fraudulent scamsters Charles Keating and Jim Bakker are among those not considered worthy of protection as victims. Just as criminal activity by corporations and the wealthy is effectively decriminalized through lax enforcement of the laws or diversion into the civil justice system, so too are the victims of predation by corporations and the wealthy "devictimized". Workers killed in accidents that result from a company's cost cutting measures to maximize profit are not victims. Consumers killed by dangerous products knowingly marketed by corporations to make more money are also not victims.

A miner killed because his employer cut costs on safety measures is not a victim. His widow who loses her life savings due to fraud by bank owners is not a victim, even having her car stolen by local thieves does not make her a victim. But, if she is robbed at gunpoint of five dollars, she is now a victim worthy of constitutional protection.

GOOD VICTIMS AND BAD VICTIMS

Various studies have shown that a majority of incarcerated sex offenders were themselves sexually abused when they were children. At what point do the sexually abused cease being victims and become criminals? When they are arrested?

Getting beyond the defining of who is an official victim and who is not, let's examine the victims of violent crimes against the person (murder, rape, robbery and assault with bodily injury). Here the key issue defining a person as a victim is not merely a matter of economic loss but the key issues of the identities of the victim and the victimizer. Or, not all victims are equal.

A point raised by some prosecutors opposed to the constitutional victims' rights amendment, which has been largely ignored by the media, is that a substantial number of violent crime victims are themselves criminals with their injuries being the result of dispute settling among members of the lower class criminal element.

Sammy Gravano was given immunity for the murder of 19 of his fellow mafia compatriots, in exchange for his testimony against John Gotti. Obviously police and prosecutors and a judge decided that Gravano's 19 murdered mafia victims were not worthy of the definition. Under a victims' rights amendment would the families of Gravano's victims be allowed to speak out against his five year plea bargain sentence? When one drug dealer shoots another in a dispute over money or turf does the slower shot now become a victim?[2]

Every day across the U.S. police and prison guards kill, beat and brutalize the citizenry. Prisoners are also assaulted, sexually and otherwise, and subjected to bodily injury by their fellow prisoners and prison staff. However, the political establishment is not calling on rights for these victims. Abner Louima, a Haitian immigrant in New York City who was sodomized with a police truncheon in a police station bathroom by New York's Finest, is not referred to as a "crime victim". We never heard the term "crime victim Rodney King" because even when police are convicted of criminal acts, to call the brutalized people "victims" necessarily implies the police perpetrators are criminals. And we cannot have that.[3]

The political problem for the advocates of "victims' rights" becomes even greater when prisoners suffer injury. The political discourse that has been created around "victim rights" steadfastly implies what it cannot openly say: "worthy" victims are nice, middle and upper class people, usually white, who are raped, robbed or killed by poor, violent strangers, especially Black or Latino strangers. If the police, media and politicians have made the universal face of crime that of a young black or Latino man, they have also strived mightily to make the face of the universal victim that of a middle or upper class white woman or child. Brutalized prisoners do not advance this political agenda. Hence, there is no concern whatsoever for the prisoners or prison staff. Not surprisingly, no one speaks of "victims' rights" for the prisoners subjected to violent crimes against their person.[4]

Then we reach the forgotten victim: people wrongfully convicted and imprisoned or executed. Whatever one says or thinks should be done with people convicted of a crime, however crime is defined, what about the innocent? Some studies estimate that 1–2% of criminal convictions each year are wrongfully obtained, not in a legal sense, but as a matter of fact: the accused did not commit the crime for which they were convicted (Wisely, 1994). Recent cases in Philadelphia where hundreds of prisoners were released after successfully showing they had been set up and convicted on false drug charges by corrupt police are but one example.[5] Whatever the actual numbers, as a matter of statistical probability, of 1.8 million people imprisoned in U.S. prisons and jails at least some are factually innocent. Few defenders of the criminal justice system claim it is infallible. '

The U.S. Supreme court has held that it does not violate the U.S. constitution to execute the innocent, so long as the condemned received a "fair trial". Justice Blackmun commented that executing the innocent "bordered" on simple murder.[6] If innocent people are convicted, imprisoned or executed for crimes they did not commit are they too not victims? Victims of a system no less, for unlike individual crimes committed by people acting alone, imprisoning and executing the innocent requires collusion by the police, prosecutors, judiciary, and sometimes juries and the media, to accomplish its end result. To call the imprisoned and executed innocents "victims" would call into question whether or not the entire criminal justice system is a victimizer.

A large part of the problem with defining who is and who is not a "victim" lies with the degree of impunity the perpetrators receive. Not surprisingly, brutalized prisoners and citizens and the wrongly convicted who suffer at the hands of police, guards, prosecutors and judges are not considered worthy of the title "victim" because the victimizing institutions of social control, prisons, police, judiciary and prosecutors, are rarely if ever held accountable for their misdeeds. People cannot become a "victim", not a worthy victim anyways, unless the social and political decision is first made by the ruling class to have a "criminal". Thus the same reasoning applies to why people who suffer economic and physical harm due to the predation of the wealthy and corporations are also not considered worthy victims.

THE POLITICS OF VICTIMS' RIGHTS

The political use of the victims' rights movement is seen by the rise of this movement as part of the overall trend towards increased state repression that began in 1968 but which accelerated markedly with the Reagan presidency. Virtually all the well funded victims' rights groups receive substantial portions of their funding directly from law enforcement agencies or groups linked to such agencies. The result, intended or not, is that these groups tend to parrot the party line of more police, more prisons, more punishment, more draconian laws. The Doris Tate Victims Bureau in California receives 85% of its funding from the California Correctional Peace Officers Association, the union which represents prison guards.[7] The union also provides the Bureau with free office space in its Sacramento headquarters. Not surprisingly, the Bureau likes what the union likes, especially things like "3 Strikes" laws which will help ensure full employment for prison guards.[8]

The net result is that those with the biggest vested interest in maintaining and expanding the prison industrial complex, police, prosecutors and politicians, eagerly use "victims' rights" groups as their stalking horses to expand regressive state police power in a manner that would seem crassly self interested if they did so directly.

It is important to note however, that not all victims' rights groups fall into this category. Murder Victim Families for Reconciliation (MVFR) and the restorative justice movement are the most notable examples of victims' rights groups that are not political pawns for those who seek to increase state repression. But, this also proves the point. Who thinks of MVFR or restorative justice when discussing victims' rights? They are neither well funded nor well publicized. Because their goal of actually helping victims of property and violent crime deal with their loss does not advance a broader political agenda for the dominant class they are largely ignored.

The current criminal justice system ill serves the victims of crime, all crime, not just that which the ruling class frowns upon, and it ill serves the criminal defendant. Most people who suffer the loss of property would prefer compensation to the thief's incarceration. Of course, those robbed by the rich usually get neither compensation nor imprisonment as satisfaction.

For the victims of personal violent crime committed by poor individuals the current system offers only punishment. (Which any discussion with the majority of victims' rights advocates quickly leads to the conclusion that no amount of punishment is ever enough). Punishment rarely gives the victim the closure or the perpetrator any type of empathy, understanding or rehabilitation. But as long as the purpose of the criminal justice system remains that of the tool of social control over the poor this is unlikely to change. Likewise, this is exactly what makes it unlikely that restorative justice will make inroads into the criminal justice system. Even less likely is that any organized voice will call for the inclusion of *all* victims of violence and theft, even if the perpetrators are agents of the state, the wealthy and corporations; even if the victims of these crimes are poor, imprisoned or socially disadvantaged.

For the foreseeable future victims will continue to be defined as the occasional white, middle and upper class person who is killed, raped, robbed or assaulted by a stranger who carries out this act in person. Unless critics of the criminal justice system begin to question and expose the current role of the "victims' rights" agenda its veneer of legitimacy and influence will go unchecked.

NOTES

1. *The Nation* and the *New York Times* have reported extensively on this amendment since it was put forth.
2. The *New York Times* and *Time Magazine* covered Gravano's deal and his testimony against John Gotti.
3. For an analysis of the Abner Louima case, see the *New York Times* coverage and *Human Rights Watch* (1998).
4. Every issue of *Prison Legal News* contains verified accounts of violent crimes against prisoners.
5. For details of this case, see coverage in the *New York Times*.
6. See *Herrera* v. *Collins*, 113, s.c.t. 853 (1993).
7. The *Sacramento Bee* and *Los Angeles Times* have reported upon this connection.
8. See also, Wright, 1995.

REFERENCES

Burton-Rose, D. (ed) with Pens. D. and Wright, P. (1998). *The Celling of America: An Inside Look at the U.S. Prison Industry. A Prison Legal News* book. Monroe, Maine: Common Courage Press.

Elias, R. (1993). *Victims Still: The Political Manipulation of Crime Victims*. Newbury Park: Sage.

Human Rights Watch. (July 1998). "Shielded from Justice: Police Brutality".

New York Times. Various, 1994–1998.

Reiman, J. (1978). *The Rich Get Richer and the Poor Get Prison: Ideology, Class, and Criminal Justice*. New York: Macmillan Publishing Company.

Wisely, W. (Oct. 1994). "The Forgotten Crime Victims", in *Prison Legal News*. Seattle: *Prison Legal News*.

Wright, P. (1995). "Three Strikes Racks 'em Up" in *Journal of Prisoners on Prisons*, Vol. 6, No. 2.

Victims' Rights: The Fallacy of the Zero-Sum Solution

Charles Huckelbury, Jr.

A great empire and little minds go ill together.

Edmund Burke

The State of Florida executed Pedro Medina in March 1997. The execution itself hardly marked a watershed; neither did the flames that erupted from Medina's head as the voltage surged through his body. The same thing happened in 1991 during Jessie Tafero's execution, and the responses to the unanticipated horror were identical. Again calls came from various public and private organizations to abolish if not capital punishment per se, then surely the electric chair itself as an antiquated method of both psychological and physical torture. At the other end of the philosophical spectrum were those who insisted on the chair's efficacy and even heralded its use as an extra measure of deterrence to would-be killers planning forays into the Sunshine State. One legislator, commenting on whether lethal injection should supplant electrocution, objected because lethal injection was too easy: it was like going to sleep.

The most startling result of Medina's execution, however, was not the accompanying argument concerning the method of putting people to death. The public's mandate seems sufficiently clear to permit the states to choose whatever vehicle suits their particular populations' tastes in death machinery. Instead, another, older argument raised its head: the question of the rights of the condemned versus those of their victims, and by extension, the perceived discordant rights of predator, prey, and society in general.

Shortly after Medina's execution, *Court TV* broadcast an installment of its popular "Cochran and Grace" show, featuring Johnnie Cochran and Nancy Grace. Cochran, of course, represented O.J. Simpson and served as the program's liberal commentator. Nancy Grace was a former prosecutor from Georgia and Cochran's conservative foil. On this particular program, Grace echoed Florida's attorney general, Bob Butterworth, by advancing the argument that irrespective of the nature of Medina's death, including whether he suffered before dying, right-thinking men and women would be better advised to put their concern for Medina's victim's rights before his.

That is, quite simply, impossible because, as I will argue, the rights of both criminals and their victims (including the families of the primary victim)

435

are identical and cannot be differentiated, either philosophically or existentially, as long as the country is governed by the Constitution.

I do not quarrel with the jury's verdict in Medina's case. I accept his guilt for statistical reasons alone: there are far more guilty than innocent people in prison. Neither will I argue Medina's mental competency at the time of his execution. I wish, rather, to address a more fundamental problem with attempting to establish a tripartite separation of rights, the same rights that are rooted firmly in the political and philosophical underpinnings of the Republic. This tactic always produces a zero-sum solution with perpetual losers.

Grace and the majority of conservative commentators insist on one group of rights for criminals (here defined as anyone convicted or even suspected of committing a crime), one for victims of crimes, and yet a third for the majority (shrinking as I write) who have had no contact with the criminal-justice system on either side. Grace et. al. complain that the criminal enjoys a distinct set of rights that not only infringes those of her/his victim and the public in general but is even more sacrosanct. Thus, there is a need to redress this grossly unfair (and impolitic) imbalance with a new declaration of rights for America's version of the *sans culottes*. What neither Ms. Grace nor anyone else can find, however, is any distinct set of rights for criminals anywhere outside the Eighth Amendment to the Constitution, which prohibits cruel and unusual punishments. These "rights" are a fabrication, the club used to beat the socially undesirable elements of society once they come under the control of the criminal-justice monolith.

Under the law, the technical definition of a criminal (notwithstanding Grace's inclusion of anyone arrested) is someone who has been *convicted* of a crime. No matter how high the mountain of evidence, how heinous the offense, how obvious the guilt, until a defendant is convicted by a jury or pleads to the charges, he or she enjoys the same protection that the law and the Constitution extend to every citizen of this country. We can hate Timothy McVeigh before his conviction if we believe him guilty of the carnage in Oklahoma City, but he did not stop being a citizen of the United States, with all the rights and privileges that status confers, until the jury rendered its verdict.

In the Declaration of Independence, Thomas Jefferson asserted that "all men are created equal [and] endowed by their Creator with certain unalienable rights, that among these are life, liberty, and the pursuit of happiness". Mr.

Jefferson naturally understood "men" to mean white males, but his point is that citizens of the United States all possess civil rights that originate from their Creator. Leaving aside the religious implications and Jefferson's racism and sexism, the greatest single mind in the country articulated a philosophy under which a government was instituted to secure those basic rights of its citizens. So fundamental were those rights that Jefferson acknowledged the duty of the citizens to overthrow any government that failed to protect them.

The Constitution became the vehicle by which those rights were secured, specifically in the Bill of Rights, something of a radical document that requires closer examination for the purpose of this essay. So subversive are these first 10 amendments that Ed Meese, a former Attorney General of the United States publicly labeled the American Civil Liberties Union a "criminals' lobby" for the organization's unqualified support of the universal application of the Bill of Rights. What provokes this kind of response and how does it bear on the current separation of rights?

Only four of the amendments arouse the ire of the proponents of victims' rights *vis-à-vis* those of criminals, with the Fourth being the perennial whipping boy. This amendment deals with search warrants and probable cause. The Supreme Court has steadily eroded the peoples' dignity to the point where the "right of the people to be secure in their persons, houses, papers, and effects" is problematic, all because of the perceived miscarriage of justice caused by the so-called exclusionary rule that prohibits the admission at trial of illegally obtained evidence. But the Fourth Amendment is designed to protect all citizens, not just those accused of crimes, against over-zealous and sometimes criminal-minded police.

The Fifth and Sixth Amendments articulate injunctions against double jeopardy and self-incrimination and mandate due process of law, a speedy trial, and assistance of counsel. Here is where the much maligned *Miranda* decision first took form. Although these two amendments pertain to criminal and civil proceedings, it hardly seems unreasonable to prevent unrestricted trials, unguided by rules of law, coerced confessions, and denial of counsel to laymen ignorant of the law and their own rights. At the risk of becoming laborious, I repeat: these rights apply to everyone, guilty or innocent. If you are asleep in your home, the police cannot enter your house, coerce a confession, and hold you incommunicado while the prosecutor prepares a case against you. At least, not yet. These are not "criminal" rights but basic rights that protect each citizen.

The Eighth Amendment, as previously noted, prohibits cruel and unusual punishments, but it — or at least its interpretation — has been vilified by politicians as infringing on a state's rights to inflict appropriate punishment on its prisoners. Perhaps some obscurantists would return us to the rack and wheel, but this amendment is necessary for a civilized society to govern the treatment of those it convicts and sentences to either imprisonment or death. If there is a criminals' right, this is it, but few would argue that the state should officially sanction cruelty at any level.

As with any section of the Constitution, these provisions are subject to interpretation by the Supreme Court, but the protections remain logical extensions of the political thought that founded the Republic and are as viable today as they were in 1789. The public would no more consider rescinding any of these civil rights than they would revoking either the abolition of slavery or the extension of the franchise to women and blacks. All are fundamental civil rights, not criminals' rights.

Why, then, the insistence that the two are distinguishable? H.L. Mencken once observed: "The trouble about fighting for human freedom is that you have to spend so much of your life defending sons of bitches; for oppressive laws are always aimed at them originally" (Quoted in Stubbs and Barnet, 1989). That describes the basis of the argument about rights today. Nancy Grace's gratuitous advice to spend more time focusing on the victims' rights than on those of the criminal's ignores Mencken's cogent analysis; namely that the rights are identical. It is the inclusion of a criminalized element beneath the umbrella of civil rights that appears to scandalize many citizens and their representatives, who think that such an inclusion is tantamount to a preferential treatment of those who ignore the laws the rest of society follows. Or, as Ed Koch, the former mayor of New York City, observed in an article for *The New Republic*, "When we protect guilty lives, we give up innocent lives in exchange" (Koch, 1985).

This is not to say that specific conflicts do not arise, especially where economic inequities dictate tough choices. Certainly a society should direct its resources to helping victims of crime, including compensation and restitution where possible from the guilty party. If a conflict exists between extending aid to a victim or his/her predator, then of course priority should be given to the victim's needs, even if that means fewer amenities for the convicted felon. But that is a long way from an endorsement of the proposition that the rights of both are any different or that one's rights should supersede the other's, at least not until the Fourteenth Amendment guaranteeing equal protection under the law is repealed.

Victims of crimes do have rights, just as any other citizen of the country. They have not been abridged by any special treatment of the men and women who harmed them. All that is necessary is for them to exercise those rights, whether in a courtroom or other public forum. Indeed, they must avail themselves of the opportunity, if for no other reason than to dispel the myth that criminals' rights have miraculously contravened their own. Unfortunately, victims and society in general tend to see the extension of any civil right to those arrested, incarcerated, or merely suspected of committing a crime as a miscarriage of justice and an affront to decent people everywhere. This ignorance of the law and avenues for redress creates a climate of fear and loathing that amplifies a specious class division, the result of which is an iatrogenic disaster.

Consider what happens when civil rights are redefined and relegated to criminals' rights.

Surveys have consistently shown that when asked if they would voluntarily submit to a search of their persons while walking down the street, most people respond affirmatively, explaining that they have nothing to hide and therefore see no inherent objection to such a search. These same individuals would consent to wiretaps on their phones and warrantless searches of their homes, all because they are not breaking the law and have nothing to hide. After all, it's only the bad guys who would object to a search. These well-intentioned citizens ignore the purposes behind the formal articulation of those rights, willing, as Dr. Franklin put it, to surrender a little liberty for a little security, a proposition that usually gains neither.

And it gets worse. Recently, the Supreme Court ruled that during a routine traffic stop, police can force everyone in the vehicle to get out. This is deemed a reasonable intrusion to protect the lives of the police making the stop. No matter what the weather or how infirm a passenger might be, forget probable cause, driver and passengers must leave the vehicle when ordered or face arrest.

Every such tactic contradicts both the spirit and the meaning of the Fourth Amendment. Yet, they are acceptable to the majority, the same majority who think that only criminals get searched or have their phones tapped, because of an erroneous distinction between civil and criminal rights. It is impossible, however, to attack one without attacking the other because both arise from the same safeguards written into the Constitution.

This insistence on two (and often three) sets of rights and the consequent reaction against the concern for the criminalized and disenfranchised is hardly new. In his *Discourses* (1950), Niccolo Machiavelli described the phenomenon. "[F]or seeing a man injure his benefactor arouses at once two sentiments in every heart, hatred against the ingrate and love for the benefactor". Citizens naturally see the state as their benefactor and equate themselves as part of it. At the very least, they commiserate with any victim of crime, because, as the same Machiavelli states in *The Prince* (1950a), "lawless acts injure the whole community". Since the rights of a victim are always grafted onto the rights of society at large, the citizen "feels that he himself in turn might be subject to a like wrong and to prevent similar evils, sets to work to make laws".

And well she/he might, but the laws, to be effective and fair, must apply to everyone. Anger at antisocial behaviour is both natural and acceptable but not at the expense of the laws that bind a people together.

It is precisely this emotional response that is most pernicious and divisive. John Locke thought that men's emotions must be restrained by the intellect. Indeed, it is the capacity to reason and control instinctive responses to prevent a greater harm that sets man apart from the beasts. The current insistence on condoning, or at least acquiescing to brutal executions because the public should pay more attention to victims' rights is a graphic example of what Locke feared. It is not whether Timothy McVeigh should be executed but rather at what costs to the national psyche and in terms of damage to civil rights?

All victims of crime have been denied their fundamental human rights by whatever predator attacked them, but society must do better than responding emotionally and creating a class of victims' rights that by its very nature subjugates other human and civil rights. We do not have the luxury of picking which laws we want to obey, at least not without penalty. Nor can we opt for certain constitutional protections for ourselves while excluding others, a tactic both illegal and immoral. It is as easy to point to interpretations embodied in, say, *Miranda* and criticize them as it was to argue against *Brown* v. *Board of Education* that ended segregation in the public schools. As unpopular as both decisions were, they each set forth civil rights that are the province of all citizens of the Republic, those arrested and those free, those in school and those out. The rights enumerated by the Constitution remain in force for every citizen, no matter what scurrilous arguments attempt to compromise or subvert them.

In 1782, Hector St. Jean de Créve-Cour published his *Letters from an American Farmer*. In that volume, he described what it meant to be an American. "We have no princes, for whom we toil, starve and bleed: we are the most perfect society now existing in the world. Here man is free as he ought to be; nor is this pleasing quality so transitory as others are" (Quoted in Lunsford, 1994). This idyllic description sounds terribly trite today, but the foundations upon which Créve-Cour's analysis rested remain as valid as they were over 200 years ago because, precisely because, the same protections this French émigré enjoyed are the same ones guarding every citizen of this country. They are not "technicalities" that free guilty felons; neither can they be subdivided into distinct classes. They are constitutional rights that must be extended in the face of inept investigations and even apparent guilt, because if those rights became preferentially enforced, then no one's rights are secure.

Should victims be compensated for their losses where possible? By all means, including fines and assessments against the perpetrators of the crimes. Should they be allowed to enter testimony at penalty phases regarding their loss and anguish? Should they be permitted to witness the execution of the individual responsible for killing their loved ones? Again, I would argue in favour of such measures, but this does not require a finding of a new set of rights. By applying existing law, or by availing themselves of possible remedies, victims can sue felons for compensation and damages, and virtually every jurisdiction permits victim-impact statements. These are fundamental civil rights, not victims' or criminals' rights.

In the last years of the 20th century, it should never have been necessary to codify separate guarantees for the protection of the rights of women, gays, and ethnic minorities. Yet it is. Victims of crimes, however, have not experienced systematic discrimination except at the hands of the most insensitive public officials. As difficult as their lives have been made by criminal activity, they have never abrogated their rights or had them denied as a matter of law. To rectify any slight, all that is necessary is to be aware of those rights and exercise them.

Oklahomans, for example, obviously feel that the verdict in Terry Nichols' trial was unfair, at least in the penalty phase. The attorney general has therefore vowed to bring Nichols back to Oklahoma, try him for the other homicides, and sentence him to death. Timothy McVeigh will likely precede him. Citizens have no right to enhance Nichols' punishment, but current law does permit them to try him separately for state and federal crimes arising out of the same incident. This is a perfectly lawful exercise of their rights that concomitantly protects the rights of the accused and is vastly superior to the unseemly lynch-mob mentality that initially heaped scorn on the same jury system that had convicted McVeigh.

No equitable way exists to create a system that protects the rights of one class and dispenses of them at will for another. The tendentious claims of politicians and advocates with personal axes to grind ignore the underlying need for nonbiased application of the laws, one that ensures equality for everyone. As Thomas Jefferson described to Colonel Carrington in 1788, universal rights are "so much the interest of all to have, that I conceive [they] must be yielded" (Koch and Peden, 1993).

The specious separation of rights into criminal, victim, and civil disparages Jefferson's and Madison's original intent to protect every citizen and plays to the natural sentiment described by Machiavelli. It subverts the Constitution by creating class divisions within society and encouraging discrimination for personal agendas. Moreover, it reduces the Republic to a three-legged stool, each leg being a separate set of rights. When one leg becomes shorter than its fellows, the stool tilts and ultimately topples over. Legs equal in length and equidistant from each other provide the strongest support. This is the underlying strength of the Republic.

There is one law that applies to all, and until something else comes along, commentators and politicians would better serve the people by following that law instead of playing to the fears, desperation, and tragedy endured by the victims of crime. Victims, like society itself, deserve the right to see justice done, to be safe from harm, and to reach some sort of closure. Finally, is that not what punishment, whether restitution, incarceration, or death, is all about?

REFERENCES

Koch, A. and Penden, W. (eds.) (1993). *The Life and Selected Writings of Thomas Jefferson*. New York: The Modern Library.

Koch, Edward (1985). "Death and Justice: How Capital Punishment Affirms Life". *The New Republic*, April 15.

Lunsford, A. (ed.) (1984). *The Presence of Others*. New York: St. Martin's Press.

Machiavelli, N. (1950). *Discourses*. Ricci, L. (trans.). New York: McGraw Hill.

———. (1950a). *The Prince*. Ricci, L. (trans.). New York: McGraw Hill.

Stubbs, M. and Barnet, S. (eds.) (1989). *Little, Brown Reader*. Boston: Scott Foresman Co.

Victimization
Dan Cahill

s a member of the underclass, having spent more than 30 years in juvenile institutions, adult prisons and impoverished neighbourhoods, I have been both victim and victimizer. I have been officially classified by the criminal (in)justice system as a career criminal. Over the years I have given a great deal of thought to the subject of victimization.

Years ago, I reflected on my criminal behaviour and through this self-analysis, I recognized that I am guilty of harming society. Although I never physically harmed anyone directly, I had to acknowledge that through my thievery and drug dealing I caused much suffering and financial loss in the community. The degree of guilt and shame experienced through this admission was tremendous and I desperately needed to make amends and pay restitution for the harm I caused. I quickly learnt that the criminal justice system is not designed to facilitate restorative justice. There would be no amends made and no restitution paid.

In the eyes of society, I am condemned forever to the underclass, to sub-citizenship. I will carry the stigma of a convicted career criminal for the rest of my life — never to be accepted by society as a person worthy of any meaningful degree of respect or dignity. The weight of shame and guilt is too great a burden to carry with me forever. Slowly, the depth and nature of my punishment became clear to me and I realized that certain elements of my punishment and stigmatization will follow me back into society and remain in place as long as I live. There will be no forgiveness.

I have been victimized by burglaries, robberies and assaults myself. I never felt anywhere near as traumatized as the victims seen on TV I may be callous in this regard but, I wonder if some crime victims do not dramatize their victimization?

When I was victimized, I wanted revenge, but, I had no desire to see the offender incarcerated. I knew first hand that incarceration is out of proportion and would exceed the crime. There is no justice in that. When my apartment was broken into, I wanted the broken door fixed and my property replaced. Sending the person to prison for 10 to 15 years would not help me get the door fixed or replace my property. I know the offender is more likely to come out of prison worse. I have no illusions concerning the prospects of rehabilitation, nor the deterrent effect of imprisonment.

Prisons have the ability to turn out "hardened criminals". A petty thief may come out of prison as a cold hearted killer. Few criminals are "hardened" when they enter the prison system since the majority of prisoners start out as non-violent offenders. We become inured to the degradation and punishment handed down by the criminal justice system. It is the system itself which hardens a criminal in most cases. The hardened offender becomes increasingly indifferent to the suffering and loss inflicted upon the victim, which enables an offender to commit even more serious and harmful offenses. It is important to understand this apathy because it is the shield that criminals use to avoid facing the pain or loss inflicted on their victims. Where does this indurative attitude come from? Is it an intricate part of our socialization? The ability to ignore and be indifferent to the plight of the less fortunate is all too obvious in our society. It is the same shield we all use to avoid facing the pain and loss our actions (or inactions) inflict on others.

For instance, a few years ago it became public knowledge that guards at the maximum security prison in Lucasville, Ohio, were handcuffing prisoners to the cell bars and beating them with steel batons. It was established in a court of law that this is a standard method of controlling prisoners deemed by guards to be "macho". There was no out-cry from the general public protesting this torture, but the U.S. condemns this behaviour in other countries. The public is indifferent to the suffering brought about by our government and uses the apathetic shield of self-righteousness. What ever happens within these prisons is considered a part of our just desserts. So, the beatings continue and criminals become "hardened".

As society condemns the criminal, so too does the criminal condemn society to his/her hatred and indifference. The ability to cause harm to society is greatly increased as a result of social apathy. It is a vicious cycle that is spiralling out of control. To slow down or possibly reverse this trend we need to understand the thought processes which enable us to victimize others through our actions or our inactions.

I can clearly remember a point in time when I came to the realization that my punishment was exceeding my crime. I made a conscious effort to sever whatever moral and psychological restraints I had which would hinder me from letting society feel the full weight of my hate and anger. I wanted to share my pain and suffering with society at large. During this process I felt some ties holding me back from the dark abyss of utter lawlessness and extreme violence.

I examined the restraints and discovered these ties which hindered me were the result of the few acts of kindness and love experienced in the course of my life. It was this emotional bond to humanity that I was trying to disregard and sever to enable me to be completely indifferent to the suffering I intended to inflict on others through violence. Luckily, I was able to break this bond. To do so would be to repay those acts of kindness with hate and violence and I could not bring myself to do that. In this manner I stumbled onto my humanity, unexpectedly.

The punishment should never exceed the offense. The news media and politicians have actually added to the problem with false or misleading rhetoric and have focused public hysteria on "street crime" and often link it to violent crime. Primarily, street crime is committed by members of the underclass; the poor and minorities. Most of the offenses committed by the underclass are drug related. Roughly two-thirds of those imprisoned are non-violent offenders whose punishment has been escalated far beyond the harm which resulted from the crime. For instance, when a person burglarizes a house, it is considered a violent offense and the offender is given a harsh sentence as if great physical harm resulted from the offense, when in fact, no physical harm took place. Law makers justify these harsh sentences by what might have happened if someone had been at home and as if physical harm had actually occurred. This is the rhetoric used to increase the length of sentences.

Sentencing is out of control and even some of the victims have protested excessively harsh sentences handed down to their victimizers. However, these victims who see the injustice and speak out against exceedingly harsh sentences are ignored by the news media, the legislature and the parole board authority. The government and victims' rights advocates give a great deal of lip service to being sensitive to the victim — as long as the victim is screaming for harsher retribution. The government and victim's rights groups completely ignore the concept of victim/offender reconciliation because it involves forgiveness and this is out of character with the current trend of vindictiveness.

Presently, I have heard of some efforts to establish restitution programs, but there is no mention of reconciliation. We desperately need restorative justice that includes both restitution and reconciliation. I do not pretend to have all the answers. However, I believe a part of the final solution to victimization would be to replace apathy with empathy on a national level. It becomes much harder to victimize someone if we are forced to face the harm we cause. A dialogue between victim and offender is long overdue and a reconciliation program would be a step in the right direction. It is time to try restorative justice.

The American Correctional Association:
A Conspiracy of Silence
Little Rock Reed & Ivan Denisovich[1]

As a member of the American Correctional Association (ACA), I believe I have a responsibility to uphold the principles set forth in the ACA's Code of Ethics. In particular, the Code of Ethics requires that as a member of the ACA I must "respect and protect the civil rights of all clients", I must "report without reservation any corrupt or unethical behavior which could affect either a client or the integrity of the organization", and I must "respect the public's right to know, and will share information with the public with openness and candor."

To this end, I am duty-bound to disclose the information contained in this article, as it reveals what I believe constitutes rampant human rights abuses against all of the ACA's clients, as well as a colossal fraud against the people of America.

My colleague and co-author who has assisted me in preparing this article also firmly believes in the ACA's Code of Ethics, but is precluded from the ACA's membership due to his status as a prisoner and unwilling "client" of the ACA.

Little Rock Reed

The American Correctional Association (ACA) is the largest accrediting agency for juvenile and adult prisons in the United States. Many citizens and organizations believe that the ACA, rather than promoting professionalism within the correctional field and protecting prisoners' rights as it claims, is in the practice of promoting the correctional-industrial complex and assisting prison officials in covering up pervasive human rights abuses against prisoners and their families.

The purpose of this article is to examine the ACA's true practices and motives.

The ACA is a not-for-profit corporation formed in the state of New York in 1954.[2] Its constitution lists twenty-two purposes and objectives, amongst which are:

8. "To promote the improvement of laws governing the criminal justice and correctional process for adult offenders. ..."

9. "... to safeguard the constitutional and other rights of personnel and offenders in the criminal justice and juvenile justice correctional process".
10. "To foster a code of ethics applicable to ... [everyone] ... throughout the correctional field".
11. "To devise, implement and promote a program of accreditation for correctional departments, agencies, institutions, programs and services".
12. "To develop and promote effective standards for the care, custody, training and treatment of offenders in all age groups and all areas of the correctional field."
13. "To publicize and interpret correctional standards to the public in order to obtain the understanding and participation of citizens".

These are purposes and objectives that all citizens, even prisoners, would concur with as noble, practical and fair if achieved and adhered to. However, these purposes and objectives have been subjectively interpreted (and in fact entirely ignored when convenient) when the interests of the ACA take precedence over the just and humane treatment of the men, women and children caught in the jaws of a voracious and ever-expanding high-profit industry called "corrections" in the United States.

As in all cases of organizational growth in a capitalistic system, money is the bottomline factor in survival. The ACA has built a profitable niche for itself on the backs of prisoners and taxpayers, priding itself as the accrediting body that safeguards the constitutional rights of prisoners and on the promotion of effective standards for the care and treatment of offenders of all ages. A standard criminal investigatory technique is to "follow the money", and as we do, it becomes glaringly obvious where the true interests of the ACA lie.

For instance, in 1989–90, the ACA reported that $1.1 million (or nearly 20%) of its income-producing activities came from accreditation fees it charged correctional agencies to evaluate and then, if "standards were met", to grant officials accreditation. With such a significant portion of its income dependent upon accreditation fees, it is in the best interests of the ACA to see its market expand in size, while also being malleable enough in its accreditation process to have the ACA's customers believe such "certification" is possible and in their own best interests as well. Public officials, as exemplified by the vast number of systems that seek certification, reason that the investment in accreditation by the ACA more than pays off as a type of "litigation insurance" when the conditions of their institutions are challenged in court. In such prison condition cases, the courts have used ACA standards and the fact that the institutions under litigation were previously "accredited" as a basis for their rulings (*Prison Legal News*, 1995). In every case in which an accredited prison was sued, the Attorney General's office prominently cited ACA accreditation in its defense of the institutional status quo.

The correctional-industrial complex is one of the fastest growing markets of the U.S. economy, and the ACA, as we shall see, has firmly established its presence in this money-making endeavor of concrete, barbed wire and misery.

Since 1980, the imprisoned population in the U.S. has grown over 300% to over 1 million in 1994 (Bureau of Justice Statistics, 1995). The national prison population is currently expanding at the rate of 1,300 prisoners per week, or an average of three new medium size prisons every seven days (Gillard & Beck, 1994). Correspondingly, the total national correctional budget to support this expansion has grown from $2.5 billion in 1972 (Halleck & Witte, 1977) to over $34 billion in 1992 (*The Nation*, 1994), one natural result of which has been the increase in the number of prisons from 694 in 1984 (Innes, 1986) nearly doubling by 1990 to 1,207 institutions (Stephan, 1992).[3]

Over the past decade, criminal justice spending has become the fastest growing budgetary item, expanding from 5.4 to 7.5 percent of public expenditures (Mandel et al., 1993). This growth in an era of relatively shrinking treasuries must come at the expense of other programs and services.[4] As criminal justice scholar Todd Clear explains, "the get-tough movement has made punishment the only growth industry in government today" (Cline, 1993). At the national level, for example, federal spending on education shrunk by 25 percent over a ten year period, while criminal justice spending increased by 29 percent (Chambliss, 1991). At the state level, California has repeatedly raised in-state tuition and cut back on post-secondary programs in order to fund its unprecedented prison expansion (Brown, 1995). In fact, states are now spending more on prisons to lock people up than on universities to educate them (Brazaitis, 1993). The hiring and training of correctional employees, observes Meredith DeHart of the

U.S. Census Bureau, is "the fastest-growing function ... out of everything government does" (Meddis & Sharp, 1994).

From this brief overview, we can see that the correctional industry is big and business is good. In 1995 at the 125th annual Congress of Correction — the ACA's jamboree — 500 "correctional professionals" of all stripes and 500 vendors gathered for what journalist Alan Prendergast (1995) called "a flag-waving, back patting, gladhanding tribute to the growing power and prestige of the booming prison industry". As Cathy Perry, the account manager for Access Catalogue Company, which sells approved personal items to prisoners, comments, "Business is great" (Prendergast, 1995). Supporting this industry as the central conduit between seller and buyer, in 1992 alone, the ACA made $1.4 million from the sale of advertising in its glossy bimonthly publication *Corrections Today*,[5] from renting its mailing list,[6] and from construction reports (source: ACA's 1992 IRS form 990), a sum representing, one-fifth of the ACA's income producing activities for the year.

Another significant source of the ACA's revenue comes from its subsidiary, the Commission on Accreditation for Corrections. The Commission was formed in 1978 and by 1990 involved approximately 80% of all federal and state adult and juvenile correctional agencies. According to the Commission (1990), the ACA's accreditation process:

> ... offers [agencies] the opportunity to evaluate their operations against national standards, remedy deficiencies, and upgrade the quality of correctional programs and services. The recognized benefits from such a process include improved management, a defense against lawsuits through documentation and the demonstration of a 'good faith' effort to improve conditions of confinement, increased accountability and enhanced public credibility for administrative and line staff, a safer and more humane environment for personnel and offenders, and the establishment of measurable criteria for upgrading programs, personnel, and physical plant on a continuing basis.

The cost for the valuative seal of approval process is nearly $8,000 for accreditation and yearly reaccreditation for prisons with populations of 500 or less.[7] For larger size institutions, the fees are determined on a "case by case basis" (Commission, 1990). This process resulted in the ACA generating in excess of $1.4 million for 1992 in the performance of 244 accreditation reviews, and in 1993 performing 236 accreditation reviews for some $1.7 million in fees, and $1.6 million in 1994 in accreditation fees (source: I.R.S. tax returns for those years). These sums represent approximately 20 percent of the ACA's yearly income-producing activities. By 1995, "... more than 1,200 jails and prisons have invested millions in training and renovation in an effort to meet ACA standards, in the belief that accreditation will improve security and staff morale, insulate them from lawsuits, and upgrade their image" (Prendergast, 1995).[8]

With all this training, upgrading, standardization and accreditation, one would believe that the nation's correctional facilities were state of the art and the envy of penology the world over. However, as we shall see, such is not the case.

The public is constantly bombarded by propagandistic articles like "Must Our Prisons be Resorts?" in the "world's most widely read magazine" (Bidinotto, 1994), and well-reported political sloganeering like Senator Phil Gramm's (R-TX) bombastic lament of "... stop building prisons that are like Holiday Inns" (Corn, 1995), manipulating the citizenry to believe that life is good behind bars.

Criminologist Kevin Wright (1987), however, maintains that "the American prison system stands in sharp [contrast] against the ideals on which it was founded, often characterized by severe overcrowding, unsanitary and even dangerous conditions, violence, brutality, and corruption". Another criminologist, Harold Pepinsky (1995) states:

> Nowhere on this continent is the battleground bloodier and more raw than in U.S. prisons, in 'control units'[9] for activist prisoners in particular. Prison activists and jailhouse lawyers are routinely receiving extended imprisonment, getting beaten and assassinated in prisons across the United States and Canada for merely asserting their legitimate first amendment rights and attempting to expose the true nature of prisons.

Assistant Attorney General of Arizona, Andrew Payton Thomas, who is hardly a "bleeding heart liberal", presents a view eerily similar to that of the criminologists: "We must wonder what the early prison reformers would say upon peering into our nation's prisons today", comments Thomas (1995), "and whether they would consider them an improvement over the houses of horror they frequented some two centuries ago".

Meanwhile, according to organizations such as the ACLU's National Prison Project and the Center for Advocacy of Human Rights, the broad majority of prisons in the United States are in violation of the Universal Declaration of Human Rights, the International Covenant on Civil Political Rights, and the International Convention Against Torture and Other Cruel, Inhuman or Degrading Treatment or Punishment (Jones, 1993; Reed, 1995). Additionally, a recent European commission found the American Prison system to be the "most barbarous" of the western industrialized nations (Vidal, 1994). It is of little wonder, then, but of major concern and marketing strategy for the ACA, that forty-two states, districts and protectorates are under court order or consent decree to limit populations and/or improve conditions (Koren, 1993/94).

Even after massive multi-billion dollar building booms, by 1990 with $11.5 billion spent on cell construction that year alone, state prisons were on average packed to 125 percent of capacity and the federal system over 136 percent of design, while California's 120,000 prisoners were serving their sentences wedged in prisons crammed beyond 190 percent of design capacity (Gillard & Beck 1994). According to Alvin Bronstein, executive director of the ACLU's National Prison Project (1995), the prison populations in Texas and California alone will exceed that of all western European countries combined within three years. It is no wonder, then, that since 1990 the ACA has "adjusted" its touted standards, reducing the minimum required cell space for prisoners "... from 70 unencumbered square feet of floor space per [prisoner] to 25 square feet, which can also include furniture — an acknowledgement that many double-celled prisons couldn't meet the higher standards" (Prendergast, 1995). It is revealing to note that the reduced floor space approved by the revised ACA standards is less in square footage than the Humane Society requires for a large dog (Stuller, 1995).

On August 6, 1982, David Bazelon, Senior Circuit Judge for the U.S. Court of Appeals for the District of Columbia, resigned from the ACA's Board of Commissioners of the Commission on Accreditation for Corrections. In his Memorandum of Resignation, Judge Bazelon stated:

> I will soon complete two years of my 5-year term in the
> Commission. ... During my tenure, I have repeatedly called on the

> Commission to make some fundamental reforms in its fact-finding
> procedures and in its relationship with the corrections community.
> The Commission has repeatedly refused to take the meaningful steps
> to guarantee its independence and to insure the integrity of its
> decisions. The Commission therefore broke faith with the public
> and has betrayed the promise of accreditation. (Bazelon, 1982)

In his Memorandum, Judge Bazelon stated that "... the history of corrections in America, I believe, is best characterized as a conspiracy of silence between corrections officials and the public". He pointed out that the federal courts "... have begun to back away from enforcing the Eighth Amendment's ban against cruel and inhumane prison conditions". In this climate, Bazelon continued, "... the concept of accreditation is especially vital, for it offers one of the few hopes for rational and humane reform in corrections. The real promise of accreditation is that the conspiracy of silence between corrections officials and the public can be replaced with a partnership for reform".

Bazelon pointed out that when he was asked to join the Commission, he believed that its accreditation program "... was fulfilling this noble promise", but that it was now apparent that it had no intention of fulfilling this promise. He explained that shortly after joining the Commission, he discovered that the ACA's *Statement of Principles'* promise of "public participation" in the accreditation process was not being kept. "The public is systematically excluded from every stage of the Commission's work", he noted. He went on to quote the ACA's executive director at the time, Anthony Travisono, who warned his colleagues at its annual meeting in 1982 that "... the Commission will fold in one year's time if this opening of the process is permitted to exist". Similarly, Commissioner B. James George warned that openness would be "sheer suicide" for the ACA. Judge Bazelon also cited Robert Fosen, the Commission's executive director, as arguing that if information about prison conditions is to be broadcast to the public, "... all kinds of persons will be critical" and this "will simply upset ... [our] integrity". Judge Bazelon (1982) correctly noted that the premise of these remarks, "... that either accreditation is run the way that prison officials want it run, or else, is an insult to the public".

In addition to criticizing the ACA's systematic exclusion of the public's scrutiny and participation in the accreditation process, Bazelon set forth detailed facts substantiating his claims that:

1. The Commission's audit techniques and deliberative procedures are inherently unreliable;
2. The Commission is unwilling to accommodate constructive criticism and the possibility of meaningful change;
3. The Commission's priorities are fundamentally flawed;
4. The Commission has pervasive conflicts of interest with the facilities it is charged with monitoring; and,
5. The Commission has permitted the accreditation movement to be transformed into a propaganda vehicle for corrections authorities.

According to the facts set forth in Judge Bazelon's Memorandum, there are no actual audits conducted by the ACA of the facilities to whom it sells accreditation. The only evidence considered by the Commission is the self-evaluation of the applicant institutions and the report of an audit team that refuses to interview prisoners unless they are pre-selected by prison officials. Moreover, the Commission has stated that its first priority is not to insure that its minimum standards of accreditation are complied with by the facilities it sells accreditation to, but to simply "... encourage as many facilities to join the accreditation process as possible". The fact seems to be that if the prison has the money, it will have the ACA's accreditation, regardless of how brutal and/or substandard the prison's conditions. Judge Bazelon noted that in the words of the Commission's own former chairman and treasurer, Gary Blake, if a more active role in investigation were played, "I think we could kiss the whole process of accreditation goodbye".

Bazelon (1982) stated that time and time again he has seen or heard of instances in which corrections officials have used their accreditation by the ACA "... to deflect public criticism and scrutiny of their management, to boost their standing with governors and legislators, to ward off judges and lawsuits, and to pat themselves on the back. They have used it to paper over the crisis in corrections with certificates of 'excellence'. They have used it, in short, for their own propaganda purposes".

Little has changed since Judge Bazelon so ethically, indignantly and publicly resigned from the ACA's Board of Commissioners on Accreditation over a decade ago.[10] It was the Southern Ohio Correctional Facility's (SOCF) accreditation process beginning in 1990, for example, that encouraged policies and conditions to become so brutal and repressive that on Easter Sunday, 1993, the prison erupted in a riot — the longest prison siege in American history, resulting in millions of dollars in damage, the serious injury of forty individuals, and the killing of ten people (Reed, 1995). [Editor's Note: See Perotti, this anthology.] By 1992, Lucasville managed to achieve accreditation on its third try (according to Commission [1990] standards, the ACA fee to accredit SOCF was then in excess of $25,000). In fact, the prison achieved 100 percent compliance with mandatory ACA standards (Prendergast, 1995). "Fourteen months later, in April of 1993, the Lucasville uprising claimed the lives of nine [prisoners] and one guard" (ibid).

While SOCF was undergoing the accreditation process, prisoners who attempted to approach the ACA inspectors with complaints of conditions violating ACA standards were threatened with solitary confinement.[11] "When the inspectors came", writes one SOCF prisoner (Freddie, 1994), "they were steered to areas where they would not come into contact with other than 'model inmates' [corroborators, informants and the like] dressed in new clothes, sanitized areas of the prison, and only the best 'politician guards' in view, rather than the Ninja Turtles — or goon squads". This prisoner also noted that the very day of the inspection, the population was fed cereal containing dead and alive roaches. Nevertheless, the prison received maximum scores by the inspectors. Another prisoner at SOCF recalls that during the inspection the ACA auditing team "never did walk into my cell block. They went to the honor block, which has telephones and privatized single-man cells that are open all day". The majority of the prisoners did not have access to even those menial conditions.

One major recommendation by an earlier ACA inspection team to accredit SOCF was that the population of the prison be lowered to 1,630 prisoners. Once this reduction was accomplished, the inspectors concluded that "... personal safety is not much of an issue as it once was ..." at the facility (Prendergast, 1995). By the time of the Easter Sunday rebellion, the population had increased to 1,819 prisoners.

Prior to, and after the inspection, the ACA received written complaint after written complaint from prisoners and outsiders such as a massive letter-writing campaign from the public interest group Citizens United for the Rehabilitation of Errants (CURE) regarding the institution's blatant disregard for ACA standards, demanding an investigation into the brutal conditions; conditions that shortly thereafter erupted into the bloody and avoidable uprising. The ACA, however, summarily dismissed those outcries, choosing instead to admonish those who protested not to interfere with the accreditation process (Reed, 1995).

Now, after the riot and after half of the state's prisons received the ACA's accreditation (Prendergast, 1995),[12] the director of the Ohio prison system, Reginald Wilkinson, has been elected to serve as the ACA's president-elect, a position that would apparently place Wilkinson in an ethical conflict of interest — at least a conflict between the supposedly independent stance of the ACA to impartially evaluate, monitor and certify the operation of Ohio's prisons to ensure standards compliance.

Then, again, such interlinked, conflicting relationships in the field of corrections in not uncommon. Fifteen of the eighteen members of the ACA's Board of Governors are primarily employed as correctional administrators, parole and probation supervisors, jail deputies, and as the chair of a state senate's select oversight committee on corrections (source: ACA's roster of 1994–96 Board of Governors). In Ohio, as a telling example, the architect who designed SOCF is the uncle of the contractor who built it (and seven other jail facilities in the state), who is the brother of Ohio Governor George Voinovich, who is the direct supervisor of the prison director and president-elect of the ACA, which certifies Ohio prisons (Prendergast, 1995) as being in compliance with ACA standards.

Yet another significant source of the ACA's income is derived from government grants: $1.1 million in 1990, $1.5 million in 1992, and $1.8 million in 1993 (source: ACA's IRS form 990),[13] averaging 18 percent of the ACA's total revenue for those years. These government grants concomitant with accreditation fees from government agencies and marketing income focusing on governmental groups amounts to nearly 60 percent of the ACA's total income, while membership dues and assessments compose only seven percent of total revenue. Many critics of the ACA note that with a constituency so heavily invested in the correctional-industrial complex's expansion, "... the association has avoided taking a stand on numerous controversial corrections issues, such as the use of control units and privatization of prisons, preferring to blandly urge the development of a 'balanced approach' to corrections" (Prendergast, 1995).[14]

A more egregious example of the ACA's failure to live up to its charter principles — specifically "to safeguard the Constitutional and other rights of personnel and offenders"[15] — involves the U.S. Supreme Court case of *Hudson* v. *McMillan*. This case involved a Louisiana state prisoner who was brutally beaten by two guards while chained in leg irons and handcuffs, all the while being observed by a lieutenant who cautioned the guards

"... not to have too much fun". A U.S. court of appeals ruled that the prisoner had no viable claim under the Eighth Amendment's ban on cruel and unusual punishment because a cracked dental plate, loosened teeth and split upper lip did not constitute a "significant injury". The prisoner's petition for writ of Certiorari (appeal) was granted and Alvin Bronstein was appointed to represent him before the Supreme Court.

On November 13, 1991, Bronstein presented Hudson's case before the court, arguing that "significant injury" should not be a requirement to substantiate an Eighth Amendment claim. "His argument was supported by an impressive group of amici [friends of the court who file supporting information briefs]. The office of the U.S. Solicitor General not only filed an amicus brief, but also argued a portion of the case ..." in support of the prisoner (Bernat, 1992). Additionally, Americans for Effective Law Enforcement, Human Rights Watch and two prisoners' rights groups also filed as amici in the case on behalf of Hudson.

Although the beating of a prisoner is in complete violation of ACA's published standards, when invited to join as an amicus on behalf of the prisoner, the ACA declined. ACA then-president Helen Corrothers wrote to Bronstein claiming that the ACA executive committee rejected the two invitations to get involved because the committee felt it was not "in the best interest of the ACA" (Bernat, 1992). Bronstein then wrote to all the members of the ACA Standards Committee expressing his consternation:

> I thought I should share with you the fact that, once again, the ACA leadership has demonstrated that ACA standards are not professional correctional standards. Rather, they are a collection of words and phrases relied on selectively by various officials when it serves their interest (e.g., as a defense to conditions lawsuits, as a means of getting funds from the legislature). The ACA Executive Committee action — non-action might be a better description — makes a sham of the whole standards and accreditation process.

It was only after the Supreme Court ruled against the Louisiana Department of Corrections, and presumably after Bronstein's admonishing letter as well, that ACA executive director editorialized that "... as corrections professionals, we are duty bound to speak out against the use of force except as a last resort" (Giari, 1992). Better late than never, as the saying goes.

Another example of the ACA's failure to live up to its claim to protect the constitutional rights of prisoners is its refusal to urge accredited prisons to respect the religious rights of Native American prisoners. The committee has received numerous complaints of the absolute deprivation of American Indian religious freedom in numerous prisons. As a general rule, the ACA's executive officers will not acknowledge receipt of such correspondence, regardless of the source.

The abuses of the accreditation process have become so widespread and well-known within the industry that in December 1994 the Center for Advocacy of Human Rights (CAHR) initiated an investigation of the ACA and ACA accredited prisons. As of mid-1995, the investigation involved the direct participation of hundreds of prisoners (primarily jailhouse lawyers) and outside supporters representing dozens of ACA accredited prisons in 43 states. The continuing investigation has revealed ongoing violations of the ACA's Standards for Adult Correctional institutions within virtually every prison that has been investigated. In many cases, these violations are also in conflict with state and federal laws, as well as international human rights law. For example, while the ACA's standards regarding "access to courts", "access to law library" and "access to counsel" expressly state that these particular standards are mandatory under constitutional law, some prisoners in virtually every ACA accredited prison being investigated by CAHR are denied such access. In fact, in many cases, such access is not only denied, but prisoners are commonly subjected to reprisals for their legitimate attempts to rectify the situation, another violation of the ACA's standards.[16]

The overwhelming majority of ACA standards are nonmandatory. Nevertheless, according to ACA policy, accredited prisons are supposed to comply with 90 percent of the nonmandatory standards. The CAHR has been unable to locate any ACA accredited prison which is actually in compliance with 90 percent of the nonmandatory standards. This is a direct result of the ACA's lack of effective auditing and monitoring procedures, as well as prison and ACA officials' willful exclusion of the public and prisoners from effective participation in the accreditation and monitoring processes. While the materials distributed by the ACA indicate that prisoners and the public will have some input into the monitoring of ACA accredited prisons, the CAHR's investigation has revealed, as Bazelon claimed in 1982, that this is quite contrary to the truth. In fact, with few exceptions, prisoners are uniformly denied access to the Standards for Adult Correctional Institutions so that they may evaluate their prison's compliance or noncompliance with the standards.

Meanwhile, ACA officials have been writing to some prisoners that if they want access to the Standards they must get written permission from the warden (which is seldom given) and then go through an attorney to obtain a copy. In one instance, Lisa Parker, representing the ACA, recently wrote to a prisoner who wished to purchase a copy of the Standards as well as ACA's policy manual. She informed the prisoner that he must go through an attorney to purchase the Standards and that under no circumstances may any prisoner see the ACA's policies. These practices are contrary to the ACA's claim that they encourage prisoners and the public to have input into the accreditation and monitoring processes. Prisoners are also denied membership in the very association that promotes the standards that govern their lives. When prisoners apply for ACA membership, either their applications are rejected outright and dues returned, or if processed and later identified as prisoners, their prorated dues are returned and they are advised that they can join the ACA when they are no longer prisoners.

The CAHR and other organizations have written the ACA seeking information, some of which the ACA is required by law to provide upon request. However, the ACA will not provide the information. For example, on May 8, 1995, and again on October 20, 1995, the CAHR wrote to the ACA's treasurer, Charles Kehoe, asking for a copy of the ACA's "... most recent financial statement, as well as the last three I.R.S. 1990 tax returns". Although state law in Maryland (where the ACA is headquartered) requires non-profit organizations to provide this information to the public within thirty days of the request, Kehoe will not acknowledge receipt of the requests nor provide the information sought. Interestingly, according to Jennifer Light (1995), public information officer for the Maryland Secretary of State, the ACA has refused to file with the Secretary of State financial statements required by law. Numerous requests by the Secretary of State to comply with the law have been ignored by the ACA (Dunn, 1995).

Another example of the ACA's failure to live up to its "Code of Ethics" — particularly its principle that "members will respect the public's right to know, and will share information with the public with openness and candor" — is demonstrated in further information it has refused to disclose to the public. For example, on September 13, 1995, Deborah Garlin, attorney and president of The Center for Advocacy of Human Rights, sent the following letter to each member of the ACA's Board of Governors and executive committee.

We address this correspondence to you in your capacity as a member of the American Correctional Association's Board of Governors. We are also sending a similar letter to each of the other members of the ACA's Board of Governors. Our reason for this is that over this past year we have addressed correspondence to some of the ACA's executive committee members, including Bobbie Huskey (President), James Gondles (Executive Director) and Charles J. Kehoe (Treasurer), either seeking information which we believe the ACA claims to disclose to the general public (or is lawfully required to disclose to the public), or complaining of human rights abuses that appear to be taking place within prisons that are accredited by the ACA. Neither Mr. Gondles, Ms. Huskey nor Mr. Kehoe have ever acknowledged receipt of any of our correspondence to them.

If this particular correspondence should be referred to someone other than yourself, we ask that you please forward it to the appropriate ACA official(s) and notify us of who it has been forwarded to for response. Thank you.

Basically we are seeking information regarding the ACA, and we will gladly pay the expenses of obtaining such information if you will notify us of the specific costs for processing. The information we seek is as follows:

1. The names and addresses of each adult correctional facility/ prison in the United States that is either accredited by the ACA or undergoing the accreditation process.
2. The names and addresses of each adult correctional facility/ prison in the United States that has ever had its accreditation revoked by the ACA for noncompliance with the appropriate Standards.
3. Is there a contract entered into between the ACA and the adult correctional facilities/prisons that the ACA accredits? If so, may we review a standard copy of said contract?
4. What are the required fees that the ACA charges adult correctional facilities/prisons to obtain and maintain the ACA's accreditation?
5. Are the prisoners in ACA-accredited adult correctional facilities/ prisons provided access to the ACA's applicable Standards and "Standards Compliance Checklists" in order to determine for themselves whether or not the ACA's auditing officials are misled by prison officials regarding compliance with the Standards?

6. When prisoners wish to complain of ACA-Standards and human rights violations within adult correctional facilities/prisons which are ACA-accredited, who are the appropriate ACA officials that should receive such complaints, and what specific action, if any, does ACA policy require be taken to determine the validity of the complaints?
7. Could you please provide the names and mailing addresses of the current members of your Committee on Legal Issues?
8. We would also like to purchase the current edition of the ACA's Standards for Adult Correctional Institutions. Please let us know what the cost will be and how to order.

We apologize for inconveniencing you with this request for information; however, we believe it is necessary as part of an investigation we are conducting regarding ACA-accredited prisons which appear to be misleading the ACA about their compliance with the ACA's applicable Standards. If and when our investigation has resulted in significant documented findings, that some ACA-accredited prisons are in fact misleading the ACA's auditing team(s) about their compliance with ACA Standards, we will promptly notify you in an effort to establish dialogue regarding the matter. If such be the case, it is our sincere desire to work in a spirit of cooperation with the ACA so that prison officials' abuses of the accreditation and monitoring processes may be corrected.

Thank you very much for your consideration of these matters. We look forward to hearing from you soon.

Two of the twenty-four ACA officers/board members who received this letter acknowledged receipt, stating that they were forwarding the letter to executive director James Gondles for response. This is apparently what compelled Gondles to acknowledge receipt of the CAHR's correspondence for the first time in two years. However, he refused to provide any of the information requested, with the exception of information on purchasing a copy of the ACA's Standards. *Openness and candor* indeed.

The CAHR's investigation has revealed and continues to reveal that prisoners in just about every accredited prison are subjected to brutal and inhumane treatment, including unsanitary conditions; sensory deprivation; denial of essential medial care which in many cases has resulted in death;

entirely ineffective grievance procedures; beatings; interference with privileged legal mail; withholding of publications which criticize prison practices and condition, etc. Additionally, the CAHR's investigation has revealed that: (1) prisoners who complain about non-compliance with the ACA's Standards are commonly transferred to non-accredited prisons in an apparent attempt to silence their criticisms; (2) prisoners and outside supporters who complain of violations are generally ignored by both prison and ACA officials; (3) alleged violations are seldom, if ever, investigated by the ACA, and when they are investigated, the investigations generally exclude interviews with prisoners who are not pre-selected by the prison officials and no meaningful corrective action is taken by the ACA.

In one recent case, a Florida prison warden actually acknowledged that his prison is in violation of numerous mandatory standards, and justified it on the grounds that the standards can be ignored since the purchase of accreditation is "voluntary". This has been found to be the standard explanation given by prison officials when they receive queries of any kind regarding the prison's accreditation, a position which appears directly contrary to Gondles' (1993) testimony that "... accreditation is based upon an applicant correctional facility's demonstration of compliance with correctional facility standards adopted by the ACA. ... ACA's sole authority is to deny accreditation to any facility found not to be in compliance with ACA standards". It is interesting to note, also, that the CAHR has been unable to locate any prison that has had its accreditation revoked once granted.

Almost every accredited prison refuses to provide prisoners with access to the ACA's Standards, and virtually every prison denies prisoners access to the prison's standards compliance "Checklist" so that the prisoners may determine whether or not the ACA is being deceived by unscrupulous prison officials about Standards compliance. Moreover, by the ACA's own admission, when complaints of noncompliance are received by the ACA, the ACA will only conduct an on-site monitoring visit after providing the prison officials with advance notice that the ACA intends to conduct a monitoring visit. This affords all prison officials who are in violation of the standards an opportunity to cover up their violations prior to the monitoring visit.

The ACA may contend that the prisons it has sold accreditation to are, in fact, in compliance with the ACA's Standards, as many of the Standards merely require that the prison seeking accreditation promulgate policies which cover the fundamental rights of prisoners. For example, the Standard regarding "grievance procedures" merely requires that "... there is a written inmate grievance procedure that is made available to all inmates and that includes at least one level of appeal". The comment which accompanies the standard states:

> A grievance procedure is an administrative means for the expression and resolution of inmate problems. The institution's grievance mechanism should include provisions for the following: written responses to all grievances, including the reasons for the decision; response within a prescribed, reasonable time limit, with special provisions for responding to emergencies; supervisory review of grievances; participation by staff and inmates in the procedure's design and operation; access by all inmates, with guarantees against reprisals; applicability over a broad range of issues; and means for resolving questions of jurisdiction.

The comment is nothing more than a comment. In other words while the comment states that the "... grievance mechanism should include ... participation by ... inmates in the procedure's design and operation", as well as "guarantees against reprisals", the fact of the matter is, no accredited prison's grievance procedure in this country has been designed with the actual input or participation of prisoners. Prisoners who utilize the grievance procedure are commonly subjected to reprisals for utilizing the procedure, including beatings, solitary confinement, etc. But these facts do not constitute a violation of the Standard itself, as the actual Standard — as opposed to the comment — merely requires that "... there is a written inmate grievance procedure that is made available to all inmates and that includes at least one level of appeal". In other words, once the procedure is placed in writing the Standard has been and continues to be complied with by the written policy's mere existence. Violation of the written policy does not constitute a violation of the ACA Standard.

But this is fundamentally deceptive. When the prison has written the policies corresponding with the ACA's Standards, then the ACA sells the prison a letter of accreditation which is then used by the prison to obtain more funding from federal, state and private sources. These letters of accreditation state that the accreditation is based on an "independent" evaluation. Independent? The ACA is not an "independent" investigator or evaluator for two reasons: 1) because the evaluators are being paid (with our tax dollars) by the prison officials who are being evaluated; and 2) because the prison officials being "evaluated" are invariably either members, associates or affiliates of the ACA, with absolutely no exceptions. As you will recall, for example, every Ohio prison that has received the ACA's accreditation is under the directorship of the ACA's president-elect. *Independent?*

The standard practices of the ACA and ACA-accredited prisons are producing what we believe to be detrimental effects on both prisoners and socio-economic conditions within the United States. It is the kind of practices described above which cause prisoners to lose all respect for the government and the people that the prison and ACA officials allegedly represent. When such respect is nonexistent, disregard for the government and the people (and their laws) logically follows, thus creating the kind of social disorder and violence that we see every day in the news and in our environments; disregard and violence that is understandably perceived by groups such as prisoners as not only justifiable, but imperative. The prisoners who rebelled at SOCF in 1993, Santa Fe in 1980 and Attica in 1971, for example, clearly believed that their actions were inevitable, as all their previous nonviolent attempts to have legitimate grievances corrected had fallen on deaf ears or had been met with administrative hostility and brutalization.

As U.S. District Judge Karlton of the Eastern District of California so aptly cautioned not long ago when considering how the Supreme Court has admonished the courts to "... defer to the discretion of prison officials" when confronted with prisoners' complaints:

> I pause here only long enough to note that such [an admonishment] does not even allow the possibility of malevolence. I know nothing in the history of prison administration in this country to provide such utter confidence. Moreover, this [admonishment] does not recognize that extreme deprivations and perceived unfairness may themselves create profound security problems, as the histories of prison rebellions from Attica to the recent incidents involving Haitian detainees clearly demonstrate. It may well be that considerations of this sort are initially for the responsible prison authorities, and that their determinations should be treated with deference. Nonetheless,

as has been observed, deference to supposed expertise may be no more than a fiction. (1987)

It is clear that ACA and corrections officials are not being held accountable to the public for their misdeeds. It could be cogently argued that the practices of the ACA are in violation of the 1970 *Racketeering Influenced Corrupt Organizations Act* (RICO). Since under the RICO Act only two linked actions are required to establish a racketeering pattern — any act or threat indictable under fifty or so state and federal laws, such as fraud of public monies — and conspiracy can be established by a wide range of circumstantial evidence, the ongoing promotion of the essentially meaningless accreditation process costing taxpayers millions of dollars apparently makes the American Correctional Association vulnerable to such an indictment.[18] In light of the apparent deception with which they have been dealing with and manipulating the public, it appears that it would be appropriate and in the public interest for Congress to conduct an investigation and public hearings on the matter. Such action is imperative if, in using Judge Bazelon's words, the "conspiracy of silence between corrections officials and the public can be replaced with a partnership for reform".

NOTES

1   Little Rock Reed is a Native American rights activist and former political prisoner. On Human Rights Day, December 10, 1995, his book, *The American Indian in the White Man's Prisons: A Story of Genocide* (UnCompromising Books, 1993), was named as an Outstanding Book on the subject of human rights in North America by the Gustavus Center for the Study of Human Rights in North America. Sponsors for the award were the National Interreligious Commission on Human Rights, the National Organization for Women, Free Inquiry, the National Conference of Christians Jews, the National Association for the Advancement of Colored People, the National Urban League, the Unitarian Universalist Association, Project Censored, B'nai B'rith, and the Fellowship of Reconciliation.
       Ivan Denisovich is the non de plume of a prisoner. For reasons of personal safety his true identity is being withheld. The name is taken from the title character in Aleksandr Solzhenitsyn's seminal work *One Day in the Life of Ivan Denisovich*, concerning existence in the Soviet gulag system.
2   The grandfather of the ACA was chartered in New York in 1871 as the National Prison Association of the United States of America. In 1909 the name was changed to the American Prison Association, and in 1954 the current title was adopted.
3   These numbers represent state prisons only and exclude federal, county and private institutions, which number into the thousands of facilities.

4   Actually, most prisons contract with private companies for slave labor. Prisoners are
    required to work full-time for little or no pay, the proceeds of which benefit private
    companies. If the proceeds were shifted to benefit the public rather than private
    corporations, prison labor would significantly reduce, if not eliminate, the need for tax
    monies to be spent on prisons.
5   Since the late 1980s, advertising revenue in *Corrections Today* has tripled (Meddis &
    Sharp, 1994).
6   Interestingly, in 1994, the ACA had to mail an apology letter to its 20,000 plus
    members, explaining the circumstances surrounding the sale of the association's mailing
    list to *Prison Life* magazine, an act that apparently many members complained of as
    inappropriate when they received a free copy of *Prison Life* (Gondles, 1994).
7   Approximately two-thirds of correctional facilities have populations of less than 500
    prisoners (Stephan, 1992).
8   The actual number of institutions that have been accredited is difficult to determine.
    The ACA has refused to disclose the figure. Estimates range from ten (Mohr, 1995) to
    twenty-five percent (Sullivan, 1995), with a higher percentage of the nation's private
    prisons receiving accreditation.
9   A 'control unit' is a specific unit within a prison or an entire prison which subjects the
    individual to severe sensory deprivation and isolation as a means of brainwashing.
    Proliferating across the country, control units were designed after the brainwashing
    chambers used on American POWs in North Korean and Chinese prison camps in
    order to achieve effective brainwashing and social control. While prison officials
    publicly state that control units are used for the most violent criminals, studies have
    indicated that they are used primarily to silence religious leaders, political dissidents,
    jailhouse lawyers and writers who are critical of prison policies and practices. The
    Federal Bureau of Prisons (BOP) established its first control unit and accompanying
    "treatment program" modeled after these brainwashing chambers with the erection of
    the U.S. Penitentiary in Illinois, following a conference in which Dr. Edgar H. Schein
    encouraged the prison officials to do so. Without exception, each brainwashing technique
    described by Dr. Schein was a violation of the constitution and international human
    rights treaties. To rationalize his position (which was adopted and implemented by
    the BOP), Dr. Schein stated, "These Chinese methods [of brainwashing] are not so
    mysterious, not so different and not so awful once we separate the awfulness of the
    Communist ideology and look simply at the methods used". In other words, it is
    politically correct to be "communists" as long as we call ourselves "democratic".
    Following Schein's presentation, then-director of the BOP, James Bennett, stood
    before his subordinates and stated that the BOP provides a "... tremendous
    opportunity to carry on some of the experimenting to which [Dr. Schein has] alluded".
    He urged them to "... undertake some of the techniques Dr. Schein discussed", and he
    assured them that BOP headquarters in Washington "... are anxious to have you
    undertake these things: do things perhaps on your own — undertake a little experiment
    of what you can do with the Muslims. ..." Indeed they did. Today the BOP and every
    state prison system has a control unit in which political prisoners/leaders are confined.
    For an in-depth examination of the origins and current use of control units, see the
    Journal of Prisoners on Prisons (1993) Vol. 4:2. Also see, T. Kisslinger (1995); and
    Part IV of this anthology.

10 As the National Advisor to the Citizens United for the Rehabilitation of Errants, Maygene Giari (1995) comments, "Most of the criticisms leveled against the [ACA's] accreditation process in the 1970s and 1980s are still as valid today as they were then".

11 During a South Carolina ACA accreditation process, two prisoners in one institution who succeeded in talking to the audit team were subsequently locked up in a control unit later that day (South Carolina CURE, 1995).

12 Accredited even though the system is crammed to 182 percent of capacity with 43,000 prisoners in system designed for 26,000 (Prendergast, 1995).

13 These figured are rounded.

14 While the ACA avoids taking a stand on controversial issues that may offend potential purchasers of accreditation, it has been known to get involved, though subliminally, in some controversial issues when its own profiteering interests and longevity are at stake. For example, in her research paper entitled "Propaganda: Misleading the Public for Political Gain", Maygene Giari (1995) pointed out that in politician's efforts to form public opinion that more prisons are necessary for public safety, a National Institute of Justice (NIJ) study by Edwin Zedlewski, "Making Confinement Decisions", drew on a number of studies "... to show that it is far cheaper to build more prisons than to use alternative penalties or early release to relieve prison crowding". As Giari points out, Zedlewski cited a Rand Corporation study (also made for the NIJ) that found inmates averaged between 187 and 287 crimes a year, not counting drug deals. He estimated that the cost of prison construction, amortized over the lifetime of the institution, amounts to about $5,000 a year. Adding $15,000 a year for the cost of imprisonment in a medium-security prison, he figured the total cost of a year's imprisonment for one inmate would be $20,000. On the other hand, with the cost of crime estimated at $2,300 per crime, the "typical" inmate who committed only the lower figure of 187 crimes per year would be responsible for $430,000 in costs of crime. Thus, according to Zedlewski's figures, sentencing 1,000 more offenders to prison would cost only an additional $25 million per year, but would prevent about 187,000 felonies costing approximately $430 million over the same period of time (Zedlewski, 1987).

Criminologists challenged the validity of Zedlewski's cost-benefit analysis. He misused the material from the Rand study, giving the impression that the "typical" criminal commits such a shocking number of crimes. The Rand study was not a survey of a typical prison population. The survey covered only robbers and burglars in prison, and such offenders represent only about 45 percent of all prison admissions. These prisoners were asked to report the number of crimes they had committed in the two years before they were sentenced to prison. Zedlewski reinterpreted this to mean the number of crimes they had committed after release. Moreover, the median number of crimes they admitted was 15 per year, not between 187 and 287.

The figure of $2,300 as the cost for each crime has been challenged as inflated, and grossly misleading when applied to all repeat offenders. Furthermore, Zedlewski under-estimated the costs of imprisonment and prison construction. In any case, offenders who commit 187 crimes a year would be more likely to be housed in maximum-security prisons which cost a lot more than medium security.

Zedlewski's study came out in 1987, but despite the criticisms leveled against it, NIJ Director James Stewart reissued it again in 1988. It was resurrected yet again in 1989 in the professional journal *Corrections Today* (published by the ACA), in an article by Richard Abell (1989) Assistant Attorney General in charge of the Office of Justice Programs. Abell [and the ACA] proposed that criminal justice professionals use Zedlewski's study as the basis for making decisions on building more prisons. Advocates of "Three Strikes" laws at state and federal levels in 1993–94 once again repeatedly cited the "savings" that would result from life sentences for third time offenders. Such claims became so frequent that Rand Corporation issued a fact sheet saying that neither the number of crimes committed by the supposedly "average" criminal nor the purported cost of those crimes is borne out by Rand studies.

15 Referring to prisoners as the ACA's "clients", the ACA's Code of Ethics states that "[m]embers will respect and protect the civil and legal rights of all clients", and that "each member will report without reservation any corrupt or unethical behavior which could effect either a client or the integrity of the organization".

16 According to the editor of the *Prison Legal News*, within days after distribution of the April 1995 edition, in which the CAHR had an extensive article published in which it urged prisoners to participate in the investigation of the ACA, an ACA representative called the publisher in an attempt to obtain *Prison Legal News'* mailing list. Although the request was denied, dozens of letters between the CAHR and prisoners who subscribe to the *Prison Legal News* have mysteriously disappeared, including correspondence between the authors of this article.

17 In fact, the ACA does enter into a contract with every agency it accredits. Prisoners are third party (direct) beneficiaries to the contracts. As such, they may bring an action directly against the ACA and the prison officials to enforce the promise made for their benefit. It was discussion of this possibility, as well as the possibility of an organized filing of numerous lawsuits against the ACA to be consolidated into a nationwide class action alleging ACA violations for fraud and other laws, which apparently concerned the ACA officials about the article CAHR had published in the *Prison Legal News* as discussed above.

18 The application of the RICO Act has consistently expanded since its inception 25 years ago. Currently, companies have employed RICO to charge unions, either trying to organize their work forces or negotiate new compensation packages, with racketeering efforts (Baker, 1995).

REFERENCES

Abell, R. (1989). "Beyond Willy Horton: The Battle of The Prison Bulge", *Corrections Today* (April) 158:160–4.

Baker, S. (1995). "The Yelping Over Labor's New Tactics", *Business Week* (Oct. 23):75.

Bazelon, D. (1982). *Memorandum of Resignation* (ACA), August 6th.

Bernet, B. (1992). *ACLU National Prison Project Journal*, Winter.

Blidinotto, R. (1994). "Why Must Our Prisons be Resorts?" *Reader's Digest* (November): 65–71.

Brazaitis, T. (1993). "Americans Brutalized by Crime Statistics", *Cleveland Plain Dealer* (Aug. 22).

Brown, J. (1995). "Jerry Brown Speaks Out on Crime Control", *North Coast Xpress* (Oct.–Nov.):18–20.

Bureau of Justice Statistics (1995). "Prisoners 1994", U.S. Dept. of Justice: NCJ-151634.

Chambliss, W. (1991). "Trading Textbooks for Prison Cells", *National Center on Institutions and Alternatives*: Alexander, VA.

Clines, F. (1993). "Prisons Run Out of Cells, Money and Choices", *New York Times* (May 28).

Commission on Accreditation for Corrections (1990). *Standards for Adult Correctional Institutions*, 3rd ed. American Correctional Association (Jan.).

Corn, D. (1995). "God, Guts 'n' Guns", *The Nation* (March 6):297–98.

Criminal Justice Newsletter (1992). "Justice Officials Call for End to Politicizing Crime Debate", (23)12: June 15.

Dunn, C. (1995). Correspondence to Central Office, ACA (Jan. 26) Annapolis, MD.

Freddie, F. (1994). "ACA Accreditation Lucasville Style", *Prison News Service* (Nov./Dec.):11.

Gatling, M. (1994). Correspondence to Ms. Jensen, ACA (July 8).

Giari, M. (1992). Correspondence to Charles Sullivan, Executive Director of CURE Pasadena, CA.

Gillard, D. and A. Beck (1994). "Prisoners in 1993", *Bureau of Justice Statistics*, U.S. Dept. of Justice (June).

Gondles, J. (1993). Affidavit of James A. Gondles, South Central Judicial District, North Dakota, Civil. No. 93-C-2078 (Aug. 3).

———. (1994). Correspondence: "Dear Valued ACA Member" (May 26), Laurel, MD.

Halleck. S. and A. Witte (1977). "Is Rehabilitation Dead?" *Crime & Delinquency* (Oct.): 372–82.

Hallinan, J. (1995). "Growth of U.S. Prisons Ensured", *Times Picayune* (March 19).

Innes, C. (1986). "Population Density in State Prisons", *Bureau of Justice Statistics*, U.S. Dept. of Justice (Dec.).

Jones, M. (1993). "The U.S. Fails to Conform to International Human Rights Tenets", *The National Prison Project Journal* (8)4:6–16.

Karlton, Judge. *Sample* vs. *Borg*, 675 F.FUPP. 574 CE.D. CAL. 1987.

Kisslinger T. (1995). *The United States Penitentiary Marion: A Case Study of the Establishment, Operation and Proliferation of Control Units as Political Prisons in America*. Unpublished Masters Thesis. Department of Criminology, University of Ottawa, Canada.

Koren, E (1993–94). "Status Report: State Prisons and the Courts — January 1994", *The National Prison Project Journal* (1)9:3–12.

Light, J. (1995). Telephone Conversation with Little Rock Reed on October 20, 1995.

Mandel, M. et al. (1993). "The Economics of Crime". *Business Week* (Dec. 13). 72–81.

Meddis, S. and D. Sharp (1994). "As Spending Soars, So Do the Profits", *USA Today* (Dec. 13).

Mohr, G. (1995). "The Easter Sunday Disturbance at Lucasville: A Corrections Perspective", *The State of Crime and Criminal Justice in Ohio*. Governor's Office of Criminal Justice Services: Columbus, OH.

Nation, The (1994). "Editorial: 'String 'em Up", (Nov. 21):599–600.

Parker, L. (1995). "Correspondence to Prisoner", American Correctional Association: Laurel, MD.

Pepinsky, H. (1995). *Review of The American Indian in the White Man's Prisons: A Story of Genocide*, by Little Rock Reed, et al., Uncompromising Books: Taos, NM.

Prendergast, A. (1995). "Inside Ohio's Booming Corrections Industry", *Cleveland Free Times* (Sept.):13-19.

Prison Legal News (1995). "Denial of Food May Violate 8th Amendment" (6)7:9.

Reed, L.R. (1995). "A Viable ACA Litigation Strategy", *Prison Legal News* (6)4:1-3.

South Carolina CURE Newsletter (1995). "American Correctional Association (ACA)", (3rd Quarter):6.

Stephan, J. (1992). *Census of State and Federal Correctional Facilities, 1990*, Bureau of Justice Statistics, U.S. Dept. of Justice (May).

Stuller, J. (1995). "There Never Was a Harder Place than 'The Rock'", *Smithsonian* (July):84–95.

Sullivan, C. (1995). *Citizens United for the Rehabilitation of Errants Newsletter* (Winter): 4.

Thomas, A. (1995). "Outdated Laws Shackle Prison Reform", *Wall Street Journal* (March 30).

Vidal, G. (1994). "The Union of the State", *The Nation* (December):789–91.

Wall Street Journal (1995). "Private Lockup", (July 11).

Wright, K. (1987). *The Great American Crime Myth*. Greenwood Press: Westport, CA.

The ACA Accreditation Fraud
Dan Cahill, Muldoon, James Pryor & Robert Woodman

For more than five years, prisoners in Ohio and throughout the U.S.A. have been condemning the American Correctional Association (ACA) accreditation program as a sham and a fraud. In 1993, prisoners at the Madison prison in London, Ohio, issued the Ohio Prisoners Rights' Union (OPRU) position paper on the accreditation program. It stated:

> ACA accreditation lends credibility to fraudulent claims by prison officials, and is used as a defence against lawsuits through false documentation. Prison officials claim that accreditation demonstrates a 'good faith' effort to improve prison conditions. In reality it's an attempt to mislead the public into thinking prisons have better living conditions than they really have.
>
> Prisoners don't have access to the ACA accreditation standards and aren't involved in the accreditation process, and have no way to compel prison officials to comply with those standards.
>
> Until prisoners are actively involved in the ACA accreditation process and have access to the ACA standards — the accreditation program must be recognized for the sham that it is. Prisoners and their outside support groups must fight the ACA accreditation program.

The OPRU position paper was distributed to all of the Citizens United for Rehabilitation of Errants (CURE) State chapters by Eunice McAllister of South Carolina. [CURE has recently become the Prisoner Advocacy Network (PAN)]. Ms. McAllister also sent evidence and reports from prisoners across the nation to National CURE exposing the accreditation program as a fraud. The evidence compiled was presented at a workshop at CURE's national convention. Indeed, Little Rock Reed and Ivan Denisovich had condemned the ACA accreditation in "The American Correctional Association: A Conspiracy of Silence" (*JPP*, 1995, Vol. 6:2, pp. 21–40) as fraudulent and malevolent.

However, in National CURE's Fall 1998 newsletter, CURE clearly supports and promotes the accreditation program. Dianne Tramutol-Lawson, Chair of Colorado CURE has even gone so far as to accept an ACA invitation to be Vice-Chair of the Volunteer Partnerships Subcommittee. Kay Perry, Chair of National CURE, is proposing ACA standards. CURE's continued support of the ACA lends credibility to the entire fraud prisoners have been attempting to expose for years. On this issue, CURE is out of touch with the movement and much worse, is working against the prisoners they claim to be helping.

Prisoners who litigate on prison issues know first-hand how detrimental fraudulent ACA accreditation can be. When a prisoner sues an accredited institution, they are faced with a mountain of documentation as counterevidence in the court. To win, the prisoner must prove that the documentation and accreditation is false or irrelevant. If he/she fails to do so, the prisoner loses the case, and the conditions which led to the lawsuit remain unrepaired.

In *Reception Perceptions* (July/August 1998) a newsletter for the Correctional Reception Center, there was an article titled "What Is ACA?". The article said accreditation is "... a defence against law suits through documentation of a 'good faith' effort to improve conditions of confinement, ... and enhanced public credibility for administration and line staff. ..." It does not seem to matter that the entire process is a sham, or that the documentation is false.

The current president of the ACA is also the Director of the Department of Rehabilitation and Correction (DORC), Reginald A. Wilkinson. Considering how much of the taxpayers' money DORC spends with the ACA each year through the accreditation program, and the purchase of ACA literature, this appears to be a serious conflict of interest. The ACA is a special-interest group which represents those whose livelihoods depend on Federal, State and County prisons and jails. Is it any wonder that they lobby legislators for larger prison budgets to continue expanding the prison systems?

During October 5–7, 1998, the Orient Correctional Institution (OCI) commenced an ACA audit for accreditation. Prior to the ACA inspection, prison officials had more than 60 dump-truck loads of what they called "junk and clutter" taken to the dump and thrown away. This "junk" consisted of hundreds of chairs, couches, filing cabinets, wooden and steel desks, unused office supplies and cleaning supplies, computers, keyboards, tape players, TVs, unused medical supplies and wheelchair padding, walking canes, crutches, file card boxes, typewriters, bookcases and shelves. Some of this "junk" was brand new and still in the original boxes. Now prison officials are in the process of purchasing supplies and equipment to replace what was just recently thrown out!

The audit team consisted of three individuals, who spent 21½ days at this prison. Most of their time here was spent reviewing policies and procedures to ensure compliance with ACA standards. No effort was made to verify that policies and procedures were actually carried out! They ignored broken windows which were covered with plastic, and made no effort to determine if showers, toilets, sink fixtures, fire alarms, or lights really worked. They ignored sewage dripping from pipes in a dorm set aside for disabled prisoners, lack of ventilation and smoke evacuation systems, an inadequate water sprinkler system (in one dorm there is no sprinkler system), and extreme overcrowding. They ignored the condemned dorms with their crumbling foundations, cracking and buckling floors, and leaking roofs. They brought no instruments to check noise levels, and in many dormitories, they did not even enter the bed areas. In 2E dormitory, only one auditor inspected, spending less than five minutes in the dorm and checking nothing. He did not even have a clipboard to take notes! Moreover, several prisoners who had previously filed complaints with the ACA had an opportunity to speak to the auditors about specific problems. All the prisoners who talked to us about their interviews with the ACA reported that the entire affair was *pro forma*. In effect, the auditors were talking to the prisoners because the rules said they had to. The auditors really did not care at all what the prisoners with complaints had to say.

It was predetermined months before this audit that OCI would be accredited. For months guards and prison staff spoke openly in front of prisoners saying "The fix is in; we'll pass the ACA inspection". This was not hard to figure out since the DORC director is also the ACA president. But were problems actually addressed? No! Problems were plastered up and painted over, but not really fixed. So called "junk" (paid for by taxpayers or purchased by prisoners' families) was confiscated and destroyed in order to meet ACA standards. However, when prisoners tried to research what those standards were, they were denied access to ACA's published guidelines and standards.

One problem in 6E dorm was (and is) water leakage. A week after the auditors left OCI, part of the roof and ceiling in B-Bay of 6E collapsed from age, rot, and water damage. Only one auditor came in 6E and never checked (much less noticed) the conditions of the roof and ceilings of 6E. Yet OCI was accredited.

The purpose of this audit was to ensure that necessary documentation is in order. The ACA was not concerned about the fact that OCI does not actually comply with the ACA standards, so long as there is plenty of documentation which SAYS they are in compliance. Moreover, just to give one example, how did the paperwork demonstrate the Quartermaster in compliance? OCI's Quartermaster does not furnish prisoners with adequate winter clothing (long johns, wool socks, water-proof boots, rain coats, adequate winter coats), and not infrequently runs out of socks and underwear. Yet the Quartermaster, like the rest of OCI, passed the accreditation. Did someone cook the books or were the auditors just not looking? This is the documentation prisoners must disprove in court if they attempt to bring about any improvements through litigation. Legislators will not force any reforms on a prison system that is ACA accredited. That is the enhanced public credibility the DORC refers to!

A prisoner who once possessed a copy of the OPRU position paper on the ACA accreditation program was charged with possession of contraband and gang activity, placed in isolation for almost two months in 1993, and has suffered many forms of reprisals over the past five years. Exposing this fraud is necessary if we ever hope to see any positive changes made in the prison system.

We know that by writing this article we may be subjected to reprisals. That fear keeps most prisoners from speaking out. Our efforts to expose this fraud, and to educate the public about intolerable living conditions are crippled so long as CURE, and people like them, buy into the ACA's lies and cooperate in perpetuating the accreditation deceit. Can we ever hope to convince the public? CURE is the nation's largest prison reform organization, and part of their mission is educating the general public and legislators about the inhumane conditions and corruption which is inherent in the prison system. In supporting and promoting the ACA accreditation program, CURE participates in the oppression of more than 1.8 million people. CURE is out of touch with the prison reform movement and should give some serious thought to the concept of "solidarity". CURE needs to condemn the ACA accreditation program for the fraud it is, help expose such activities, and stop working against prisoners.

OCI will be accredited, along with all Ohio prisons. We stand by what we have written and challenge the ACA to prove otherwise! We also ask all thoughtful people on the outside of the fences to contact their legislators and ask them to stop accepting the accreditation lies from the ACA. Are your tax dollars well-spent by letting prisons and the ACA cover up serious problems with a blizzard of fraudulent paperwork?

Pell Grants for Prisoners Part Deux:
It's Déjà Vu All Over Again
Jon Marc Taylor

Perhaps the most asinine amendment to the already mulish United States Omnibus Crime Bill (Currie, 1994) was submitted by Senator Kay Bailey Hutchison (R-TX) three days before the Senate overwhelmingly approved H.R. 3355. On November 16, 1993, the junior senator from Texas stood before the most exclusive millionaires' club in the world and lamented that prisoners serving sentences "for offenses like carjacking, armed robbery, rape and arson received as much as $200 million in Pell [higher education] funds, courtesy of the American taxpayer" (Congressional Record — Senate, 1993). She explained to the august assembly that although the year before they had approved the *Higher Education Reauthorization Act* (HERA), which in part stipulated that prisoners serving death and life without parole sentences were prohibited from receiving Pell Grants, the current reduced prisoner eligibility was still "not right". Thus the senator's solution was to prohibit all state and federal prisoners from receiving Pell higher education grants.

The senator was not alone in her discontent, nor the only legislator moved to action. Three weeks before, waving a copy of the Pottstown, PA *Mercury* above his head, Representative Timothy Holden from Pennsylvania fulminated before the C-SPAN cameras that he was appalled to learn from the newspaper's report that prisoners were receiving $200 million in Pell Grant funding, allowing them free college educations (Berkey, 1993A). "There is an obligation to do the best you can to give incarcerated people a chance, but certainly not from a program that has been earmarked for low-income people to educate their children", explained the representative. This, he argued, was "an outright abuse" (Berkey, 1993A).

The abuse the congressman referred to, besides the fact that prisoners were receiving this grant, was that colleges listed bogus students, inflated tuition bills, and submitted fraudulent housing charges for already "housed" prisoner-students. He also accused the understaffed office administering the grant program of negligence. Holden then declared that he was planning to co-sponsor Representative Bart Gordon's (D-TN) Amendment 1168, which would exclude prisoners from Pell Grant eligibility. At the conclusion of his speech, the congressman was barraged by other House members questioning him about his proposal.

476

In the immortal words of that great uniquely American philosopher, Yogi Berra, "It's Déjà Vu all over again". Over three years before the Hutchinson Amendment, Senator Jesse Helms (R-NC) initiated what became an annual Capitol Hill exclusion-fest to effectively eliminate prisoners' post-secondary opportunities. In early 1992, Representative Thomas Coleman (R-MO) and Bart Gordon (D-TN) introduced a joint resolution (1168) that would prohibit, "any individual who is incarcerated in any Federal or State penal institution" from qualifying for Pell Grant funding (Congressional Record — House, 1992A).

Both the Senate and House proposals were eventually defeated after extensive, though low-keyed lobbying in committee hearings (Taylor, 1993A). In the spring of 1993, Gordon (sans Coleman) reintroduced H.R. 1168, only to see it languish and fade away in committee backwaters during the session, never to see a floor vote (Taylor, 1993B). Gordon, obviously a politician not to be deterred by failure or facts, re-submitted his Amendment for a third time, with it so sensationally spotlighted by Congressman Holden. Finally, on April 20, 1994, the day after the broadcast of a highly biased and inflammatory report on the topic by the news magazine *Dateline NBC* (Taylor, 1994), the House (in a vote of 312 to 116) added its own expulsion amendment to the crime bill. When President Bill Clinton signed the Crime Bill in September 1994, prisoners became ineligible for Pell Grant disbursements.

What was lost in all the smoke and mirrors of the grandstanding rhetoric was the purpose of the Pell Grant program, the very real crime fighting effectiveness of higher education. Coleman, Gordon, Helms and others who supported Gordon's amendment used specious reasoning and disingenuous pronouncements which culminated in descriptions of dire predicament that bore no resemblance to reality.

Senator Hutchinson (1994) rationalized her proposal for citing the federal government's expenditure of $100 million a year on education and training available only to prisoners. She stated that the Pell Grant program was created, "in order to help the children of the poor and working class families to have a chance to go to college" (Congressional Record — Senate, 1993), and that was more than one million students were denied grants because there was not enough money to go around. To punctuate the point of this ongoing injustice, she used the example of an exasperated police officer whose daughter could not qualify for a Pell Grant. The Senator quoted his trite retort that, "maybe I should take off my badge and rob a store" (Congressional Record — Senate, 1993).

To begin with, the Senator was a few dollars off in her claim of the amount the federal government spends on prisoner education and training. The Department of Education's Office of Correctional Education, which coordinates the dispersal of federal dollars to state correctional systems, reports that less than $70 million is passed on to educate prisoners (Schwartz and Koch, 1992). In addition most of these federal correctional education funds are dollars dedicated to particular literacy and adult basic education opportunities such as the G.E.D. program, allowing administrators limited discretion in how to spend them. Less than six percent ($1.3 billion) is spent on offender education, vocational training, substance abuse counselling and programs of all types (Lillis, 1993A). With this amount of funding, it should come as no surprise that the median education of those paroled in 1990 was at the 10th grade level (Perkins, 1993), while 70 percent of prisoners have drug problems (Krammer, 1993). One state (Nevada) even reported no educational budget item at all (Lillis, 1993A).

For years, educators have noted that there has been and continues to be considerable need for improvement in correctional education programs (Quay, 1973; Partlett, 1981; Rousch, 1983; Corcoran, 1985; O'Neil, 1990). National surveys (Bell et al., 1979; Conrad, 1981; Hovarth, 1983; Ryan and Woodard, 1987; Lillis, 1994) have all found that the major problem facing correctional education programs was the lack of funding. By 1993, Jamie Lillis, a research assistant for the *Corrections Compendium*, noted that "budget cuts continue to whittle away at the quality and perhaps even the very existence of many education and training programs for incarcerated offenders" (1993B). With only 15 percent of the adult prison population enrolled in formal education programming and three times as many eligible (Lillis, 1994), it is a fallacious assumption by the senator that correctional education is already adequately supported in the United States.

In 1968, when Congress created the Basic Education Opportunity Grant program, later called Pell Grants in honor of Senator Claiborne Pell (D-RI) who sponsored the legislation, the purpose was to assist the poor and working class to have a chance to finance a college education. This goal has been (and still is) being largely achieved. In 1993–94, 70 percent of the Pell Grants went to students from families who earned less than $15,000, with 95 percent of the grants going to those whose families earned less than

$30,000 yearly (Congressional Record — Senate, 1993). Reversing the Bush administration's policy of pushing eligibility levels ever lower (Toch and Slafsky, 1991), Congress began in 1992 to expand the program's parameters to include more middle class families by raising the maximum family income ceiling from $33,000 to $42,000 (Krauss, 1992). By the 1993–94 academic year, over 4.3 million students received $6.4 billion in Pell Grant disbursements (Berkey, 1993B; Berkey, 1993C).

Even with this level of funding, over a million students were denied Pell Grant assistance in 1994. The short-fall in assistance was a result of a combination of inflation, overall reduced aid, and swollen enrolments. Between 1980 and 1990, the annual tuition at a four-year public university rose a whopping 141 percent, and tuition at private colleges rose even higher (*The Washington Spectator*, 1992). The cost of higher education, as a share of median family income rose from 12 to 16 percent of the family budget when the student attended a public school and to nearly 40 percent up from 26 percent when the student attended a private institution. Yet as tuition increases surpassed those of even the much vaunted medical inflation rate, state and federal financial assistance increased by only 50 percent, barely covering more than a third of the ballooning costs (Wagner, 1993). Combine the two factors of tuition inflation and relative aid reductions with the 34 percent jump in college enrollments beginning at the start of the recession in 1991 (Berstein, 1993A), and you have a national enrollment of 14 million students (Berstein, 1993B) many of whom and their families struggle to pay tuition bills. Since four out of five American families' real income declined during the 1980s (Sanders, 1993), with full-time working families of four existing below the poverty line growing from 12 to 18 percent of the population (Hitchens, 1993), the crunch to give junior or daughter (God forbid, both!) a college education has never been greater.

A significant point omitted by the promoters of the exclusionary legislation is that every student applicant to the Pell Grant program that *qualifies* receives a grant. The yearly Congressional appropriation, which has never been enough to fulfill the program's established spending parameters, is divided on a sliding, need-based scale amongst those who receive grants. Therefore, not a single Pell Grant qualified student has ever been denied a Pell Grant *because* a prisoner received one. With the elimination of prisoners from the Pell Grant program not a single additional student will receive a grant, but rather the funds that had gone to eligible prisoner-students will be distributed amongst the rest of the millions of recipients. If evenly disbursed, this means that grant recipients in 1995 received less than an additional $5.00 a semester, while some 30,000 prisoner-students were no longer able to go to school (Sullivan, 1994).

*****

In *Who Goes To Prison?*, the researchers reported that 65 percent of prisoners had not completed high school. A like number had no specific job skills, and half had never been employed. A national survey a decade ago defined between three to four-fifths of the prison population as functionally illiterate (Bell et al., 1984). All the while, *Workforce 2000* observes that the majority of new jobs will require a skilled and college educated workforce, with the majority of this labour pool to be drawn from female and minority populations. With their gross lack of educational attainment, 60 percent of the prison population composed of minorities (Stephan, 1992), and 70 percent having existed below the poverty line the year preceding their incarceration (Perkins, 1993), does the question that prisoners are needy or deserving students even need to be asked?

It seems evident that even with the inclusion of prisoners the Pell Grant program is fulfilling its stated objective; assisting the poor and working class to finance a college education. This is especially so when considering the opinions of those voting for the *Higher Education Reauthorization Act*, who represent a wide range on the political spectrum. "One of the central goals of this legislation was", thought to be by Senator Edward Kennedy (D-MA), "to increase access to higher education for all Americans" (Congressional Record — Senate, 1992). Senator David Durenburger (D-MN) observed that "we do need to make higher education more accessible for every American student. And we do need to be accommodating to the changing nature of the student population" (Congressional Record — Senate, 1992). On the far right, Senator Phil Graham (R-TX), Hutchinson's senior, stated that "ensuring access to higher education for all segments of society helps to equalize opportunities for all people to pursue and achieve the American dream" (Congressional Record — Senate, 1992).

Senator Hutchinson's lamentation over the one million applicants who were denied grants is a specious point. The already noted economic and demographic impact of double digit tuition inflation, single digit aid increases, and exploding enrollments coupled with families' shrinking real incomes, places a strain on an admittedly wallowing bureaucracy (Associated Press, 1992). Additionally, those "denied" assistance did not qualify for it in the first place. As a matter of due course, financial aid counselors advise students to apply for anything and everything possible, and then use the evaluative reports to assist in their own aid disbursement decisions. Furthermore, in the 1994–95 academic year, an additional 324,000 grants were awarded, totalling 4.7 million students (over one-quarter of the national collegiate enrollment) helped by the Pell Grant program (Berkey, 1993C).

Finally, the dramatically quoted police officer's frustration is a little disingenuous to cite, and perhaps his is a hypocritical ire to boot. The family's annual income exceeded $46,000 and they admitted that they did not save for their daughter's education because they adopted her late in their lives (Berkey, 1993C). Not only did the family income surpass the grant program's Congressionally set ceiling of $42,000 by $4,000, the father was eligible for over $30,000 in forgivable federal education loans through the exclusive Perkins Loan Cancellation Program for law enforcement and correctional officers; a program not available to the average citizen. Thus while the average prisoner-student earns a skill related Associate degree costing less than $3,000 in Pell Grants (Sarri, 1993), the irate cop can receive ten times as much federal money to improve his skills, advance his career, and raise his income at the public trough. The ironic aspect of these (supposedly antithetical) two tax-funded programs is that they both end up fighting crime.

*****

Representative Holden's arguments against prisoner Pell Grant participation was based on the Pottstown *Mercury*'s sensationalized series (Gauker, 1993), which in turn was substantially furnished with facts and figures from Congressman Gordon's office. Yet analysis of Gordon's objections still do not hold up. He complains that prisoners unjustly take a large number of grants away from traditional students, some schools unfairly provide, "prisoner-exclusive scholarships" that are not available to other students, no one tracks prisoners to see if they use their educations "properly" upon release, and other funds should be used to provide these opportunities so as not to unnecessarily duplicate government services.

During the original House debate over Amendment 1168, Gordon's side kick in that ignoble misadventure, Coleman, claimed 100,000 prisoners received Pell Grants each year (Congressional Record — House, 1992). It turned out to be an interesting statistic. It would have meant that one out of every eight prisoners at the time (there were 800,000 prisoners in the United States during that year) were college students (Bureau of Justice Statistics, 1992), while just a few years earlier only one out of every one hundred prisoners had a college education (Greenfield, 1985). Now Gordon "estimated" that only half of the number cited by Coleman (50,000 prisoners) received Pell Grants totalling some $200 million in funding (Berkey, 1993b). In the same breath, however, Coleman admitted that Pell awards for prisoners averaged only $1,400, which if multiplied by 50,000 equals only $70 million in funding. The ludicrousness of both sets of figures is that they bear no resemblance to reality.

In 1993, Lillis (1994) reported there were approximately 38,000 prisoner-college students in the nation while other studies (Berkey, 1993d; Sarri, 1993) revealed that at most 80 percent of these students received Pell Grants. In other words, at best just over 30,000 prisoners received Pell Grants in 1993 (Pell, 1994) at an average of $1,400 per grant for approximately $42 million. Approximately six-tenths of 1 percent of the $6 billion in Pell Grant funds distributed in 1993 went to prisoner-students; all told, far less than the 50,000 recipients and $200 million in aid, cited by proponents of the exclusionary legislation.

The Representative was also critical of schools giving prisoner-scholarships to cover the differential between the Pell Grant award and standard tuition schedules. Gordon believes that since these prisoner scholarships are not available to non-incarcerated students, they are discriminatory in nature (Berkey, 1993B). The schools that provide these in-house tuition stipends can do so because of the reduced costs involved in educational programs in the penal settings. Classrooms, utilities and maintenance are provided at no expense, and student services ranging from marketing to counselling to placement are greatly reduced as well (Blumenstyk, 1991). If these scholarships were not provided, in many cases there would be no other way for prisoner-students to pay tuition, even reduced tuition, since they are excluded from even minimum wage jobs, barred from loan programs, and excluded from other grants and scholarships. And now the honorable representative from Tennessee objects to schools who are able to pass along their reduced expenses as student assistance in the process of lowered tuition charges.

A point consistently stressed by Gordon is that prisoners need to be tracked to see if higher education does indeed pay off upon their release (Berkey, 1993F). Never mind that no other Pell Grant recipients are tracked to see if they "properly" utilize their college educations; prisoners are a special class that must be continually tracked. Howard Petters III (1993), director of the Illinois Department of Corrections, emphatically states that, "statistics have proven that investing in correctional education reduces the likelihood of recidivism, enhances employability upon release and thus taxability, and even benefits the prison environment for all who live and work there".

Even with some mixed results, during the 1970s studies from New Jersey (Thomas, 1974), Alabama (Thompson, 1976), Maryland (Blackburn, 1979) and Pennsylvania (Blumenstein and Cohen, 1979) reported substantial reductions in recidivism rates amongst college students. During the 1980s, a plethora of evaluations from Texas (Gaither, 1980), Michigan (Haviland, 1982), New Mexico (*Psychology Today*, 1983), California (Chase and Dickover, 1983), Ohio (Holloway and Moke, 1986), Washington, D.C. (*Lorton Prison College Program — Annual Report, 1990*) and in Canada (Duguid, 1981) revealed either reduced recidivism rates or at least reductions in the seriousness of new offenses. By 1990, two massive studies of nearly one-thousand prisoner-students each were concluded in New York and Michigan. The New York Department of Correctional Services reported that earning a college degree while incarcerated was positively linked with successful post-release adjustment for students who completed the program (Clark, 1991). In the Michigan Department of Corrections — Jack Community College program, it was learned that not only were graduates, who were identified as, "some of the most hardened criminals to be found in the United States", returned to prison significantly less than the average convict, but when they did it was for less serious offenses (Wreford, 1990:62).

Peter Drucker (1989) observes that in today's world, education, especially post-secondary education, is the major determinant of an individual's employability, career prospects and future. For decades it has been shown that there is a correlation between unemployment and dysfunctional behaviour including crime (Robinson, 1990), with unemployment itself being a significant contributor in parolee recidivism (Lawyer and Dertinger, 1993). Reports from New York (Wolf and Syles, 1981), Ohio (Holloway and Moke, 1986) and Canada (Duguid, 1981) during the recession of the early 1980s found graduates of prison college programs were employed up to twice the rate of other ex-prisoners. The Pennsylvania Business Institute, which operates a program at the state's Graterford Correctional Facility, reported that of the 55 prisoner students released so far, only a few have returned and nearly all are employed (Berkey, 1993G).

A 1988 study concluded that society receives financial benefits of at least 12 percent on its total public and private investment in higher education (Bernstein and Magnusson, 1993). A recent National Bureau of Economic Research study reported that for each year of college a student completed, they earned 5 percent more than a high school graduate (Samuelson, 1992), and *U.S. News and World Report* recently reported that over a working lifetime, a college graduate can expect to earn 1.9 times the likely earnings of a high school graduate (Zuckerman, 1995). Conservatively figuring a tax burden of 30 percent (Gergen, 1992), the prison college graduate more than pays for his incarceration and education just through taxation, not to mention law abiding behaviour as opposed to the norm of continued criminality.

As demands on governments exceed their fiscal capabilities, it is more necessary than ever before to invest in "smart" programs that not only reduce ever greater demands, but also add to the economic strength of the society. Over the years, several studies (Seashore et al., 1976; Haber, 1983; Greenwood and Turner, 1985) have commented on the cost-savings that post-secondary correctional education programming can provide through reduced recidivism and increased taxation. My analysis of the possible cost-savings from increasing the number of paroled offenders with a college education to a level of 60 percent parity with the national rate of adults with a like amount of education (approximately 25 percent), revealed cost-savings of non-incurred reincarceration costs of $120 million annually (Taylor, 1992). Taking the model a step further, I found that by using two different crime-cost formulas, that the cost-savings to society of crime *not* committed by rehabilitated ex-offenders ranged from two to twenty billion dollars (Taylor, 1992). An IBM computer program called "Tax Users vs. Tax Generators" produced a report that only a 1.6 percent reduction in recidivism over a 15 year time span in Alabama would increase tax revenues from that subpopulation by 30 percent, while decreasing the demand for correctional spending by over 40 percent (Chancelor, 1992). Chris Marschner, the Hagerstown Junior Community College prison program coordinator, states simply that, "the rate of return on educating a prisoner is so great that [only] an idiot wouldn't do it" (Money, 1992). This is a comment that makes one wonder about those who backed the legislation to eliminate the funding for such opportunities.

A final objection by the Congressman to the use of the Pell Grant program by prisoners is that other federal programs offer rehabilitative training and literacy education, and, "mixing the roles of the federal student aid and prisoner rehabilitation leads to a wasteful service duplication" (Berkey, 1993G). As noted previously, the "other programs" that exist are grossly underfunded, limited in scope, and are not applicable to college programming. Furthermore, higher education is a highly efficient means to reduce offender recidivism. Without Pell Grant financing these opportunities simply cease to exist (Lohman, 1992). Senator Pell comments that he does, "believe prisoners should be able to use a Pell Grant to achieve a college education. Other programs are not the answer. They are very inadequately funded" (Berkey, 1993B). David Evans, Pell's staff director, scoffs at Gordon's suggestion to use other appropriations to fund the prison college programs. "I don't buy that answer", Evans says. "It's the way of getting out of it. Take the money from here and get it from somewhere else. There are no excesses of money at the federal level" (Berkey, 1993H).

Evans also disagrees with the assumption that prisoners deprive traditional students of Pell Grants. He claims prisoners are not doing so (Berkey, 1993H). Dr. Gary Rizzo, associate dean of Montgomery County Community College, who has been monitoring the school's prison program for a decade, is even more adamant in his objections to this assumption. "Those traditional students are taking money away from prisoners", Rizzo argues. "There's no compelling reason to deny [prisoners]. Their logic is flawed" (Berkey, 1993H).

Dr. Steven Steurer, the executive director of the Correctional Education Association and himself a prison teacher, openly wonders why correctional populations are continually treated so differently than the rest of society. In referring to the exclusion of whole state prison populations from Pell Grant eligibility because of the "states'" violation of the supplant/supplement rule imposed by the 1992 Higher Education Reauthorization Action (HERA), Steurer observes that everywhere else students apply for Pell Grants at their colleges and are declared eligible if they meet the criteria. In his opinion, "the policy is rather inconsistent and, to say the least, unfair" (Steurer, 1993).

   In the final measure, perhaps the strongest reason to allow prisoners Pell Grant eligibility comes from the simple words of a graduate of these programs. Commenting on earlier Congressional attempts to exclude prisoner grant participation, the ex-prisoner reflected that, "I would hate to think what would have happened to me if there was no college program while I was incarcerated — without it I would have joined the ranks of repeat offenders and become another addition to the escalating figures of recidivism" (*Justice Watch*, 1992).

*****

The real issue behind the smokescreen thrown up to obscure the problem is not the relative infinitesimal use of Pell Grants by prisoners, rather it is the overall higher education funding crunch coupled with stagnant if not declining family incomes. The attack on prisoners receiving Pell Grants amounts to shopping around for scapegoats. As political analyst William Greider (1991) explains, it is, "a way to change the subject from what is really hurting people". So that, "whenever people are losing their jobs and social decline is visible, it's easier to blame the troubles" on minority segments who seem to be, "getting more than their share". The fact that politicians avoid addressing substantive issues with positive actions, leaves little wonder why a recent Gallup Poll found that law makers rank below lawyers and even talk-show hosts in public esteem (Wildstrom, 1993). The rogues gallery assembled, in effect, to perpetuate crime through assuring high rates of recidivism by denying prisoners access to Pell Grants is a classic example of the hypocrisy emanating from Washington in the guise of governance.

   Very few of us would even think to question the lack of moral integrity possessed by prisoners; it seems to be a given. However, should we not at least question the political integrity of those obtusely promoting the exclusion of prisoners from Pell Grant assistance?

   Senator Hutchinson represents the great state of Texas, which brought the nation the macabre spectacle of dueling gubernatorial candidates outbidding one another on the number of prisoners they would fry if elected (Minton, 1993), proposed state legislation to ship prisoners to China as a cost-savings measure, the perennial bill to punish thieves by cutting off their fingers (*Parade Magazine*, 1994), and 56 prisons currently under construction (Heines, 1994). From this wellspring of criminal justice philosophy, the senator not only voted for the most repressive and bloody (adding over 50 new death penalty crimes) legislation in U.S. history, but in addition proposed the elimination of funding for the most effective crime fighting program in corrections today. And all the while she was busy lethally injecting convicts and expelling prisoner-students in the senate, Hutchinson was battling her second indictment at home for misusing State property and employees to conduct personal business and political campaigning (Irvins, 1994). Perhaps it was the senator's alleged misappropriations of public funds that sensitized Hutchinson to what she myopically viewed as another theft on the public purse when she sponsored the prisoner Pell Grant ban. Hutchinson should be cautious, though, for some day she may need something to occupy her time when she is in one of those new Texas prisons.

Then we have everybody's favourite troglodyte, father of the prisoner Pell Grant exclusion and self-admitted bigot, Senator Jesse Helms, whose state of North Carolina outranks even Texas on the Justice Fellowship's Criminal Justice Crisis Index scale (*Inside Journal*, 1993). It was Helm's proclaimed concern over student college funding that supposedly prompted his original prisoner exclusion legislation; though, later, hypocritically, the senator cast the single vote against the *Higher Education* (Pell Grant) *Reauthorization Act* (Krauss, 1992). Even his past ghost-writer [Leonard, 1992], the conservative national columnist George Will (1994), recently considered the proposed funding ban and felt it was, "grandstanding and chest thumping", and came out in support of prisoners receiving Pell Grants.

Another in the lineup was Representative Thomas Coleman from Missouri. This state shuttered all of its prison college programs early in 1994 because it had reduced its funding for prisoner education and treatment from 3.3 percent of its 1983 corrections budget (Ryan and Woodard, 1987) to only 1.2 percent of its 1993–94 budget (*Corrections Compendium*, 1993). The specific elimination of state funding for its post-secondary correctional education program triggered the 1992 HERA'S supplant-supplement rule, which caused the entire state prison population to be declared ineligible for Pell Grant assistance as the state dropped below its 1988 prison higher education funding level as the Show-Me-State did. So as Coleman ludicrously fulminated about 100,000 prisoners receiving Pell Grants, he sent out 255,000 postcards to constituents at a cost in excess of $50,000 proclaiming that he was outraged by the Congressional checking scandal, and, that he did not bounce a single draft (*Insight*, 1992). Pete Sepp of the National Taxpayers Union (NTU) commented that, "the money he spent on that would probably rival anything he could have bounced in the bank" (*Insight*, 1992). The NTU identified Coleman as among the top seven percent of the users of the Congressional frank (free postage), which cost the taxpayers $80 million in 1992. Coleman defended his use of the franking privilege claiming the House Banking Scandal was the number one issue among his constituents, and, "the people of my district need to know their member of Congress still has integrity and didn't bounce any checks" (*Insight*, 1992). He also spent enough in the single mailing to furnish over 33 students with $1,400 in Pell Grants.

All in all, the near bumbling efforts of Hutchinson, Helms and Coleman pale beside the pernicious actions of Holden and Gordon in the debate. Though it is possible that Representative Timothy Holden's remarks on the House floor were made out of ignorance that does not lessen their deleterious effects including arousing the feelings of those who listened to him because of the erroneous information he conveyed. Regurgitating and misrepresenting the information reported in the *Mercury* series, Holden cited a litany of abuses ranging from school-based fraud to inadequate oversight of the grant programs, to "lifers" receiving free college educations (Berkey, 1993A). The Congressman's ire was not only misplaced, but exposed either his lack of reading comprehension, knee-jerk reactionism, or deliberate misrepresentation of the facts.

Abuses of the Pell Grant program were sadly rather common during the tenure of the Reagan administration. More than 1,600 schools (mostly fly-by-night trade schools teaching skills such as cooking and trucking (Foust, 1993) have been closed during a recent two-year Department of Education fraud investigation (Berkey, 1993F). Focusing on corrections, only a handful of propriety schools with prisoners composing 100 percent of their enrollments were found to be guilty of abuses. These abuses ranged from charging prisoner-students for room and board to filing claims for non-existent students. Meanwhile, some three dozen ultra-orthodox Jewish seminaries in the New York area alone were accused of illegally bilking the Pell Grant program for as much as $40 million (Fenyvsi, 1993); more than the annual total disbursements to prisoner-students. Yet, no one was calling for the banishment of would-be cooks, truckers or rabbis from the Pell Grant program for what their schools did, only prisoners.

The allegations of the DOE's Office of Post-Secondary Education (OSPE) of mismanagement of the federal grant and loan programs are reasonable charges. Instances of store front schools, non-resident students, and non-enrolled students receiving millions of dollars in aid supported the mismanagement charges. However, this is another legacy of Reagan staffing cuts that left only 3 administrators to police 800 schools in the southwest (Toch, 1993), for example. To accuse the DOE of negligence in administering student aid programs is the same as berating the wheelchair basketball league for not having a team in the NCAA's Final Four. In none of these "fixes" to the Pell Grant program are there DOE-OSPE staffing increases. So even with the more stringent regulations that helped to convict the fraudulent schools the department will still occasionally drop the ball.

The really insidious, inflammatory charge made by Holden was that prisoners on death row and serving life without parole sentences were receiving free (i.e., worthless) college degrees. This simply was no longer the case and Holden knew it if he actually read the newspaper story he waved above his head. The 1992 legislation took a number of steps to rectify existing problems in the Pell Grant program relating to prison education. Besides the discriminatory supplant/supplement rules, housing allowances were eliminated from prisoner grants, only one-quarter of a school's enrollment could be prisoners (although a waiver could be granted to non-profit degree granting institutions) and the political concession was made that death row and life without parole prisoners were ineligible for grants (*CURE*, 1992). By the time Holden pontificated before the C-SPAN cameras, the "abuses" he cited out of ignorance or spite to antagonize a membership terrified of being seen as "soft on crime" had been a moot point for over a year.

Representative Bart Gordon, though, is by far the worst offender in not only the misinformation campaign, but in essentially promoting a racist agenda. Since the introduction of his Amendment 1168, the Congressman has been furnished with numerous evaluation studies and reports (including many of those cited here) detailing the effectiveness of post-secondary correctional education programs in significantly reducing participants' costly and painful cycle of recidivating through the system time and time again. His continued objection to prisoner Pell Grant funding because no one has tracked Pell Grant funded prisoner-students' post-release behaviour is a totally disingenuous allegation. No matter where the financing originates, it is the education, not the dollars that pay for it, that effects the change in the students. Ignoring numerous studies by the representative, some of which indeed noted Pell Grant financing, is particularly obstreperous. Along with the myriad of other erroneous "facts" cited by Gordon, his credibility on the issue, to say the least, is suspect.

Finally, Charles Sullivan, the executive director of the Citizens United for the Rehabilitation of Errants public interest group, explains that Gordon's legislation smacks of racism since the majority of the penal population is composed of minorities (Berkey, 1993I), and thus minority groups will be disproportionately affected by banning the Pell Grants for prisoners. In fact, several studies (Blumenstein and Cohen, 1979; Haviland, 1982; Holloway and Moke, 1986; Wreford, 1990) have noted that post-secondary correctional education enrollments largely reflect the ethnic composition of prisons. Beverley Coles, director of education and housing for the NAACP, observes that the higher education shortfall has made college education increasingly inaccessible for African-American students, 85 percent of whom receive some type of aid (Del Valle, 1992). And with more young black males in prison than on college campuses (Maurer, 1990), Sullivan (1991) wonders, as absurd as the concept is, about having to go to prison to receive a college education, are we now going to close that avenue off, as well?

Lillis (1993B) in the *Corrections Compendium*, comments on financing correctional education. She points out that "voters and legislators around the country must choose between inmate rehabilitation or inmate recidivism". By playing to the "cheap seats" in the rhetoric of getting tough on crime and fighting government waste, the advocates for excluding prisoners from Pell Grant participation are only exacerbating the agony perpetuated by the continued criminalization, victimization and reincarceration plaguing our society.

In the final analysis, piercing the fog of how many grants, how much money, how else to fund, et cetera, the elimination of prisoner Pell Grant eligibility affects the closure of post-secondary correctional education opportunities in the United States. Questioning the wisdom of the ban when it was still a proposal, Fernando Garcia, a 21 year-old prisoner at the Camp Hill Penitentiary in Pennsylvania, wondered, "Why stop me from becoming a better person?" (Berkey, 1993F). With all the factors considered, "Why indeed?"

REFERENCES

Associated Press (1992). "Pell Grants Ran Over Budget". (August 25).

Austin, A. & Irwin, J. (1990). *Who Goes to Prison?* San Francisco, CA: National Council on Crime and Delinquency.

Barker, E. (1986). "The Liberal Arts in the Correctional Setting: 'Education Befitting Free Men' — For Those Who Presently Are Not Free", Presented at the Correctional Education Association Conference, Cincinnati, OH.

Bell. R., Conrad, E., Lafley, T. Lutz, J., Miller, P., Simon, C., Stakelon, A. & Wilson, H. (1979). *Correctional Education Programs for Inmates*. U.S. Department of Justice, Washington, D.C.

Bell, R., Conrad, E. & Suppa, R. (1984). "Findings and Recommendations of the National Study on Learning Deficiencies in Adult Inmates", *Journal of Correctional Education*, V. 35, N.4:129–137.

Berkey, K. (1993A). "Holden Takes Articles to the House Floor", *The Mercury* (October 28):A1, A4.

———. (1993B). "College Grants Meant for Students go to Cons", *The Mercury*, (October 24):A1, A4.

———. (1993C) "Policeman's Daughter can't get Pell Grant", *The Mercury* (October 26):A1, A4.

———. (1993D). "Inmates learn — the Hardway", *The Mercury* (October 25):A5.

———. (1993E). "More Pa. Jails, More Pell Grants", *The Mercury* (October 25):A1, A4.

———. (1993F). "Commit Murder, Go to College", *The Mercury* (October 27):A1, A4.

———. (1993G). "P.B.I.: Pottstown, Prison Business Institute", *The Mercury* (October 25):A1, A4.

———. (1993H). "Pell Grants Never Meant for Inmates", *The Mercury* (October 24):A1, A5.

———. (1993I). "Drugs Led to Prison & College", *The Mercury* (October 26):A1, A5.

Bernstein, A. (1991). "Is Uncle Sam Shortchanging Young Americans?" *Business Week* (August 19):85.

———. (1993A). "The Young and the Jobless", *Business Week* (August 16):107.

Bernstein, A. & Magnusson, P. (1993). "How Much Good Will Training Do?" *Business Week* (February 22):76–77.

Bureau of Justice Statistics (1992). "Bureau of Justice Statistics: National Update", U.S. Department of Justice (January) V. 1, N3.

Blackburn, F. (1979). *The Relationship Between Recidivism and Participation in Community College Associate of Arts Degree Program for Incarcerated Offenders*. Ed.D. Dissertation, Virginia Polytechnic Institute and State University.

Blumenstein, A. & Cohen, J. (1979). "Control of Selection Effects in the Evaluation of Social Problems", *Evaluation Quarterly*, V. 3, N 4:583–608.

Blumenstyk, G. (1991). "Use of Pell Grants to Educate Inmates Provokes Criticism", *The Chronicle of Higher Education* (June 5):A1, A20.

Cauchon, D. (1992). "Lock 'em up Policy Under Attack", *USA Today* (September 1).

Chancelor, F. (1992). *A Study of Alabama Prison Recidivism Rates of Those Inmates Having Completed Vocational and Academic Programs While Incarcerated Between the Years of 1987 thru 1991*. A special report by the Department of Post-Secondary Education, Alabama Department of Corrections.

Clark, P. (1991). *Analysis of Return Rates of the Inmate Program Participants*. Albany, NY: New York Department of Correctional Services.

Clark, R. (1970). *Crime in America*. New York: Simon & Schuster.

Congressional Record-House (1992A). "Amendment Offered by Mr. Coleman of Missouri", (March 26):1892–98.

Congressional Record-Senate (1992). "Higher Education Amendments", (February 21):1947–1969.

———. (1993). "Amendment No. 1158", (November 16):15746.

Conrad, J. (1981). *Adult Offender Education Program*. Cambridge. MA: Abt Associates, Inc.

Corcoran, F. (1985). "Pedagogy in Prison: Teaching in Maximum Security Institutions", *Communications Education*, V. 34, I.1:49–58.

CURE Newsletter (1992). "Prisoners will CONTINUE to Receive Pell Grants", (Summer): 1.

Currie, E. (1994). "What's Wrong With the Crime Bill?", *The Nation* (January 31):118–121.

Cutler, B. (1989). "Up the Down Staircase", *American Demographics* (April):32–41.

Del Valle, C., Schine, E. & McWilliams, G. (1992). "A Lot Less Moola-Moola On Campus", *Business Week* (October 5):114–115.

Drucker, P. (1989). "How Schools Must Change", *Psychology Today* (May):18–20.

Duguid, S. (1981). "Rehabilitation Through Education: A Canadian Model", in Lucian Morain (ed.) *On Prison Education*. Ottawa, Canada: Canadian Publishing Centre.

Farrell, C. (1993). "Time to Prune the Ivy", *Business Week* (May 24):112–118.

Fenyvesi, C. (1993). "Washington Whispers: Tuition Fraud", *U.S. News & World Report*, (September 27):21.

Foust, D. (1993). "Student Loans Ain't Broke. Don't Fix 'Em", *Business Week* (April 5): 74.

Gauker, J. (1993). "Irresponsible Pell Grant/Prisoner Sensationalism", *Graterfriends*, V. 11, N.8:1.

Gergen, D. (1992). "Welcome to Great Society II", *U.S. News & World Report* (August 1): 42.

Greenfeld, L. (1985). "Examining Recidivism", *U.S. Department of Justice, Bureau of Justice Statistics*.

Gaither, C. (1980). "An Evaluation of the Texas Department of Corrections' Junior College Program", Huntsville, TX: *Department of Correction Treatment Directorate, Research and Development Division*.

Greenwood, D. & Turner, S. (1985). *The Vision Quest Program: An Evaluation*. Santa Monica, CA: Rand Corporation.

Greider, W. (1991). "The Politics of Diversion, Blame It on the Blacks", *Rolling Stone*, (September 5):32, 33, 96.

Haber, G. (1983). "The Realization of Potential by Lorton, D.C. Inmates with UDC Education Compared to Those Without UDC Education", *Journal of Offender Services, Counseling and Rehabilitation*, 7: 37–55.

Haviland, J. (1982). *A Study of the Differences Between Prison College Graduates and the Total Released Inmate Population on Recidivism by Risk Category*. Unpublished Doctoral Dissertation, Western Michigan University.

Heins, V. (1994). "Governor Helps Break Ground for San Diego Prison", *The Caller-Times* (February 26).

Hitchens, C. (1993). "Minority Report", *The Nation* (August 9/16):164.

Holloway, J. & Moke, P. (1986). *Post-Secondary Correctional Education: An Evaluation of Parole Performance*. Wilmington, OH: Wilmington College.

Horvath, G. (1982). "Issues in Correctional Education: A Conundrum of Conflict", *Journal of Correctional Education*, 33:8–15.

Hutchison, K. (1994). "Should Inmates Get Student Aid? NO: Deserving Pupils Lose Out on Pell Grants", *USA Today* (March 17):13A.

Innes, C. (1988). "Profile of Inmates 1986, Special Report", U.S. Department of Justice, Bureau of Justice Statistics: NCJ-109926.

Inside Journal (1993). "Criminal Justice Crisis Index Compares States", (Nov/Dec): 1, 3.

Insight (1992). "Frank Words" (June 1):29.

Ivins, M. (1994). "My Friends, the Time is Not Yet", *The Nation* (February 7):159–161.

Justice Watch (1992). "From a Concerned Citizen" (Spring):4.

Koretz, G. (1993). "Community College Educations Pay Off in the Labor Market", *Business Week*, (May 24):22.

Kozol, J. (1985). *Illiterate America*. New York, NY: Anchor Press.

Krammer, M. (1993). "Clinton's Drug Policy Is a Bust", *Time* (December 20):35.

Krauss, C. (1992). "Senate Votes to Expand Aid to Needy College Students", *New York Times* (February 22):6.

Leonard, J. (1994). "Our Life and Times", *The Nation* (February 21):238–242.

Lillis, J. (1993A). "DOC Budget Nearly $22 Billion", *Corrections Compendium*, V 18, N. 9 (September):7, 10.

———. (1993B). "Cutbacks May Endanger Inmate Education", *Corrections Compendium*, V. 18, N. 9 (September):1–4.

———. (1994). "Prison Education Programs Reduced", *Corrections Compendium*, V. 19, N. 3 (March):1–4.

Lawyer, H. & Pertinger, T. (1993). "Back to School or Back to Jail?" *Criminal Justice* (Winter):21, 51–52.

Lorton Prison College Program — Annual Report (1990). Division of Continuing Education, University of the District of Columbia (November).

Mauer, M. (1990). "The Sentencing Project Receives National Attention", *The Sentencing Project* (Summer).

McNamee, M. (1994). "Robert's Rules of Order", *Business Week* (January 24):74–75.

Minton, J. (1993). "Crime Prevention Keys Lies in the Next Generation", *The Advocate* (January 19).

Money, J. (1992). "Pell Grant Bill May End Prison Programs", *Hagerstown Morning* (April):A-1.

Parade Magazine (1994). "The Best & Worst of Everything" (January 2): 5.

Parlett, T. (1981). "The Benefits of Advanced Education in Prison", in Lucian Morain (ed.), *On Prison Education*. Ottawa, Canada: Canadian Publishing Centre.

Pell, C. (1994). "Should Prisoner Get Student Aid? YES: Pell Grants Dramatically Reduce Recidivism", *USA Today* (March 17):13A.

Perkins, C. (1993). *National Corrections Reporting Program, 1990*. Bureau of Justice Statistics, U.S. Department of Justice (May).

Peters, H. (1993). "Letter to Members of the International Correctional Association", Illinois Department of Corrections (April 13).

Psychology Today (1983). "Learning Maketh an Honest Man" (April):77.

Quay, H. (1973). "What Corrections Can Correct and How", *Federal Probation* (June).

Quinn, J. (1992). "The New Rules for College Aid", *Newsweek* (September 21):74.

Robinson, W., et al. (1990). *Prison Populations Cost Illustrative Projections*, 1980. Washington, D.C. G.P.O.

Ryan, T. & Woodard, J. (1987). *Correctional Education: A State of the Art Analysis.* National Institute of Corrections (July 7).

Samuelson, R. (1992). "The Value of College", *Newsweek* (August 31):75.

Sanders, B. (1993). "Clinton Must Go to the People", *The Nation*, (June 21):865–867.

Sarri, R. (1993). "Educational Programs in the State Department of Corrections: A Survey of the States", Paper presented at the American Society of Criminology, Phoenix, AZ (November).

Schwartz, G. & Koch, C. (1992). "U.S. Department of Education's Correctional Initiatives", *Issues in Teacher Education*, V. 1, N. 2:100–108.

Spillane, M. & Shapiro, B. (1992). "A Small Circle of Friends", *The Nation* (September 21):278–281.

Stephan, J. (1992). *Census of State and Federal Correctional Facilities, 1990.* Bureau of Justice Statistics, U.S. Department of Justice (May): NCJ-137003.

Steurer, S. (1993). "Legislative Accomplishments", *CEA News & Notes*, V. 15, N. 3 (July):6.

Sullivan, C. (1991). "Correspondence: Dear Board Members", *CURE* (August).

Sullivan (1994). "FACT SHEET", *CURE*.

Taylor, J. (1992). "Post-Secondary Correctional Education: An Evaluation of Effectiveness and Efficiency", *Journal of Correctional Education*, V. 43,1. 3 (September):132–141.

———. (1993A). "Pell Grants for Prisoners", *The Nation* (January 25):88–91.

———. (1993B). "Deja Vu All Over Again", *Indiana Defender* (September):23.

———. (1994). "Should Prisoners Have Access to Collegiate Education? A Policy Issue", *Educational Policy* V. 8, N. 3 (September):315–338.

The Washington Spectator (1992). "FYI, Items of Interest from Spectator Files", V. 18, N. 20 (November):4.

Thomas, F. (1974). "Narrative Evaluation Report on the Institute for Educational Media Technology", *Burlington County Collect*, NJ.

Thompson, J. (1976). *Report on Follow-up Evaluation Survey of Former Inmate Students of Alexander City State Junior College.* Alexander City State Junior College, AL (July).

Toch, T. & Slafsky, T. (1991). "The Great College Tumble", *U.S. News World Report*, (June 3):50.

Wagner, B. (1993). "The High Cost of Learning", *U.S. News & World Report* (June 21): 58.

Wildstrom, S. (1993). "Washington is Becoming a City of Amateurs", *Business Week* (October 11):42.

Will, G. (1994). "Prisoners. Pell Grants and Public Safety", *Washington Writers Group* (January 31).

Wolf, J. & Wylves, D. (1981). *The Impact of Higher Education Opportunity Programs: Post Prison Experience of Disadvantaged Students: A Preliminary Follow-up of HEOP Ex-Offenders*. Albany, NY.

Workforce 2000: Work and Workers in the 21ˢᵗ Century. Hudson Institute, Indianapolis, IN.

Wreford, P. (1990). *Community College Prison Program Graduation and Recidivism*. Unpublished Doctoral Dissertation, University of Michigan.

Where Have All the Superpredators Gone?
Jon Marc Taylor

> For every complex problem, there is a solution which is short,
> simple, and wrong.
>
> H.L. Mencken

Nearly two years ago, in a *St. Louis Post-Dispatch* featured editorial, Ph.D. candidate T. Markus Funk joined the litany of foreboding prognosticators giving admonition of the states' failures in addressing the growing wave of juvenile delinquency.[1] He was echoing what professors James Alan Fox of Northeastern University, James Q. Wilson of UCLA, and John J. Dilulio of Princeton — a prolifically vocal triumvirate of the "lock 'em up and throw away the key" school of criminology — had been advocating since 1994.[2]

This trio considered the rising teenage crime rates beginning in 1985 — along with the maturing of the baby boomlet into their most crime-prone teenage years, which in 2016 will crest at four million more than the post-WWII baby boomers did in the mid-1970s[3] — as cause for concern of an impending tidal wave of dangerous, violent "superpredators" terrorizing an unprepared nation. Professor Fox went so far as to coin the soap-operatic sound byte, labelling this predicted scourge as the "young and the ruthless".[4]

Politicians who never miss an opportunity to "fight crime" jumped on the bandwagon passing laws to quash the rampaging youth. "When it comes to crime", Fox cogently quips, "politicians believe in the three Rs: Retribution, Revenge, and Retaliation, which they think takes them to the fourth — Re-election".[5]

In a flurry of bills, all the state legislatures passed laws allowing for kids from sixteen to ten — with twenty states setting no minimum ages — to be prosecuted as adults.[6] Amnesty International recently estimated that 200,000 children are prosecuted in adult courts every year, while 7,000 are held in adult jails and 11,000 are serving time in adult and other correctional centres.[7] Thirty-eight states already house adult-adjudicated juveniles in adult prisons with no special or separate programs.[8] Currently there are seventy men on death rows for crimes committed as juveniles, with a dozen more since 1976 already having been put to death.[9]

In Washington, as well. Congress tried to hitch their own buggy to the national caravan of childhood punishments. The recently failed *Juvenile*

Crime Control Act would have: economically blackmailed states with federal grant money, requiring them to open juvenile records to the public; permitted prosecutors (not judges, as current practice) to determine whether to prosecute thirteen-year-olds accused of serious drug or violent crimes as adults; and allowed states taking federal funds to imprison juveniles with adults — an action that, ironically, the federal largesse presently prohibits.[10] Even more revealing than its particular elements, the bill's sponsor Rep. Bill McCollum referred to violent juvenile offenders as "the most vile human beings on the face of the continent". His prescription is that they "should be thrown in jail, the key should be thrown away and there should be very little or no effort to rehabilitate them".[11]

All in all, it would be difficult to argue that we are not tough on crime, juvenile or adult. The only problem with the Four Horsemen of the Delinquent Apocalypse's remonstrations is that the teenage assault against the ramparts of our civilization never materialized. Looking back on his dire finger-waving, T. Markus should be in a funk. As the "ticking demographic time bomb" was being pontificated upon,[12] stirring a plethora of punitive penal amendments, a funny thing happened on the way to the hoosegow. The felonious flare-up never erupted. In fact, the opposite occurred.

From 1993 to 1997, juvenile arrest rates for murder dropped by nearly half,[13] and in just the two years between 1994 and 1996, juvenile arrests for all violent crimes decreased by almost twenty percent.[14] The whole time these crime rates were declining, teenage populations were steadily increasing.[15] Moreover, according to the Office of Juvenile Justice and Delinquency Prevention, only one-half of one percent of youths between ages ten to seventeen were arrested for violent crimes.[16] As William Schulz, executive director of Amnesty International observes, "the image that we now have of huge numbers of murderous juveniles who need to be taught a harsh lesson by society is a myth".[17]

Attempting to explain the early decline in juvenile crime rates in November 1995, Dilulio called the dip "the lull before the crime storm". Two months later, writing for the Council on Crime in America (an organization of prosecutors and law enforcement experts), the Princeton professor warned of the delinquent time bomb set to detonate in a few years. If this modified forecast had been correct, comments Franklin Zimrig, a professor of law at the University of California at Berkeley, "we should have our umbrellas open right now" in 1999.[18] Instead we have been slathering on sunscreen, heading to the beach under increasingly peaceful, clearing skies.

Yet the terrible costs to our children and eventually ourselves by the needlessly harsh lessons we are handing down can never be fully tolled. Nationally, two-thirds of juveniles waived to adult courts were non-violent offenders. Juvenile drug offenders were waived to adult court at one-third greater rates than were violent offenders, while the rate at which youth drug offences were shifted to adult courts doubled between 1992 and 1998.[19] More specifically, by example, since Ohio permitted teens as young as fourteen to be charged as adults in 1995, the number of juveniles so tried has increased seventy percent in just two years.[20]

And what result are we achieving by this excessive punitiveness? Youth in adult facilities are five times as likely to be raped, twice as likely to be beaten by staff, and horrifyingly eight times as likely to commit suicide as adult prisoners in the same institutions.[21] The physical and psychological trauma incurred by youth in adult prisons is so endemic that the Children's Defense Fund scornfully retitled Congress's proposed Juvenile Crime bill as the "Child Rape Opportunity and Criminal Mentoring Act".[22] Not surprisingly, in separate studies the National Institute of Justice, and the National Council on Criminal Delinquency, found that juveniles processed through the adult system were thirty percent more likely to recidivate, committing more crimes than like youthful offenders held in the juvenile system.[23]

"Simply put", comments Vincent Schiraldi, the director of the Center on Juvenile and Criminal Justice, "adult institutions are a nightmare".[24]

*****

Some may contend that it has been the very actions of the state's "cracking down" on wayward youth that has nipped the perennial weed of crime in the maleficent bud. Fox's colleague at Northeastern, Jack Levin, makes this very argument claiming the doomsaying criminologists deserve credit for raising the plague flag in containing the contamination.[25] There are a few problems, however, with this assumption.

First, juvenile crime rates began declining before most of the legal changes became effective. The rates dropped sooner and even faster than the most optimistic draconian advocates could have divined. And as we have seen, the harshness of the penalties indiscriminately sweep up tens of thousands, contributing more to perpetuating the anti-social mindset than rehabilitating the errant kids punished as adults.

Secondly, the waning of juvenile violence has more to do with changes outside of the legal system than anything else. A study released by the Justice Department concluded that the most significant reason for the decline in homicide rates was the dissipation of the crack epidemic. Another study of 142 cities found that the "emergence and proliferation of crack cocaine is responsible, at least in part, for the increase in violent crime", especially robberies in the 1980s.[26]

Alfred Blumstein, a criminologist at Carnegie Mellon University, observed the connection between the marketing of crack and juvenile violence was especially strong.[27] "You had a lot of kids recruited to sell it", he said, "they armed themselves, and then their friends got guns, too, to protect themselves", setting off a bloody arms race on the streets. Professor Rosenfeld, of the University of Missouri, also adds that the pharmacological effects of a short intense high crashing to paranoia created a volatile, urgent demand. He comments that combined with legions of armed youthful sellers, buyers and bystanders, "this generates lots of competition and greater levels of violence".[28]

Since peaking in 1988, overall crack cocaine use has declined by more than seventy percent,[29] while general drug abuse has increased slightly. Complementing this change, concerted community efforts combining focused social and employment services, church activism, and community policing strategies have had a massive impact on preventing teen delinquency. For example, Boston's model Ten-Point Coalition — which contributed to the lowering of juvenile homicides in that city to a single one in the past three years — has been highly successful in achieving across-the-board reductions in offending.[30] All the while, Massachusetts maintains the second-lowest juvenile incarceration rate in the country.[31]

So much for the clarion call for secure cells in the quest for safe communities.

*****

Two years ago, Marcus Funk warned us that "today's optimism about declining crime rates may soon fade".[32] Last month, James Wilson admitted that "so far, it clearly hasn't happened". Self-deprecatingly, he continued, "this is a good indication of what little all of us know about criminology".[33] What we do know is that politically popular efforts calling for more prisons and pushing more people into them for longer periods of time is an end game that eventually punishes us all. As an adult, the loss of freedom is a terrible thing. As a child, the loss of innocence is a tragedy. What we should remember when reading the pronouncements of overly-assured soothsayers such as Fox, Wilson, Dilulio, and Funk is that statistics are not destiny.

NOTES

1   Funk, T. M. (6-10-97) "Forgive-and-Forget Approach Won't Halt Juvenile Crime", *St. Louis Post-Dispatch.*
2   Steinberg, J. (1-3-99) "Teenage crime rate down despite prediction", *New York Times.*
3   Zinn, L. et al. (4-11-94) "Teens: Here Comes the Biggest Wave Yet", *Business Week.*
4   Johnson, K. (10-3-97) "Young and the ruthless never materialized", *USA Today.*
5   Gregory, T. et al. (4-27-98) "It's 4:00 pm: Do you know where your children are?" *Newsweek.*
6   Puente, M. (4-1-98) "Law getting tougher on children", *USA Today.*
7   (11-18-98) "Amnesty rips juvenile justice system", *L.A. Times.*
8   (11-18-98) "Report: More incarcerated teens abused", *Associated Press.*
9   Jones, C. (4-13-98) "Old enough to pay the ultimate penalty", *USA Today.* (1-28-99) "Condemned killer loses bid for clemency", *Associated Press.*
10 Wickham, D. (2-10-98) "Avoid jailing juveniles with hardened adults", *USA Today.*
11 (9-97) "A Matter of Fact", *Prison Legal News*, p. 9.
12 Zuckerman, M. (4-1-98) "Scary kids around the corner", *U.S. News & World Report.*
13 (11-20-98) "Arresting of youths for crimes of violence fall, Reno says", *Associated Press.*
14 Puente (4-1-98).
15 Zinn et al. (4-11-94).
16 Peterson, K. (9-29-98) "Public Clamors: Get-tough at a tender age", *USA Today.*
17 *L.A. Times* (11-18-98).
18 Steinberg (1-3-99).
19 Snavely, K. (Summer, 1996) "States Catch Waiver Trend", *The Drug Policy Letter.*
20 *Prison Legal News.*
21 (11-18-98).
22 Wickham (2-10-98).
23 Puente (4-1-98). Butterfeld, K. (10-27-97) "Drop in Homicide Rate Linked to Crack's Decline", *New York Times.*
24 Peterson (9-29-98).
25 Johnson (10-3-97).
26 Harden, B. (10-23-97) "Boston's Approach to Juvenile Crime Encircles Youths, Reduces Slayings", *Washington Post.*
27 Stewart, R. (Summer, 1996) "Alfred Blumstein: Youth, Guns and the Drug Trade", *The Drug Policy Letter.*
28 Harden, B. (10-23-97) "Boston's Approach to Juvenile Crime Encircles Youths, Reduces Slayings", *Washington Post.*
29 Ibid.

30 Fields, G. (10-25-96) "Boston hasn't had a juvenile homicide in '96", *USA Today*.
31 Harden (10-23-97).
32 Funk (6-10-97).
33 Steinberg (1-3-99).

Life and Death in America:
The Killing of Amadou Diallo
Charles Huckelbury, Jr.

Justice is the end of government.

James Madison, *The Federalist* #51

It is the madness of folly to expect mercy from those who have refused to do justice.

Thomas Paine, *The American Crisis* #1

A little after midnight on February 4, 1999, Amadou Diallo was standing in the entry to his apartment in New York City. Mr. Diallo had committed neither felony nor misdemeanor; he was a West African immigrant and street vendor without criminal history who had come to the United States believing the promise of Emma Lazarus's poem engraved on the Statue of Liberty. He was not wearing a mask, and he was not displaying a weapon. In short, he was not doing anything remarkable to distinguish him from any other citizen. He had not, however, considered two liabilities that put his liberty in danger and ultimately cost him his life: he was black and living in the wrong part of the city.

As Mr. Diallo stood in his vestibule looking out on the street in front of his apartment, he was approached by four white policemen — all were members of the Street Crimes Unit, a special tactical squad emphasizing the identification and arrest of neighbourhood thugs. None of the police officers were in uniform, and all were large, intimidating, muscular men with the requisite attitude for doing their job — which is to say, they looked for trouble, expected to find it, and did not mind so much when they did.

As testimony subsequently revealed, the police officers were looking for a black rapist, and Diallo had the misfortune to be black and living in the same area where the suspect committed his crime. Moreover, one of Diallo's neighbours had called police and reported that he (Diallo) was acting "suspiciously". Thus, when the four officers approached Mr. Diallo, they were primed.

When all four were within approximately ten feet from Diallo, they reportedly identified themselves as police officers and ordered him not to move. Unaccustomed to being accosted by the police, Mr. Diallo responded reasonably to the officers' presence and verbal order by attempting to withdraw his wallet from his hip pocket, presumably to offer identification. As soon as the wallet was out of his pocket, one of the police officers yelled "Gun", and all four men drew their weapons and opened fire on the unsuspecting immigrant. Forensic evidence revealed that the officers fired forty-one times, with nineteen rounds striking Diallo, at least two of which entered the bottom of his feet as he lay on the floor of the vestibule. He was dead in seconds.

In and of itself, the killing of Amadou Diallo would have been tragic enough. Four police officers gunning down an unarmed and totally innocent man, while not unheard of in this country, certainly should have provoked enough outrage and re-examination of police policy to ensure that such a profound blunder would not happen again, or at the very least, that the chances for such a catastrophe would be greatly diminished. The tragedy was compounded, however, by the subsequent testimony at trial of the four officers indicted for Diallo's murder. Not only was Amadou Diallo sent to a premature grave by representatives of the government, he was made complicit in his own death, and the men who killed him walked out of the courtroom and returned to their families and jobs.

Revisiting the accounts of Diallo's behaviour that night, it is noteworthy that during the initial investigation, he was not accused of doing anything that might have provoked such a vicious fusillade. He was not a wanted criminal, and he had no prior record. He earned a living as a street vendor, and he was doing nothing more threatening than standing in his own vestibule looking at the activity in the street. A rational person would think that anyone standing on his or her own property, observing the street, would not present a threat requiring forty-one rounds of ammunition. Diallo was simply a reportedly "suspicious" person.

The vestibule where Diallo stood was well lighted, and he attempted to do what any right-thinking citizen would do when confronted with four aggressive police officers; he unhesitatingly tried to present identification, a standard but offensive requirement when demanded in this day of no-nonsense law enforcement and unrestricted police license. That is, by any objective standard. Amadou Diallo did absolutely nothing to precipitate his death. Indeed, so innocent was Mr. Diallo that one of the police officers at the scene cradled his head after the shooting and begged him not to die, a rather disingenuous request, considering that same police officer had just done everything in his power to kill him. And then came the trial testimony.

The police officers all took the stand in their defense and described a series of events that night that shifted the blame for the tragedy directly onto Diallo's cold, dead shoulders. It was the felonious equivalent of finding him guilty of the tort offense of contributory negligence in his own death. By the time they got to trial nearly a year later, the police officers told a cohesive version of what had happened that night. Now the vestibule became "dimly lighted". Diallo was acting like a suspect, here defined as being black and looking first in one direction, then the other. When the four officers approached him, at least one held out a badge for identification and "asked" to talk to Diallo. (Only in Colorado after JonBenet Ramsey's murder have the police ever *requested* an interview.) According to the officers' trial testimony, Diallo responded by moving back into the recesses of his apartment's vestibule and reaching for his hip pocket. Ignoring shouted commands to show his hands, Diallo adopted a "combat stance" and pulled his wallet.

As soon as the wallet was visible, one of the officers mistakenly identified a firearm and screamed a warning to his companions. At this point, one of the other police officers apparently tripped and fell to the ground, thereby, according to testimony, leading the other officers to believe that he had been shot by Mr. Diallo. It was never sufficiently explained how the police officer who tripped could have been shot when there was neither sound of a gunshot nor sign of a muzzle flash from a weapon. Nevertheless, all four officers began firing wildly at Diallo. Only after he was dead and a search begun for the weapon did the police discover the magnitude of their mistake. Thus began the futile attempts to stanch the flow of blood from the nineteen holes in Amadou Diallo's rapidly cooling body.

The officers also tried to explain away the number of shots fired by testifying that the sparks from the many ricochets from their own gunfire made them believe that Diallo was returning fire, thus provoking an even more intense response from the police officers. For those who have watched action movies starring Mel Gibson or Sylvester Stallone, ricochets perhaps do spark off everything from car fenders to modeling clay, but that is Hollywood's version (like the laser duels in *Star Wars*) and bears no resemblance to reality. Amadou Diallo's building was brick and wood. Lead striking wood is absorbed; lead striking brick is indeed deflected but without producing a spark that would indicate the bullet's striking another metal. In other words, there could not have been any sparks that night because wood and brick do not generate them when struck by expended pistol rounds.

Did the police lie or were they simply mistaken in their abject terror in the presence of what they thought was an armed adversary? Twelve men and women heard the testimony, twelve men and women who had never been close to a shoot-out and would not know gunfire from a backfire, and they held that the killing of Amadou Diallo was justified.

It is not the purpose of this essay to determine whether the police officers embellished their story or if they truly believed a lone unarmed man was attempting to kill them by firing even more rapidly than four of them in concert were capable of. What I would like to explore here is another, more pernicious explanation that runs parallel to the truth about the shooting and involves the attitude instilled and nurtured in police departments in general and in tactical units specifically that promotes tragedies like the killing of Amadou Diallo. It is the intense militarization of the police over the past two decades that has culminated in the belief by the men and women who work the streets that they are indeed soldiers operating with the same rules of engagement that govern armed forces overseas. And it is this precise attitude that causes police officers to view citizens of this country, citizens who have done nothing illegal, as threats in the domestic equivalent of a free-fire zone.

Like any competent combat unit, police tactical squads develop an *esprit de corps* that promotes overreaction when confronted with a hostile or dangerous situation. The tactical advantages of massive firepower are currently taught in police academies, and the officers in the Diallo killing testified that they had been instructed to empty their weapons in a gunfight. Tactical officers also *expect* trouble, similar to soldiers on a combat patrol. And, if the truth is not too harsh, these men and the occasional woman not only anticipate confrontation — they look forward to it. After all, it is why they train, and like any good combat unit, the training is only preparation for the real thing, in this case, armed confrontations on the street. Compounding the situation is the racial distribution of these tactical squads; most are predominately or exclusively white, while their anticipated adversaries — and this is fundamental to the results — are predominately or exclusively people of color. Add to that the adrenaline surging during such an encounter, and you have a recipe for disaster.

Tragedies like Amadou Diallo's killing, therefore, are virtually guaranteed, given the number and nature of these tactical units deployed in police departments around the country. But the John Wayne attitude is not limited to members of SWAT teams. In Louisville, Kentucky, for example, two white police officers shot and killed Desmond Randolph, a black teenager, for revving the engine of the stolen car he was driving.[1] In California, police officers surrounded the car of a sleeping teenager, also black. After first trying and failing to wake her, the police then attempted to break the driver's window. The teenager instinctively reached for the pistol lying in the seat beside her, which provoked the police into shooting her more than a dozen times in the head and upper torso.[2]

The officers who work the tactical units are volunteers, all of whom undergo both physical and psychological training in preparation for their mission, and notwithstanding the professed remorse of the defense witnesses in the Diallo case, these officers see that mission in the same terms that infantry units in the armed forces approach theirs: maximum firepower in the face of armed resistance, or in Amadou Diallo's case, suspected armed resistance.

This is not to say that police officers should be naïve enough to trust exclusively in the good faith of the men and women they are hired to protect and serve, if I may be permitted such an anachronism. Indeed, "bad guys" still roam the streets in certain areas, and all law enforcement personnel should be alert to the potential for danger. The stark facts, however, demonstrate that the risks are exaggerated and criminal defendants usually surrender rather than engage in shoot-outs with police. In fact, in any given year, police work is consistently absent among the top ten jobs in terms of mortality and injury rates. Cab drivers, lumberjacks, firefighters, and commercial fishermen all have higher rates of on-the-job deaths than police officers. Indeed, in 1999, the latest year for which statistics are available, cabbies suffered on-the-job deaths at a rate of 30 per 100,000.[3] Police officers, by comparison, died at a far lesser rate of 6.8 per 100,000, slightly less than retail-sales clerks at 6.9 per 100,000.

Moreover, the percentage of police officers actually killed by armed assailants generally comprises about half of all deaths, the others coming as a result of heart attacks, traffic accidents, suicides or other causes. So a simple statistical analysis demonstrates that the dangers purportedly inherent in police work are overrated, even in the face of counter-claims by police organizations and television shows like *COPS* and *America's Most Wanted*.

So why have police departments militarized their tactical units, and even their traditional patrol units, to such an extent? What is the justification for going among innocent citizens with a gunfighter's mentality, not only expecting to engage an armed adversary but welcoming the showdown? The answer lies partially with the self-interested promotion of politicians and certain law enforcement executives, but the other half of the equation is a confluence of public and law enforcement opinion that marginalizes individuals like Amadou Diallo and sets them up for victim status. And, sadly, American society as a whole has participated in an invidious particularism that contributes to the mutual animosity between the police and certain ethnic groups.

The particularist school of political theory allows each group (like the police) within society the right to promote its own self-interest without regard for the interests of other groups, no matter how large or small. The emphasis is therefore on group survival, rather than a stronger, healthier gestalt. Pluralism, in contrast, recognizes each group's development within a larger framework of common society. As Diane Ravitch explains it, "Instead of promoting reconciliation and a sense of shared community, particularism rekindles ancient hatreds in the present; its precepts set group against group. [Adherents] learn that it is appropriate to think of others primarily in terms of their group identity".[4] That is, individual merit and identification are subsumed within the group to which that individual belongs, relieving the "foreign" observer and group member of the responsibility for objective assessment of any other group's members.

To demonstrate, hyphenated Americans have now become the rule rather than the exception, and although ethnicity can and should be a source of pride, it can often function as a line of demarcation, separating citizens of heterogeneous backgrounds who would normally form a cohesive unit. Black Americans and immigrants of African descent, like Amadou Diallo, tend to close ranks in what they see as a self-preservation effort to stave off assimilation by a biased (and often oppressive) Eurocentric culture. That is, as society has become more ethnically self-aware, *de facto* segregation has become resurgent as racial and cultural enclaves seek to distinguish themselves and their values from mainstream lifestyles, situations in which they feel at once alienated and mistrustful. It is this fragmentation of contemporary American society that permits an unexamined subculture to avoid accountability and encourages the police, acting within their own group, to engage in the same kind of particularist philosophy as the people they observe on the street. Given their training and indoctrination in terms of this particular *zeitgeist*, police officers could hardly be expected to react to hostile situations, either perceived or actual, with other than immediate and deadly force against a particularized enemy, notably people of color.

Contrary to the almost apathetic attitude of white respondents, black Americans consistently identify racism as a primary concern and expect it in their daily encounters with white society. The deplorable condition of many predominantly black schools versus upscale white facilities; the lack of health care for the working poor and those on welfare; and the disproportionate number of black and Hispanic citizens in prison all contribute to an us-versus-them mentality, displayed in anti-establishment music, dress, and behaviours, whether in the street or on the athletic field. Conservatism, whether compassionate or the other more common variety, encourages this separation with its retrenchment or elimination of affirmative action, for example, and its perceived favouritism of the more affluent (read "white") members of society.

Law enforcement therefore becomes, in the eyes of the multicultural segments of society, a tool of the affluent, of the same constellation of predominately white males who make the laws that minorities see, rightly or wrongly, as depriving them of both their rights and their identities. Minority populations react by withholding the traditional respect extended to the police that white society (and the police themselves) expects and often demands. The police concomitantly view these autonomous displays as a rejection of the mores (and often the laws) that define the majority, which in turn produces the suspicion and anticipation that makes firearms the first response in the field. The corollary, of course, is that the police begin to reflect the majority's response to the minorities' demands: they see themselves as under-appreciated and misunderstood. They become resentful, aware of the latent hostility they face each day and paranoid in the face of any encounter, especially with people of color. They close ranks within their group and identify, as Ravitch described, other group members on the basis of external factors relating to that group's membership. A recent study of the Miami-Dade (Florida) police department confirms this analysis.

Geoffrey Alpert and Roger Dunham (1988) examined use-of-force reports for the years 1996–1998 and classified the incidents according to the race of the officers and civilians involved. The statistics demonstrate that when both police officer and arrestee were white, force was used in twenty-six percent of the reported cases. When the officer was black and the arrestee was white, force was required in sixteen percent of the cases. The study further disclosed that white police officers used force against black arrestees in forty percent of incidents, compared to sixty-seven percent when both officer and arrestee were black.[5] Chuck Wexler, the executive director of the Police Executive Research Forum, hailed the results following the Diallo trial as proof that use of force occurred more in *intra*racial arrests than during *inter*racial confrontations, thus putting the lie to accusations that the police were inherently racist.[6] After all, if police officers were more prone to use force on members of their own race, then Amadou Diallo's killing could not be characterized as a racist response by white police officers.

Wexler, however, misses the point. Although intraracial force was more common than interracial force, the ineluctable conclusion of the study, a study accepted by Wexler and his organization, is that black arrestees were subjected to the use of force far more than their white counterparts in similar situations. The racist or particularist response to this study would be that blacks are more violent and tend to resist arrest in more statistically significant numbers than whites. The more obvious conclusion is that black suspects are more likely to *evoke* a forceful response from the police, and that distinction is crucial.

The intuitive leap is therefore to assume that the police expect violent confrontations with black defendants and in general diminish the importance of black lives, thus leading to unnecessary fatalities like the killing of Amadou Diallo. But what if the *police* are victims of a psychological campaign to isolate them from society in general and minority society particularly? Consider: in 1999, forty-two police officers were feloniously killed in the line of duty, *fewer than in any other year since the FBI began keeping statistics in 1963*. But instead of welcoming the good news that America's streets are steadily becoming less violent, James Pasco, the executive director of the Fraternal Order of Police, the nation's largest police union, responded by asserting, "It's not getting safer for law enforcement. Absolutely not. There is a far greater disposition to attack law enforcement officers than there ever has been",[7] this at a time when overall crime has decreased for eight consecutive years. In other words, the police officers in the street are not being told the truth, not even by their own; they are being manipulated for personal benefit, a pernicious and vicious abuse of power that advocates an apocalyptic view and places those officers at higher risk for escalating confrontations in which they could be injured or killed.

Thus, statistical analyses such as those by Alpert and Dunham prove what the prisons confirm: that society and its judicial enforcement arm have also been the victims of a massive disinformation campaign. Americans, after all, love illusions, whether in their movies, televisions, or print media, and vested interests, including law enforcement, respond by identifying, cultivating, and maintaining an audience in order to provide what that particular group desires. This is the result of the current fragmentation of American society, a Diaspora of sorts that banishes people of color to the fringes and keeps them there, not necessarily economically or even socially constrained, but in a perceptual sense that they are somehow not one of us.

To eliminate this mutual, reactive misunderstanding, it will become necessary to drop the shields each side instinctively carries and to move toward a more pluralistic social environment, that is, one in which police and civilians look beyond group identities to establish common ground. The current emphasis on community policing is a correct step in promoting empathy, a quality sadly lacking in police academies and minority neighborhoods. But simply putting police in certain geographical areas will not eliminate the problem; the four police officers who killed Amadou Diallo were on the street in a very real sense but unconcerned with establishing community relations, and the anonymous caller who described Diallo's behavior as suspicious clearly was hostage to a stereotypical bias.

As the start of a remedy, there needs to be a dialogue between the majority and the minorities with the police as an active participant. Without some sort of regularly held symposia, in which all sides voice their concerns in an atmosphere of candor and trust, and in which accurate information is available to all, the fragmentation I have described will continue apace, all sides refusing to accept responsibility and declining to treat each other as worthy but fallible human beings. We are not combatants staring at each other's battle lines across some DMZ; it is time everyone stopped playing these dangerous roles.

The militaristic, confrontational attitude of today's urban police departments is anachronistic and does more harm than good. Although it focuses on quickly overcoming armed opposition and preserving the line officers' lives, it has resulted and will continue to result in needless civilian casualties in a specious war whose justification has expanded incrementally over three decades. The tragic paradox is that as America's streets have become progressively safer for everyone, contacts between civilians and police have become increasingly deadlier, due largely to subjective evaluations encouraged by disinformation campaigns like that of James Pasco.

America is not and never has been the "melting pot" of its reputation, but surely it must remain a republic in which, as James Madison observed, justice is the end, and in which citizens of any color or creed can safely walk the streets without fear of urban predators on either side of the law. If American society is a weave of ethnic and religious patterns, then we are all part of the same tapestry, deserving of the same respect and recognition. Just as it is certainly wrong for citizens to fire on the police, it is not unreasonable for all law-abiding citizens, no matter what their color, to demand the same consideration in return.

NOTES

1   The officers fired twenty-two times at Randolph, killing him instantly. The chief of police praised the two officers during an awards ceremony (Exceptional Valor Award) for their prompt reaction. The chief was subsequently fired by the mayor for his "insensitivity" ("Fatal shooting, delayed fallout roil Louisville", *USA Today*, March 29, 2000, v. 18, n. 139, p. 8A).

2   The officers were subsequently cleared of the shooting. They all claimed they were in fear for their lives, although they did admit they could have found a less alarming way to examine the young woman, Tyisha Miller ("Fatal Judgement", *People*, October 11, 1999, v. 52 n. 14, p. 143–9).

3   "Cabbies face fears with every fare", *USA Today*, May 2, 2000, p. 3A.

4   Quoted in David Shipler, *A Country of Strangers, Black and White in America* (New York: Knopf, 1997), p. 225.

5   "Measuring and Assessing Police Use of Force and Suspect Resistance", 1998. United States Department of Justice.

6   *USA Today*, March 13, 2000, p. 4A.

7   "Number of police slain drops to record low", *USA Today*, May 16, 2000, p. 4A

Prison Violence: How Society Can Profit from Videotaping Attacks Behind the Walls

Joe Miceli

Since rehabilitation has been completely abandoned in New York State penitentiaries, and the sole purpose for prison expansion seems to be a means to garner votes by pumping billions of dollars into the economy, I've come up with an idea. After endless nights tossing and turning in my bunk, and countless days contemplating various options, I decided to draw up this presentation for you. Commissioner Goord. Hopefully society will profit from its execution.

Although I am a prisoner, and you may at first be somewhat skeptical of my intentions, I hope you will put your feelings aside for a moment, and weigh the possibilities I now offer you. For your information — and I assume you presently do not have my folder in front of you to evaluate my credibility — I have 20 years experience behind the walls. Who is more familiar with the treacheries of life in the penitentiary? That's why I feel confident the deal I am about to share with you and your colleagues will make you reassess current policies and implement new ones. As a rule I am particularly concerned that New York State officials — you, Senator Nozzolio, Governor Pataki — receive my recommendations (and perhaps help me regain parole in return), but I think my plan could benefit corrections systems everywhere.

Before I begin, let me stress I do not anticipate your having financial difficulties, especially considering Governor Pataki's popularity among his constituents, and recent program cuts in corrections. As a matter of fact, cutbacks undoubtedly make available necessary funds that will help make this project possible. And once it's underway, education, drug addiction counseling, job skills, or the need to worry about inmates' transitions back to the street will all be irrelevant. Of course there are other areas in the Department of Corrections that can be scaled back if more money is needed. So I shall address those questions to the best of my ability. As for funds and your associates, let me say this.

If you wonder where you will find the initial cash to begin this operation, perhaps the State can appropriate a portion of the 25 million dollars a year it generates from prisoners' phone calls. If so, I predict you'll be able to repay the loan in the course of a year. In addition I suggest you abolish pay wages for prison jobs; convicts will be more than happy to work for free to get out of their cells for a few hours. You could also jack up the prices in the vending machines in the visiting rooms, increase penalties for misbehavior reports from five dollars to ten, and make prisoners pay the State for room and board.

My suggestion will ultimately accumulate more cash in one day than prison industries do in a whole year. I am not one given to bragging or making exaggerated claims. So I urge you to evaluate my recommendations carefully, and to grant them the same attention you would officers' concerns. Rest assured I make these assertions with a certain degree of confidence after conducting several studies that back them up. Primarily after consulting with a team of financial analysts at Cornell's business school, and particularly with a friend of mine there who happens to be the chief economist — and, I might add, advised me to sink every dollar I own into this venture.

As part of my analysis I conducted a "Monte Carlo Simulation", a study that predicts how much your endeavor is expected to earn over a given time period. The report predicted earned annual growth rates of 350 percent. Quite enough to stir public interest and appeal to savvy investors. So I submit to you with all honesty, Mr. Goord, this project will unquestionably pay for itself.

As I mentioned earlier, costs do have to be considered at the outset. And after discussing this at great length with my mentor at Cornell, I was assured start up expenses would be just over 12 million dollars. I realize this might seem a bit high, but I'm convinced — and the figures I have enclosed prove — that projected profits for the first month of operations will be ten times greater than the outlay for the entire production.

Financial gains aside, my game plan not only has numerous advantages for society, but also for its participants. Incidentally, you will probably have to contend with prison activists who will object to my scheme. Frankly, I welcome criticisms. They allow me to formulate new strategies and improve my agenda (although I have taken great pains to calculate a multitude of variables already). Still, I'm confident once you air the first telecast ... that's right, I'm talking about the most spectacular program in the history of television ... the event will be so successful the cries of your detractors will be drowned out by the cheers of your supporters.

Before I continue let me digress for a moment. Perhaps it's presumptuous of me to assume all your associates know precisely what goes on in our penal institutions. So with your permission, allow me to enlighten them on the bitter reality of prison life.

Every day COs (corrections officers) risk their lives when they enter correctional facilities. If a riot breaks out they are the first to be raped or killed. They can surely attest to how dangerous jails are, and how often inmates brutalize each other. It is this that makes a program like mine necessary.

Today the widespread availability of heroin in our penitentiaries and the increasing use of all sorts of drugs are not only an explosive mixture with potentially deadly consequences, but also the source of most, if not all, violent episodes. There seems to be no end to the number of men who are victimized by drug dealers they cannot pay. Besides attacks related to narcotics consumption — and I remind you the unusual incident reports included support my contentions — petty differences escalate into unbelievable acts of brutality.

One reason for this is that men are forced to house together in double bunk cells. Case in point: Two inmates at Upstate's special housing unit clashed in their cell in May. Not surprisingly the battle was over something as meaningless as a fluorescent light. *Associated Press* reported that one prisoner liked to sleep late and stay up at night to read, while the other was an early riser who liked to go to sleep early. The dispute ended when the larger and stronger combatant used his hands and feet to pummel his cellmate to death. This illustration supports my position perfectly. So for your consideration, here is my proposal.

On any given day in New York State, convicts are being killed, assaulted, burned with hot cooking oil, stabbed, bludgeoned, disfigured, raped, and slashed to ribbons. Few, if any of these battles are recorded. If hidden video cameras had been installed at Upstate do you suppose it would have been interesting to watch from the comfort of your living room? I do. That's why I urge you to video tape all assaults and market them world wide.

The inspiration for this occurred to me one night after skimming through an old *Gallery* magazine. Inside was a story about Ultimate Fighting Championships (UFC) in New York. Several photos depicted wide eyed, musclebound contestants, squared off hand to hand in blood splattered octagonal cages. The bouts were described as "The hottest pay-per-view sport on television". According to the article, men fight in no-holds-barred matches until one either gives up or is knocked out.

I immediately saw striking similarities between UFC competitions and the combats in our facilities. Soon I realized that people all over the world are dying to see this type of entertainment. The popularity of shows like *Jerry Springer* and Reality TV prove this. So I thought, why not provide the public with authentic, gory, gladiatorial contests. The Romans packed stadiums full of thousands of fans eager to see Christians devoured by wild beasts and slaves hacked to pieces.

As you see by the incident at Upstate, penitentiaries breed hostility. On an average day hundreds of prisoners are ripped with razors, and even more are victimized by one of the several unpleasant methods I described earlier. Of course since security is woefully inadequate, and video cameras are not in place, disturbances like these are neither documented nor exploited. So for that purpose, and considering UFC's success, I contacted a man who could tell me how to turn the prison carnage into dollar signs.

Mr. John Markowitz, the president of New-York-based Spartacus Entertainment, found my idea fascinating. He said: "It has the potential to be immensely profitable". Mr. Markowitz explained: "Tough man competitions in New York and Europe have been sensational ... customers paid fifty dollars and up for tickets and they were always sold out". He emphasized that UFC subscriptions jumped from 80,000 to 350,000 in two years, and added: "There's a lot of money to be made in this business; however, there are obstacles you will have to overcome. Particularly opponents who will seek to ban your events the same way they outlawed the UFCs".

Chief among the pointed accusations hurled at Mr. Markowitz and the UFC was that his affairs were nothing more than "Human cockfights ... savage, barbaric skirmishes that unraveled the moral fiber of humanity". The most vociferous critic was a Senator named John Goodman (R-Manhattan) who stated: "This sport has no place in civilized society and I will do everything in my power to ensure it is banned forever". Mr. Markowitz hinted the Senator was motivated by political interests because later, in response to "community leaders concerns" (it was election year), Goodman wrote several articles for the *Daily News* condemning the UFC. In one dated October 28, 1985 he said: "New York cannot and will not become a haven for this type of bloodthirsty activity".

Political considerations aside, I believe Mr. Goodman is out of touch with reality. The fact is that countless acts of uncivilized cruelties occur every day in the corrections facilities of Mr. Goodman's home state that make tough-man competitions look like *Snow White and the Seven Dwarfs*. My intention is to showcase these incidents, and use them to aid society.

Regardless of how citizens view violence, it still flourishes in our institutions. Remember Corcoran State Penitentiary in California? Officers there pitted Black and Latino gang members against each other and wagered on the outcome. The fights were aptly described by the *L.A. Times* as "Blood Sports". The special report said several men at the jail were allowed to knife their enemies to death and were themselves shot and killed by marksmen in gun towers. Amazingly, every one of the triumphant combatants had received a single bullet wound to the head. After the F.B.I. had received complaints from prisoners about human rights violations at Corcoran, questions surfaced and investigators demanded to know why warning shots had not been fired first. Soon after the F.B.I. got involved several officers were arrested, and ultimately convicted in federal court. One, a captain suspected of being the master mind of the brutalities, committed suicide before he was scheduled to go on trial.

The lessons of Corcoran and the UFCs were not lost on me and I incorporated them into my strategy. During my research I dissected the mayhem and assessed the feasibility of capitalizing on prison attacks. I felt certain my idea's time had come. If citizens enjoyed seeing prisoners battle each other, imagine how much more thrilled they would be watching snipers gun them down. I decided "Blood Sport" entertainments were precisely what the public wants and needs. I could think of no better way to satisfy society's primal urge for revenge, while simultaneously performing a great service to humanity by eliminating its human waste. Here was a way, I realized, to make good use of criminals; a way to make their cruelties work for us; a way the savages could redeem themselves by titillating the passions of millions of viewers world wide.

After consulting with several electronic specialists I determined that setting up this project would require some changes in DOC's current system. Video cameras with zoom lenses would have to be positioned in strategic locations everywhere, especially in Special Housing Units, not to detect and prevent barbarity, but to exploit it. Obviously if prisoners continue to kill each other in double bunk cells, and my arrangement is approved, video taping assaults will enable officials to charge assailants with new crimes. Toss in a bunch of gangs, lax security, incompetent personnel, lots of narcotics, plenty of weapons, and you have the whole recipe. The inmates will take care of the rest.

Imagine the entertainment value. I am convinced the average citizen wants to see bloodshed. It's satisfying to sit home, turn on your television, and watch real life and death drama unfold before your eyes. Instead of opening with a catchy tune called "Bad Boys", Prison TV (PTV) would begin with the sound of slamming steel gates, the squelching of walkie talkies, the echoes of raw hateful profanities reverberating through cell blocks, and images of hard-eyed convicts, peering through cell bars with mirrors, or hanging on gates, glaring at officers during mandatory counts.

The appeal of PTV would stem from its ability to capture unadulterated film footage of gang attacks, stabbings, slashings, assaults and murders. The public has no idea about what goes on in our prisons. This type of program will satiate their curiosity. I'm positive viewers will be gripped by a sense of fascination as they watch the events in living color.

For instance: a camera pans the yard and concentrates on a group of inmates huddled around a television. All eyes are focused on a basketball game. The Lakers and Knicks are tied and there's five minutes left on the clock. The crowd is mesmerized, cheering their team, unaware of what is about to happen. Several men in hoods are paying close attention to a man at the rear of the pack. They nod to each other and disperse. Two advance like Ninjas; silently they creep closer to their target. The audience at home knows that something is wrong. They can tell the thugs who have approached the cluster are up to no good. Their body language has betrayed their intentions. The pair slide up on the unsuspecting victim from the left, one circles to his right. The designated hit man turns and aims a glance at an officer in his guard booth. His chin is resting on his hand, he's staring off in the distance; preoccupied with who knows what, oblivious to what is about to occur.

The three men nod to each other, each drawing courage from his cohorts. Instantly, spurred on by their solidarity, they act as a single unit with ruthless, military precision. One bumps his prey; it's a diversionary tactic. The mark turns left and looks at the man that bumped him. Suddenly in a flash of blinding cold steel a hand shoots out from the right and rakes a razor across his face. Blood pours from his wound and the crowd sways and rolls in panic. All eyes are wide and scanning the perimeter now. Shock and terror are etched on the expression of the man gripping his torn, flapping cheek. His assailants have scattered in several directions. The officer in the wooden shack realizes something is wrong now; the cluster of prisoners are not watching the game. He eyes the mob and spots a man bleeding profusely from his face and summons help. A swarm of cops arrive and toss several men on the wall and rush the injured man to the hospital. Real life in the penitentiary brought to you by PTV.

Of course there are some disadvantages to consider. Even prisoners dumb as nails know getting more time for killing is bad business. So sooner or later the incessant brutalities will cease and the opportunity to increase prisoners' existing sentences will be lost. Yes, convict populations will shrink and become less violent, but packs of young thugs weaned on "Gangsta Rap", eager to become TV stars, will burst through penitentiary gates to take up the slack.

First and foremost my primary concern is, and always has been, society and its victims. That's why I suggest we use a portion of the profits from PTV for both law enforcement and the crime victims associations. Our police could use these funds to improve the quality of investigative techniques and put more cops on the street. The police could also offer handsome rewards to snitches for information regarding crimes. This would diminish the number of undesirables in our communities, and fill our prisons with new, prospective combatants culled from the underclass.

Eventually PTV will serve the public by ridding it of its monsters; burying those killed during incidents (at a cost to their families) and preserving the futures of those lucky enough to be "scared straight". As a result, New York State will eventually become crime free and a much safer place to live. As Mr. Markowitz said, I realize we will have to overcome massive protests; that liberal minded bleeding hearts will say this is insane. But I'm convinced if prisoners are given the choice between dying and doing life, they will certainly choose death every time.

Skeptics may question the logic of my premise, but the fact is for some prisoners the sorrow, the pain, the loss of freedom, and the separation from loved ones, is unbearable. I can attest to that having been behind bars for the better part of twenty years, and especially after having been present in the visiting room last week and observing the following scene.

A young man rose from his table after his visit ended, kissed his teary eyed wife good-bye, and struggled to pry his tiny daughter's pink fingers from his shirt as she cried: "Daddy, daddy, please don't go".

The psychological strain of doing hard time, with absolutely no chance of ever going home, as opposed to the freedom of dying, seems, if not understandable, at least preferable. No one wants to spend his life living in fear, or suffer the interminable pain and heartache associated with being incarcerated forever. So I assure you: PTV will improve society and help inmates as well.

Theoretically crime must decrease considerably within the first five years of PTV's inception. Indeed security officials will regain control of their prisons, and bedlam should all but cease. And for most of the elderly prisoners like myself who live within the rules? We will undoubtedly live out the remainder of our time, and die peacefully of natural causes at a ripe old age. So whether or not you help me make parole, I will still reap the rewards of this program the same way society and its good citizens will.

For all the reasons listed herein I trust you will find my proposal worthy of realization and let the games begin.

PART VII

APPENDICES

This catalogue includes thematically organized and more general issues. Howard Davidson edited the first issue (1988), which focused upon prison abolitionism and included papers presented at ICOPA III. This issue introduced Jo-Ann Mayhew to the *JPP* and included her contribution of our motto, "allowing our experiences and analysis to be added to the forum that will constitute public opinion could help halt the disastrous trend toward building more fortresses of fear which will become in the 21st century this generation's monuments to failure" (*JPP* 1:1, i).

Over the next two issues, Little Rock Reed, Mumia Abu-Jamal, and Jon Marc Taylor became contributors. Volume 2:2 (1990) focused upon the imprisonment of North America's First Nations peoples and featured cover art by Norval Morrisseau and an essay by Art Solomon.

Volume 3 (1991) took the form of a double issue and focused upon two related themes — capital punishment and Prison Justice Day. Howard Davidson completed his sojourn as editor with two thematic issues for Volume 4 (1992–93). The first issue (Vol. 4:1) focused upon education programs in prison and is a companion volume to Davidson's (ed.) (1995) *Schooling in a Total Institution*. Volume 4:2 focused upon maximum-security prison regimes and the development and spread of "marionization" across the U.S.A. This large issue was edited from inside the maximum-security penitentiary at Lucasville, Ohio, by Little Rock Reed, with the help of Lisa Morgan. This issue analyzes behaviour-modification experimentation in a carceral setting, focusing especially upon the intent of close confinement regimes, and the institutional order and relationships put into place to achieve them. The contributors to this discourse were serving time in United States Penitentiary Marion, Illinois, or similar supermaximum facilities.

There was a change in editorial group responsibilities in 1993, with Bob Gaucher and John Lowman stepping in as editors. Volume 5:1 introduced Victor Hassine and included John Perotti's "Sunday, Bloody Sunday" on the Lucasville prison riot and our first report on the fugitive status of Little Rock Reed. Gayle Horii and Liz Elliott edited Volume 5:2, which addressed women's imprisonment and featured Gayle Horii (including photographs of her sculpture and drawing), Jo-Ann Mayhew, Melissa Stewart, and Norma Stafford, among others. This issue includes an in-depth discussion of the increasingly tumultuous situation at Kingston Prison for Women (P4W), which eventually led to the Arbour Inquiry (1996) and the closing of this facility in 2001. The events that unfold throughout the 1990s at P4W are also explored in subsequent volumes.

The two general issues of Volume 6 (1995) focused upon the current prison conditions and the emerging prison-industrial complex in the U.S.A. This included Victor Hassine's analysis of prison overcrowding ("Runaway Prison or Mr. Smith Goes to Harrisburg") and James Morse's deconstruction and exposure of the racial bias of the United States' crime-control industry. An interview with David Milgaard, conducted at the founding conference of the Association in the Defense of the Wrongly Convicted (AIDWYC) in Toronto, and a major "Prisoners' Struggles" section on capital punishment in the U.S.A. completed Volume 6:1. In Volume 6:2, Paul Wright, Jon Marc Taylor, and Little Rock Reed examine components of the expansion and industrialization of penal control for the "dangerous classes" in the U.S.A., including three-strikes laws, prison labour, and the conspiracy of silence of the industry's elite ACA. The "Response" essay on the Kingston Prison for Women, "Arbour Inquiry" by Kim Pate (Canadian Association of Elizabeth Fry Societies), brought us up to date on the situation at P4W addressed in Volume 5:2 (1994).

Kiernan McEvoy, in Belfast, with the help of Brian MacLean, produced our first European volume (1996–97) with issues representing Republican and Loyalist political prisoners in Northern Ireland. Mícheál Mac Giolla Ghunna, a Republican prisoner, composed and edited the Republican issue (Volume 7:1) and Brian MacLean edited the Loyalist issue (Volume 7:2). The breadth of the Republican writing is well represented in this anthology. John Lowman stepped down as co-editor after this issue.

Volumes 8:1/2 (1997), edited by Bob Gaucher and Curtis Taylor, were dedicated to Claire Culhane, the Canadian social justice activist for whom "prisons were the best fight in town". Claire's combative spirit is represented in the issue's discourse on the intended degradation of the incarcerated and the ultimate expression of that degradation — capital punishment. Claire stressed the importance of self-awareness and general and political education for surviving the prison; she relentlessly exposed the careless disregard for the suicide and self-destruction of Canadian federal women prisoners at P4W, many with extensive histories of physical, sexual, and social abuse; and she fought against the stigmatization and abuse experienced by prisoners' families and friends in their interactions with prison authorities. These issues are all addressed in a volume that features the writing of regular contributors to the *JPP* (Steven King Ainsworth, James V. Allridge III, Victor Hassine, Charles Huckelbury, Jo-Ann Mayhew, Melissa Stewart, and Jon Marc Taylor).

Liz Elliott (replacing John Lowman as co-editor) and Stephen Reid edited Volume 9:1, a general issue that featured articles by Mumia Abu-Jamal on American law, Thomas Mann's interview with Donald Marshall, and Ian Miller on Japanese prisons. Little Rock Reed's continuing battle as a fugitive from "injustice", was detailed in the "Prisoner's Struggles" section.

The prominence of victims' rights initiatives in the United States and Canada, and the political use of the "crime" victim issue by police associations, politicians, political parties, and their allied policy and mass media representatives, prompted us to do a thematic issue that addressed criminal victimization and criminal justice. In deconstructing the narratives and political usages of the so-called crime victims' movement, Paul Wright provides a political economy of the construction and utility of the "designated crime victim". Charles Huckelbury extends the discourse through his deconstruction of the ideological and legal contortions lodged in the punitive justice lobby's claim that prisoners' rights delimit and undermine the rights and care of "crime victims". The contributors to this issue reorder the working definition of victimization so as to include victimization by the state and the role of the crime victims' rights initiative in perpetuating the cycles of violence and inequity that characterize revenge-driven criminal justice policies. They also note the existing inequities and biases in criminal justice, which add to the "distributive injustice" that victimizes the disenfranchised and marginalized.

To celebrate our Tenth Anniversary (1999), Volume 10 was devoted to an exploration of the purposes and understanding that *writers in prison* bring to their work. It was dedicated to the memory of long-time contributors, Jo-Ann Mayhew and Robert Brydon. Victor Hassine, Charles Huckelbury, and Gregory McMaster discuss becoming a writer in prison, and the understandings and purposes that surrounded their development as observers and writers. Paul Wright, in "The History of *Prison Legal News*: The Samizdat of the American Gulag", discusses the editing and production of *PLN* as political action. Thomas Mann and Richard Stratton addressed post-carceral encounters with being a writer "on the streets". To exemplify the spirit of the *JPP*, Seth Ferranti, Gerald Niles, and Gregory McMaster presented a "what else can you show me" take-up of the "horrors" of carceral life. All confront the prison as the dominating context, the reality of their lives, the place of their being and knowing, the driving force of their art. The punitive criminal justice ideology that presently dominates public and academic discourse is a focus for their counter-inscriptions and is presented as a motivating factor in their need to talk back.

With Volume 11 (2001) we came to an agreement with Canadian Scholars' Press Inc., and changed our production from a biannual to annual status. Liz Elliott and Jay Jones produced a general issue for this volume that included Stephen Reid on prisoner classification in the postmodern industrialized prison; Ed Poindexter on the relationship of stigma, self-esteem, and recidivism; and Gregory McMaster on coping with long-term incarceration. John McKenzie, Jon Marc Taylor, H.D. Blake, and Charles Huckelbury discuss state repression and the loss of human rights as it extends from capital punishment for minors, to the police shooting of Amadou Diallo, and the legitimation of coercive juvenile justice legislation through the punitive justice lobby's incorrect prediction of escalating youth violence and the emergence of juvenile "superpredators".

A number of themes run through Volume 12 (2002), which includes the journal's first contributions from Australia. Debbie Kilroy of *Sisters Inside* addresses the assaultive nature of strip searches of women prisoners in Australia, and Tracey Leivers describes the inadequacy of the medical services they are provided. Craig Minogue continues the analysis in "Human Rights and Life as an Attraction in a Correctional Theme Park", arguing that "it has been routine practice of prison authorities in the Australian state of Victoria to display prisoners as one would display animals in a zoo". Joe Miceli (Auburn, New York) extends this vision with suggestions for profit-reaping "Reality TV" shows featuring prison violence. Karamoko Akpan-Patches and Charles Huckelbury discuss the geopolitics of the prison-industrial complex. This volume also features an essay by the historian and professor emeritus, Peter Brock, on the "Prison Samizdat of British Conscientious Objectors in the First World War".

The tables of contents of these issues may be accessed through the *JPP* website at www.jpp.org. Back issues for most volumes are also available.

ABOUT THE CONTRIBUTORS TO THIS ANTHOLOGY

Mumia Abu-Jamal
A noted journalist and recognized political prisoner in the U.S.A., Mumia spent almost twenty years on death row in Pennsylvania before his sentence was commuted in 2002 to life without parole. He is the author of a number of books, including *Live from Death Row* (1995) and *Death Blossoms: Reflections From A Prisoner of Conscience* (1997), and numerous articles. He has been a regular contributor to the *JPP*.

Steven King Ainsworth
Steven began serving time in California in 1968. In 1979 he was sentenced to death and spent more than twenty years on death row. His sentence was commuted to natural life in 2001. Steven's writing (fiction, nonfiction, and poetry) and art has been published and exhibited in the U.S.A., Canada, and Europe. Steven has contributed articles and cover art to the *JPP*.

James V. Allridge III
A noted artist and writer, James has been imprisoned on death row in Texas since 1987. A regular contributor to the *JPP*, his art work has been featured on the covers of three issues. His art has also been exhibited throughout the U.S.A. He may be contacted and his art viewed at http://www.lightexpressions.net.

Robert Brydon
From the age of seventeen, Robert spent more than twenty years in federal penitentiaries in Canada. A poet and a writer, he was a long-term contributor to the *JPP* and member of the editorial board from 1993 until his death in 1999.

Johnny Byrd
At the time his article was written in 1994, "ByrdDog" was on death row in Ohio.

Dan Cahill
Dan spent more than twenty years in juvenile and adult prisons in Ohio. A prisoner's rights activist and regular contributor to the *JPP*, he was released from prison in 2001.

Ms. Cree
Ms. Cree was an Aboriginal prisoner in Kingston Prison for Women, Canada.

Jacqueline Dana
Jacqueline is an American academic and political activist whose work focuses upon Republican prisoners' issues.

Ronald Del Raine
Ronald was sentenced to 199 years in the late 1960s and has spent the subsequent years in supermaximum facilities such as Marion, Illinois and Leavenworth, Kansas. Over the decades his writing has been recognized by PEN (U.S.A.) awards and through publication in numerous magazines.

Ivan Denisovich
Ivan is a long-term prisoner in the U.S.A.

P. Dunford
Ms. Dunford was a prisoner at Kingston Prison for Women, Canada.

Dawnya Ferdinandsen
For the past decade, Dawnya has been imprisoned in Ohio. Her article was written two weeks after the death of Carol Ann Bell. In her own words, "I wrote it from the heart".

Seth M. Ferranti
Seth is a federal prisoner of the U.S.A.'s "war on drugs". In 1993, after two years as a fugitive, he was arrested and at the age of twenty-four (under mandatory sentencing guidelines) was sentenced to twenty-five years and four months for running a "continuing criminal enterprise". He has no chance of parole.

Ned Flynn
Ned is a Republican prisoner in Belfast, Northern Ireland.

Amy Friedman
A writer and playwright, Amy currently lives in Los Angeles.

Bob Gaucher
Bob is a founding editorial member of the *JPP* and has been general editor since 1994. Bob has taught in the Department of Criminology at the University of Ottawa (Canada) since attaining a doctorate at the University of Sheffield (U.K.) in 1982.

Eddie Griffin
A long-term prisoner, Eddie was shipped from the federal prison at Terre Haute, Indiana, to Marion, Illinois, in the 1980s. He is currently serving his sentence in a federal prison in Pennsylvania, where he continues to research and litigate against penal inequities.

Victor Hassine
Shortly after completing a law degree, Victor was sentenced to life without parole in Pennsylvania in 1981. He won his first PEN writing award in 1993, and is the author of *Life Without Parole: Living in Prison Today* (1996; 1999). His litigation activities have resulted in major changes in Pennsylvania's prisons.

Danny Homer
Danny is of Cayuga/Mohawk descent. Currently forty-three years old, he has been serving a life sentence since the age of seventeen. He enjoys reading, writing, and playing sports. Danny is the father of two young children and his immediate goal is to join them as soon as possible. He credits the Creator for his talents as an Aboriginal drummer and as a writer. While incarcerated, Danny completed a university undergraduate degree.

Charles Huckelbury, Jr.
Sentenced to life imprisonment (thirty-five year minimum) at the age of twenty-seven, Charles has spent the last twenty-eight years in prison. Awarded second place in *Prison Life's* fiction contest in 1995, he won the PEN first prize for fiction in 2001. A regular contributor to the *JPP* since 1997, Charles joined the editorial board in 2001. He was one of four featured writers in Shawn Thompson's *Letters From Prison* (2001).

Mícheál Mac Giolla Ghunna
A Republican prisoner in Belfast, Northern Ireland, Mícheál edited the *JPP* issue on Republican prisoners of war (1997, 7:1).

Mary McArdle
Mary is a Republican prisoner at Maghaberry Women's prison in Northern Ireland.

Gregory J. McMaster
Gregory has served more than twenty years of a life sentence, fifteen years in maximum security in U.S. prisons, before being transferred to Canada. He has won numerous writing awards, including first prize in the *Prison Life Magazine* (1995) and in *Prison Arts Foundation* (1997) contests. Since returning to Canada he has been a regular contributor to the *JPP*.

Seán McMonagle
Seán was a Republican prisoner who spent four years in Long Kesh in the 1990s.

Jo-Ann Mayhew
Jo-Ann served a life sentence at Kingston P4W, which was commuted to time served after she had been paroled. As editor of *TightWire Magazine* in the 1980s, Jo-Ann was successful in exposing the plight of (federal) women prisoners in Canada. A major contributor to the *JPP* from its inception, after her death in 1998, she was recognized and eulogized by women's groups across Canada.

Joe Miceli
Joe is a long-term prisoner in New York State.

John H. Morris III
John is a prisoner in California.

James Morse
James was a prisoner in New York State. His contribution is an essay from his book, *The Expendable*. His writing has appeared in numerous publications in the U.S.A.

Gerald Niles
Gerald was sentenced to a life sentence (twenty-five years minimum) in Florida in 1991. Because of his litigation and political agitation he has been

constantly transferred (ghost trained) to Special Handling Units in maximum security prisons across the U.S.A. He has been a regular contributor to the *JPP* throughout his travels.

Paddy O'Dowd
Paddy is a Republican prisoner in Northern Ireland.

John Perotti
An anarchist and recognized political prisoner, John was sentenced to twenty-two to sixty-six years in 1982. Since that time he has been imprisoned in supermaximum facilities, and for the last fifteen years has been caged in Special Handling Unit isolation. John continues to litigate against prison conditions suffered by Ohio's prisoners.

Prisoner's Wife
Prisoner's Wife is the spouse of a Northern Ireland Republican prisoner.

James Pryor
James is a prisoner in Ohio.

Little Rock Reed
During the more than ten years he served in prison in Ohio, Little Rock fought for Aboriginal prisoners' rights to access to elders and spiritual ceremonies. After release he edited and wrote *The American Indian in the Whiteman's Prisons: A Story of Genocide* (1993). Shortly thereafter he became a "fugitive from injustice" because of his political activities. He died in a traffic accident in January 2000 in Taos, New Mexico.

Stephen Reid
Since Stephen's memoir, *Jack Rabbit Parole*, was published in 1986 while he was imprisoned, he has established himself as a writer; he has taught creating writing courses inside and outside prisons, and he has been an active member of PEN (Canada). In the 1990s, he was instrumental in defeating federal legislation aimed at stifling prison writing in Canada. In 1997 he joined the editorial board of the *JPP*. He is currently "writer in residence" at Williams Head penitentiary in British Columbia.

Juan Rivera
Juan was a prisoner and educator in New York State prisons, where he was involved in the creation of the "Conciencia and Resurrection" study groups, and was also a member of the Community Justice Institute in Albany, New York.

Susan Rosenberg
A noted political activist and political prisoner in the U.S.A., Susan was a defendant in the *Resistance Conspiracy* case.

Melissa Stewart
Melissa served six years at Kingston P4W, during which time she helped to create "Project Another Chance" — a support group and crisis line for women prisoners.

Jon Marc Taylor
Jon Marc has served more than twenty years in prison, during which time he has completed undergraduate and graduate university degrees, authored more than one-hundred articles and been the recipient of numerous writing awards, including the Robert F. Kennedy Journalism Award. A major contributor to the *JPP*, Jon Marc joined the editorial board in 1998. The second edition of his book, *Prisoners' Guerrilla Handbook to Correspondence Programs in the United States and Canada*, was published in 2002.

Robert Woodman
Robert is a prisoner in Ohio.

Paul Wright
Paul was sentenced to 304 months in Washington State in 1987. In 1990 he helped to found *Prison Legal News*, which he edits and produces. A regular contributor to the *JPP*, he co-edited *The Ceiling of America: An Inside Look at the U.S. Prison Industry*. His most recent book, *Prison Nation*, is scheduled for publication in 2003.

One of the most enjoyable editorial tasks is choosing the art for *JPP* covers. Prison arts and crafts have been prized for centuries, from the ship models and letterboxes produced on prison ships during the Napoleonic Wars to the Aboriginal carvings, and airbrush and acrylic paintings of today. The cover art images have been created in a number of mediums. Puerto Rican political prisoner Elizam Escobar's *A Weltanschaung* set the standard with the first issue, and once we were established, we had a wealth of materials from which to choose. In the interim I composed covers for Volumes 1:2 and 2:1 from the artwork in my collection of Canadian penal press magazines. On the covers of Volume 2:2 we were honoured to present two works by the celebrated Aboriginal artist Norval Morrisseau, *The Shifter* and *Red Bird.* For the next three issues (Volumes 3 and 4) we used drawings to illustrate issue themes: Canadian Peter Collins's *Prison Justice Day August 10th;* Briton Tony Bashforth on education; and American Mark Harris on marionization. We used a *Cree Shield* by Dennis Okanee as the image for Volume 5:1 and Gayle Horii's sculpture *En Nom de Dieu* for Volume 5:2. Gayle's artwork was included throughout this volume on women's imprisonment.

In 1995, Volume 6:1 introduced James V. Allridge III (death row, Huntsville, Texas) with his award-winning coloured drawing, *Piano Wave.* Bryant Ross's Pacific Northwest mask, *Chilcot Moon,* was featured on the cover of Volume 6:1. Micheál Doherty (Long Knesh, Belfast) illustrated the issue by Irish Republican political prisoners, and James V. Allridge III returned with *Wolf Woman* for Volume 8:1/2. We featured an ink drawing, *The Polka Dot Keed,* by Steven King Ainsworth (death row, San Quentin, California) on the cover of Volume 9:1. A past contributor to the *JPP,* in this edition Ainsworth's talent as an illustrator, as well as a writer, are evident. Andre Latouche's award-winning airbrush and acrylic *Lifer's Dream* portrays the chaos and dilemmas of doing a life sentence and visibly introduces Victor Hassine's "Monochromes from Over a Prison's Edge" in Volume 9:2. For our anniversary issue, we assembled a display of *JPP* cover art from past issues. Bryan Seymour's haunting *Searching* (acrylic) introduced our first annual, Volume 11. The latest addition (Volume 12) is a piece by James V. Alldridge III, entitled *In the Limelight.*

ABOUT THE COVER ARTISTS

Steven King Ainsworth

Steven spent twenty years on death row in California before his sentence was commuted in 2001. His pencil and ink drawings have been exhibited in galleries and published in books and magazines in the U.S.A. and Europe. A self-taught artist he states:

> During my quarter century of confinement, I have always been drawn to creative endeavours in order to alleviate the boredom and stress of incarceration. The therapeutic value of creating something positive in the negative environment of prison is immense.

James V. Allridge III

James was sentenced to death on June 9th, 1987, at the age of twenty-four. He developed his artistic talents while on death row. In light of his confinement, James is a "copy" artist who relies on photographs, cards, and magazines for inspiration. His ink and coloured pencil drawings have been exhibited in art galleries in the U.S.A. and in numerous books, magazines, and newsletters. James produces greeting cards and note-cards to finance his legal defense. He now uses "dramatic contrasts of light and darkness to symbolize his hope that even in the darkest situations, beauty can still be found, if only we look towards the light". His work can be seen at http://www.lightexpressions.net.

Tony Bashforth

Tony was from Sheffield, England, and realized his artistic talents while serving a borstal sentence. He won his first Arthur Koestler Award for Prison Art in 1975, at the age of nineteen. Later, while serving an eight year sentence, he won three successive Koestler awards (1982–84). His art has been exhibited at the Crucible Theatre in Sheffield, and the Hayward Gallery in London. His work is represented in the prestigious "Outsiders Collection" in London. Tony passed away in the mid-1990s.

Peter Collins

Peter is from Ottawa, Ontario, where he was sentenced to life imprisonment in the 1980s. His interest in drawing was apparent throughout his childhood, and while imprisoned, he developed his skills.

Ralph Danton
Ralph was an editor and illustrator for *Mountain Echoes*, a Canadian penal press magazine from Stoney Mountain Penitentiary, Manitoba, Canada. His drawing *Mountain Echoes* (1960) graced the cover of *JPP*, Volume 1:2.

Micheál Doherty
Micheál was a Republican prisoner in Northern Ireland.

Elizam Escobar
An illustrator and art teacher in New York City, in 1980, Elizam was accused of belonging to the Armed Forces for the National Liberation of Puerto Rico and sentenced to sixty-eight years in prison for seditious conspiracy. His paintings have been exhibited in Puerto Rico and the United States. In the catalogue of an exhibition of his work in Chicago, entitled *Art as an Act of Liberation*, Elizam stated:

> Art and poetry and their discourses, if they are for real, are always critical of Power: their politics is to transform reality and not to merely ideologize it. We should not pretend to possess truth or to have the only unique truth. But an artist or a poet with a critical consciousness is always uncompromising with Power in relation to truth, in order to be for a revolution and real democracy.

Mark Harris
Mark was a prisoner in Ohio. Since his release he has made a career as an artist.

Gayle Horii
Gayle is from Vancouver, Canada. Her art includes sculpture and drawing. Her work in Volume 5:2 was created while serving a life sentence in Kingston Prison for Women and in Matsqui penitentiary. She says of her sculpture *En Nom De Dieu*:

> The rationale used for torturing and burning women at the stake for witchcraft is identical to the patriarchal need for controlling all women. Each black flame signifies the many assaults directed towards the sexuality of women, particularly towards women in

prison. Her body is cut signifying the pain she has already endured and the injuries she inflicts upon herself when her despair and rage turns inward. The state is invisible as are the ties that bind her, which signifies the covert manner used to impose added punishments upon women. She asks: Why? Still?

André Latouche

André was born in Quebec City in 1956. While serving a life sentence he achieved a D.E.C. in Arts. Working in pencil and ink, oils and airbrush, he has been awarded numerous prizes in painting and design. He says of *Lifer's Dream*:

> I consider this art as a voyage in the symbolism of a dream. The dream of a life sentence. I dream void of all logic and order. A detached imagination, a vision unfurling, confused in time and space. As a whole, give the feeling like the crying out of a spirit which pours forth its love, its hate, its nightmares, its lost dreams: drowned in the true to life carceral system where the abnormal becomes the normal. This art demonstrates the negative transformation of the inner self and of the deterioration of a personality by the system.

Norval Morrisseau

An Ojibway artist of international importance, Norval's work was first exhibited in 1962, in Toronto, Canada. A "shaman-artist", his work has had a major impact on the development of Aboriginal artists in Canada and the U.S.A. In his own words:

> My art reflects my own spiritual personality. Driven from birth by the spirit force within, I have always been convinced I am a great artist. Only the external and commercial society around me which has caused interruptions and deviations to occur has attempted to dictate to me and establish false values and ideals. The path through this maze has not been easy ... fortified by my grandfather's spiritual teachings during the first nine years of my life, I make peace with the external world, and I recognize the higher powers of the spirit. (Quoted in *The Art of Norval Morrisseau*, 1979, J. Pollock and L. Sinclair)

Dennis Okanee

Dennis is a Cree artist, born on the Thunderchild Band's territory in Alberta, Canada. He developed an interest in traditional Cree culture and art as a child. He started to produce art while incarcerated.

Bryant Ross

Bryant was born in Manitoba in 1951, and is of Scottish-Canadian ancestry. His friendship with Norval Morrisseau reawakened his need for creativity and led him to open Coghlan Art Studio in Aldergrove, British Columbia, in 1988. His artwork draws inspiration from his respect for traditional Aboriginal culture and from his love of primitive and contemporary Aboriginal art. His carvings and sculptures have been exhibited in galleries in Canada and the U.S.A.

Brian Seymour

Brian was born in Ontario, Canada, in 1956. He developed his youthful interest in art while imprisoned. His work in acrylics and silkscreen is inspired by the more somber aspects of his persona, while his carving reflects the lighter side of his life. He relates:

> There are many facets to who we are. We can pick up different pieces of who we are and find things about ourselves that we don't like. But if we throw them away, it affects who we are. In this painting, I was searching for the different aspects of myself, the many facets of my personality. This is a reflection of my soul-searching phase.

LISTING OF THE COVER ART AND ARTISTS FROM 1988–2002

1. Volume 1:1 (1988), Elizam Escobar (1986) *A Weltanschaung*
2. Volume 1:2 (1988–89), Ralph Danton (1960) *Mountain Echoes*
3. Volume 2:1 (1989), Bob Gaucher (1989) *Composition of Canadian Penal Press Cover Art*
4. Volume 2:2 (1990), Norval Morriseau (1989) *The Shifter* (front cover); (1989) *Red Bird* (back cover)

5. Volume 3:1&2 (1990–91), Peter Collins (1989) *Prison Justice Day August 10th Never Forget*
6. Volume 4:1 (1992), Tony Bashforth (1992) *Untitled*
7. Volume 4:2 (1993), Mark Harris (1993) *Untitled*
8. Volume 5:1 (1993), Dennis Okanee (1993) *Cree Shield*
9. Volume 5:2 (1994), Gayle Horii (1989) *En Nom de Dieu*
10. Volume 6:1 (1995), James V. Allridge III (1991) *Piano Wave*
11. Volume 6:2 (1995), Bryant Ross (1994) *Chilcot Moon*
12. Volume 7:1 (1996–97), Micheál Doherty (1996) *Untitled*
13. Volume 7:2 (1996–97), (No cover art)
14. Volume 8:1&2 (1997), James V. Allridge III (1994) *Wolf Woman*
15. Volume 9:1 (1998), Steven King Ainsworth (1993) *The Polka Dot Keed*
16. Volume 9:2 (1998), André Latouche (1997) *Lifer's Dream*
17. Volume 10:1&2 (1999), Bob Gaucher (1999) *Composite of Past Covers*
18. Volume 11 (2001), Bryan Seymour (1998) *Searching*
19. Volume 12 (2002), James V. Allridge III (2001) *In the Limelight*